To the memory of Vera Katz and Nick Fish, former New Yorkers who personified what the Flight for Freedom was all about:

Mayor Katz overcame her fears, faced her personal trauma, and defied death threats to bravely and joyously lead 1,000 Oregonians on a mission of caring and support

Nick Fish, who was not initially invited to participate but when he read about the trip, like all the other Freedom Fliers picked up the phone and volunteered, putting his life on hold and giving his heart and soul to make the Flight for Freedom as powerful and professional and compassionate as possible

And to the courageous Freedom Fliers themselves who brought open wallets, open arms, and — above all — open hearts to a place engulfed in pain . . .

. . . and made a difference.

n those days, we finally chose to walk like giants & hold the world in arms grown strong with love

& there may be many things we forget in the days to come, but this will not be one of them.

— "awakening" by Kai Skye*

* When the Flight For Freedom was over, Loen Dozono gave the employees of Azumano Travel the poster with this quotation created by Kai Skye after 9/11 in response to the attacks.

TABLE OF CONTENTS

Author's Note. vii
Introduction. 1

WHERE THEY WERE: GEOGRAPHY AND EMOTIONS 1

The Seven Regions of Oregon 3
By the Numbers: Oregon and New York. 15
Lisa Sokoloff: Surviving the September 11 Attacks 19

THE FLIGHT FOR FREEDOM .33

An Idea Becomes Reality. 35
Why They Went. 125
The Adventure Begins 167
Mourning, Feasting, and an Unexpected Challenge 203
America Wakes Up to Oregon 239
Ringing the Bell. 251
I Love a Parade! 259
All-Oregon Reception 289
Last Moments. 297

IN THEIR OWN WORDS 317

Ground Zero 319
Bearing Witness 361
The Impact 415

TIMELINES: 9/11 AND ITS AFTERMATH. 457

A Timeline of the September 11 Attacks. 459
As It Happened: September 12–26 469

SOME NOTES ON OREGON OR IF OREGON CAN DO IT, ANYONE CAN! . 499

The Land 501
Economic Transition 507

The Most Politically Polarized State 511
Water 513
Lewis and Clark 521
The Oregon Trail 527
Immigrants of Color in Oregon .531
Acknowledgments 555

APPENDIXES 561

Appendix A: The Aftermath 561
Appendix B: Former New York Governor George Pataki 581
Appendix C: Oregon's Senators Praise the Flight for Freedom 585
Appendix D: Letters of Acclamation 589
Appendix E: Nick Fish (1958–2020) 595
Appendix F: Leo Nadolske 603
Appendix G: Organizers, Supporters and Volunteers 609
Notes 611
Bibliography 647
Participants and Other Notables in This Book 673

AUTHOR'S NOTE

The focus of this book is, of course, the Flight for Freedom. To fully understand the Flight for Freedom, I believe historical context is necessary, particularly for those who are too young to remember 9/11 and its aftermath, as well as for those who know little about the state of Oregon and its history.

As a result, I created three sections of the book that I feel are essential if you fall into either of those categories.

Where They Were: Geography and Emotions

Following this note, you will find a section that provides some introductory context for Oregon geographically and for New York emotionally. You will find a map of Oregon and a short overview of the seven very different regions of the state, which range from wet, urban and liberal to dry, rural and politically conservative. You will find an interview with Lisa Sokoloff, who recounts her experience on September 11 and how she escaped Battery Park alive, which will give readers an indication of the emotional state of New Yorkers when the Flight for Freedom participants arrived. In addition, you will find a short comparison of Oregon and New York by the numbers, which indicates how seemingly different those two places are—which will help to demonstrate how, when you read about the experiences of the Freedom Fliers, differences melt away when people connect at the level of shared humanity.

Some Notes on Oregon

When I began this book, knowing it was for a general audience, I assumed that most people would not know much about Oregon. People might assume it's only rain, hippies, the Trail Blazers, and

Portlandia. I wanted to include some information to explain the state's wide geographical diversity and some of its history so readers would understand how varied the state really is.

Oregon's history is far more contentious and complex than I'd realized—and Oregon is representative of the rest of the country in far more ways than I could have imagined. What I had envisioned as one introductory essay ballooned into multiple essays; all have been peer-reviewed by the leading expert in Oregon history, Oregon State University Professor Emeritus William G. Robbins.

Oregon's racial history has been particularly problematic. Oregon is the only state to enter the union—to actually become a state—with a law in its constitution prohibiting Black people from living there. (Simultaneously, Oregon prohibited slavery.) In addition, from the Native Americans to the Chinese to the Japanese to the Latinx communities, Oregon has been on the front lines of every racial conflict this country has experienced. Loen Dozono's father was incarcerated in the World War II internment camps, and Loen herself was born in Utah at the end of that period. Her father, George Azumano, made a point that he was traveling on the Flight for Freedom and recruiting fellow Japanese American veterans—yes, he served the federal government in the U.S. military and that same government put him in a camp—"in hopes of reminding Americans of what can happen if we turn to racial prejudice in times of war."

In 2004, Nate Silver of 538 found that Oregon was the most politically polarized state in the country. This fact makes the ability of Oregonians to come together for the Flight for Freedom even more inspiring.

I also wanted to shine a bit of light on issues in rural Oregon; water rights is a major one. In 2001, one of the first major standoffs between the government and supporters of local farmers near Klamath Falls in Southern Oregon, escalated into an armed confrontation that ended only with 9/11. Organized via the internet, groups from across the West sent representatives to defend what they saw as their rights. These issues have arisen repeatedly over the years. With a record drought looming in 2021, conflicts over water are likely to recur.

After reading this section, my hope is that readers who are longing for the United States to work on mending divisions today will say, as many in Oregon said when I told them about this part of the book: 'If Oregon can do it, anybody can!"

Timelines: 9/11 and As It Happened

This section has two parts:

- **A timeline of the events of September 11, 2001.** Particularly for people accustomed to being able to find instant answers on the internet, I hope that this timeline can provide a bit of insight into the experience of that day, as people watched television and the tragedy unfolded. Nobody knew what was going to happen next. Above all, nobody thought that those buildings, the fifth-tallest in the world, could collapse because commercial airliners had penetrated them.

- **"As It Happened": excerpts, primarily from _The New York Times_, that provide a day-by-day glimpse into what people were learning about the attacks at the same time the Flight for Freedom was gestating and being planned.** This section shows how understanding of the aftermath unfolded step by step, and the incomprehensible (at the time) idea that this attack was carried out by people openly living in our own communities. I hope this section also conveys the uncertainty and the pain of not knowing—for weeks—the fates of the 60,000 people in those buildings, not even knowing how many were missing, discovering that many had been vaporized, crushed with no trace. And the eventual journey toward some kind of comprehension of what had happened in little more than an hour at that site. This section I hope will also provide at least an inkling of how so much of Lower Manhattan and its people were affected; and why almost everyone across the New York metropolitan area knew someone who had died in the attacks.

I hope, too, that you will find here some small sense of the enormity of the loss of so many firefighters and police on that day. Three hundred forty-three firefighters died on September 11, going into danger to help get everybody out. Sixty police were killed there in the line of duty. This is why the New York fire stations became shrines.

This is why Portland firefighters slept at the airports until planes were flying, so they could work "the pile" and help sift through the rubble to find evidence of their brothers. And it's why visiting fire and police stations was a priority for most Freedom Fliers.*

Notes on Style

If a city is in Oregon, the state will not be listed.

In order to minimize the number of footnotes, when only one source for a person's quotation exists, I have decided not to include a footnote. You will find the original source for that person's contribution under their name in the bibliography.

And, you ask, why is the state name—"Oregon"—spelled so many different ways in this book? Answer: Quite frankly, New Yorkers do not pronounce "Oregon" correctly. Think of it as an American dialect. Smile as you read these cockamamie Oregon phonetic spellings and hear those grateful New Yorkers.

---

*In the years since, the illnesses caused by 9/11 have far outpaced the nearly 3,000 deaths on September 11 itself. About 40,000 people have conditions linked to 9/11, including thousands with respiratory illnesses and mental health issues, says Dr. Michael Crane, who directs the World Trade Center Health Program at the Icahn School of Medicine at Mount Sinai in Manhattan. This includes 10,000 people who have developed various cancers associated with exposure to the toxins, with 50 to 80 new cases of cancers associated with 9/11 toxins certified each month. Exposure to the toxins in the atmosphere—which includes the area's residents—may have affected 80,000 to 90,000 people. In 2019, the 9/11 Memorial Glade at the World Trade Center site was dedicated, which is a tribute to those who are sick or have died from their recovery work. Diane Herbst, "9/11 Still Claiming Victims: 10,000 With Cancers, Thousands More With Other Illnesses," *People*, September 11, 2019, https://people.com/human-interest/9-11-still-claiming-victims-10000-with-cancers-thousands-more-with-other-illnesses/.

INTRODUCTION

> Good and kind people outnumber all others by thousands to one. The tragedy of human history lies in the enormous potential for destruction in rare acts of evil, not in the high frequency of evil people. Complex systems can only be built step by step, whereas destruction requires but an instant. Thus, in what I like to call the Great Asymmetry, every spectacular incident of evil will be balanced by 10,000 acts of kindness, too often unnoted and invisible as the "ordinary" efforts of a vast majority.
>
> We have a duty, almost a holy responsibility, to record and honor the victorious weight of these innumerable little kindnesses, when an unprecedented act of evil so threatens to distort our perception of ordinary human behavior. — *Stephen Jay Gould**

On September 26, 2001, the morning the Flight for Freedom was announced in Portland, Oregon, *The New York Times* published an essay Stephen Jay Gould was inspired to write when he saw the reaction to the warm apple brown bettys he brought rescue workers at the World Trade Center site. Gould captures my motivation for writing this book.

I write this at a time of enormous division in our country, enormous racial strife, and a time when we have had to be physically isolated from one another.

I felt a need to do what I could to let the world know about what some courageous, selfless, and highly competent people did to help others when help was needed. The Flight for Freedom was a historic event, but I would not have felt compelled to spend my off-hours—I

---

*Stephen Jay Gould, "A Time of Gifts," *The New York Times*, September 26, 2001, A19.

do have a day job—documenting this event if it had been "only" 1,000 Oregonians getting on planes to go to New York City in October 2001. This at a time when, as one Oregonian said, "People were afraid to go to the Dairy Queen," when the travel industry was in tatters, and New York City's economy was in the toilet. As much as these things alone were historic—Oregon was the first to step up, and although others intended to surpass them, nobody else did—it would not have been enough.*

But let me stop a moment and stress this point because even though as you read this book you'll see that putting the Flight for Freedom together took a lot of effort, it's worth making the point: *nobody else* in the country pulled off this kind of feat. No other state, no other city, no other county. Nobody.

I wanted to make sure this story was told because I was there in 2001—I covered the Flight for Freedom for the *Chicago Tribune* and *The Boston Globe*—and I saw that the Flight for Freedom was about infinitely more than just having the courage to get on the same kinds of planes that had just weeks earlier been used as missiles, though God knows that was plenty. It was about infinitely more than the money spent, though in that one weekend organizers estimated that they pumped $1 million into New York City's struggling economy.

I wanted to let people know about the Flight for Freedom because it is a story about the best of the human spirit. I was there, and I experienced it and, like everyone I've met and spoken with who was part of it, it was a deeply meaningful experience for me. Every person involved, from the organizers at the top to all the rest of those people who put their lives on hold to participate in it brought the best of themselves to the effort. And *every single person* made a difference by being part of the Flight for Freedom. Those of us who were there all know it, too. And I want others to know that this is possible. It is possible to make a difference even when the chips are down, even when they are way down.

---

*A group in Irvine, California, assembled 5,000 persons from around the country who went to New York in November 2001. While it was enormously valuable to the New York economy, the trip's purpose was very different. That's the only similar kind of effort I have been able to discover in my research.

It came at a moment when the United States was unified; the country had come together when faced with almost unfathomable tragedy.* And countries across the world were overwhelmingly behind us.

Here's what didn't matter, and never even came up among those who participated: race, class, religion, politics, gender identity, urban or rural origins. The trip's organizers created an opportunity for a highly diverse and democratic group to help New York and New Yorkers, by making it affordable, by providing scholarships, and by naming former Governor Vic Atiyeh, an Arab American, and State Sen. Margaret Carter, an African American, to head the group's diversity committee, in an effort to make the group as racially diverse as possible.

One in every 3,000 Oregonians, from remote Crescent Lake (pop. 400) to mighty Portland, stepped up. Many who signed on had never been to New York City before, some had never been on an airplane, some had never traveled alone.

In New York, people kept asking, "Is this some kind of a club?" No.

Kristen Dozono describes it perfectly: "It was the biggest display of random people you could ever find."[1]

In the "Notes on Oregon History" section of this book, you will learn that Oregon has quite a racist history; and in 2004, presidential exit polling data showed it to be the most politically polarized state in the country. That Oregon accomplished this amazing effort demonstrates that even in places marked by conflict and distrust—like the United States today—coming together across those things that divide us is possible. Or, as people in Oregon said to me when I brought this up: "If Oregon can do it, anybody can do it!"

What they knew about the trip when they signed up was this; sometimes they knew even less, depending on when and how they heard about it:

---

*That said, anti-Muslim hate crimes arose, and anyone with dark skin with features that could be interpreted by those predisposed to such crimes were vulnerable. Also, with the bombing of Afghanistan that began during the trip (to everyone's shock), that international and domestic togetherness began to change.

The mission has several goals, both practical and symbolic. Participants want to show New Yorkers that Oregonians support them at their time of grief. They also want—albeit in a small way—to give a boost to the New York economy by filling the hotels, restaurants, theaters and taxis that provide jobs to many New Yorkers.

Among tentative plans are a visit to the memorials for victims in Union Square, religious services on Sunday, a visit to Wall Street and a possible meeting between Giuliani and Katz, who is paying her own way.

The trip costs $379 plus tax for airfare and two nights lodging, or $434 for three nights.[2]

Azumano Travel took no commissions and made no money on the trip. They asked the airlines and hotels to offer low rates. Delta stepped up first and United followed, and Hilton offered its New York crown jewel, the Waldorf-Astoria, for basically the room tax, and covered the cost of receptions, too. And when the numbers of travelers kept growing and growing, the corporations stood by their prices. Because of the Freedom Fliers they were able to keep people employed; the Oregonians ate at their restaurants and bought from their gift shops, but nobody was making any money from this. Still, the $379 price meant that people like the Portland cab driver who saved his tips to pay his way would be able to go.

Even though New York's mayor had put out the word for people to come to New York, to not be afraid, nobody was flocking there. As a consequence, thousands of New Yorkers had lost and were losing their jobs due to the 9/11 attacks. America was locked in fear.

But only a week after the attacks, in "little bitty Oregon," Loen Dozono had the idea of a "reverse wagon train," a caravan, to provide relief and help to the city that had just experienced the largest attack on U.S. soil in our history. Two 110-story buildings that were landmarks of modern engineering had, inconceivably, come crashing down as we watched—and as we watched in horror we saw, though at first we didn't know what we were seeing, people jumping to their deaths. We saw others try to outrun an opaque cloud that was surrounding them, running for their very lives.

From the beginning, the idea was not just to spend money, although Oregonians certainly did that. Loen's instinct was more humanitarian. The message became, "We gave our blood, we gave our money, now we're going to give ourselves."

That's why I wanted to make sure this story was recorded, and remembered, because the Flight for Freedom proved what it can mean to put yourself on the line for another person. Someone you don't know.

The Oregonians who went on the Flight for Freedom didn't know what they were getting into, really. All they knew was that there was this trip. They felt that by going, they could show the terrorists that they hadn't won, that Americans were not going to live in fear; and they could show New Yorkers that they cared about them.

They were simply people who cared. And that was enough.

What they did not—could not—have conceived of was the raw pain they would encounter when they came into face to face contact with New Yorkers. Neither could they have anticipated the depth of gratitude.

From New Yorkers? They were the cold, gruff, rushing urbanites who won't give anybody the time of day. Everybody knows that.

The overwhelming emotion of the New Yorkers, the shock and surprise and appreciation that somebody would show up for them was expressed over and over and over again. My college friend Lisa, who had escaped with her life from her apartment in Battery Park City,* was going to be inducted as head of the Jewish Lawyers of New York at the end of October, an event the group had decided to hold despite the attacks. Her own father would not venture from New Jersey to attend it. But these people from 3,000 miles away showed up.

This group made a difference to some people's very survival. Housekeepers, bellmen, and other hotel staff were called back to work; and so they could feed their families and pay the rent. Waitstaff, cab drivers, and baristas got work and tips. Actors on Broadway had larger audiences because of Oregonians—and the cast of Kiss Me Kate autographed 100 programs just for them, and met with them after the show.

---

*By one of the coincidences that marked this trip, Lisa was homeless and living in the Waldorf-Astoria. She told her story to the Freedom Fliers there.

This was a self-selected group. When asked why they went, most people told me, "I just knew I had to do it." Simple as that.

When they got to New York, they were present for these strangers in whatever ways they were needed—and these hundreds of everyday encounters, between New Yorkers and Oregonians, meant a lot to the people on both sides of the interaction.

With their conspicuous brilliantly white Oregon ♥ NY T-shirts and buttons, especially in a city known for chic black couture, the Oregonians couldn't be missed. And New Yorkers went out of their way to thank them. This book is filled with the stories of these encounters. New Yorkers needed hugs, too, and they got them.

Sometimes New Yorkers needed more: to tell their stories, to cry, to be held. Not one Oregonian ever shied away, no one ever thought it was "too much." Instead, they moved into the pain and into the need in a spontaneous, and deeply warm and human way.

They came away knowing they had made a difference.

The people who organized this trip, beginning with Sho and Loen Dozono—were Republicans, Democrats, businesspeople, nonprofit executives, media professionals—and all volunteers. All of them, like all the participants, dropped everything and put their lives on hold for two weeks to make this happen, to create an opportunity for a wide range of Oregonians to go to New York. Community leader and attorney Bruce Samson had the same idea as Loen at almost the same time, and that realization gave the project its instantaneous acceleration.

Sho had the contacts needed, and he called them—"persistence" is the word most commonly used to describe him. He told Loen he thought this could be a "big idea" and he did not hesitate to pick up the phone, send an email, or make a quick decision to keep the project moving.

Campaign strategist Elaine Franklin brought understanding of how to organize, plan, and execute a winning campaign—and she knew that being the first ones there was critical. Native New Yorker Jack McGowan, former media personality and executive director of the Pacific Northwest's largest environmental volunteer group, SOLV, channeled his own personal suffering over what had happened to his hometown into serving as an inspiring, camera-ready spokesman for the group. Elisa Dozono, who was working in communications at the top levels of Portland's government at the time, not only guided the project at its conception but brought on John Ray, and was instrumental in securing Portland Mayor Vera Katz's participation. Former New Yorker, political strategist Len Bergstein, who, as Sho Dozono describes it, was the moral center of the project, thought the idea was "electric" the moment he heard it. Another New York transplant, then private attorney Nick Fish, made all the difference by bringing in New York's Governor George Pataki, stars from *Phantom of the Opera* and *Les Misérables*, and pulled together a memorial service at Union Square that could not have been more honorable and moving. Journalist John Ray relentlessly used every connection he had and anybody he'd ever crossed paths with to generate a local, state, regional, national, and international media blitz that showed the world not to be afraid. The Oregonians were a media sensation.

Mayor Vera Katz, another former New Yorker, tirelessly went from event to event and represented the city in national media and in events across the city; she gave the trip a credibility it would not otherwise have had. In a variety of interviews, Katz generously shared her own personal and emotional journey from Holocaust refugee in New York to leading an American city in the Columbus Day parade almost sixty years to the day of her arrival on our shores. Her commitment and dedication brought a tender humanity to viewers' perception of the Oregonians in the media and everywhere she went. Like everyone else, she gave her heart and soul to this effort. And she showed New Yorkers the best that Portland, and Oregon, had to offer. On top of that, she was utterly terrified of flying and she did it anyway.

Unlike the other organizers who were asked to help, Fish, a relative newcomer to Portland who belonged to a renowned New York political family, offered his help when he read about it in the paper, almost a week after organizers had begun to meet. He called Sho Dozono and offered his help. His creativity and his New York connections gave the trip some of its most meaningful and most spectacular moments. In one of the synchronicities that marked the trip, Fish's home church, the Cathedral of Saint John the Divine, was having its annual Blessing of the Animals the weekend of the trip, which meant that choirs, the Paul Winter Consort music group, all manner of animals—which that year included the dogs working "the pile" at the Trade Center site—and Fish not only made it possible for Mayor Katz to attend the service, but to speak at it. She had lived in the neighborhood of the cathedral while growing up in New York, but as a Jew had never had the temerity to enter it. "The place rocked" when she spoke, Fish said.

It's been twenty years since then. Though many of the people who participated in it are gone now, many are still around and available to tell their stories. It's been an honor to record them.*

What needs to be made clear is that this was a moment in which 1,000 persons' paths crossed. Except for the organizers of the trip, most of whom knew one another, everybody else signed up on their own and showed up on their own. And while those who traveled alone were "adopted" by their fellow travelers, and people of course met one another at various events, I have heard of only two people who stayed in touch for an extended period of time after the event.

It was a moment in time when all of us brought our best, all of us gave our all. Just to help New Yorkers. Just to help fellow Americans.

This is a true story. America came together in 2001 on the Flight for Freedom. It's possible to do it again.

---

*I believe very strongly that this book is only a beginning. Building on the Freedom Fliers identified for this book and many others whose memories are not included here, an effort should be made to capture the oral histories of those who participated in this trip so that Oregon's, and America's, 9/11 history can be fully documented and preserved.

WHERE THEY WERE: GEOGRAPHY AND EMOTIONS

When 9/11 happened, everyone put down their swords and shields and sort of embraced each other emotionally, if not actually, and we saw how as Americans we have so much more in common than in difference—and Republicans and Democrats did it, too . . . .

As difficult a moment that that was in our nation's history, it was ironically one of the best because the better angels of our nature were hung on every flagpole and on every American heart. Flags were everywhere. We were out of the "Pluribus"; we were "Unum."

—Oregon Senator Gordon H. Smith

THE SEVEN REGIONS OF OREGON

Geographically, culturally, politically—in more ways than you might expect, Oregon is a microcosm of the United States.

The state is extremely diverse geographically, a characteristic that brings with it a variety of climates that could not be more different. While Portlanders may be growing moss between their toes, east of the Cascades it's dry and it's what we think of as the American West: wide open spaces, cattle rangelands, mining, wheat, and more mountains. The state is composed of seven diverse regions: the Coast, Portland Metro, Mount Hood and the Columbia River Gorge, the Willamette Valley, Eastern Oregon, Central Oregon, and Southern Oregon. In these regions you'll find the ocean, mountains, valleys, high desert, cities, small towns, and just about everything in between, everything except the tropics.

THE OREGON COAST

Oregon's coastline is 363 miles long and encompasses everything from the Oregon Dunes—forty miles of sand that roll into hills up to 500 feet high—to majestic rock formations and picturesque beach towns like Manzanita, which a century ago inspired Oregon Gov. Oswald

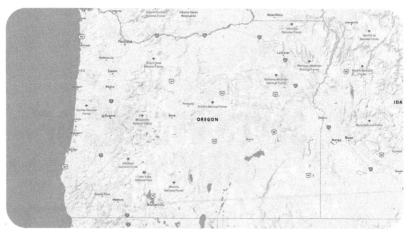

Oregon map courtesy of Mapbox.com.

Heceta Head Lighthouse first shone its light, whose lens traveled to Oregon from England in a barrel of molasses for safety, in 1894. The lighthouse stands 205 feet above the Pacific Ocean on a bluff carved out of the west side of 1,000-foot-high Heceta Head, which is twelve miles north of Florence. The 56-foot-high tower shines the most powerful light on the Oregon Coast, a white beam that flashes for eight seconds every minute and can be seen 21 miles from land. Heceta Head was named in 1862 for Spanish Basque explorer Bruno de Heceta y Dudagoita, who sailed along the Oregon Coast in 1775 in an effort to claim the Pacific Coast for Spain. Heceta Head is one of the best places on the coast to watch whales during their spring and fall migrations. Source: Cameron La Follette and Douglas Deur, "Heceta Head Lighthouse," *The Oregon Encyclopedia*, https://www.oregonencyclopedia.org/articles/heceta-head-lighthouse/#.YLgXRkwpAc8, last updated May 22, 2020 Photo: Oregon Parks and Recreation Department.

West to declare that Oregon's beaches should always remain free and open to all. And so they have. (Read about what it took to keep that promise in the chapter "The Land.")

Swimming in the Pacific off the coast requires a bit of intestinal fortitude, though; Oregon's dynamic waters seldom reach temperatures higher than fifty degrees.

PORTLAND METRO

By 1843 two New Englanders owned a land claim (on lands used by Multnomah Chinook Native tribes), but Portland did not have a

Twin spires, Oregon Convention Center against the Portland Skyline. First opened in 1989 with a LEED Platinum renovation completed in 2019, the Oregon Convention Center is on the east side of the Willamette River in Portland's Lloyd Center neighborhood. Sho Dozono states that he worked with the president of Pacific Power to acquire the lights, which cost $75,000 and were made in Venice, and have them installed. On September 11, 2002, the twin spires were lit in observance of the first anniversary of the attacks. Photo: Anne Haugen on Unsplash.

name until 1845. Its naming story is famous and the penny whose flips gave the winner, Francis Pettygrove of Portland, Maine, naming rights, is now in the Oregon Historical Society. Its first "few dozen" English-speaking settlers arrived in 1846. During the 1850s, the city with the port that could welcome seafaring ships that was on the Willamette River and near the Columbia, surpassed Oregon City to become the largest city in Oregon, and it has stayed there ever since.

In 2010, Portland proper had a population of 583,776, with 2,226,009 in the seven-county metropolitan area, twenty-third largest metro area in the United States. Portland has the last remaining commission form of government among large cities in the United States, in which power is spread across six elected officials: four Commissioners, the Auditor, the Mayor, who all comprise the City Council. Interestingly, U.S. government policy toward Native Americans has contributed greatly to the ninth largest Native American population in the United States residing in Portland. Portland is known for its coffee, micro-breweries, rain, gardens (thanks to the rain), civic engagement, and quirkiness.[1]

MOUNT HOOD AND THE COLUMBIA RIVER GORGE

If you're within 100 miles of it, you can see Mount Hood. At 11,239 feet, Mount Hood is the highest mountain in the state—but it's actually a dormant volcano. This majestic natural edifice, which has eleven glaciers and is the second-most climbed mountain in the world, can be found in the Mount Hood National Forest only about twenty minutes from Portland. Mount Hood National Forest is bounded on the north by the Columbia River Gorge that separates the states of Oregon and Washington, and encompasses more than a million acres of forests, with lakes, streams, and eight designated wildernesses.

The Columbia River Gorge National Scenic Area is the nation's largest. It was established by Congress in 1986 to both preserve beauty and maintain a stable economy. The area extends eighty-five miles along both sides of the Columbia River, from the Sandy River to the Deschutes River and one to four miles inland. Its unique and representative management partnership includes the U.S. Forest Service; four Native American tribes; and the Columbia River Gorge Commission

Mount Hood. Photo: Jean Beaufort.

made up of representatives appointed by the governors of Oregon and Washington and the six counties it spans.[2] Oregon is fortunate that retired lumberman and hotelier Simon Benson purchased many scenic spots, including its most famous, Multnomah Falls, and donated them

The Columbia River Gorge. Photo: NPS/Dunbar.

to the state for preservation. Completed in 1922, the seventy-four-mile Historic Columbia River Highway is designated a National Historic Landmark, not because it was the first paved highway in the Pacific Northwest but because its design preserved the landscape while also making it accessible; nature took priority over economics in its construction. The National Park Service took the highway as a model for its "Lying Lightly on the Land" philosophy in developing parks and trails. Engineer and landscape architect Samuel C. Lancaster, who was the highway's primary designer, said that if built as planned, the highway "will rival if not surpass anything to be found in the civilized world."[3]

WILLAMETTE VALLEY

The Willamette Valley was home to at least twenty Native American tribes, including the Kayalupa, Molalla, and Chinook peoples for at least 14,000 years, where their culture was based on hunting, fishing, and gathering.[4] In the nineteenth century, it became the "land of milk and honey" that inspired "Oregon Fever" for many on the Oregon Trail, which led to the Willamette Valley being the most highly

Vineyards, Salem, Oregon. Photo by Dan Meyers on Unsplash

populated area in the state, aside from Portland. You'll find the state capital, Salem, here. With the coming of the Euro Americans, an agricultural economy based in rich soils, rainfall, and sunshine—yes, a modified Mediterranean climate in the growing season—that continues to this day. Willamette Valley farmers produce more than 170 fruit and vegetable crops and livestock products. It is the nation's top producer of hazelnuts, blackberries, boysenberries, and marionberries, which were developed there. Today, the region may be best known for its more than 500 wineries, and particularly its Pinot Noirs.[5]

EASTERN OREGON

Sparsely populated Eastern Oregon is fondly known as Oregon's Wild West. In the northeastern corner of the state is Pendleton, where for more than a century some of our nation's finest woolen products have been made and cowboys have been bucking broncs at the Pendleton Round-Up. Also near Pendleton, the Tamástslikt Cultural Institute on the Umatilla Indian Reservation is the only tribal-run museum devoted to the history and culture of Native Americans along the Oregon Trail. Bordering Southeastern Washington and Western Idaho Eastern Oregon is dry, and some places may receive only five inches of rain annually; the spectacular natural beauty of this region is of a completely different variety than that found west of the Cascades. This is the land of high deserts, rivers, the Blue Mountains, and the Wallowas. The Blue Mountains were the site of Oregon's Gold Rush and many of the region's ghost towns are remnants of mining's boom-and-bust cycle. With the coming of the railroad, Baker City became a major trading center by 1900, with a mix of miners, ranchers, cowboys, shepherds, gamblers, and dance hall girls that could be as explosive as what was used in the mines nearby.[6] [PHOTOS P. 10]

CENTRAL OREGON

Bordered by the Cascade Mountains and the Deschutes River to the west, Central Oregon has become one of the most popular centers of leisure and tourism in Oregon. It's Oregon and it's sunny! East side

John Day Valley Rock Formations, John Day Fossil Beds National Monument. Colorful rock formations at John Day Fossil Beds preserve a world class record of plant and animal evolution, changing climate, and past ecosystems that span over 40 million years. (See also note 6.) Photo: NP Photo.

The Painted Hills on a Stormy Day, John Day Fossil Beds National Monument. Located about nine miles northwest of Mitchell, Oregon, the Painted Hills are the most visited part of the National Monument. Affected by light and moisture levels, their appearance is ever-changing. A sequence of climate change is preserved in leaf fossils 30–39 million years old and animal fossils from 27–30 million years ago. Source: National Park Service, "Painted Hills," nps.gov, https://www.nps.gov/joda/planyourvisit/ptd-hills-unit.htm, last updated May 16, 2020. Photo: NPS Photo / Scott Ritner.

of the Cascades, you find are 300 days of sun and an arid, high-desert climate. Former lumber-town Bend, one of state's fastest-growing cities, is its center. Much of the story of this area is the transformation from lumber country to recreation country with other towns like Redmond, Prineville, and Sisters making the transition as well. Home to many resorts and second homes, Central Oregon offers opportunities for both winter and summer sports. Rivers and lakes offer paddling and fly fishing, with snowboarding and winter activities at resorts like Mt. Bachelor, where you can ski from November to May. The 1,800,000-acre Deschutes National Forest and the 850,000-acre Ochoco National Forest draw hikers and bikers. Central Oregon is also filled with caves and more than 500 lava tubes, the empty tunnels left behind when lava stopped flowing through them. With the transition to tourism, development for subdivisions, recreational activities, and luxury homes has boosted the demand and price of land in Central Oregon; farmers and ranchers who want to maintain agricultural production and stay on their land have turned to Oregon's renowned land-use planning laws to keep development at bay and maintain the affordability of local lands.[7]

Smith Rock. Many of the rocks and mountains are remnants of a volcanic past. Smith Rock State Park outside Redmond attracts rock climbers eager to navigate its 30 million-year-old formations. Photo: Oregon Parks and Recreation Department.

SOUTHERN OREGON

Eastern Oregon may call itself the "Wild West," but Southern Oregon, perhaps the state's most remote and isolated area until the early twentieth century, may deserve that title, too. Some of Oregon's most bloody nineteenth-century conflicts with Native tribes occurred here when Euro-Americans immigrants arrived. Seeing itself as sometimes neglected by the state's power centers, this region celebrates the independent spirit of its pioneer heritage, and in recent decades, the history of Native Americans (Klamath, Modoc, and Coquille), Latinos, and others has gained a more prominent place.

The Klamath, Siskiyou, and Southern Cascade mountains inform this region, as do the Rogue River and the mammoth Klamath Basin straddling the Oregon-California border, and the landscape encompasses high deserts and low, open valleys. Mining, logging, and irrigation agriculture were the region's first economic base.* The Rogue River Valley is still known as "pear country," and wineries and vineyards benefit from the sunny, mild climate.[8]

Ashland's Oregon Shakespeare Festival (OSF) has played a key role in economic renewal as timber and flour mills declined. Founded in 1935 using the walls of an abandoned Chautauqua theater, the Tony Award-winning OSF is among the nation's oldest and largest professional, non-profit theaters. Originally three days and two plays, the festival now draws 400,000 people in an eight-month season with up to eleven Shakespeare plays, plus classics, musicals, and contemporary plays, in seven performance spaces.[9]

---

*Please see the chapter "Water" for the conflicts over water in the Klamath Basin that have escalated throughout the past century.

Crater Lake in the Cascades is one of the most popular natural sites in Oregon. Native Americans witnessed the volcanic crater's formation 7,700 years ago, when a violent eruption more than forty times the size of Mount Saint Helens' in 1980 blew the top off Mount Mazama, which now cradles the lake. Known for its blue color, it's the deepest lake in the United States and one of the most pristine on earth. President Theodore Roosevelt created the Crater Lake National Park in 1902. Source: Stephen R. Mark, "Mount Mazama," *The Oregon Encyclopedia*, https://www. oregonencyclopedia.org/articles/mt_mazama/#.YLml30wpAc8, last updated March 17, 2018. Photo: Elisa Zercoe/National Park Service.

BY THE NUMBERS: OREGON AND NEW YORK

W e're living in a time that almost seems to worship numbers. "The numbers tell the story," we hear a lot. As if numbers are truth. When you compare Oregon—looking at the whole state because Freedom Fliers were from the entire state—with Manhattan, the only New York City borough they visited, you'll see just how different these two places are—on the surface. And then I'm going to tell you to pretty much throw the numbers away.

Two big differences: very few people per square mile in Oregon; and New York? How do they squeeze so many people into such a small space? The second thing that's very apparent is that Oregon is a lot whiter than Manhattan. That is, there are a lot more white people per capita in Oregon. A little more than half the people in New York City are white, but more than 85 percent of Oregon is lacking mela-tonin in a big way.

So how could these people possibly connect? And that's where we'll see that numbers don't tell the story—the connection is deeper than race or religion or color or politics or economic status or any other cat-egory. The Oregonians felt that they, too, as Americans, were bombed, and that's why they went. They knew they hadn't experienced what the New Yorkers experienced, but they cared because they're Americans, too. That's all. It's that simple. As you will discover in these pages, none of those categories mattered. The healing that took place and the connections that were made happened on a human level.

It's shared humanity, a story no numbers can ever tell.[1]

	Oregon	
Population—2000 Census	3,421,399	
Square miles	95,988.01	
Pop. per square mile	35.64	
Racial Composition		Percent
White	2,961,623	86.6
Black or African American	55,662	1.6
American Indian and Alaska Native	45,211	1.3
Asian	101,350	3.0
Asian Indian	9,575	0.3
Chinese	20,930	0.6
Filipino	10,627	0.3
Japanese	12,131	0.4
Korean	12,387	0.4
Vietnamese	18,890	0.6
Other Asian	16,810	0.5
Native Hawaiian and Other Pacific Islander	7,976	0.2
Hispanic or Latino	275,314	8.0
Mexican	214,662	6.3
Puerto Rican	5,092	0.1
Cuban	3,091	0.1
Other Hispanic or Latino	52,469	1.5
Some other race	144,832	4.2
Two or more races	104,745	3.1
Largest City	Portland—529,121	
Achieved statehood	1859	

Note: Numbers related to race may add to more than the total population and percentages may add to more than 100 percent because individuals may report more than one race.

	New York City (Manhattan only)	
Population—2000 Census	1,537,195	
Square miles	22.96	
Pop. per square mile	67,454.50	
Racial Composition		Percent
White	835,610	54.4
Black or African American	267,302	17.4
American Indian and Alaska Native	7,617	0.5
Asian	144,538	9.4
Asian Indian	14,620	1.0
Chinese	86,974	5.7
Filipino	8,654	0.6
Japanese	14,325	0.9
Korean	10,848	0.7
Vietnamese	1,370	0.5
Other Asian	7,737	0.5
Native Hawaiian and Other Pacific Islander	1,069	0.1
Hispanic or Latino	417,816	27.2
Mexican	30,391	2.0
Puerto Rican	119,718	7.8
Cuban	11,950	0.8
Other Hispanic or Latino	255,757	16.6
Some other race	217,383	14.1
Two or more races	63,676	4.1
Largest City	New York City– 8,008,278	
Achieved statehood	1788	

LISA SOKOLOFF: SURVIVING THE SEPTEMBER 11 ATTACKS

Lisa Sokoloff is my friend. We attended Vassar College together and by 2001 had lost touch in the twenty years since we'd graduated. Knowing she was in New York City, I contacted her after September 11 to see how she was doing and was astonished to hear that she was directly endangered by the attacks—and that she was living in the Waldorf-Astoria, where the Flight for Freedom participants were staying. The first night we arrived, Lisa came down to the lobby and met us and told her story. Even now, twenty years later, she says it was "cathartic" and enormously important that these people from Oregon listened.

"It was like they were witnesses," she says.

Lisa told me, in 2021, as I was preparing this book, that at the time, it was all about the people in the planes, and I would add also that it was about the first responders. These are my words, but my sense is that the other people who were affected were overlooked, perhaps because so much was happening and their losses were not as final. Of course, that's understandable. But the pain was there, the trauma was real, the damage had been done.

What Lisa told me was a surprise. Because after speaking with 70–80 Freedom Fliers, that was something I had never heard. No Freedom Flier ever said that what the New Yorkers told them, the hugs they needed, were not important or were not merited. What Lisa told me has only served to make me understand how important the role the Freedom Fliers played, listening to those who maybe had not been considered at that time of chaos and overwhelm.

Lisa was generous enough to recount her story here so readers can understand what it meant to live through the attacks and the emotional situation the people from Oregon walked into. And after the Freedom Fliers arrived and understood why they were there, instead of rejecting the trauma and grief and sadness that surrounded them, they immersed themselves in the opportunity to be of service and comfort.

As Mary Platt of Portland said after hearing Lisa's story, "That's what we came for."

I include a short narrative of Lisa's professional accomplishments below so you can understand, too, what it meant for people to move on with their lives. As you read her September 11 story, knowing what she has achieved in the twenty years since the attacks, be inspired by Lisa herself and by the strength that lies in each one of us. Despite the trauma of September 11, Lisa fulfilled her dream of being elected a New York County Civil Court Judge. She was married in 2013 and she and her husband live in Manhattan.

Lisa Sokoloff is an Acting Supreme Court Justice in New York County. She serves on the New York Women's Bar Association Elder Law Committee Committees. She is a co-chair of the annual Martha E. Gifford Summer Program entitled, "What It's (Really) Like to Practice Law as a Woman." She is co-chair of the Women's Bar Association of the State of New York (WBASNY) women judges committee. Justice Sokoloff is currently a member of the New York Supreme Court gender fairness committee and a former co-chair of the gender fairness committees of the Manhattan Civil and Criminal Courts. She is also a past President of the Jewish Lawyers Guild and the New York Women's Bar Association, and a past officer and current Advisory Board member of Judges & Lawyers Breast Cancer Alert (JALBCA).

Before being elected to the bench, Lisa practiced law for twenty-eight years, all but one of them in New York City. Justice

Sokoloff earned a J.D. from Boston University School of Law, where she was an editor of the *International Law Journal*.

This is her story of escaping Battery Park City and the attacks:

In September 2001, I was employed by an insurance defense law firm. I wrote most of the significant dispositive memos of laws and appeals, motions for summary judgment, and appellate briefs. The day before the 11th, I was researching and writing a memo of law for one of the senior partners who was trying the case [in legal terms, who was "on trial"]. I had come close and finally, sort of late in the evening—7:00, 8:00, 9:00—I finally found the cases that I needed in order to advocate for the position that he wanted. I did not finish the memo, which I always regretted, and I left to go home, thinking that I would come back in the morning and just finish it up.

I woke up the next morning and I felt like I had a little bit of a migraine; my head hurt, and I think that I was woken up by the first plane hitting, but I didn't realize it. I got into the shower and washed my hair and showered. I had gotten out and was toweling off when the second plane hit.

I knew immediately that it was something sonic. I could feel the pressure of it. And then almost instantaneously I heard screaming and I ran to my windows, which faced north in Gateway Plaza and I could see people running from right to left towards the cove, the marina just north of Gateway.

And there were all these people running, they looked like little mice running and they were screaming. And I could see to my right that one or both of the towers were on fire and smoke was billowing. Some of my view was obstructed by the smoke. I then tried to get my television on and they said that they were small planes that had hit. And because they didn't say jetliners or anything like that, I didn't think it was going to be such a big deal.

My sister in California called me and I was surprised she was up because it was three hours earlier and she generally is not an early morning person. She was like, "Get out."

Then I spoke to my mother, who didn't say that much; I don't think people comprehended the danger. I started getting dressed to get out of there. I poked my head out to the hallway, and most people said they were staying; some were saying they were going. I put on some black leggings and a big, orange T-shirt, my favorite from the Sonoma Mission Inn, and I tried to blow my hair, but the circuit breaker flipped and I couldn't get my hair dryer to work.

I said, "This must be a sign from God. I should get out of here."

I stupidly did not turn off my air conditioners, I didn't take my medicine with me. There are a lot of stupid things I did. I did have my ID and my bank card and a few things like that. I had a cell phone at that point. And then I made my second stupid mistake, which is that I took the elevator down.

I'm the niece of engineers and, in fact, my uncle on my father's side was one of the engineers that built the Bathtub for the World Trade Center. The Bathtub is a cement structure that keeps the river from flooding the towers and making them unstable. And in fact, it was the only part of the Trade Center that did not collapse. He told me that where I lived was built on landfill that they had taken out in order to build the Trade Center. He slept over there and I thought, if it's good enough for him to spend the night—he and my aunt stayed with me at least once—then it's OK.

But I know better than to get into an elevator in an emergency because the power can go off and you can get trapped. And when I got downstairs I saw my doorman. And he was like, "Oh, Lisa, I didn't realize you were upstairs. They told us to clear."

Nobody came around and knocked on our doors. And I knew that some of my neighbors were still upstairs.

One of my friends had been raised in Israel, and was part of the Israeli defense forces and he knew about a wheelchair-bound person on the twenty-eighth floor and he carried her down—there were only emergency lights in the stairwell, but they were very dark. He took her down the whole twenty-eight floors. One of our friends, it was days before he was rescued. The building did not go door to door and tell people to get out and to get them out.

The doorman said, "Go stand in the courtyard," which is this pretty, landscaped area with some little walkways between six buildings. And we literally faced the World Trade Center, a half a block away.

We could see people jumping from the towers. It was horribly upsetting. You would see the ties of men flying up and hitting them in the face on the way down. Some people held hands as they jumped.

Little did I know that I knew people who were on the top floor because there was a conference going on in one of the restaurants.

Maybe Windows on the World, but it may have been a different event space.

And I knew it was dangerous to be out there. I had the key to my synagogue, which was on the first floor of another building, and so I told people, "Get out of here, it isn't safe. You can come with me, I'm going to open up this space. You can stay in there." And a lot of people did come with me.

We went in and people said, "Turn on the TV so we can see what's going on."

They asked, "Can I use the hardline to get in touch with my mother?" And of course I said yes.

We were not there a couple minutes when we heard a rumbling preceded by this sound. It sounded like kachunk-kachuk-kachunk-kachunk. And each kachunk got faster. And that was the floors collapsing when the first building went down.

And as that happened, the ground under us undulated. You couldn't see it moving, but it felt like the earth had like a tidal wave under it and it was very frightening and our fight-or-flight instinct kicked in and we all ran. I did not lock or I'm not even sure if I closed the door to the synagogue, which I had tremendous guilt about because the synagogue's two Torahs were in there and if something happens to them, it's very terrible and I didn't want to be the person who brought that about.

And we ran out of the door to a courtyard on the other side of the building, the other grassy area that led into a restaurant, I think it was called "Steamers," and that restaurant was on the walkway that leads from the top of Battery Park City down to the bottom.

When we got onto the walkway, we were overcome by the cloud. Although on TV it looked white and it was white on our clothing, when you were in it, it was black. I couldn't even see the tip of my nose. I couldn't see my fingers held up to my face so I closed my eyes and people were running into me. I opened my eyes a couple of times to check, and I didn't want to move until it had lifted enough.

When it did, first I pulled my T-shirt over my nose, exposing my stomach and the bottom half of my breast and later I got smart enough to pull it up by the neckline to cover my nose and my mouth. But what we saw were people climbing over the railing to the water to a boat. Those railings were specially designed to prevent people from jumping because they didn't want people to commit suicide by going over them. So they were incredibly hard to climb over.

Originally, I thought it was a construction boat because they had been doing work on the underside of the pilings that held up the walkway. But in fact it was a fireboat and the firemen were screaming, "Women and children only!"

The first time I got the ladder to climb down someone literally ripped it out of my hands. I couldn't blame them because I understood.

We all thought we were going to die.

We didn't know what had happened, if more planes were coming back, we had no clue. If there were bombs, we didn't know. All we knew is that the buildings we lived in could collapse and we were scared.

I got the ladder on the second try. It was actually a straight wooden ladder. I guess that these officers used them in certain types of rescues, but it wasn't even tall enough to go to the area of the railing that we were hanging onto. So it was very precarious getting on it. And as soon as I started climbing on it, somebody else pulled it over so they could be next and slammed me onto the concrete of the walkway.

So I was hurt, I was scared, I was climbing down this thing and this amazing fireman, God bless him, was able to get me and bring me down to the boat. I'm not going to tell you how big I was, but I was big. I know they have to carry [things] over their shoulders, but I don't think they expect to have to lift with their arms outstretched, but that's basically what he was doing.

I tried to get in the inside of the boat to get as much cover from the stuff that was coming down from the air and what was going on. I saw a man in the boat who was screaming whose leg had been broken in several places. You could see the bone coming out of the calf.

I saw one of my neighbors. I later found out his wife was away. He has his infant daughter strapped to his chest and they were telling him, "Walk down to the bottom of the park and there will be boats there." But he wasn't taking a chance with his infant daughter. He threw his dog into the boat and he jumped 25 feet. Amazingly, neither he nor his infant daughter was hurt. I saw him once [after that], in Hoboken—or it could have been Jersey City—and talked to him for a few minutes and that was it. I also saw a woman that

I knew named Jan, and that was it; I didn't know any of the other people in the boat.

There was a ferry terminal, not exactly directly across, but fairly directly across in Jersey City—and halfway there, they find out that the boat we were in was too deep for the ferry terminal and they had to turn our boat around to go to the pier in front of the Colgate clock tower.

So they turned the boat around and as they did it, we all saw the second building go down. We were screaming. It was unbelievable that those towers could come down. It was just surreal.

We were pretty far away at that point. We were more than halfway across the Hudson. I didn't hear anything. You saw it go down and it was, one minute it's there and the next it's not. There's a plume of smoke. That had to have been the second building because the first came down when we were evacuating.

So they had to use wire cutters and cut the wire around the pier to get us off the boat and onto the pier. And then the side of the boat was very high and I'm very short. And my legs are short. And I could not on my own get off the boat and onto the pier and some very nice fireman literally held me up so I could get off.

And as we were walking off the pier, I suddenly doubled over and threw up some of the stuff I had inhaled or breathed in or whatever, I don't know. People were taking pictures of us. I said, "Stop, that's not right. This is the worst day of our lives."

But of course everybody thinks that they're a newsperson and they didn't stop. There was a bus there and they offered to take us to a convention center and I said, "No, I'm injured. I really need to go to a hospital."

They said, "No, we're not going to have [medical attention] there. You walk up this way, there's a hospital about a mile away, the Jersey City Medical Center."

So I started walking and I was all by myself and most people, their phones didn't work because a lot of the cell phone towers had gone down on top of the Trade Center. A couple people invited me into their homes, but being by myself I did not want to go.

And at one point I saw a young man speaking in Spanish and I said, "Do you have reception?" And he said, "I do." I asked him who he's speaking with and he said his father.

I said, "It's very important. I just came from the Trade Center and it's very important that I get in touch with my family so they don't think I'm dead. Would you write down a couple of numbers and say a few words to them?"

I had them call my mother, my father, and my office. At that point, my office had already shut down and everybody had left except one friend of mine who was waiting to hear what was going on. But I didn't give him her extension and the central number was just taking voice messages so she never heard that I was OK and she had to walk all the way back to Brooklyn. My father was just very, very upset. He just cried. But I was so grateful to that man and his father who did that for me because at least my family knew I was OK. I told him to say, "Lisa's alive and in Jersey City and going to the hospital."

So I started walking. Traffic was not moving that fast and I was exhausted. And I literally talked my way into two cars to help me, to take me to the hospital. These people were so nice because I was completely covered in fiberglass. I looked like a fuzzy white person, with little streams coming out of my face, my arms, but mostly my face. They graciously took me in . . . .

But eventually I had to get out because they were blocking the way [road] to the hospital. [She kept walking to get to the hospital.]

There's a long line outside. A person with a broken leg, a very pregnant woman, and I'm thinking to myself, "Oh my God, I'm never going to get seen."

I knock. They say, "I'm sorry, we're closed for an emergency."

I said, "I just came from the World Trade Center."

They literally pulled me inside and started working on me immediately, flushing out all the stuff on my skin, all the stuff in my eyes. They were amazing. And they asked me for the names of people who I was looking for, and I [told the names of some of my friends from my building].

They came back to me and said that [my friends] were not in the hospital. As they'd done as much for me as they could, they put me in a room with reporters and I didn't want to speak. It was just terribly unfair.

There was a man in the emergency room and he was on his stomach and he had a gigantic flaming pattern of an "I" on his back and it was from an I-beam that obviously had fallen on him. I cannot imagine what happened to him and the incredible scar that he probably bears from that. He is likely a fireman, but I don't know.

Eventually, we were taken up to the doctors' lounge and we stayed there for a while. We went out on a patio and tried to get a cell signal and we couldn't. But they let us into the doctors' library and we all got on computers and wrote to the people we knew and loved. I got in touch with one of my friends.

Eventually, of course, we wanted to get out of there. I think they gave me a top of a doctor's uniform and I don't remember what I had on my legs.

I was in touch with my father and stepmother, who lived in Mahwah, New Jersey, twenty-five to thirty minutes away on a good day. They were going to try to come down and pick me up, but a lot of the roadways were closed. At that time we didn't know it, but there was a threat of a truck with a bomb, and they were closing the tunnel and bridges. Eventually, I found out that there was someone in the Accounting Department of the hospital who lived a town or two away from my father and stepmother. I begged my stepmother to get me some clean underwear and a T-shirt to sleep in and a couple of little things. And that twenty-five to thirty-minute ride took us hours because we were stopped along the way.

I'm not sure that man from Accounting would have gotten home without me—he said, "She was at the Trade Center. I'm taking her home." Everybody could see the pockmarks from the fiberglass strands and they let us go.

I got there and my father had a small, two-bedroom apartment, my half-brother slept in the second bedroom and they put me in the storage room in the back. Their dog stayed with me the whole time. My stepmother had just been diagnosed with breast cancer, but they didn't tell us. Things were very tense there and I could tell and I had to get out. Plus, my father, he watched every bit of news coverage about everything. He's a softie like me he just bawled like a baby. So one day a friend who lived nearby picked me up and took me to a shopping center either in Jersey City or Spring Valley or someplace nearby and I bought a few things.

Somebody gave me a tiny little roller [suit]case, it looked like a kid's case. It was weird for me because when you see people shopping and there's no respect for what's happened. These people were happy and just being themselves and it was hard to see, for me it was very hard to see. And so at some point one of my father and stepmother's friends was going to Connecticut, I think to Stamford, and agreed to give me a lift so I could stay with my mother.

She was almost in denial: "I have some work to do, I have a closing," she said. [She was a realtor.] It wasn't like her. It was such a weird response for a parent—I think she couldn't handle it. I desperately needed to be able to talk about my experiences. My mother and I were so close and she was so loving and caring about me, and she was just treating it like, "You're here a couple days, no big deal."

And I ended up going over to visit my mother's best friend's children just so I had someone to talk to. That was very healing for me. And I desperately needed to be able to talk because it was a harrowing escape. We didn't know if we were going to make it. We really weren't in that much danger, but it didn't feel like it when we were going through it. And there were still people from my community who were listed as missing and nobody knew where they were. And I felt really alone and she wasn't really there.

The whole thing happened right around Rosh Hashanah and I really wanted to go to synagogue. One of my mother's best friends, oldest friends, was able to secure a ticket for me. They brought me over to their house and she and her husband took me to synagogue because my mother never went, didn't believe in it. It was weird because I was used to having a special meal to celebrate it.

And I do remember, at some point there were people in my community, Battery Park City, who were getting hotel rooms because you still couldn't be where we lived. There was someone in our community who worked for the hotel chain that included the Waldorf. All these well-heeled, big white-shoe firms had rented out most of the rooms for their employees, but my synagogue got me a room. When they said they got me a room, about ten days after the attacks, I got on a train and got right in.

It was not fancy, not what you'd think of when you hear "the Waldorf-Astoria." I'm not even sure I was able to secure a microwave, but it had a mini-kitchen with a tiny little refrigerator off this one room; it was literally just a bed and dresser and television. All the rooms in the city were the same price. It didn't matter if you were at the DoubleTree Inn or the Waldorf. It was $100 a night.

I felt a lot safer, but when I heard the subways or the trains run underneath Park Avenue, they reminded me of the way the ground felt when the buildings were collapsing and it would just trigger an emotional response for me. Plus, I don't know why, I was watching that Tom Hanks movie *Band of Brothers* [World War II series], so I just emotionally was a basket case.

And of course I had to buy all my meals. At that point, they didn't have a microwave for me. So whatever I could get [had to be] premade. I didn't even have forks and spoons and things like that. It was really weird. It was a weird time.

I had excellent insurance, Chubb, that paid for it. For a long time they paid. I stayed there because it was a block or two blocks from my office at the time, 570 Lexington Ave.

I wasn't making money. My job was "of counsel" so I only got paid when I worked. I was sort of an hourly employee and things were very difficult. I applied for assistance and the Red Cross asked me what my annual salary was, and I said it's approximately "X." They said, "You make too much money, we can't help you."

Meanwhile, they were helping plenty of people in Battery Park City [which had certain income requirements to live there]. The rents were so high that no one could pay them if they [earned] the cutoff that the Red Cross set. I applied to Safe Horizon* and they did give me money once or twice, and it was a lifesaver for me.

I had to rebuild my wardrobe to go to work. I got one visit for fifteen minutes and then I didn't get another visit until the whole complex was opened up. It was a tough time.

I have to say, even when I got back to work, I couldn't work. I would sit at my desk and I couldn't concentrate. It was months before I could even eke out a little work because I was so traumatized. I had PTSD. I saw a counselor. I kept dreaming that me, and one of my best friends who had been in World Trade Center 5 at the time, that we were trapped in a burning building and we were trying to find our way out.

A few months later, I was supposed to become the president of the Jewish Lawyers Guild. We decided to have the event even though all of this terribleness had just occurred. I'm not sure why we did.

---

*Safe Horizon is a victim assistance organization, operating a network of programs across New York City communities and systems. Safe Horizon works with survivors of all forms of violence, including racism, to "move from crisis to confidence." After September 11, through partnerships with the September 11th Fund, the 9/11 United Services Group, and Project Liberty, Safe Horizon acted as a conduit, distributing funds and emergency services.

I'm sure I was included in the decision since I'm the incoming president, I honestly don't remember any of the discussion, but it was a big thing for me. I felt incredibly proud to have been elected to that post, to lead a big, august group of lawyers.

And I asked my parents if they would come and my father said, "No." He said he would not cross a bridge or go through a tunnel. The only time he did was to see his dying uncle who he considered like an older brother because when he was a child his parents had taken this uncle in.

But my mother took a train in, stayed with me at the Waldorf overnight and came. And it was pretty amazing. I think it was late October.

After about sixty days they said we could go back [to Battery Park City]. I don't remember exactly, but I didn't feel it was safe. I worked with a lot of our clients' construction firms; they said, "If you were my daughter, I wouldn't go back [unless] this was done, that was done." Cleaning out vent shafts [was one thing they said should be done]. The fiberglass that you didn't want to inhale [could still be] brought up and down by vents in the building. Nobody involved in the cleanup could say that [the vents had been cleaned].

They had cleaned out my apartment. I mean that literally and figuratively. They took a lot of stuff from me. At one point, we were allowed to go in and I found my jewelry box and some photographs and I took it. But a couple years before, I had gone to Italy. They took my leather jacket. Somebody [had given] . . . me an amazing magnum of champagne. Worth $250 probably. I had these brand new beautiful cotton knit sheets and pillowcases. They took them or they cut them up and used them to clean. They didn't take my dirty old towels that I'd used for ten years. They took the finest things I had.

All my plants had died and I really felt like [that was] a second insult. And I didn't want to go back to that apartment.

Also, one of the days when I was let in so I could collect some stuff, my phone rings. My house line, it was my house line. It was Macy's with a collection call with something I bought a few days after so I'd have something to wear. I said, "Do you understand where you're calling? I'm right next to Ground Zero. We don't have access to our mail, I haven't gotten any mail in months. When I did get mail, it was covered in the stuff you're not supposed to touch so I threw it out."

I was so offended by them, but I did pay it off, and of course I was going to. I cut up my Macy's credit card and I think maybe since then I have shopped there two or three times, period.

The temperature in the area was boiling hot [the 11th]. It was outrageously hot because there were all these fires and they were literally across the highway from us. One of my friends . . . was at home with her children. Her husband was at work and she, like me, had just gotten out of the shower. Her windows blew in because they face the Trade Center. She was lucky that none of them got seriously hurt.

I had a very close friend. She worked in No. 5 World Trade Center. She was smart enough to get out of there. She lost everything in her office, she had thirty pairs of shoes, and things like that. Maybe a week later, some period later—she was estranged from her sister and her sister's family, [and] they called her husband to see if she was alive. Not because they were interested in whether she was alive, but because they wanted her things. I found it to be an interesting—like when she told me that story, I was pretty appalled.

Very luckily the husband of one of my best friends, his mother had an apartment in Riverdale [the Bronx] and she only came up for the summer. The rest of the time she lived in Florida. She was a snowbird and they said, "You can have the apartment until she comes back."

. . .

Another close friend rented or borrowed a car and they helped me get my little, tiny bit of stuff and that's where I stayed until she came back. I paid for my apartment until my lease was over, but I never lived there again. They charged me for service in some certain things when we couldn't even live there. But that's over.

I took the things I felt had survived, others I didn't, like my grandmother's old feather chair. The feather stuffing had to go—the chair had to go. I eventually bought new furniture. And I did come back to Manhattan in 2003.

I went to live on the Upper East Side for a while, that's where the least expensive apartments were. I went to a building that was run by the same landlord that owned a building I lived in in Riverdale . . . .

I always think of that as this incredible gift [that I saw you and] I was able to tell my story. It was very cathartic. I went through—I had a great counselor, a wonderful counselor who I got through some survivors' organization. I think she was an art counselor and so we connected on that level. She was wonderful and very helpful, but still . . .

You don't ever lose this. You go through certain horrible traumas. I remember finding out when President Kennedy was shot. I was five years old, I can recount that day like it was yesterday but it's not the same. I don't have nightmares about it.

But seeing you was so wonderful and hearing that people came [from Oregon], to support us was so wonderful. Particularly after I had seen people just going on with their lives and doing nothing. To see people who dropped everything to be here and to support all the people whose livelihoods were in danger, it was wonderful . . .

I will never forget the Oregonians. I got to meet and speak to a whole bunch of them down in the lobby of the Waldorf and they were all lovely and supportive . . .

It was like they were witnesses.

It's remarkable that people were interested in what happened to me. [At the time, attention was paid to] . . . mostly what happened to people who died on the plane. And of course, that's 100 times more important, but it was very cathartic for me. It was extremely cathartic. To have people interested, because I wanted to talk about my experience, to get it out of me, so I could not think about it or talk about it again.

THE FLIGHT FOR FREEDOM

We were doing something significant because we were bringing people back to work again. Time and again, people at the Waldorf said, "I wouldn't be working right now if you weren't here." I felt like a pioneer with bringing tourism back to New York.

—Sandra Kempel, Freedom Flier

AN IDEA BECOMES REALITY

> " We were a small place that everybody discounts. We're just everyman. We're not California that's got lots of money, we're not Seattle high-tech people, we're just folks, and I felt that that was the right message to be sending, and that we ought to be the first ones, to hopefully get others to follow in our footsteps and do the same thing. —*Loen Dozono*

TUESDAY, SEPTEMBER 11, 2001

The weather in Brussels was relentless. Downpour after downpour. After downpour. The weather seemed to echo the economic downturn that had caused most major airlines to cut flights.[1] In Brussels, travel agency execs were being wined and dined at the annual AAA Travel Conference. The travel-agency sector had already started a decline that would accelerate enormously as internet-based reservations companies came to the fore in the following two decades.

Sho and Loen Dozono, owners of Portland-based Azumano Travel, one of Oregon's largest travel agencies, were among the group. Sho had grown his father-in-law's business to 250 employees and $150 million in annual sales, and was chair of the 1,700-member Greater Portland Chamber of Commerce, the first minority person to hold that position.[2] In Portland in 2001, the Dozonos were movers-and-shakers, known for combining business acumen and devotion to social causes.

The name "Azumano" was well-known in Oregon and held in high esteem; Loen's father, Portland native George Azumano, had lost everything in the incarceration of Japanese Americans during World War II and had come back to become a trusted adviser to governors and a pillar of the Japanese/Japanese-American community. Azumano Travel was an institution. As Sho tells it, when he entered the business, many travel agencies employed the wives of professionals who wanted to work part-time, liked to travel, and did not see travel as a career but as a short-term job.

The Azumano agency was not necessarily one of those; its four employees catered to the Japanese-American community and so it had experts in that field. But the soft-spoken and iron-willed Sho—don't mistake "soft-spoken" for shy and retiring—had ambitions for the company, to grow it beyond that category. He expanded the employee base to people who wanted to make travel their career. In turn, they brought their experience to serving customers. This enabled Azumano Travel to handle sophisticated needs, including for government and business travel. He also was the first, he says, to put travel agency offices in Portland high-rises, potentially 2,000 customers in a building. Convenience and easy access to travel experts spurred the growth of the business. Over the year, the Azumano Travel staff became known for their service to lone vacation travelers, as well as to corporate and government contracts, and large groups for leisure travel.

In the travel business, says Sho, you have to get it 100 percent right. A wrong date, airport, hotel destroys an entire trip. It was that standard that the staff at Azumano Travel lived by. Azumano staff were known for getting things right.

Earlier that day at the AAA trade show, Sho and Loen had worked in the Pacific Gateway display, which was the reason they had participated in the trip. Then they'd spent a rainy afternoon at the Château de la Hulpe (Solvay Castle) where they drank champagne and Belgian coffee, ate Belgian chocolates, toured the chateau, and visited the nearby Fondation Folon, a museum created by artist Jean-Michel Folon to display his paintings, prints, and sculptures.

"We hurriedly scramble back into the buses, a feeling of trying to cram in as much luxury as we can during an hour or so's time," Loen wrote in her journal. But as soon as the doors were closed "and as the bus pulls away, a[n] AAA spokesman begins with, 'Well, I guess we just can't keep it from you, we have to tell you what's happening.'"[3]

An hour and a half before, the World Trade Center and the Pentagon had been attacked. Brussels is six hours ahead of the East Coast of the U.S., and nine hours ahead of Portland on the West Coast. Loen recorded the moment in her journal:

> It takes a while to understand the gravity of what he's saying. Several women next to us begin panicking, reacting in terror with the realization of a relative who works there. We begin to try to let our minds sort things out, to think through our situation of being an outside spectator to the horror, with our isolation in a foreign country, why is this happening, who is it, how will we get home?

They would later learn that within twenty minutes of the first attack, the Federal Aviation Administration banned airplanes in the United States from taking off. Twenty minutes after that, all aircraft in U.S. airspace were grounded. And forty-five minutes after that, all transatlantic flights into the U.S. were diverted to Canada. No word on when air travel could begin again.

"As we re-enter the hotel," Loen wrote, "the staff behind the front desk are all observing us with shocked but sympathetic eyes. We go to our room to watch CNN and try to deal with the magnitude of what has happened."

In 2001, communication was very different than it is now, twenty years later. While the internet was by then an essential part of many people's lives, particularly via websites and email, it was not where people got their breaking news. Many people used cell phones, but making international calls was difficult with most cellular networks. Pagers, or "beepers," which received calls and alerted the owners to call back, were in wide use. Fax machines, which used phone lines to transmit documents, were in wide use to provide instant information. And the broad use of social media was not yet a thing, although the first groups on the internet were active conversation spots for cutting-edge techies.

The Dozonos could not get through to Portland. Their right-hand man, Bill Harmon, was in Canada and they could not reach him.

Back in Portland, Assistant Vice President Jeri Hunt was notifying Azumano employees at headquarters and branches about how to handle the calls that were beginning to come in from "distraught clients,"[4] and distributed a memo that went out to corporate accounts. "We have been able to confirm that there were NO Azumano or Azumano/Away passengers on any of the four flights (United 175, United 93, American 11 and American 77) which were confirmed as having crashed today." They were also "responding to calls from stranded passengers, doing our best to assist with reaccommodation of car and hotel reservations as needed." In addition, they had identified those with scheduled flights so they would be prepared to process refunds, exchanges, rescheduling, and other actions that would be required.[5]

In Brussels, the Dozonos ended up jury-rigging a system of using a wireless keyboard that enabled email through the television set in their hotel room; this allowed them to get into Sho's Azumano email account and send an email to the office, and one to their son.

Sho immediately realized that the family business was in jeopardy. On returning to the hotel, he devised a five-day plan that would be in place until he returned on Sunday. He requested voluntary furloughs of his employees to help the company stay afloat, asked all nonessential employees to leave the payroll for five days, and stopped certain checks from going out. Seventy-eight people departed voluntarily.

In a memo that went out to their employees the following day, he also wrote, "I must prepare you for the inevitability and imminence of a substantial reduction in staff. This is not a step I take lightly nor without a heavy heart . . . . This news is not pleasant to deliver, but I know it is much more difficult to receive."[6]

"I had $150,000 worth of checks going out, I said, don't let them go out," said Sho, who would develop a more detailed plan on the plane back to Portland. Later that evening, he was able to get through to the office by phone and convey the plan to his employees. He and Loen were also able to reach family. They watched the attacks "in horror, over and over and over," said Loen, as did Americans back home and others around the world.

Overwhelmingly, in 2001 people learned what was happening in New York and Washington by planting themselves in front of the TV. In Brussels, the hotel's large conference area was turned into a CNN-watching space, and buffets and briefings for participants were held there. All the planned conference events were canceled. Not only did attendees have to figure out how to get home and what they would do next, but the hotel needed to let travelers who had planned to stay there in the coming days know that the current guests would be filling the rooms. For the next forty-eight hours, AAA would provide buffets and briefings to the stranded Americans. That first night a primary theme was reassurance that the travelers would have help to get home. The hotel also provided an access code so that they could call home from their rooms. It was a "lifeline to home," Loen wrote.

WEDNESDAY, SEPTEMBER 12

September 12 was the day the Dozonos began the journey that birthed the Flight for Freedom. Being abroad when this happened was significant, Loen said. "That we were out of the country, it gave us a different kind of perspective of what was happening."

This day was also the beginning of a series of synchronicities that would occur throughout the Flight for Freedom journey, up until the final All-Oregon Reception at the Waldorf-Astoria on October 8. "There are so many things that I felt like we were in the right place at the right time to hear," Loen said.

That morning *Le Monde*'s front-page headline read, "Nous Sommes Tous Américains" ("We are all Americans").

While it may not have had a direct impact on their thinking, that the Dozonos were at the headquarters of the European Union and the North American Treaty Organization (NATO), cannot have helped but to shape the atmosphere. Both organizations met in special session under flags flying at half mast, to chart their responses to the attacks. The Dozonos had a front-row seat to the world coming together in support of the United States.

The evening of September 11, the North Atlantic Council, NATO's principal political decision-making body, met in special session and released an official statement, which stated, in part:

> At this critical moment, the United States can rely on its 18 Allies in North America and Europe for assistance and support. NATO solidarity remains the essence of our Alliance. Our message to the people of the United States is that we are with you. Our message to those who perpetrated these unspeakable crimes is equally clear: you will not get away with it.[7]

The next evening, September 12, NATO's Atlantic Council made history by invoking for the first time Article 5 of the Washington Treaty of 1949, which states that an act of war against one member is an attack against all and commits the members to responding with force, if necessary. Almost equally notable, perhaps, was the organization's statement that it considered an act of terrorism equal to an act of war.[8]

The Council of the European Union also expressed solidarity with the people of the United States and extended their sympathy. The foreign ministers declared that Friday would be a day of mourning in all fifteen member nations and asked that all Europeans observe three minutes of silence on at noon Brussels time (6 a.m. U.S. Eastern Daylight Time).

In an exceptional move, NATO Secretary General Lord Robertson attended the meeting. "We have to stand together," he said. "We are two organizations that speak with one voice, one strong voice, that will not stand for terrorism."[9]

This stand of solidarity with the United States was a change in world attitude toward the U.S., in fact. Anti-American sentiment had been on the rise, especially since the Bush administration had taken office in January. Issues of contention were the death penalty, the environment, American plans for a missile defense shield, genetically modified food, and the extent of American cultural and economic power.

"I truly believe this will drive the U.S. and E.U. together," Richard Morningstar, the departing American ambassador to the European Union, said in Brussels. "The key issues on which we demonstrate our common values will take precedence over what I think we can all agree today are some of the lesser issues on which we have been concentrating in the last couple of years."[10]

It was an extraordinary moment of universal goodwill, an opportunity that the U.S. government could choose to leverage for good.

World air travel was in chaos. Armed police patrols could be found in airports around the world. Were the U.S. hijackings just the beginning of a worldwide epidemic? The shutdown of flights to the United States—500 westbound Atlantic crossings each day, each flight carrying about forty passengers[11]—had a ripple effect. Stranded and diverted travelers were everywhere.

- Many flights to the Middle East from Europe and Canada had been canceled. In Canada, where more than 100 transatlantic flights had been rerouted, 30,000 people were being housed and fed, often by townspeople in their own homes.
- Mexico City had received about forty diverted flights, mostly from South America to the United States.
- One of Asia's busiest hubs, Hong Kong's international airport, had canceled all flights to the U.S., as had China and Taiwan.
- Tokyo's Narita International Airport said a combined 170 flights—both arrivals and departures—were expected to be canceled.
- In Brussels where Sho and Loen were, commercial flights over the city had been banned.

When air travel to the United States would begin again was unknown, although New York's Mayor Rudolph Giuliani had said late Tuesday night that he had heard perhaps around 2 p.m. on Wednesday.

That day, conference organizers offered tours for participants, but the Dozonos declined. Numb, and needing a break from the barrage of televised tragedy, they began their morning with a walk to the Grand Place de Bruxelles, considered one of the most beautiful squares in Europe, which had been named a UNESCO World Heritage Site just three years before. The cobblestone plaza is surrounded by mostly seventeenth-century government and commercial buildings on a site that had been important to the city's political and economic life for nearly a thousand years.

Without warning, a parade of about twenty-five elderly veterans and widows crossed the square. The Dozonos surmised they were World War I soldiers wearing the hats of their old companies and marching behind their flags. Their dignity of bearing despite the infirmities of age inspired and moved Loen greatly. "They survived all that, and here they are. . . . It's that struggle, and people go on." Tragedy, loss, recovery, continuity.

As they continued their walk, they walked through a large cathedral on a hill. "I had the feeling we ought to do this today, that it is appropriate to be in a place of worship," Loen wrote.

They made a point of stopping at a well-known chocolate shop they'd learned about "to have some *omiyage*," in the Japanese custom,

a gift or souvenir (often edible) to give friends and family after returning home from a trip.

Much of the rest of the day was spent with CNN and emailing,
and wondering when they could return to Portland. At a comfort-food
dinner of hamburgers and milkshakes at the hotel—"the best hamburgers I've had in such a long time," wrote Loen, they learned of a
prayer vigil at a nearby Anglican church. A little before 8 p.m. they
and a few others "slipped out" to attend.

The candlelit chapel was a counterpoint to the televised river of
images of death. Loen:

> There are just a few people inside, but we are warmly greeted with hand-
> shakes and smiles. The service is simple, an organist, two ministers, two
> hymns ("Oh God, Our Hope in Ages Past" and "The Lord is My Shepherd"),
> two periods of silence, a time of sharing, which was so special. Each volun-
> tary speaker offered a different perspective.

There they gained a glimmer of equanimity and to her great
astonishment, Loen found herself led to a place of inner peace by one
of the speakers.

> The first man was one who had greeted us at the door with a firm handshake
> and welcome. He spoke of this time when outstretching hands, people
> reaching out to others, is important. He had lost a relative in one of the ter-
> rorist plane crashes a few years ago . . . .
>
> Another woman . . . spoke almost joyously as she said it was a day of "cross-
> ing over" for thousands of souls who had died, that she knew they were all
> right because she had seen in a vision a huge flash of golden light.
>
> . . . And as I sit now writing this at 4:30 a.m. on September 13, the wind is
> howling and rain pelting the windows.[12]

"She said that soon after the WTC towers fell, she saw this huge,
golden light and all of a sudden she knew everything was all right,"
Loen remembered. "It was for me very jolting, it was totally unexpected to have someone say that at that point in time."

In that moment, Loen remembered another moment, a moment
from the day before. She had taken a break from television. "It
had been storming and storming and storming once we arrived in
Belgium, torrents of rain," she said. "I looked outside and it was all

clear and I thought, 'Isn't that just strange, the peace and the serenity that there is now?'"

It's human nature, she said:

> You fall into a pattern of dealing with things . . . but if someone presents to you a different way of looking at it, takes you out of it, you're not so caught up in it. You understand how horrible it was, you understand there was all this terror, but you can get out of it . . . . Her little testimonial gave us such a different way of looking at things.

The way the service ended also inspired hope, she wrote:

> Then we were invited to light candles to symbolize the spirits who were moving to the next life. We went up, lit our candles and placed them on a pedestal then turned. My eyes were amazed to see how many had quietly joined us in the room, a diverse mix of races, ages, backgrounds, come together. We were bade to go in silence. And as we walked out, I was so thankful to them for the opportunity to participate, to feel like I could do some small thing in the wake of the tragedy at home.

Maybe, she said, "Maybe this wasn't the end of the world, maybe this wasn't the worst thing to happen. Those people were okay in a greater sense, in a spiritual sense. That was really surprising. And then we proceeded to try to get back home."*

Home was Portland, of course, and both Dozonos had deep roots there. Since events would continue to move swiftly for the Dozonos and, within two weeks, for the rest of Oregon, so at this moment of peace, perhaps now is the best time for me to introduce you to the Dozonos, and for you, the reader, to become familiar with their heritage.

Sho and Loen were high school sweethearts. "It was youthful hormones," says Loen, about her attraction and marriage to the charismatic Sho, who took center stage as their family grew to include five children, and Loen moved from her teaching job to focusing on home and family.

---

*In May 2021, Loen would put it this way, that they saw another perspective. "You're not just defeated." And her thought was, "What can we do?"

A second-generation native Portlander, Loen's well-known compassion and commitment to public service existed, like that of many
Americans, despite her family's experience of internment in post-Pearl
Harbor America—a front-row seat to one of America's lowest ebbs
of bigotry. Loen was, in fact, born in Utah during a work detail that
allowed her father George, and his wife to leave the Minidoka camp
in Idaho.

Ironically, their incarceration was caused by the Japanese attack
on Pearl Harbor on December 7, 1941, the historic antecedent to
which the September 11 attacks were most commonly compared.
At the time, Pearl Harbor had been the [largest] attack on U.S. soil,
with 2,400 deaths, until the September 11 attacks. No one incarcerated
in the camps was accused of a crime, and no accusations were ever
made; these incarcerations took place purely on the basis of race—
and approximately 60 percent of those incarcerated were native-born
American citizens.*

Loen's father, Portland-born Ichiro "George" Azumano had
received his business degree from the University of Oregon the year
before, and was serving in the U.S. Army in San Francisco. He was
discharged due to his Japanese heritage. He arrived in Portland
the day his father was taken away by FBI agents. Japanese and
Japanese-American families were forced to dispose of everything
they couldn't carry with them, including their pets, within days. The
Azumano family was forced to sell their Fuji Grocery for 10 cents
on the dollar and, like all other Japanese, to report to the "Portland
Assembly Center," which was the Portland Stockyards. Livestock
stalls had been whitewashed and a plywood floor placed over the
manure-caked dirt floors. Families would live there for months before
being moved to more permanent facilities. The Azumanos ended
up in a camp in Minidoka, Idaho.[13] George remained at the camp
until 1944, with intermittent releases for work that included labor in
nearby sugar-beet fields and in an Ohio automobile battery manufacturing plant. Despite the hardship, he and his college sweetheart, Ise
Inuzuka, were married in Twin Falls, Idaho, in 1943.

---

*Learn more about Japanese incarceration during World War II in the
"Immigrants of Color" chapter.

Despite lingering anti-Japanese sentiment after World War II, by 1949, Azumano had started over, founding an insurance company devoted to Americans of Japanese ancestry; this company ultimately became Azumano Travel. As he built his business, the serious and hard-working Azumano became known for considering his role in the community just as important as the bottom line.

Azumano spent his life caring for the Nikkei (Japanese-American) community in Portland, building U.S.-Japan relations, and making Oregon a destination for Japanese tourists. In 1962, Gov. Mark Hatfield tapped him to take part in the first Oregon trade mission to Japan, which was the first trade delegation by any state government to that country. Between 1963 and 1974, the region's exports of wheat tripled, and exports of potatoes grew six times. Later, as a U.S. senator, Hatfield asked Azumano to serve on the Region 10 Civil Rights Commission.

In 1974, on the occasion of the Japanese ambassador's visit to Portland, *The New York Times* reported:

> The Pacific Northwest, which was virulently anti-Japanese only thirty years ago, is now so pro-Japanese that Ambassador Yakusawa was given two standing ovations at the crowded conference recently on this region's agricultural trade with Japan.[14]*

In the following decade, Gov. Vic Atiyeh appointed Azumano to the Oregon Tourism Commission. Azumano organized a luncheon for Atiyeh with Japanese travel agents during the governor's first trade mission to Japan in 1979, a meeting Atiyeh credited with helping to put Oregon on the map in Japan as a tourist destination. In 1982, the Japanese government awarded Azumano the Emperor's Medal of the 4th Order of the Rising Sun for his work improving US-Japan relations.

When Azumano died in 2013, Joe D'Alessandro, former president and chief executive of the Portland Oregon Visitors Association (POVA), told *The Oregonian*, "So many travel agencies were just

---

*Coincidentally, the ambassador was made to feel more at home, said the *Times*, by the surprise reuniting with his high school teacher, whom he had not seen for forty-six years; that was none other than Asazo Dozono, Sho's father.

focused on selling tickets" for outbound travel. "What was different about George was that he really did care a lot about the state and about economic development and focused on bringing people into Oregon."[15]

Public service was merely one aspect of George Azumano's life. As his family wrote in his obituary, the "overall theme of his life" was "responsibility for family, his church, civic duty, equality and justice for all."[16]

So Loen came by her compassion and commitment to others honestly. *The Oregonian* described her well-known father as "quiet but influential," words that could equally apply to her. She was at the table for every Flight for Freedom meeting, and those present credit her for bringing the group back to the task at hand and focusing on getting things done. She also kept meticulous records of the Flight for Freedom's progress and development.*

Loen has a brilliant mind, an enormous heart, a passion for social justice, and a bent for action. Add to that a profound spiritual connection and a pragmatism that she does not hesitate to express.**

Loen was long active in the Ikoi no Kai (Meeting Place) founded for senior citizens of Japanese heritage where they could receive a healthy lunch; it is now a place for all Nikkei recreational and educational activities have been added to the meals served. Sponsored by the Japanese Ancestral Society, it is located at the Epworth Methodist Church, which has been an important community center for Portland's Japanese community since the late 1890s. It is the only Japanese Methodist church in the state, and one of only sixteen in the nation. The *Oregon Encyclopedia* entry on the Epworth Methodist Church was written by George Azumano.[17]

Sho arrived in Portland from Japan in 1954 with his father, Asazo Dozono. His mother, Nadyne Yoneko "Meema" Dozono, had been born in Portland and was sent to Japan as a teenager in 1931, to spend two years learning the Japanese culture ("and maybe find a husband," says Sho). That two years lasted more than twenty. When

---

*Ray said, "Ideas would be exploding and [Loen would say] I thought we were talking about the parade." (May 13, 2021)

**Loen proofread my 2003 book on the Flight for Freedom before it was published, taking the time to make sure everything was right.

the family united in Portland, both of Sho's parents actively served the community.*

While this was the beginning of the years in which Asians aspired to be the "model minority," concentrating on assimilating by focusing on education and career achievement, and not making waves, Sho realized that for him, the pursuit of high grades wasn't his path. For him, status and popularity were the way to get ahead. He says today that because he spent his first ten years mostly in Japan, he did not absorb the feeling of being "less-than" that Asians who spent their formative years in the United States internalized.

While he came to the United States knowing no English, he learned it in about six months. By high school, he was junior-class president at Cleveland High School in Portland.

At the University of Washington, Sho was the first member of a racial minority accepted into the Alpha Delta Phi fraternity. The fraternity, which was founded as a literary society, is described as "one of the most distinguished of the original American college fraternities. It has retained its focus on its literary roots, by attracting only the best students at only the more prestigious colleges and universities in Canada and the United States."[18]

He was still naïve about being Asian, though, he says. When about twenty members came to interview him for membership, he was elated. He thought so many had come because they were so excited to have him. He learned later that just the opposite was true: because of his race, it was felt that he needed extra-careful vetting. And he remained the only minority member of the fraternity throughout his time at the University of Washington. Later on, in Portland, when members of all-white, Protestant country clubs (Catholics and Jews

---

*In 1934, Yoneko married Asazo, a Tokyo University graduate who later became the youngest high school principal in Japan. After the war, she served as an interpreter for the Atomic Bomb Casualty Commission in Hiroshima and for Jean MacArthur, Gen. Douglas MacArthur's wife. After returning to Oregon, where her family had been incarcerated during the war, she worked for the Portland Public Schools. Asazo worked as a technical adviser for the Japanese consulate general's office in Portland and received the Emperor's Award in 1975. Yoneko Dozono's life is extensively documented as part of the Japanese American Oral History project: Nadyne Yoneko Dozono, 1998 January 23-February 5. archiveswest.orbiscascade.org/ark:/80444/xv820889.

were prohibited from membership in many country clubs.) invited him to join, he refused. "I don't want to be an exception," he said.

Following a stint in the Army, while stationed in Vancouver, Washington, he earned a master's degree in education—the "family business"—at Portland State University. College advisers had discouraged him from the law, he told *The Oregonian*: "They said you could not get hired by law firms because the jury system would not favor a person of color."[19]

For five years, he taught social studies at Portland's Grant High School and coached the wrestling team. But he was not a teacher for long. In 1976, he joined the four employees in Loen's father's business, Azumano Travel, and became president in 1981. George Azumano had been key to building Oregon's exports to Japan and Sho continued and greatly expanded that work. He developed a close relationship with Japan's Fuji Television, ultimately encouraging its producers to come to Oregon in the 1980s to shoot the *From Oregon With Love* TV series, which boosted Japanese tourism in the state.

Civic involvement was as much as part of Sho's life as it had been of his father-in-law's. Over the years, he would serve on the boards of organizations across the state: the Portland Art Museum, the Museum at Warm Springs, Portland State University Foundation, and many, many more. He served as co-chair of the Oregon League of Minority Voters, the US-Japan Council, the Portland Metropolitan Chamber of Commerce, and the Portland Oregon Visitors Association, among other organizations.

But the event that first put Sho on the broader community's radar screen was the 1996 "March for Our Schools," which was the largest political event in Portland history up to that time. It drew 30,000 people from across the state and raised $11 million dollars, saving the jobs of hundreds of teachers in the city's ailing school system. The way Sho made it happen, quickly and achieving more than others thought possible, foreshadowed the turn-on-a-dime mobilization of the Flight for Freedom.[20]

The "March for Our Schools" was a watershed event that demonstrated Sho's strengths in mobilizing the civic and business communities, along with the state's citizenry, for a greater social purpose. He would continue to organize such projects beginning with the Flight for Freedom and later, after other natural disasters:

Hurricane Katrina, the tsunami in Thailand, and the earthquake in Japan. He never looked back.

Unlike Loen, whose documentation and records are orderly and accessible, Sho's records are "somewhere"—Azumano Assistant Vice President Jeri Hunt was integral to keeping that part of his work life organized—and reviewing them is of little interest to him. Sho focuses on the future.

THURSDAY, SEPTEMBER 13

When they returned to the hotel after church the night before, AAA was briefing the attendees and said they'd work to get everyone's travel arrangements made and "break camp" on Friday. Hertz offered everyone cars to drive home, if they were unable to reach their home airports in the United States. The Dozonos decided that rather than changing their plans and trying to go to the States immediately, they would continue with their scheduled itinerary, which would take them to Dublin for a day.

Some attendees simply killed time, watching and waiting for air travel to begin opening up. The Dozonos took advantage of an opportunity to visit nearby Bruges, what Loen called "a fairy-tale contrast to all the ugliness of the week—it was an escape from reality."

Back in Portland at Azumano Travel, it was chaos. Which airports were open? Which flights were happening? What were the new security restrictions? When should people be at the airport? If someone's flight had been canceled, could they get their money back?

The emails came in droves from airlines, airports, the American Society of Travel Agents (ASTA), American Express (an Azumano partner). Each one provided needed information—but the situation was so fluid that the answer might change in the next minute. ASTA was asking its members to contact their Congressional representatives to request that federal recovery funding include travel agencies.

And the calls—from stranded customers, and customers who wanted to cancel reservations.

In two days, world travel had dropped dramatically. Sho saw the massive domino effect this incident could have, and the economic devastation a continued decline in travel could create worldwide.

And he was angry, said Loen. "He was asking, 'How can you get them to understand that they're playing into the hands of the terrorists, they're doing exactly what the terrorists want them to do?'"

Plus, added Sho, "People weren't flying anywhere and my business was gone. It's like nobody's eating at the restaurant. In the next six months, you're out of business."

The New York Times backed up Sho's fears. Hotel analyst Robert Mandelbaum of PKF Consulting predicted "the largest single drop in 40 years" in revenue per room for hotels "for an industry that was already hurting so far this year."[21]

The attacks had exacerbated an economic downturn that was already in progress. The day before, Raleigh, North Carolina-based Midway Airlines had announced that it was shutting down, suspending flights immediately, and laying off 1,700 employees.[22] Ansett Airways, Australia's second biggest airline (after Qantas), filed for the equivalent of Chapter 11 bankruptcy protection but said that it would continue flying.[23] A poll of companies found that 88 percent of employees said they could cut back on travel in the coming weeks, and many companies said they would ban travel.[24]

In Congress, airline representatives were asking for legislation to limit their financial liability in the attacks. The Chubb Corporation had already started paying claims.[25]

Airlines began flying again that afternoon, although with only limited service, after Secretary of Transportation Norman Y. Mineta cleared the way for airports to reopen. New security restrictions were in place (including bans on knives; on curbside check-ins; and greater scrutiny of luggage, planes on the ground, and vehicles near terminals). And the National Guard had been called in to patrol airports.

"We have taken every precaution to make sure it is safe to fly in America," President Bush said. "If a family member asked if they should fly, I would say yes."[26]

FRIDAY, SEPTEMBER 14, AND SATURDAY, SEPTEMBER 15

September 14 had been designated a day of mourning by the European Union, a declaration that grew to include all forty-three member states of the Council of Europe.[27] Across the continent:

At the stroke of noon Brussels time, in cities and towns, urban and rural areas, people stopped what they were doing—farmers stood in their fields, traffic came to a halt. Shops, offices, schools, factories, railway stations, airports and city centers fell quiet. Television and radio stations suspended programs. Stock exchanges ceased trading. Court cases were halted. Buses and trains stopped. Pubs stayed closed until it was over. In Berlin, more than 200,000 people packed the avenue that leads to the Brandenburg Gate. The tolling bells of Notre Dame echoed through Paris. Schoolchildren in Bhopal clasped their hands in prayer, while people in Brussels linked hands to form a human chain before that city's World Trade Center towers. In Italy, race-car drivers practicing for Sunday's Italian Grand Prix silenced their engines in unison, and Pope John Paul II knelt silently in prayer. In Tehran, thousands of people attending a World Cup qualifying match between Bahrain and Iran observed a moment of silence.[28]

Sho and Loen experienced the observance at the Brussels South Charleroi Airport, and Loen recorded it in her journal:

As we entered the airport, exactly at noon, we were surprised to hear an announcement that it was a National Day of Mourning and a request for three minutes of silence to honor those killed. It was a small airport, but nevertheless an amazing thing that everyone stopped short, stood absolutely still—phones ringing were taken off the hook, not a sound . . . . . . except for a few children who didn't understand, crying or shouting.

We felt so moved that in a foreign country this would happen. Emotions that had not risen began to well up as we bought a paper and magazine which commemorated the fact that Europe wanted to stand with America, encouraged people in the UK to fly American flags! We were not sure if the silence at the airport was a result of a Belgian proclamation or an Irish one, as Ryanair is an Irish carrier.

(Sho had checked the Internet Thurs. evening and gotten onto Ryanair and found that as a result of the terrorism, no hand baggage would be allowed so we packed accordingly. Sure enough, they carried out this procedure. He was unable to even carry his briefcase on board.)

That the Dozonos spent September 14 in Dublin was another of the synchronicities that would mark the day. The impact of their experience in Dublin not only demonstrated how personally people around the world felt the attacks, but how quickly the unfolding news of the tragedy could spread.[29]

Ireland was one of only three countries to set aside the entire day as a National Day of Mourning for the victims of the U.S. attacks, and Dublin was the scene of the nation's largest observances.* Schools, government offices, businesses and shops, and pubs were closed and all sports and entertainment were canceled. Every parish and diocese held religious services.

Two thousand people tried to attend a service at St. Mary's Pro-Cathedral in Dublin, which holds 1,500, where Taoiseach Prime Minister Bertie Ahern, President Mary McAleese, and many other cabinet members were present. Many stood outdoors.

"We arrived in Dublin and got into a taxi," wrote Loen. "The driver had the radio on to a station broadcasting a memorial service for the N.Y. victims—it seemed to be an Irish service—with moving poems and beautiful songs in Gaelic and with pipers."

"The cab driver mentioned that we wouldn't find anything open because of the National Day of Mourning throughout Ireland," said Sho. "We almost couldn't believe it. And then we saw people standing on line for three hours at the U.S. Embassy to sign a book of condolences. I was so inspired." [PHOTOS 1-3]

Ultimately, more than 4,000 people would sign the condolence books at the U.S. Embassy, which also received almost 30,000 condolence messages. Its fence became a shrine of flowers, teddy bears, candles, and messages. At 3 p.m., the Dublin Fire Brigade bagpipe band led 250 firefighters from across the country to the Embassy to lay floral wreaths in tribute to their lost New York colleagues.[30]

---

*By coincidence, the first certified casualty of the September 11 attack was the Irish-American chaplain of the New York City Fire Department, Father Mychal Judge, who was killed while giving last rites to a firefighter. Three thousand people attended Judge's funeral mass on September 15, 2001, at St. Francis of Assisi Church, which was presided over by Cardinal Edward Egan, the Archbishop of New York. The Father Mychal Judge Walk of Remembrance takes place every year in New York on the Sunday before the 9/11 anniversary.

Loen wrote in her journal:

When we went there we were totally overwhelmed. Our eyes were full of tears. We wished we could tell them all how much we appreciated their actions.

A Nigerian family stood on an intersection island with a poster. We thought it was maybe a protest, having seen one apparently disgruntled woman with a cardboard sign being moved away by an embassy official. But Sho stopped to read it and it was indeed a sign of support. We told them thank you . . . . Later, we saw the official carrying the sign. He apparently had accepted it from them and held it under his arm as he attempted to direct people to open books so the process would go more quickly. Maybe it was a response to Sho's suggestion earlier when he caught the attention of a man posted at the gate to ask whether more books could be brought out so people wouldn't have to wait so long. We walked around the corner and up to the end of the block several times, trying to capture in pictures the magnitude of this demonstration of caring. The books are to be here twenty-four hours a day until Monday morning.

The most moving poem I saw was by a young girl of about twelve or thirteen who had slept with "Peachy" for three years, and in this loss of innocence, exposed to the ugliness of the real world, was leaving her teddy bear now in front of the US Embassy.

There were sorrowful notes of people who knew the police officers who'd died, notes from children hoping that the moms and dads of the victims' children might be able to return—candles lit, flags, mementos—just a huge outpouring of sympathy.

When Sho and Loen returned to the hotel, they called Bill Harmon at Azumano Travel, who was "surprised" at the national shutdown because "at home it was pretty much business as usual," Loen wrote. "We are wondering and feeling that there is a big lack of leadership in an important way."

Loen said later:

We knew when we talked to our family at home that that wasn't happening, yet here was this whole country closing down because of respect. We were just so moved and so then, I don't know if it was more of a world kind of an aspect—[we saw that] it's not just Americans who are suffering.

If we were home, [coverage] would just be looking at us . . . . The whole world was involved, they were trying to [show] respect. It was a bigger picture kind of a thing. It was really impactful to us.

In other notes, she wrote that the time they spent in Dublin was "important to give a world perspective . . . . a domino action which will precipitate financial as well as emotional crisis."

In the United States, September 14 had been designated a National Day of Prayer and Remembrance. The observance began in Washington, D.C., in a nationally televised service at the Washington National Cathedral. The service was attended by former Presidents Clinton, George H.W. Bush, Jimmy Carter, and Gerald Ford, as well as former Vice President Al Gore. Members of Congress, the Cabinet, chairman of the Joint Chiefs of Staff and other military leaders, and dignitaries and officials from all over the nation and the world also attended. Only Vice President Cheney was absent, for security reasons.

"In every generation, the world has produced enemies of human freedom," the president said, glancing at his father, who was a fighter pilot in World War II. "They have attacked America because we are freedom's home and defender . . . . "Our responsibility to history is already clear. To answer these attacks and rid the world of evil."

But the day would be remembered most for what happened that afternoon, when President Bush, accompanied by Mayor Rudolph Giuliani, Gov George Pataki and members of Congress, traveled to Ground Zero, where the search continued for survivors in the rubble. Standing atop a charred fire truck, someone yelled out that they couldn't hear him. He grabbed a bullhorn, and what he said became a rallying cry for the country and sent his popularity soaring: "I can hear you. The rest of the world hears you. And the people who knocked down these buildings will hear all of us soon."[31]

On Saturday, the Dozonos did sightseeing in Dublin, which Loen thought was busier than London, Tokyo, or New York. They saw Trinity College and the Book of Kells, and prepared for their departure the next day. They learned from Bill Harmon that their original plan, to fly to JFK and then to Portland, had changed. Instead, they would be flying to London, then to Vancouver, British Columbia, and then—fingers crossed—a flight would be available to Portland. "We're still unsure if the last leg is a possibility," wrote Loen.

In Portland, in an act of service to the community, the Oregon Symphony gave a free concert, "In Memoriam." Mayor Vera Katz introduced the performance and led the audience in a moment of silence. The orchestra played to a full house of 2,700 inside the flag-draped Arlene Schnitzer Concert Hall, and those outdoors in candlelight listened via speakers installed for just that purpose. Many were at the symphony that night for the first time; many had come to grieve collectively. No longer able to give blood or money, what could they do? Carried live on television and radio, the concert reached 250,000 people.

"It is, perhaps, the finest hour for the symphony and its conductor, James DePreist," wrote the *Oregonian*'s longtime music critic David Stabler.[32]

The field producer was a longtime KOIN-TV reporter, John Ray, who, after twenty-three years, had been laid off by the station a few weeks before.

Murry Sidlin, who was the Oregon Symphony's resident conductor, remembers the genesis of the concert, which was as remarkable as that of the Flight for Freedom. In a time before the internet was streamlining ticketing and reservations, everything, was put together in seventy-two hours. Management, unions, broadcasters, civic leaders all worked together to give the community this opportunity for collective grieving.

"On the evening of the day of the attack we performed a scheduled concert in Salem, OR. We had debated whether it was the right thing to do, but knowing the ability of music to comfort, we decided to perform. Music Director James DePreist conducted. Normally, we had a packed house for our concerts in Salem, but predictably on this night we attracted half our normal audience.

"At intermission, Jimmy said he was too heartbroken to continue conducting, and asked me to complete the concert, which I did. (Beethoven's Seventh Symphony, a composition of hope, fate, and longing.)

"On the drive home, Jimmy and his wife, Ginette, came up with the idea for the Friday night concert and the next day Jimmy put into motion all the parts for a memorial concert to be held in just three days, and televised statewide. The concert was announced that day.

"Much of the technical personnel and equipment for the broadcast were donated by Oregon Public Broadcasting. Paul Allen, who owned the city's basketball team, the Portland Trail Blazers, donated the broadcasting van.

"By Thursday morning, tickets had been printed. When I arrived at the concert hall for rehearsal at 8:30 a.m., the line to obtain free tickets, and the tickets, were gone within two hours.

"Jimmy then insisted that huge speakers be placed outdoors so that people could gather on the park blocks and hear the music being made inside the concert hall. Jimmy also insisted that no speeches be presented with the exception of an introductory few words given by Mayor Vera Katz. No commentary, no applause. A spiritual and contemplative evening wherein the music did all the communicating.

"Those of us who have great confidence that music will reflect hope, faith and longing for the good in mankind understood Jimmy's intent to let the music speak and touch each of us personally, deeply, and significantly. I assisted the non-musical television directors and John Ray in the TV truck calling the camera shots, though with my eyes covered by tears of great pain for the entire event, I wonder if I was at all helpful."[33]

SUNDAY, SEPTEMBER 16–MONDAY, SEPTEMBER 17

The Dozonos arrived home on Sunday. "Because we were in Brussels and we had to come home, we couldn't deal with any fear, we got on the plane and we went home," said Loen.

Interestingly, she noted "not even huge relief on being back in Canada, then landing in PDX [Portland airport], just familiarity," she wrote. "Every day Sho agonizes over job loss but feels he has work situation under fairly good control—not worried about survival—Gulf War, other close calls provide experiences in handling travel crises."

Sho estimated a thirty percent loss in business. To recover what he could, Sho decided to lay off thirty-five employees, and cut the remaining employees—including himself—to eighty percent time, or a thirty-two-hour workweek. "We all worked thirty-two hours. There wasn't a job for everyone forty hours, so 250 people were on 80 percent," he said.

He learned that Portland Chamber of Commerce trip to Japan scheduled for October had been canceled.

The nation was moving away from the period of shock and disbelief. American leaders began to speak about the need to move on.

The news was filled with a plea from New York City Mayor Giuliani: "I encourage people from all over the country who want to help, I have a great way of helping: come here and spend money. Go to a restaurant, a play . . . . The life of the city goes on."

On Sunday, September 17, *The Oregonian* began publishing *The New York Times'* "Portraits of Grief" on page A2 (inside the front page). These profiles appeared a few days after they first appear in *The Times*.[34] This is an example of one of those Pulitzer Prize-winning stories:

WINE BY NIGHT
Matthew Picerno

Try, now, to envision a municipal bond broker, in his 104th-floor office, who dreams the green and bacchanalian dream of being a winemaker. That was Matthew Picerno, 44, of Holmdel, N.J. By day he worked at Cantor Fitzgerald, rising at 5:30 a.m. Six months of the year, when the day job ended, he headed over to Jersey City, to his Bacchus School of Wine franchise, and worked there until 11 p.m. It was a former two-truck garage, well scrubbed, with Italian flags and piped-in Sinatra. The students turned out 200 barrels of wine a year, the school only broke even financially, but what does money matter in an affair of the heart?

"This was a hobby," said his wife, Petrina Marie, "but he really enjoyed it. Municipal bond broker at day, winemaker at night. He was pretty wild, very loud. This was a man if you told him this was a rule, he would try to break it just because it was a rule. Anything. Driving. He lost his license at least twice in his lifetime."

Mr. Picerno, who leaves three children, aged 9, 12 and 14, had planned to pursue winemaking full time when he left Wall Street.[35]

TUESDAY, SEPTEMBER 18

Sho sent out an "Update for Staff," which let them know he was back on U.S. soil and provided additional information regarding what they could expect in the days to come.

[W]hile it was both wrenching and frustrating to be so far away from home and from you, I was provided with a unique perspective in terms of reaction abroad . . . . [T]he outpouring of sympathy for our country and the victims of this senseless tragedy was truly moving . . . .

There is no doubt that by moving quickly last week to initiate a temporary cutback in staff, we were able to stabilize the company. I am most appreciative of all those who volunteered to take leave without pay . . . .

In the next few days, we will be fine tuning an aggressive strategy which will placed into effect for the remainder of the year in order to sustain our company. I must tell you, however, that each of us will be called upon to sacrifice . . . .

By the end of the week, I will announce the measures to be taken . . . . We must endure and calmly go on. Never forget that a strong will, a settled purpose, an invincible determination can accomplish almost anything.[36]

Azumano staff were busy cancelling reservations, says CI Azumano Travel* vice president and general manager Nancy Parrott, who was leisure sales manager for Azumano at the time. It was depressing. Parrott herself had just spent the weekend at a wedding in New York. "I was determined not to have the events of 9/11 impact our travel and ruin our wedding," she said, adding that many people had canceled. Later on, it would give her insight as they prepared for the Flight for Freedom. "I kind of had a feel for what was going on in the airports."

The Harmons and Parrott would be instrumental in taking a completely random assemblage of passengers and turning them into a group, as would the head of Azumano's Group Department, Gregg Macy. Other elements, like the shirts, buttons, and logo, would be critical, but without understanding the structure of a leisure travel group, with welcome and closing receptions, a hospitality table, and other support, the Flight for Freedom would not have been as successful as it was.

That Parrott was an operations woman would also be essential in taking a project that would normally require six months, and getting it done in less a week. In a time before internet ticketing, when tickets were still all on paper and reservations required phone calls, filling

*CI Travel acquired Azumano Travel in 2013.

out forms, and faxing credit card information—all while the FAA was putting in place new, unprecedented security requirements, getting 1,000 people onto sixty-two flights within a week was no small feat. On top of it, they were building the group identity visually, and everything they needed—T-shirts, buttons, parade banner, hospitality signs—had to be ordered and shipped to New York and then unpacked there in time for the travelers' arrival.

WEDNESDAY, SEPTEMBER 19

That night, Sho wrote the Chamber of Commerce's monthly newsletter, focusing on the devastating effect the World Trade Center bombing could have on the national economy. The message: "We need to get back to the business of business." The title was, "This Land Was Made For You and Me."

Loen remembered "some concern" over the theme of moving on: "[I]s it too soon to push for this? But his reply is always the urgency of jobs lost."

> For many, the events of September 11 will forever change our lives, but we must move on and try to put the horror of that day behind us. We must not let the terrorists win . . . .
>
> We have already felt the impact in Portland. Boeing's announcement of 30,000 layoffs hit all too close to home and will surely impact the Boeing operation in Gresham . . . .
>
> Our economy, already in a decline before the 11th, will surely be sounded as the death knell unless we begin the process of recovery and restore consumer confidence to the point where we all feel safe again. We must get back on our feet and start living our lives as we did before. Of course we'll continue to feel sad and be distracted at times, but we must go on . . . .
>
> Only by refusing to allow fear to grip and immobilize us, only by celebrating our diversity and respecting our ethnic, cultural and religious differences, only by turning our attention to the future, can we ever hope to recover from the past . . . .
>
> Believe in each other and this great land of ours . . .

THURSDAY, SEPTEMBER 20

10:00	While editing the Chamber newsletter, Loen has New York caravan idea
1:00	Loen shares her idea with Sho
2:00	Sho tests idea with travel professionals
3:00	Sho sets meeting for 1:30 p.m. Friday in his office with community leaders to explore idea

While Loen was editing the newsletter on the computer, she had an idea: a car caravan to "grow attention and participation of ordinary citizens to move on." It would be a five-day trip driving to New York, then flying back. "Reasoning: at this early stage, everyone is very gun-shy of planes—we can be cautious by only going one way."

Loen, who seldom came to the office, brought the plan to Sho.

"She had this piece of paper," he remembered. "I told her that this could be a really big idea," said Sho. "My imagination was all the people who are losing their jobs, bellboys and restaurant workers."

The question was, was there even availability?

"I called Dave Zielke at Delta Airlines to see if I could arrange for one-way flying back because we didn't want to drive both ways." Loen noted that Sho asked Dave about 100 tickets. Dave said yes.

Sho called Joe D'Alessandro, president and CEO of the Portland Oregon Visitors Association (POVA), who loved it. They set up a meeting on Friday at 1:30 p.m. to discuss the idea further.

"The idea was to do something personal: physical, emotional, spiritual," said D'Alessandro, now president and CEO of the San Francisco Travel Association. "The emotional and spiritual was the most important piece—how it made you feel. And that it wasn't passive, it was an active effort on the part of people . . . . The idea was to give New York a real good hug and show the empathy Oregon has. It was a simple act of kindness."

D'Alessandro also called Todd Davidson, the state of Oregon's tourism director. They'd known each other since Todd began working as international marketing director in the Office of Tourism in 1994. Together they had worked on promoting Oregon in Japan.

When Davidson heard the idea, he said, "This is brilliant, this is necessary. The travel and tourism industry should be at the fore in terms of showing Americans that it is safe to travel, and we need to be there to support our fellow Americans in New York during this time."

President Bush addressed the nation and a Joint Session of Congress, and made his case for U.S. actions in response to the attacks in New York and Washington. He provided an overview of who the attackers were, organizations and names that very likely were new to many/most Americans—Al Qaeda and Osama bin Laden—their goals, and his plan for using the $40 billion provided by Congress on what he called the "war on terror." He explained how this war would be different than other wars, that it was a new kind of war, not for territory, not against one nation. He explained the Taliban's repression in Afghanistan and pledged an attack unless Afghanistan surrendered bin Laden.[37]

As Sho and Loen discussed the feasibility of the idea, the idea changed from a car caravan to a bus because, among other things, it would have been too difficult for Sho to communicate to all the cars. Recalling President Clinton's bus tours that were in large part media campaigns, Sho thought, "We could be communicating and telling everyone in America to come to New York." (Sho had ridden on the candidate's bus in Oregon for a short time.)

The idea was to take five days crossing the country, stopping in major cities with announcements to spread the message. But by evening, the bus trip was in doubt, said Sho. "By Thursday evening we said, 'I don't know if we have that many friends who'd go with us on a five-day bus trip. I could see us doing it, riding on the back of a bus . . . .'"

It was barely a week since the terrorist tragedy.

FRIDAY, SEPTEMBER 21*

9:00	Chamber Board meeting—float idea
10:00	Loen and Jeri Hunt create project info sheet
11:00	Call Bruce Samson—he has a "great idea."
	Test idea on other business/political leaders

1:30	Meeting: Azumano Travel office
	• Purpose: Is this a good idea?
	• Attendees include:
	  – Joe D'Alessandro (Portland Oregon Visitors Bureau, [POVA])
	  – Elisa Dozono, Port of Portland Corp. Media Manager, former Communications Director for Mayor Vera Katz
	  – Jeff Hammerly, Travel Oregon, former student of Sho's
	  – Val Hubbard, VH Productions
	  – Gregg Kantor, vice president of public affairs and communications, NW Natural Gas Company
	  – Debby Kennedy, Port of Portland public affairs director
	  – Kim Kunkle (*Oregonian* freelance writer, married to Rich Read, *Oregonian* Pulitzer Prize winner)
	  – Randy Loveland, city manager, United Airlines
	  – Suzanne Miller (Port of Portland)
	  – Brian McCartin, vice president of marketing and sales, Portland Oregon Visitors Bureau
	  – Bruce Samson, former chairperson of the Portland Chamber of Commerce and former general counsel, NW Natural Gas Company
	  – Craig Thompson, general manager at 5th Avenue Suites hotel in downtown Portland and on POVA board

5:00	Ruth's Chris Steak House, Dozono family • Kristen • Elisa • Tom
7:00	*Heroes* Telethon • Jack McGowan • Gerry Frank

On Friday, the dream would become a plan. The day was devoted to vetting the idea, and even the first meeting was weighted toward actually making it happen—and quickly! Sho's gift is taking an idea he believes in and quickly assembling the people who can implement it.

---

*Calendar times for narrative purposes only, not necessarily accurate.

But keeping Azumano Travel afloat was painful. That day, "The Plan," the next steps that had been promised to employees on September 18, was distributed. Twenty-three employees (of about 250) were placed on a thirty-day temporary layoff without pay.

"In no way is this action meant to reflect negatively on these individuals, and we hope that we can welcome them back should conditions improve," the memo stated. All staff were placed on a thirty-two-hour work week for thirty days beginning the next day, September 22, and a number of strategies to cut expenses were implemented.[38]

That morning, Sho floated the idea for the trip to New York at the Chamber of Commerce board meeting. President and CEO Don McClave didn't think people would go.

Meanwhile, Loen was working with Azumano Travel Assistant Vice President Jeri Hunt to create an information sheet. Jeri added language and created a covered wagon with the "New York or Bust" theme.

While the information sheet shows that the first concept showed a covered wagon and proposed thirty-five cities nationwide sending people to New York,* the essential elements of the Flight for Freedom, which would not change, were already in place: liberating people from fear, the leadership of Portland Mayor Vera Katz, grassroots participation, group activities, and identifying buttons or pins for participants.

Above all, it stressed, "So many are working to flood the relief effort with dollars, but at this point, it is more important to get people there."

In the next four days, the project and its messaging would be honed, but the fundamental purpose of the trip—for grassroots people to show that they would get on a plane and courageously put their bodies in New York City—never wavered.

When Sho returned to the office, a phone message was waiting for him from Bruce Samson, a Portland business and community leader, who had recently retired from his position as counsel for Portland Public Schools and had served as chair of the Portland Chamber of Commerce. The message: he had a "great idea." "Call back by 11 a.m." he urged.

---

*With 100 planes, each with 100–150 persons on board, that would total 10,000–15,000 people descending on New York to help. If each person spent $1,000, it would be a $15 million boost to the city economy, money that would get people working.

"Sho said, 'Loen, did you call Bruce? I've got a message from Bruce—*Great idea—call before 11 a.m.*" . . .

She hadn't talked to Samson; she had no idea what his idea was. And while the New York idea was inspiring them, the pain of the situation at Azumano was very real. Sho shut his office door to confide that office morale was bad. People had received their termination notices and the four-day work week was set to begin.

The roller-coaster of what would become the Flight for Freedom may have begun at this moment, when, surrounded by loss, Sho called Bruce Samson back.

Samson had worked extensively with Sho on the March for Our Schools and many other civic projects. He told Sho:

> I was concerned about our reaction to the 9/11 thing and how it was inhibiting our willingness or ability to—it was changing our lives in ways that I didn't think were very healthy, and particularly with respect to air travel. I'm an old Navy pilot who loves flying and was very angry that flying was being used against us. I also felt that it would be nice to figure out a way that we could support New Yorkers and what they were going through . . . .
>
> I read that air travel was down and that visiting New York was down and then I thought, wouldn't it be neat . . . if a few of us could go to New York to show our support? I thought there's one guy that I could call that's in the travel industry that's a civic leader and that I've known for years and if he thinks it's a good idea, then it's probably something worth pursuing . . . .
>
> When I talked to him about it, Sho was just quiet for a minute and he said something like, "This is unbelievable. This is what Loen and I were talking about yesterday." And he said, "I have put together a meeting," . . . and wondered if I could be there.

"He said, 'Whatever I can do, count me in," so he was one of the first people who came on board," said Sho.

This was a game-changer.

"We kind of went into a crisis mode," said Loen. "When Bruce came up with the idea, all of a sudden I felt this urgency that we won't be the first ones if a couple of us had already been thinking about it so we pushed a little harder to go a little faster to get it done."

Sho again called David Zielke at Delta. He also called Randy Loveland at United Airlines to ask about seats, Brad Hutton, general manager of the Portland Hilton, and Terry Lee of Marriott Hotels, regarding room availability in New York. He asked Hutton if it would be possible to get reasonable pricing on a Hilton property around Times Square. Hutton said he thought it would be possible, that he'd call headquarters.

Known to have one of the best Rolodexes in town, Sho began making calls and sending emails to test the idea, and faxed out the newly created information sheet. "I called the people who were important to me as a businessperson to make sure they were going to be supportive," he said. He made it clear that he was contemplating this project as chair of the Greater Portland Chamber of Commerce and stressed that Azumano Travel would be taking no commissions.
[PHOTO 4]

But that was just the beginning for this man known for his persistence. He contacted Phil Knight, who owned Nike; George Passadore, head of Wells Fargo Bank; Lucy Buchanan (Portland Art Museum director of development); former Gov. Vic Atiyeh (who was immediately on board); and Mark Dodson (President and Chief Operating Officer, Northwest Natural Gas Co.).

Responses were mostly positive, although one negative response surprised him: *Oregonian* publisher Fred Stickel, a World War II Pacific theater Marine veteran. Sho had expected him to be all for it, but Stickel was against the plan, saying that his wife would not fly for "a million bucks," Sho remembers.

At 1:30, the Dozonos held the first meeting to talk through the concept. Unable to get a babysitter, Kim Kunkle brought her son, Nehalem, who worked on the computer across the hall while Azumano Travel executive Tina Harmon babysat. Sho and Loen's daughter Elisa came; she had worked in communications for Mayor Vera Katz until just four months before; she was now heading communications at the Port of Portland.

With the information sheet as a guide, the group discussed the idea of organizing a trip to New York. The response was clear.

"People are positive, say it's a good idea," Loen noted in her record of the planning, "but decision is pretty unanimous it needs to be a plane trip. How do we make our mark on NY?"

Lucky for them, POVA vice president of marketing and development Brian McCartin was already on it. He had brought stickers that POVA had used in a campaign to demonstrate economic presence. The stickers could be put on bills at restaurants and hotels; they read, "POVA was here."

"It was a marketing campaign; whether a movie theater or a Broadway show or a restaurant or wherever, we ["Freedom Fliers"] were to put a sticker on there. If I were the server, it would drive me crazy to put that on my ticket," McCartin laughed, thinking of how the stickers blocked lots of the information on the restaurant checks.

By meeting's end, an initial consensus was in place. VH Productions' Val Hubbard said, "It sounds interesting. Let me know when you get an okay on the trip, maybe I can send a few people to help." Later on, Hubbard's unsung help would be instrumental in getting people ticketed.

Suzanne Miller went back to her office and vetted the idea. The Port is "on board" she told them. That the Port saw the idea as a good one was important; the Port of Portland is the city's port district and oversees not only marine activities but general aviation and the Portland International Airport. Any group project that was going to fly would need the Port's support.

Mark Dodson and NW Natural are "on board," wrote Loen, adding that Mark was going to Saturday's University of Oregon game in Eugene, where he and Bruce Samson would try to talk to former governor/US Secretary of Transportation Neil Goldschmidt and Nike founder Phil Knight.

Sho arranged for a large meeting on Monday afternoon with members of the Chamber of Commerce and other big players in the state. But moving forward wouldn't wait until Monday.

That night, at dinner at Ruth's Chris steakhouse with their children (Elisa and her husband, Tom Turner; and Kristen), Loen and Sho discussed the idea further. Kristen remembered that her mother's idea was "this wagon train that would provide relief and assistance."

Elisa was already "on board," and Tom and Kristen were enthusiastic as well. Tom, a photojournalist at KATU, the local ABC affiliate, would end up assembling one of the most complete video and photo records of the event available. Kristen, who had recently graduated from Portland State University with a degree in communications, with a concentration in diversity, would devote seemingly all her waking hours to the project in the coming weeks.

After dinner, as chair of the Portland Chamber of Commerce, Sho appeared on the local NBC affiliate's portion of *America: A Tribute to Heroes*, a benefit concert to raise money for the victims of the September 11 attacks and their families, especially New York City firefighters and police officers. The program was produced by the four American broadcast networks (ABC, CBS, Fox, and NBC), and was shown on thirty-five networks simultaneously in the United States and Canada, commercial-free. Actor George Clooney organized celebrities to perform and staff the phones to take pledges. (The show raised $200 million, which was donated to the United Way.)

Organized like a telethon, the show had breaks for local appearances. Sho's message to KGW viewers was clear: America was consumed with grieving and crying, but he was convinced that America needed to do something to shake off what could end up as a crippling paralysis.

Off-camera, he ran the idea of the trip by professional golfer Peter Jacobsen, who was very supportive; his wife was in New York and even had photos of the smoke from the disaster. Sho also spoke with Gerry Frank, Sen. Mark Hatfield's longtime chief of staff, who had spent much of his life in New York and written a guidebook to the city. Frank did not think New York was ready for such a thing.

The show's host was Jack McGowan, a well-known local television personality who had been press secretary to Portland Mayor Bud Clark, and hosted the news and covered Oregon issues on KGW, along with other programs. For the past decade and more, he had served as executive director of SOLV (originally conceived by Gov. Tom McCall as "Stop Oregon Litter and Vandalism"). With his wife, Jan McGowan, grew the environmental organization into the largest volunteer nonprofit in the Pacific Northwest.*

McGowan was immediately supportive and wanted to help. Popular and charismatic, this native New Yorker would become the group's spokesman.

---

*Under McGowan and his wife, Jan, SOLV would grow from a staff of one to thirty-four, a budget of $28,000 to $2.3 million, with up to 90,000 volunteers in more than 250 Oregon communities.

What people did not know, as McGowan gamely presented the show and expressed his grief for his place of birth, was the true depths of despair into which the attacks had thrown him.

> It put everybody in America back on their heels, but what happened to me was I went into a depression. And my wife, Jan, . . . was the one that got me through this. Our son was fourteen years old and it affected Travis so much—here's a fourteen-year-old kid . . . [who] saw what I was going through and saw what the world was going through, and he asked if he could sleep on the floor of our bedroom.

McGowan thought the trip was a great idea and was willing to help in any way he could, but actually going on the trip was out of the question, he said. SOLV was known above all for its annual "Beach Cleanup," in which tens of thousands of volunteers spread out across the entire 362-mile Oregon coast and often collected about thirty tons of trash. The fall cleanup was scheduled on the weekend they were discussing for the trip to New York.

> I came back from KGW with Sho and Loen and we [Jan, Travis and Jack] started to talk about what this could be, I said, "I don't think I can go, we've got the beach cleanup, I've got to be with you to coordinate the beach cleanup. Jan was adamant. She said, "You have to go."
>
> I thank my wife for saying "no ifs, ands, or buts; you have to go." She was absolutely right. That to me got me through one of the most of the trying times of my life.[39]

For the first time, McGowan would be absent from SOLV's flagship project. John Ray would later call McGowan the "spiritual head" of the core group of organizers; to Flight for Freedom he brought that same heart and soul that had helped SOLV to blossom.

SATURDAY, SEPTEMBER 22

10:00	Meeting: Azumano Travel office • Purpose: Is this a good idea? What shape should it take? • Attendees include: – Sho – Loen – Elisa – Tom Turner – Len Bergstein – Bruce Samson
1:00	University of Oregon football game—Bruce Samson and Mark Dodson to speak with Neil Goldschmidt and Phil Knight
6:00	Interfaith Day of Prayer and Healing • Elisa Dozono recruits former KOIN-6 journalist John Ray
7:00	PSU plays Grambling State University. Idea shared with PSU and other leaders.

The group of supporters had now expanded to include one of Sho and Loen's closest and most trusted friends: Len Bergstein, who Sho would come to describe as the "moral center" of the project. Another native New Yorker who, like McGowan had immigrated to Oregon in the early 1970s, fallen in love with the idealism of the place, and the natural beauty. An urban creature, for Bergstein it was the opportunity to live in a lovely urban environment that kept him in Portland to marry and raise his family. In the 1980s, he had opened a consulting company, Northwest Strategies, and became a Democratic political consultant, lobbyist, and political analyst who embraced the liberal ethos of the city while recognizing the issues around racial equity that had plagued the state. Bergstein was media-savvy, and his perspective would be highly valued in that area as well.

When he heard the idea, he said, his reaction was "electric." Immediately inspired, he was integral to shaping the project, although he was unable to go on the trip himself. (Years later, though, he would laughingly remember his strong need to get rid of the nineteenth-century covered wagon image when the world needed to get back in the air again.) [PHOTO 5]

"It was human-to-human outreach because it was rooted in a genuine human effort to support New York," he said, emphasizing that "the real heartbeat" of the trip was "reaching out to people in need, even across the country."

The Oregonians, he said, were out to "break the spell. The bad guys weren't going to keep us from the freedom we had." People were on a special mission.

"Loen gave us the vision," he said, and it was his job to help craft the media message; he knew how it had to appear.

Bergstein also brought the perspective of a New Yorker who had chosen Portland, and this is what, in 2021, he said he'd found in the city, and what it was like, even twenty years ago:

> [Portland] was an insular, receptive place. People cared about their neighbors. They weren't here because they wanted to be at the top of a social pyramid. People came into the neighborhood and got attached to it, they put themselves into the things they cared about. It wasn't just about writing a check. [In Portland] caring for neighbors was an important ethic.[40]

Elisa brought to the meeting a refined version of the information sheet from the day before. Loen's notes documented the primary outcome of this meeting: "Len and Elisa help us understand that the focus should not [be] to cover the whole country—but that just limiting it to Oregon, to pare down what the camera can see is best."

As they put together position statements, goals, and messages, they floated names for the effort: "Stand Tall America," "America on the Move."

That evening, after walking in a march for the Interfaith Day of Prayer and Healing with their friends Betsy Ames and her husband John Ray, Elisa had a proposition for John, who recently had been laid off after twenty-three years in news at the local CBS station, KOIN 6.

"Elisa asked me if I could attend a meeting at her father's office the next day to talk about this idea he had of trying to help the people in New York after September 11," Ray remembered. "I'd met Sho only at Elisa's wedding. I'd seen him at other things and I just knew that he was one of the big movers and shakers. To me, he was kind of a towering figure in the city."[41] John Ray too would be integral to the effort's success.

At the Portland State University vs. Grambling State University game at PGE Park, Sho and Loen were doing more "market research"—and receiving more positive feedback. They "recruited" PSU President Dan Bernstine, State Sen. Margaret Carter, and Metro Councilor Ed Washington, all African Americans, to join the effort, along with Jim Rudd, a principal at Ferguson Wellman Capital Management. They were all invited to the Monday meeting Sho had arranged at the Hilton.

SUNDAY, SEPTEMBER 23

Noon	Meeting: Azumano Travel office
	• Purpose: Is this a good idea? What shape should it take?
	• Attendees include:
	– Sho
	– Loen
	– Elisa
	– Tom
	– Brian McCartin
	– Bruce Samson
	– John Ray
	– Speakerphone
	  • Gerry Frank
	  • Jack McGowan

With McGowan and Frank on speakerphone, the group met to explore the idea one more time before the big Monday afternoon session with Chamber of Commerce members and other high-level Portlanders. Elisa introduced John Ray to the group as someone who could help with the media. Frank, McGowan, and Ray were new to the group, so the ideas that had been discussed in previous meetings were run by them.

"I got a sense that this was a second or third meeting," said Ray. "They wanted to know could they convince enough people to do this—was it worth doing?"

First, they talked about a bus trip—Loen's idea, said Ray, and they walked through all the stages of evolution they'd discussed with other groups: a Berlin airlift to free New York, the covered wagon and the slogan, "New York City or Bust!"

The organizers wanted to coordinate flights from Los Angeles, Seattle, and Portland. "We want to get as many people going as we can," said Sho. "We were trying to make a statement that it was okay to not be fearful of travel."

"Originally, our hope was that maybe fifty or 100 of us could go," said Samson, but the idea was never that only dignitaries would travel. "We thought we could tap into people who felt like Sho and Loen and Jack and I did . . . . We thought that there is probably a group of people out there that want to show the terrorists that we can't be pushed around."

Parameters were nailed down quickly, said Ray:

> We pretty much had kind of decided by the end of the meeting that we needed to have a personal convoy, maybe one flight, two flights, that it was important to have the mayor involved, Vera Katz, and the governor, that we would try to see if we could get these two people to lead a delegation, and we were thinking that we could convince enough people to get 150 people on a flight. [Gov. John Kitzhaber already had an Asian economic development trip scheduled so he could not attend.]
>
> I was asked because of my media experience, what kind of media would this attract? I told them that I thought that we could convince all the TV stations to do something, convince a couple of them to come along, but it was important to have a news conference, to sit down with the local media and to convince them to be a part of the spirit of the thing.

They discussed dates. Wanting to be the first, and to do it as soon as possible, they had talked about September 29 and 30, but neither Frank nor McGowan were available then. Frank continued to express his concern that New York was not yet ready for visitors. He also suggested that perhaps they could raise money for a scholarship, a way to make the trip be more substantive than simply buying things.

Frank, the Salem-based Meier & Frank heir and eighth-generation Oregonian, "had a love affair with New York." The Meier & Frank department stores had an office in New York so he had traveled there every other week during his business career. Throughout the three decades he had lived in Washington, DC, he spent every other weekend in the city. Out of his intimacy with the city had come his *Where to Find It, Buy It, Eat It in New York* guidebook.

> They knew that I'd spent a lot of time there. They asked me lots of questions about what to do and I was happy to give them information. It cemented my relationships with a lot of my friends and fellow Oregonians. My friends in New York were so pleased that they could meet people from Oregon. Oregon seemed like a long way away.[42]

They began to recruit additional leadership, and a campaign to recruit Portland Mayor Vera Katz, which would be one of Samson's personal projects. Sho knew that logistically Azumano Travel's staff could handle it; political and financial support was what was needed at this point.

Ray stressed that the trip should include a Monday, which is usually a slow news day. He also thought he could get national exposure through his connection with NBC *TODAY* show host Ann Curry, with whom he had gone to college.

By meeting's end, October 7–9 or 19–20 were their options. They also needed to determine when and where to stage the announcement.

"We left the meeting and it wasn't unanimous," said Ray. "There were some who wondered whether it was worth doing, but it was clear that Sho wanted to do it very badly and thought it was the right thing to do.

"I'm a big believer that when the boss wants to do something, let's talk about why we can, not why we can't."

It had been eleven days since the World Trade towers had fallen.

MONDAY, SEPTEMBER 24

10:00	Meeting: Azumano Travel office • Purpose: Prep for afternoon meeting with Chamber members • Attendees include: – Sho – Loen – Len Bergstein, Democratic political strategist – Elaine Franklin, Republican political strategist – Jack McGowan, executive director, SOLV – John Ray, media consultant – Bruce Samson, counsel for Portland Public Schools (retired)

	Meeting: Portland Hilton Conference Room
	• Purpose: Is this idea feasible?
	• Elaine Franklin names it: "Flight for Freedom"
	• Attendees include:
	– Sho
	– Loen
	– Scott Andrews, president, Melvin Mark Cos. Commercial real estate
	– Former Gov. Vic Atiyeh
	– Len Bergstein, Democratic political strategist
3:00	– Dan Bernstine, president, Portland State University
	– State Sen. Margaret Carter
	– Kristen Dozono
	– Elaine Franklin, Republican political strategist
	– Bill Harmon, Azumano Travel
	– Tina Harmon, Azumano Travel
	– Roger Hinshaw, president, Oregon and Southwest Washington, Bank of America
	– Brad Hutton, general manager, Portland Hilton
	– Gregg Kantor, vice president of public affairs and communications, NW Natural Gas Company
	– Debby Kennedy, Port of Portland public affairs director
	– Bernie Kronberger, vice president of community development, Wells Fargo Bank
	– Randy Loveland, city manager, United Airlines
	– Don McClave, president and CEO, Greater Portland Chamber of Commerce
	– Jack McGowan, executive director, SOLV
	– Nancy Parrott, leisure travel manager, Azumano Travel
	– Dylan Rivera, *Oregonian* (covered Port of Portland/airlines)
	– Jim Rudd, principal, Ferguson Wellman Capital Management investment advisors
	– Bruce Samson, counsel for Portland Public Schools (retired)
	– Ron Saxton, Republican gubernatorial candidate
	– Jay Waldron, president, Port of Portland Commission
	– Ed Washington, Metro councilor
	– Linda Wright, vice president, US Bank
	– David Zielke, district sales manager, Delta Air Lines
After meeting	Elaine Franklin pulls Sho aside: "death by 1,000 ideas"
5:00	Small group meets, and assignments in smaller group delegated

On Monday the project moved into high gear. Only two days later, the press conference would announce the still-nameless project, and the first Freedom Fliers would leave for New York in little more than a week.

On the Azumano Travel side, Sho wrote to all the company's corporate accounts to encourage them to keep traveling: "I have no doubt that Corporate America will eventually realize it needs to engage the world again and move on." He also let them know that he had taken action to keep Azumano Travel viable and "have the least adverse effect upon both our employees and our customers," which included "a temporary reduction in staff and cutback of hours." He ended with: "I trust you know how much we value your business!"[43]

A small group met at Azumano Travel that morning to prep for the afternoon meeting, which would pull together many representatives from the top echelons of Portland's government, academia, and business, particularly the travel and banking fields.

A new volunteer joined that morning, Republican political strategist Elaine Franklin.

"I was surprised to see Elaine come in. I was pretty intimidated," Loen wrote. "I didn't realize Sho had asked her to come via Ron [Saxton, then-Republican gubernatorial candidate]."

Like other members of what would become known as the "core" group, Elaine Franklin's participation would be pivotal in the conception and execution of the project. The statuesque, Great Britain-born Franklin, who twenty years later has left the Republican party and is an independent, was known for her take-no-prisoners ability to win political campaigns. She was also known as the wife of former Oregon Senator Bob Packwood (1969–1995), to whom she had served as chief of staff.

> I knew Sho Dozono and I think he recognized—my background is running campaigns—and to his credit, I think, Sho recognized that if we were to pull this off at all, it needed to be a very, very short, intense campaign. And it needed some political people because we were going to need some political endorsements and support.[44]

As they honed their presentation, the group agreed that the handsome, articulate McGowan would be their spokesman.

Sho marveled at the group around the table. The caliber of the organizers was so high, he said. "I couldn't hire this staff."*

---

*"I'm sure you're asking us to do certain things, not telling us," one of the high-level volunteers said. "You did all the hard work behind this," said Sho.

That afternoon, at 3 p.m., in a conference room at Portland's Hilton Hotel, the attendees numbered up to as many as thirty-five.

Sho began by thanking them for coming on such short notice, then talked about the economic toll the attacks were taking on the country, with airlines laying off 106,000 employee, Boeing laying off 30,000 workers, and the cancellations in the hospitality industry.

> The reverberating effect will surely cripple all kinds of businesses in all sorts of industries if we don't take **decisive** and **immediate** action. We don't have the luxury of waiting for people to work through the fear that has gripped them, indeed paralyzed them, putting lives on hold since September 11. With each day that passes, another business teeters on the brink of ruin. More lives are devastated.

> New York may be 3,000 miles away, but what occurred on the other coast of our great land is being felt right here in our own backyard. **Let's do something about it!** Let's summon Oregon's Pioneer Spirit and organize a delegation of Oregonians to lead an airlift of support that will get the blood flowing again in the veins of this once-vibrant city and jump start its shell-shocked economy.

> Let's assemble a diverse group of Oregonians representing the leadership of sectors from corporate, to government, to the working men and women whose jobs are now at risk, and make it a call to action for other cities to follow suit. More than just a charity event or a vacation I the Big Apple, this is a way to get New York and all of America back on her feet and on the move again—physically, economically, and emotionally.[45]

"Around the table were some of the big movers and shakers of Portland," Ray remembered. "They all said, 'That's a wonderful idea, how can we help?'"

Also important, said Franklin, was that the people Sho pulled together "had a lot of really good contacts."

Brian McCartin, who had worked for Brad Hutton in Hilton Hotels for years, had become vice president of sales and marketing for the Portland Oregon Visitors Association (POVA, now Travel Portland) at the end of January. Like many in the room, he knew only

---

"I just went for the ride." (Group meeting April 29, 2021. Meeting notes in author's files.)

a few people, but also like many in the room, he wouldn't realize that many others didn't know one another, either, because when they came together, their shared purpose was paramount.

> They were all important people and I came to kind of figure that out. It did not matter [though] because all that got checked in the [Azumano] boardroom. They were all there for Sho. I didn't realize he'd led the March for Schools and he got known for that.... My sense of all those people in that room that they were all friends and trying to figure out what they could do. Sho's not one to hold back and [he'll] give you something to do that would seem insurmountable.

The group also expressed a concern about part of the concept, noted Loen: "Concern about doing something for NY—just shopping too frivolous."

Kristen Dozono made what Loen called a "significant comment" about the "little people" who were affected, those who had lost their jobs and were struggling, a reminder of both the economic and emotional pain the average New Yorker was experiencing.

Two questions arose as well, one of which Ray recalled as being "somewhat ancillary" but still relevant if they were to attract coverage: "Who cares about little dinky Portland, Oregon? And what difference was it going to make to send people with open arms and a willing hug?"

Ray countered that this perceived weakness could also be a tremendous strength:

> That also became what was the good story about that, which was, what an extraordinary statement from one of the smallest states in the country, the farthest you could get from New York except for Alaska and Hawaii. We thought because nobody was flying that it would be an extraordinary statement. As we grew and grew and grew, obviously, it became a huge deal.

For Franklin, one thing was essential: to be there first, just as Loen had instinctively felt from the moment Bruce Samson had called them with his "great idea." Franklin remembers:

> I can remember sitting in that room thinking this is sort of a visionary project and effort, but unless we could be the first state to

get on those planes to New York and publicize it, it would probably lose some of its effect. We had to be the first state.

Part of that instinct comes from my background. It's not fun to come in second. If we're going to really be effective, we need to be the first ones out of the box.*

And then, as the thirty people around her brainstormed, she eliminated the chaff and, as is her practice, cut to the next bottom-line requirement:

I'm going in and out of this meeting and in and out of these ideas and thinking, "How would I approach this as a campaign?"

First of all, a campaign needs a slogan. I'm half listening and I'm thinking, "What is a catchy slogan and quite frankly it came into my head: [Flight for Freedom].

What had been taken away from those two planes went into the towers? Clearly, freedoms were very much taken away and freedom was being attacked. I literally came up with the slogan, wrote it down, "Flight for Freedom," passed it along to Sho Dozono who was probably listening to fifty ideas.[Sho thinks she gave it to Don McClave first.] And he glanced down and said, "Well, we've got a name."

And that, quite frankly, was what we needed in the group—someone who could make decisions quickly and instinctively . . . .

The whole point was to urge people to get on planes and go to New York. It was also, "Hey, we're not scared. We are not going to have somebody impact our lives like this. This is our freedom, this is our democracy."**

When Franklin presented "Flight For Freedom" to the group, it resonated, and the response was unanimous. "Everyone said, 'That's what it is,'" said Sho.

------

*In an email to me three years later, Mayor Vera Katz agreed: "The excitement that was created by Sho's team and the fact that we were first to go made it successful." July 30, 2003.

**Loen Dozono's meeting notes made in 2001 state that the trip's name was coined the following day at the media meeting, but this is Franklin's memory and, frankly, Franklin's is a much better story. Sho also thinks the naming may have happened during this day's meeting.

"We decided . . . to open it to all of Oregon," said Ray. Sho assigned Azumano executives Bill and Tina Harmon to work on the travel portions of the project. As the next week would demonstrate, this was no small assignment. Nancy Parrott, head of leisure travel, managed operations and made it possible for 1,000 people to be spoken with and ticketed within days—pre-internet days!

"The team at Azumano was used to my dad having these things that run wild," says Kristen almost twenty years later.

But more than that, the ability for this to be an "every-person" trip was essential, and the Azumano Travel staff kept that awareness at the forefront of their approach to the work. Brian McCartin, who has devoted his career to travel and tourism and represented the Portland Visitor's Bureau on this project, explained:

> A travel agent like Azumano Travel who knows how to package things and pull them together, they knew how to bundle that at a price where it would work for a lot of people from around the state, not just the big businesspeople in Portland. To make it more reasonable was important.

But even with very reasonable pricing, would enough Oregonians want to participate to make the trip worthwhile? McCartin:

> That would be a real statement for Oregon to go there. You have to get them to be courageous enough to get on an airplane. A lot of people in the tourism industry were losing their jobs because people weren't traveling . . . It was a part of finding the Oregon spirit and people believing in it.

Former Governor Vic Atiyeh, an Arab American, and State Sen. Margaret Carter, an African American, would become the Diversity Committee, ensuring that the travelers included a diverse cross-section of Oregonians. In biographies of organizers, George Azumano's role is tied to his internment experience in World War II:

> George was in his 20s when he was forced to live in an internment camp, along with tens of thousands of other Japanese Americans during WWII. Azumano has taken a special interest in the Flight for Freedom, organizing a number of Japanese American veterans to

also take part in the Flight, in hopes of reminding Americans of what
can happen if we turn to racial prejudice in times of war.[46]

By meeting's end, those in attendance had reached consensus that
the idea had merit, and that it was feasible. Subgroups were identified, and Gerry Frank was named honorary chairman.

The next step, the media team—Elisa, Ray, Franklin, and
Bergstein—explained to the group, would be to schedule a news
conference. It was decided the press conference would be held on
Wednesday.

Another thing everyone agreed on was that one leader's participation was essential.

"Could we get the mayor?" said Ray. "And if we didn't get the
mayor was that going to derail the trip?"

Mayor Katz had sent no representation to the 3 p.m. meeting.
Elisa Dozono had spoken to the mayor's chief of staff, San Adams,
over the weekend. Mayor Katz herself was opposed to going, but her
staff was very enthusiastic.

Samson had stopped by the mayor's office that morning.

> I remember going up to her office and the first time I talked to
> her, it was fairly early on . . . . And her initial reaction was, it was a
> great idea, but she didn't think it was right for her to leave Portland
> in a time of crisis. And frankly, she doesn't like flying anyway . . .
>
> I said, "For most of us, this isn't an act of courage, but for you it is
> because you don't like flying anyway."
>
> She laughed about it. She said, "You think I'm a coward."
>
> I said, "No, I don't. I think you're brave."

Katz herself sensed there was another reason she was waffling,
but it was more visceral and she would need a few days to figure out
exactly what it was.

When the meeting was over, Franklin pulled Sho aside and told
him two things with the frankness for which she is known. That the
project was doomed to die by "a thousand ideas" and that Oregon
had to be first:

"Campaigns are all about preparation, organization, execution, and luck. And with this project when I was at that first meeting, I thought, "Yeah, this is going to be a very short time to actually have the preparation phase, a very short time to organize and then you've got to have people who can really execute and deliver." . . . I bet he had at least thirty people around that table—and I'm sitting, going in and out of all of the ideas that are coming up and thinking, ah—this project could really suffer death by 1,000 ideas . . . .With a short campaign you've got to have a committee of people that can make decisions and execute and we don't have much time to bring 1,000 ideas down . . . . I'm a bottom-line person. It's a great idea—how do we make it happen and with whom can we make it happen? Sho to his credit analyzed exactly who could make it happen and what their strengths were, and what strengths were needed to make it happen.

I told Sho that "Hey, this can only be effective if we do it first, and therefore, let's form a smaller group than we had in the room this afternoon."

Sho literally invited a very few people to meet. I think the next day or the day after and that core group—give or take some people who couldn't come—that small group began a whole organization phase of the campaign.

And we met—as many of us as we could, we met every other day, maybe some of us every day.

They may have been on opposite sides of the political fence at the time, but Democrat political strategist Len Bergstein said something similar twenty years later about execution. "There was a mix of people and they had good ideas, and it was fun to blue-sky, but the devil was in the details."

A smaller group was selected that would include Franklin, McGowan, Bergstein, Elisa Dozono, Ray, and they agreed to meet at 5 p.m., after work.

At the 5 p.m. meeting, Elaine was assigned to interact with Gov. George Pataki and Mayor Rudolph Giuliani to begin building a relationship with the project.

The group also decided a logo was needed to go with the slogan. "It was a great idea, we now had a slogan, a logo, but it would all be for nothing unless we were the first," Franklin stressed.

"The smaller groups met so many times," said McGowan. "Everyone forgot about anything else they were doing. This was all-consuming, not only for the immediacy but the logistical—it could have been a logistical nightmare."[47]

TUESDAY, SEPTEMBER 25

10:00	Media team meeting: Azumano Travel office
	• Purpose: press release, press conference
	• Attendees include:
	  – Sho
	  – Loen
	  – Elisa
	  – Len Bergstein
	  – Elaine Franklin
	  – Jack McGowan
	  – John Ray

Morning	Sho goes to Chamber meeting, then visits Vera Katz to make pitch for her to lead trip. She does not say yes.
	"Vera not yet on board—take Belgian chocolates."
	Brad Hutton calls to say that the Hilton organization will offer the Waldorf-Astoria at the same price ($55/night) that it could offer a Times Square hotel.
	Oregonian columnist Jonathan Nicholas calls Sho to ask about the trip.
10:30 p.m.	Sho and/or Loen drop off Belgian truffles with Elisa so she can take them to Mayor Katz's ("Vera's") office early Wednesday morning "to help influence a positive decision."

In Washington, DC, the Travel Industry Association met with the Secretary of Commerce to plead for government action to try to restore confidence in travel. "Our industry is in dire straits," said Betsy O'Rourke, the trade group's senior vice president. "If the American people don't get back to traveling, to normal life, a number of these companies won't be there to serve them."[48]

In the first two weeks after the attacks, New York City had lost an estimated $163.27 million in visitor revenue.[49]

In Portland, Sho sent his staff a memo that thanked the employees for their performance and for their support of him and of one another, provided an update on the company's status, and echoed the

Chamber newsletter's "move on" message. The company had even acquired "a couple of new accounts" since September 11. "It is natural to be afraid," he wrote, but I urge you to keep your fears from others and instead, show your courage to all. As John Wayne once remarked, 'Courage is being scared to death . . . and saddling up anyway.'"[50]

"We hear Gerry is not happy, feels date is wrong, he may jump ship," wrote Loen. "Mayor still doubtful."

The media group held its first official meeting to plan the press conference that was to take place the next day, where and when still to be decided. In large part, these were not people who knew each other well or who had worked extensively together.

From the vantage point of twenty years later, two people who worked very closely together on this project and under great pressure were from different sides of the political aisle: Elaine Franklin (a Republican) and Len Bergstein (a Democrat). "We've been on opposite sides of a lot of things," said Franklin, "but I've worked in a professional way with Len Bergstein."

Demonstrating how collaborative the team members from opposites of the aisle were, that day, in a memo to the "Communications Team," Bergstein shared "some great themes from Elaine Franklin—which should be worked into our 'media release' and 'talking points,'" and which did, in fact, appear in the press release.[51]

With a philosophy that seems to have disappeared by 2021, Franklin spoke about how she brought her political *modus operandi* into the Flight for Freedom sphere:

> In politics, I worked from the premise that yesterday's enemy may have to be tomorrow's friend. You can be on opposite sides on so many things, but work together [on shared] goals and solutions. So we were a group of professionals who respected each other's strengths and we all had a lot of strengths. We were all, most of us anyway, pretty secure so that we didn't mind throwing out ideas that might be completely idiotic and wouldn't ever come to anything, but we were comfortable enough in that room to brainstorm and push ideas out and trap the ones that [had potential]."

The main agenda item was the press conference, which was set for 10 a.m. the following day, but where should it be? Elisa proposed the airport. While some were against that idea, Sho supported it. And it was decided: Port of Portland Commission President Jay Waldron would open and host the press conference at the airport.

Then came the press release:

FOR IMMEDIATE RELEASE

September 26, 2001

CONTACTS: John Ray, Len Bergstein, Elisa Dozono

Oregonians Organize "Flight For Freedom"

Summoning Oregon's pioneer spirit, state business and civic leaders today announced that they are organizing a "Flight For Freedom" the weekend starting Saturday, October 6. A delegation of 200 Oregonians will fly from Portland to New York City that weekend.

Oregon's "Flight For Freedom" is both symbolic and practical. "We send a message to the world that we will not be cowed by atrocity," said Sho Dozono, Chair of the Portland Metropolitan Chamber of Commerce. "Mayor Giuliani has asked us to come to New York, so in the spirit that brought pioneers west on the Oregon Trail, Oregonians now will journey back east to put a face on freedom," said Bruce Samson, Portland business and community leader. Jack McGowan, Executive Director of SOLV, stated, "We'll stand tall with New Yorkers to show that the economy may have been knocked down, but it hasn't been knocked out."

While in New York, the first stop will be Union Square to pay their respects at what has become a makeshift citizens' memorial. The group will participate in other activities and then individual members plan to make personal contacts with New Yorkers in all walks of life. A university president and school board member will meet with educators, the President of the Urban League will meet with her counterpart, public safety officials will meet with police, fire and emergency workers. Businesspeople who have connections with New York will re-establish the commercial ties that are an important part of the connection between Oregon and New York.

Oregonians interested in joining this Flight For Freedom are asked to contact the Flight For Freedom committee at (503) XXX-XXXX or via e-mail at flightforfreedom@azumano.com.

Sho attended the Chamber of Commerce meeting that morning. There he saw Portland Public Schools Superintendent Jim Scherzinger, who said he'd bring his whole family.[52] Jim Rudd, who had agreed to work on sponsorships (including his investment banking firm, Ferguson Wellman), would not be able to travel himself, but he was sending his wife Cathy and daughter Hilary.

Brad Hutton called to let the organizers know that the Hilton would be providing its flagship Waldorf–Astoria Hotel, and for the same price, $55 per night, as it would have offered for a Times Square property. "They said, 'If you're going to stay with us, you're going to stay at the Waldorf-Astoria,'" Ray remembered.

Located on Park Avenue between Forty-Ninth and Fiftieth Streets, the Waldorf-Astoria had been the residence of Cole Porter, Frank Sinatra, President Herbert Hoover, and many others, and its role in politics and Hollywood had earned it a secure seat in the history of world affairs and glamor in the twentieth century. The $55 a night rate was basically the room tax.

Azumano Travel had "a really strong Groups Department," said Nancy Parrott, who ran the Leisure Department. "The head of our Groups Department, Gregg Macy, got busy negotiating with the airlines and the hotels."

Oregonian columnist Jonathan Nicholas called Sho and asked him about the trip. Exactly how Nicholas learned about it has so far been lost to history, but given the number of people in town who knew about it by then, that a reporter worth his salt would find out it was in the works is no surprise.

Sho talked to him about the "New York City or Bust" concept, about sharing airfares from $250 and rooms from $50, and the hope that hundreds, "and then thousands" of Oregonians would travel. "We can't stay away because we're afraid," Dozono said. "And if enough Oregonians spread the 'Meet Me in New York' message to friends and family across the country, this could become a national movement."

Nicholas ended his column with:

Tough call here for Vera Katz.

Does the Portland mayor accept the invitation to take wing and lead the delegation lending support to her second-favorite city?

Or does she listen to those whispering in her ear that the place for her to be encouraging citizens to jump-start an ailing economy is right in her own back yard?

2

The column would appear in Wednesday morning paper.

That morning, Sho had called on Mayor Katz to personally invite her to lead the trip. She had not yet come to a decision.

She had spent the previous days sorting out her confusion. The source of her hesitation, she discovered, reached almost as far back as she could remember. She recounted her story for *The Oregonian*, whose reporter, Courtenay Thompson followed her throughout the trip.

Vera Pistrak was born a war refugee in Dusseldorf, Germany, on August 3, 1933. Her Jewish parents, Lazar and Raissa Pistrak, had been politically active Mensheviks, who opposed the Bolsheviks.

When she was just two months old, her parents again fled with her and her older sister, Zena, this time from Hitler's rising power. They went to Paris, leaving behind aunts, uncles and cousins who, reluctant to leave Germany, later perished in death camps.

In Paris, Vera was unhappy. She remembers once, at age four or five, refusing to eat for a week. She drank only the liquid from the wet washcloth she'd suck in the bath, a child's comfort.

When she was six, the Nazis invaded France and the bombings began. She remembers going three or four times a week to the bomb shelter down the street from her family's Paris apartment. They'd emerge to find sections of buildings, or entire homes, in rubble.

The rest of her war is a child's blur of images:

A little white dog running after her to a shelter. He didn't make it.

Her sister being forced to give the Nazi salute at school.

And Paris streets filled with hundreds and hundreds of people, carrying little, saying nothing, walking silently away from their homes and their lives.

Sculptor Aristide Maillol hid the Pistraks in southern France for a night as they once again fled the Nazis in 1940, when the Vichy government gave foreign Jews one day to get out of the country.

They walked across the Pyrenees. Vera was seven.

When they arrived in New York, she remembers a loudspeaker announcing to their waiting sponsor, "The Pistrak family, with no belongings."

They first moved to the Lower East Side but then moved to the

Upper West Side, where her mother worked in sweatshops knitting sweaters for soldiers and sewing evening bags at night. Her father had left them soon after they arrived. When Vera was ten years old, she and her mother became naturalized citizens . . . .

"I thought I'd gotten beyond all that," Katz said on the flight out to New York on Saturday. "It has all become very, very real again.

"Seeing the planes hitting the towers is such a psychological and emotional shock to the psyche."[53]

In New York, the little girl who'd been running finally could rest. But when it came to the trip, "The more I thought about it," Katz said two years later:

> . . . the more I realized that it was a replay of personal history for me, that [the bombing of the World Trade Center] was the realization that all my hopes and dreams were shattered by the fact that New York was not safe anymore. The reason I left and struggled by crossing the Pyrenees by foot, to get to America and to get to New York, that was all shattered for me and I couldn't deal with it emotionally . . . .

> "It wasn't safe anymore, the one place in the world that we came, that we came with nothing, absolutely nothing, was safe anymore."[54]

WEDNESDAY, SEPTEMBER 26

After she realized that her reluctance had come from a very deep place in her past, Vera Katz had come to a decision.

> My heart broke and then I said to myself, "Well, that's a little selfish, and if you can give hope to New Yorkers and show that at least one place around the world, in America, was willing to extend itself, you ought to be there. And you're the mayor of the city and the idea came from people living in the city and people who are my friends . . . .

> That was kind of the beginning of the emotional trip and as it ended, it was probably one of the most positive experiences I've had in my life, both personal, and as part of a community that went to assist, or at least to send a message.

Early that morning, Elisa Dozono went to the see the mayor. "And in that time," said Katz, "I had already figured out why I was so adamant not to go. I realized it and I said, 'OK, I understand, I'm going.'"

Nearly twenty years later, former Oregon Senator Gordon H. Smith says, "I remember talking to Vera Katz and saying what a wonderful idea this was. She was from New York and I thought her response was wonderful, to lead the city at that time with that kind of outreach."[55]*

From that moment until the last reception held in New York, the pace would be flat-out for everyone:

7:15 a.m. KXL radio called Sho; they'd seen the Jonathan Nicholas column. Could Sho do fifteen minutes during morning drive time?

7:30 a.m. Elisa called Sho. Vera had agreed to go. Sho swore Loen to secrecy. The media team rewrote the press release to include the mayor.

7:40 a.m. Sho on KXL: "This is just a symbolic gesture by a group of us to tell America, 'Wake up, do what you were going to do September 10, just don't let this terror stop us from enjoying life in our own community.'"

By 10 a.m., the Portland International Airport conference center was jammed with reporters from all the city's media, along with State Sen. Carter, Portland Oregon Visitors Association's Joe D'Alessandro, the Hilton's Hutton, and the other key players.

When Loen and Sho arrived, McGowan greeted them excitedly: "Did you hear? Vera's going!"

"So much for secrecy!" Loen wrote.

Gerry Frank arrived with investment banker Jim Rudd's wife, Cathy, a sign that he was maybe not as disgruntled as they had feared,

---

*On October 15, Smith would stand on the Senate floor and celebrate the efforts of the Flight for Freedom participants in an eloquent speech, which is preserved in the *Congressional Record* and you will find in the Appendix.

though he did mention to some people that he thought the date was wrong and he wouldn't be able to participate personally.

As planned, Port of Portland Commission President Jay Waldron kicked off the event. "It has been a rough couple of weeks, with the entire airline industry suffering immensely," he said, adding that 14 million people come through PDX every year. "Our message is we want them to keep flying, and we want even more to come from out of state and see our beautiful new concourse—which the public will see eventually."

State Sen. Margaret Carter, who had served in the Oregon House of Representatives with Mayor Katz and Rep. Darlene Hooley, who was serving as a U.S. Congresswoman, read the mayor's official statement:

> It is fitting that the pioneering spirit of Oregon joins the nation on restoring the path to economic health.
>
> As a former New Yorker, I am looking forward to leading this delegation, as Portland demonstrates their support for New York, not just financially, but in a human sense.
>
> New York took care of me sixty years ago, when the citizens of the city embraced me and my family as we emigrated from Europe.
>
> Ironically, it will be almost to the day that I will return to the city to offer my support in return, this time as a mayor—proof that the American dream does happen.
>
> Mayor Giuliani's asked for people to come back, to help the city move on economically and emotionally. I am proud to be a part of what I hope will become a national movement.

It was only two weeks since the tragedy, and the excitement in the room was contagious. State Sen. Carter stressed the need to put vitality back into the daily existence of Americans: "We will not be defeated by anything that is happening in our country, and hopefully this movement will generate activity in the minds of other people to want to get back and join life, live life at its fullest, and that's what's important.

"Plus," she added, "For me, I'm going shopping. I'm buying shoes."[56]

Sho spoke about the purpose of the trip:

> This effort has been an extraordinary meeting of some very great
> minds and a pulling together of some cosmic-like forces to accom-
> plish a single critical goal: to free America from the grips of fear and
> get us back on the move again . . . .
>
> I want to stress that this isn't about my company. To be sure, [Flight
> For Freedom] involves a plane trip to New York, but this isn't about
> the airline industry or the travel industry. This isn't even just about
> New York. This is about America. It's about freedom. It's about
> our fellow citizens, not just in Oregon but all around the country,
> who have become paralyzed with fear. It's about the thousands of
> working men and women in all walks of life who have lost their jobs
> because of what that fear has done to our economy.
>
> And so, I speak to you this morning as chair of the Portland
> Metropolitan Chamber of Commerce . . . .Let's make sure New
> Yorkers get the message that the rest of the country is with them, not
> just because we say so, but because we're doing something about it.
>
> We're going to New York to connect with New Yorkers, one on one—
> on both a personal and a business level. We're going to New York
> to put the shine back on the Big Apple, to show how very much we
> care, to show the rest of the country, indeed the whole world, that
> Americans will not be cowed by atrocity, intimidated by fear . . . .
>
> Our trip to New York is not a vacation. It's a call to action.[57]

"We announced this idea we had and all of a sudden it became
the hottest thing around," said Ray. "The local media was a wonderful water carrier for us . . . . We took care of about ten media requests
[to go on the trip] within an hour of our news conference."

"The media was hungry for the good news story," says Bergstein,
and the Flight for Freedom "had authenticity to it. Because it was so
authentic and the people who were part of the flight were moved—
you can't make it up."

"It was all death, search for survivors, hatred of attackers,
economy collapsing," says Ray, who added that at the same time the
Flight for Freedom was there, a group of about 150 from Jamaica was
there, and "we took pains to say they were in town in our messaging."
It was positive; "In every story you saw, we said, 'Giuliani said please
come and we did. We're going to see New York.'"[58]

Going to New York was a no-brainer for KXL radio, remembered reporter Chris Sullivan:

Azumano was a big sponsor and everybody knew Sho. Once he decided this was something that was going to happen, our management was, "He's a big sponsor, let's tag along." . . . I was there to be a fly on the wall, but I spent most of my time tagging along with the dignitaries because that's what they wanted [me] to do.[59]

KPAM radio's Bill Cooper remembers things a little differently.

Three [radio] stations in town were doing news: KPAM AM 860, KXL, and KEX. I had friends at both KXL and KEX, Chris Sullivan and Neal Penland over at KEX. [They were the main reporters.] The three of us got together and we'd been told by our bosses that there was no money in the budget to send a reporter on the trip and so we all lied to our bosses.

I told my management that KXL and KEX were sending Chris Sullivan and Neal Penland. Penland said that Sullivan and Cooper are going . . . . So all of our management at the time didn't know that we'd cooked this up and we all got to go. [PHOTO 6]

There's a lot of competition in radio news, and there was at the time, and well strived to get the story first, but this was a case if we all three didn't go, none of us were going. So we went.

It was a great trip.

The reason they did what they did was that the three newsmen understood that the Flight for Freedom was major news, says Cooper:

We had this historic attack on our country, 9/11, and then less than a month later, here you have a prominent businessman in Sho Dozono and Vera Katz joining forces to put together a trip to New York with 1,000 people just to show the city support? It was a no-brainer, it was something we had to cover. It was the biggest news story around that time other than the attack itself.[60]

"I didn't hesitate," said KGW television's Krista Vasquez, who told station management that they should cover the trip. "I was so amazed by the outpouring of support and the whole premise behind the trip. I wanted to go and see Oregon support New Yorkers. It was an amazing trip, one that I will never forget." She would capture interviews on the plane, accompanied by photojournalist Scott Williams, camera in tow. [PHOTO 7]

The cost was $379 plus tax for airfare and two nights lodging, or $434 for three nights (and $55 per person per night for extra stays at the Waldorf). Travelers could depart daily between October 4 and October 8, and return October 5 through October 11, though the main activities would take place from October 6 through October 8. Azumano took no commissions and received no revenue from the project.

"That's unheard of," said Travel Oregon Executive Director Todd Davidson about the rates. "It tells you that there was a tremendous amount of support, that there was goodwill that the Azumano Travel company had obviously accumulated and they were able to utilize that. Even twenty years ago, that was very inexpensive, crazy inexpensive."

"We had the right contacts, and the airline partners—Delta in particular—when we went to Delta and said we want to do this, we were able to negotiate incredible airfares because their planes were all flying empty," said Nancy Parrott, who was leisure sales manager at the time.

> Something is better than nothing, right? Delta really came to the table and helped us with the seats and gave us incredible airfares.
>
> And the same thing happened at the Waldorf-Astoria. They were empty; they had nothing but cancellations. The rate we had there was completely unheard of. It really was monumental, being able to secure as good a rate as we did. They had just laid off a lot of their employees so they saw this as an opportunity to bring their employees back for a period of time. They realized that the Flight for Freedom travelers were going to use the restaurants and the bars and they were going to use housekeeping services.

By day's end, Azumano Travel was swamped. "Frankly, it was going so fast, we wondered if we should cut it off. Calls and emails came in from everybody," said Ray. "At no time do I remember anyone saying, 'I'm really afraid.'"

At Azumano Travel, the staff set up the phone system mechanics to take all the calls, and the Flight for Freedom website was put in place. Assistant Vice President Jeri Hunt worked with Mo Denny, the contractor who managed the website and, in this case, donated her time, to design and implement the site with contributions from Tina Harmon as well. In a short time, this site became the crossroads for a random assemblage of people who shared the bond of the Flight for Freedom travel.

From the beginning, the website clearly explained the Flight For Freedom's mission: "(1) to show the world that the skies are safe for travel again and that terrorists cannot keep us grounded due to fear; (2) to encourage Americans—and people around the globe—to begin healing our economy by investing in our communities; and (3) to bring symbolic, yet heartfelt, economic and emotional support to the citizens of New York." Even though it had been created quickly for a single project, this site was used for many years and served as the hub for subsequent Flight for Freedom trips that Azumano Travel organized. The site also included a page where people could record their thoughts and feelings and receive messages from all over the country. [PHOTO 8]

As the media inundation began, Elaine Franklin worked with Ray to develop disciplined messaging so that everyone would be "singing from the same hymnal." In one of his first opportunities as spokesman, McGowan conveyed the main message, which would be repeated throughout the trip:

> We, individually and as a country, need to get back on the horse. We need to move on, for not to do this would send a message that acts like these will work . . . not only at crippling our airline, convention, tourism and other business infrastructures, but even more important, affecting our psyche as Americans.

Mayor Katz released a statement that put her firmly in place as the Flight for Freedom's leader, and she revealed the personal elements that would add even more resonance to the project.

That afternoon's organizational meeting saw a seismic introduction, though nobody would know it at the time. They needed a logo to go with the twenty-four-hour-old name.

NEWS   NEWS   NEWS   NEWS

News from the office of
Vera Katz
Mayor Portland Oregon The City That Works

NEWS   NEWS   NEWS   NEWS

FOR IMMEDIATE RELEASE
September 26, 2001

CONTACT: Sarah Bott
Phone: (503) 823-3442
Pager: (503) 323-1041
E-mail: sbott@ci.portland.or.us

STATEMENT BY PORTLAND MAYOR VERA KATZ REGARDING VISIT TO NEW YORK CITY

"It is fitting that the pioneering spirit of Oregon joins the nation on restoring the path to economic health.

"As a former New Yorker, I am looking forward to leading this delegation, as Portland demonstrates their support for New York, not just financially, but in a human sense.

"New York took care of me 60 years ago, when the citizens of the city embraced me and my family as we emigrated from Europe.

"Ironically, it will be almost to the day, that I will return to the city to offer my support in return, this time as a mayor – proof that the American dream does happen.

"Mayor Giuliani's asked for people to come back, to help the city move on economically and emotionally.

"I am proud to be a part of what I hope will become a national movement."

###

Photo courtesy of Jackie Young.

Elaine Franklin suggested Oregon ♥ New York, and Loen suggested the shadow of the twin towers with two Douglas Firs standing in for the destroyed buildings. Franklin volunteered to work on the button design and had a designer friend implement it. This logo and especially the button that bore it turned out to be perhaps the most important contributions to the Oregonians' on-the-ground experience in New York. [PHOTO 9]

The buttons and T-shirts that carried that logo made Oregonians instantly identifiable and, in New York City, not only opened doors for the Freedom Fliers but opened arms as well. (McCartin of POVA remembered hearing a story of Oregonians who visited New York again three months later and wore their shirts—a police car pulled up at the corner and said, "Are you guys still here?")

Nancy Parrott remembers the generosity of the group's vendors:

> We had people who had to do the creative—the T-shirt and the logo and the buttons and they were working with printers and we're trying to negotiate the best deals possible to make everything very affordable. Everybody wanted to help. When we started talking about what was going on, even suppliers wanted to help. Everything we got was at cost, pretty much. That was a contribution from a lot of the suppliers . . . .

At this meeting, another new member joined the team, Karen Winder, who was on loan from the Portland office of The Collins Group, a consulting firm that assisted nonprofit organizations with fundraising. Winder helped with media, stickers, shirts, and many other elements of the project; as with others, she was a volunteer, with the full support of her employers.

Despite the joy and enthusiasm shared by everyone working on the project, the reality was that arranging for Mayor Katz's travel presented challenges unique to her.

"We didn't know what was going to happen," said Sarah Bott, her communications director. "She was getting death threats for being Jewish. She was brave, man."

"Vera hated flying, refused to fly," said McGowan, who was, like Katz and her husband, a former New Yorker. "I remember at one of the advance meetings, Vera and I became close and I hugged her and I held her hand, and I said, 'Vera, if you want me to sit next to you and hold your hand the entire flight, I will do it. This is not only for Portland, Vera, this is for you.' . . . You forgot about your personal safety. And things could have happened."

While Mayor Katz received support in the press and from the public, both in Oregon and in New York, she also was the target of criticism.

She was called "a shameless opportunist" for spending taxpayer money on a "vacation to New York." Mayor Katz and those on her staff paid their own way; the city did not foot the bill. Not only that, but they worked throughout the trip, far more than the usual eight-hour day.

Some voices in the media expressed the belief that Portlanders, with the mayor in the lead, should be spending their money in Portland, where the economy was in decline. The mayoral staff responded by pointing out that one of the trip's goals was to encourage tourism to Oregon.

Brian McCartin, who was vice president of sales and marketing for the Portland Oregon Visitors Association at the time, remembers that in doing market research in that period, they discovered that when you asked consumers about Portland, nothing would come to mind for 35 percent or more of respondents—that was first place. Rain ranked second and the city's basketball team, the Portland Trail Blazers, third. At that time—shortly before Gov. John Kitzhaber's administration boosted the tourism budget in response to the recession—Oregon ranked forty-eighth in tourism funding, said McCartin. "Mississippi had a lot more than Oregon."

Sho Dozono had his critics, too. "Governor Atiyeh advised me to 'Watch out for land mines,'" said Sho. "He warned me that people will think the wrong thing no matter how I do this."

His response to the critics was, "If they don't get it, it's their problem. I'm making no profits, no commissions from this. If people want to make sure [about that], they can call the hotel, they can call the airlines. Will it cost me money? Yes. Do I care? No."

Atiyeh was right. As with everything, there were critics. In November, Oregon would be the first state to announce it was officially in a recession. People said the money should be spent locally. Others said that spending money as an act of patriotism lacked a moral foundation.

Still others criticized the Oregonians for not spending enough. Mitch Goldstone organized the National Economic Patriotism in Irvine and Coast to Coast trip in November 2001, a 5,000-shopper pilgrimage to New York with people from 173 cities, including about 140 from his hometown of Irvine, Calif. *The Christian Science Monitor* reported that Goldstone reserved particular moral indignation for Oregonians, calling it a "moral imperative not to spend a little more but to spend a lot more."

"I fail to see the economic patriotism in that," said Goldstone, a New York native. "We paid full price for airfare, hotels, everything.

The city asked if there was anything they could do for us. We said, 'No. This isn't about us. It's about you.'"[61]

Interestingly, this was a change of tune for a man who had written to Dozono the month before (October 11) praising the Flight for Freedom and sharing the Irvine effort, which was called, at that time, "Economic Patriotism in Irvine and Coast to Coast" (EPICC), and whose website had been developed the day before:

> A giant congratulations on your group's campaign to support NYC.... The goal is to run with the Oregon Flight for Freedom campaign and challenge the entire nation to join Irvine.... Our goal is to create less of a junket atmosphere, as we are seeking to buy full-fare tickets and provide as much sentimental currency by purchasing full-price theater tickets, etc. and vouchers for restaurants, etc....
>
> Your comments are so valued and welcome. Thanks for everything you have done, and hopefully this EPICC campaign will take the mission national, and just in time for the holiday season.[62]

Sadly, Goldstone missed the point. Even though organizers estimated that the Flight for Freedom group pumped $1 million into the city that weekend, its purpose was different than that of the Irvine trip. By making the trip affordable, Flight for Freedom organizers made it possible for courageous people without great means to participate—which made it possible for one in every 3,000 Oregonians to help, including those who had never been to New York or even traveled on an airplane.

The Flight for Freedom made it possible for people who would have lost work, whether they were those on the sixty-two flights that transported Oregonians or the hundreds of staff at the Waldorf who would have been laid off, to go back to work. The actors and crew of Broadway productions, cab drivers, and restaurants, also made money. Less than a month after the attacks, when the city was empty, 1,000 Oregonians showed up.

Former Gov. George Pataki said the Flight for Freedom's symbolic importance was enormous:

> The hotels were empty, workers unemployed, restaurants were empty, and theaters were dark. Tens of thousands of people had lost their jobs through no fault of their own because after the attacks,

people were afraid to come into the city because they were afraid to be attacked again.

So when so many people from Oregon said we're going to go, and in a highly visible way go to the restaurants, stay in hotels, walk on the streets, let the rest of the world know that it's OK to be in New York, the meaning of that act was far beyond the economic benefit of the people who came, although that was significant. The symbolic commitment to be a part of the recovery of New York from these horrible attacks meant a great deal to all New Yorkers and sent a very positive message to the entire country. It will always be remembered by New Yorkers because it was courage and graciousness and a time of uncertainty, to get us to build back to where we are today.[63]

"If we're the grief-busters, that's OK," Sho told *The Oregonian.* "We want to bust through this, for each other."[64]

THURSDAY, SEPTEMBER 27

While the organizers were in the media, the real activity was happening at Azumano Travel, where ticketing began at noon. A banner was posted for the "Command Center." [PHOTO 10]

Sho estimated that a trip of this scale usually requires about six months of lead time, but they had put it together within a week — working nearly around the clock. Nancy Parrott said that despite the very demanding hours, this project was good for staff morale:

We needed something positive to do and this was because everybody stopped traveling completely; all we were doing was canceling reservations and refunding airline tickets. Having something else to focus on was a real positive for the employees and everybody in the company. That's basically what happened. It was all hands on deck for about a week and a half while we pulled it together.[65]

Calls were heavy. By 7:30 a.m. the firm had received 125 emails alone, plus innumerable voice mails. Staff, who were donating their time, worked well into the night processing reservations. This was the "execute" stage Franklin had outlined in her elements of a successful campaign. The group that had felt it would be lucky if it could get 200 participants soon found itself overwhelmed beyond all expectations.

And the Azumano Travel staff and the volunteers they quickly trained executed superbly.

The Flight for Freedom was successful because every person—all of them highly skilled and highly experienced—executed in every aspect of the effort, or "campaign," as Elaine Franklin would describe it. Whether it was media or event-planning or reservations and ticketing or building a logo and creating a brand or hospitality, all the many, many elements of the project were executed right and everyone performed. Every aspect was important, every contribution mattered, and the people who contributed understood that, were capable of delivering, and did.

Most of this book will focus on the participants and the organizers. But understanding the truly unsung heroes of this trip is essential: the people who sat at desks and answered phones, who stood by the fax machine, who put together documents and made itineraries—"You're in Bend? Let's see where you can leave from and which connecting airport will work best for you"—worked individually, "by hand," so to speak, for 1,000 persons in a little over a week. "Fortunately, this is what we do," said Parrott.

Today, as a vice president of CI Azumano Travel, looking back at the Flight for Freedom with thirty-two years in the field and an expertise in operations, Parrott describes what it took to accomplish what they achieved in that week:

> I'd say we had a team of at least twenty, twenty-five people, and they were employees—many [volunteers] were from the Dozono family . . . . And then it trickled through rest of the company. Back then we had a lot of branch offices. So the receptionist and the staff were all getting phone calls about how do I sign up? Everybody in the company helped with those. We got them versed on reservation forms to fill out, and they'd come to headquarters [by fax], we'd get them into the system and get them booked.

> Initially, it took a lot of us with that industry experience to be able to pull it together as quickly, securing the hotel, the airline seats. Building an itinerary, securing the transfers and so forth. We did that first thing . . . At that time the internet wasn't prevalent and there was no way to book all this online so people on the committee and the volunteers . . . helped get the word out to the community and the press, and they helped man the phones.

We spent about a week and a half taking reservations from people and then the rest of the travel team would take those requests and confirm on the air, prepare their itinerary, prepare their documents and send everything out. We did the bulk of this in about seven days.

. . . Since we didn't have any other business going on, we literally pulled a team of leadership together from within the company.

. . . And then of course we had to pull all the pricing together, get it to market and then we set up a team, a phone bank to start taking requests from people.

Our phone lines were so busy that we had to take messages and call people back in a lot of cases. But then from that point, we called in a lot of our administration staff and they were pulling other travel manifests and name lists, and we had all these tickets to issue.

Logistically, we were prepared to do that because that is our business . . . .

Of course, it wasn't just preparing to get everyone booked, then we needed staff and people in New York to work there, too.

We had a lot of meetings in those days. "We're going to meet at 10 a.m. and again at 2 p.m. and figure out where everybody is, make decisions, what staff will go with the group, who will be coordinating departures at the airport."

I ended up flying out with the very last group. Then when we were in New York we manned a hospitality desk /area for the entire time. It was a challenge but it was kind of a fun challenge. It was fun because everybody knew the impact of 9/11 and it was fun because there was something to do. We couldn't just wallow in how bad our industry had been hit.

It was very exciting because the people that traveled with us were so motivated and they were thrilled to have the opportunity to do this, to show the world that we're going to New York, we're going to support those New Yorkers, not just through travel "and showing everyone else it's OK to travel," but supporting them economically by shopping and going to the restaurants and so forth. That was the fun part, hearing all of those travelers getting ready and preparing for the trip itself.

A little bit of it happened on the fly, but all of the travelers were very understanding and understood it. The Flight for Freedom was such an amazing thing . . . everybody was flexible and understood that it was a big complex pulling it together. There may be a glitch here or there, but it all worked . . . .[People left from airports all around the state.] It didn't start out that way, but we were getting demand and getting requests from throughout the Pacific Northwest and as a result, there were flights available so we just started taking group space on a variety of flights and it worked. But it was all based on the overwhelming demand.

I don't think any of us ever anticipated that we were going to end up with 1,000 people. Initially, our goal was that 300 would be great. But it kept growing and growing and it got bigger and bigger so we needed to add. We needed to meet the demand.

Chaotic as it was, it was exciting chaos. And our fax machine, because people were faxing these forms, too. We had one person just standing by the fax machine. They were coming from everywhere. And some of them were probably coming from our offices in Tigard and Albany and Corvallis and so forth, too.

Rick Love of Azumano Travel was one of the people who had been working long hours to organize the trip. He was exhausted. He remembered that "very late" one night:

Sho came in and said, "We can use your help in New York, and that was how it all started. At first, after working all the hours I had already worked, I thought, "What have I just done?" But once we got there—Sho was kind enough to allow me to bring my wife, Pam—I knew we were in for something.[66]

POVA sent volunteers to Azumano Thursday and Friday. "Thank God," wrote Loen, who was helping with coordinating volunteers, answering phones, and facilitating ticketing.

Employees who had been laid off returned to help. People even walked in off the street to volunteer. Soon, the Flight For Freedom on-site staff was half composed of "fill-in" workers. It took almost fifty people, with twenty-five Azumano staff and about twenty volunteers, to get phones answered and people ticketed.

LaVonne Scheckla, whose husband was a retired firefighter, had signed up for the trip and then volunteered for days. Scheckla remembered another a volunteer who had just moved to Portland from Cincinnati who walked in off the street to help.

Loen's notes from that day provide a glimpse into the highs and lows those working the phones experienced: "Tina [Harmon] is devastated by mean-spirited phone call, then a little later receives one of most heartening calls from school board member in rural N.Y. offering home stays."

"Some of the most wonderful comments were the older people, who had been through World War II, who had been through the Depression, and they said, 'My gosh, we're not afraid, we're going to go,'" Loen remembered in 2003. One elderly couple that was coping with cancer and had never been to New York decided that it was time to make the journey. Some of the "Freedom Fliers," as they came to be known, had never flown before. Sho remembered hearing about a Portland Radio Cab driver who saved up his tips to pay for the trip, and some people cashed in their 401(k)s to go.

Kristen, recently graduated from college, was amazed at the cross-section of people she spoke with on the phone:

> Bartenders that just decided to go. There were a lot of individuals who called: "I need to do something, I need to go." I can't say how much taking that trip meant. You could have donated to the Red Cross, but showing up, showing up means something. Standing on the same ground and being there for people.

"We have sent blood, we have sent money. Now we have to send ourselves," Jack McGowan would tell the media.

"Up until this time, I'd not seen what can happen when one man has a dream and pursues it without concern as to outcome," said Samson, who was recruiting people from around the state, to ensure that the trip included schoolkids, teachers, union people, Muslims, representatives of city and county governments on the flight. He called it putting "a face on freedom."

McGowan:

> It was the culmination of a cause. And the cause manifested itself instantaneously. All of a sudden, look what happened. Everyone remembers—our parents remember where they were the day of infamy [Pearl Harbor]. Every single person of a generation or multiple generations know exactly where they were when 9/11 occurred.
>
> And so I think for all of us it was the sense of—it became such an overarching, all-encompassing mission—and it built and built and built so all of a sudden, we were all swept up into this mission.

Whether it was coordinator or whether it was participant, it was this whirlwind that we were all caught up in this shared experience and the emotional outlet was so dramatic because we lived every moment of it.

Debra-Diane Jenness, in tiny Crescent Lake (pop. 400) in the Deschutes National Forest, was one of the people who had to "do SOMETHING." She told her story in 2002:

The events of September 11th, 2001, hit our family very hard. Living in Crescent Lake, Oregon, we are at a distinct disadvantage to hear about things; no radio stations come in, no "local" TV reception; in fact, if you don't have a satellite, you don't know much about anything. We put in a satellite only three years ago so we could at least get the news. Only newspaper is from Eugene, no "local" coverage. Our son is home-schooled, and he started his school year on Monday, September 10th. He was fourteen years old at the time, and in ninth grade.

On Sept. 11th, we both got up early as usual, he to start his work, and I headed down to the post office to collect our mail. (There is no mail delivery in Crescent Lake; we don't even have a street address!) The post office is in one of our two local gas station/mini-marts. As usual, the TV was on in the grocery store part, and as usual, I paid absolutely no attention to it when I walked into the post office. I got my mail and chatted for a few minutes with the postmistress, who said her daughter was quite upset; apparently a friend of her daughter was not able to reach her Dad, who works for Colin Powell.

I asked what the problem was and the postmistress looked at me and said, "You don't know, do you?" (I do not turn the satellite/TV on in the mornings when I get up.)

I said, "Know what???"

This was at 8:45 a.m. our time, 11:45 a.m. in New York. So she told me what had happened. I stood there with my mouth hanging on the floor, looking to the TV in the store. Of course by this time, the Twin Towers were already reduced to a pile of rubble. I remember saying, "Gee, I guess I better go home and turn on the TV" and left. As I walked in the door, my son was coming down the stairs and I told him what had happened, and to go get his Dad as I turned on the TV. I also told him "no school today" as we stayed glued to the TV for the next several hours . . . .

How does a person put into words the feelings of seeing the devastation in New York and the anger at whomever did it? At that time, we didn't know. I asked my husband, "Who did we piss off?" and he also had no guesses. We were just dumbfounded, as most of the country and world was.

Being "glued to the TV" was the nation's activity that day. In the coming days, in a state of shock, the Jenness family was certain of one thing:

> . . . [W]e still had the urge to do SOMETHING, but what? We wanted to do something that we KNEW would help, not just send money to an organization and hope it got there (we did that also), but wanted to do something more "hands-on", but WHAT? Then my husband read a blurb on the Internet about the "Flight for Freedom" and shared it with me, and we felt we had our answer. The three of us were going to New York.

> I contacted Azumano Travel via the email they had set up on a Thursday to get more information about the project. By Monday, we had our reservations for Friday's departure, even though we did not receive our actual confirmation and e-ticket information until Thursday. It was a very hectic week getting ready for this trip; for us, we did not consider this a "vacation" so it was difficult to know how to pack, other than we didn't want to take much . . . .[67]

Loen remembered:

> I don't know if it's a testament to how well people in Oregon can work together, and I think that's the message also of the trip, it's just [that] regular people can do something, it doesn't have to be big-whoever-it-is. That's what was so wonderful, don't you think? It was just this amalgam of everybody, a hodgepodge, and it was the most wonderful thing.

At 4 p.m. Sho, Bruce Samson, Chamber of Commerce President and CEO Dan McClave, State Sen. Margaret Carter, POVA's Brian McCartin, and Port of Portland Communications Director Elisa Dozono met with the *Oregonian* editorial board. The next day, the newspaper would do a story quoting many of them: "Oregonians Will Travel to N.Y. to Lend Support."

In addition to local coverage, within twenty-four hours Ray had confirmed spots for Mayor Katz on both the "Today Show" and "NBC Nightly News." MSNBC had picked up a local story on the effort. "I spent pretty much all of my time of calling every source that seemed to make sense and asking anybody they knew if they had friends or connections," said Ray. "My former brother-in-law knew someone at *People* magazine." (*People* ultimately covered the trip at the end of October, and a *People* magazine reporter came to the welcome reception at the Waldorf.)

By day's end, 500 people had signed up and the waiting list seemed astronomical.

FRIDAY, SEPTEMBER 28

"It astounds me how this coalesced so shortly; we were just thrown into a maelstrom together. We had never met before," said McGowan. Ultimately, what happened on this day would epitomize what can be achieved when egos and the need for individual credit are set aside for a greater purpose. Nick Fish, a relative newcomer to Portland, was welcomed in and his volunteer effort would add enormously to the experience and impact of the Flight for Freedom. Fish, says his wife, Portland State University Professor Patricia Schechter, "only did things that were in the alignment that fit him emotionally and gave him joy."[68] Little did he know what joy volunteering for the Flight for Freedom would bring him and how beautifully this would fit his ability to build bridges and build relationships in both his old hometown of New York and in his new one.

The organizing committee was meeting three times a day. During the morning meeting, Sho received a call from Nick Fish, a local attorney who had read a piece in *The Oregonian* about the project. The two had met at Japanese American Society of Oregon events and had spoken about putting together a benefit trip to New York that would exclude the clichés and focus on the "real" New York.

This "local attorney" was actually a member of a New York political dynasty. His father had served in the U.S. House of Representatives from 1969–1995. The original Hamilton Fish had served in Congress, and was New York's governor, and secretary of state under President

Ulysses S. Grant. Another ancestor, Nicholas Fish, began a family tradition by naming his son after his Army pal Alexander Hamilton, and the first of four Hamilton Fishes went to Congress in 1843.

Fish had arrived in Portland from New York City five years before when his wife, Patricia Schechter, became a professor in the history department at Portland State University.

"9/11 for me was devastating," said Fish, who knew many people who were directly affected. When he read in *The Oregonian* that Dozono was organizing the trip, his first reaction was,

"'Why didn't Sho call me?' And then, when I got over that and realized that these things happen quickly and who the hell am I, I called Sho."

Fish's contributions to the Flight for Freedom would exemplify and epitomize what was best about everyone who volunteered. Not only did he volunteer, but he put his life on hold and gave his *everything*. The humility, zeal, creativity and effectiveness he showed around the Flight for Freedom are a tiny indication of what he brought to everything he did throughout his life. Throughout this book, the name "Nick Fish" will appear; he had connections and he used them. He also had a perceptiveness and the imagination to pull together people and events that gave the Flight for Freedom a great deal of the impact it had.

Sadly, Fish's life was cut short: he died in 2020 at age sixty-one, but he had spent nearly twenty years after the Flight for Freedom becoming a respected and beloved public servant and member of the Portland community. Upon his death, *Willamette Week* wrote, "An ex-New Yorker, he came to symbolize the best of Portland."[69]

Fish became the longest serving member of the Portland City Council (2008–2020), and was so respected that the City of Portland maintains a web page in honor of him to this day.* He was known for building consensus and for fighting for the underdog, with a particular interest in homelessness and public parks. He had been recruited for a role in housing in the Obama administration, but he turned it down to stay in Portland.

---

*"Nick Fish (In Memoriam)," https://www.portlandoregon.gov/fish/47686. A housing complex has been named for Fish as well.

"It is impossible to quantify just how better off Portland is because of his contributions," Multnomah County Chair Deborah Kafoury wrote on her Facebook page, *Willamette Week* reported. Kafoury told Oregon Public Broadcasting (OPB), "In this day and age when our country is so torn apart with divisive politics, Nick really tried to bring the best out in everyone."

"For him, it was important that people treat each other with respect and dignity," Zari Santner, who worked for Fish for several years as Portland parks director, told OPB.[70]

It would be no accident that one of Fish's contacts at this stage in his life as a Portlander was a leading light in Portland's Black community as well as at the top levels of state government, Baruti Artharee. Nick invited his friend Artharee, deputy director of the Portland Development Commission (PDC) and the board chairman of the Urban League of Portland, to increase the diversity of races and voices of the trip.

Fish had three ideas for Flight for Freedom events: a memorial service at Union Square, which already had become a makeshift memorial site. Because Fish had chaired the local community board, he was able to quickly pull together the pieces for a first-class observance there. Also, the world's largest cathedral and Fish's home church, St. John the Divine, would be holding its annual Blessing of the Animals service that weekend, something Fish himself tried to attend every year.

"I mentioned to Sho that there was this extraordinary service and I had a sense that it was going to be a big event this year because of 9/11."

And finally, Fish stated that if they wanted a big gala at the Waldorf, he had connections with the theater community and in Governor Pataki's office. (His stepmother, Mary Ann Fish, worked for the governor.)

> So I said, "If you want to get the governor there and you want to get some stars from Broadway, that could be helpful.' That was just nervous energy, I just threw out three ideas that came to me.
>
> And typical Sho—and it's one of the things that makes him a gem— he said, "We're having a meeting this afternoon, can you swing by?" Or he may have said, "We're having a meeting in five minutes."

I walk into the room and it's filled with people whose names I was familiar with but had not met . . . . So for me, it was pretty new and very exciting.

Sho chaired the meeting, going around the room, each person outlining what they were doing. Then, in his typical, low-key style, he introduced Fish and said, "Nick has some ideas, why don't you share them?" Fish offered his thoughts.

Dozono responded, "That sounds good, Nick. I want you to work on those."

"I quickly realized that I had been drafted and I had my assignment," said Fish. "It was a little daunting, not because I didn't think I could deliver." But he was the new kid on the block, and he didn't know the people he was working with.

"I had to figure out protocol." And he found himself among these talented, competent, dynamic people "because of a little box in *The Oregonian* and I put two-and-two together and got excited."

"This core group of people were absolutely amazing," says Loen. "People gave the best of themselves unselfishly and that's what made it so beautiful. You don't get into a situation like that very often, where people don't have outside interests. And boy, it was really nice."

Franklin concurs:

> I think it worked because Sho had an original great idea and we as professionals knew what it would take were able to form a team and deliver. It sounds very cold, but that's absolutely what happened. Once we had decided it was a great idea and definitely worth doing, we analyzed we've got to do it first, what it's going to take, and then the rest of it came . . . .
>
> We were both pragmatically and emotionally involved in making it work.

Bergstein adds another ingredient that contributed strongly to success: the number of former New Yorkers who were organizers. They understood how New York worked; Bergstein is credited on the media side with understanding how important local contacts were to getting coverage, just as Nick Fish used his New York contacts to make possible the events that simply could not have been accomplished by Oregonians alone. Fish also opened doors for Ray with local New York media, along with the *Forward*, an important Jewish newspaper based in New York, and the Greenwich Village paper.

"Nick's understanding of working New York neighborhoods resonates with the Oregon style," says Bergstein. "Others would have started top down, but Nick had a feeling for the streets and an appreciate for the people."

That day, *The Oregonian* reported that buttons and T-shirts that said "Oregon loves New York" were on order and that Oregonians would hand out stickers to New Yorkers to let them know Oregon had been there. Tentative plans for a visit to Union Square, religious services on Sunday, a visit to Wall Street, and a meeting between Vera Katz and Mayor Giuliani were under discussion. The effort had grown so important that *The Oregonian* assigned a reporter to it, Courtenay Thompson, whose sensitive stories still provide the strongest continuing print coverage available.

Organizers had worked to recruit leaders from around the state. Dignitaries who had signed on included Eugene Mayor Jim Torrey; Republican gubernatorial candidate Ron Saxton; John Rickman, head of Oregon operations for U.S. Bank; Roger Hinshaw, president of Bank of America, Oregon (who brought his whole family); Baruti Artharee, deputy director of the Portland Development Commission, and incoming president of the Urban League; and Jim Scherzinger, interim superintendent for Portland Public Schools.

Sponsors at this point were the Port of Portland, the city of Eugene, the Portland Oregon Visitors Association, Wells Fargo Bank, U.S. Bank, SOLV, Portland State University, and the Bend Chamber of Commerce.

Writing now, in 2021, from the vantage point of one of the most divisive times in American history, the story of the Flight for Freedom's genesis is even more instructive than it might have been in the past. People put their differences aside and in many cases the differences never even came up. Ann Nice, vice president of the teachers' union, lived it and described it nearly twenty years later:

> I thought, "You know, there are times when there are things that are bigger than politics." And I loved the fact that probably there were a lot of people with a lot of different opinions and it didn't matter on that trip. We found commonality. And not only did we find it, but there was a lot of respect for everybody.

I never heard an unkind word towards one another on that trip from anybody who normally might not have gotten along super well. I have to remind myself today that that's a possibility.*[71]

"It was a search for common ground . . . . the common humanity of [the Flight for Freedom]. After a horrendous situation, it brings out the best in people. Not only did that happen then, it's part of the American story, it's who we are," says Bergstein.

The core group of volunteers was now complete: they were Vera Katz, Sho and Loen, Len Bergstein, Elisa Dozono, Nick Fish, Elaine Franklin, Brian McCartin, Jack McGowan, John Ray, Bruce Samson, and Karen Winder.

Those who volunteered on the staff side were Maureen "Mo" Denny, Bill and Tina Harmon, Jeri Hunt, and Lynn Porter. Val Hubbard answered the phone herself, and provided people from VH Productions to help during the rush to ticket the passengers. Loen asked Hubbard to handle special requests. Portland State University Director of Marketing Jan Woodruff also joined and helped in many ways both before and throughout the trip.

SATURDAY, SEPTEMBER 29

Ten days into the planning, and less than a week before the first Freedom Fliers were to depart, the call volume remained heavy. "People had to be so patient," says Loen, who was helping to answer the phones. "All of a sudden we found ourselves looking at the days and saying, "We've got to cut this off because people are leaving on Wednesday, and we haven't been able to ticket them."

Delta, United, and the Waldorf-Astoria agreed to stand by their discounts for as many Freedom Fliers as Azumano could book.

---

*Nice added, "I'm a fairly liberal person and I've always been pretty political and there were some people on the trip that were of a different political persuasion than me. Some of them—Vera Katz, for instance—I have had a love/hate relationship for a long time. I thought, 'Vera and I, we have had some less than pleasant conversations and I wonder how this will be.' Elaine Franklin, Bob Packwood's wife, who I only knew of in a negative way. And I found her to be so nice and so charming and so helpful."

Eventually, the Oregonians would fill the Waldorf. And for the first time in months, full flights would leave PDX for New York.

"At the time, I read that they were expecting a few hundred and they kept calling the hotel and the hotel said 'Yes' and 'Yes,'" said Betsy Holzgraf of Portland almost twenty years later.

"They had some cachet to be able to do that. And the cost, that made it much easier for more people to be able to go."

The Oregonian ran an editorial, "Portland ♥ New York," in support of the trip and celebrating the bravery of those who were going. "I'm afraid to fly," they quoted one Freedom Flier's website comment, "but we'll fly with you for America."

And, wrote the editors, "We may not be back to our happy-go-lucky selves anytime soon—there are still more tears to shed—but just hearing about this expedition is enough to make you smile."

The editors also noted that organizers were hoping to encourage tourism to Oregon as well. The sector had brought $2.6 billion into the state and nearly 25,000 jobs to the three-county Portland metropolitan area in 2000.

Scheckla, the Freedom Flier who signed up and then spent five days volunteering at Azumano, said that most of the people whose calls she took said they were going to let New Yorkers: [PHOTO 11]

> . . . know that Oregonians are supportive . . . . It's like losing part of your family, no matter where you are. I thought it would be a grieving and honorable experience, but just talking out and handling some of the intake and the people who are calling in who are participating, it's already a very uplifting experience. It's already a kinship.

Of the hundreds of people with whom Scheckla had spoken, only three mentioned the price. "Being affordable has been a helpful factor, but it's mostly the enthusiasm about being able to go as a group of Oregonians for this mission," she said, adding that those interested were of all ages and all walks of life. "It's a true cross-section."

Scheckla herself was going to go with four others, a group that grew from her phone call to a friend—whose husband wanted to go. "It mushroomed," she said. "I've heard those [kinds of] stories before from other people."

Val Hubbard joined with the volunteers again, and Lynn Porter from West Linn Travel also donated her time. Local TV covered the volunteer effort.

Elisa Dozono and her husband, Tom, spoke with their parents by cell phone from the Mariners game in Seattle. Loen noted that the last time they'd spoken from a Mariners game was September 9 "as we were en route to Brussels—the world would change two days later."

At the same time, organizers were raising funds for scholarships, and they sent several students from schools. Bruce Samson, who had been counsel for the Portland Public Schools, was key in this initiative. Thanks to scholarships, Police Activities League (PAL) Activities Director Beth Faulhaber of Molalla in Clackamas County south of Portland was able to bring two students and a colleague.

The connection with PAL was a strong one and organizers used it in biographies of participants shared with the media. Organizers had invited Cliff Madison, a Portland Police Bureau Captain on executive loan to the Portland Public School District Police serving as their Chief of Police, who had founded the PAL program in Portland.* "The program impacted many community youth and I'm proud of the work that was done by law enforcement personnel and community volunteers," says Madison, who is now retired.

Madison, who is African American, was a New York City Police Athletic League (PAL) kid, and participated in the boxing program, basketball, football and other sports, when his father was stationed there during his military career. "It was the first place I remember playing with police officers and it took the fear factor away and made me really respect them," says Madison. "I still believe that those experiences helped me choose law enforcement as my career."[72]

The story was building in the media. "I learned message discipline from Elaine," said Ray. "Early on, from Elaine, we agreed as

_____

*When Madison was selected to help form a community youth program to serve at-risk inner city youth and overall Portland youth, Madison recommended a PAL program. The organization was created as a nonprofit organization with the theme of "Kids, Cops and Community." PAL joined with the Multnomah County Sheriff's Office and other local area criminal justice agencies to try to break down the walls among PAL, Portland youth, and law enforcement. PAL offered football, basketball, boxing, and many more sports and activities as well as a summer camp.

the core group that we would say things specifically the same all the time and what surprised me was that there was a lead story on the "NBC Nightly News" on that Saturday and everybody who was interviewed said exactly what we said. It was because Elaine said we've got to say the same things over and over and over again . . . .

"The message there was that we can't be afraid. Elaine said it, Jack said it, Sho said it. It was why we went from 150 on the Wednesday of the news conference [to so many people signing up] so quickly."

"We looked terrorism in the face and we did not blink," said McGowan.[73]

That night, Mayor Giuliani appeared in a cold open on *Saturday Night Live* with several firefighters and police officers to say that New York and the show would go on as normal. As they prepared, Producer Lorne Michaels had asked Giuliani, "Can we be funny?" and Giuliani famously replied, "Why start now?"

SUNDAY, SEPTEMBER 30

That day's press release said that less than a week after announcing the "Flight for Freedom," the website had received about 23,000 hits, and 625 people were booked to fly on sixty-two flights with the group."[74] John Ray:

> I always remember when we would get to the end of the day when we were getting closer to the trip and I'd get a sense from how many requests they'd received and how many reservations. I would report to the media a high number. One day I'd say, "We're up to 600 now."
>
> I remember Jack McGowan saying, "We can't put out that high of numbers, we'll look foolish." The funny thing was by the time we were done, with 1,000 people, I never reported to the media a number that was off by that much.

Flights were departing from Portland, Medford, Eugene, and Bend. (Portland had one nonstop flight to New York, on Delta.)

Elaine Franklin joined the ranks of the volunteers answering phones and filling out applications.

MONDAY, OCTOBER 1

Organizers announced they were closing the reservation books. "We were all stunned by how many, once the word got out, how many people wanted to be involved in it," said Samson.

Loen noted, "Calls are up to about 800 confirmed tickets—we are so behind in ticketing. We must close offer as of 5:30 p.m." Val Hubbard continued to volunteer ten to twelve hours a day, this time shifting over to the Group Department with Gregg Macy.

"We had to cut things off because of our commitments to the airlines and also the Waldorf," said Parrott. "They needed a room count and a manifest so they could make sure they had personnel in place. And there really wasn't that much more time anyway."

Though not yet announced publicly, receptions at the Waldorf-Astoria had been arranged, as had a dinner in Chinatown hosted by U.S. Rep. David Wu (D-Ore.), the first Chinese-American member of Congress. Business in New York's Chinatown, which is very near the World Trade Center, Wu told Sho, was "desperate."

"We need to go down there," the Congressman said, and said he found sponsors to feed 600 people. Organizers also learned that in New York things cost far more than in Portland. The double-decker buses that shuttled Freedom Fliers back and forth from the Waldorf-Astoria to the Harmony Palace Restaurant in Chinatown, for instance. A couple thousand dollars, the Oregonians assumed. It was quadruple that.

Port of Portland Commission members were scheduled to meet with the acting Executive Director of the Port Authority of New York/New Jersey, whose organization had occupied part of the World Trade Center and had lost seventy-four employees in the attack. The Port of Portland offered assistance to the New York Port, including the possibility of loaning the assistance of one of its executives. Commission President would present the Port Authority with a Made-In-Oregon gift basket—the first of the seventy-four to be distributed to families of those who had been lost.

Usually official trips rank right at the top on the "Big Snore Meter," said a Eugene *Register Guard* editorial, but Mayor Jim Torrey's upcoming visit to New York was different. Torrey was scheduled to read to students in two New York elementary schools where some of the kids' parents had been killed in the bombing. He would bring gifts, including a banner made by Fern Ridge Middle School students reading, "We Appreciate Your Courage," packets of flower seeds from a local business, letters from Springfield first graders, and an American flag that had been flown at half-staff at the Eugene Airport.

The items McGowan was bringing included a 20-foot card of condolences and well-wishes signed by more than 100 people attending *The Newberg Graphic*'s September 13 block party. The card included a letter to Mayor Giuliani and a copy of the September 15 *Graphic* that included coverage of the party.

"This is not a Portland event. This is an Oregon event," said McGowan.

In addition to crab fishermen and schoolteachers, bank presidents and homemakers, the list of participants had now grown to include U.S. Representative Darlene Hooley, State Treasurer Randall Edwards, State Senator Ted Ferrioli, delegations from local police and fire bureaus, Multnomah County Chair Diane Linn, and Multnomah County Commissioner Maria Rojo de Steffey.

John Ray and the media team also conducted a statewide email campaign targeting chambers of commerce. Representatives from the Bend (central Oregon), Hermiston (northeast Oregon), and Medford/Jackson County (southwest Oregon) chambers of commerce had signed on.

Oregon native Amy Solomonson, senior communications manager at NYC & Company, the city's tourism bureau, said, "All the other groups [who have come to New York] are forty and fifty people. Seven hundred fifty people, sixty-two flights sold out is phenomenal. That's above and beyond anything else we've seen so far."[75]

Behind the scenes, Nick Fish hit the phones:

> I just carved out some time, kind of dropped what I was doing and started working with the governor's office [New York Governor Pataki] and Mary Ann Fish, my stepmother, to work on the governor's piece; called both the head of Actors' Equity and the head of the League of Theaters and asked them if they would consider supplying some stars from Broadway to a gala. My community board covered the theater district so I was deeply involved.* They were bullish, which was good because I was calling friends.

---

*Fish had spent a decade on Community Board Five, said his wife, Patricia Schechter (May 13, 2021).

In the Fourteenth Street Union Square Business Improvement District, the president was a dear friend of mine. He listened to me for about five minutes and said, "It's done, we'll make it happen."

Then I called my friend Stephen Facey, executive vice president of programs at St. John the Divine, and when I told him that we had this delegation that may include the mayor and may come to the service on Sunday, he said that Bobby Kennedy [Jr.] was going to be speaking, the guide dogs from the search and rescue process were going to be part of the processional and that the mayor of Portland, a former New Yorker, would come speak, would be the icing on the cake. Steven and their people worked together to work out some of the kinks.

I had some friends in the mayor's office that I was able to touch base with. It kind of quickly fell together and because again, because of Sho's leadership style and because of the extraordinary people he pulled together, everyone was focused on getting things done. He had delegated this to me. I think my enthusiasm in pitching . . . people got on board.

TUESDAY, OCTOBER 2

With the public count now at 850, Ray told *The Seattle Times*, "We thought 150 would be a great response."

The group announced they had purchased blocks of tickets to see *Kiss Me Kate* and *Proof*. With theaters dark on Sunday night, some actors may perform at a reception at the Waldorf-Astoria, Ray told *Crain's New York Business*. He hinted that they might even have a dinner *en masse* in Chinatown. But he stressed that *en masse* events were not the purpose. "The average group size will be parties of four to six, up to as many as twelve."

In an email, Cristyne L. Nicholas, president and CEO of NYC & Company, responded to POVA's request to attend the Monday night reception with, "This is amazing! . . . I can't wait to greet them on Monday night at the Waldorf . . . . So many funerals and memorial services . . . ."

WEDNESDAY, OCTOBER 3

"Panic City," read Loen's notes for the day. "We are trying to keep up with calls, people who leave [tomorrow] haven't gotten notice of flight times."

When the trip was over, Freedom Flier Paula Becks of Scappoose, made a point to email Azumano Travel and thank them: "The Azumano staff and volunteers taking our reservations were the greatest. Soooo gracious and calm, when I might have been tearing my hair out!!"[76]

As those in the office were immersed in ticketing people who were leaving as early as the next day, the first of the organizers left for New York.

For the Azumano Travel party, Bill Harmon, Gregg Macy, and Val Hubbard were the advance party. Among the organizers, Nick Fish, Elaine Franklin, Jack McGowan, and John Ray were also on their way to New York.

Ray was pushing to get more national coverage, and this would be the day he broke through. *USA Today* put the Dozonos on the front page of its "Living" section under the headline, "Tourist spending defies terrorism Portland, Ore.'s Flight for Freedom sends patriotic dollars to New York."

The first, small number of Freedom Fliers were scheduled to leave the following night, and Ray left early to set up a media room with Jack McGowan and prepare the New York press. He left PDX on a relatively empty plane before *USA Today* had hit the stands:

> That was an amazing day. My flight was to go from Portland to Chicago. By the time I arrived in Chicago, I was beaming, it was so cool to see that our effort had finally paid off. I turned on my cell phone after I picked up the paper to call Sho and I already had ten messages on my phone from New York people trying to lock us down . . . .
>
> [He was trying hard to get ABC.] I had already gotten some tentative okays from CBS and NBC, and it was weird, when I landed in Chicago, there was all of a sudden this bidding war of people who wanted to put Vera on the air. I finally got a booking from "Regis and Kelly" for Vera and all of a sudden, the *USA Today* thing gave us credibility that we were trying to build.

Everybody thought it was a nice, sweet gesture and when it hit the media, it became bigger than that . . . . Everyone locally had done such a great job to try to follow the story that there were a lot of regional papers picking it up.

It became not only national but international.

The role Ray's media work played in the trip's success cannot be overstated. Mayor Katz gave Ray's efforts the highest marks:

> We were treated like royalty and the prices were depressed anyway, but because of the work done on the media, they all knew who we were and that "My God, there's a group of 1,000 Oregonians from 3,000 miles away coming to literally give us hope and heart."

McGowan and Fish flew out together. McGowan had had a long and very public career in Oregon as correspondent and on-air host for NBC affiliate KGW-TV 8, KINK-FM Radio, the Mt. Hood Festival of Jazz, and as assistant to Portland Mayor J.E. Bud Clark.

Flying with Jack McGowan, said Fish, showed him what it must have been like "to be with The Beatles. The people I was sitting next to asked to sit next to him."

The two men had not known each other before they were thrown together on this project. On the flight, Fish learned that they shared a strong bond: "I experienced a tremendous range of emotions. Jack McGowan and I returned as sons of New York who had relocated to Oregon." In fact, they would share that range of emotions throughout the trip.

The flight itself foreshadowed the welcome they would find from New Yorkers. "The captain came on and thanked us for flying Delta," McGowan remembered. "Then he said he was a native New Yorker and he gave us his deepest thanks for coming. The entire plane broke out singing 'God Bless America.'"

On virtually every plane carrying Freedom Fliers, the crew made some sort of public expression of gratitude.

Fish and McGowan met a woman from Nike on the plane, who was going to a movie premiere in New York and offered to drop them at the Waldorf in her limo. ("We crashed somebody's limo that was sent by the studio," said Fish.)

When they arrived, Fish hit the ground running. At the Waldorf, "there was a war room. I got on the phone to firm things up; the Pataki thing was not yet firm. We were pushing, pushing, pushing, pushing and we got things firmed up."

While business seemed to be picking up a bit in Manhattan, the loss of tourist revenue had been huge. From September 11 to 22, the city lost a total of $163.7 million in visitor spending, according to the visitors bureau. New York's restaurant association reported losses of $20 million daily. Hotel occupancy rates, normally around 89.5 percent during this, their busiest season, had climbed from an immediate post-September 11 level of around 40 percent to about 65 percent, said Joseph E. Spinnato, president of the Hotel Association of New York City. "This contingent is an emotional reassurance for shaken New Yorkers as well. Right now everybody needs reassurance, especially us here. They're still cleaning up, still finding people. It's just a boost that everybody needs."

Of Battery Park City's 9,000 residents, only about half had been able to return to their homes, he said.[77]

Over the next three days, the Freedom Fliers would come to experience how prophetic Spinnato's statement was.

THURSDAY, OCTOBER 4

On this day, the Flight for Freedom experience began with the first group of travelers leaving from Portland International Airport—and on the other coast the organizers preparing for them at the Waldorf-Astoria.*

Meanwhile, on the East Coast, the reality of what they'd signed up for was setting in. That morning, the advance group met with all the departments of the Waldorf-Astoria to firm up the logistics of the 1,000 persons who were about to put their lives and safety in the hands of the people in that room.

Bruce Samson:

---

*The story of the departures will be told in the next chapter, "The Adventure Begins."

Here we were, a little group from Oregon and they set up a large square table that must have been 50 feet across, four-sided, and all of the heads of all of their departments were at the table telling us what they planned to do for us while we were there. The manager of the hotel, there must have been twenty of their staff department heads that were there, and it was like a peace meeting at Versailles or something like that. It felt very strange. The Waldorf-Astoria treated us well.

Jack McGowan:

The general manager had set up a meeting with line staff to try to help coordinate what was going to be a major, major national event. I walked into this anteroom, which was almost like a small ballroom, and there must have been twenty people easily; the head chef, the head of housekeeping, security, maintenance, the general manager, the assistant general manager, secondary management crew, and so there must have been twenty people and everybody there with placards and white damask tablecloths — typical Waldorf. The reality then hit me as I walked into that room: "Oh man, this is big." . . . Even the Waldorf is taking this very, very seriously. And everybody's credibility was on the line.

I remember the seriousness of the head of security for the Waldorf talking about the security aspects and what they were going to do. We were always serious about it, but then the magnitude of what we were bringing people into. [We didn't know this at the time.] With the 9/11 Commission, New York was absolutely scared, literally scared that there was going to be another terrorist attack, that there was chatter on the air, that it could be a dirty bomb, that it could be in midtown Manhattan, and New York City cops, the Police Dept. was concerned. I still remember that discussion and the seriousness of it, not only the emotional aspect of it, but all of us were putting not only ourselves into but also the 1,000 people who were joining us. That was a lasting impression.[78]

The Waldorf's media team offered to help Ray with media at all levels (local, international) because they are such an important brand.

"All of a sudden we realized we had an international media tiger we put together," said McGowan.

The Waldorf had been very empty, but they did have a wedding reception for a very wealthy family and they agreed to move that group to the Renaissance Hotel nearby for a night.

Ray remembers that he, Samson, and McGowan all wore suits, as did Elaine Franklin. Nick Fish showed up in a jacket with a T-shirt underneath. When they asked him what was up, Fish laughed, "This is my city!"

For McGowan, the boy from Jackson Heights, Queens, it was one more stage in an emotional tsunami.

> It brought back so much to me. The thirty-one years that I had been in Oregon and creating my own life was a maelstrom for me and I didn't think much about New York City. All of a sudden, it came back to me, here I am in this remarkable position, the honor of being part of this advance guard. It shocked the hell out of me, here I am at the Waldorf-Astoria.
>
> I went into the Waldorf and sat on the bed, and what the—the juxtaposition of horror, sorrow, remembrance, life passing in front of your eyes—it was all of these things. The emotional ties of being in New York are all coming back. The horrors of what we'd experienced, watching the World Trade Center go up [he'd lived in Greenwich Village while it was being built].
>
> I took [my wife] Jan and [my son] Travis to New York and a buddy of mine got us a beautiful table at Windows on the World [the restaurant at the top of the World Trade Center].
>
> Bam-bam-bam-bam one emotional remembrance after another.
>
> And here you are sitting with the senior staff of the Waldorf planning this immense event, [and] Security talking about what we're going to do in the event of some kind of terrorist event.
>
> It captured the nation's eye. The nation was looking for something positive. Giuliani was still America's mayor . . . . So all of a sudden, every single emotional trigger that could be pulled was being pulled.

With much of their staff in New York, but the Dozonos themselves not scheduled to leave until the sixth, Sho contacted the Waldorf about simple refreshments for the Saturday night reception. Organizers had budgeted $2,000.

"They told us $24,000," Sho laughs. "I told our staff to approach the general manager cautiously, to have him just give me his bottom line. He said, 'We'll sponsor it.'"

The Waldorf covered the entire cost of a sumptuous dessert buffet.

That day, Portland US Bank representative Pete Sinclair explained the trip's purpose in *The New York Times*: "It's a statement, it's not really a trip. It's people saying we're not going to change our lives and the way that we live."

Almost twenty years later, Marla Nuttman of McMinnville stresses the atmosphere in the United States in late September 2001:

> At that time we were still unified as a country; we were still collectively grieving. We were still one country. . . . even the flyover states, we're all part of the same country. We'd all been attacked on that day. it was us going to support our brothers in new York. Later it became blue state and red states and we became so divided. At that time we were still one country.[79]

And on the floor of the United States Senate, U.S. Sen. Ron Wyden (D-Ore.) honored his constituents' pending accomplishment:

> This weekend a number of strong-willed people of my state are mounting an operation they call "Flight for Freedom," answering the national call for all of us to get on with their lives and come to the aid of those hurt in the attacks of September 11.

> In a show of solidarity with their fellow Americans, more than 700 Oregonians are making a statement to the nation this weekend by heading to the hotels, Broadway shows, and restaurants in New York City that are fighting for economic survival in the aftermath of the attacks. Oregon's Flight for Freedom, with the people of my state standing shoulder-to-shoulder with the citizens of New York, is an effort to make clear that no terrorist can break the American spirit.

> I want to congratulate Sho Dozono and the other organizers and participants in Oregon's Flight for Freedom for their generous efforts.

> I urge all Americans to follow their example. Oregonians are showing this weekend that we're going to stand against terrorism by reaching out to their fellow citizens and enjoying what American life has to offer in our centers of commerce all across this great nation. Because of these kinds of efforts, we can send a message that terrorists can't extinguish the American spirit.[80]

1. Line outside the U.S. Embassy in Dublin, Ireland. Photo courtesy of Sho and Loen Dozono

2. Floral tributes outside the U.S. Embassy in Dublin, Ireland. Photo courtesy of Sho and Loen Dozono

3. Signing the guestbook at the U.S Embassy in Dublin, Ireland. Photo courtesy of Sho and Loen Dozono

4. Kids, this is a Rolodex. Each card has a person's name and contact information on it and it's alphabetized. This is a big one, like Sho's, and you can easily add cards as you add contacts. Electronic power and charging not necessary. Photo by Liorpt

NEW YORK CITY OR BUST!
An Airlift to New York

Americans have been grieving during the aftermath of the terrorist bombings of September 11. We have all taken a defensive stance as a consequence of these events—canceling plans, staying glued to the TV, cowering in the corner.

Let's turn that around and adopt the pioneering spirit that brought people West along the Oregon Trail, and move back across the country—encouraging any "brave souls" to join us. We'd like to begin with an "airlift" to New York, reminiscent of the Berlin airlifts of the 50's. Our immediate goal would be to fill a plane with leaders from communities around Oregon to spend the weekend of October 4 re-exploring New York City, rediscovering all it has to offer, liberating it from the grips of fear which have emptied her hotels, restaurants and theatres.

We would like the Oregon delegation to be led by Mayor Katz, a native New Yorker. We would also like the participation of cultural leaders such as Arlene & Harold Schnitzer and Peris & Mary Mark in acknowledging the need to continue preserving cultural resources. It would also be desirable for the group to include many grass roots folks—members of Chambers of Commerce from cities of all sizes, Veterans groups, retired police, firefighters, anyone who wants recognition as an entity of support.

Our overall hope would be to see this "bandwagon" grow to 100 planes with 100-150 passengers each from about 35 cities nationwide. This would result in a contingent of 10,000-15,000 people descending upon New York. If each person were to spend $1,000, it would be a $15 million boost to the New York economy. So many are working to flood the relief effort with dollars but at this point, it is more important to get people there.

- Organize an evening in Central Park—a hootenanny with folk songs from the 60's—in particular, "This Land is Your Land." Need to have uplifting songs that reminds the American spirit.
- Create pins or buttons for participants bearing an appropriate slogan—"Free New York," perhaps, but this is only a means to our end which is really to free all of America from the grips of terrorism.
- Create a "commemorative medal" of some sort for tourists to be able to gather from each state. You'd have to visit the state to get it. Would encourage travel and tourism.

5. Early Flight for Freedom concept sheet. Courtesy of Brian McCartin

6. "The Three Amigos," Chris Sullivan of KXL, Bill Cooper of KPAM, and Neal Penland of KEX. Photo courtesy of Bill Cooper.

8. Flight for Freedom website, 2001. Archived website

7. KGW's Scott Williams and Krista Vasquez. Photo: Betsy Ames

9. Button courtesy of the author.

10. Sho Dozono in the "Command Center" at Azumano Travel. Photo property of Oregonian Publishing Co.

11. LaVonne Scheckla marches in 2002 Rose Parade. Photo property of Oregonian Publishing Co.

WHY THEY WENT

> If you had to think about it, it was too late. —*Loen Dozono*

Deciding to fly across the country at a time when, as realtor George Haight of Woodburn said, "most people were afraid to go to Dairy Queen" was an immediate yes for most Freedom Fliers.

Which means that one in every 3,000 Oregonians shared that impulse and put themselves and their safety on the line to bypass the Dairy Queen and fly across the country—to help.

That no other place did this at this scale—and so soon after the worst attacks on U.S. soil in our history—says that something was unique about this place and these people.

From the beginning, the concept was a democratic one. The Dozonos began with the idea of enabling lots of people to participate. The leaders and corporations that joined in made that concept into reality.

But just because leadership had created the opportunity, would people come? And, of course, the answer is yes. It was a perfect marriage.

Maybe that's the "Oregon Spirit" the state proudly proclaims.

Still, this was a self-selected group. What they shared is that they all volunteered in an instant and then became the Flight for Freedom. They had a variety of reasons for signing on, some ineffable; but listening to them talk about it now, decades later, can reawaken the reactions and emotions of twenty years ago, and remind us of the way many Americans were feeling after the attacks. While they share common elements, their stories are also uniquely individual and— perhaps somewhat ironically, in the context of 3,000 dead—remind us of the value of each human life.

Barbara Shaw, 49, Scio (Pop. 695)* [PHOTO 1]

On September 11, 2001, Barbara Shaw was in a hotel in Portland, where her son had been married two days earlier. Like much of America, that morning she woke up to a telephone call: "Turn on your TV."

> On 9/11/01 the phone rang about 6:30 a.m., or so in our hotel room. It was my oldest son, Scott, telling me to turn on the TV. At that point we saw a plane crashing into one of the twin towers in New York. And that was the beginning of something so beyond belief that I would spend the rest of the week glued to the TV.
>
> We went home. We wondered how, why, and who could do this. I bought a *Time* magazine so that I could see the chronological order of events. The plane crashed into one tower, then another plane crashed into the second tower. Then a plane crashed into the Pentagon, then another plane crashed into the ground. There were sounds of sirens, people screaming, people coughing from the dust, and towers falling. Planes crashing, people crying, the total disbelief of it all. There was dust everywhere, debris, and firemen and policemen trying to help. Hour after hour, day after day. Why? Why? Why? What kind of people could be filled with such hatred? We would soon find out, as Mayor Giuliani seemed to have some control of the situation.
>
> My sister was supposed to fly home to Newark, New Jersey, and my brother and his fiancé were to fly to Denver. But the airports were closed. We all sat and watched and waited in shock at the aftermath that had occurred. We would never be the same. We looked to see if there were many survivors. There were few.
>
> My husband's company was on strike, so as a supervisor he had to work 12-hour shifts on graveyard. It was a sad, frustrating, scary

---

*All places are in Oregon unless otherwise stated. Census numbers based on 2000 U.S. Census.

week. By the end of the week, some of the airports had opened. My brother and his fiancée flew back to Denver, and my sister flew back to Newark. One of the planes that crashed had flown out of Newark. How eerie. After another week, my parents flew back to Arizona.

Then around October 1, I saw on the news: Would you like to go to New York for a very reasonable price? Oh yes, probably. I was born in New York, at Mitchell Air Force Base on Long Island. My parents were born in Brooklyn. It was my home state. I needed to go. I needed to let the people of New York know that here in Oregon, we feel some of their pain. We care. We love you New York. Of course I'll come.

I called Azumano Travel, which was sponsoring the trip along with Delta Airlines, and left a message.

None of my friends wanted to go. They thought I was nuts. But my kids, my wonderful, supporting, loving kids and their wonderful wives thought it was great. My husband just said, "OK." He was tired from the wedding, family, and the strike at work.

It was only a week and a half away. I would have to go by myself to the "Big City" of New York and stay in a hotel by myself for the first time. I'd been married thirty-one years, and had two grown and married sons. Scott, twenty-eight, and Mike, twenty-six. And I'd never stayed in a hotel by myself before.

When my reservation was confirmed, I had a week to get ready.

I wanted to bring something from Oregon to comfort the people in New York. I wanted to make a homemade quilt. First I needed a plan, then a design, then a pattern. There wouldn't be much time. I went to the local fabric store and bought the white fabric for the top. Then I bought a dark green sheet for the back.

The pictures on the front of the quilt would show the things that Oregon and New York have in common. They both are coastal states, they both get snow in the winter, and have fir trees. They both have areas that produce fruits and vegetables. And after all, New York is known as "The Big Apple." So the quilt would have pictures around the edges of seashells, fruit, and trees.

Also on the front would be the words "To New York from Oregon with Love 9/11/01."

There would also be two flags: the New York flag, and the flag of Oregon, that was made by my friend Peggy Alex from Tangent, Oregon.

It was a busy week. I worked feverishly every evening to get the quilt done. I assembled each square by appliquéing satin pictures: trees, a pear, an apple, a sailboat, and a shell. I realized a little late that the sailboat represents a more fun time in New York. But I didn't have much time, and I was working alone. So I made a dove square, but I didn't have time to interchange the squares. (I still have the dove square at home twenty years later). It was fairly big, 60 x 72 inches. Everything had to be laid out on the floor, pinned then stitched.[1]

When Shaw arrived in New York, she placed the quilt in the Flight for Freedom hospitality area at the Waldorf-Astoria and invited participants to sign it.

Cecil Pulliam, 60s, Lebanon (Pop. 12,950)

Cecil Pulliam was a volunteer fireman in his hometown of Lebanon, in the Willamette Valley. "It really came home when I saw guys go in those buildings, and the number that didn't come out."[2]

Connie Hawk, 56, Salem (Oregon State Capital, Pop. 347,214)

For Connie Hawk, making the trip was about self-healing as much as about helping New Yorkers.

> I was in Virginia Beach on September 11, and it took two weeks for me to get on a plane and come home. I was very afraid to fly. Once I got home, I decided that I wanted to go to New York so I knew that I was in control, not the bad guys.

State Sen. Margaret Carter, 55, Portland (Pop. 529,121; Metro Area Pop. 1.9 million) [PHOTO 2]

State Sen. Margaret Carter, Mayor Vera Katz, and U.S. Rep. Darlene Hooley had all served in the Oregon State Legislature together and had become "great friends." Carter, who was the first African-American woman to serve in the legislature, remembers that Katz:

> . . . had called us and said, "Carter, you need to go on this. I'm going to go and Darlene Hooley needs to go." Of course as my friend and mentor, I would do exactly what she said. This would be a great trip.

We needed to show the people of New York compassion and help with their economic base. Stores were closed, people afraid to get out to work. We decided to take extra money to shop . . . .

We were just looking forward to having a hallelujah time. Portland was going to show our love to New York and we were joyous and happy about the opportunity to be in New York, but most of all to try to lend to the economics of the day in the city. We were all too excited about helping to be afraid.

I have nine kids and I bought nine kids gifts while I was there.

But for Carter, the impetus went back to her Shreveport, Louisiana roots, and it influenced her choice to attend as many funerals as she could, too.

I moved here [to Portland] in 1967 as a result of domestic violence. I had a dream that I was in this faraway place that had beautiful, red flowers. I could not identify the type.

And I had just gotten out of the hospital with a broken jawbone from where my husband had violated me. I talked to a friend I hadn't talked to in ten years and it happened to be Portland, Oregon. She said, "We have the most beautiful red roses. We grow most of the roses of the Rose Parade. They're red, they look velvety."

And she asked me if I would come to see them. I said, "Yeah."

She said, "Bring the kids with you, we'll put all of the kids up." Three days later I packed myself and five little children.

When you're talking about being afraid. I thought if I could go through what I've gone through, I know what it is to show compassion, to show people from across the country compassion.

Melissa Goodwin, 23, Toledo (Pop. 3,472)

Melissa Goodwin, a caregiver for the elderly, had donated her German Shepherd Chance's used shoes after hearing that the dogs working at the World Trade Center site had to wear burlap bags on their feet. A five-year-old seeing-eye dog, Chance works with Goodwin "for my help, and also for the patients' comfort. First and foremost, he is my working guide dog," she told me. Chance works on Goodwin's left side because she lost her vision in her left eye and has low vision in her right eye. I spoke with Goodwin just a few days before she left for New York:

> I heard about it on the five o'clock news last Thursday and I knew immediately, I called and got the voicemail, and they called me back the next day . . . . It's hard to imagine all the way in Oregon what happened; you can see it on TV, but to actually go there and see what happened, I'm guessing it's going to be a lot different.
>
> I've always wanted to go to New York. I'm from Phoenix. I'm used to the big city and I kind of miss it.
>
> I want to see the Statue of Liberty, go shopping—I want to say that I went shopping in New York. I'm kind of a go-with-the-flow type of person . . . . The touristy things, that's excellent. Everybody needs that now. It impacted our whole nation. To know that Disney World in Florida is empty . . . . Everybody's been hit really hard.
>
> I think if people decide to go somewhere, I think it should be New York . . . . that New York really needs support.[3]

Chance went to New York with Goodwin on her plane—"He's excellent at flying"—and roomed with her at the Waldorf. This was Goodwin's first trip to Manhattan. For Goodwin, the trip went beyond paying respects to 9/11 victims and human rescuers. "I'm showing my support for the working dog," she said.

Joe Weston, 63, Portland

The principal of Weston Investment Co., LLC, brought his family on the trip. It was a "moral obligation," he said. "All Americans would understand. It was like when JFK got shot. It was such a shock."[4]

Martin and Kerrida Fisher, 30s, Bend (Pop. 52,029)

Martin Fisher went with his wife and six-year-old daughter. He saw the story in the newspaper on Saturday, signed up through the website on Sunday, Azumano Travel called him back on Monday and they made their reservations; and the family left from Redmond at 4:30 a.m. that Friday.

> A lot of people were donating blood . . . but it seemed like the problem was that people weren't going there [to New York City].

And it seemed like an opportunity to be part of something big . . . . I've been to the Arizona Memorial [in Pearl Harbor] and it seemed like the opportunity to be part of something like that. [The Flight for Freedom] looked like something that: a) was actually afford-able and b) was a real way of doing something, although frankly, I just thought, people probably wouldn't notice and my thought was, when it was over, we would have probably made more of a personal statement than any kind of large social statement, which I guess was the huge surprise when we got there . . . .

It was something you just had to be a part of . . . . Over here, we all watched it on TV that morning and it seemed important to turn it into something other than a news highlight. And also, you know, I kind of had a feeling that for our daughter it would be a very import-ant event. She's only six, but she saw it also, and I think to be able to say when she's older that she was a part of something like this is important.

Another reason that I think I felt obligated to do it is I felt inclined to give the finger to the people that did this and short of standing outside and doing it, that was a way of telling them, screw you. It was probably to tell them that I'm not afraid and partly because I so was so incredibly angry . . . .

You probably couldn't have picked a safer time to fly.

Portland Firefighters [PHOTO 3]

Allen Oswalt and his firefighter colleagues paid their own way. They had a conversation on the topic, Oswalt remembers:

> After we bought the tickets . . . we had dinner and talked about, "Why are we going?"

"To support the New York firefighters."

But we had another draw. Some of our coworkers had gone back there on their own time, like Wes [Loucks,] and created relationships with people there so we went knowing firefighters. There was that aspect of it, just supporting the New York firefighters and meeting with them, the ones that we knew.

For me as a public citizen, I might not have taken advantage of the opportunity, but as a firefighter knowing that 343 firefighters had died that day, and that they're brothers in New York. I can go into any fire station in America and walk up to their door and stick my hand out and say, "Brother."

Once they know I'm a firefighter, even retired now [in 2021], we are brothers and he'll do whatever he can to help me.[5]

Michael Lee, Portland

For Vietnam veteran Michael Lee, going to New York was the beginning of starting to feel things after many years of having shut down emotionally.

> Vera's call to arms raised feelings and beliefs I had long lost in a dark forest of my own making . . . . Those were my brothers in those planes and in those towers. They were my daughters, my children, and I wanted New Yorkers to know you are not alone. I took my oldest daughter in the hopes that I could get her to see what patriotism really means. That freedom is not free . . . . It's the young whose blood will be spilled now. There is no glory in war and the young more than ANY of us besides the vets know that.

Merritt Marthaller, 73, Gresham (Pop. 90,205)

> Never would I believe my September 18, 2001, Friendship Force Mission to Iran would be canceled for this reason. I instantly knew I must participate in the "Flight for Freedom" trip to comfort, give hope, listen to the people of New York and help their economy.[6]

Al O'Brien, 64, Portland [PHOTO 4]

Born in Buffalo, New York, this was Al O'Brien's first trip to the Big Apple. His family had moved to Oregon when he was in the fourth grade. Al worked as a "fuel jobber," contracting with gas stations to do their upgrades and branding, which allowed the gas stations to benefit without having to pay the cost of the upgrade.

> I didn't know if I was going to go or not because I was single and didn't have anyone to travel with. Then I thought, "Oh the heck with it, I'll do it anyway." I called [Azumano Travel] and they didn't know if they had enough tickets or what so I went downtown to Portland to their office. They put me on hold that day; they didn't know if they had any room.

The next day they said to come down and pick up the ticket so I was going to be leaving right away. I picked up the ticket and packed. I got one of the last ones. At the time, they were going to do 250, but they did 1,000 people.

I did it because I'm from Buffalo originally. Here we are 3,000 miles away, and I wanted to let people know that we're one country. I'm not patriotic or anything, but 3,000 miles away, maybe they'd like to know that people care.[7]

Betty Long, 64, Aloha (Pop. 41,741)

This was Betty Long's first time in New York. "When I look back, I believe my primary reason for really wanting to go was the title of the trip. 'Flight for Freedom' was sort of like 'FIGHT for Freedom' and I felt like it was my duty to go."

Baruti Artharee, 48, Portland [PHOTO 5]

For others, the trip would be personally sad. Baruti Artharee, deputy director of the Portland Development Commission (PDC) and the board chairman of the Urban League of Portland, had been invited by Portland attorney Nick Fish of New York's Fish political dynasty, who was organizing many of the high-profile Flight for Freedom events in the city. Artharee would speak at a wreath-laying at Union Square and participate in the official events, but he would also attend a memorial service for a colleague's nephew. Artharee told *The Oregonian*:

> Americans, we are like a big family. We have squabbles, and we disagree. But when someone attacks us, it's as Americans we're being attacked. They weren't trying to kill white people, or brown, yellow or red. They were there to kill Americans.[8]

From the vantage point of twenty years later, Artharee says:

> My success in the corporate sector, in the community, working for two governors and two mayors was one thing, but the bell to fight back was rung for me as I left on the trip. Today I feel the same way about the whole right-wing militia and white supremacist movement. They are attacking Americans and the bell has been rung.

As I have talked with family and friends there is a collective feeling of, as Americans we are being attacked by misinformation, false propaganda, and actions contrary to the Fourteenth Amendment that guarantees equal rights and protection. So it is the same thing all over again, use our freedom to stand up, show up, and speak up.

In June 2001, Artharee had had colon cancer surgery and spent the summer recuperating and receiving treatment.

Many of my friends and family members tried to convince me not to go on the Flight for Freedom. There were concerns about my health and the personal safety of those on the trip.

My illness had brought to the surface strong emotions related to death and the fragility of life. Prior to my cancer surgery I had been blessed to be strong, healthy, and high energy. I was devastated and it felt like going into a dark tunnel and not knowing if you will come out the other side.

During my recuperation, I became emotional at times and my sensitivity to suffering heightened. When the bombing and death happened in September, I thought about the impact and grief on the lives of so many people which multiplied exponentially my own experience. That made me even more emotional leading up to departure for the trip.

After the bombing on 9/11, local civic leaders started talking about traveling to New York to show strength and support the locals. My invitation to join the group might have been based on the fact that I was known as one of the few Black guys that got respect walking on both sides of the river. Meaning that I had grassroots credentials on the east side community [Black area of Portland] from working to address police shootings, the shortage of affordable houses, and pushing for economic opportunities. On the west side, in downtown I was known as a senior official working at PDC and having served on the cabinets of two Oregon governors, Kitzhaber and Roberts.

When Nick Fish invited me to be a part of the contingent going to New York, I quickly agreed because I felt a need to do something, and I was grieving for the thousands of lives lost and their families. My reaction could be attributed to my growing up in Compton, California. There it was understood that if you want respect you have to give respect. If not, there would be consequences and repercussions. You learn not to take stuff and fight if necessary. That philosophy served me well in my corporate and public sector careers. Most people would say I am the same person in all situations.

Some Black folks questioned my participation in the trip because of the belief that I was getting involved in white folks' business. Meaning that we have far too many issues related to our survival to get involved in issues such as conservation or climate change, concluding these types of issues were white folks' business.

So, with the Flight for Freedom, the people that went on that trip were those that had some means in order to take time off and be able to afford the cost. Many other folks were home just trying to make ends meet.

In spite of the naysayers, regardless of the risks for health and safety, I recognized there are times you have to show up, stand up, and speak up![9]

Philip and Kathleen Peters, 40s, Wilsonville (Pop. 13,991)/Fairlawn, New Jersey

Philip and Kathleen Peters, who own a wellness marketing business, weren't even in Oregon when they heard about the trip. The fifth-generation Oregonian and his New Jersey-born wife lived on both coasts and had lost colleagues and neighbors in the attack. From their home in Fairlawn, New Jersey, Philip said they could "see the tower, the plume of smoke, going up into the sky for days, and it was like being in Portland and watching a forest fire on the horizon."

Kathleen had been working across from the towers in New Jersey. That morning, when the second plane hit, a woman collapsed in Kathleen's arms, knowing her brother who worked at the location of impact must be dead.

"We had cinder all over. It was probably like Mount Saint Helens, it was like a giant incinerator," Kathleen remembered. Just as people had seen the clouds of smoke and ash on Wall Street, ash was covering the New Jersey side as well.

One of the most poignant memories of that time for the couple was the park 'n' ride parking lot. "When I went by in the morning, I didn't realize what I was seeing," said Philip. "When I came back out in the afternoon, there were little tags on the windshields of almost all those cards—and I noticed there was dust. I realized that those cars were cars nobody was ever going to pick up."

The Peters heard about the trip within days of its launch. Kathleen saw the trip on the news in a Delaware hotel where she was on a business trip. "I dragged Phil out of the shower and said, 'You have to see this. We have to be a part of that.' I thought it was so empowering."

From their car, on the way back to New Jersey, Kathleen phoned everyone she could think of to find out how they could be part of the trip. Philip kept telling her the information would be in the newspaper, but she said, "That's not good enough. We're supposed to be there. If there's anyone who's a part of Portland and loves Portland, it's Philip Peters. I'm going to keep trying until we hit a dead end."

She finally reached Flight for Freedom organizer Elaine Franklin in New York, where she learned the details of the trip.

Though they weren't officially part of the trip, they stayed at the Waldorf-Astoria and participated in every activity. "We paid full price for the Waldorf and it was worth every dime because we were part of something special," said Kathleen, who sang for Gov. Pataki at the Monday night reception. "It was one of the highlights of my life . . . . It was such a pure intent, of why people came, and then to be there and to connect with the people in New York."[10]

Patty Deines, 59, Portland; Betsy Holzgraf, 51, Portland [PHOTO 6]

"In Oregon, we like to say we have this pioneer spirit," says Patty Deines, a retired schoolteacher who was also bravely traveling alone. "We'll fly all the way across the United States to show we care about what these people have been through."

This would be Deines's first trip to New York City. She had heard about the trip on the radio and decided to fly without her husband to support the New Yorkers who had been through "an atrocity." She usually traveled with her husband, but she changed her plans to go with him on a hunting trip in Eastern Oregon. "I was going to eat granola in the woods," she said.

For her, traveling alone, much less flying across the country, was an act of courage.

Little did Deines know that separately, a former colleague from the Bilquist Elementary School in the North Clackamas School District had felt the same need to help.

"Somehow something strikes you and you just have to act on it. I was teaching at the time and fortunately, my principal was sympathetic and she let me go. It just felt like something I needed to do," says Betsy Holzgraf. She told friends about it and they went as well, but after Holzgraf ran into Deines at the Welcome Reception at the Waldorf the first night, they ended up spending much of the trip together. (Holzgraf's husband had decided he couldn't take off from work, which "will be one of the biggest mistakes in his life," she says.)

Lana Cupper, 50, Portland

Lana Cupper was Betsy Holzgraf's assistant in the library at the Bilquist Elementary School.

> In 2001, our son had moved to New York City and he was going to the Twin Towers for his CEO job. He had meetings there and so we were sick when it happened. It was two or three hours into the whole drama of what was happening back in New York before we could touch base with him. I think the phone system wasn't working where he was at the time. I think it was before texting.*

> . . . So when this opportunity came up for the Flight for Freedom, we jumped on it . . . .

> We wanted to be part of it, not just to see our own kids and stuff, but the whole thing, the whole background. The principal was nice enough to give us the time off and their blessing for us going.

> The flyer we got on it, we said, "We've got to do this." There was just no doubt. I'm very, very, very glad we got to do that. That was such a horrendous time . . . .

Jane and Steve Ditewig, 50s, Longview, Washington [PHOTO 7]

Jane is a sorority sister of Betsy Holzgraf. She was a Fulbright scholar, a high school French teacher, and she leads student trips to France every year. Steve worked for the pulp and paper company Crown Zellerbach.

> **Jane:** The idea that it was something you could do. And it was because of my friend Betsy finding out about it. We were having dinner and she told us about this experience and we said we want to do it. We weren't sure if we could do it; we weren't living in Oregon.

---

*She is correct; this is before people used their phones for texting.

But just to experience it and knowing what you see on the news and what you see on TV, you don't really know it until you experience it yourself. That's why we did it, and to give support.

I think we asked if they would let us go since we're not Oregonians. I went to Oregon State. Steve was born in Portland, went to Willamette University. And the whole identity thing, that's part of what all this is. We're supporting things for the right reason. That's something we checked on when we first started . . . .

We were just really excited to get in. There was a rush. We were able to do it. The whole experience. It was so well-planned, all the experiences that we got to have. . . .

We didn't have any hesitation. We were thinking that if anytime is a safe time to fly, now is. It was odd getting on a plane.

[At the time] you did, too, talk to people who probably would not have done it, people who were too worried about what would have happened to them.

Jean Andersen, 79, Portland; Kevin Martin, 48, Portland; Julie Andersen Martin, 48, Portland; Kelley Martin, 19, Portland

Jean Andersen brought her daughter Julie and son-in-law, Kevin, and her granddaughter Kelley Martin, who they took out of Willamette University. "She'll get more education on this trip than in a day in class," said Jean.

George Haight, 52, Woodburn (Pop. 20,100) [PHOTO 8]

When realtor George Haight decided to go on the Flight for Freedom, he contacted the mayor of Woodburn, the city council, and the Woodburn Area Chamber of Commerce, who wrote letters to Mayor Giuliani, which Haight hand delivered in New York. Haight also brought extra money that he collected from friends—more than two hundred dollars—so that he could do some extra tipping. While in New York, he was one of the Oregonians who "adopted" Barbara Shaw so she didn't have to participate in activities alone. Before he left, he told *The Woodburn Independent*:

We all wanted to do something and this is the only thing that I could come up with that would really mean something besides donating blood. When I saw this, my wife said, "Absolutely do it." I was a little hesitant at first, but she said I'd be a darn fool if I didn't, and she wouldn't live with a darn fool.

Frankly, I'm not sure how I'm going to react. To be at ground zero and seeing what in essence is a mass grave for 5,000 people, I don't know how I'm going to react. I know I get goosebumps whenever I think about it.

I'm tickled that Oregon is the first state to organize something like this. We'll fly across the continent and spend a little money and show that we will persevere.[11]

Haight and his wife had actually visited New York twenty years before and stayed at the Waldorf-Astoria, and toured the World Trade Center. "It's kind of eerie," he said. Soon after he returned, he told the *Independent*:

I was on the flight to New York and was being interviewed by KOIN. They asked me what I was going to be doing and I told them I was going to be "tipping." Other people heard that and decided that was something they'd do, too.

The whole trip was kind of a way to show that little symbolic things can really mushroom and make a difference.[12]

Genevieve and David Voorhees, 70s, Portland; Kay and John "Jay" Voorhees, 70s, Tigard (Pop. 41,223); Pete Sinclair, 51, Portland
[PHOTO 9]

David and Genevieve Voorhees, who had retired from the Portland Tupperware franchise they had owned for twenty-five years, wanted to do more than sign a check—and they were too old to give blood (though their kids all did). They went with a family group of brothers and sisters-in-law. Genevieve spoke with me about the trip in a phone conversation before they left:

It just kind of filled a need to do something. It seemed to be a pro-active move to support them back there, to fill up some hotel rooms and give some waiters and waitresses something to do, and get the airlines flying again . . . . I just hope that we can make a difference to some of the people back there . . . . We're all in our seventies, we're not kids anymore—

At this point, David interrupted, calling out from the background, "I am!" Genevieve continued: "I just hope that we can make a difference to some of the people back there."[13]

"Sure, I'd like to see the Empire State Building, the Statue of Liberty, all those things. But just to let the people in New York know we care, that's my main reason for going," said Kay Voorhees.

As a twelve-year member of the Tualatin Valley Fire and Rescue's Board of Directors, Kay's husband, John "Jay" Voorhees, was bringing pins from the Tualatin Valley firefighters to the Fire Department of New York City (FDNY).

> It's really, really hard sitting out here and seeing what we see happening back there to those people and it gives you a feeling of inadequacy. I can't help but think that if there's any way in the world that we can help them by taking this Freedom Flight that we should do it . . . . We jumped on it right away . . . .
>
> We have never lost a firefighter through fighting a fire or trying to rescue someone. It's really hard to say how I would have felt being on the board, knowing one of my firefighters had died. You listen to the radio and read in the paper where there's 160-some of them that died and eight or ten of them in one firehouse, it gives you a really weird feeling in the pit of your stomach to think that that could have happened out here . . . .

A friend who lived near the twin towers told them that it would be gut-wrenching. "We know that . . . there will be more tears than laughter," said Jay. "We're trying to prepare ourselves."

Pete Sinclair, a Portland-based executive with U.S. Bank, fit the trip into his schedule by returning to Portland late Tuesday night and catching a 6:30 plane to Minneapolis the following morning. Sinclair was going with four other family members, including the Voorhees, and the trip had a number of objectives.

> It's an opportunity for my wife and I to visit New York City with some relatives and experience a city in healing . . . . We have five kids and five grandkids, and what kind of example is that to be afraid of people who treat other people like that. We're not going to let a terrorist rule our lives. It's our way of making a statement. This is our way of fighting back. It's a statement, it's not really a trip.

Elaine Edgel, 41, Tualatin (Pop. 22,791)

Like Mayor Vera Katz, for some Freedom Fliers the trip was a very personal one. Elaine Edgel's son, Josh, a Marine, was stationed at Quantico, Virginia, just outside of Washington, DC, and was planning to be at the Pentagon on September 11. When a co-worker told Elaine that the Pentagon was hit:

> I knew I needed to leave for home. I left the room and started to walk down the hallway. About halfway down the hallway I just started to cry. I fell back against the wall and slid down it, crying uncontrollably, grateful that I was alone. I started to get myself together, found my manager to let her know that I needed to leave.
>
> I have never been able to remember the forty-five minute drive home.
>
> Shortly after I arrived I saw the second tower go down, I got down on my knees crying and praying to Heavenly Father that he would be with all of us, to please let those trapped in the towers not suffer.

Hours later, her son phoned to say he had never left Quantico. "That night when I was getting ready for bed I didn't sleep much at all, I kept thinking of those that still were wondering about their loved ones and the sadness I had for them. I knew exactly what they were going through; even though my terror was only for a few hours, it was like an eternity."

Josh met Elaine at the Waldorf during the Flight for Freedom. "When I saw my son we both embraced each other for a very, very long time as I cried."

Alexia Halen, 39, Portland; Jane Meskill, 41, Portland [PHOTO 10]

Social worker Alexia Halen is originally from New Jersey and had many friends who were directly affected by the World Trade Center attacks. One friend hid in the bushes in Battery Park for hours. She knew people on the streets below who had run, not knowing what was happening but just to escape. "I think it really hit home just hearing our friends' stories of the absolute terror," she said.

Halen's husband was in school at Cornell in Ithaca, New York. She had not been able to reach him when the attacks were happening and it was frightening.

People may not realize today, twenty years later, that during the time these attacks were in progress, nobody knew what exactly was happening. Was this just affecting New York and Washington, DC? Would other cities be targets? Almost immediately, the Sears Tower in Chicago was shut down, and tall buildings and landmarks around the country were evacuated. In 2021, Halen remembers her fear for her father, who worked in a Portland high-rise office building:

> I remember thinking we were going to get attacked, all of us. That morning of 9/11 my dad worked at the US Bank Tower, the big pink building. He was up towards the top of the building and he was at the office and I said to him, "You need to go home. We don't know if there are more planes flying into tall buildings." His response, because he was in World War II, was, "I'm not worried. If it happens it happens." . . .
>
> We all came together. Going into grocery stores. Anywhere you went, you looked in people's eyes, there was this . . . knowing, and community, and everyone was feeling the same thing.

Halen, who had worked with Portland City Commissioner (city councilman) Dan Saltzman on children's initiatives, knew immediately that she had to be part of the Flight for Freedom—even though she had a one-year-old son:

> It was one of those things where I felt like I have to get there for lots of reasons. Of course I'm going to go on this trip because this is what we do. I was not afraid.
>
> But it's kind of crazy that I would leave my one-year-old son. My husband took a bus down to New York and I met him there . . . .
>
> It was absolutely insane—family friends took care of my son. Why would I leave my one-year-old son? . . .
>
> It is one of those moments in my history when I'm thinking, "What was I thinking?" I was really driven. There was no question that I would be a part of that.
>
> I just wanted to be there and support people there . . . to support the restaurants or stores that were open and to show we're here, and it's safe to come here. The main thing—to show others, it's safe to come here now. And we need to because this city is so hurting. The people,

everything they've gone through, to be right there . . . . You can bring the city back to life again.

And I think just walking—I love just wandering around New York City. I just wanted to see the impact and see people and try to support people . . . .

I'm Lebanese so I have darker skin and my brother looks like the men that did the 9/11 attack. He could fit in that lineup. He's very dark, dark-haired.[14]

Halen's friend, Jane Meskill, was also originally from the East Coast, from Alexandria, Virginia. Having young children had kept her from participating in other efforts, but the Flight for Freedom she felt she could do.

There were all kinds of tragedies happening. Sarajevo was falling apart right before then and I wanted to do something to help, to do some art therapy with kids who were traumatized, but because I had the kids I couldn't go and provide relief. I always had this idea to help in a tragedy. It was just something we could do. It was just a short trip, I could leave my kids for a short time, it was economics . . . . The sadness, you want to do something to take care of it . . . .

I think it's sort of like making sure they were going to be all right. I think that's what I needed, to see for myself that life goes on and things were going to be OK.[15]

Don Yule, 71, Portland

Retired cofounder of Century 21 Real Estate Corp., Yule brought his fiancée. He had moved to Portland about a year earlier to live near a daughter there, and he had a daughter in Manhattan who had lost friends in the attack. He also wanted to support the city, where he'd kept an office on the World Trade Center's seventy-third floor with a view of the Statue of Liberty. Yule knew immediately that he would go. "There was hardly any thinking about it." He volunteered at the Portland Red Cross, and had seen the effects of the attacks across the continent.

The next day was my day at our central headquarters for the Northwest, and I just felt I ought to go in a couple hours early. I got there two-and-a-half hours before normal and people were already lined up in the street. It's a very large center; we were just over-whelmed. Many donors also wrote checks the same day. I've been a witness to the responsiveness of Oregonians to this horrible thing.[16]

Thomas Wiebe, Portland

On 9/11, and for the next few days, the response from New Yorkers, and from surrounding cities, was to look for any way to help those in the World Trade towers. Volunteers rushed to help, shelters and emergency clinics were set up, teams were organized to locate and help survivors. It became terribly clear within a few days that, unlike many past disasters, there were almost no survivors to find and to aid. Our President rallied the country, but it seemed that everyone I knew was in shock.

After a couple of weeks, Cindy and I heard from my parents, Tony and Celia Wiebe, of an effort by a local travel agency owner, Sho Dozono, to organize a group of Oregonians to visit New York, as a sign of support. That soon after the disaster, many people were too spooked to fly or take vacations, with immediate economic effect: Airlines were bleeding money, hotels were empty, and restaurants were already starting to shut down. The group was called Flight for Freedom, and grew to around 1,000 people; we joined them three weeks after 9/11 to visit New York City, to spend four days there. Cindy and I had never traveled to New York together before that.[17]

Jackie and Phil Young, 60s, Happy Valley (Pop. 4,519) [PHOTO 11]

Jackie owned SWIMBABES infant and toddler swimming school. As chief estimator for Precision Construction, a subsidiary of Hoffman, Phil handled many big builds in Oregon.

Jackie: The way it all came together was crazy. I got a call from my friend and she said, "Have you heard about the trip to New York? About 250 of us are signed up."

And I said, "I'm going."

Phil was at work. It was like a Tuesday that I did this. He comes home from work and our son greeted him—"Guess where you're going! You and Mom are going to New York on Friday!"

I said "Phil, we're going. It's the least we could do."

We had no idea that that whole group of people would swell to at least 1,000.

And then I had bought a big, huge beach bag. It had blue and white stripes and on the bottom of it was circled with red and all the stars. I thought, "Everywhere I go I will wear my T-shirt and carry that big bag." I was trying to make a statement and say we're going to get this economy going.

Everybody was afraid to go to New York and go in the shops. And all the people were devastated.

There's a lot of similarities with now [2021, COVID]. But just the whole thing was amazing . . . . It was just an amazing time, and no one talked politics. [PHOTO 12]

Michael Phillips, 30s, Portland

Portland playwright and professor Michael Phillips, whose play *Voices from a Sunlit Shadow* came out of his experiences in the Flight for Freedom, also got involved:

> . . . out of a sense of helplessness, really. I have many, many friends in the New York area. And, I was feeling like I needed to DO something, anything, but being all the way across the country I had no idea what that could possibly be. I was feeling the same shock that everyone else was, I suppose, and with that came a sense of complete helplessness—almost an inertia. The Flight for Freedom suddenly gave me a way to get involved that made sense, on a number of levels.

Bill Cooper, KPAM Radio, Portland [PHOTO 13]

Bill Cooper went because it was an important news story, but when he discusses the effects of the 9/11 attacks nearly twenty years later, he embodies the moving-forward-with-life idea that was a major purpose of the trip:

> After seeing Ground Zero in person [it] gave me a sense that the United States was no longer invulnerable. We had had a terror attack hit our country very hard, and that really there was no safe place on earth. Terrorism could happen anywhere and I think that hit the hardest with me and it scared me. I realized that because of the way this attack happened nobody had any ability to protect themselves from that. I had a wife and two young daughters and I realized that

if there was another attack like this and we happened to be in the wrong place at the wrong time, there was not a snowball's chance in hell that I could protect them from that.

I don't think it's had an impact on how you lived your life. Because there's nothing you can do. There's nothing that you can do to really protect yourself from an attack like that. And there's no change in your life that you can make. You can't make any change in your life that's really going to make a difference in that respect other than yes, I was scared about what that meant. But then you just have to go on and live your life. Because you can't do anything [about it]. You shouldn't let it paralyze your life.[18]

Glenn Kloster, 49, St. Helens (Pop. 10,019) [PHOTO 14]

When I heard about the trip, I yearned to go, to say, "I'm not afraid to fly on that plane." If I can donate some money and employ people and get them back to their jobs in New York in that big industry of tourism and all the shows and everything, I just want to do it. It's a simple thing.

By evening, Glenn Kloster grew crystals for the semiconductor industry. Since 1997, he had also worked with Weyerhaeuser and the wood products industry, designing fiberboard kits for model villages for kids to assemble and color. The buildings were about one-foot square and two-feet tall, with doors and windows that open, and places to park cars and trucks and—in sync with the times, to place beanie babies inside. After September 11, Kloster specially designed New York police and fire stations with logos and captions that read, "We Love NY Police Department" and "We Love NY Fire Dept." printed on the buildings. The project took "a lot of hours, and sometimes unemployment benefits," Koster said. He had planned to send them to New York with one of the Freedom Fliers, to be signed by trip participants and donated to a New York police or fire station.

But Kloster deeply wanted to go himself. To raise travel funds in pre-crowdfunding times, Kloster created an announcement that made it clear that his village was going to New York regardless:

While [Kloster] plans to send the village with another traveler, he's hoping to make the trip himself and searching for sponsors. Kelly Services has already signed on.

Ultimately, Kloster's trip was sponsored in part by the Portland district office of Kelly Services. One of Kelly's executives had lost a son in the Twin Towers, who remained unaccounted for. Kloster took the weekend off and used vacation time to go. "My boss said, 'You can go, just take vacation time.'"

Before he left, Kloster betrayed his tech roots in the way he characterized his impulse to be part of the Flight for Freedom: "It's not programmed or anything, it's from the heart. It's just, 'Let's go!'"[19]

Jos Anemaet, Corvallis (Pop. 78,158); Joy Schertz, Corvallis

Jos Anemaet was to begin her retirement from her position as a librarian at Oregon State University on October 1. Instead of relaxing, she and her partner, Joy Schertz, found a cat-sitter and packed their suitcases.

"That whole feeling of giving, the feeling that we have to let life go on," was among the reasons behind the trip, said Anemaet. "We want New York to know: Even though we're on the other side of the U.S., we want to support you."

New York City held special meaning for Anemaet, who had come to the United States forty-two years before as a Dutch refugee from Indonesia. "The first view I had of America as a twenty-year-old, not speaking the language, was New York," she said.

Sandra Kempel, 53, Portland; Pamela Getty, 53, Portland [PHOTO 15]

Sandra Kempel knew immediately that she would go. She kept trying Azumano Travel and "every number I could possibly find for 'Azumano'" until she got through. It would be her first trip to New York City.

> It was instantaneous. I didn't care if I had money, it was going on the credit card and I could pay it off in four years. There was no doubt in my mind that I had to do this for [New Yorkers]. I'd gotten the call and I was answering it. I wasn't thinking like, this is my perfect opportunity to get to New York. No, this is the time I have to go to New York.
>
> I felt so strongly that the terrorists would not intimidate Americans and prevent them from having the freedom to travel that they'd always had. I just made up my mind that no matter what happened,

I was going to make the trip. And my first instinct was when the Twin Towers went down, when they were attacked, I said, "Not my New York!" I'd never visited there, but it was someplace I'd always wanted to go and it just wounded me, like millions of others all over the world.

I'm tremendously empathetic so I felt a lot of pain, although I didn't know anyone personally who had died there.

It's old, it's one of the first populated areas in the country, and it just represented so much of what is America. I know that it's a melting pot, the Irish immigrants came there, the Italian immigrants, and that's just about where everybody landed to begin this new life of freedom, whether or not they realized at that time or not, but still they came here and years later, we're still opening our doors to immigrants and it's been a place of freedom, and that just represented the influx of immigrants to this country.

Even though it did not have a bearing on her decision to make the trip, Sandra's sister and brother-in-law were on vacation on the East Coast and might have been in New York on that day; they had been at the top of the World Trade Center's South Tower and the Pentagon just the week before.[20]

Kempel's Point West Credit Union colleague, Pam Getty, the credit union's mortgage manager, went, too; together they became a credit-union envoy, which resulted in "a [lovely] day with the colleagues at the Actors Equity Credit Union in New York."

"We're so far away from New York, but the devastation, and all those lives that were lost just touched us and we felt we had to do something," said Getty. "So when our Mayor Vera Katz sent a message that the best way to help is to travel and spend money in New York we leapt at the chance."[21]

Georgette Brown, 59 Josephine County (County Pop. 75,726)

Originally from New York, Josephine County Clerk Georgette Brown wanted "closure. You see all the pictures, but it doesn't really seem real." Later, when she went to Ground Zero and thought it was raining, she realized that ash was still falling from the sky. People coming home from work had an "unnatural, glazed look." It became real.

Dave and JoAnn Dewey, 50s, Bend (Pop. 52,029)

"It was thumbing our noses at the terrorists," says JoAnn Dewey, who went with her husband Dave. "It said: 'You can't put us down. We're going to keep on coming.'"

Eric and Sara Christenson, 20s, Portland

Married August 25, the Christensons, were on their second honeymoon. "We came for the same reasons as everybody else," said Eric, who worked at a high-tech firm. "There is no freedom in fear."

"That whole feeling of giving, the feeling that we have to let life go on. We want New York to know: Even though we're on the other side of the U.S., we want to support you."

—Jos Anemaet, Corvallis

Organizer Karen Winder.
Photo: Betsy Ames

Joy Cavinta, 50, Tigard (Pop. 41,223) [PHOTO 16]

Joy Cavinta, who worked in a custom film processing lab and volunteered for the sheriff's department, heard about the trip only once, when she just happened to stay up late and heard about it on the Channel 8 news. She says that "the price helped" to make it possible for her to go. For her, traveling to New York was the strongest statement she could make about terrorism and fear.

> I'm not going to let them win. I was very, very angry at the whole situation that it had happened, that as many people had died and it didn't matter that they were firefighters, police officers, workers in the World Trade Center, they were human beings and they didn't deserve to die like that.

Debra Minchow, 44, Newport (Pop. 9,532); Bryan Coleman, 39, Newport

"I'm very anxious about flying now, and I'm not usually a very anxious person. I have a bit of concern about it. But I'm going anyway," nurse Debra Minchow told the Newport *News-Times*. The newspaper followed her and Bryan Coleman, an Oregon State University Hatfield Marine Science Center computer systems professional, both before and after the trip. For both of them it would be their first trip to New York City.

Minchow's generosity perfectly captured the spirit of the Freedom Fliers; she even asked that the newspaper publish their phone number: "I'll be leaving Saturday morning from Portland. If anybody wants me to put something there for them, some kind of memorial, please call me . . . . I'd be more than willing to do so."

Coleman, who said the trip was "an opportunity to see history," brought a card from the Newport Fire Department to deliver to a New York fire station.[22]

Alice McElhany, 70s, Portland

Alice McElhany made her first trip to New York—only her second airplane ride—with the Flight for Freedom. She also went back to New York on the anniversary visit in 2002.

> The news stations around town reported about the upcoming trip on the evening broadcasts. I thought that it was a very nice way that people could help New York City. The next evening, as I heard again about the trip, I thought I would like to go (But me go to NYC?—not likely!) By the third evening of the news reports I was thinking I really want to go on this trip!
>
> I had watched the news so much since the attacks on September 11. But it was not enough to pray and send cards of encouragement; I wanted to do more. The trip was a way to help and encourage the people of New York City—just what my heart yearned to do.
>
> . . . Though friends were worried about additional terrorist attacks I was most worried about muggers and rude New Yorkers. And though many frequent fliers were frightened out of flying, I excitedly anticipated my second airline trip. I had no idea of what New York was like. I bought a laminated map, borrowed a book, and studied them both.

Brad and Kimberly Hicks, 30s, Medford (Pop. 63,154)

Many people felt apprehensive, though not necessarily about flying. Brad Hicks, president of the Medford-Jackson County Chamber of Commerce, went with his wife, Kimberly, and paid with their own funds, though he planned to focus on business while there.

"If I have any anxiety, it's about what we're going to see in New York. I haven't felt like this about anything in my life. It's impacted me in a deep way and I've felt compelled to go there since September 11 and see how we can be helpful," he told Medford's *Mail Tribune*.

The Medford/Jackson County chamber had already sent offers of help to the Manhattan chamber, and had received a request that they join the organization for a year to help with the financial crisis caused by the deaths of many members in the World Trade Center bombing.

On a more personal level, Hicks said, "I want to be as available as I can to help New Yorkers. I don't look at it as a fun trip."

Ann Nice, 52, Portland

Ann Nice, vice president of the Portland Association of Teachers (PAT), participated as the association's representative. Sho Dozono had worked with the education community in Portland and wanted to make sure that the union was part of the group.

> They were looking for a core group of people, ordinary people from various walks of life, and Richard Garrett, the president, couldn't go so he asked me.
>
> I wanted to go in the worst possible way, but I have an adult developmentally disabled daughter whose seizures were bad at the time and I just knew I couldn't leave her and go. There wasn't any way and so I told him I just didn't think I could, but I'd think about it overnight.
>
> I was talking to my sister and I told her about it and by the time I got off work that day, she called and said, "You're going. We will take care of Angie. We'll get her to work, get her where she needs to go, and if you want to go, you go."
>
> And I called Richard and said, "I'm in."[23]

As the PAT representative, she brought cards from Portland's students, along with posters she hung on the fence at Ground Zero; and she made sure to use her per diem money to support the New York economy and show people that it was safe to enjoy New York.

Beth Faulhaber of Molalla, 20s, director of the Police Activities League (PAL), and **Portland School Police Officer Jerry Cioeta, 20s,** brought Portland middle school students **Alisha Santos, 12, and Sarah Loftis, 11**. Azumano Travel had suggested to one of PAL's board members that "some of the PAL kids go," Faulhaber told *The Molalla Pioneer*. "This was like last Sunday . . . . five days before we were supposed to go."[24] Azumano Travel sponsored Santos and Loftis, PAL sponsored Faulhaber, and Cioeta went along as a chaperon.

Lance and Marla Nuttman, 20s, McMinnville (Pop. 26,499) [PHOTO 17]

The Nuttmans, who had gotten married in June and never had a honeymoon, decided the Flight for Freedom would be the perfect opportunity. They worked the swing shift at the Native American-owned Spirit Mountain Casino in Grand Ronde in the table game. Business had been slow after 9/11, so taking off five days on the spur of the moment was no problem.*

"There were a lot of people who were locals who didn't see that [9/11] was a big deal at the time. People weren't coming here from other places," said Lance.[25]

Lance and Marla were on the cutting edge of technology—they were on the internet when they heard about the attacks.

> **Marla:** When the first plane hit, we were up and on the internet. I was playing games on Pogo and somebody said something in chat. There was no Google then, and you couldn't search for things. You had to

---

*At this writing, it is not known that any members of Oregon's Native tribes participated in the Flight for Freedom. Marla and Lance still work at the casino. In 2021, Marla outlined the casino's progress. "I always think of them as the owners' kids," she says of tribal members. "I grew up in a family business and that's what they are. And especially at that time [2001], our casino was really young and it's different twenty years later, twenty-five years after it opened. It's different for them because they've had time to mature and help their people. At their time they were still pretty oppressed. It's better now. They were still struggling at that time to find a place for their people." Marla Nuttman, interview with the author, January 24, 2021.

follow links through pages or you had to know a web address. So it wasn't like we were getting our news from the internet . . . .

I think we were some of the first people who signed up because we didn't have any trouble getting on that trip. On September 10, we had just said, "We should go to New York sometime and go see Conan, and the next day the thing happened and so we were very anxious to go.

Lance: It was twofold. Like Marla said, we had discussed going somewhere and I remember when she said that, terror struck me. Not because of 9/11, not because of New York City—because I didn't travel. I had only been on a plane once before—going to Yuma [Arizona] on a plane to see her. Since then [2001], we travel . . . . The other thing was, New York needs help. It was a city we'd never seem, this famous city. We literally went, "They need help. We can do this. We're lucky enough to have money to do this. And the time. When are we ever going to have this chance again?"

Marla: It was an excellent opportunity as far as the cost goes.

Lance: It was very affordable. I'm always thinking of that, too.*

Toni Epperson, 55, Josephine County

Toni Epperson, candidate for Josephine County commissioner, told the *Daily Courier* in Grants Pass that death could happen at any time, so people should travel and just look at the odds. "I can walk out in my street and get run over by a car," she said, adding, "the country needs to stick together and show that it believes in what it stands for: freedom."

Artie Rene Knight, Linda Daugherty, and Eileen Wiedrich, Portland
[PHOTO 18]

Mt. Tabor Middle School teachers Artie Rene Knight, Linda Daugherty and Eileen Wiedrich brought a wreath made by their students, some of whom had lost family members in the attack, and a check for $7,300: donations that had been collected by the students.

---

*Lance put together an extensive website about the trip, with both serious observations and witty takes on their experiences, many of which are included throughout this book.

They hoped the trip would help them explain the disaster to their students.

Gary Fuszek, 48, Corvallis (Pop: 78,158); Kimberley Rockwood, 34; Ashley Fuszek, 17; Amanda Martinez, 11

USA Today reported that Ashley Fuszek, 17, brought a banner made by her classmates at Crescent Valley High School, and her step-sister, Amanda Martinez, 11, brought one from her fellow students at Highland View Middle School. They planned to hang them in Union Square, which had been transformed into an *ad hoc* shrine by New Yorkers starting on the afternoon of September 11.

"I know it's going to be emotional," Kimberley, who had accompanied the girls with her husband, Gary, had said. "I know we'll be seeing the effects of what's happened. I'm looking at it as a very positive experience. But it's going to be hard." It was Fuszek's first trip to New York.[26]

Stephanie Hinshaw, 15, Portland

Roger Hinshaw, president of Bank of America, took his wife, Margaret, and their two teenage children. After the trip, Stephanie wrote an essay capturing her intellectual and emotional journey, which was infinitely longer than the 3,000-mile plane flight. Margaret sent the essay to Azumano Travel. The essay is excerpted throughout this volume.

> I love going places. Sterile airplane silverware, Styrofoam pillows, copious gift shops, and tiny bathroom samples. This was my heaven. It doesn't matter the destination, but the further the better. That's why I didn't hesitate a second when I was told I had the opportunity to go to New York City. My heart raced at the thought. I had never been to the East Coast. I'd been all over Asia, but never New York.
>
> "Weren't you afraid to fly?" someone asks. I wasn't scared at all, though is that insane? . . . Did I think about our plane getting hijacked by terrorists? Yes, but it didn't bother me. I wasn't going to hang on to some possibility of danger and pass up an opportunity.
>
> I love flying . . . . I love it when my ears pop. I love looking out the window at the clouds. When you go to someplace different what's really you has the opportunity to separate itself from what only

appears to be you. When I travel, it's interesting to see what parts of me stay with me, and what parts are left on the clouds as I fly by.[27]

Randall Edwards and Julia Brim-Edwards, 30s, Portland [PHOTO 19]

Randall Edwards said that even though he was state treasurer "it was suggested to go, but I went as a citizen of Oregon . . . . I just went."[28] Edwards was also carrying a financial message to New York, that the economies of both states have a symbiotic relationship. The state of Oregon has a direct connection to the financial and economic centers on the East Coast, and it pumps millions of dollars into the markets annually. And of course, Oregon relies on national financial markets in order to provide essential services in Oregon.

The fact that the market was up and operating so soon after the attacks was a testament to the strength of the country's financial system, said Edwards, who planned to convey the message that Oregon still had confidence in the market, and would continue to use it:

> We use the market to manage state investments and regardless of last month's tragedy, we are not deviating from how we invest the state's money. In fact, during the first week the market reopened, we reallocated $1 billion of the state pension fund back into the equity markets. There are undoubtedly some opportunities there and we waited to buy until it was prudent to do so.

On August 31, 2001, the state's total portfolio was $47.3 billion, $36.5 billion of which is the Public Employees Retirement fund.[29]

As a member of the Portland School Board, Julia Brim-Edwards focused on meeting teachers and students in New York. She brought cards and messages from Portland's schoolchildren to share with children in New York schools to let them know that Americans cared about them.

Ron Saxton, 46, Portland

Republican gubernatorial candidate Ron Saxton captured his sense of purpose in an essay in *The Portland Tribune*:

> We were comrades armed with renewed spirits, quiet determination as well as eager pocketbooks. Our mission: to show our brothers and sisters in the Big Apple that Oregon cares.

We are here to comfort where we can. To support this great city and her people so horribly wounded. With every handshake, every hug, we celebrate our common bond of humanity.

To prove to the world—ourselves—that we are "one nation" and that our collective will cannot be broken. That we can face our challenges united.

We are reminded, again, that our strength as a nation is often best represented during adversity.[30]

Ed Washington, 64, Portland

Ed Washington was the first African-American councilor for the Portland Metro Council, a regional government entity that serves the Portland Metropolitan Area (Clackamas, Multnomah, and Washington counties). Founded in 1979, Metro was the first directly elected regional government in the United States.

Washington joined the trip because, he said, it was time to show we could start moving again after being stopped on September 11th. "But we're not stopped forever," he told KGW. "This isn't a time to be afraid. This is a time to stand tall."[31]

Rachel Gerber, 48, Beaverton (Pop. 76,129)

I heeded the call—the call to shake off fear and go to the Big Apple. Took me but a New York minute," Rachel Gerber, former chairman of the Oregon Government Standards and Practices Commission, wrote in *The Oregonian*. "Up until that time, I'd not seen what can happen when one man has a dream and pursues it without concern as to outcome."[32]

Cathy Rudd, 47, Lake Oswego (Pop. 35,278); Hilary Rudd, 12, Lake Oswego

Cathy Rudd and her daughter, Hilary, had visited the World Trade Center together once before. "She remembers being in Windows on the World," said Rudd, about the famous restaurant on the 106th and 107th floors of the North Tower. Hilary wanted to go to New York, added Rudd. "She knows there's a tremendous amount of hurt back there. She told me that when people are in need, you need to go to their aid."[33]

Cameron Platt, 16, Portland

I loved traveling and still am a big traveler and that was all I wanted to spend my allowance or saving or summer job money on. I remember hearing—I think it was an article in The Oregonian about the trip to New York and . . . as soon as I found out about it, I went to my parents and said, "We should totally do this."

I was very independent at that age and I suggested that I would go myself and pay my own way and they expressed interest in going as well and it turned into this family group. "I'll pay my own way"— that was a strategy of mine . . . . I think they probably paid for me in the end . . . .

[On September 11] I remember hearing the news on the radio and turning on the TV and processing it all day in school. I think when I heard of an opportunity to go there, I felt like that was so important in terms of the understanding and the next steps. I don't know if I had the consciousness of healing or thinking of it more in depth at the time. I think everybody felt so helpless at the time, that was a concrete step—"Sure, we could do that."

It's such a big. global thing, it's like, you feel like how am I going to play any role in this at all? And that was a tangible, immediate action.[34]

Mary Platt, 50, Portland

September 11 is Mary Platt's birthday. She was on Cycle Oregon and heard about the attacks and saw no television coverage for days.

We came back and we hadn't been bathed in that over and over again . . . . We came back trying to catch up . . . . We didn't see any of the images live at all until we got back. That was pre-cell phone . . . . I felt much more protected emotionally than most people and I think it contributed to my wanting to do the Flight for Freedom also because I'd had this chance to be on this wonderful ride while the whole nation was reeling in it, and we were spending the rest of the week in beauty. I think it did contribute to my wanting to go back and to help.[35]*

---

*Mary Platt's husband, Rob, was on a motorcycle trip across the state. In Service Creek, an unincorporated "stake shop" (pop. 4) in eastern Oregon. Platt encountered a "rural reaction. It's a big city, whatever. Which was a very surprising reaction but understandable."

Kathi Karnosh, 51, Lake Oswego [PHOTO 20]

"I just felt compelled," said Kathi Karnosh, who was a dental hygienist at the time.

> I just wanted to be part of something that was bigger than me— it was an historic event, and it was an opportunity to be witness to some sort of healing for what the city had gone through. And I just remember saying, "Boy, I want to go."
>
> It was so sudden because we were there three weeks after 9/11. There was still steam coming out of the ground, and it was like we're going to get this trip together and we're leaving in a week . . . .
>
> My brother-in-law at the time was in the Army and he had an office at the Pentagon, but it was a Wednesday and—
>
> —My daughter was married on September 8, and she flew to Hawaii and her birthday was September 11 and I remember calling her and leaving a message: I said, "Amy, turn on the news."
>
> And, of course, Hawaii shut down and their honeymoon was not as expected;, but my brother-in-law decided not to go into work that it day [the Pentagon] was hit. I don't recall just why he didn't go in, but that was pretty significant . . . .
>
> At the time, our nation came together as one and the churches were filled and people were softer and kinder to each other and it was sobering, but it was kind of a time for healing and I was just really proud of that trip, very proud.[36]

Joyce Willing, 38, Portland

"The country came together," says Joyce Willing, remembering the effort twenty years later. "We were clear across the country, but we still felt the need to help our families and friends."[37]

1. Barbara Shaw displays her handmade New York/Oregon quilt. Photo courtesy of Barbara Shaw

2. State Senator Margaret Carter. Photo by Bill Cooper

3. Portland firefighters at the Waldorf-Astoria. Left to right: Greg Strech, Mark Walkley, Mike House, Allen Oswalt, James Kirkendall. Photo by Betsy Ames

4. Al O'Brien and Portland Mayor Vera Katz at the Welcome Reception. Photo by Al O'Brien

5. Baruti Artharee speaking at Union Square on October 7, 2001. Photo courtesy of Baruti Artharee

6. Betsy Holzgraf and Patty Deines on the set of "The View." (See "Last Moments" for the story.) Photo courtesy of Betsy Holzgraf

7. The Ditewigs at the Flight for Freedom hospitality tables at the Waldorf-Astoria Hotel. Photo courtesy of Jane and Steve Ditewig.

8. George Haight at the Waldorf-Astoria. Photo by Barbara Shaw. Letters from Woodburn mayor and city council chair and the Chamber of Commerce . Letters courtesy of George Haight

9. Kay and Jay Voorhees arrive at the Waldorf-Astoria Hotel. Photo property of the Oregonian Publishing Co.

10. Alexia Halen and Jane Meskill at the Flight for Freedom hospitality tables at the Waldorf-Astoria. Photo courtesy of Alexia Halen

11. Jackie and Phil Young at the Waldorf-Astoria. Photo courtesy of Jackie Young

12. The Youngs went with their friends, Don and Jeanine Ford (right), together at the All-Oregon Reception on Monday, October 9, 2001. Photo courtesy of Jackie Young

13. Bill Cooper and Mayor Katz at JFK Airport. Photo courtesy of Bill Cooper

14. Glenn Kloster's "New York Village" at the Welcome Reception, where Flight for Freedom participants signed it. Kloster later donated the model to Engine 54, Ladder 4, Battalion 9, the firehouse that lost the most members on September 11. Photo by Betsy Ames

15. Sandra Kempel and Pam Getty in New York's Little Italy, where, as everywhere in New York, Oregonians were warmly welcomed. Photo courtesy of Sandra Kempel

16. Joy Cavinta. Photo courtesy of Sho and Loen Dozono

17. Marla and Lance Nuttman in Times Square. Photo courtesy of Lance and Marla Nuttman

18. Mt. Tabor Middle School teachers Artie Rene Knight, Linda Daugherty and Eileen Wiedrich. Photo by Betsy Ames

19. Left to right: Portland Public School Board Member Julia Brim-Edwards (seated), Multnomah County Chair Diane Linn, and Oregon State Treasurer Randall Edwards. Photo by Betsy Ames

20. Kathi Karnosh (at right) with Freedom Fliers Mary and her husband, originally from Brooklyn. Photo courtesy of Kathi Karnosh

THE ADVENTURE BEGINS

THURSDAY-SATURDAY, OCTOBER 4-6, 2001

The first 180 Freedom Fliers got on planes at Portland International Airport—PDX—on Thursday, October 4, 2001. [PHOTO 1]

Before the Oregonians left their state, they were simply people on their way to New York to help out after the September 11 attacks. By Saturday night in the Waldorf-Astoria's Starlight Ballroom, they had become the Flight for Freedom.

It's hard to imagine how little anyone on the trip knew what it would be all about when the adventure began.

Betsy Holzgraf, a teacher from Portland,* captured most people's state of mind: "It wasn't a social trip. It wasn't a party, *per se*, and when we went into it—I had no idea what to expect."

That morning, the trip's organizers had sent out a press release announcing for the first time that official activities for the participants in this adventure had been planned: that Portland Mayor Vera Katz would lead the Oregon delegation in New York's Columbus Day Parade; that U.S. Rep. Darlene Hooley and State Treasurer Randall

---

*Unless otherwise stated, all cities and towns are in Oregon.

Edwards would "Wake Up Wall Street;" or that that Rep. David Wu, the first Chinese-American to serve in the House of Representatives, had invited everyone to dinner in New York's Chinatown.

With flights leaving in the early morning—the three-hour time change means it's an all-day trip across the country—Azumano Travel staff were at the airport at 4 a.m. hanging banners and preparing for the group.

Passengers were unsure of what exactly they would find at the airport. Security practices that are commonplace today were unprecedented less than a month after 9/11. While security was tighter than ever, streamlined processes were yet to be put into place. All these passengers knew was that they needed to get to the Portland airport (PDX) extremely early, two hours in advance, and that there was a new list of carry-on contraband, which included such heretofore benign implements as nail files.

Flight for Freedom participants were not left on their own in Portland; Azumano Travel helped them check in for their flights, and made sure they were comfortable. Leisure Sales Manager Nancy Parrott:

> There was security, [but] we didn't have TSA checkpoints. There were really long lines because nobody really knew what they were doing yet.
>
> There was a lot of media there obviously, saying good-bye to the Flight for Freedom travelers and doing a lot of interviews. And of course we had signage at the airline ticket counters and special check-ins for the Flight for Freedom travelers and so forth.

Everything was even slower than anticipated. Loen captured the morning in her notes:

> We run between Delta and United. Security gates are maddening—lines four across reaching to "Made in Oregon" shop. People barely making flights.
>
> Everyone is excited. I meet Roy Stilwell checking in . . . .his wife says he brought a violin, is retired Oregon Symphony violinist and will perform anywhere. I mention to Bruce [Samson] to contact him for Memorial Service.
>
> Group departure reception room set up—people appreciate service. Media covering departure. Kristen, Mary Ellen Hanson, Jessica Brown, gets on TV with Bonnie Dillon, embroidered black coat "Flight for Freedom." [PHOTO 2]

Meeting Roy Stilwell was another of the synchronicities that marked the trip, and one of the most memorable. Nick Fish had contacted him to play at the Union Square service, and that turned out to be one of the most memorable moments of the event. "Fortune shined on us," Fish would say later. "Everything seemed to fall into place, I think because it was meant to," said Loen. "There couldn't have been a more perfect way of those things coming together, but it was all last-minute little things, the right people at the right time being there to do those things, to say what they said."

On the next day, Friday, October 5, Loen would experience a different glitch than the new security processes: arranging for a Muslim participant, Portland Imam Shaheed Hamid and his wife. In her notes, she wrote: "It was strange trying to allow a late addition; the airline was frantic for the name, probably for security. It seemed tense, but we would see what happened." (Hamid and his wife traveled.)[1]

Portland's Royal Rosarians were there, too, to give all of the Freedom Fliers a warm, celebratory send-off.* In this case, as they saw the travelers off, the Royal Rosarians were performing the opposite of their mayoral mandate: to serve as "Official Greeters and Ambassadors of Goodwill for the City of Portland." But in a way, that rare task (for them) aligned perfectly with the concept of the trip, as Sho had described it to *Travel Weekly*: "We have a pioneer spirit here in Oregon. This would be like the Oregon Trail, but backwards."

Cornelia Wilkes of Entity Entertainment and her partner, Jeff, made dove pins that they donated to the Freedom Fliers to wear. She had moved to Portland from New York only two months before, and her father was still there. They had brought 300 of the pins to Azumano Travel the day before and, learning of the great numbers of people that were going to New York, they were at PDX the next morning with 500 more that they had stayed up all night making.[2] Some lucky Freedom Fliers also received the "Oregon ♥ NY" pins, but most of those were not ready yet. [PHOTOS 3-5]

Portland radio and television personality Rebecca Webb recounted her Flight for Freedom experience in the *Portland Tribune*.

---

*The Royal Rosarians are a Portland institution, founded in 1912 to promote the "best interests" of the city and its Rose Festival.

> The call had gone out, and I answered: Yes! This was a mission for which I qualified. They weren't asking for doctors or ministers. This time they needed shoppers, diners, and audience members.

Still, a flood of doubts hit me in the days before I left . . . . Was I crazy to fly? Potentially leaving my children motherless? Blindly answering a government command to "spend money"? Would I notice the ethnicities of other passengers?

Packing was different this time. I removed my Swiss Army knife from my purse, where it had always come in handy on trips. And instead of pushing the limits of carry-on (as I usually do by boarding with roll-on suitcase, hanging bag, waist pack and purse), I checked my suitcase—having tucked potential weapons (tweezers and nail scissors) inside.

I was surprised to see hordes lined up at the airline terminal. This was going to take time, it was clear, but I had allowed the recommended two extra hours to get through security. Despite the repeated questions and requests for photo ID, nearly everyone seemed to be making a special effort to be pleasant and cooperative.

"Three lines, 200 feet long, stretched out in front of the x-ray machines," said Jack Kostel, materials acquisition coordinator for the Oregon Museum of Science and Industry, who had awakened at 3:45 to catch his flight. "Three people near me in line, who were scheduled to leave at 7:30 a.m., did not make their flights." Kostel had brought five new white T-shirts and red and blue felt-tip pens. He passed out the shirts and pens and found "artistic volunteers," who decorated them and he displayed them at the Waldorf-Astoria when they arrived. [PHOTO 6]

For *Gresham Outlook* reporter Rob Oster, the trip to New York was a trip to his native city, a gift from his mother-in-law.

> Unarmed National Guard personnel wandered amid four extremely long lines for the metal detectors. Armed policemen were also out in force. As I neared the entry point to the gate area after a 35-minute wait, security personnel barked out instructions. "Take all keys and coins out of your pockets and put them in your carry-on baggage. Remove all laptops from their cases and place them in the X-ray machine by themselves." All tickets were scrutinized with great care. Random searches with hand-held metal detectors were conducted. Bags were sporadically opened and inspected. None of

these procedures, however, could dampen the spirits of Flight for Freedom members. [PHOTO 7]

Fifteen-year-old Stephanie Hinshaw of Portland was a frequent traveler, but this was her first trip to the East Coast:

> Yes, there were longer lines to allow for tightened security and armed guards at each gate, but they didn't change anything. You really have to rely on yourself when your world gets so upside down that camouflage-suited men with rifles patrol every airport. I have a strong admiration for men who are so strongly and bravely devoting themselves to our protection. It made me question myself, how much of my life was so trivial. On the way home there was a larger number of national guards. Going through security we had to take off our jackets and belts. At every desk we stopped at we had to provide picture I.D. There was tenseness in the air, everyone's radar was on high alert. I didn't want to go home to my simple life that now seemed so protected and false. I missed the rawness of the city already.[3]

"The Other"

The terrorists who conducted the attacks were Middle Eastern men. Issues around skin color and those who may have appeared Middle Eastern resulted in a spike of anti-Muslim hate crimes during this time. Some Freedom Fliers had related experiences.

Alexia Halen of Portland:

My dad, whose parents are from Lebanon and came through Ellis island, he lives in West Linn and somebody had written some letter to him threatening him. Everyone was flying their flags and my dad was in World War II, very patriotic, but his flag had some kind of rip in it and he didn't want to fly it and he couldn't buy one because they all were sold out. So he didn't have a flag out for the first couple weeks because he couldn't find one.

[The letter said] "We know who you are, we know where you come from. You better fly a flag or you go back where you belong." Someone sent him a letter. I think that was also this interesting theme around "the other," people being "other." That was an interesting part of the trip, to experience that.[4]

Baruti Artharee, deputy director of the Portland Development Commission (PDC) and the board chairman of the Urban League of Portland:

I got profiled so many times during that because my name is Baruti L. Artharee. My name, which was African and Arabic, this happened before I went on the flight. People would see my name, people would look at me side-eyes, "Who are you?" I'm not Muslim.

I was concerned about my Muslim friends and afraid they'd be profiled. I found myself in Portland being profiled as a potential terrorist. When we went on the Flight for Freedom, when we got to the airport, I was walking with [State Sen.] Margaret Carter and [Portland Mayor] Vera Katz. We all ended up at check-in and we were chatting and checking bags and luggage, and walked towards the gate. Margaret at that time was one of my mentors. I think I worked with Vera at the time, and I'm walking slightly behind them.

We go in, we check our bags, we get our boarding passes, we're walking towards the gate, and very quickly, a couple guys walked up to me who were some kind of government officials, one on one side, one on the other side. "We want to talk to you."

"What?"

"We just want to ask you a couple questions."

I didn't even get a chance to say to Margaret, "Hey!"

We went into a room and they asked me a lot of questions. Initially, I wasn't offended by it, I understand, OK, but then that started happening on a regular basis. Even on the return flight of the Flight for Freedom.

It got to where even the people on the plane—I was telling them the story.

I'd say, "My name must be random. Every time I go through, they'd say, 'We're just doing a random check.'"

And it was this black guy who was FBI, he started fast talking, "Where did you go to high school?" Trying to get me to say something of value to them.

I said, "I went to Compton, I'm not from New York, I'm from Compton."

Leslie Krueger—now Leslie Parker—worked for the state government in Salem; she was so excited that she "actually drove to the Portland airport and stayed at a hotel there." She could leave her car at the hotel, get a shuttle to the airport, and not have to pay for parking. "I thought since my flight was very early anyway, I'll go the night before, get myself in the rhythm of this thing." After the attacks, she had decided to go to New York in the spring, but when she heard about the Flight for Freedom she said, "Why wait until then? They need support now." The flight she was on had very few people.
[PHOTOS 8-9]

Martin Fisher and his family from Bend in Central Oregon were surprised to find "five or six others doing the same thing" [Freedom Fliers] on their 4:30 a.m. flight to San Francisco, where they would change planes on Friday, October 5. The manager of the Redmond Airport had made beaded American flag pins for everyone on the flight.

> We connected in San Francisco and ended up meeting lots of other people going there and that was maybe the first sense you got that something large was going on. When we got on the plane in SF, it was absolutely packed. There wasn't an empty seat. And it was full of people from Portland and Eugene, and they told us that GMA ["Good Morning America"] had come out, the Rosarians had come out. Before that, we didn't really have any sense at all that this was big. Because over on this side of the mountains, it wasn't covered at all. It didn't show up anywhere. From what I had seen in The Oregonian and had heard, I was thinking maybe there were 100 people total, it was not that large and so I was just really surprised that there was a lot of people.

The Jenness family also left from Redmond, though they were on a different flight than the Martins; they would change planes in Portland. "As we left Portland, the flight attendants were overjoyed to have people on the plane; it was nearly full, and they told us that the day before there had only been nine people on the same Portland to Chicago flight."[5]

Community leader and former attorney for the Portland Public Schools Bruce Samson had discussed the fears of pilots and crews as they returned to flying after the attacks with his brother, who was an airline pilot.

> We packed the plane, and it was the first packed plane that the flight crews had seen and they were so jubilant. They were just delighted that we were there and we were not going to take it lying down, so to speak. Their attitude was just marvelous.

Webb remembered the general air of tension.

> Tension was palpable as we boarded the plane, since most of us were flying for the first time since the world changed September 11. Trying not to look too long at dark-skinned passengers, I found my seat.

> It was impossible not to imagine what it would have been like to be aboard one of the hijacked planes of Sept. 11, since we were on a 757—a model used in the attacks. I envisioned an Arab-looking passenger rising from his seat, threatening an attendant, setting off a terrifying chain of events. The struggle would seem so close to me— might involve me. Would I be able to think, to react, to join other passengers in any form of defense?

Jane and Steve Ditewig of Longview, Washington, kept a journal. On this day Jane wrote: [PHOTO 10]

> Saturday, October 6, 7:05 a.m. A bit eerie to enter the plane and think of the blanket as an anti-hijacker weapon. This is the first time I can remember being asked to be quiet for the safety video and complying.

> Everyone in the airport appeared friendly yet wary. We all seem to look our fellow passengers in the eyes and attempt to look into their souls. National Guard . . . .

> Lots of reassuring smiles. I wonder if I would feel the same way if my pallor wasn't in the majority—hmm.

Twenty years later, Jane remembered:

> It made me think—at the time, I wouldn't say it was the first time, but it made you very aware of skin color and your feelings about that, as far as looking at somebody that might be Middle Eastern

that's getting onto the plane, which is absolutely horrible. And that's the same thing that continues today in our country. That was—I think that made me more aware . . . . It's inbred in us and all of that and it also made us more think about life, too. Things were so unsure during that time.

The Ditewigs were on the same flight as Mayor Katz, the Dozonos, and most of the organizers, who held a news conference. *Good Morning America* (GMA) covered their departure live. [PHOTOS 11-13] Before boarding the plane, Mayor Katz declared "Flight for Freedom Day" in Portland and gave her official proclamation to Sho Dozono. State Treasurer Randall Edwards and Sho Dozono spoke. Dozono:

> This is a simple grassroots effort, and a symbolic gesture to the rest of the nation that it is "We the People" who, by not traveling, are causing hundreds of thousands of people to lose their jobs. It is not the terrorists. They only did one act, on September 11th.

Port of Portland director Jay Waldron then read a letter from Secretary of Transportation Norman Mineta wishing the group well.

By evening, nearly 1,000 Oregonians would converge on Manhattan.

On board Delta flight 1056, a flight attendant thanked the passengers: "We appreciate your patronage," she said. "Thank you for restoring the confidence of all of the people in New York City."

A few hours into the flight, *Oregonian* reporter Courtenay Thompson sat down with Mayor Katz. Remembering the trauma of arriving in New York as a Holocaust refugee with absolutely nothing decades before, the mayor said, "I thought I'd gotten beyond all that. It has all become very, very real again."

But she was looking forward to talking with New Yorkers. "Share with them their grief. Comfort them. I'm a little nervous about all the memories that will come back, but we'll get through it." [PHOTO 14]

KPAM Radio's Bill Cooper came equipped with the latest technology: a digital camera with floppy disks and wifi. The plane, he remembers, even had wifi. "This was one of the first planes that had a wifi connection and it had power. I could power my laptop and I did a short little video—I don't remember if I fed this from the plane or when I landed—with Mayor Katz. 'Hello Portland, from the Flight for Freedom,'" she said. Cooper still has the video.[6]

Baruti Artharee was interviewed by Thompson on the flight as well. Artharee, whose schedule would include attending the memorial service of a colleague's nephew was quoted by Thompson as saying "I liked the powerful symbolism of the trip as a statement to the world." And he continued:

> This is an outrage. Americans, we are like a big family. We have squabbles, and we disagree. But when someone attacks us, it's as Americans we're being attacked. They weren't trying to kill white people, or brown, yellow or red. They were there to kill Americans. I hope this Portland delegation may be the first of many trips, and be an example to other cities around the world. "Hey, if Portland did this, we're going to step up and send a delegation."' We're not going to let this destroy us as a country.[7]

On the following Monday alone, ABC's "Good Morning America" and "Live with Regis and Kelly," CBS's "The Early Show" and NBC's "Today Show" all planned to have Freedom Fliers as guests. ("Today" would later back out, stating that they would host the Flight for Freedom only if they could have an exclusive.)

When the mayor's flight arrived at John F. Kennedy Airport, Congressman David Wu was there from Washington, DC to meet the contingent, carrying an "Oregon Loves New York" T-shirt as a gift for the mayor.[8] The New York press was there as well. [PHOTO 15]

Rebecca Webb:

> We were close to beginning our descent into New York's LaGuardia Airport, the pilot announced. A buzz generated among the passengers, as people in the aisle seats craned for a glimpse of the city's altered skyline. A collective gasp. A hush fell when we finally saw it, with the Empire State Building now more prominent, no longer overshadowed by the Twin Towers. You could still see the haze of pollution caused by their collapse.

> As we gathered our personal belongings and waited for the pilot to turn off the seat belt sign, the flight attendant hoped we would all enjoy our visit to New York. She extended a special welcome to the goodwill ambassadors "from Ore-uh-gone."*

---

*Throughout this book you will find "Oregon" spelled in a variety of ways to capture the way New Yorkers pronounced it. "OR-a-gun" is the way

Perhaps feeling our new closeness to New York, we gave her a round of applause.[9]

Jackie Young of Happy Valley says she will never forget "getting off the plane and walking down through the airport and I could hear my footsteps; it was that empty."[10]

And Kathi Karnosh of Lake Oswego remembers being greeted by a reporter.

> When we landed, it was so funny because a reporter came up to me—he said, "What brought you to New York?" I don't know why I said this, but I said, "I'm here to do my patriotic duty and shop till I drop." We checked into our rooms and after a while we came downstairs to the lobby, it was about dinnertime and somebody said, you were just on TV. I didn't see it—but oh golly . . .

Mary Platt, an occupational therapist from Portland who went with her husband, Rob, and her son, Cameron, says that one of the first amazing things that happened took place when they got off the plane in New York.

> The airport was just empty and we'd gotten our bags and we were walking towards the exit and there was a police officer off standing in the middle by himself and wanting to talk to us. We were worried—did we do something wrong? He said, "I just want to thank you for coming." That was the first interchange that we had about the recognition of who we were as a group.[11]

Debra-Diane Jenness, her husband, Gordon, and their fourteen-year-old son, Tyler, took their first trip to New York from Crescent Lake, Oregon, population 400. Debra-Diane's account of landing in the city shows just how much courage it took for Oregonians to make this trip—and how deep the caring was that had brought them to New York.

> Upon arrival at LaGuardia, we retrieved our luggage and tried to figure out how to get to the Waldorf-Astoria. I called the hotel and

---

Oregonians pronounce it. New Yorkers said a version of "Or-a-GONE."

they advised either taking a cab or the shuttle from the airport. So I proceeded to the airport information counter. They said the shuttle would take about thirty to forty-five minutes to get there, and would cost the three of us thirty-nine dollars, or thirteen dollars each. The taxi cabs were right outside, could take us right away, and would cost between twenty and thirty dollars. The airport man said the cab drivers really needed the work, since many of them were Middle Eastern and no one would ride with them since the attack. So, since we were there to try to help stimulate the economy and help those who needed it, we decided to take a taxi.

We went outside and joined the taxi line. A cab pulls up, pops his trunk from inside, and you load your own luggage in. This was interesting to watch, since ahead of us in line were three older ladies who struggled to get their bags in the trunk of the cab, but the driver did not come out to assist them. Next was our cab; it pulled up, the trunk lid popped open, and the driver got out to assist us.

First major shock: he looked like Osama bin Laden's twin brother!! Long beard, turban around the head, long gown.

My husband turned to me and mouthed, "Holy shit!" and gave me a "What do we do?" look. The man's cab had American flags all over it, and signs that said, "Proud to be an American and a Sikh."

I said to him quietly, "Get in the cab!"

The driver helped us with our bags, we snuggled up in the back seat, and were off. He drove quickly but carefully and had us at the Waldorf in an eighteen-dollar cab fare, much less than we were expecting. One of the things that the "Flight for Freedom" organizers had told us was to tip as generously as we could, and so we did. The driver had tears in his eyes; he thanked us over and over for riding with him, and for the extra tip.

Staying at the Waldorf-Astoria has been a lifelong dream of mine. We were totally treated like royalty there, and anything we needed was immediately at our disposal. They were very, very gracious to help out in this endeavor by granting the low rates to make it all possible, as were the participating airlines. We got checked in, dropped our things off in our room, and decided to go for a short stroll outside. I told my husband not to go too far, I didn't have a map and being lost in New York late on a Friday night was not my idea of a good thing! We walked outside, and then it hit you: the smell. You could smell the disaster. It didn't smell "dead," it smelled very sulfurous, like being around the volcanoes in Hawaii, like a huge electrical fire.

From our room, we had a view of the top of the Chrysler Building, all lit up; beautiful.

For many who'd never been to New York, the city seemed busy and loud. But for those who had spent time there, it was a very different place than before.

Elaine Franklin, political strategist, former chief of staff for Sen. Bob Packwood, and now his wife says, "What I mostly remember when I first stepped out onto the streets of Manhattan was complete silence. There were no cabs honking, no loud voices—just stressed, shocked faces."[12]

And Todd Davidson, executive director of Travel Oregon remembers:

> Inconsequential and telling. As someone who's traveled quite a bit. I've been in New York City several times. The unwillingness of the taxicab drivers to honk their horns—[usually] they're laying on their horn right away when the light turns green. I remember coming in from the airport and commenting to the taxi driver, "This is a little surreal to me."
>
> The streets were fairly empty . . . there was so much courtesy. "You've got your bike, you come up off the curb." It had changed them [New Yorkers] as well, it had changed their perspective about what it was that matters. They went from being that cab driver who had to make a buck, had to make a fare, to that these are my fellow New Yorkers and I have to look out for them. It just jumped out at me because it—was so much different than any other trip I'd had to New York City.[13]

Playwright and professor Michael Phillips of Portland considered New York his second home, even though he'd never lived there. He was grateful that the Flight for Freedom gave him a way to *do* something; his most distinct memories were not the five plays he saw but the city itself. He wrote a long letter to friends when he returned from the trip.

> There is a great sadness there. Even with its activity, its attempt to get back to normal, there is an underlying pain that is so very palpable. It's a quieter city; the cabs were honking their horns again, but

not nearly as much as I remember, and the further south you go the quieter it becomes.

John Webster of Hood River even found Times Square empty.

Leslie Parker arrived late Friday, October 5. It was her first trip to New York. She and another woman on the flight went out to have something to eat. It was quiet on the street. "The hustle and bustle—I'd only seen it in movies and on TV—but we knew something wasn't quite right."[14]

Native New Yorker Vic Rini of Aloha, Oregon, wrote an essay, "The City of Heroes," when he returned.

On the Queens-Midtown tunnel approach to Manhattan there is a large billboard that reads: WELCOME TO THE CITY OF HEROES. In Times Square in front of a tall building, there is another sign, this one is of a large red, white and blue apple and states YOU DO US PROUD, NEW YORK, NEW YORK. Farther down the street another one reads GIVE PEACE A CHANCE."

And Rob Oster of Gresham noted, "Even the graffiti has turned patriotic."

For myself, arriving in New York and walking around Midtown near the hotel I had one of my clearest and most heartbreaking experiences. Midtown is far from downtown, far from the World Trade Center, and yet even here, families had posted "missing" flyers. That we saw these this far uptown testified not only to families' desperation but to the generosity of places like Kinko's. The Kinko's near the hotel—again, quite far from the World Trade Center—had signs notifying people that they could get free photocopies made there.

The walls of the store were filled with photocopies, and closer inspection of them showed what the free copies would be used for: they were all announcements about lost loved ones. And that's what was most painful. The somber quality of the words was in direct conflict with the emotions conveyed through the pictures. These were snapshots of people, happy people, often shown enjoying vacations, weddings, bar mitzvahs, Fourth of July celebrations, accompanied by sobering headlines: "Missing," "Have You Seen?" I had not been downtown yet. If it was like this in Midtown, what must it be like at the site of the devastation?

By Friday night, another 350 Oregonians had arrived, and as one Freedom Flier put it, the Waldorf's elegant Art Deco lobby had been "Oregonized." "No longer is it the ultra-chic, sequined-gowned establishment, but rather it's filled with our "Oregon loves NY" T-shirts, Duck sweatshirts, Nikes, and (gasp!) jeans."[15]

More significant than the casual attire the Oregonians brought was their vitality and energy. While it was tragedy that had brought them to New York, they couldn't help but also bring with them the excitement of travelers who had actually made it cross-country as well. "We did it, we're here!" The lobby was literally abuzz with excited Oregonians who'd just met. Their joyful energy was infectious.

Back in Portland, the staff at Azumano Travel, still pushing to get people ticketed, got in on the festivities vicariously when John Ray phoned them from the Waldorf and said, "Listen to this . . . " To those back in Portland, the background noise sounded like the cheers at a football game.

"What is it?" Sho asked.

"The Waldorf employees are clapping for the Oregonians," Ray told Sho, who turned on his speakerphone for everyone in the office to hear; and he kept it on throughout the welcome. [PHOTO 16]

As they entered the Waldorf, the Oregonians found the employees applauding—when they looked over their shoulders to get a glimpse of the dignitaries they assumed were being so welcomed, they had a sudden realization: "It's us!" they realized. "They're clapping for *us*!"

Across the lobby and throughout the registration process, seventy-five or more Waldorf-Astoria employees clapped and sang "New York, New York" in welcome. General Manager Eric Long said this had been the employees' idea; they were so grateful for the business the Oregonians brought with them. By filling the hotel, Oregonians had given them at least five days of work. Without them, the only business the hotel would have had during that period was one wedding.

As she entered the building, Alexia Halen of Portland burst into tears.

All of the staff were lining the stairway on either side and they just clapped as we walked up the stairs . . . . You really didn't know what to expect. You knew you were going [there] to support them, but you didn't realize what the people there were feeling, the level of emotion,. and that this really did mean so much to them.

Back at the Azumano Travel office they were all in tears, too. Every person who experienced it recounted the moment to me.

"Chefs, housekeeping, a whole cross-section—bellhops, elevator operators, all there cheering," said Jack McGowan, executive director of Oregon environment nonprofit SOLV and spokesman for the Flight for Freedom. "The visual aspect of that was extraordinary. It wasn't just senior executives doing the clapping, it was the entire cross-section of the Waldorf. They were cheering and cheering."[16]

I remember OMSI's Kostel singing to the accompaniment of the Waldorf's pianist Daryl Sherman, "Yankee Doodle came to New York just to eat at restaurants," he sang, while the couches overflowed with conversation.*

I spoke with Sherman, who usually played jazz standards apropos of Cole Porter's former residence, and he said, "I think the energy is contagious. It's restorative to see the spirit of the human condition. New Yorkers are resilient and it is essential to understand that we all share a bond. Some people came from London one weekend in the last few weeks to show their solidarity, too." He added, "Music is a universal healer."

Joy Schertz of Corvallis remembered "Staying at one hotel helped us form a real connection, as did the organized activities. Even the buttons helped us identify each other."

And New Yorker Veronica Jaeger, amid the Oregonians in the lobby, said, "It's a little sugar shock. This is not normal. I guess it's nice, but livin' in New York, I'm not used to this."

Phillips said, "When I checked in at the hotel, I told the young man my name, and that I was with the Oregon contingent. He stopped what he was doing, turned to me and said, "Thank you so much for

---

*Kostel would go on to participate in many of the subsequent relief and support trips organized by Azumano Travel.

doing this. We had to lay off half of our staff last week, but because all of you are here we had to call them all back in."

Sandra Kempel, an administrative assistant at Point West Credit Union in Portland, remembered that "The bellman who helped us with our luggage the first day said, "Thank you for coming here. I was laid off for two weeks with no hope of coming back to work here . . . until youse from Oregone came.' And then there was a guy in a deli, he hadn't a clue who we were or what we doing—he said, "What's that button? Oregone loves NY?" And so I told him that a group of about a thousand of us had come from Oregon to support New York and give a little relief to the economy. He said, with his New York accent, "Well, that's really nice. Yeah, way to go."

After chatting with a couple from New Jersey as I waited in the check-in line at the Waldorf, I asked naively, "Were you affected by the World Trade Center tragedy?" As the woman turned away, the man answered, "We knew eight people . . . ."

As a freelance journalist with an article due the next morning, I set to interviewing Oregonians. I met with the Platt family in the hotel lobby. When sixteen-year-old Cameron had told his parents that he wanted to go to New York, and that he would pay his own way, his parents agreed to join the Flight for Freedom.

As I was talking with them, my college friend Lisa Sokoloff, a Manhattan attorney, joined us. I had lost touch with her since we'd graduated from college about twenty years earlier, but I contacted her to see how she'd fared on September 11 when I knew I would be coming to New York. I was flabbergasted when she said it would be easy for us to get together since she was temporarily living at the Waldorf. She was one of about 9,000 New Yorkers who had become homeless when her Battery Park City neighborhood near the World Trade Center was devastated by the blasts. The Waldorf would be her "home" until her apartment building was deemed safe. (Months later, when her building was again approved for occupancy, she did not feel assured that the building was safe and moved out of Manhattan temporarily.)

That night, to a rapt group of Oregonians, she recounted how she had become one of Manhattan's homeless and displaced.* Sokoloff described her escape from the Trade Center disaster, about being surrounded by an opaque black cloud of debris, and about negotiating fences and ladders to reach a fireboat to New Jersey, where she walked three miles to a hospital for eye and skin treatment.

Telling her story, Lisa said, was healing. After listening to her, Portlander Mary Platt noted that although they had flown in to support New York City by spending money, they also hoped to connect with New Yorkers in some way. Hearing Sokoloff's story, she said, was "what we came for." (See "Lisa Sokoloff" in "Where They Were.")

Almost twenty years later, what Mary's husband, Rob, remembered hearing about Lisa's experience:

> The thing that struck me most was the confusion. Nobody knew what to do and nobody knew what to tell them. There were conflicting directions. It's like the beginning of COVID, only 100 times worse.

> I remember it being a very heart to heart. Obviously, she was in a very vulnerable spot and she opened up quite deeply to us. She'd never met us. I just remember being struck by how intensely emotional and vulnerable she felt in the conversation itself. We'd just gotten off the plane.

> That was the theme of the trip. Sitting in a chair talking about it kind of brings tears to my eyes, not in the sense of 911 per se, but the sense of the people that we talked to.

> We went to get coffee and a croissant at a coffee shop and everybody was talking about this stuff in the same way Lisa was; it was pretty much right down the road. Every place we went people were totally open and vulnerable and tell us what happened. They knew who we were, some of them didn't, a lot of them didn't.[17]

Azumano Travel had set up what it modestly called a "hospitality desk" at the south end of the Waldorf's lobby. It was, in fact, many tables that were staffed all day, every day, by Azumano employees and by the Dozono family, including Sho and Loen themselves—with

---

*See Lisa's story of survival at the beginning of this book.

the day's itinerary posted, along with opportunities for theater tickets, Gerry Frank's book, free copies of Zagat's guidebook, and many other activities.* [PHOTO 17]

The Dozonos' daughter Kristen had arrived on Friday, October 5, and she worked the table along with friends she'd recruited to help. They checked people in, gave them T-shirts, told them about the activities. Above all, they were friendly faces that helped the Oregonians get the lay of the land. Kristen:

> My two girlfriends volunteered with me and we were stuck working so much—twelve hours straight at first. It's like working on a campaign or something like that. It's like a war room, you're on a natural high. They sent a couple of us back to New York later because we never left the hotel. People would come back and tell stories . . . .
>
> I remember we got the dress code from the Waldorf. We had country folks and elephant garlic farmers from Canby. These are people that wear jeans and Pendleton shirts and tennis shoes. They [the Waldorf] had a dress code that was like, no jeans. We had to tell people we can't dress like Oregonians.**

Most important was the table with the free "Oregon ♥ NY" stickers, buttons, and T-shirts. Azumano Travel's Nancy Parrott:

> I spent a lot of time in the hospitality area . . . . I had been at the airport—the first group left Thursday so I was at the airport like at 4 a.m. on Thursday, and again on Friday getting all those flights out, and then I left on the last flight Saturday morning and as soon as I got to New York, I got my group on the bus and as soon as I got to the Waldorf, I immediately started working in the hospitality

---

*Nearly twenty years later, Marla Nuttman of McMinnville says, "It was a great trip they put together. We'd never before took a tour trip like that and we haven't since. I would be open to it in the future to do another thing like that. Because it had enough events and things planned that we could involve ourselves in, but we also got to do what we wanted to do. We weren't stuck on a bus going place to place."

**The Waldorf-Astoria was the only hotel in New York with a dress code. No jeans, T-shirts, tank tops, or casual hats in the Main Lobby, Park Avenue Lobby, restaurants, or public areas after 6 p.m. Hotel management relaxed those guidelines while the Oregonians were there.

area. People were signing up for tours and getting their T-shirts and wanting to make dinner reservations and I was answering questions. It was just jam-packed with people milling around and getting to know each other. I spent a lot of time over those next few days working the hospitality desk. A lot of times I'd stay back [rather than going to an activity] and do that and prep for the next day.

The stickers were an ingenious idea suggested by the Portland Oregon Visitors Association's Vice President of Sales and Marketing Brian McCartin, and they were there for the Oregonians to give away too—especially on restaurant checks and credit-card receipts and cash, to make the Pacific Northwest dollars that were being spent as visible as possible. Oregonians gave out those stickers everywhere they went, and lots of New Yorkers ended up wearing them. [PHOTO 18]

Even almost twenty years later, the stickers are a strong memory for Lance and Marla Nuttman: "We walked by a fire department and that was another very stunning moment because I remember that in their garage where the rigs are, there was an Oregon loves NY T-shirt," says Lance. "It was either hanging up or it was on the grill [of the truck]. It was neat going anywhere in the city seeing us—a T-shirt or a button or a handmade sign."

"The stickers were everywhere," says Marla. "People put them on the edges of the subway entrance—everywhere, so that was pretty cool."[18]

Journalist Glennis McNeal wrote in *Galley Proofs*, a local journalism newsletter, that they had what seemed an unlikely encounter in the hotel lobby:

> It was late Saturday night, October 6. The men, in tuxedos; their wives, floor-length gowns. My friend Joyce and I, wearing denim, walking shoes and logo T-shirts, stepped aside to let them pass. I have a guilty feeling that our presence tarnishes the glamour of their upscale Saturday night. One of the women glanced at my T-shirt. She turned abruptly. "Thank you for coming to New York," she said, her voice husky with tears. The men with her stopped and offered handshakes. "Yes, we appreciate this so much. Thank you for coming," they repeat. Again, our "Oregon loves New York" T-shirts melt stereotypes. Oregonians are more than rubes. New Yorkers are more than highly-varnished, hard-shelled sophisticates. We are all Americans.

By Friday night, the Freedom Fliers were already gaining celebrity, thanks to the media team. CBS Evening News, CNN. and many local TV stations had aired stories about the first wave of travelers, and the Flight for Freedom had been covered by what the team called "dueling network morning shows," with GMA covering the 450 travelers who were departing PDX, while McGowan and Brad Hicks, president of the Medford-Jackson County Chamber of Commerce, were guests on the CBS's "The Early Show," backed by some of the enthusiastic, T-shirt-clad Flight for Freedom participants who were already in New York.

At nearly 1,000 strong, the Oregonians were by far the largest contingent to make New York City a post-September 11th destination. The previous weekend, eighty-nine senior citizens from Rochester, Minnesota, had come to the city on a "Patriot Tour," and on October 4 a group from Jamaica had arrived; some of them were staying at the Waldorf, too, according to the *New York Daily News*. Led by Jamaica's famed Olympic bobsled hero Tal Stokes, the 150 primarily tourism and business officials from Jamaica would be the second-largest group from a single locale to organize a similar effort to support the city.[19]

But on that program, McGowan explained to the nation that the Flight for Freedom wasn't only business and community leaders, it was a grassroots effort: "It's not just the numbers of people, it's the type of people," he said, explaining that this group was overwhelmingly composed of hundreds of everyday citizens. "The whole thing just caught the interest of so many people. Only in Oregon I think, and Oregon proved itself to be the only state to amass a group of people with no common thread; it wasn't a business group, it wasn't politicians, it was Oregonians from a cross-section of the state who coordinated the effort. It was incredible."[20]

"Everybody in New York is talking about the Flight for Freedom," said Eric Long, Waldorf-Astoria general manager. "New Yorkers are overwhelmed by and grateful for the efforts that Oregonians are making to come to New York to support us."

Beth Faulhaber, Police Athletic League Activities Director, from Molalla, Oregon, made the trip with a group of students, a trip made possible through scholarships because the organizers felt strongly about enabling young people to participate. "I was very excited, but very nervous," she says. "The welcome we got was totally amazing.

People kept saying, "Oh, you're those people we saw on TV from OreGONE."

The trip's organizers had scheduled a welcome reception for 10:30 p.m. Saturday night, by which time almost everyone would have arrived. (With the three-hour time difference and the long cross-country fight, the trip took an entire day.) In one more surprise, that event cemented in participants' minds the fact that there was more to this journey than they had expected.

People learned about the reception from Azumano's lobby board, and at the appointed hour, people began streaming into the Starlight Room. The line reached all the way to the elevators. Inside, tables heaving under the weight of elaborate desserts and hors d'oeuvres were spread under the elegant, gilded ceiling, with its Austrian crystal chandeliers, and magnificent views of New York City.

On the way in, the guests admired the work of St. Helens modelmaker Glenn Kloster, who had made models depicting a New York fire station, police station, and other buildings, which he had brought on the plane for Flight for Freedom participants to sign at the welcome reception. On Monday afternoon, he and others from the group would deliver them to the Engine 54, Ladder 4, Battalion 9 fire station on Eighth Ave., which had lost an entire shift of firefighters, the most of any firehouse in the city. (See Kloster in "Why They Went" and "Bearing Witness" for photos.)

The Starlight Room was electric with the excitement of hundreds of Oregonians embarked on this effort to do what they could. On the dais were the politicians and organizers. [PHOTO 19]

"It really didn't hit you until you got into that hotel, just to see all the people," said Oregon State Treasurer Randall Edwards." I knew a woman in Salem who worked in the basement State of the capital and I somehow said, 'Are you guys going to go to New York?' She said, 'We're going to do it.' They were in the ballroom. They made it."
[PHOTO 20]

Sarah Bott, Communications Director for Mayor Katz:

 We were so protective of Vera and she had a security detail that included an on-duty Portland police officer and off-duty New York City police officers. We were so afraid something was going to happen to Vera because she'd already received death threats [because she was Jewish]. [PHOTO 21]

Her security detail says he's going to get the mayor a cold drink and could I watch her. I thought, "Don't get out of my sight." I was like—it was that feeling of, Oh my God. Somebody has to go to the bathroom, and they say, "You watch her now." The terror that something bad could happen. . . .She was this iconic leader, spiritual leader of this trip. She showed such leadership to pull people together like that to do something that was so important and meant so much to the country . . . We couldn't buy flags in Portland [because the city was sold out]—she went on television and told people how to draw with crayons an American flag that you could paste in your window.

McGowan welcomed and rallied the crowd, inspiring greater heights of emotion when he invoked the Oregon State Motto, "She Flies With Her Own Wings."

Then Mayor Katz spoke, thanking everyone and naming all the towns represented. It was no accident, it turns out, that the first place she mentioned was "Sweet Home," south of Salem. Before the speeches, Dave and Linda Holley of Sweet Home had talked with the mayor. "That's when we found that another couple (Chuck and Penny Farrington) from Sweet Home was here," said Dave.

As the mayor listed towns, the audience responded enthusiastically. John Webster, who would be transferred to New York within months, proudly wrote in his local paper, "Throughout the crowd, people would shout out the towns they were from and, of course, being up front I yelled. 'Hood River.' That got on the local news channel by my little plug for us."[21]

Mayor Katz also read letters of congratulations and thanks from President Bush, Mayor Giuliani and others (Appendix D). President Bush's letter said:

Your efforts to contribute to New York's economy and assist with relief efforts represent the generous and caring spirit of America. You also show the world that the strength of our Nation is not only in our economy or in our buildings. America's strength lies in her people.

Members of the NYPD and FDNY also spoke. "It was all from the heart," wrote Kostel. [PHOTOS 22-27]

The importance of the trip made itself felt that night. Nearly 1,000 Oregonians had given of their hearts, their time and their money to be here. They had courageously boarded planes when many Americans were (understandably) still afraid to do so. The organizers made sure that the nation knew about it, and that the participants themselves recognized the importance of what they had done. [PHOTOS 25-29]

Dave Holley, Sweet Home:

> Our focus changed because of that reception. We decided to drop some of the sightseeing plans and go to where we could meet regular people. Lots of glamour and furs around the Waldorf, Rolls Royce limos and the like everywhere, but that's not why we came.

> When you were able to see over 900 people in this one room, Oregonians from small towns and large cities together to say, "We aren't afraid to come see New York," it made me feel good about our decision to make the trip.

Nancy Waples, a radiology technician at Mt. Hood Medical Center, went to New York with her mother and niece, and met her brother and his wife there; his wife is originally from New York and they had traveled in from Dallas. They also saw friends: a woman who worked at St. Vincent's Hospital, which was the closest to Ground Zero, and a friend who worked for an insurance company, whose office was three blocks away and who saw a plane hit. For Waples and her family the Flight for Freedom began "as a trip to New York at a great price." But once they arrived, their perspective changed.

Debra-Diane Jenness from Crescent Lake remembered the shift that took place that night:

> We felt such an amazing part of such an amazing group of people who went and I was so proud of Oregonians and so proud to be a part of that group.

> I think [our concepts changed] actually right at the reception that night, at the hotel. At that point, I felt a part of a group. And I realized really the impact of what the trip was. And then, of course, as we walked around New York and people would come up to you and

grab your hand and shake your hand and hug you, and say, "I can't believe you people did that"—and cried as they did it . . . . From TV newscasters to Scott Thomason, the auto dealer, all of us, were united in a common cause.

Almost immediately upon arriving, the Oregonians would learn that listening would become one of their most important activities during their stay in New York.

Merritt Marthaller of Gresham spoke with "and listened to" a Waldorf employee. "I was given this penciled poem she had written soon after the attack. It was given as a thank-you token for coming. Our tears were flowing as we hugged. Of all the emotional experiences I encountered while in New York, this moment touched me the most."

Victims In Mourning

Who am I
Where am I
Waiting to be redeemed
Longing to be loved
My heart aches
My cries unheard
Who am I
Where am I

Heroes, Council, Clergy
Parents, children, husbands
Wives, friends, neighbors
Supporters of my world

Flags, flowers, prayers
Holding onto hope
Silence, chill consume my
body. Faith has no end
Love cries from beyond
Who am I
Where am I

Justice is divine
Awake!! the world is
you, you are here everywhere
Peace be with you always

—Valerie S.

Azumano Travel's Nancy Parrott:

The thing I remember the most is, we were so busy getting ready to get to New York, it never occurred to me what it was going to really be like when I got there. And the very first night it was probably midnight when we shut down the hospitality desk and a couple of us went to a restaurant right near the Waldorf and we walked in there and of course everybody knew the people from Oregon. But we sat down and had a late dinner and the serving staff was terrific. They had nothing else doing going on.

I remember this one waiter sat down and talked to us. He personally was acquainted—some he knew better, others he knew of—four people that lost their lives. And those were the stories and things that I hadn't even quite wrapped my arms around yet. Talking to these people and how they'd been impacted. That was pretty overwhelming.

And that's just one story. That one just hit me so hard because it was the first night and we were all exhausted. I'm thinking, "Don't complain. These people are going through so much, and they're just trying to move on." That was pretty amazing to me. That particular experience I won't forget. And there were others that would stop us and thank us for being here. But that first one was—just caught me completely off guard.

And Jean Andersen, of Portland remembered, "I spent most of my time talking to New Yorkers. They cried, they were so moved that 1,000 of us came here. They were really shaken and scared by what happened. It was like they needed to talk."

The Waldorf

Lance and Marla Nuttman were newlyweds on this trip, which was their honeymoon (sort of). In their twenties, they both worked the swing shift at the Spirit Mountain Casino in Grand Ronde, Oregon, sixty miles southwest of Portland. Lance created a website for this trip. The commentary below is based on his

The Nuttmans' swanky room at the Waldorf-Astoria. Note the personal fax machine on the desk. Photo: Lance and Marla Nuttman.

website commentary and on a 2021 interview with the couple.

Caption: The view from the balcony. In their white T-shirts, the Freedom Fliers are in line for buses to Chinatown. Photo: Lance and Marla Nuttman

Marla: We were in fleece and Birkenstocks and we're like we're totally not New York people. We all looked like Oregonians because we didn't look like New Yorkers. We were the fattest people on the island.

Lance: It was on the itinerary—we're staying in the Waldorf. Then we got there, and I was like, I don't think this is right. We don't belong here. There was marble everywhere, beautiful fixtures and gigantic flower bouquets that they had in the lobby.

Marla: This was the nicest room we ever stayed in.

Lance: Room 1629. King-size bed, REAL down pillows, tiled bathroom, in-room fax, the works. While we take turns making phone calls to home, Marla makes an interesting discovery: we have a terrace. That's right, 16th floor, 35'x12' brick, open-air terrace. We could look down on Park Avenue on one side, Lexington on the opposite side, and 49th Street between the two. Plus, on the clear days you could see the East River.

1. Loen Dozono and volunteer Karen Winder help people departing from PDX. At left is Jamie Lim, the 62-year-old publisher of the Asian Reporter newspaper in Portland. He left Portland on Thursday with his wife, Dory. While in New York, they would be attending a memorial service for their twenty-six-year-old nephew, Arnold Lim, who had worked on the 97th floor of the World Trade Center. Arnold had gotten engaged a month earlier; he loved traveling to the Philippines, where the Lims had family. "He was just getting ready to get his life started," Lim told The Oregonian. "They have finally come to the realization that we'll probably never find him. We held out hope to hopefully find parts of him. I don't know that that will happen." Photo is the property of Oregonian Publishing Co. (Courtenay Thompson, "From Oregon, with Love," October 7, 2001)

2. Bonnie Dillon's embroidered black coat became known to every Freedom Flyer. After she booked her flight, Dillon hastily had "Flight for Freedom Portland, Oregon loves New York City" emblazoned on her back, so that all New Yorkers would know about the trip. Travelers didn't know that a logo, buttons, and T-shirts would be provided. They were an unexpected bonus. Photo by Betsy Ames

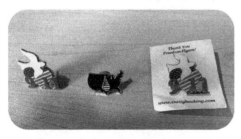

3. Pins designed, manufactured, and given to Freedom Fliers by Cornelia Wilkes. Center: Pins received in New York by Freedom Fliers. Photo courtesy of Flight for Freedom participant

4. The Delta Airlines counter celebrated the Flight for Freedom. Photo by Betsy Ames

5. Azumano Travel staff and Royal Rosarians (in straw hats) assemble at PDX to kick off Flight for Freedom departures. Front row left to right: Loen Dozono, Sho Dozono, volunteer Karen Winder, who helped with media and other tasks, and others. Photo by Betsy Ames

6. The T-shirts Jack Kostel, materials acquisition coordinator for the Oregon Museum of Science and Industry, invited his fellow travelers, "artistic volunteers," to decorate on the flight to New York. He displayed them at the Waldorf-Astoria. Photos courtesy of Loen Dozono

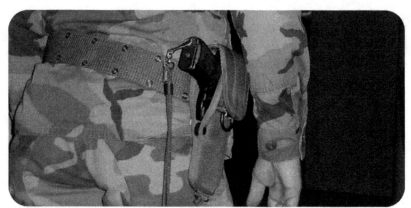

7. Armed National Guardsman at PDX. People had been told not to take pictures of the military, but KPAM reporter Bill Cooper took seriously his role as a representative of the free press and recorded what he saw. Photo by Bill Cooper

8. Photo by Betsy Ames

9. University of Portland students on their way to New York. Photo by Betsy Ames

Oct. 6, 2001

7:05 a.m.

Excited emotional + the double entendre of anxious. We're in the waiting area preparing to board the Flight for Freedom to New York City.

7:45

A bit eerie to enter the plane + think of the blanket as an antihijacker weapon. This is the first time I can recall being asked to be quiet for the safety video and then complying. Everyone in the airport appeared friendly yet wary. We all seemed to look

10. The Ditewigs' Flight for Freedom journal. Photos: Jane and Steve Ditewig

11. Mayor Katz at PDX Airport with the Royal Rosarians. Photo by Bill Cooper

12. An apprehensive Mayor Vera Katz on the plane to New York. Photo is the property of Oregonian Publishing Co.

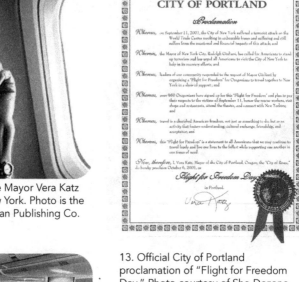

13. Official City of Portland proclamation of "Flight for Freedom Day." Photo courtesy of Sho Dozono

14 Reporter Courtenay Thompson interviewing Freedom Fliers on their way to New York. Thompson's *Oregonian* series, which appeared every day of the trip, would be the most complete account of the trip in print. The local broadcast media sent back generous, constant feeds as well. *The Oregonian* also listed where locals could find their friends on television and radio during the trip—which was pretty much all over the national airwaves, thanks to the media team. Photo by Betsy Ames

15. Congressman David Wu with T-shirt for Mayor Katz. Photo by Chris Sullivan.

16. The staff at the Waldorf-Astoria applauds the arriving Freedom Fliers. Photo by Betsy Ames

17. Azumano Travel's Flight for Freedom "hospitality table." Photo by Betsy Ames

18. Photo courtesy of Brian McCartin

19. Left to right: Rep. David Wu, SOLV Executive Director Jack McGowan, Rep. Darlene Hooley, State Sen. Margaret Carter, Political strategist Elaine Franklin, Chamber of Commerce Chairman and Azumano Travel Owner Sho Dozono. Photo by Betsy Ames

20. The Welcome Reception. Photo is the property of Oregonian Publishing Co.

21. Mayor Vera Katz surrounded at Welcome Reception. Photo by Betsy Ames

22. Honorary Flight for Freedom Chair Gerry Frank speaks at the Welcome Reception. Photo by Betsy Ames

23. The three friends who had known one another in the Oregon House of Representatives sing "America the Beautiful." Left to right: Portland Mayor Vera Katz, U.S. Rep. Darlene Hooley, and State Senator Margaret Carter. At far left, U.S. Rep. David Wu; at far right, Jack McGowen. Bill Cooper of KPAM Radio is front and center with a microphone. Photo courtesy of Loen Dozono

24. Singing "This Land Is Your Land." Photo by Betsy Ames

25. Terry Dorsey in his "Rose City Corvettes" jacket. Photo by Al O'Brien.

26. The Waldorf-Astoria donated the dessert reception for 1,000 Oregonians. Photo by Betsy Ames

27. Oregonian Derek Ewell plays at the opening reception. Photo by Al O'Brien

MOURNING, FEASTING, AND AN UNEXPECTED CHALLENGE

&&Every restaurant we walk into they say, "You guys are from Or-E-gone?" They can't say it right, but they greet us with open arms. —*Medford City Councilman Ed Chun*

Flight For Freedom participants didn't know it when they signed up, but their trip coincided with a milestone in American history, a time when the United States would begin its journey out of its post-9/11 introspection, shock, and grief and move toward retaliation. On Sunday, October 7, the bombing of Afghanistan began. If the Freedom Fliers had thought security was as tight as it could possibly be before that, it became even more restricted afterward. For the organizers, whether the following day's Columbus Day parade would still be held was once again in question. How dangerous was it to be in New York? How dangerous were large gatherings? The 9/11 Commission would reveal later that federal intelligence was aware that New York was still a target, and that the concerns about large public events were very real.

The bombing of Afghanistan on Sunday morning and the escalated increased security was, in fact, another test of the Freedom

Fliers' resolve. Those already there stayed the course. And when the last forty-seven Freedom Fliers arrived on Sunday night they were ebullient, ready to spread their good spirits around Manhattan.

Already their presence was felt in the city. In Courtenay Thompson's October 7 *Oregonian* story, she met New Yorker Debbie Lowenthal, who was on the plane with Saturday's travelers. Lowenthal's friends had joked about the T-shirt-clad Oregonians sprouting up on the streets of Manhattan. But she said, "Despite their laughter, they were touched."[1]

Some Oregonians began their day at church. [PHOTO 1] The first official event was a wreath-laying ceremony at Union Square, which began at 9:30 a.m. The Union Square event was the inspiration of Nick Fish, the recently transplanted New York leader who was connected to those who could make events like this happen. It also happened that Fish had chaired the local Union Square community board, so he knew the area intimately.

That Union Square was the site of the service could not have been more meaningful; nor could it have demonstrated more clearly that the Oregonians understood where and how New Yorkers were grieving. Since the afternoon of September 11 Union Square, the southernmost public space accessible to New Yorkers, had been the most prominent place of public mourning in the city. Its southern boundary, Fourteenth Street, was the demarcation of the crime scene and going beyond it was prohibited.

Just hours after the bombings, nineteen-year-old student Jordan Schuster brought a sheet of blank butcher paper to Union Square to allow people to share their grief. The next day, two Armenian immigrants arrived at Union Square carrying an eight-foot concrete-covered column with what *The New York Times* described as "a wire-mesh Christmas tree on top." They had stayed up all night making it, their tribute to the victims of the attacks. Within two days, more than 100 sheets of paper had been filled and the base of the column was covered with flowers, candles, and photos of those missing. In the beginning, the only things known to be gone for sure were the Twin Towers; the missing people were hoped to be just that.

Photos and mockups of the Towers themselves were also in place. Lorna Dolci, an orchestra manager from North Plainfield, New Jersey, brought postcards of the World Trade Center. "It's the loss of so many people, and the loss of something that's been considered such a sign of stability," she said.[2]

Who could imagine that two 110-story buildings could disintegrate almost instantly, in less than two hours?

If the sixteen-acre hole downtown was the epicenter of the destruction, Union Square became the epicenter of grief. Nightly candlelight vigils were held there. People needed to be in the presence of others.[3] *The New York Times* reported:

> Television is supposed to have created a global village, but person after person said yesterday that staying home and watching images of destruction on television only made them feel alone. And so, as if desperate to escape the keening within, people took themselves to public places and community institutions, from parks to churches. Many people also went to the firehouses devastated by loss, bearing flowers, food and simply good wishes.

"I don't know why I've been coming here, except that I'm confused," Mario Lucero, a twenty-six-year-old technician at Lucent Technologies told a *New York Times* reporter. "Also a sense of unity. We all feel differently about what to do in response, but everybody seems to agree that we've got to be together no matter what happens. So you get a little bit of hope in togetherness."[4]

This impulse to be with others, to find solace through communing, was shared by many of those who volunteered for the Flight for Freedom. The *Times* story described the multiplicity of needs that drove people to Union Square: the need to believe it had really happened, the need to find a missing friend or family member, the need to encourage those whose loved ones were missing, the need to honor the dead, the need to vent, the need to mourn, the need for human contact, the need to not be alone. While the Freedom Fliers didn't know they'd find emotion this raw in New York, when they encountered those in need, they met them by being present, by stepping up to the pain, by comforting them when invited, and by opening their hearts with simple human decency and kindness.*

---

*Writing this in May 2021, after more than a year of the COVID-19 pandemic, I realize that while many similarities with the trauma of 9/11 exist, one sad difference stands out: in this time, we have been deprived of the very thing

The scene at Union Square became a phenomenon. Within days, Washington's boots were colored pink, and his horse was covered with antiwar graffiti. The floral tributes, the posters of the missing, the venting, the assembling, all grew exponentially. Some people even lived in the park, and votive candles burned continuously. On September 20, the site was dismantled.

But that did not stop the continuous flood of flowers and posters and tributes. When the Flight for Freedom arrived for its ceremony, Union Square was filled with flowers and messages and flyers for the missing, but George Washington had returned to his pre-psychedelic bronze. The Flight for Freedom wreath-laying ceremony would be one of the last 9/11 memorial events in the flower-bedecked park. When the Rinis of Aloha stopped by a few days later, the memorial was gone. "We were told that it had all been cleaned up, taking three days to remove the wax from the pavement." [PHOTO 2]

Arriving at Union Square that morning, Nick Fish found that his friends and colleagues, who included the Chief of Police in Lower Manhattan, had, as he knew they would, "set up an amazing event."

The Business Improvement District had built a sound stage and cordoned off the northern part of the park. Eric Petterson, who headed the effort, had even set aside space in his iconic New York/ Brazilian diner, Coffee Shop, for speakers to make final plans. (Fish noted that Danny Meyer of Union Square Café was also "very supportive.") Nick's friend, former New York City Parks Commissioner Henry Stern, volunteered to officiate.

"One thing about New York," said Fish, "when the city and those various entities commit to doing something right, it's pretty remarkable because of the high caliber of people working on these things. They had it, with a sound system, to the flowers, to a podium with "City of New York," to the press management—and there were two or three people there making sure that it was being done as a professional thing. It didn't hurt that I had developed a strong relationship with the chief of police at Lower Manhattan."

Union Square offered: physical communion and congregation. For most people, the many technological platforms for communication we now have available cannot replace the need to congregate with others physically.

As with the Flight for Freedom itself, organizers who had never before met had to trust each other. Any fallout, any dropping of the ball would be a very public fiasco, Fish remembered. Organizer Bruce Samson, a powerhouse Portland attorney who was leading the service, "walked into this thing thinking 'Good God, I hope this works out,'" said Fish, adding, "[Bruce] doesn't know who I am, hasn't worked with me; but everybody stepped up and it came together in ways that nobody anticipated."

One of those ways was the musical accompaniment. As Loen saw off one of the flights departing from Portland, a woman pulled her aside and said that her husband, Roy Stilwell, was retired from the Oregon Symphony; he had brought his violin and was willing to play if needed. Fish found Stilwell in New York and booked him.

The Jenness family from Crescent Lake were the first to arrive at Union Square that morning:

> We were greeted by the Park Manager with open arms, a tight hug, and tears in her eyes, for thanking us for coming. She directed us to the area where the services would be but said we had about an hour if we wanted to walk around. We did, looking at a lot of the makeshift memorials people had left; signs, candles, flowers, pictures of those lost. Again, the raw emotions.[5]

Fish was astounded when he saw the hundreds of Freedom Fliers in attendance. The crowd also included leadership and representatives of the Pacific Northwest National Incident Management Team 2, who were supporting the recovery efforts at Ground Zero. "We had a mob, plus we had all this press," he said. "At that point, for me, that was the first taste that this thing was huge, that there was something happening here beyond just Oregonians coming to New York. There was a connection that was being made, and we were in the middle of this media frenzy." [PHOTO 3]

Despite the hundreds who were there, the park was silent. The grief was palpable.

It was an especially poignant moment for Jack McGowan, onstage with fellow daughter and son of New York, Mayor Katz and Fish.

> I looked and I thought, here, "My god, here we are three New Yorkers." Nick and I native born and Vera in her heart. And I thought

to myself how interesting it is that this occurs and that this tragedy brought three old New Yorkers together. And Nick and I, we shared stories. [McGowan was already old friends with Vera Katz.]

This was an emotional thing for everyone, of course, and especially just because of an added dimension for Vera and Nick and me. And that Oregon brought all of our live in focus and together and yet here we were as the New Yorkers going back to our, if you will, our hometown.[6]

That morning, Portland Police Bureau Captain Cliff Madison, along with his colleague, Portland Police Public Schools Director of Security Frank Klejmont, were wearing their dress uniforms and having breakfast with those participating in the service. One of the organizers asked Madison to say a few words at the ceremony. [PHOTO 4]

Madison led the series of speakers: "I . . . just said some things from the heart—and I see people in tears. I had to thank the people for coming and spending the money to come. The emotions are hard to describe."[7]

When New York Police Deputy Inspector William Callahan took the podium, he was nearly moved to tears by the crowd's size and the palpable emotional response.

As a native New Yorker, I can speak on behalf of the police officers and certainly the rescue workers and New Yorkers in general. We're very touched by the support we've seen from all around the country, especially when folks like yourself come from Portland, Oregon, such a distance. It touches us. It's the one positive thing that I've seen in all of this.[8]

Stern spoke next, and he lightened the mood by telling about how close he had come to moving to Oregon as a young man. He also told the crowd that, perhaps to people's surprise, New York was home to 28,500 acres of parkland, including not just natural areas but wetlands and woodlands.[9] [PHOTO 5]

Like Cliff Madison, Baruti Artharee, deputy director of the Portland Development Commission (PDC) and the board chairman of the Urban League, had received the call to speak on short notice. He remembers: [PHOTO 6]

" The night before the event, Nick Fish cornered me and asked would you be one of our speakers? This was a ceremony to recognize the first responders, the firemen and policemen who had perished. Their families, colleagues were there, there were hundreds of people there.

The reason I got asked was because Nick and Sho were some of the major organizers. And they had somewhat of a steering committee who would get together [in New York] and lay things out. What had happened was that there was a black minister from Portland who had committed to going on the trip and they had penciled him in to be a speaker [and he didn't end up coming] . . . . I've got a big mouth, been a motivational speaker.

And I was shocked—I was like, "What?"

I prayed about it the night before. What am I going to say? And I made some notes.

The next morning when we got there and when my turn came, I had gotten resolution in my soul with my comments.

I said along the lines that what had happened is going to result in consequences and retaliation, and I actually said that as Americans, this is not something that we're going to take laying down, and [my comments] had a pretty aggressive tone. In my soul, I can't rest with this. Someone do you injustice, you've got to deal.

And interesting enough, that same day, when we got back to the Waldorf-Astoria hotel, the U.S. started dropping bombs. The hotel went into lockdown, you had to show ID and your key to get into the room. Within a couple hours of my having said that we as Americans are going to retaliate.

"He was roped into it at the last minute, very graciously agreed to do it, but you could tell that he was moved by the moment," said Fish, who paraphrased Artharee's talk:

" When they attacked the World Trade Center, it was indiscriminate, and the people that paid the price were black and brown and yellow . . . . When America responds to this attack they will do it, black and brown and yellow working together.

As she would throughout the weekend, Mayor Katz spoke from the heart. "To hear [her] speak of her childhood and what she went through to get to America and what it meant to her, and then how this situation dealt in with that, it nearly broke your heart," Jenness wrote.

At the end of the ceremony, each Oregonian filed by and placed a sprig of Oregon cedar below the wreath, in honor of the lives lost. The crowd's silence had lasted from the moment they first assembled until the last sprig was placed. [PHOTOS 7-12]

In placing the boughs, said Jenness, "You felt so noble but so humble."

After the ceremony, the dignitaries were taken away in police escorts to the world's largest cathedral, The Cathedral of St. John the Divine in Upper Manhattan, for St. Francis Day and the annual Blessing of the Animals. Through his connections and because of his own love of the event, Fish got New Yorker-turned-Portland Mayor Vera Katz a spot on the dais. Katz was scheduled to address the crowd after Robert F. Kennedy, Jr., son of the man whose example had led her into politics. The cathedral's capacity was at its limit.

Not only was Mayor Katz on the same program with the son of her idol, but the cathedral was only "steps away" from her girlhood home, "where she had played with her friends and raided the corner candy store for long pretzels in tin canisters and the fizzy delight of sipping a chocolate egg-cream."[10]

She saw the edifice every day on her way home from school, but she had never dared enter the cathedral's portals, feeling that she wouldn't be welcome because she was Jewish.

But on this day, Vera Katz was met at the door and escorted to VIP seats at the front of the sanctuary by Stephen Facey, the cathedral's executive vice president and friend of Nick Fish.

Those in attendance had a rare treat in store. At St. John the Divine, the Feast of St. Francis is celebrated differently than anywhere else in the world. "The service is a very unconventional thing, filled with gospel and jazz and dance and poetry and theater and it is the highlight of what the cathedral does. It's just a gem and it's probably my favorite event, period," said Fish. [PHOTO 13]

Praised be You, my Lord, with all Your creatures,
especially Sir Brother Sun,
Who is the day and through whom You give us light.

And he is beautiful and radiant with great splendor;
and bears a likeness of You, Most High One.

Praised be You, my Lord, through Sister Moon and the stars,
in heaven You formed them clear and precious and beautiful.

Praised be You, my Lord, through Brother Wind,
and through the air, cloudy and serene, and every kind of weather,
through whom You give sustenance to Your creatures.

Praised be You, my Lord, through Sister Water,
who is very useful and humble and precious and chaste.

Praised be You, my Lord, through Brother Fire,
through whom You light the night,
and he is beautiful and playful and robust and strong.

Praised be You, my Lord, through our Sister Mother Earth,
who sustains and governs us,
and who produces various fruit with colored flowers and herbs.

—*From St. Francis of Assisi, "Canticle of the Creatures"*[11]

The Blessing of the Animals is held in many churches in the United States, but the Cathedral of St. John the Divine was among the first, if not the first, to hold this service. The idea had started in 1981 when Paul Winter, resident artist in the cathedral, wanted to create a modern mass that celebrated God's creation. He incorporated songs of the whales and wolves into the composition, with musical instruments echoing the natural music. Four years later, they decided to allow animals into the cathedral and by 2002, they hosted 6,000 people and 4,000 animals. After the service, the cathedral holds a fair and the clergy blesses all the animals brought by their owners, along with memorabilia people often bring of pets who are deceased. On this day, not only do they celebrate the natural world, they elevate and honor the relationship between families and their pets.

Saint Francis (1181/82–1226) is the patron saint of not just Italy (with St. Catherine of Siena) and animals but of ecology. Ecology was added, in 1979, when Pope John Paul took the unusual step of naming a Saint of Ecology.[12] St. Francis famously was the "natural" candidate for this role. The son of a cloth merchant and former soldier, he had rejected his family's wealth and embraced a life of poverty when he heard God's call to rebuild the church.* He spent much of his life in prayer in nature, where he heard God clearly, and in preaching to animals, plants, birds, rivers and other elements of the natural world.** While St. Francis's legacy contains many, many colors, it is the bond with nature and animals that is the focus of many churches on his feast day, which is October 4 on the Catholic calendar. (Saint John the Divine is an Episcopal church.) [PHOTO 14]

At the time, Kennedy was a well-known environmentalist. He had founded the Environmental Litigation Clinic at Pace University School of Law, where he served as a professor of environmental law. He was perhaps most recognized as co-founder of the Waterkeepers Alliance and protecting the Hudson River. In 1997, he had collaborated with John Cronin on *The Riverkeepers*, which had become a primer for water protection. A perfect fit to speak on the feast day of the Patron Saint of Ecology—and in fact, he told the congregation, St. Francis is his patron saint. He began by referring to the Bible verses they had just heard, which included the parables of the swallows and the mustard seed and the lilies of the field. [PHOTO 15]

> Throughout history, in every religious tradition, the great leaders and our great religious thinkers and theologians have used parables and allegories drawn from of nature to teach us the difference between right and wrong and to teach us what the face of God looks like. Whether it's the ancient pagan philosopher Aesop, to the modern Christian theologian C.S. Lewis with his Narnia Tales, and everybody in between. Confucius and Buddha; the Upanishads and Hinduism; the Koran, where all of the prophets came out of the

---

*"Go, Francis, and repair my house which, as you see, is well-nigh in ruins," which at first Saint Francis took literally, beginning his life of dedication to God by repairing multiple churches in Assisi.

**"He called all creatures his 'brothers' and 'sisters,' and, in the most endearing stories about him, preached to the birds and persuaded a wolf to stop attacking the people of the town of Gubbio and their livestock if the townspeople agreed to feed the wolf." Brady, Ignatius Charles Grady and Lawrence Cunningham, "St. Francis of Assisi," Encyclopedia Britannica, https://www.britannica.com/biography/Saint-Francis-of-Assisi, retrieved June 19, 2021.

desert and all of them were shepherds and that daily immersion in nature gave them a special access to the wisdom of the Almighty. The Old Testament, where the seminal events of the Garden of Eden, which is a mandate for stewardship. God didn't give nature to Adam and Eve to destroy . . . . They were supposed to be gardeners in the garden and take care of nature. Noah's Ark, which is a mandate for biodiversity. God didn't say to Noah, "Just bring two of every creature that can demonstrate a current economic value." He said, "Bring them all on board because they all have a value because I created them and they're good." And the New Testament where Christ is born in a manger surrounded by animals, and that's not an accident.

And where he discovers his divinity for the first time is while he's spending forty days in the wilderness communing with nature, and that incidentally– the wilderness is the place in every religious tradition where the central revelation occurs . . . .

Human beings have other appetites besides money. And if we don't feed them, we're not going to grow up. We're not going to fulfill ourselves, we're not going to become the kind of beings that our creator meant us to become.

He went on to say that New York after the attacks was a paradigm for all of America in its struggle to see how God takes the chaos visited on us by evil and creates something good out of it—because He always does, said Kennedy.

One of the things that I sense as we learn to cope with this tragedy is that across America we're finding common ground with each other. For the first time in many, many years, and we're finding a sense of community. And understanding that we're all one people.

And that's always been a challenge for our country. More than any other nation on earth because we come from all over the place. A Frenchman doesn't have to worry about his Frenchness . . . . But for our country, we don't share a common language or culture or religion or race or color. And so what allows us to call ourselves a community? What allows us to call ourselves a people? There's two things. One is shared values, and that's really a commitment to constitutional democracy. And the other is the land. And when we treat the land with contempt, what we're saying is this isn't really about community, this is just a commodity it's just real estate, upon which a bunch of strangers have to increase the size of their own piles and then to keep moving. It's about self-interest. And whoever dies with the most stuff wins . . . .

This country has a special mission in history and it's to teach the rest of the world what all of these diverse human beings when they're put together in one place, that we can create communities, and those communities can be a city on the hill and a lamp to all the other nations on the earth about what human beings can accomplish if we try to live and work together in communities and maintain our focus on a spiritual mission . . . . The essential question about whether or not our democracy is working is how it distributes the goods of the land, the fresh air, the clean water, the abundance of fisheries, the things that we own in common . . . . [Allow our children to] connect themselves with the seasons and the tides and the things that connect all of us to the 10,000 years of generations of human beings that were here before there were laptops. And ultimately that connect us to God . . . .

In my view, therefore, and I know this is what St. Francis believed, that when we destroy these things [creation] that it's sinful. We're diminishing our children . . . . That's what we're celebrating today, the gift that God gave us of these creatures who bring so much joy and enrichment to our lives, and we owe them back the obligation to preserve their habitats and the creatures themselves. Thank you.[13]

"All I needed to do was close my eyes and I could hear Robert Kennedy speaking—the same sound, the same passion," said Katz, who described his presentation as "incredible."

She then took her place behind the carved Gothic lectern adorned with sunflowers, set aside her prepared notes and told the New Yorkers before her how much she loved New York, why she and 950 other Oregonians had come, and how much it meant that she was able to come back and reach out to New Yorkers.

"We prayed for you, cried with you," Katz said. "We decided to bring ourselves, to give our love and to comfort you." [PHOTO 16]

This speech was perhaps her most personal of the trip. She talked of the insights she had gained during her recent bout with breast cancer, *The Oregonian* reported:

She learned the power of human-to-human contact—the power of a simple hug—last year, when she underwent radiation treatment (for breast cancer). A longtime public figure who sharply guarded her personal life, she shared her story publicly, comforted other women privately and learned to "give a little more of myself to other people."

"To think at my age I'm still beginning to learn what this is all about," she mused. "What surprises life brings."

To the 4,000 New Yorkers in the cathedral, she said, "You will recover. You have friends all over the country who will help you make that happen."[14]

"It was worth the whole trip to go to that service with her and see the way that New Yorkers responded to her," said Samson. "It was beautiful."

"She spoke from the heart—and the place rocked. It was staggering," said Fish. "Vera gave the speech of her life." For Fish personally, the event was monumental:

> Howard and Alice Shapiro, Peter and Mary Mark, and Betsy Ames*—to be there with someone who had roots in New York but now called Portland my home. It was one of the most emotional moments I can think of in my life, really, and [then] the guide dogs and other animals came through.

The cathedral doors were thrown open and in flooded the light and the procession of the animals began, a dignified procession accompanied by and imbued with Winter's sacred music, as the animals walked the two football fields in length that is the Cathedral of St. John the Divine sanctuary. As always, each animal was adorned with a garland of flowers and each handler wore a red robe, from the children leading the cow to the beekeeper with his hive. A bald eagle led the procession to the altar, followed by a camel, a cow, goats, lizards, a tarantula, and even an ant farm.

---

*Howard Shapiro was chairman of the Housing Authority of Portland. Native New Yorker Melvin "Pete" Mark was chairman of the Melvin Mark Cos., a commercial real estate firm that managed more than 3.1 million square feet of office space at his death in 2017, and who fell in love with his adopted city. Betsy Ames was assistant ombudsman/policy director for Mayor Vera Katz and later became chief of staff for Nick Fish, who was elected city councilor.

But that year, the guests of honor were the NYPD and their rescue dogs who were working at the World Trade Center site.[15]

"The service was the best of New York," said Loen Dozono, for whom, as for her husband, this would be the only non-working event of the weekend. [PHOTO 17]

> A church service in New York is like a theatrical production. People can bring their pets, but in New York, they had camels and cows, dancers, people from the plays on Broadway, singing, an orchestra—and then the parade of the animals was a menagerie of every single animal you could think of.*

"I just cry and cry when I think about it, it was so emotional," said Loen.

And then they found out that we had all been taken across the Rubicon.

Loen: "And then, at the end of the service, the bishop said, 'I have to tell you this, the bombing has started.'"

The United States had begun its military strike on Afghanistan, its first retaliation for the September 11 attacks. The bombings of October 7 began a new phase in what would become known as the "War on Terrorism."

Loen continued:

> I was just devastated. It was like, everything that we came here for, and this is happening. It was like at the highest high, thinking of this incredible experience we're so fortunate to have and all of these beautiful things and Vera had spoken amazingly after Robert F. Kennedy, Jr. had spoken and then, can you believe this?
>
> And we went outside and all of a sudden everything was in a panic. The mayor had to be whisked away with her bodyguards, had to be taken by herself . . .

---

*"By the way," wrote Kostel, "don't ever sit beside a young lady with a stressed-out cat on her lap. My hand was approximately eighteen inches from the cat, who looked up at one point and sprang onto my hand, claws bared. When she pried her pet off my hand and the bleeding stopped, she excused herself and left. I gave God a little extra thanks for her speedy departure!" (Kostel, "Flight for Freedom Memories.")

That day was the reality of the situation and it was—don't get such a big head, don't think this is all euphoric—this is what's really happening.

In the midst of the post-service chaos, a well-dressed man approached Bruce Samson and his family and friends.

> He thanked us over and over again for coming and one of us said, "This is nothing for us. The sacrifice is the people like you that is so important and impressive." And this guy was a stockbroker and he said, "Yeah, it's not been easy. My wife was on the 107th floor. I think she died immediately." The thing about it was, all he was going through and the way he was reaching out to us as if we were doing something special.

Mayor Katz did not let herself be distracted by the bombing. "I had not visited that address in all the years after we left, and we left in 1964," she says of the home where she had grown into young adulthood. When her contingent got on the bus to leave, she said, "Let's scoot around and see where the apartment house is."

> And it was gone, it was ripped down. The area was being gentrified. The apartment house next to me where my girlfriends lived was still there. Mine, which was a little less glorious in stature and architectural significance was down so it was like, not only did they rip my heart out for the city, but my home as well, and that was really where I grew up. I got over that part, realizing that change does happen, and that's life and move on . . . . It was sort of a closure to my childhood in New York.

Every Freedom Flier remembers where they were when they heard the news of the Afghanistan bombings.

Nancy Parrott was, as usual, working the hospitality table at the Waldorf:

> The Waldorf management came get us, and they said, "This is"—it hadn't hit the airwaves an awful lot yet—they just said, "We want to make you aware that the United States has just invaded Afghanistan and there are threats, maybe just rumors—they're concerned about security here in New York as a result. We're going to be

locking down the Waldorf and only the main entrance will be open. There may be some other security measures taken."

I think we had a group that was going to go to the Empire State Building. Some of the landmarks were being closed because they were worried about security.

That was the only time when I was there when I was a little concerned. I thought to myself, "Gosh, I kind of wish I was home with my family right now."

So I called and everything was fine. But that was a little bit alarming, too. But you just keep moving on.

We had a couple people who went back. There weren't a lot.

For nurse Debra Minchow and computer analyst Bryan Coleman of Newport, it was very clear that something had changed since they had entered the Metropolitan Museum of Art several hours before. "When we got out, it was all quiet, subdued. Then we learned the bombing had started. The people on the subway we rode down to Wall Street had such a look of resignation on their faces."

I was just devastated. It was like, everything that we came here for, and this is happening. It was like at the highest high, thinking of this incredible experience we're so fortunate to have and all of these beautiful things. . . . That day was the reality of the situation.

—Loen Dozono on learning of the bombing of Afghanistan

George Haight of Woodburn had run out of film near Canal Street:

I went into one of those camera shops. There were two Mideast fellows and me in the store and they were huddled around a little transistor radio. I could tell that they were really intent and I asked what was happening.

It was when our first rocket attacks hit Afghanistan. They had relatives there and just this kind of bewilderment on their faces. It really spooked me out, frankly.

I asked if I could take their picture so I would know where I was when this began. They were very accommodating . . . .

Every time I look at that picture, I get a real lump in my throat. The ramifications of this tragedy got spread around the world. Totally innocent, disconnected folk that became very involved and very connected to this incident [the bombing of Afghanistan], all over the world. It really kind of brought it home to me.

Jane Ditewig of Longview, Washington:

[My husband and I] went to the 42nd Street play and at intermission we found out that there was a bombing in Afghanistan. I remember that was a pretty eerie feeling, going back and seeing the rest of this play. Your mind wasn't always on the play.

There was a little bit of concern during that time, too. Everything was so up in the air. It was so uncertain. It was less than a month [after 9/11].

When Baruti Artharee returned to the hotel from Ground Zero with Robert Hinshaw, president for Oregon and Southwest Washington for Bank of America; Jesse Carreon, president of Portland Community College; and Bernie Kronberger, head of Wells Fargo Bank's community relations, he was shocked: "To come back and to see the police cars parked around the building, barricades up, the guards around the door, it was, 'Wow, this was real.'"

Mayor Katz's public relations person, Sarah Bott says, "When we started bombing Afghanistan, I remember we were in the hotel and Vera's having a drink with Congressman Wu and I was like, "Holy shit, here we are—"

Al O'Brien of Portland:

I had read a book about the Waldorf, and it talked about the bar downstairs. [On Saturday night] I thought I'd go down and have a cocktail—there was a marvelous stairway that went down and there was nobody in this really beautiful bar. The bartender was this really elderly guy and he said he'd been there for thirty-five years. I ordered Smirnoff on the rocks, He said the Waldorf has every liquor in the world, but I can't find Smirnoff . . . .

We got to talking about fishing and hunting. [He said he fished in the] Hudson and East River. I said I could go down to the Willamette in downtown Portland and catch a salmon and go back and eat it.

The next day . . . Mike [Getsiv, whom he'd met on the plane] and I went down to Ground Zero and we couldn't get anywhere close because the criminal investigation was going on. I don't know what happened with Mike, but I took the train back to the Waldorf. I was going to get dressed up and go someplace else.

When I got [to the Waldorf] we had bombed Afghanistan and so I had to go through all the security.

So I went down to see Johnny [the bartender] and he had a bottle of vodka there for me. He poured me a drink, gave me the bottle and said, "Pour yourself a drink, son." He filled the glass with way more.

"Let me know when you want to eat."

"I'm ready to eat."

He pulled a table right behind me. [Al didn't even have to move from where he was sitting having a drink.] There was nobody in there.

I had one of the best meals I've had in my lifetime that night. I had a New York steak and a salad and a glass of wine. The steak came and there was nothing with it. It was all à la carte.

When I finished my meal, I brought my wine up [to the bar]. [Johnny] asked me all kinds of questions about Oregon. I wanted him to come to Oregon. He would have gone crazy here—Oregon's so great for fishing. I can't even imagine going out on the Hudson River and trying to catch a fish.

Like many on the trip, Bridget Flanigan of Portland was at Ground Zero when the news came. "I thought it was classic justice and classic timing. I thought it was an incredible spot to be. I will remember forever where I was when we finally paid them back."

Reporter Chris Sullivan of KXL Radio was also near Ground Zero:

> [People were saying]"Hooray, we're bombing the bastards who did that to us."

> That was the first day that the bombs started going and I remember it spreading through the crowd. We were a couple of blocks away, but the people in the buildings were like, "We're bombing Afghanistan."

> But it was like—at Ground Zero, the sense of retribution or revenge or accountability spread through the crowd and people were excited about that.

> I don't think they expected to be there twenty years later. I won't forget that, in addition to the devastation.

> Those [things] are etched on my soul.

Cherryl Walker, a state representative from Murphy, Oregon, and Medford City Councilman Ed Chun were at Ground Zero as well. The Medford *Mail Tribune* captured their story:

> Walker and [Chun] said they visited the ruins of the World Trade Center—nicknamed "ground zero"—Sunday. They were shocked by the enormity and the smell.

> "The pictures and television images aren't the whole picture," Chun said. "There's the smell of smoke and debris and this odd odor. You know what it is, but you don't want to admit it."

> "I literally broke down."

> Walker said she cried when she saw a single steelworker working on a fragment of the remaining structure—a flag was flying above his head.

> As they were looking on, police backed up the crowd by a block. The police officers said they didn't know why. Later, Walker came upon some officers and asked again.

> "When they found out I was a state legislator, they said, 'You should know we attacked Afghanistan an hour ago,'" Walker said.

> As she walked back to her hotel, Walker saw a small antiwar demonstration in Union Square.

"I think it ran out of steam pretty quickly," she said.[16]

Former Long Islander Rob Oster was flying back to Portland that night. As he wrote for the *Gresham Outlook*:

> When my brother Steve turned on the New York Giants football game early Sunday afternoon at my mother's house and Dan Rather's concerned face appeared instead of Terry Bradshaw's, I knew my 5:30 p.m. flight back home had just become a lot more interesting . . . .

> Most of the passengers on the return flight that I spoke with said they still felt comfortable flying, but the day's military action against Afghanistan definitely cast a pall over the flight home and, on a personal note, left me with a mild case of the jitters.

Security at Newark airport was tight. Two hours after the bombing was announced, Martin Fisher of Bend and family arrived there, and waited in security lines for four hours:

> That was the first day that the National Guard showed up, which was kind of an eerie experience. We're standing in line and all of a sudden a line of soldiers come in carrying rifles. They've got their M-16s ready instead of just slung over. That was kind of odd. I never thought I'd see that.

Lance Nuttman summed up the Rubicon Crossing that it was and that has informed the lives of America ever since:

> It was a turning point. We landed the plane the day they started bombing Afghanistan. We were all so thrilled when we landed; it was this sobering, slap upside the head. Shortly after that the whole patriotism thing went from one thing to another.[17]

Like the other Freedom Fliers, the trip's dignitaries put on a brave front. Congressman David Wu told the press, "The right thing to do at this point is to carry on with what we're doing. Osama bin Laden said that America is struck with fear from north to south and east to west. I don't know about north to south, but all the way from Oregon to New York City we are not fearful. We will prevail."[18]

The Dozonos had immediately returned to the hotel in triage mode; they found the Azumano staff was panicked at the thought of hundreds of immediate returns. Sho phoned the airlines to see if planes were even operating: they were. The big question was whether people would panic and say they were going home.

One person returned to Oregon to be with her son, and five others inquired about leaving early.[19] The desire to be with one's children and explain what was happening was something Portland School Board member Julia Brim-Edwards, mother of three children, understood well. "I'm worried about my kids. It's times like this when you need to be with your kids."[20]

"Everyone seemed a notch lower than yesterday," said John Ray, who ran Flight for Freedom media relations. "It's like the whole city is subdued."[21]

The Youngs from Happy Valley weren't sure whether to stay, Jackie wrote me in 2003:

> We certainly did not feel like we wanted to be in any parade. But there was the meeting in Chinatown that night with Rep. Wu . . . . When we saw how all [at the dinner] were so glad we were there we realized that this was about enduring . . . . and so it has become.[22]

The trip's whole point was to go on with life. The Freedom Fliers had come 3,000 miles to make that point; why would they let a massive bombing thousands of miles away do what the September 11 attacks could not: paralyze them with fear, make them change their plans? Even though, in the wake of the bombings, the Waldorf closed all but one door, now required ID to get in, and had security guards search bags before anyone could enter, the Oregonians remained unbowed.

"Some people even extended their visits," said Sho.

Kristen Dozono, who was, as usual, working the hospitality table, remembered "hundreds" of people asking about extending.

Loen Dozono:

> It was just the best of humanity. You could be so proud of the people in Oregon who were dealing with that crisis.

> The most incredible thing was . . . just as we got back to the hotel there was a whole planeload of people who were arriving and had just gotten in from Oregon, and they said, "We came to New York to see what we're going to see. Tell us what there is to do."

Among the new arrivals were Lance and Marla Nuttman of McMinnville. They checked into their room and, Marla recalled:

> We had this balcony . . . . We went outside there and we watched our buses down there and we didn't know they were for us. We were like, "Look at those tour buses." I'd been to New York before on a tour bus. And you get on all at the same time. I didn't know that any of that was going to be part of this trip.[23]

In the extensive 2001 website scrapbook Lance made, which, sadly, no longer exists, he recounted the tale of their trip:

> *After making the necessary phone calls, we head down to the lobby to check out the "hospitality desk." . . . We're heading towards one of the tables when a girl grabs us and asks us if we're with the Oregon group. Since we were, she practically threw us onto one of about six tour buses headed for a banquet in Chinatown. Oregon Congressman David Wu was treating everyone on the Flight for Freedom to a ten-course Chinese dinner.**

Kristen Dozono just may have been that "girl." Almost twenty years later, she remembers:

> We had all these tour buses at the last minute to get people to Chinatown. And we were going to Chinatown and it was fairly cold and we had to get people to sit on the upper decks of these things and usher people out. And trying to sell people to get on the top deck to take photos.
>
> And then at the end of that, one of the tour bus drivers was like, "Where did you get that voice?"
>
> Because I was yelling. There were like six of us on the last bus. We were so worried.

Everyone got there on time and there was plenty of room on the buses. In fact, Kristen had done her job so well that when she, Bill and Tina Harmon of Azumano Travel, and her two cousins got on the last bus, they were the only people on it. The problem with room happened when they got to Chinatown and the first restaurant was so packed they had to sit in a restaurant across the street.

---

*"With wine yet!" Jack Kostel noted in his "Flight for Freedom Memories."

As the only Chinese-American Member of Congress and chair of the Congressional Asian Pacific American Caucus, Wu was especially sensitive to Chinatown's plight. Being near the World Trade Center and barricaded to traffic until earlier that week, the neighborhood, "which is not a well-heeled community," he said, was struggling economically. This dinner would be a financial boon for them.

Born in China himself, Wu knew authentic Chinese food. Wu's father had first come to the United States as a thirty-four-year-old exchange student. Given U.S. law at the time, the family could not come with him. David, his two sisters, his mother, and his grandmother, would wait six years to be reunited with his father, who did not return to them because he was not sure if he would be allowed to leave the country again. As a boy, Wu remembered staying in touch via aerograms, and his father sent gifts "a couple times a year." The boy and his family were allowed into the United States under an Executive Order early in the administration of President John F. Kennedy, who updated the number of immigrants who could come in from different countries, so that they no longer reflected the disproportionately high number of Western Europeans from fifty years earlier. Under these new quotas more Chinese could come into the country. (See "Immigrants of Color in Oregon.")

Wu, whose candidacy had been supported by the Chinese community nationwide, said he had made many calls to raise the funding for the dinner and buses. Sponsors included Intel Corp., Nike, Inc., Columbia Sportwear, and Evergreen International Airlines.

"Investment capital firms have capital they can survive on, but the moms and pops in Chinatown—Chinatown was bisected; half the town is closed. People couldn't make a living," says Wu, who had been to New York twice since September 11.[24]

The dinner was at the Harmony Palace at 98 Mott Street. For the Oregonians, it was a great culinary opportunity. "Chinatown has some of the most authentic Chinese food in North America," says Wu, who, at the time said, "I look forward to hosting Oregonians in one of my favorite neighborhoods in New York City—a neighborhood that is vibrant and welcoming."[25]

Even the bus ride was an exciting introduction to the city. [PHOTO 19] Lance Nuttman:

After passing through Times Square, Union Square, even happening upon the building that's the front of the show "Will & Grace,"
we come into Chinatown. Fish markets and lots of lights, elderly
Chinese women selling fresh fruit on the sidewalks, lots of things to
see. Traffic is pretty stop-and-go, partly because of the Chinese Lion
Dancers who had come to welcome us, partly because it's New York,
and that's what traffic does.

And then they went into the restaurant, where they joined "at least
a couple hundred other Oregonians looking for a free meal." [PHOTO 20]

Being in the right place at the right time and open to anything
could pay off. On the bus, realtor George Haight of Woodburn chatted
with a woman who, he learned, owns the Beachwood Ocean Front
Motel in Lincoln City, Oregon, and was leaving for Russia the following morning. As they walked to the restaurant:

Here came Jack McGowan and said, "Follow me." He pointed
at us. She looked at me and I looked at her and so off we went and
two blocks down—he was grabbing people as we went—there were
fifteen or twenty of us probably, and we walked through a Chinese
parade with dragons, dragon dancers, and up this little narrow stairway into a building into a conference room.

It was the city council chambers for Chinatown, and the mayor of
Chinatown was thanking Congressman Wu for being a part of the
trip and being the first Chinese-American in Congress. It was really
cool.

Judi Henningsen of Portland:

We had just enough time to do a little souvenir shopping, before
preparing for the reception and dinner at Chinatown.

We boarded a double-decker, English style red bus. Susan and I were
on the upper deck just behind the windshield. Thank goodness, since
it was cold and breezy. What a great vantage point to see the city!

Soon we arrived in Chinatown. I couldn't believe my eyes and ears.
There in the street was a band in bright red uniforms, playing just
for us!

We walked about a block to a Chinese restaurant, where seating for about five hundred of us was waiting. Two hundred more of us dined across the street.

As cocktails were being consumed, in came the dragon dancers. One was white, the other dragon [was] red.

We were served in traditional style . . . ten courses!

"I had my first lobster there," said Lance Nuttman. "The duck was the whole duck with its head chopped off and braised and chop, chop—so delicious."

Rep. Wu thanked the group for coming, then introduced U.S. Representative Nydia Velázquez, who represented Chinatown in Congress, whom he had invited. Rep. Velázquez addressed the group, thanked them for the effort, and stressing what their visit to Chinatown and New York meant to the city. [PHOTOS 21, 23]

Eric Marcus, since 2016 founder and host of the *Making Gay History* podcast, was at the time an author of many books, including the groundbreaking *Making Gay History*. He and I had gone to college together and I'd invited him to meet us in Chinatown. In 2003, Eric shared his recollections of joining our table of Oregonians and another New Yorker:

> When I first heard about the idea—on the news—I thought what a lovely thing [for Oregonians] to show their support for New York and at the same time I thought they're out of their minds to get on a plane and come to New York at that moment.
>
> If I'd had my choice, I'd not have been on a plane. It was a very, very surreal time to be in New York and to be a New Yorker. People were so frightened by what had happened . . . . It meant a lot to me and I know to others as well that there were people willing to demonstrate in a very real way their love and support of the New York at a time when people were still in shock.
>
> Chinatown was badly hit because of the power failures and people were not traveling downtown because smoke was still pervasive and so it meant a lot to me being there sitting there at a table with Oregonians who came here at a time that was really difficult.
>
> A lot of the people at my table had not been to New York before or had only been once and so for them, they were pretty wide-eyed

about the city in general. My impression was that people had not necessarily come from Portland, they had come from areas outside of Portland and were just amazed by being in a big city and I felt like something of an ambassador being at the table, being asked questions . . . .

The fact that people were coming from Oregon was striking because it was so far away and the effort was so heartfelt. I was impressed by how strongly people felt about this and how strongly they felt to demonstrate solidarity with the people of New York. I don't know how disconnected people felt, but I imagine that coming here made it all the more real.

. . . The city, which is normally full of tourists, was devoid of tourists. Normally, we're so used to having tourists here it's no big deal. But the Oregonians seemed to be ubiquitous, they were incredibly cheerful or upbeat and it was nice to see it. It was as if hundreds of goodwill ambassadors had swooped down on New York from a faraway place; we're thinking about you and supporting you.[26]

Nearly twenty years later, Marcus's emotional memory of the Oregonians' presence is strong: "It was such a lovely and brave gesture at a time when people were terrified of the thought of getting on the airplane," he says. "It was so unexpected. You came from far away to say we'll be OK and that was very comforting. I remember your visit very well.[27]

For the organizers, the Chinatown dinner was chaotic. They were already thinking of the next morning, when Mayor Katz was scheduled to appear on "Good Morning America" and "Regis and Kelly."
[PHOTO 22]

Decisions and negotiations were ongoing that afternoon, as Sho remembered:

We were afraid that the parade was going to be canceled . . . . We wanted the program to happen like clockwork, then the bombing started, we didn't know about the parade, and Jan Woodruff was talking to ABC, saying, "We're going to send 100 people down to Times Square," and ABC was afraid of mass gatherings so they said, "We'll put you in the studio."

Loen said, "That's exactly what the terrorists want us to do . . . to go inside out of fear."

Jan was under the table in the Chinese restaurant trying to talk on the cell phone so she could get her message across, hollering away because the room was so noisy.

We said, "Hey, we're not backing down."

The question was asked to me, "Do you think you could get 500 people?"

"Absolutely."

So that's when we made an announcement at the dinner to get people to meet in the lobby at 6 a.m. to go down there.

Like most Freedom Fliers, Judi Henningsen didn't think twice about a mass gathering:

> By the time I got to course number eight I was so full I didn't think I could eat another bite. Besides, I think I had worn my chopsticks down to toothpicks by then.
>
> This was a full day. Have to get home and to bed. We have to get up at 5:30 to prepare to walk to Times Square for the ABC-TV "Good Morning America" show.[28]

The day may have been over for most Oregonians, but it wasn't for the Nuttmans. Marla recalls:

> We went out in the middle of the night looking for a McDonald's. The streets were empty in the middle of the night. I don't know if that was good or bad. There's like a McDonald's every few paces; we had to find them on our map. I think we were too embarrassed to ask the concierge "Where's a McDonald's?" I didn't know it then, but I know it now that it would be totally legit to ask the concierge.

But despite their nocturnal food-finding mission, they were up and ready for *Good Morning America* at 6 a.m.

Azumano Travel had arranged for a block of tickets to Sunday matinees of *Kiss Me Kate* and other Broadway shows. The *Kiss Me Kate* performance was especially touching. Gubernatorial candidate Ron Saxton:

A very special remembrance came when a group of about one hundred Oregonians attended the Broadway show *Kiss Me Kate*. During the curtain call, cast members came out with "Oregon Loves New York" stickers on their costumes. The cast had autographed one hundred playbills and came back onstage after the show to thank Oregonians for coming to New York.[29]

Playbill courtesy of Brian McCartin.

Portland Area Theatre Alliance President Julie Stewart:

I went to four musicals in two days and was treated like a celebrity, as I wore my "Oregon Loves NY" button. The cast of *Kiss Me Kate* gifted us with cast autograph Playbills and asked us to come to the stage after the show so they could thank us for coming to New York.[30]

And at *The Producers*, Terry from Portland [last name unknown] and his wife and friends went backstage and all the actors and actresses signed their programs, too.

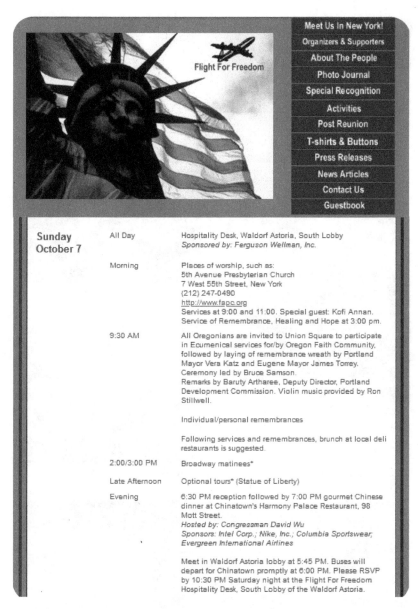

Meet Us In New York!
Organizers & Supporters
About The People
Photo Journal
Special Recognition
Activities
Post Reunion
T-shirts & Buttons
Press Releases
News Articles
Contact Us
Guestbook

Flight For Freedom

**Sunday
October 7**

All Day	Hospitality Desk, Waldorf Astoria, South Lobby *Sponsored by: Ferguson Wellman, Inc.*
Morning	Places of worship, such as: 5th Avenue Presbyterian Church 7 West 55th Street, New York (212) 247-0490 http://www.fapc.org Services at 9:00 and 11:00. Special guest: Kofi Annan. Service of Remembrance, Healing and Hope at 3:00 pm.
9:30 AM	All Oregonians are invited to Union Square to participate in Ecumenical services for/by Oregon Faith Community, followed by laying of remembrance wreath by Portland Mayor Vera Katz and Eugene Mayor James Torrey. Ceremony led by Bruce Samson. Remarks by Baruty Artharee, Deputy Director, Portland Development Commission. Violin music provided by Ron Stillwell.
	Individual/personal remembrances
	Following services and remembrances, brunch at local deli restaurants is suggested.
2:00/3:00 PM	Broadway matinees*
Late Afternoon	Optional tours* (Statue of Liberty)
Evening	6:30 PM reception followed by 7:00 PM gourmet Chinese dinner at Chinatown's Harmony Palace Restaurant, 98 Mott Street. *Hosted by: Congressman David Wu* *Sponsors: Intel Corp.; Nike, Inc.; Columbia Sportswear; Evergreen International Airlines*
	Meet in Waldorf Astoria lobby at 5:45 PM. Buses will depart for Chinatown promptly at 6:00 PM. Please RSVP by 10:30 PM Saturday night at the Flight For Freedom Hospitality Desk, South Lobby of the Waldorf Astoria.

1. October 7 Activities. From archived website, http://www.azumano.com/ flightforfreedom/activity.html, downloaded by the author February 23, 2021

2. Photo by Betsy Ames

2. Photo by Barbara Shaw

2. Photo by Betsy Ames

2. Photo by Betsy Ames

3. Freedom Fliers at the Union Square Memorial Service. Photo courtesy of Loen Dozono

4. Portland Police Captain Cliff Madison addresses the Union Square audience. New York Police Deputy Inspector William Callahan is at his left. Photo courtesy of Loen Dozono

5. Vera Katz with Parks Commissioner Henry Stern. In the background from left to right: Eugene Mayor Jim Torrey; Baruti Artharee, deputy director of the Portland Development Commission (PDC) and the board chairman of the Urban League; Flight for Freedom organizer and Portland power attorney Bruce Samson. Photo by Barbara Shaw

6. Baruti Artharee addresses the Union Square crowd. Photo by Barbara Shaw

7. Eugene Mayor Jim Torrey addresses the crowd. Photo by Betsy Ames

8. Retired Oregon Symphony Orchestra violinist Roy Stilwell. Photo by Barbara Shaw

9. Eric Petterson, co-owner of Coffee Shop, speaks to the crowd. Photo by Betsy Ames

10. Laying the Boughs. Photo courtesy of Loen Dozono

11. Laying the Boughs. Photo by Betsy Ames

12. Laying the Boughs. Photo by Barbara Shaw

13. Blessing of the Animals celebration, Cathedral of St. John the Divine. Photos courtesy of Loen Dozono

13. Photos courtesy of the Archives of the Cathedral of St. John the Divine, 1047 Amsterdam Ave, New York

15. Robert F. Kennedy, Jr. speaks at the Cathedral of St. John the Divine. Photo courtesy of the Archives of the Cathedral of St. John the Divine, 1047 Amsterdam Ave, New York

14. Rt. Rev. Mark S. Sisk and friend. Sisk had been installed as the Bishop of the Episcopal Diocese of New York the week before, on September 29, and served in that position through 2013. Photo courtesy of the Archives of the Cathedral of St. John the Divine, 1047 Amsterdam Ave, New York

16. Mayor Vera Katz addresses the congregation at the Cathedral of St. John the
Divine. Photo courtesy of the Archives of the Cathedral of St. John the Divine, 1047
Amsterdam Ave, New York

17., 18. Rescue dogs and their partners from the World Trade Center site honored
at the Blessing of the Animals at the Cathedral of St. John the Divine on October 7,
2001. Photos courtesy of the Archives of the Cathedral of St. John the Divine, 1047
Amsterdam Ave, New York

19. On the bus to Chinatown. Photo courtesy of Loen Dozono

20. A lion dance and a marching band greeted the Freedom Fliers in Chinatown. Photo by Betsy Ames

21. U.S. Rep. David Wu and U.S. Rep. Nydia Velázquez. Photo courtesy of Loen Dozono

22. Enjoying Chinatown dinner. Photos courtesy of Loen Dozono

23. U.S. Rep. David Wu chats with the guests. Photo by Barbara Shaw

AMERICA WAKES UP TO OREGON

[I]t's not always dollars and cents that rebuilds a community. It's caring folks willing to share the emotion of a moment, willing to be the wall others lean on, willing to simply say "you are not alone in this," that will help New York, and this country arise from the terrorist attacks of Sept. 11 . . . . In the end, the large acts will get the publicity, but it will be these small acts of kindness that will mend the hurt we all feel. — *The Woodburn Independent*[1]

That they went to New York was an act of courage. That they stayed even after U.S. bombings of Afghanistan began showed they meant what they said about the terrorists not destroying America's way of life.

On Monday morning, the Freedom Fliers awoke to a new chapter in the "War on Terrorism," as it would be labeled by the president. The United States was now making war and the Oregonians would spend the first day of this new reality in some of the most attractive targets in the country: Times Square, the New York Stock Exchange, and the Columbus Day Parade, where hundreds of thousands of people were sure to gather.

Sho had told the press the week before, "We're doing this to ourselves."

Alerts had been posted for Americans around the world. On Sunday, the State Department issued a worldwide alert about the possibility of "strong anti-American sentiment and retaliatory actions against U.S. citizens and interests throughout the world."[2]

New York City was on its highest security alert. The Associated Press reported that "armed National Guard troops, New York [City] Police and the State Police were out in force Monday, blocking intersections with giant sand trucks and squad cars. They blocked off-ramps and access to key Manhattan Buildings. There were checkpoints at every bridge and tunnel."

"We're clearly at an enhanced level of security," said Gov. George Pataki, "and we will be for some time."[3]

While the extra security made him feel safe, New York tour guide Joseph Svehlak captured the atmosphere succinctly: "It feels like a war zone."[4]

During morning mass at St. Patrick's Cathedral, prayers for combatants and innocent civilians in Afghanistan were added. The service concluded with 'The Star-Spangled Banner."

The Oregonians remained public cheerleaders for New York—and for letting go of fear. "I urge you to take a trip to New York City and see for yourself," KPAM talk-show host Sheila Hamilton told the folks back home from her remote broadcast at the ABC Radio studio on West End Avenue. "It is staggering."[5]

At the World Trade Center site, U.S. bombing in the Middle East had changed nothing:

> [H]uge cranes continued to dip into a mountain of smoldering rubble, lifting several-ton sections of what were once support beams. The movement of debris released 100-foot-wide plumes of smoke from fires within the ruins. At least one body was pulled from the ruins and draped in an American flag.[6]

City officials said 4,979 people remain missing; 393 people were confirmed dead and of them, 335 had been identified. Three hundred forty-three Fire Department members and twenty-three police officers [were confirmed dead/missing]. By day's end, the death toll would rise to 417, the *New York Daily News* reported, and the discovery of bodies continued:

Rescue workers pulled the body of another firefighter and two civilians from the Trade Center wreckage. They also found a firefighter's gloves and oxygen tank in a stairwell of 2 World Trade Center; spurring hopes more bodies would soon be recovered . . . .

The number of missing fell by 158 to 4,815 as police found more duplication in paperwork. No survivors have been found since the day after the Sept. 11 attacks.[7]

For many Oregonians, the top priority was still getting up before dawn to appear on "Good Morning America" with Mayor Vera Katz; this would be the first of two major media appearances for her that morning. (She'd been booked on the "TODAY" show, but they had canceled when they learned of the GMA booking; they wanted an exclusive and Media Relations Director John Ray did not consent. Ray later said he felt especially bad about it because he'd gone to college with native Oregonian and TODAY co-host Ann Curry, and he knew she had nothing to do with the decision by the show.)

While GMA producers wanted the Oregonians to all be inside the studio in order to not attract attention (of would-be attackers), so many Oregonians showed up that that would be impossible. Times Square was filled with white T-shirts.

Organizers had realized that they would need help to ensure that the Freedom Fliers, many of whom had never been in Manhattan before, could get to Times Square by 6:15 a.m. "Somebody miraculously asked for guides and they had guides to lead us all the way down there," Loen remembered. Later she learned that Val Hubbard, who had volunteered countless hours helping the Azumano Group Department, made the call.

Joe Mauriello of WineDineNY Inc. and NYCTourGuides.com provided tour guides at no charge, helped take the press around the city in a trolley provided by New York University (NYU) and provided the escorts to Times Square that morning.[8] Mauriello himself lost friends in the attacks and his brother was almost killed in Building Six. When he learned that the Oregonians were coming, he immediately offered his company's services by submitting an email to the Azumano Flight for Freedom website: [PHOTO 1]

THANK YOU, as a 3rd generation New Yorker I commend Mayor Katz and all involved in this forward thinking project. Myself and many other licensed tour guides extend a welcome to all current and future visitors to New York. If at any time during your visit you need information or tour guides (YES . . . many tour guides are offering free or discount services) PLEASE CALL ME . . . God Bless You All, and thanks for the moral as well as financial support.[9]

After learning what organizers needed, Mauriello got in touch with the president of New York University (NYU). The NYU president told Mauriello: "Whatever you need." When asked why go to all this trouble at a traumatic time for people he didn't know, he said:

It wasn't trouble, it was something I felt had to be done and at the time I had a lot of good contacts and I took advantage of them. It was a time no one could say no. I had restaurants that were willing to feed them [the Freedom Fliers] for free. They said, "Yeah, we'll just send them in and we'll do X amount of meals." It was an outpouring. Everybody had a stake in this.[10]

After the trip, Mauriello again posted on the Flight for Freedom website. His efforts were inspired by gratitude, he wrote: "Between 9/11 and today I have witnessed extraordinary examples of support, but one thing I will remember is that your group was the FIRST to help us get back up."[11] [PHOTOS 2-3]

And with nearly twenty years of perspective, Mauriello still says, "It was an amazing thing."

Not only were guides available for those who walked, but buses provided rides as well, and Judi Henningsen of Portland took advantage of them:

Oh, it is so cold. The wind is blowing. It feels like it is cutting right through me. Oh goody, they have provided a bus for those who are unable to walk. Another open air double decker bus! There was lots of room so Susan and I filled a couple of empty seats topside in the breeze, as opposed to hoofing it.

We arrived after the walkers. Some of them made it inside the studio, but most of us were to stand outside the window waving. It is colder now, wind blowing, hands in pockets to keep them warm. Our purpose here is to be visible to the media. We want to let New York know we are here for them.

Sandra Kempel of Portland:

It was, maybe we'll be on TV, but it was also, take a look! I'm proud to be an American, I'm proud to be from Oregon, and look at what we've done we're here, so pay attention, America![12]

After twenty-four hours in the city, Lance and Marla Nuttman of McMinnville knew the ropes:

Well, Marla at this point knows the maps very well, so we decide to get a head start on the group. On the way, we stop at a convenience store (which we will frequent every day we are in the City), and buy a CINNAMON BUN (he stared blankly at me when I asked for the Pershing) from a Middle Eastern gentleman manning a pastry cart. After we snarfed down breakfast, we arrived at the Good Morning America building.

After standing three rows deep in Oregonians, some of us are ushered into the middle island of Times Square, awaiting our moment in the spotlight. Thing about Times Square is it's the intersection of three streets.

"Funny, Times Square wasn't as big as I had expected either," wrote Henningsen. "I was imagining what it must feel like to stand in this spot on New Year's Eve, watching the ball drop. There were huge electronic signs on buildings recognizing us."

About 100 of the T-shirt-clad group got into the studio—Debra-Diane Jenness of Crescent Lake next to Mayor Katz—and the rest waited on the island in the middle of Times Square "freezing our Oregon Grapes off," wrote Lance Nuttman. (It was in the thirties [Fahrenheit]). Still, he looked on the bright side: "[A]t least it ain't raining. If we were back home, it would've been raining." [PHOTOS 4-6]

Meanwhile, inside the studio, hosts Charles Gibson and Diane Sawyer wave at the group and point them out on camera:

DIANE SAWYER: They came to New York, as they said, to make a point. The 700 [sic] Oregon tourists who flew here last week to fight back against the fear that has devastated the tourist trade, and we'll be going out to see what they have to say. And—and is there an Oregon song? Think of an Oregon song down there, if you can hear us, by theme we get there. We'll sing it together.

CHARLES GIBSON: They came from Oregon, and it is cold here in New York. I feel so badly for them . . .

And then Mayor Katz did the weather report with GMA's Tony Perkins: [PHOTO 7]

TONY PERKINS: And this Columbus Day is a special day for you in New York.

VERA KATZ: In 1940, my family fleeing from the Nazis arrived on the shores of New York City with big dreams and hopes for everybody.

TONY PERKINS: And, obviously, things have worked out for you.

VERA KATZ: Yes. I'm the mayor of the city of Portland, Oregon.

TONY PERKINS: You guys had a good time this weekend?

VERA KATZ: We had a wonderful time. New Yorkers were wonderful.

TONY PERKINS: We are happy to have you here. Now, Madam Mayor, please take a look at the map and give us the forecast for the fair city of Portland, Oregon . . . .

DIANE SAWYER: Thanks, Tony, and thanks to the mayor, too. When we come back, the travelers on a mission to rescue New York's tourism industry. They come from Portland, Oregon, here to help. Portland serves when GOOD MORNING AMERICA continues.

In the next segment, ABC News's Elizabeth Vargas reported on her weekend covering the Oregonians in New York.

DIANE SAWYER: As we've been telling you, the mayor has said that New York has been losing $30 million a day in hotel and restaurant money. Well, the people of Oregon decided they knew what to do about this. Nine hundred and fifty of them came, and they spent the weekend going wild and shopping, and Elizabeth Vargas is going to show you a little of what they did.

ELIZABETH VARGAS: Taking care of business is why they were here. A mission of mercy: shopping, dining, putting some cash into Manhattan's pockets, to show the world "Portland loves New York." Tourism has taken a hit here so they checked into the hotel and then spent their way from Fifth Avenue to Times Square—everything from a $5 cab ride to $200 shoes, seeing the sights, buying tickets for a Broadway show.

Vargas showed the Oregonians enjoying New York, and even evangelizing for it. As one unidentified Oregon woman told her: "I would definitely recommend that everyone from the entire United States puts aside any fear they may feel."

At the dinner in Chinatown right after the Afghanistan bombing started, Congressman David Wu had reiterated the point: "We were concerned about having this dinner tonight but we decided to go ahead because that's what this trip is all about, about carrying on with a stiff upper lip."[13]

While initially Sawyer had suggesting the Oregon state song, the song selection was changed because, as Gibson stated, "The words are a little strange. We have them here, but for this weekend, the Oregon song is":

OREGONIANS (Singing in unison): "Start spreading the news. I'm leaving today. I want to be a part of it. New York, New York."

CHARLES GIBSON: You can tell all of these people were self-selected for their musical talent. These are the outstanding voices for the state of Oregon.

DIANE SAWYER: All right. But we have to do "if I can make it there."

OREGONIANS (Singing in unison): "If I can make it there, I'll make it anywhere. It's up to you New York, New York."[14]

Despite the cold and the security levels, Gibson and Sawyer had promised to meet the crowd outdoors. While they waited, George Haight of Woodburn went across the street for a cup of coffee:

> The street sweeper, an almost elderly fellow with a broom that worked for the city, stopped me and said, "May I shake your hand and thank you for being here?" And I lost it. I just stood there—that's

the other nice thing about the trip. Grown men can cry in public. Watching some of the police and firemen in the parade with tears just streaming down their faces, Oregon cops hugging New York cops . . . . But that street sweeper got me. Just a guy, you know.

The Nuttmans got antsy in the cold:

> 7:50 comes, and they tell us we'll be on at 8:00. Unless you've got some kind of funky wide-screen TV, you just missed seeing us. Lance screamed out "Pan left, PAN LEFT!" while Marla shivered.
>
> Then they say Charlie (Gibson) will be coming out at 8:15. 8:15 comes; they tell us Diane will be out at 8:30. The camera scans the crowd again, and our heroes (that's us, eh) are stuck behind a woman with the biggest hair in the world. At 8:30, we don't see Diane, so we decide to go check and see if we can get us some Conan O'Brien tickets.
>
> (It's not until two days after our return that we find out indeed BOTH Charlie and Diane showed up ten minutes after we left.)[15]

Barbara Shaw of Scio got an on-camera hug from Diane Sawyer. Azumano staffer Rick Love had his picture taken with Sawyer, a photo he hung proudly in his office—alongside Sho Dozono's of course, he laughed.

Judi Henningsen: [PHOTOS 8-11]

> Diane Sawyer . . . is so darling. She thanked us all for coming and gave Susan a great big hug. At last, the nation knew the Oregonians were here.
>
> We wore our T-shirts. We wore our pins.
>
> We wore our coats.

GMA was just the first stop for Mayor Katz that day. She had to go the ten blocks from ABC's Times Square studios to "Live with Regis and Kelly" at Lincoln Center in what would normally be unheard of: thirty minutes. With the city in semi-lockdown, it became possible.

The mayor planted a kiss on Regis and called the Flight for Freedom "wonderful."

The Freedom Fliers were on hand to provide support, as always. Connie Hawk of Salem even gave her T-shirt to a stagehand there.

The former New Yorker surprised and charmed everyone by showing that she hadn't forgotten the blunt approach of her first American home:

> We said, "We're going to come to New York, we're going to honor New York, we're going to pay tribute to New York, we're going to spend some money. Because the mayor of New York said, 'Get off your butts and come and fly.'"[16]

John Ray:

> A high point for me was because my wife at the time worked for her, I was real proud of the work that we did and what a great public face for our city that Vera was. To get her in front of so many venues and to see her being so approachable and enjoying the whole thing. It's so hard to talk about it as enjoyment . . . .[17]

Jean Andersen of Raleigh Hills in Portland won the trivia bonus: $250 worth of steaks! She made it into the show because she'd tipped the Waldorf concierge.[18]

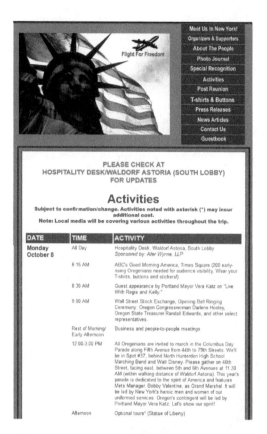

**PLEASE CHECK AT
HOSPITALITY DESK/WALDORF ASTORIA (SOUTH LOBBY)
FOR UPDATES**

Activities

Subject to confirmation/change. Activities noted with asterisk (*) may incur additional cost.
Note: Local media will be covering various activities throughout the trip.

DATE	TIME	ACTIVITY
Monday October 8	All Day	Hospitality Desk, Waldorf Astoria, South Lobby. Sponsored by: Ater Wynne, LLP
	6:15 AM	ABC's Good Morning America, Times Square (200 early-rising Oregonians needed for audience visibility. Wear your T-shirts, buttons and stickers!)
	8:30 AM	Guest appearance by Portland Mayor Vera Katz on "Live With Regis and Kelly."
	9:00 AM	Wall Street Stock Exchange, Opening Bell Ringing Ceremony: Oregon Congresswoman Darlene Hooley, Oregon State Treasurer Randall Edwards, and other select representatives.
	Rest of Morning/ Early Afternoon	Business and people-to-people meetings
	12:00-3:00 PM	All Oregonians are invited to march in the Columbus Day Parade along Fifth Avenue from 44th to 79th Streets. We'll be in Spot #37, behind North Hunterdon High School Marching Band and Walt Disney. Please gather on 46th Street, facing east, between 5th and 6th Avenues at 11:30 AM (within walking distance of Waldorf Astoria). This year's parade is dedicated to the spirit of America and features Mets Manager, Bobby Valentine, as Grand Marshal. It will be led by New York's heroic men and women of our uniformed services. Oregon's contingent will be led by Portland Mayor Vera Katz. Let's show our spirit!
	Afternoon	Optional tours* (Statue of Liberty)

**PLEASE CHECK AT
HOSPITALITY DESK/WALDORF ASTORIA (SOUTH LOBBY)
FOR UPDATES**

Activities

Subject to confirmation/change. Activities noted with asterisk (*) may incur additional cost.

	6:00-8:00 PM	No-host "All-Oregon" Cocktail Reception for Flight For Freedom flyers and friends, relatives and business associates in the New York area. Waldorf Astoria, Grand Ballroom
		Host Sponsor: American Express
		Oregon Sponsors: Ater Wynne, LLP; Bank of America; Ferguson Wellman, Inc.; IBM-Oregon Division; Advantage Sales & Marketing; PacifiCorp; Regence Blue Cross BlueShield of Oregon; RB Pamplin Corp.; US Bank; Wells Fargo.
		Entertainment by: Broadway performers from Les Misérables and Phantom of the Opera.
		Remarks by: Eric Javitz, US Ambassador to Disarmament Conference, and Christyne Nicholas, President and CEO, NYC & Company.
		Special appearance by: New York Governor George Pataki.
		Presentation of American Express "Great Performers Award" to Azumano Travel.
	Evening	Broadway show* (optional)

1. October 8 Activities. From archived website, http://www.azumano.com/flightforfreedom/activity.html, downloaded by the author February 23, 2021

2. Joe Mauriello, owner of of WineDineNY Inc. and NYCTourGuides. com, contacted Azumano Travel to volunteer his company's services and secured a trolley for the press. Photo by Bill Cooper

3. KPAM Radio's Bill cooper does a live shot from the trolley. Photo courtesy of Bill Cooper

4. Organizer Bruce Samson enjoys the "Good Morning America" experience. Photo courtesy of Loen Dozono

5. The Freedom Fliers outside the *Good Morning America* studio. Photo courtesy of Loen Dozono

6. Mayor Vera Katz and the Freedom Fliers in the GMA studio. Photo by Betsy Ames

7. Mayor Vera Katz with GMA weatherman Tony Perkins on the Times Square jumbo screen. Photo by Betsy Ames

8. GMA hosts Charles Gibson and Diane Sawyer with the Freedom Fliers. Photo by Al O'Brien

9. Photos courtesy of Loen Dozono

10. "Some of the people who work for ABC were up in another building and they made a sign that said 'We love you too.' Everyone started cheering," said Molalla resident Beth Faulhaber, who was representing the Police Activities League. Photo by Betsy Ames

11. "We were appreciated," Celia Wiebe, who went with her husband Tony, emailed friends and family on October 11. "I wish you all could have heard what the ABC crew had to say. It touched us all in so many ways." Wiebe shared her note with Azumano Travel on October 11, 2001; retrieved from company website by the author on July 24, 2003. Photo by Betsy Ames

RINGING THE BELL

Millions of people watched the opening bell around the world, so not only were we able as a group to reach out to New Yorkers as we did individually walking the streets; but we symbolically showed the world that we were there and doing something. [That was] the whole thread of genius of the trip. —*Oregon State Treasurer Randall Edwards*[1]

While Mayor Katz was charming the morning shows in Midtown, U.S. Congresswoman Darlene Hooley and Oregon State Treasurer Randall Edwards were leading a group downtown to leave Oregon's mark on the New York Stock Exchange (NYSE). The stock market had reopened on September 17, but the bombing of Afghanistan had raised new concerns, and security had been heightened.

That morning, three Port of Portland Commissioners met with the New York/New Jersey Port Authority Acting Executive Director Ron Shiftan to offer New York their help. Commissioners Jay Waldron, Cheryl Perrin, and Mary Olson met with Shiftan at his temporary office, the Granite Capital International Group.

The Port Authority had occupied several floors of the downed World Trade Center. Shiftan was "Acting" director, because their executive director was one of seventy-four Port Authority employees lost in the collapse.[2]

Since ringing the opening bell is an honor reserved far in advance for movers and shakers, for the Oregonians to be placed on the agenda with little notice was a real coup; Hooley had arranged the ceremony as a member of the House Financial Services Committee. Making room for the Oregon delegation meant bumping the Senate Majority Leader and Speaker of the House, said Nick Fish.[3]

Teacher's union Vice President Ann Nice, "the girl from Powder, Oregon," found herself in the group:

> I like to spend money and I kind of like having it, but that's about it. It was so nice of [Randall Edwards] to ask us so we went down and got to walk on the floor of the stock exchange. Because the stock exchange is not very far from where those planes hit, it was maneuvering to get down there.
>
> A company sent these beautiful black town cars in front of the Waldorf-Astoria and we all got in and got our little rides down like we were really something.

Edwards also remembers that "just getting down to Wall Street was a trip in and of itself" and that it was especially moving crossing over Canal Street:

> There were about twenty of us and when we went over the demarcation, it was like entering a war zone. There were barricades, security—it was still. I've traveled a fair amount in my life, but it was just strange. You were entering a place where something big had happened.
>
> There was still a lot of dust around. It was a big event, but you could only imagine something like what happened in Japan after a nuclear bomb . . . . Or what happened in Dresden, the bombing that totally devastated the city.[4]

Knowing that the September 11 attackers had focused on the centers of both government and business in the United States, security at the Exchange was at its highest level ever:

> They sent anyone who was carrying a bag bigger than one for coffee and a bagel to another entrance. Behind them, workers with briefcases were standing in a second line, one forty people deep, to be searched outside in the fresh October chill . . . . Several deliverymen

were turned away because they did not have the direct telephone extensions for the intended recipients of their packages.[5]

Gaining security clearance to be among the Oregon contingent had been tough from the beginning, Sho remembered. Each participant was required to provide identification the week before, and only ten of the group could be on the balcony when the bell was rung. The Oregonians were ushered into NYSE President Dick Grasso's office, the Exchange's inner sanctum, where they were to sign the guest book, which included the signatures of U.S. presidents. Then came the part Sho told with a twinkle in his eye:

> We'd just gotten done signing this book and there's this cute young gal standing in the room with an "Oregon Loves NY" T-shirt and I thought, "Oh, someone already gave T-shirts to a couple of staff people" and so I said, "Where'd you get the T-shirts?"
>
> They were a couple of gals from Blue Cross/Blue Shield that were on the trip with us and somehow they got in. They talked themselves into this room. We had to give our Social Security Number, get security clearance, only ten of us could be in there. I thought, "These two gals are going to go somewhere."
>
> They had a lot of spunk, so that's the kind of people we took to New York.[6]

For former New Yorker Jack McGowan, the NYSE trip resonated on a deeply personal level. The September 11 attacks had devastated him emotionally; being in the city brought up complex emotions and ultimately, some healing, but the trip to the stock exchange brought him back to his former workplace. Just as Vera Katz was living her sixty-year anniversary of arriving in New York as a Holocaust refugee, McGowan experienced a synchronicity that might not be believed were it not true:

> When I was in my senior year of high school, I really didn't want to go to college (and truthfully, my grades weren't that good). And my buddy in Queens, Richie, and I decided we'd go work at the New York Stock Exchange. So we got jobs there as traders and he and I worked there about four years. I wanted out. Richie didn't feel the same way and he stayed and we lost touch.

I left New York in 1970. And a funny thing occurred, I've told quite a few people this, but the way I found Oregon was a serendipitous way. I was living down in Greenwich Village, a friend of mine had sublet his apartment to me. I was living on Bleecker and MacDougal, and you can't get more of the epicenter of Greenwich Village than that. I was living in a seventh-floor walkup and I could look out my window and watch the World Trade Center being built. It was probably a third of a mile away, something like that.

So I decided to leave New York, I was so disillusioned with New York and Wall Street, I thought there had to be some place that I could change the trajectory of my life. I had decided that I was going to go to California. I had never been west, so that was what I was going to do.

June 26, 1970 was my last day on the New York Stock Exchange. I left New York for the last time, probably around the second week in July. Around July 9 or so, a buddy and I were on Sixth Avenue at 61st Street and all of a sudden I looked and coming out of the Columbia Studios was Paul Simon. This was when he was with Simon and Garfunkel.

We could not believe it. Like every young person, he was a hero, the eloquence of his songwriting and the messaging. We both came up to Paul, and the light happened to change. And Paul was so approachable and so self-effacing. We spoke for probably fifteen, twenty minutes. My friend Steve, who now calls Portland his home—we were so embarrassed that we were the ones that ended the conversation.

But I was the one, when I poured my heart out, we were talking about the [Vietnam] War, Martin Luther King, Kent State, all of the horrors that were going on, and I just said I was going west and I had never been west before. Paul suggested that before I made California my home that I might try the Pacific Northwest.

He said, "Portland is a town that thinks it's a city."

That totally changed my trajectory. I spent a brief period of time in San Francisco, didn't like it, and came to Portland, without a job, no friends, no family, and created a new life for myself. It's because of Paul that I found my Oregon.

I hadn't set foot in the New York Stock Exchange for thirty-one years. A lot of emotions came up going into that building.

And then we're in Dick Grasso's office and I hear, "Jackie McGowan."

"Richie."[7]

The two boys from Queens swapped stories of growing up and the old neighborhood before the group went to the podium, where Grasso asked "Jackie" to stand next to him. Two banners showing in green McGowan's chosen home, the state of Oregon, hung from the podium.[8]

> The emotional thing of seeing my childhood friend [Dick Grasso], who I hadn't talked to in thirty-one years, and all of sudden for Dick to recognize me, to have me stand next to him at the opening bell, looking at where I used to work: there's the phone that I answered on the floor, there's where I was receiving orders.[9]

"Up in the rafters" covering the Oregonians at the podium were Chris Sullivan of KXL, Chris Penland of 1190 KEX News Radio, and Bill Cooper from KPAM Talk Radio. With the stock bell ringing at 6:30 a.m. Pacific Time, they could do live pieces during the morning news.[10] [PHOTOS 1-3]

The New York Times was there to cover the NYSE on the second day of U.S. bombings in Afghanistan. Edwards, they reported, had come to New York "as part of an emotional support mission with more than 900 other Oregonians." The Stock Exchange visit was supposed to be "a pinnacle of the traveling pep rally."

While the floor was noisy compared even to right after 9/11 the previous day's bombings had an effect:

> [T]he workers milling about on the floor seemed newly somber. Notably absent were efforts to cheer on the stock market, exhortations for some sort of patriotic rally like those heard on September 17, when Wall Street reopened after the terrorist attacks on New York and the Pentagon.[11]

On the floor, "people were nervous for sure," said CNBC reporter Maria Bartiromo. "On [September] seventeenth, people were very emotional. They came to the floor feeling sad and yet strengthened. That excitement is still there, but there's a lot of uncertainty."[12]

Or, as Representative Hooley put it, "Let me just say they weren't happy."

One hundred fifty million people were watching and Edwards, who had been in the visitors' gallery but never on the floor of the exchange, admitted to being a little nervous—and it was more than mere stage fright: "The day before, we started bombing Afghanistan, and I thought this could be really bad. Who knew what the market was going to do?"[13]

At 9:29 a.m. Eastern time, Grasso asked for a moment of silence and prayer for the troops. Edwards remembered:

> That was amazing because you're standing up on the podium and it's just a buzz of noise before the bell rings, but then Grasso asked for a moment of silence and you could have heard a pin drop. It was a phenomenal contrast.

Oregon's state treasurer felt the weight of the group's responsibility at the podium. He was well aware that they were representing not only the 1,000 Oregonians in New York, but the entire state. And opening the market was a powerful image, he told *The New York Times*, "symbolizing our confidence in the marketplace."

At 9:30 a.m., Hooley and Edwards rang the bell—forty-three times in four seconds; one worker on the floor managed to make the Sign of the Cross between clangs twenty-five and forty.[14]

From the silence of one minute before, "it just became a wall of noise," said Edwards. "That . . . was really amazing."[15]

Then Hooley and Edwards worked the floor, handing out "Oregon ♥ NY" stickers.

"I pretended like I knew what I was doing as I walked around the stock exchange," said Nice. "Everyone you walked by thanked you for coming."

"It was just a great experience, not only for me personally but for the entire state and the delegation symbolizing our confidence in the marketplace," Edwards told KXL Radio. "We've been treated so well here in New York. This has been another capstone of the whole trip."[16]

1. Floor of the NYSE. Photo by Bill Cooper

2. From left to right front: Portland Chamber of Commerce Chairman, Azumano Travel CEO and owner and Flight for Freedom organizer Sho Dozono; SOLV Executive Director and Flight for Freedom organizer Jack McGowan; New York Stock Exchange Chairman and CEO Richard "Dick" Grasso; U.S. Representative Darlene Hooley; Oregon State Treasurer Randall Edwards; Portland School Board member Julia-Brim Edwards. Back row: unidentified; Portland Chamber of Commerce Chairman Don McClave; unidentified; Port of Portland Commissioner Cheryl Perrin; Republican gubernatorial candidate Ron Saxton; Bank of America Oregon and SW Washington President Roger Hinshaw; U.S. Bank President and Manager of Commercial Banking, Oregon John Rickman. Photo source unknown.

3. After the bell, left to right: Eugene Mayor Jim Torrey; SOLV Executive Director and Flight for Freedom organizer Jack McGowan; unidentified, Oregon State Treasurer Randall Edwards; U.S. Representative Darlene Hooley, New York Stock Exchange Chairman and CEO Richard "Dick" Grasso; unidentified; Portland Chamber of Commerce Chairman, Azumano Travel CEO and owner and Flight for Freedom organizer Sho Dozono; unidentified. Photo source unknown.

I LOVE A PARADE!

A large contingent of Oregonians, who traveled to New York in response to the mayor's pleas . . . appeared to be the most popular group in the parade. —*Long Island Newsday*

"You can give blood, you can give money, but to go there in person and let people know one-on-one how much you care . . . . We can't presume to know what they've been through, but we know what we've been through. —*Molly Cunningham, Milwaukie, Oregon*[1]

Many Freedom Fliers might have awakened on October 8 expecting their moment on ABC-TV's "Good Morning America" to be the day's highlight. Little did they know that the afternoon, marching in New York's Columbus Day parade, would surpass it infinitely, and be a major life experience.

Instead of the traditional Italian-American focus, this year's theme was "Columbus Day Parade Celebrates America." A number of groups had pulled out after September 11, and for a time city officials and parade organizers had debated whether to even hold the parade—would it be another target for terrorists? But Charles A. Gargano, the state's commissioner of economic development and president of the parade's sponsor, the Columbus Citizens Foundation, said that the parade would not only help the city get back to normal; it would also allow those lost in the Trade Center, the firefighters, and others working at the site to be honored.

The shift in theme was plainly evident. *Newsday* called it "more a display of American patriotism than a celebration of the life of its namesake explorer."[2] The Stars and Stripes outnumbered the Italian red, white, and green flags.[3] For the first time, the city's Bravest and Finest did not march; a single fire truck and a police cruiser took their place instead. They were otherwise engaged.

The crowd lined up three and four deep near the start of the parade at 44th Street, and thinned out north of Central Park South to the end of the parade at 70th Street. Organizers would later estimate that about 300,000 spectators lined the route, far more than at the usual Columbus Day parades. John Scruggs, a Portland police officer, said the parade route was as packed as Burnside Road during the Portland Rose Festival.[4]

Up to ten officers were posted at intersections. Some news sources called this a "heavy" presence; others said it was normal for the parade.

Back at the hotel, the somber mood of Sunday was gone as the Freedom Fliers sang in the lobby as they gathered to march. Sho Dozono had told people they could give away their "Oregon Loves New York" T-shirts to New Yorkers and later get replacements, so people were prepared to find just the right recipient. That they should be afraid, especially on the second day of U.S. attacks in Afghanistan, occurred to no one, it seemed.

At noon, they assembled at the parade's beginning, on 46th Street between Fifth and Sixth Avenues: at least 400 Oregonians, in a loose formation of rows of ten. [PHOTO 1]

"Now I feel alive again," Patricia Craugh, 78, told *The Oregonian*. Diagnosed with cancer, she had returned to the city where she went to secretarial school "1,000 years ago." Craugh came with her niece, Colleen Kruse from Vancouver, Washington, a 38-year-old mother of seven. Kruse had brought her aunt, who had become depressed after watching the nonstop coverage of the attacks on television. Now, as she walked to the starting point of the parade, Craugh sang along with a tune coming from one of floats: "You're a grand old flag, you're a high-flying flag and forever in peace may you wave . . . ."

Loen Dozono asked Kathleen Peters of Oregon (and New Jersey) to come to the front to help lead them in singing "God Bless America" and "Oregon, My Oregon," the state song, along with other patriotic tunes they came up with along the way. [PHOTO 2]

The Flight for Freedom marchers had been placed in front of rescue workers from Fort Myers, Florida, who had been working in the rubble.

"The place of honor that we were given was totally overwhelming to me," said Sandra Kempel of Portland.

The Oregonians were behind a marching band whose green-and-gold colors reminded them of the colors of the University of Oregon in Eugene. "They had talked before the parade about singing the Oregon and Oregon State fight songs, and found themselves walking behind a green-and-gold marching band," Doug Irving of KGW reported.*[5]

The band was New Jersey's North Hunterdon High School band, which, unlike one-third of high school bands, had not pulled out of the parade.** Rachel Boyle, a sixteen-year-old trumpet player in the band, told *The Oregonian* that seeing the Flight for Freedom participants made her less afraid of an upcoming band trip to Italy. [PHOTO 3]

"It's made me feel not so afraid to go, seeing all of them," she said. Many parents of the students at her school worked in Manhattan, and some had died on September 11.

Interestingly, when *The New York Times* reported on people assembling despite the nation's fear, the newspaper spoke to a New Yorker and an Oregonian:

"I think it's important that we aren't afraid," said Tim Amuchastegui, 50, a contractor from Klamath Falls, Ore. "Osama bin Laden has done what he's done and he may do more. We came all the way across the country to show support for New York."[6] [PHOTO 4]

The group waited at least an hour before they began to move. Newlyweds Lance and Marla Nuttman of McMinnville handled it their own way:

---

*When asked about his memories of the Flight for Freedom nearly twenty years later, New York Gov. George Pataki, who would speak to the group that evening and be showered with Oregon memorabilia, found that the green-and-gold combination stuck with him. "I remember green and gold. I've never been a great fan of the combination of green and gold, but I remember seeing it so much during that time, the fond memories give me an affinity for the color scheme that didn't exist before." (Interview with the author, May 13, 2021.)

**Some were fearful of being a target in such a large gathering. Others felt that a parade should not be held in a place that had become a funeral home.

❝We rush down there, late as always, and find a pretty organized bunch of Oregonians standing in seventeen rows of ten.

At this point, we're running on one half-liter of Mountain Dew and a CINNAMON BUN, so while everyone else stands in the middle of the street for the next hour or so, we grab a sub sandwich and chow down on the curb.

The groups were staged on side streets and then fed into the main parade so the group began their march on 46th Street, toward Fifth Avenue.

Initially, the parade was relaxed, and to the participants it just seemed like a fun thing to be doing on a gorgeous fall day. Every few steps they paused to sing.

But at the end of the block, turning from 46th Street onto Fifth Avenue, the Oregonians met with an emotional tsunami.

"I came around that corner and broke into tears," Deborah McGuire, wife of Portland Police battalion chief Mike McGuire, told *The Oregonian*. "I was completely overcome by the love."

"The crowd was going crazy. We thought, 'Who's behind us?'" said Jackie Young of Happy Valley, who then realized the New Yorkers were cheering for them. "And people were reaching out with their arms over that barricade."[7]

"It's beyond what any of us anticipated—Can you hear the people clapping?" Pamela Treece asked above the clamor of the crowd. "That's for us. That's for Oregon."[8]

Vera Katz leads the Flight for Freedom contingent. Photo by Betsy Ames

The rows had been pretty loose to start with and it didn't take long before the Oregonians had broken ranks to shake hands and share hugs and kind words with the New Yorkers on the sidelines.

To say the group "marched" would be a stretch. The New Yorkers who had courageously shown up in a time when any mass gathering was considered a terrorist target, were reaching out very literally to the Oregonians. It didn't take long before the Freedom Fliers had broken ranks to shake hands and share hugs and kind words with their fellow Americans on the sidelines.

"It was more of a ramble," said Betsy Holzgraf.

Kristen Dozono, who'd spent most of the trip inside the Waldorf at the hospitality table, remembered her experience at the parade vividly almost twenty years later:

> Everybody said, "We love you, Or-e-gone." Nobody could pronounce it. To march in the Columbus Day Parade, and people holding up signs that said, 'Oregon.' They knew we were coming and they said, "Thank you for coming."
>
> I could cry right now. That was tear-jerking.
>
> There were families. I think there was picture of me with an African-American family and I think they had a sign. I think I gave them my shirt.
>
> And my dad was like, "Everybody who gives away a shirt, we'll give you another shirt."
>
> We didn't have a budget for shirts. He would do things and figure it out later. And he would just spend it and find a sponsor. There was no pre-existing fund or budget or anything for these T-shirts, for those stickers everybody put everywhere.[9]

Nancy Waples gave her T-shirt to a young boy about fourteen years old just two blocks into the parade. "He said, 'Can I have your shirt?' And I said, 'You bet you can.' So I gave mine away right away."[10]

"We talked about it ahead of time, and we each looked for just the right person along the parade route to give it to," said Molly Cunningham of Milwaukie. "I mean, I could have given it to 500 different people. The streets were totally lined with New Yorkers, all of whom, it seems, were saying, 'Oregon, thanks for coming, we're so glad to see you. Thank you, we love you.' It was overwhelming."

Barbara Shaw felt the same way. "I could have given away 200," she said. "When I gave the T-shirt away, it was hard. If I'd known, I'd have bought ten . . . . They [New Yorkers] were so loving. They needed a lot of love." [PHOTO 5]

Amidst the cheers and exuberance, Portland School Police Officer Jerry Cioeta saw a woman crying at the curb and went over to give her his T-shirt. As he and Police Activities League (PAL) Director Beth Faulhaber chatted with her, they learned she had lost her husband in the September 11 attack.[11]

Waples estimated that in crisscrossing the street they walked eight miles instead of the two of the actual route:

> I thought we'd march along in a parade, that sounds like fun. But the minute we got down there and people started screaming at us and hugging us, we had so much fun. That was probably the most fun thing I've done in my life, was that parade. We had people call us over; you just walked back and forth . . . .
>
> "Hey, Oregone, come here," they'd say. Oh yeah, we were called "Oregone" all the time.
>
> You'd start to shake hands and they'd say, "No, give me a hug." And they'd say, "I just thank you for coming." One lady says, "I've never been to Oregon, but I'm going now. Next vacation I'm going to Oregon." . . .
>
> It was funny because my sister-in-law's from New York and she said, "New Yorkers are not like that, I don't get this. They don't go up to people and hug 'em on the street. I don't understand this."

Native New Yorker Vic Rini of Aloha:

> They shouted over and over again, "We love you, Oregon" and "Thank you, thank you, Oregon."
>
> Someone yelled out in a deep New York accent, "Orygone rules!"
>
> Three different times, someone sincerely asked. "Where is Oregon?"
>
> Many of us hugged and shook the hands of policemen and spectators. Some had tears in their eyes, as they yelled out, "We're glad you came!" and "Thanks for coming!"

Many of us also had a few deep swallows. We trudged up the street, young and old, waving flags and carrying banners. It was an emotional trip up Fifth Avenue that day.[12]

"Being able to look back for well over two blocks at the people from Oregon who were marching in that parade—it was amazing to me," said Philip Peters.[13]

"To a person, they said, "You are great." That was what was just amazing to me," said Betsy Holzgraf. One New Yorker told her, "I just found out where Oregon is and I want to move there!" Betsy particularly remembers the sea of white Oregon T-shirts. "That was so cool looking back, all those white shirts. Just because we were the first ones. To people in New York City, we were like a foreign country, that we came so far, and so many of us." [PHOTO 6]

"It's a real boost for us New Yorkers and it shows people out of state care for us," said Robin Merlo, a public relations representative from Manhattan, who yelled out a thank you to an Oregonian who passed.[14]

"Handing out pins, and giving hugs—the time went so fast that I hardly knew my feet were sore," said Judi Henningsen of Portland.

Flight for Freedom travelers got involved from the sidelines, too. In famous Harry's Bar "We stood up when the Oregon group went by," said Roger Meier, who was celebrating his fiftieth wedding anniversary with his wife Laura, along with another golden-anniversary couple, Mary and Melvin "Pete" Mark, chairman of the Melvin Mark Cos. commercial real-estate firm. "The whole restaurant stood up with us." Laura Meier was a native New Yorker and Roger, a fourth-generation Oregonian and descendent of the founders of the Portland-based Meier & Frank department store chain.

"It's one of the most fantastic experiences I've ever had," said Mark.

Along one block, viewers chanted, "Oregon, Oregon, Oregon," State Rep. Cherryl Walker reported to her local paper, Medford's *Mail Tribune*. "It was a tear-jerker."

"Even the transient people, the people sitting on the sidewalks, they said 'Thank you for coming,'" said Colleen Kruse.

Portland Police Frank Klejmont and Cliff Madison split the street, giving out lapel pins and police patches and saying hello to the police and firefighters. "The guys were thankful and appreciative," said Madison. [PHOTO 7]

At one point, the parade's grand marshal, New York Mets Manager Bobby Valentine, was on Klejmont's side of the street, and the Archbishop of New York was in front of St. Patrick's Cathedral, on Madison's side of the street. Madison asked Klejmont, "Frank, you want to switch sides of the street?" So Frank had great pictures of him with the reigning New York Catholic official and I got a picture of Bobby Valentine with me."* [PHOTOS 8, 9]

By the time she got to St. Patrick's, Michele Longo Eder of Newport found that one of those church officials had been "Oregonized." She wrote: "One bishop, atop his raiment, wore an "Oregon Loves New York" T-shirt that one of us had given him. Perfect."[15] [PHOTO 10]

Madison remembered another poignant moment: [PHOTO 11]

> There was a fireman in uniform pushing an old-fashioned baby carriage. He goes, "You know what saved my wife's life?" He showed me his new baby boy in the stroller.
>
> His wife worked on the 101st floor of World Trade Center and started her maternity leave that day. She wasn't in the tower when the explosion happened. You feel the eyes watering and the tears when you hear that story. There's things out there that bless you.[16]
>
> We're out there shaking hands, people are thanking us, it's heartwarming, and I see a tall, lean, black vet of the NYPD, and I say, "Hey, I just wanted to say thanks and let you know we're thinking about you." A guy was wearing an "Oregon Love NY" T-shirt and said, "Could I get a picture of you guys together?" He kept saying to me, "Come on, come on." He got in and someone else took the picture. And the guy gave him the shirt. And I look over at him and tears are running down his face.

Lance and Marla Nuttman: [PHOTO 12]

> Finally, an hour after we were told to congregate, we enter the parade. And it's totally worth the wait. New Yorkers line the streets

---

*Bobby Valentine was also the recipient of Jack Kostel's Oregon ♥ NY button, Jack Kostel reported in his "Flight for Freedom Memories." Kostel marched in the parade with Robert Skipper, retired Multnomah County Sheriff.

as far as the eye can see. Everywhere you look there's an American flag or Italian flag or Mexican flag, and everyone, everyone has a smile on their face. All of the sudden we go from overwhelmed country-mice to celebrities. New Yorkers screamed at us. Not what you would think, though . . . lots of "We love you Oregon!" and "Thanks for coming!" and "Yeah, Oree-GONE!" No one bothered to correct their pronunciation.

I gotta tell you, being in the center of a crowd and having hundreds of people shout their love and support for you is pretty darn emotional.

Mar and I were both struck with the diversity in the crowd. It's pretty cool looking into a crowd, at a chunk of fifty people standing on the sidewalk in a parade. And in that little microcosm, you could pick out every race, every religion, so many different walks of life. All brought together in this city, this immense city. Standing together on the sidewalk, a sidewalk they more than likely walked down a day ago on their way to work, watching a parade. We're talking Melting Pot, people. We've seen it. It's real. It's called New York City. It's called America.

New Yorkers get a bad rep. Sure, we were there under special circumstances, and we were having adoration spewed at us in stereo, but we were treated very well by the citizens. Shop owners and employees would find out we were from Oregon and spend five minutes asking us how our trip was. With the exception of one guy who mentioned his machete, we never felt unsafe. And I don't think he was threatening us specifically, I think he wasn't quite right in the head, so that's OK. It didn't matter, because he was a New Yorker, too.

So this brotherhood they report on the news, and how the City has changed, and how everyone is so much nicer to each other there: Yeah, that's all true . . . .

Something we both noticed in the city was the patriotism. Everywhere you looked, anywhere you looked, was an American flag. Or three. Or forty. At any point in our trip, in any neighborhood, you could close your eyes, spin around a couple of times, and when you opened your eyes you'd be staring straight at something red, white, and blue.

The parade route took us up 5th Avenue, from 46th St. up to 81st St. Half of the parade route took us parallel to Central Park. Coming out of the fashion stores on 5th Ave. and walking right into beautiful, lush deciduous trees blowing in the wind was a wonderful contrast. The huge park, which runs from 59th St. to 110th and is three blocks wide, brought just enough green (and fresh oxygen, no doubt) to make us just a tad homesick.[17]

Todd Davidson, executive director of Travel Oregon, nearly twenty years later:

> Of all my experiences—the reception, dinner in Chinatown, the opportunity to visit Ground Zero—of all the experiences, the one that has stayed with me the longest—it's become part of who I am—is the story of us marching in the Columbus Day Parade. And we had been invited to do that. There were T-shirts—I love NY—and 1,000 Oregonians in the parade all wearing their T-shirts *en masse*.
>
> The word had gotten out in the New York City media what these crazy Oregonians were doing. The people that were lining the parade route ... were yelling to us, "Thank you Oregon," "We'll never forget you, Oregon," "We'll come to see you." Constantly throughout the entire parade route, we'd hear shouts of how they'd never forget Oregon and what we'd been through in New York City.
>
> For me personally, I was near the edge of the group walking along that curve and there was an elderly woman who was standing there who was probably 4 ft. 9. She was sweet and she was shaking everybody's hand, all the Oregonians who went by, to stay thank you—a double handshake.
>
> Because I was near the back, when she took my hand, she didn't let go. She just hung on. She—all of a sudden, she pulled herself into me and I just put my arms around her and she started crying. She was sobbing, I'm crying.
>
> The parade is going by and I don't care. That was our moment together and she just kept saying, "You have no idea what you mean to this city, you have no idea what you've done for me. What you've done for this city."
>
> I've never forgotten that.
>
> That to me has become the emblem of the importance of travel, the power of travel. At its core, it's about forming new relationships. I have no idea how who she was and I'll never forget her, and that was twenty years ago.
>
> Sharing the moment with you, I started to choke up. It happens to me whenever I use this story in a speech. I just think about what it means.

My memory really does get eclipsed by being in that parade and that moment with that woman. At least—knowing where I was and how I lost all the Oregonians.

We stood there for twenty minutes together at least. She was really crying and I wasn't going to leave her that way. I was crying, too. I think we were there for each other.

The parade just kept going by and suddenly it didn't matter. Time just stood still for the two of us there, a New Yorker and an Oregonian grieving for what was lost and what we still had.

I'm looking back over a thirty-three-year career in the tourism industry in Oregon and if you were to ask me to name the most memorable moments, this is one of those most memorable moments. This is one of those times that it all came together.[18]

The Oregonian:

New York Police Detective Vinnie LaPenta, who was doing crowd control after two weeks of searching through the rubble at the World Trade Center site told *The Oregonian*, "It's sixteen acres of hell, that's what it is. The gap in the skyline is incredible. It can't ever be replaced. But we'll bounce back with the help of people like you in Oregon." . . .

Charles Brown, a 65-year-old New Yorker from Queens, was three floors under the World Trade Center when the first plane hit. "It was terrible, terrible. I'm so glad to be alive," he said, after cheering for the Oregonians . . . .

Oregonians spared no energy in hugging New York's finest—and one woman even attempted to correct an officer's pronunciation of "Orygahn."

The officer, Sidro Carrion, laughed with her—"I can't say 'Oregun,'" Carrion said. "I'm from New Yawk." . . .

Annette Belloni, 54, a lifetime New Yorker, stood near her East 62nd Street home and said she'll take her next vacation in Oregon. "It's really uplifting," she said. "It's the happiest part of the parade."

She was moved after Southwest Portland resident Jeanine Ford ran over to hug her . . . . "I could cry. I love New York, and now I love Oregon."[19]

Oregon State Treasurer Randall Edwards:

As a politician, I've been in a lot of parades, I literally have, and there was nothing like this parade.

Not only because the Columbus Day Parade's a massive parade, but the response people were giving this group was incredible and being one of the, at times, people who held the banner or walked next to the banner, it was just incredible. It was so emotional, exhilarating. Even though I was the state treasurer and it was suggested to go, but I went as a citizen of Oregon . . . .

I'm walking in the parade and somebody yells out my name from the sidelines. I yell, "What?" It's my chief of staff's daughter who started her freshman year in upstate New York, happened to be down in the city. So I guess the world is very small . . . .

That whole experience has proved to me that there was a real connection between a world-class, multimillion-populated city and a state that's on the far reaches of the same country. And for those who'd never been to New York or even those who had, the fact was, the event drew us together and I think that was really the intent of the whole trip.[20]

Columbus Day was the sixty-first anniversary—to the day—of Vera Katz's arrival in America. Two years later, she remembered:

I didn't realize that the parade was attached to the visit, so, we're assembling to get ready for the parade and I'm just standing there, and I'm, "My God, I came to this country sixty years ago as a refugee, an immigrant, with absolutely nothing, no hope, no future, except what we're going to make of it—and leading the delegation down Fifth Avenue." . . .

It was just mind-blowing for all of us, but I had that little extra personal piece.[21]

Debra-Diane Jenness and her family were determined to carry the state flag, which had been adorning the Waldorf's lobby: "It meant so much to us to be able to do that, to carry the flag of our State in representation and celebration of what was happening!"[22]

Mayor Katz: [PHOTO 13]

> There were a lot of Oregonians standing [along the sidelines] of the parade—there was an Oregonian that was holding up the state of Oregon flag and we left the parade and we hugged, we hugged anybody in uniform. It was a pure love and emotion that was shown both ways and I think that was the surprise for us, that they were as emotional about it as we were.

> You're walking down Fifth Avenue . . . . The fact that they even allowed us to be in the parade, and how people felt carrying the banner. Republicans, Democrats, there were people that ran for office and didn't make it, there were people who ran for office and made it, and all together and proud to be an American and proud to have made the trip and made the decision to make the trip. It was one of those extraordinary moments—that you could turn somebody's life around a little bit more, at least acknowledge that there are people in this world, and feel their pain.

Former mayor of Hermiston (pop. 13,154) Frank Harkenrider said the parade was the highlight of his life. In New York for the first time, Harkenrider marched with his wife, Bev,* hugging New Yorkers. "I'm just a little kid from the sticks," Harkenrider said. "It's the most unbelievable thing."[23] [PHOTO 14]

Nearly twenty years later, Baruti Artharee remembered the parade as a "peak experience."

> We had our T-shirts on—I still have that T-shirt, Oregon with the big heart Loves New York.

> There was so much pride in our group. The welcome, the reception, the appreciation that we were getting from the people on the street, both in the parade and as we moved around the city, patronizing the restaurants. We were the largest group at that time. We were there, we went out, we went to restaurants, even in the cabs, we were spending money, people were so enthused.

---

*At that time, Hermiston proclaimed itself the Watermelon Capital of the World. Bev wore a watermelon pin on her lapel throughout the trip. The couple were happily recognized by all the Freedom Fliers as two of the most enthusiastic and happy people in the group.

So walking in the parade, I remember the sun shining, and I was just beaming, seeing all the people on the side.

"Marching in that parade was something I'll never forget. And just the amount of love that I felt from New Yorkers from us being there," said KGW reporter Krista Vasquez. In addition to interviews with New Yorkers, she and colleague Scott Williams covered the parade as they were marching and captured sound bites from the crowd: "We love you, Oregon." "Thank you so much for coming." "We appreciate you so much." "You're New Yorkers now."

Twenty years later, Vasquez still has her "Oregon ♥ NY" T-shirt. Scott Williams, also looking back from the vantage point of 2021:

> The Columbus Day parade—I think that made the folks from Oregon, that really tied the knot, just because people from New York were so knocked out that that many people came from Oregon to support them. I really felt like that was a nice moment. The police officers and clergy, the fact that this little old state on the West Coast mustered all these folks to come—they're regular folks, they came to spend their money and do their darnedest to let folks in New York know that "Hey, we're all in this together." . . .
>
> You could see it on people's faces . . . . You can see some of those folks, they're that quintessential New Yorker, who is super hard and in a hurry or who looks like somebody who is in a rock band or a fashion designer . . . .
>
> New Yorkers, they've seen everything, but the level of emotions and emotional sort of outpouring was really, I don't know that I've seen anything like that since. It's year thirty-five in TV for me and I've seen a lot of stuff. I think it just broke down barriers, it broke down any sort of restraint.[24]

Mary Platt of Portland remembers being interviewed by a television reporter:

> . . . to tell our story and then—the sense of expressing with our physical being our support and to be able to see people and talk to people. On the West Coast, Oregon feels like such a safe harbor compared to what they had dealt with. To be able to come forward and step to the center of what they had dealt with.[25]

As if handing out T-shirts, buttons, and stickers wasn't enough, some Freedom Fliers brought other gifts for the onlookers. Vic and Dodie Rini of Aloha and their family handed out sympathy cards. And—Jackie Young of Happy Valley brought 100 copies of a post-September 11 poem by Max Lucado that she had received before the Flight for Freedom was organized.

> I had gone on the Internet, and I saw the poem by Max Lucado ["Do It Again, Lord!"]. And my dad was a pastor and I shared it with him and gave it to Daddy and he loved it.
>
> As I was praying and thinking what am I going to take, I thought, "I'm going to print out at least 100 copies of that prayer."
>
> We were just going along and hugging people, shaking their hands, just mostly listening. And the only thing I had in my bag in that parade was all 100 of those prayers. I'd see somebody, maybe three people that were up close and they would be crying, I could see the tears. I'd just point out that person and the crowd would shove them up in the front.
>
> I would say . . . "When you have a quiet time, [this] might help you."
>
> I gave out all 100 of those prayers. And prior to that, I didn't feel moved to give anybody a prayer. We didn't know we were going to be in that parade. And I could have given out 100 more easily. I came home and I was so amazed and I thought that was a godsend for sure.[26]

When the parade was over, the Freedom Fliers estimated that they had shaken hands and hugged about 400 people during the two-hour-plus event.

"Some people wouldn't let go of your hand," said Al O'Brien of Portland. "Some were even sobbing."

New Yorkers' losses were real, New Yorkers themselves were broken. Of course, everyone knew that, everyone was inundated by it. It was on the radio, on TV, in the papers. But the Freedom Fliers didn't just read about it. Instead of avoiding tragedy and sadness, they decided to go directly into the emotional trenches. They knew by taking the trip they were giving of themselves; but they had no idea how much they would be asked to give while they were there.

"There was one Italian gentleman in his seventies. He was standing at the side of the road, just sobbing," Medford City Councilman

A New Yorker Remembers

On Columbus Day 2001, *Oregonian* reporter Courtenay Thompson found Nancy Mechaber in the crowd:

"Hey Oregon, thanks for coming!" yelled Nancy Mechaber a Fort Lee, NJ, middle school teacher . . . . [She said that] on September 11 her sixth-graders had a clear view of Manhattan as the World Trade Center collapsed . . . . "These wonderful people from Oregon care about us."[27]

Nearly twenty years later, that day remains etched in Mechaber's brain. On her refrigerator, she still displays the photo her mother took of her on her way to the parade in the red, white, and blue earmuffs she'd made. "I wanted to go over to the Columbus Day parade. None of my friends would go with me because it was a terrifying time."

Nancy Mechaber of Fort Lee, NJ, on her way to the Columbus Day Parade. For twenty years, including a move to Florida, Nancy has kept this photograph on her refrigerator. Photo courtesy of Nancy Mechaber.

She and her students had watched the first plane hit the tower.

When the first plane hit it was just smoke. The kids in my class were like, "What's happening?" We told them we didn't know. When the first plane hit it could have been an accident because there was a small plane that ran into the Empire State Building years and years ago.

When the second plane hit, I let the children look out the window. This was something—a once-in-a-lifetime tragedy that happened. I just sat at my desk and cried. They were looking at me and some of them also cried, it was that emotional.

I had the radio on in the classroom. The library had a television and we could have gone in there, but I didn't want them to see it . . . . It's one of the first times that the school ever really went on a lockdown.

One of the children in my class, his mother worked in the ferry boat; they didn't collect any fares, they evacuated people. He didn't see his mother for two days. She just stayed at the terminal and slept and continued to work. One of the teachers in our school system lost her son in the plane that crashed in Pennsylvania.

The other thing was, living in Fort Lee, that's where the George Washington Bridge is and since they closed the bridges and the tunnels, no vehicle traffic was going in and out. They were walking from Wall St. All transportation was stopped from the city. They were walking to the GW Bridge and were triaged at Fort Lee H.S. It was a tragic thing.

It was really very strange to live there in this semi-warfare type place . . . . And we could smell the twin towers, the fires in the six months after.

Mechaber, who has visited Oregon—"so I know it's a beautiful state"—still has her "Oregon ♥ NY" T-shirt, too. "It was a nice thing to see, that other people cared about New York."[28]

Photo: Nancy Mechaber.

Ed Chun told the *Mail Tribune.* "We went up and gave him a hug and he said, "God bless.

"I guess you can call me a hug therapist," Guy Markham told *The Oregonian.* "We're not strangers anymore, we're all in this together."

"The parade, that was something I'll take to the grave with me," said George Haight of Woodburn. "We were definitely the hit of the parade. It was just thrilling."

When she got to the end of the parade, Betsy Holzgraf still had her extra shirt. In 2021, she recalled:

> I looked at this woman and she was about my age and she was all by herself. She cried and she said "You'll never know how much this means to us that you did this." I thought, "You're right."

> "I still get choked up thinking about handing my shirt to the woman.

> . . . "[H]ow divisive things are now and how mean it is. It's OK to be rude and cruel and say things—even if it's not really terrible things—the way people treat strangers in parking lots.

My impression of New Yorkers, in a hurry, rude, and I know some of that is true—it's a big city and rushing around, but how they became so human and went out of their way to thank us, the appreciation that was shown by everybody, from the taxi driver to the police to the homeless person and how amazed they were that we came so far and that so many of us came—their impression was [it was] the whole state.

"After the parade," remembers Nancy Waples, "we were just standing at the end of the parade by Central Park and this young Japanese man walked up to me and he spoke English, but it was very broken, and he said, "I wish I could talk to you, but I cry.

"I see so many bad things. This is first beautiful thing."

Barbara Shaw and Mary Mueller met a couple who thanked them for coming. Their maid's husband was killed in the attacks.

After the parade, the Oregon delegation assembled on the eastern side of the Metropolitan Museum of Art, on the marble steps, to have their picture taken. They unfurled their banners and flags in the brilliant sun of a clear fall day. Before dispersing into Manhattan, they sang a rousing chorus of "God Bless America!" and let out a cheer. Nearby another group spontaneously began singing "God Bless America," too. [PHOTOS 15-16]

In the following months, Mayor Katz would receive many letters and emails from New Yorkers. Some were about the parade:

Onlooker Susan Mollo: "One of the marchers ran over to me, threw her arms around me and held me. She then gave me her 'Oregon Loves New York' T-shirt—literally the shirt off her back! I also received a card from a 'Caring Family in Oregon.' On behalf of New York, I cannot thank you all enough for your love and support. I look forward to meeting you when my husband and I visit Portland."[29]

"You put a big plug in the hole in my heart," another parade-goer wrote.[30]

New Yorker John Barell sent Mayor Katz his perspective on the Oregonians' effort:

... "We sent our blood; then we sent our money. Finally, we had to send ourselves and here we are!" said one Oregonian. "We're about one thousand from all over Oregon; we're farmers, business folks, students, teachers, from all walks of life."

Led by Portland's Mayor, Vera Katz, the Oregonians walked proudly under a cloudless, deep blue sky. "We have to go to New York!" she said. They were marching in the middle of the Columbus Day Parade up New York City's Fifth Avenue—the grand parade route of all the cultures that came to America through Ellis Island.

. . . "Everybody has been out going to shows, shopping and eating in restaurants," said Jack McGowan, one of the organizers. "Our message is to get people back to flying, to leading their lives and doing the business of America. We wanted to show our fellow Americans living in New York that we are with them and, by this example, encourage others to follow our lead."

. . . "This is what it is, our flight from Oregon to New York, a Flight for Freedom," said one marcher . . . .

Before dispersing out onto the quiet and somewhat restive streets of Manhattan, they sang a rousing chorus of "God Bless America!" and let out a respectful cheer.

"This is America, right here!" exclaimed one of the organizers. The face of America shown brilliantly in the diversity of our armed forces marching in formation up Fifth Avenue, in the uniform services honoring those fallen in the line of duty at ground zero and in the smiles of the men, women and children of all ethnicities from Oregon.

New Yorkers at the parade shook their hands warmly and said, "Thanks for coming!" and the Oregonians beamed with the joy of having visited and for making the lives of New Yorkers brighter for their visit. The pioneering spirit of Oregon made New Yorkers realize that we are not alone, that we live in community and brotherhood with millions of Americans from the broad Atlantic across the great plains of wheat out to the Cascades bounded by the blue Pacific.[31]

Another New Yorker wrote: "I thank all of you for coming to my City, my home, and for letting the rest of our country know what true spirit is. I reflect so fondly at the memories of the parade especially when a kind woman took my hand and simply said, 'I love you. New Yorkers are such good people.'"

Oregonian Casey Walker forwarded this email from a former client in New York:

It was a big parade as usual but not as well-attended as in years past due to the Twin Tower tragedy. The news is there were 800 people from Oregon in the parade. . . . . Supporters of New York after the disaster . . . . It was one of our greatest moments . . . . I asked a marcher for an Oregon sticker . . . . He didn't have one, but we were so enthusiastic . . . . they found us a "big" Oregon Loves New York pin and gave it to my wife . . . . Meanwhile they were all laughing and crying at the same time. Soooo I was thinking of you because you are one of the few people I know in Oregon. I was also more than moved at the spirit of our country . . . . That these people would travel 3,000 miles to support this town in so much need of moral support . . . . I have always said and firmly believe that we were the greatest country in the world and we prove it every day. So this is a salute to your great state of "Oregon."

Thanks so much, and please spread the story around. It's something we will never ever forget.[32]

With the parade behind them, only one more official Flight for Freedom event remained, a reception at the Waldorf that evening. With the hourglass looking emptier, the Oregonians made the most of the time they had left.

"Another woman and I went through Central Park because I wanted to see the John Lennon Memorial," said Sandra Kempel:

We were on the east side of the park. We needed to go to the west side so we were trekking across the park, absolutely amazed at the small number of people out. It was incredible, it was a beautiful, sunny day, beautiful weather, perfect day to be in the park and yet there were very few people out.

The thing that impressed me the most was that we saw no fewer than six weddings going on and that was just in our trek going from east to west via Central Park, and just on our path. It wasn't a special spot.

I couldn't help but think that maybe some of these weddings were rushed so that they could actually . . . there was some impact on them personally realizing, some urgency that says, life is precious, maybe we should just—the park's perfect, let's do it.[33]

The Nuttmans, too, headed for Central Park:

While we're deciding where to go in the park, an NYPD cop comes up to us. He talks to us for a couple of minutes, telling us how great he thinks it is that we came to New York, how it really means a lot to everyone in the City. At this point, all three of us are tearing up. Marla and I were very touched by the sincerity of the officer, his wonderful welcome. The officer then asks if he can have our "Oregon loves New York" buttons, which we received from the Flight for Freedom hospitality desk. Sure, we say, and hand him both of ours. In return, he reaches into a pocket and gives us both a real-life genuine NYPD sew-on badge. After a few more teary interchanges, we take our really cool souvenirs and head into the park.

. . . [W]e get to the Great Lawn, a huge grass lawn where people throw Frisbees, baseballs, spar, or just take a nap in the sun. We're greeted once again in the Park by a few locals, who yell at us, "Hey, you two from Oregon? We saw youse on TV!"

The office buildings, apartments and stores overlooking the Lawn just add to the wonder, the amazing contrast and coexistence.

. . . . We then continue west to Central Park West, and see the Dakota, where John Lennon lived and died.

A short walk from there is the John Lennon memorial, in a part of the park called Strawberry Fields. A beautiful mosaic lies in the middle of the walk, where many different paths converge. This seemed one of the quietest parts of the park, where every few minutes someone would walk up to the memorial and pay their respects, or simply reflect quietly. No one steps over the memorial, and the flowers and candles which lay upon the mosaic look like they are placed there daily. A dozen or so people sit quietly, reading, thinking, and resting. In light of the state of the world, this was one of the most poignant sights we visited.

The incredible mosaic reads "Imagine."

. . . On our way out of Central Park, we heard hip-hop being played rather loud. Once we tracked down the sound, we discovered a group of Roller disco-ers. It reminded me that we were still in New York City. One thing can be happening on a street corner or a section of the park, and not 50 feet away something totally different is going on. There's so much culture everywhere.

We left the park then, and wearily trod to FAO Schwarz, the world's biggest toy store. OK, that was a bit of a disappointment (Vegas's was much better) . . .

Food was a priority, so we stopped at a little diner/ burger joint a block away from the hotel, which was recommended in our travel books. Good eats, but Marla noticed one thing. A burger in New York is pretty much a bun, cheese, and meat. We're pretty much burger connoisseurs, so the lack of condiments was shocking. We also didn't come across mayonnaise until McDonald's.[34]

Because I was researching an article for *The Oregonian*, I missed the parade. I wore my "Oregon ♥ NY" button and spent Monday in Tribeca, which, like Chinatown, had been devastated economically. There, I hoped to contact my friend Denise, whose phone had been down since the bombing. Unfortunately, her building's security was connected to the phone system so I couldn't buzz her.

In the meantime, I spoke with a man working to fix the phone network [Robert Fighera of the Bronx]. The Red Cross had given him two shaving kits from children. His voice broke as he showed me the newest one, from "Modile, Alabama," according to the carefully printed card inside. He'd already written a thank-you note to the first child and would do so for this little girl as well.*

I met a doorman, who said, "I want to thank you for spending the weekend here. We really needed it. It makes me feel terrific. It shows the best that people have to offer, and we're happy to get it."

Happening on the Tribeca Grill, well-known because actor Robert DeNiro is a co-owner, I asked if someone could speak with me briefly for my article. Director of Marketing Tracy Nieporent spent forty minutes with me. He and his brother Drew were Tribeca "pioneers" and they owned many downtown restaurants, all of which had lost business dramatically. The World Trade Center was the Nieporents' TriBakery's biggest customer. "We lost a lot of friends we saw every day," Nieporent told me.

The restaurant had concentrated on feeding workers for the first two weeks after the bombing, but that day New York Police Commissioner Bernard Kerik was having lunch there. Stretchers were stacked outside the restaurant, which had been a makeshift respite center for workers. "Things are beginning to return to normal," Nieporent said.

---

*This was part of a care package from Holy Family Catholic School in Mobile, Alabama.

PARADE

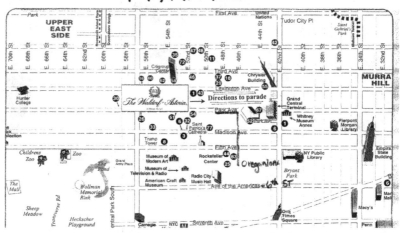

Parade: If you want to walk as a group, we are meeting in the lobby and leaving at 11:00 a.m.

For those of you going on your own…..Leave the hotel on the Park Avenue side. Turn left and walk down to 46th Street. Cross Park Avenue and walk west two blocks and cross 5th Avenue. We will be in spot #37, behind Walt Disney behind North Hunterdon High School Marching Band and Walt Disney. Gather on 46th Street, facing east, between 5th and 6th (Avenues of the Americas) at 11:30 a.m.

1. Courtesy of Sho Dozono

3. The Freedom Fliers found themselves before New Jersey's North Hunterdon High School band, which shared the school colors of the University of Oregon: green and gold. Photo courtesy of Loen Dozono

2. Betsy Holzgraf's travel journal. Her friends, the Ditewigs, wait for the parade to begin. Photo by Betsy Holzgraf

4. Tim and His Son, Tahn Amuchastegui. Photo courtesy of Tahn Amuchastegui

5. Elaine Franklin wasted no time before giving away her shirt. Photo by Betsy Ames

6. Photo by Betsy Ames

7. "I could tell them I worked in the 75th Precinct," said former New York policeman Klejmont in 2021 (at right). "So we immediately—just being a cop with other cops you have a bond. Here I was, I used to be a New York City cop. [Nearly twenty years later] It's bringing up all those emotions." Photo by Cliff Madison

8. Vera Katz and Jack McGowan speak with New York Mets Manager Bobby Valentine. Photo by Betsy Ames

9. The Klejmonts with the archbishop of New York. Photo by Cliff Madison

10. Monsignor Eugene Clark dresses up his vestments with an Oregon Loves NY T-shirt. Photo is the property of Oregonian Publishing Co.

11. *We're out there shaking hands, people are thanking us, it's heartwarming, and I see a tall, lean, black vet of the NYPD, and I say, "Hey, I just wanted to say thanks and let you know we're thinking about you." A guy was wearing an "Oregon Love NY" T-shirt and said, "Could I get a picture of you guys together?" He kept saying to me, "Come on, come on." He got in and someone else took the picture. And the guy gave him the shirt. And I look over at him and tears are running down his face.* Cliff Madison at right. Photo courtesy of Cliff Madison

12. *Mar and I were both struck with the diversity in the crowd. It's pretty cool looking into a crowd, at a chunk of fifty people standing on the sidewalk in a parade. And in that little microcosm, you could pick out every race, every religion, so many different walks of life. All brought together in this city, this immense city. Standing together on the sidewalk, a sidewalk they more than likely walked down a day ago on their way to work, watching a parade. We're talking Melting Pot, people. We've seen it. It's real. It's called New York City. It's called America.* Lance Nuttman of McMinnville. Photo courtesy of Lance and Marla Nuttman

13. Mayor Katz greets a New Yorker. John Ray is to her right. Photo by Betsy Ames

14. Frank Harkenrider hugs a cop. Photo by Betsy Ames

15. On the steps of the Metropolitan Museum of Art. Photo by Betsy Ames

16. A FLIGHT FOR FREEDOM PHOTO ALBUM

Photo by Thomas Monaster/New York Daily News/
TCA

Loen Dozono gives away
a T-shirt. Photo courtesy of
Loen Dozono

Mayor Katz and KPAM's Bill Cooper at St.
Patrick's Cathedral

Photo courtesy of Loen Dozono

Nobi and George Azumano. Photo
courtesy of Loen Dozono

Nadyne Yoneko "Meema" Dozono (Sho Dozono's
mother). Photo courtesy of Loen Dozono

16. A FLIGHT FOR FREEDOM PHOTO ALBUM

Photos courtesy of Loen Dozono

Photo by Betsy Ames

Photo by Betsy Holzgraf

16. A FLIGHT FOR FREEDOM PHOTO ALBUM

Bruce Samson takes a photo. Photo by Betsy Ames

Photo by Betsy Ames

Photo by Betsy Ames

Left to right: Loen Dozono, Elaine Franklin, and Karen Winder get in a little choreography. Photo by Betsy Ames

Photo by Lance and Marla Nuttman

Bruce Samson and Sho Dozono. Photo by Betsy Ames

16. A FLIGHT FOR FREEDOM PHOTO ALBUM

Photo courtesy of Loen Dozono

Photo by Betsy Ames

ALL-OREGON RECEPTION

"I don't know that I'll ever have an experience that comes close
to the intensity of that experience outside of having my daughter.
—*Organizer Nick Fish, 2003, on the Flight for Freedom*

The Monday night reception in the Waldorf-Astoria's Grand Ballroom
was yet another serendipitous event that surpassed any participant's
expectations.

Attorney Nick Fish had left that afternoon to make a court appearance in Portland the following day. In 2003 he said, "I was so focused
on my piece [of organizing] I couldn't see the forest for the trees . . . .
To this day, I kick myself for having that conflict." Before he left, Fish
confirmed that the Broadway stars he had lined up would be at the
reception—and he learned that Gov. Pataki had rearranged his schedule to be there as well. "At that time, the governor was managing the
crisis and he was in the middle of the firestorm himself . . . for him to
change his schedule so he could be at the benefit at the Waldorf was
huge. I think it would have been easier to get the president at that
time."

Nearly twenty years later, Gov. Pataki told me that he recognized
immediately the value of the Oregonians' effort. "Mary Ann Fish [Nick
Fish's stepmother] is the one who made me aware that Oregonians
were considering this and trying to put it together. She and I had been
friends more than thirty years at the time that this happened and she

was inspired by it and her enthusiasm certainly helped me to share that enthusiasm, but I knew right away that it would be an important event for the entire city."[1]

The KGW reporters didn't want to miss this event, which started at 6 p.m. and was scheduled to last until 8 p.m. "We ran ten blocks [to get there]," laughs Williams. "We had five minutes to get down to the hotel. I was running with the camera and we made it in time."

American Express sponsored the "All-Oregon Reception," and Jack McGowan served as master of ceremonies. Nick Fish wasn't kidding when he said Broadway "stars": Michael Crawford and Sarah Brightman, the stars of *Phantom of the Opera* and *Les Misérables*, performed.*

Speakers included Cristyne Nicholas, CEO of NYC & Company, New York's tourism entity; Mayor Katz; Cheryl Perrin, Port of Portland commissioner; Randall Edwards, Oregon State Treasurer; Organizer Bruce Samson; and a very special guest.

Native Portlander-turned-New Yorker award-winning bassist Mike McGuirk brought his jazz band. [PHOTOS 1-2]

American Express Vice Chairman Jonathan Linen presented Sho Dozono and Azumano Travel with the American Express Great Performers Award in recognition of "unparalleled customer service."

Guests were welcome, especially Oregonians who were living in the New York area. In 2003 Oregon State Treasurer Randall Edwards remembered:

> I had a good friend in New York who I called and asked, "Do you want to come to the closing?" . . . I had told her that we were coming and she saw some media things, but she works for MoMA [the Museum of Modern Art]. I had called her and said, "This

---

*Lance Nuttman wrote, "We're ushered in just in time to see two Broadway performers, one from *Les Misérables* and the other from *The Phantom of the Opera*. They sang "I Dreamed a Dream" and "Music of the Night," respectively. I've heard "Music" sung many a time, but this guy was by far the best.

"I looked into getting tickets to *Phantom* through the hotel's concierge, but after being quoted a $150 per ticket price through the hotel, we decided to just put on some nicer clothes and go get some hot dogs and pretzels at the banquet." Lance Nuttman, "Lance and Marla's Website, and www.geocities. com/lmnyc7. No longer available; printed out by the author in 2003.

group's coming out. Is there anything MoMA could do to offer to help? Could they give them a pass or get them into the museum?"

They gave them passes and they gave these gift bags. Then I said, "Why don't you come to the last dinner?"

She had no idea the size, the scale [of the group], I think she had seen a little bit on the TV that this group was in town, but she was just amazed at the size, the spirit, she was moved by the whole thing. She had no involvement, other than I called her. She hadn't really experienced it until she got to the reception.[2]

George Haight of Woodburn:

They probably had about ten stations of finger food around the perimeter of the ballroom and then tables set up. There was a little bit of milling around, but people seemed to already have their groups and being alone there and nobody [else] from Woodburn, I just kind of worked the crowd a bit.

There were a couple there from Hermiston. He was the former mayor of Hermiston and this was their first time in New York. Their eyes were about the size of dinner plates, sitting there in the middle of the Starlight Room . . . . This couple from Hermiston, they were all over the place. They got the biggest kick out of the glamor and the chandeliers and the hoopla, and then to have the governor of New York make his appearance . . . .

I visited with a fellow that was serving the hot dogs and sauerkraut and he said he was so glad to get the extra work, that in fact, he had come in directly from a funeral.

He had lost a relative in the towers and he had come to work after the funeral because he needed the money. There he was standing there serving us hot dogs and he lost it. He absolutely broke down and I put my arm around him and we walked around one of the big pillars so he wasn't in the direct line of eye contact and we both just stood there and wept.[3]

When Gov. Pataki arrived, Sho presented him with an Oregon Loves New York T-shirt, and Randall Edwards presented the Oregon state flag. Pataki put on an Oregon Ducks baseball cap, expressed his gratitude to the Oregonians, and talked about the hope they'd brought to New Yorkers.* [PHOTOS 3-4]

"When we New Yorkers were just a little down, a little bruised, the people of Oregon showed up to give us the boost we needed," he said.[4] Then he added:

> I want to thank all of you ordinary citizens from Oregon who understood that this was not just an attack on New York. This was an attack on America. By your presence, you're showing that America stands together. We're not going to give up our freedom. We're not going to give up our confidence . . . .
>
> While New Yorkers are proud of the spirit we've shown, we're incredibly proud of all of you. We are going rebuild our great city and make it better. We're going to rebuild our great state and make it better, and with the help of people like you from Oregon and around this great country. The best of America is ahead of us. We will win this war, and we will win the fight for the future of our children and their children's freedom.[5]

As with so much of what happened on that trip, everything fell together at the last minute. Kathleen Peters was asked to sing "right there on the spot," she said. "It was just a matter of flying and winging with it and everybody loved it and it worked out great. It was an honor to do it. Everybody was crying, too.[6]

Lyrics had been distributed to the crowd and together they sang "America the Beautiful" and "New York, New York." [PHOTO 5]

"I remember everybody holding hands around the room," said Kristen Dozono. "It was just—it was a feeling of unity in a time when the world was torn apart."

---

*Three years later at the Republican National Convention, Gov. Pataki began his speech by asking the Oregon delegates to stand: "The past few evenings we've spoken of September 11th, of our heroes and of those we lost. But there's a part of this story that has never fully been told. I'd like to tell it. After September 11th, our tourism industry was hit hard. Do you know what the people of Oregon did? A thousand people from Oregon came to New York and rented 1,000 hotel rooms so our workers and desk clerks and waiters could keep their jobs." ("Speeches from the 2004 Republican National Convention: George Pataki, New York, September 2, 2004," PresidentialRhetoric.com, http://www.presidentialrhetoric.com/campaign/rncspeeches/pataki.html.)

The hope was that many other cities and states would do the same or surpass Oregon in bringing people to New York City. "What a night," wrote Judi Henningsen. "California has stepped up to the challenge and are attempting to send 10,000 people to NYC. We will see."*

---

*No other city or state sent 10,000 persons. Irvine, California, mounted a group of 5,000 in November. See "An Idea Becomes Reality." After the trip, many cities and states contacted Azumano Travel to learn how to put together a similar effort and Azumano responded, but none of them to the author's knowledge mounted a trip.

1. Native Portlander Mike McGuirk and his jazz band. Photo courtesy of Loen Dozono

2. American Express Vice Chairman Jonathan Linen presented Sho Dozono and Azumano Travel with the American Express Great Performers Award. Photo courtesy of Loen Dozono

3. Oregon State Treasurer Randall Edwards presents New York Governor George Pataki, wearing an Oregon Ducks baseball cap, with Oregon state flag. Sho Dozono at back. Photo courtesy of Loen Dozono

4. New York Gov. Pataki addresses the All Oregon reception audience. Photo courtesy of Loen Dozono

5. Photos courtesy of Loen Dozono

5. Photos courtesy of Loen Dozono

Azumano Travel's Tina Harmon (far left) and Bill Harmon (far right).

Azumano Travel's Rick Love.

Mayor Vera Katz and U.S. Rep Darlene Hooley.

LAST MOMENTS

Thank you, Oregon.—Ellis Henican, *Newsday*, October 9, 2001[1]

TUESDAY, OCTOBER 9

Although the Flight For Freedom's official events were over, many participants still had a half-day before flying out. Here is how some Freedom Flyers filled those hours.

For the organizers, it was time to close up.

Almost twenty years later, in a meeting of the organizers, Elaine Franklin remembered: "It was a great team. Right at the end of this trip, everybody was gone and everybody was saying good-bye to each other and John [Ray] and I just looked over at each other went to each other and hugged, and burst into tears. The adrenaline. It was an exhausting trip, but it was so emotional and we just burst into tears.

"Two people who probably don't cry very much in their lives were just hugging and sobbing."

To which John Ray responded, "I remember telling Elaine, 'You're not so tough after all.'"[2]

When asked in 2003 why they had been able to pull off the Flight for Freedom when nobody else did—and many other entities had written to Azumano Travel with great enthusiasm to replicate the effort—Sho Dozono responded that:

> We in Oregon do believe that we, or in some instances, one can and do make a difference. Look at our history—the initiative and the referendum process was started in Oregon. The pioneering spirit that carried people across the plains and across the Atlantic and the Pacific Oceans still lives within us all. Whether they be old immigrants (came many generations ago) or new arrivals, we are the same. We believe that we have made a choice to be here and that we are part of that pioneer heritage.
>
> Secondly, we are a community—small enough to be in touch with each other. With a single call to action, we can all respond. And we are a caring community that responds well to others' needs or call for help.[3]

Portland-based Point West Credit Union Mortgage Manager Pam Getty and Administrative Assistant Sandra Kempel had arranged to visit a "sister" credit union, the Actor's Federal Credit Union in Times Square on Tuesday, October 9, in support. Like many New York-based businesses, the credit union was suffering as a result of the September 11 attacks. Kempel and Getty treated their New York peers to a pizza lunch and brought along Made-in-Oregon items ranging from maple syrup and cheese to a Point West CD opener, and a card signed by the entire Point West Credit Union staff.

"We heard that a lot of actors had been out of work since the tragedy, we know how it can impact the credit union, and we just wanted to show them that they are not alone," Getty told *Credit Union Times*.

"The unexpected visit from the people of Oregon was deeply touching," said Actors Federal Credit Union President/CEO Jeff Rodman. "More than once it brought tears to our eyes. Seeing people care enough to set aside their daily lives, pack up their bags and come here on a moment's notice to show support—I can't tell you how much it means to us."

For their part, the New Yorkers surprised Getty and Kempel with dessert—and an even better treat, an array of stars to thank them: Dominic Chianese, who played Uncle Junior in *The Sopranos*, Jason Danieley of the Broadway show *The Full Monty*, Hope Davis from the

Hearts in Atlantis movie, and TV series actors Gil Rogers, who played Hawke Shane in the *Guiding Light* and Ray Gardner of *All My Children*.[4]

Almost twenty years later, Kempel remembered clearly:

> Hope Davis told a story that really, really touched me. She went down and was working every day at a canteen that fed relief workers. She said she remembered specifically one man who would come in, he wouldn't talk, he was tired from working at the site, and dirty. He would point at the baked potato, wouldn't ask for salt, pepper, nothing, just pointed at the baked potato, went in the corner and ate, then went out and worked at the site.[5]

Kempel also remembered her major regret; they had to turn down Chianese's offer to take them to lunch or for drinks because they had to catch a plane. In the new post-9/11 world, they had to get to the airport three hours early![6]

AFCU also showed them a rehearsal hall, an audition studio, and introduced them at an Actors' Equity Association Eastern Regional board meeting, where they received a standing ovation.

"I'm a big Broadway fan, so for me to be able to meet and speak to these people and then for them to give us an ovation—it was just so emotional," said Getty. "After Dominic Chianese helped load our suitcases in the cab and as we were pulling away from AFCU I just burst into tears because everyone was just so good to us. This has truly been such an inspirational, meaningful trip."[7]

A trip to P.S.1, the Alfred E. Smith Elementary School downtown (8 Henry Street), brought together educators from Oregon and New York in a school with a full view of the Twin Towers and where children had witnessed the attacks and had been out of school for a period. Portland Association of Teachers Vice President Ann Nice, Portland Public Schools Board Chair Julia Brim-Edwards, teacher Diane Teelan, Oregon State Treasurer Randall Edwards, Ann Nice's niece, two children from Oregon, and others, brought gifts for the New York children. Nice brought cards, notes, and pencils from classrooms in Portland, while Brim-Edwards had gathered T-shirts with logos from schools in Portland. The group visited multiple classrooms.

This visit is a noteworthy example of people coming together from vastly divergent vantage points: the School Board and the teachers' union. "We didn't see eye-to-eye at all," said Nice, but as with the Flight for Freedom as a whole, they put aside their differences. "It didn't matter that Julia was from the school board and I was from the teachers' union. We went there because we really wanted to connect with these kids and let them know people in Oregon cared."[8]

Randall Edwards:

> It was really good talking to these kids. Obviously, they had been through a lot . . . . You could literally have seen the towers burning . . . . It was pretty horrific . . . .
>
> They had been impacted by the tragedy of the World Trade Center, but they were more interested in us. They were wanting to know where Oregon was, who we were, and why were there. And they were pretty impressed that we would come 3,000 miles to, in essence, be with them . . . .
>
> We were sort of an oddity . . . but I've got to say, it was really fun to see that they were pretty much normal kids, but you could tell that they had gone through something. There school had been closed so it had bene a little challenging for them. These kids had seen way too much . . . .
>
> We were prepped by their teachers. There were a lot of kids from— we were close to Chinatown and there were a lot of—I think one of the teachers told us that a lot of these kids' parents were illegals and so they didn't—they had been affected in a myriad of ways, finan- cially, and weren't able to get a lot of help. They were sweet, nice kids, and kids are kids, and they were pretty resilient.[9]

Ann Nice:

> I think it was one of the students [from Oregon] started talking at the beginning and said that—and she showed him [New York child] we flew from here to here to show people it was safe. And that people in Oregon and all over really care about people in New York and want you guys to know that we're sorry that this happened. The kids related—the kids related to the younger kids in a really neat way . . . .
>
> We weren't there a long time because they were trying to keep school as normal as possible, but I went over and talked to one of the teachers. Because the teacher was letting us talk to the kids and stuff, I asked her about [her 9/11 experience]. She had tears in her eyes and she said, "I was here until really late because we had to get

our kids to their families. I had to walk across the Brooklyn Bridge to get home because I didn't know if my family was OK." There were moments like that that took your breath away.

Other Oregon teachers were honored on network TV. Retired teacher Patty Deines's daughter was dating the producer of the ABC morning talk show "The View." Her former colleague, Betsy Holzgraf, joined her:

> Everybody was so welcoming. The cab driver wasn't sure which building, and we are double-parked and there is a policeman on the corner. He leaves the cab, goes kitty-corner, talks to the policeman, comes back, finds out where to take me. Nobody was honking and I thought, "It's going to go back to the way it used to be. Now, it feels so good."

The celebrity continued during the taping. Holzgraf:

> It's funny because a friend of mine was home and just happened to watch it. I'd never heard of "The View." We weren't in the bleachers; we were on the floor on some folding chairs and midway through they had us stand up for the cameras, just Patty and I, and we had our badges and again, just the gratefulness of everybody.[10]

Mount Hood Radiology Tech Nancy Waples of Gresham:

> On our last morning there, our brother and sister-in-law and Mother and I and Michelle wanted to go to St. Patrick's Cathedral. When we got there, they were setting up for a memorial service for a fire chief. We saw some people going in, but the street in front of the cathedral was lined up—hundreds, across the street along Fifth Avenue, so we knew it was fairly soon for the memorial service to take place.

> We walked up to the door and a policeman stopped us and said, "The building's closed." . . .

> Then we heard, "Oregone, what are you doing? I just want to thank you for being here."

> We said, "We were hoping to go to the cathedral, but it's closed."

And this man said, "Not for you. You're Oregone, and you get what you want in my city. Come with me."

He took us around to the side door. The policeman said, "You can't go in."

He said, "Yes, they can, they're with me." He spent about a half hour with us. He showed us some places that people don't usually get to see. He pointed out some special stained glass windows and behind the altar, where the crypts are, he showed us all around . . . .

When we went to thank him, he said, "You don't thank me, I thank you."

His name was Officer Beggins. He was a New York cop, but his beat was the cathedral, and he'd been there for about ten years.

At the same time, they were setting up for the memorial service. After we came back out, we stood there and watched the procession. After the high of the parade, it kind of brought us all back to why we were there, watching that funeral procession.

From outside, the thing that really struck me is, you know how long the blocks are north and south? The block across the street from the cathedral was lined five, six, maybe eight deep with firemen. There were hundreds of firemen lined up along the street and right in the middle they had a fire truck with a tall extension ladder and a big flag hanging from that and then the procession started about a block away.

They had bagpipers playing "America." First, there was a motorcycle escort and then the bagpipers and then Knights of Columbus group and then the long limousine with his wife and two or three kids. The limousine pulled up in front of the church, they were escorted in, and we had to leave because our plane was leaving. The streets were blocked off for three blocks long for the procession.

We think we even saw Mayor Giuliani real briefly. He pulled up on the side door.

That was another thing that [our New York friend] Ellen said, that she had been to six or seven memorial services the week before. When you think of how many people and how many funerals . . . .[11]

After the closing reception, the Jenness family had two more days in New York, which they wanted to fill with visits to the police and fire stations and spending time with New Yorkers. Tuesday was filled with adventures and a synchronicity that marked everyone's experience in the city:

> Tuesday we got up and my husband decided he just HAD to ride the subway. So, since we could not get out to Ellis Island (it was closed), we decided to go down and take the Staten Island Ferry so we could at least go by it and get some pictures. So we took the subway to do this.
>
> Now this was a true New York experience!! Purchased a "pass" for the three of us, and then could not figure out how to use it in the little swipe it thru thingie. No one around to ask, of course. Finally got it to open the gate, and I went in, and found myself stuck half-way thru the turnstile! Eventually we figured it out, got all three of us through and on to the subway.
>
> Man, it's dark underground there!!! Twisting and turning all over!
>
> Seemed like we were going on forever—which, we probably would have, if we hadn't said something. We were on the right train, but going the wrong direction! So, we got off at the next station, crossed over the tracks, and got back on the train going the CORRECT direction to Staten Island. The New Yorkers seemed amused by our mistake but were happy to direct us properly.
>
> We waited about fifteen minutes for the next ferry to come in and hopped on board; this is a free ride, and one of the best attractions in New York. There was a Coast Guard ship guarding the Statue of Liberty, but we were still able to take some very good pictures. There were also the barges going back and forth hauling debris from the World Trade Center site over to the New Jersey site where it was being sorted for recycling. Again, a very emotional scene . . . .
>
> [At the New York Stock Exchange, where they were unable to get into the visitors gallery.] We were visiting with a police officer, who then said he personally would walk us back up to the subway so we'd get on the right train going the right direction. This was very nice of him.
>
> We got off at Grand Central Station and decided to walk the last four or five blocks to our hotel, but we wanted to see all of the remodeling in the main station. All you can say is: WOW!!! It was beautiful, stores, restaurants, all pretty neat.
>
> We left there to walk back to the Waldorf, and as we went to cross the street, this huge Lincoln Towne Car turns the corner, and the

driver is yelling at us, "Hey Oregon, Hey, Oregon, come over here a minute!"

He pulled over to the curb, so I walked over to the passenger side of his car, where the window was open. He said, "I've got these two tickets for the Knicks/Spurs game tonight in Madison Square Garden and I can't use them, I want you to have them, it's my little way of saying THANK YOU for having come to New York."

I thanked him and he said, "NO, Thank YOU, Oregon!" and he drove away.

These were $150 tickets each, about six rows off of the floor! And the game was in a few hours. Well of course, it was sold out and we could not get a third ticket for our son; we have a family rule, we do things together, but we were not going to let these tickets go to waste.

So, we walked back inside Grand Central Station and my husband started talking to one of the police officers there. He said they'd been working fourteen-hour days, six days a week, and he was just getting ready to end his shift. So my husband asked him if he was a Knicks fan. He said he was a HUGE fan! So my husband asked him how he and his wife would like to go to the game tonight, and offered him the tickets.

The Officer couldn't believe it. He whipped out his cell phone and called his wife to check with her; she said, "You can't get tickets, that games been sold out for weeks!" (We could hear her through the phone).

He said, "No there are some nice people here from Ora-Gone that want to give us two tickets for the game!" She said she'd be ready in ten minutes, and he said he was on his way home. It was a great feeling, someone wanted to do something special for us, which he did, but because we also couldn't use only two tickets, we passed the kindness along to someone who probably needed the night out more than we did. So the good continued to circle around.

We left Grand Central and headed back to our hotel, stopping via the United Nations Building. You could not get close, it was all blocked off with trucks full of sand. But the three police officers guarding one entrance said if we sort of walked down behind this planter and wanted to take a picture, he wouldn't be able to see what we were doing, you know. So we walked on down there and shot a few pictures, and then walked back to visit with him and his two buddies.

We were all wearing special pins, one of a flag, of course, and one with flag decor on it but it was in the shape of the USA. One officer asked me where I had gotten that one; I told him at one of the gift shops inside the Waldorf. He said he wanted to get one for his wife, as she had lost her sister in the Tower attacks. I took my pin off and gave it to him to give to her.

He said, "No, No, I can't let you do that, I'll just tell her where to get it, she comes into town every day anyway." I insisted, saying to take it home and tell her it was from someone from Oregon.

He said, "OK, but let me pay you for it."

I said "NO!!! Just take it home to your wife and tell her it's from someone from Oregon who came to New York because they cared." This big, burly police man then wrapped me in a bear hug and cried. Of course, I cried, too.

That pin was meant for his wife, I knew I could get another at the hotel. So we finally went back to the hotel. I went to the gift shop and guess what? They were all sold out!!!! I said, "Oh well, my pin went where it needed to go."

The shopkeeper told me to come with her to one of their other stores in the lobby, she thought she may have some more there. So I did, and she did, so I was able to replace it. I also bought all the rest of the ones like that and have shared them since we returned. It is things like this, a hug from a police officer, tears, that made this trip so worthwhile . . . .[12]

On their last final, full day, the Jennesses felt they "needed" to see St. Vincent's Hospital in Greenwich Village, the trauma center nearest to the Twin Towers. At St. Vincent's medical teams had waited for bombing victims on the morning of September 11, the World Trade Center victims that never came (although hundreds of the injured did arrive there). The hospital had been, in fact, superbly prepared, having put in place a crisis plan designed after the 1993 World Trade Center bombing. St. Vincent's became known for its "Wall of Remembrance," the twenty-five-foot south wall of the facility on 11th Street, on which were posted the flyers of the missing. In 2010, *The New York Times* recorded some of them in its tribute when St. Vincent's made the decision for financial reasons not to create a permanent display:

Have you seen Elizabeth Holmes? She was in 2 World Trade Center. How about Lindsay Herkness? He was on the 73rd floor. Maybe you know of Lucy Crifasi? She was wearing a striped blouse, black and olive green. Please, please, what about Thomas Edward Galvin or Harry Glenn or Joan Donna Griffith? "Still searching, never forgotten," said the flier for David Marc Sullins, a paramedic killed while trying to rescue injured people.[13]

The flyers would stay up, under plexiglass, until 2005. When they came down, the loss was commemorated in 2008 by an Oregonian in a short story, "Bern," for *The Georgia Review*. Tracy Daugherty taught writing at Oregon State University and was doing research in New York. "I get shocked by my own reaction," said Daugherty "Why did I feel the loss so. keenly? I don't know why. But I did."

Jenness captured her experience at the Wall of Remembrance:

We had to see "The Wall" . . . . the Wall of notes, photos, the "have you seen ???" messages . . . . took our breath away, it was so LONG. It took me 12 photo images to get it all in, and even then, that wasn't enough. A time for prayerful remembrance.[14]

Barbara Shaw and Mary Mueller, who had met on the trip, spent time near the World Trade Center site. They passed the McDonald's on Chambers Street where the store's owner operator, Lloyd Frazier, saved a police officer's life by opening the door and pulling the officer in when the towers came crumbling down and the streets were engulfed by blackness. It became known as "Hotel McDonald's" because hundreds of fire fighters found refuge there and even rested on the floor and throughout the store. Frazier and his employees volunteered their time in his mobile unit outside the store and served over 700,000 free meals to fire fighters, police officers, emergency responders and rescue workers. (Frazier died due to 9/11-related lung cancer in 2006.)[15]

Shaw and Mueller also stopped at St. Paul's Chapel, the little church built in 1766 across the street from the Twin Towers that had earned the nickname "the little chapel that stood." St. Paul's, which was unharmed in the attacks, was engaged in a relief ministry to rescue and recovery workers that lasted for nine months.

Memories of St. Paul's remained vivid to KGW Videographer Scott Williams nearly twenty years later:

> The entire church ground was full of papers that had come from the surrounding buildings—papers were blown out the window from fire and they'd all landed in this one churchyard. That's a really surreal thing to walk into. And until you get to a place—and let's face it, nobody else has had that sort of incident, you can't really imagine, and there wasn't a lot of video shot of surrounding buildings that I saw. Until later. I went back and looked for the aftermath, because it was so chaotic. But just the amount of damage to surrounding buildings and neighborhood places that were closed.[16]

St. Paul's was also the site of an ongoing presence of the Flight for Freedom, thanks to Tahn Amuchastegui and his father, Tim: [PHOTO 1]

> As we were walking around Ground Zero, we passed St Paul's Chapel of Trinity Church. There were banners and all manner of remembrances hanging on the fence and there were a few NYPD officers near the fence. My dad felt compelled to speak with the officers and ask if he could hang his Oregon (Hearts) NY shirt along with the other items. They said, "Sure," and I snapped photos from across the street of him hanging the shirt and with one of the officers. He had a good chat and thanked them for their service and we went on our way . . . .
>
> My dad passed in 2015 and this trip was one of the best memories he and I shared for many years.[17]*

When Lance and Marla Nuttman went to St. Paul's, they were surprised to see an "Oregon Loves New York" shirt on the fence and captured it on film. [PHOTO 2]

That night, Lance and Marla fulfilled one of their top priorities: seeing "Late Night with Conan O'Brien." They'd begun the day in line (or "on line," as they say in New York) at NBC and "snagged" some tickets for a show with Snoop Dog, Edie Falco, and Trisha Yearwood. Before the show, they had dinner at the Hard Rock Café, whose staff left something to be desired in the rock 'n' roll knowledge department.

---

*Read the rest of the saga of Tim Amuchastegui's shirt in "The Impact" chapter.

We chowed down at the Hard Rock Café, where the manager didn't know who any of the members of Queen were. We asked him if there was any Queen memorabilia, to which he responded, "I think there's something from that singer upstairs somewhere." Sheesh.

Then off to the show:

But the second sketch featured the one and only Preparation H Raymond. You see, Preparation H Raymond wanders the globe handing out Preparation H to those in need. Basically, a guy in big, funny ears comes out, throws boxes of Preparation H into the crowd, sings about inflammation and the like. The cool part was that one of the boxes found its way into Marla's hands—Raymond actually threw it right to her.

After seeing the taping of the show, we stowed our really cool (and soothing) souvenir and walked to the Hard Rock Café for some grub.[18]

Twenty years that Preparation H is in Marla's souvenir box. "I'm happy to say we never opened it and used it," she says.[19]

On the return home, at the airports what had been new and unfamiliar security on the trip east had been stepped up. Nancy Parrott of Azumano Travel remembered "more security, especially on the return trip. In New York in particular—even arriving there, you saw military personnel with guns. It was very apparent, very military style."[20]

A HOT SPOT

Tahn Amuchastegui and his father, Tim, lucked out. One night they:

. . . finally found a place that was open to eat as it was kind of late. We waited quite some time to be seated and then they sat us right next to the bathroom. After a while we noticed folks were looking at us as if to try to figure out who we were. Then groups of two to four women would stand and walk by us to get to the ladies room. We noticed after a while that a great majority of the women seemed to be models. Somehow we had wandered in to one of the hot spots and we ended up having one of the best seats in the house. :)[21]

When they returned, Lance Nuttman created a website recording their trip, his first to New York City. Here are just a couple of Lance's observations of the details that make the city the city.

The Subway. The subway is just plain cool. Once you get the hang of it, it's really the best way to travel. It didn't seem unsafe or intimidating. You just keep your head down, and go where you want to go. The subway cars didn't seem any more dirty than a MAX train in Portland or a bus, and the graffiti was minimal. I quite liked it, and could see myself commuting to work that way. I found myself wishing they would put them in back home.

Metrocard, if you're not using one, you're a chump.

Lance also got the lingo down: "We ride the #4 Green Line uptown to Grand Central. OK, I'll admit, I don't need to be that specific, but talking like that makes me feel really cool. So you got a problem with that?"

"No Standing" Signs. You'll also notice the "No Standing Anytime" signs. These signs are all over the City, downtown, uptown, midtown, everywhere. No one is allowed to sit down anywhere, it seems. Ever. Maybe that's why it always seemed so busy there, no one can ever stop and just stand around and look at things. So next time you see footage of New York City on the news, and all the people are walking intently down the street, just remember.[22]

At the airport, the United Airlines ticket agent recognized Jack Kostel from his appearance on TV the night before—Oregonians were on TV a lot during this trip:

> . . . so after she charged me $100 for changing my ticket, she gave me two coupons worth fifty dollars each. All is well with the world. After check-in she took me up to the Red Carpet area where I could relax for about thirty minutes. I visited with a lady from upstate New York and then recognized the man working on a crossword puzzle as George ("The Paper Lion") Plimpton. As he was getting up to go, I went over and introduced myself and got a picture with him, which the lady from upstate New York kindly took for us.[23]

When Betty Long of Aloha's watch and pin were misplaced going through security at a New York airport, she responded with kindness, which led to some much-needed fun:

> I had to speak with the Security Supervisor who looked very tired — stressed — sad. (A lady in her forties, attractive, dark hair — wish I knew her name) She found them in a drawer at Security and gave them to me and she said, "That will be $5,000!!" in a Brooklyn accent with a dry sense of humor.
>
> I started to walk away and then stopped and said to her, "Wait! I do have something for you." She looked at me as I pulled out an "Oregon Loves New York" T-shirt that was on top of my carry-on bag. I held it out to her so she could read the front and she took it — held it up as high as she could, facing the lettering out towards all the people coming through security and said really loud, "GOD BLESS OREGON!!"[24]

Barbara Shaw was lighthearted about leaving her camera at La Guardia. "The cannolis made it, but the camera didn't. My kids said, 'You can get another camera. The cannolis are great.'"[25]

And then there was the turtle at LaGuardia. Jane Meskill of Portland:

> When we came back to the airport that's when things really changed. I had like a little live turtle I'd gotten in Chinatown. You used to be able to carry things on the plane . . . .
>
> We had to put everything on the conveyor belt, go through a check-point. The National Guard was there with machine guns. I burst into tears, too.
>
> When we got on the plane in Portland that wasn't there. I don't remember having done that before. I don't think we'd had the shoe bomber yet. We weren't taking off shoes, weren't putting things on conveyor belts.
>
> They put him [the turtle] in a little plastic box. He was in a plastic box on this conveyor belt.[26]

For the Jennesses, the flight home would be a challenge, given the new, supposedly tight security:

They had seated us together in the last row of the plane. No problem. We showed our photo ID's and boarded . . . . . . .only to find three people already sitting in our seats. They were all elderly and appeared Hispanic.

We got a flight attendant and showed her our boarding passes. She asked the people seated for theirs, and was given them. The boarding passes THEY gave her had OUR names on them!!

Now, tell me this; in light of everything and the added security, how did three other people get on the plane with boarding passes with MY family's names on them? Obviously their photo ID's would not have matched???? And they still had their original TICKETS!!! Something was very, very wrong here! . . .

Normally the rest of the flight would be uneventful, but things were not done "happening to us" it seems. We had been in the air about fifteen minutes when a woman seated two rows behind me went into a Grand Mal Seizure and went unconscious. They called for medical help, and a Dr. came to assist. She would not come to; stayed out cold. Then had ANOTHER seizure. The Dr. stayed with her, and then the Captain came back to check on things. (Our flight was from LaGuardia to Chicago to Portland to Redmond) Next thing we know, we are told we are being diverted to Buffalo, NY, so this ill person can be taken off the plane.

I hate to say this, but the thought did cross our minds: is this person really sick, or is this a diversion?? We never would have thought anything like that before Sept. 11th. We landed safely in Buffalo to a waiting ambulance, who immediately off-loaded this lady and the people with her.

Accompanying Mayor Katz's group on the way back to Portland, KXL reporter Chris Sullivan recounted his last moments in Manhattan:

We sang "God Bless America" one last time as we approached PDX. Our whirlwind, four-day trip to New York is over, but the memories, friendships and emotions will last a lifetime.

. . . Arriving at Kennedy Airport for the flight home, I thought they had reinstated curbside check-in. There was a line of people with luggage outside the terminal, but this was the line just to get in. If you didn't have a ticket, you didn't get in. Soldiers with M-16's just inside the door watched over the x-ray machines and metal detectors. We were searched and patted down. Security is definitely the priority in New York.[27]

On the return trip, Loen Dozono observed a lighter, freer Mayor Katz: [PHOTO 3]

> We all went home on the same plane together. On the way over [to New York] she was very reserved and protective because she'd get besieged by people wanting to talk to her. On the way home, the flight attendants passed out pillows and Vera was passing out pillows to everybody on the plane. It was that much of a release and it was a beautiful thing—very, very special.[28]

Portland Playwright Michael Phillips:

> New York City is truly amazing. The people I met were out and about—going to theatre, eating in restaurants, going to work. There is humor in New York, there is music, art, compassion. There is hope. And for me, it was an extraordinary, life altering experience to be there, to share my time with them, to hear their stories.
>
> In the midst of worrying about war, about possible breaches of civil liberties, about uncertainty of where this will all lead, let us all remember those who died one month ago today, and think of those who were left behind, yet changed forever.[29]

Lance and Marla Nuttman had adventures, too, which Lance captured on the couple's website:

> We had been craving Mexican food the whole trip, and we'd spotted a Chevy's (our favorite in any state). So we hailed a cab (our first) and headed out.
>
> That's where the trip got real interesting.
>
> We took the time to admire some artist's work, done in spray paint. Marla was just about to buy a cool skyline picture, when she noticed that she no longer had her wallet. Left it in the hotel room? Nope. Dropped it in the street? Nope. Fell out in the cab? Well, at first that's what we thought, but after putting everything together, we're pretty sure her wallet was "lifted." It was 9 p.m., Times Square, and as much as we'd like to think we'd been acclimated to and integrated

into the City, we're still a couple of easy marks. We never did get our Mexican food.

"I could live with the loss of $100 out of my wallet, and we stopped my debit card, but it was my driver's license to get back on the plane. We were "NYPD Blue" fans at the time so it was kind of cool."

. . . The lost money and cards were minor worries, however. The biggest horror was the fact that in less than eighteen hours, we had a plane to catch. Couple that with the fact that we were leaving on a jet plane on the one-month anniversary of the 11th, toss in a healthy dose of incredibly tight security, and we've achieved Problem. Word was from the travel agency that they weren't allowing people past the terminal without picture ID, let alone on an airplane. The travel agency told us we were pretty much SOL, good luck.

The airline suggested we file a police report, and get as much information as we could, birth records, the works. So we enlisted help from Marla's sister, Lisa, who scanned about and sent us a faxed copy of every form of ID (badge from work, Costco card) anything with a picture, every credit card . . . even her library card. Marla's dad, Leon, got on the phone with the DMV, airline, and anyone else he thought might be able to help us.

Then we headed down to the 17th Precinct.

So we walk into the 17th to inform the guys on the job that some dirtbag skel is out there roamin' the streets and we want the whack-job brought in. They helped us out, told us we needed to head over to the 14th, the Precinct where the wallet was lost. Apprehensively, we hail another cab, this time making sure we get a receipt (which was asked for in the first cab, but denied due to a feigned language barrier). Just shy of midnight, we pull up to the 14th Precinct.

The 14 is in a much seedier part of town. Times Square area again, a bit southwest, Midtown South, 35th Street. We step in, and it's like something out of NYPD Blue, complete with the unwashed junkie being booked at the front desk and tiled walls. We were asked if we needed some help by a pretty young beat cop (not without the strong Brooklyn accent) who looked like she walked right off the set. We're taken into the PAA's room and we meet PAA Barksdale. She was very helpful and informative, and calm, which helped us out. We filled out the report, got ourselves a case number, and bade our farewells to the helpful NYPD. They were being extra nice to us, extra patient because we were tourists.

What fate awaits our heroes?

Will they be allowed passage home?

Will they have to rent a car, forcing Lance, the only one with ID, to make the cross-country pilgrimage?

Will Conan O'Brien hear of their trials and come to their aid?

Will Lance and Marla have to revive their Vaudeville routine one last time to earn gas money?

Escape from New York

Four pages of faxed info awaited us at the hotel's business center.

We bought a few final souvenirs, chowed some fast food, and a guy in an elf costume handed us some coupons. All in all, your typical New York City morning.

A nice man named Jim asked us if we'd like to share a cab to the airport with him and his father, Jerry. We had actually crossed paths with Jim two weeks earlier, in the Travel section of Borders in Salem.

A fifty-foot line of travelers three deep awaited us at the Delta terminal. I'm not sure if this is still true, but at this time they were only allowing ticketed customers into the terminal. This was the first place they wanted to see picture ID. Our first test, so to speak. When we reached the front, we explained our situation to the girl, and were allowed in without incident.

Whew.

Check-in. We again explained our situation, presented our documents, looked upon the strapping young buck in Delta-blue with the full weight of our hopes gleaming in our bloodshot eyes . . . and he smiled and wished us a good flight.

[Marla in 2021: I think the TSA guy, they weren't what they are now. That was right at the beginning of that and so much has happened since then. They were still getting used to the added security. They wouldn't let me on now, even with all that faxed stuff.][30]

WOO HOO!!!

To be truthful, we got the feeling they really didn't want to deal with something like that at that point. It was pretty much easier to just let us through. Plus, we did have a police report, four pages of info, everything they could have possibly asked for. Unscrupulous types usually don't come so well-documented.

We were way early, a couple hours, so we ate lunch at a golf-themed airport restaurant and chatted with other Oregonians.

Our trip. Our vacation. Our adventure. Our honeymoon. The feeling of patriotism in a crowd of thousands who come together on a crisp fall day to see a parade. The constant bustle of the traffic on every street, that first view from the airplane of the City's monstrosity, that same view's absolute beauty, brides and grooms at Bethesda fountain, worshipping at the NBC altar, stepping onto that first subway car, Chinatown at night, pictures and flowers taped to a streetlight, a guy salsa-dancing with a mannequin for spare change, a NYC Police precinct, the Staten Island Ferry.

So much more, so many signal experiences. I really think everybody should see New York City at least once. This trip widened our view of America and our fellow citizens. We're so glad we were able to see the Capital of the World.

1. Tim Amuchastegui hangs his "Oregon Loves New York" T-shirt at St. Paul's Chapel. Photo by Tahn Amuchastegui

2. When Lance and Marla Nuttman went to St. Paul's, they were surprised to see an "Oregon Loves New York" shirt on the fence and captured it on film. Photo by Lance Nuttman

3. An exuberant Mayor Katz passes out pillows on the flight home. Photo by Betsy Ames

IN THEIR OWN WORDS

The psychological barriers that separated Oregonian from New Yorker, us from them, human from human, disintegrated. Soon we were holding perfect strangers in our arms. In those moments, we shared tears, hurt and fear, but we also shared hope. In those moments, we saw that our similarities eclipse our differences, we knew that human spirit could triumph over hatred, and we understood that compassion heals souls.

—Jan Woodruff, Freedom Flier and director of
marketing at Portland State University

GROUND ZERO

"Ground Zero's everywhere." —A New Yorker's response when asked by a Flight for Freedom participant if he'd been to Ground Zero

When the Flight for Freedom participants arrived in New York, smoke was still rising from the huge chasm that had been the 110-story World Trade Center. Workers were still hoping to find bodies—or parts of them—or personal effects, at least. As they moved the rubble, which was up to ten stories high, the smoke plumes reached 100 feet in the air. Because it was an active crime scene, the area directly around the 16-acre site was completely cordoned off. It would be seven more months of work twenty-four hours a day, every day, until the initial clean-up was complete.

Many of those workers were firefighters and police officers, who were searching for remains and evidence of their fallen colleagues. The attacks had left FCNY and NYPD devastated. The Fire Department lost 343 members and twenty-three police officers were confirmed dead. Memorial services—memorials because bodies were never found—of Fire and Police Department members took place every day. Freedom Fliers would, in fact, remember what seemed like "constant" services.

"None of the news channels are close enough to show what it's really like," a man who worked "the pile" told Portland playwright Michael Philips, testimony he captured in his play, *Voices from a Sunlight Shadow*.[1]

Fewer than 400 deaths had been confirmed and official counts, which were dropping daily, listed nearly 5,000 missing. (The final death total, not known for months, would be 2,977.)

Downtown Manhattan remained barricaded, though the police were slowly decreasing areas restricted to vehicular traffic. Freedom Fliers, like the rest of the public, could walk within two blocks of Ground Zero. Portland Association of Teachers Vice President Ann Nice brought posters and signs from Oregon classrooms and posted them on the fence around the site. The area around the Trade Center site was a modern-day, ash-encased Pompeii—or as Oregonians would quickly recognize, reminiscent of Mount Saint Helens explosion twenty years before.

Portland firefighter Wes Loucks, 51, Gladstone (pop. 11,438) [PHOTO 1]

The Flight for Freedom was our second trip. Four of us from Portland Fire Department went three days after 9/11. We went on the fourteenth. We had a friend back there who was a New York City fireman and we went back to help him. We were going to help anybody do anything because we knew they would be in chaos. We ended up being a handful of people that were allowed to work on "the pile." Moving debris, finding victims, so we were back there doing that, living in the fire station. [The firemen never called it "Ground Zero," Loucks said.]

The fireman we went back to visit, probably one of the most famous and decorated firefighters in the city, Billy Quick, had a lot of influence back there. We snuck onto the site a couple different times. We were spotted by some of the fire chiefs and politely asked to leave the site which we refused to do and they just gave up to us . . . .

I have a T-shirt that says "Portland Fire." [A guy] says, "Anybody not New York Fire Department or Police Department has to leave now." I just kept staring at him.

"If you're not from friggin' New York get the hell off the pile. OK, I've said it, back to work."

We weren't leaving. We came all the way from Oregon. and it was an odyssey getting there.

We were there for about a week. And were accepted back there. First they thought we were from Portland, Maine, and thanked us for coming from Maine. We said, "Hell, we're from Oregon."

What we did at the pile, we would just take five-gallon buckets, fill it up on one end, pass it down 100 people, dump it on the ground, people sifting through it and constant, constant circle of these buckets, going up one line and down the other. It was literally searching by hand. One hundred different people will touch that bucket and then dump it and then other people will be looking through it . . . .

. . . I don't know if I'm imagining this or if it really happened, but the morning of the attack, I'm sitting in front of the TV and I'm watching the first collapse of the South Tower, I see my friend running for his life down the street with this dust cloud chasing him. I said, "My God, that's Billy."

That's when four of us almost simultaneously decided were going. When the phone rang, I said, I'm goin'." I knew why he was calling.

We sat out at the Portland Airport for three days trying to get a flight out. We had offers of private pilots in their Lear jets would fly us out there as soon as the flight restrictions were lifted. We ended up flying TWA. I'm still friends with the pilot today. We're Facebook friends.

We found out that TWA was flying. We said, "We want to buy some tickets."

"It's $1,200 one way," they said.

We said, "We're going to do it. We're prepared to pay this exorbitant price."

And one of my friends said, "Hold on a minute." He made a phone call to the headquarters of TWA in L.A. and got to talking to a vice president of the company and explained what we were trying to do and they flew us back there round-trip for $250 first class.

There were only about twenty, twenty-five people on the plane. We were in civilian clothes. We didn't announce who we were, didn't want to bring attention to ourselves.

But the pilot/co-pilot came out. They had a delay because they had to bring in machinists to reinforce the cockpit doors. And she comes out and she broke down in tears because everybody was so emotional about what was going on and welcomed us aboard and then people knew who we were and what we were doing. They held a flight for us in St. Louis to get on that connecting flight because we were running late.

We got into LaGuardia midnight on a Saturday and it was a ghost town. There was no one there. It was spooky. And we landed in there and were met by some other friends who picked us up. One of the guys worked for *The New York Times* and he got us to the fire station and that's where it started and next morning we were out on the pile.

We'd go out there 7:00 or 8:00 in the morning and be there until after 6:00 or 7:00 in the evening. We wore face masks. One of our first observations was—the towers were made up of all glass—110 stories. There was no glass. It was pulverized. Everything was dust. It just crumbled.

There were fire engines lined up and down the streets. Dozens of fire trucks and engines. They were demolished, had been crushed. They just pulled them out of the pile and lined them up orderly until they could get them out of there.

You'd find just, like firemen turnout coats but nothing in them. But it was a pile of dust. When you have 110 stories of concrete on you, you're being shredded like a cheese grater all the way down. You're hitting every hard object you could imagine: steel, concrete, glass, with everything landing on top of you. There were fires burning there for six months later underground.

We were there again when you were on the Flight for Freedom.

On St. Patty's Day or the day before or after, the four of us went back over to Ground Zero and gave a whole day of searching again. We found a firefighter's gear. When you found somebody, they had a big procession. They'd call the company in that he was a member of. They'd escort him to a temporary morgue that was set up on site there.

The group I was with recognized a coat, a fireman's turnout coat (a bunker coat, but it has a name on it). I found a lot of pieces of ID, driver's licenses, and other identifying paperwork and stuff, and you'd turn that in so they'd get an idea that they were here. But they weren't finding anybody alive.

It definitely affected us emotionally—how can it not?

There were millions of pieces of paper. Letter-size paper, legal-size paper. That stuff survived better than the glass because it would just be floating in the air and it could have landed blocks and blocks away.

Almost a year later, I was sent an actual piece of the tower, a glass piece of the tower they found on Staten Island on Fresh Kills [Landfill], where they took all of the debris and they had forensic pathologists, the FBI, searching through this stuff.

I learned back there that it affected people back there so much more than we felt it out here.[2] [PHOTOS 2-3]

Mary Platt, 50, Portland* (City Pop. 529,121, Metro Area 1.9 million)

I remember making our way to Ground Zero and it was just horrific, just seeing the empty buildings and all the ash and then cars that were halfway out of the carparks above us and the sensing and people's notices and flowers and all of it was just horrific.[3]

Michael Phillips, 30s, Portland

We leave the Wall Street subway station, walk up Broadway about three blocks to the corner of Liberty, and then suddenly there it is. Or, there it isn't. Instead, there is a building with its entire side sheared off. Across the way, in a place that used to be completely blocked by the trade towers, is a building which looks intact except for five or six huge steel girders sticking out of it like straws sticking out of a milk shake. Girders from the towers that were projected into the building. Below, the remaining skeleton of the towers is still visible.

The air isn't as bad as I expected, but the smell of dust and smoke is still strong. The relatively small crowd is almost completely silent. And no one, and I mean no one, is able to stand there and look at it without tears. We all know that it still remains a huge, devastating, unthinkable crypt for thousands of people. And, it's very hard to be there.

Mayor Vera Katz, Portland; Portland Public Schools Director of Security Frank Klejmont; Portland Public Schools Police Captain Cliff Madison**

---

*Cities listed are where Freedom Fliers lived in October 2001.

**To be accurate, Cliff Madison was a Portland Police Bureau Captain on executive loan to the Portland Public School District Police serving as their Chief of Police.

Within an hour of arriving at her hotel that evening, Mayor Katz journeyed to Ground Zero with Portland Public Schools Police Captain Cliff Madison and Portland Public Schools Security Director Frank Klejmont, who had arranged the experience through his friend and former colleague, NYPD Sergeant Joe Williamson, who escorted them.

On the flight to New York, Mayor Katz had confessed to *Oregonian* reporter Courtenay Thompson how personally traumatic the World Trade Center attacks had been, how they penetrated deep, over sixty years of her history.

"She had feared this moment since agreeing to head up the "Flight for Freedom" trip," wrote Thompson. She was, she said, "Afraid to see what I know exists."

Klejmont was the director of security for Portland Public Schools, which was part of Portland's Police Bureau. A native New Yorker, Klejmont had started his career as a New York cop:

> I was a cop there 1974–1975 and I was in 75 Precinct, which was East New York. It was terrible. It was dangerous. They put you where they were needed so I just happened to go there. It was a great place to learn because you learned quick.

Layoffs of 5,000 police in the midst of New York's financial crisis in 1975 led Klejmont to Portland, where the police force was hiring. He asked some friends from Oregon, fellow Vietnam vets, about the place. They told him, "You can come here because you're cool, but don't tell anybody else."*

> I went to Portland in 1977. I went, "Wow." I remember this guy was driving us to the 911 Center, one of the people that hired you, and I was sitting next to him, a couple people in the back.

"What do you think of our ghetto?"

I went, "What ghetto? That's nicer than where I grew up."

---

*Klejmont has the sad distinction of being the second casualty of the Vietnam War in 1972; the first casualty, his friend Dale Farris, didn't make it.

It was a culture shock for me, in a good way. Much more laid back. It was nowhere near the intensity of New York City police work.

As the beat cop in her neighborhood, Klejmont had known Vera Katz since her days as speaker of the Oregon House of Representatives. "She would speak softly and carry a big stick," he said. "She was very personable and when she had to do her legislative or mayoral duties, she would make sure she got it done. She could be tough."

The delegation included the mayor and her bodyguard from Portland; Joe Williamson; Klejmont and his wife, Peggy; Madison and his wife, Melody; and two plainclothes dignitary protection escorts from the New York Police Department. "They treated us like royalty," said Klejmont. [PHOTO 4]

Captain Cliff Madison:

To stand there and not see the towers . . . One chunk of the World Trade Center speared into another building. I just said a prayer. It was sadly amazing to see the destruction and the evil.

The building that was bowed, but the windows' glass are still in and everything was up against those windows. You think about the people that must have been in there. It was like someone took the building and shook it . . . .

We're in hard hats, but you knew how hard people were working and you felt horrible for what they were going through.

We were at the food cart in our jackets and people said, "You're part of that group from Oregon. Have some food."

"No, no." We couldn't do it.

They said, "We're serious."

I wish everybody from our group had that same sight just because it really sinks home how hard-hitting and how devastating that was and how evil evil can be.

You could chew the air out there, the smell. It was a seven-story high debris pile. Dump trucks come by and realize that the tires are almost as tall as you are and it looks like a Tonka truck . . . .

You want to be there, you want to try to help, you want to, in your mind, find that one person. Even if they tell you it's burning 1,000 degrees, you know there are six or seven stories underground . . . .

I think a lot of people working around Ground Zero are numb. Their emotions have to be in check. You work twelve on, twelve off, it's got to be an emotional drive. I still think there are a lot of tears being shed.

We understand because we were there, but it's not the same because it didn't happen to us . . . .

Some of our firemen worked back there. In tears, one man called his seventeen-year-old daughter to say he loved her . . . .

Klejmont:

It was heart-wrenching to be down there in Ground Zero. We were there about a half-hour to an hour. Joey got us into Ground Zero. And when you were down in there, you can't imagine what it was from watching TV. There was no comparison. They were still working on it and they had huge—the biggest earth moving machines I had ever seen on top of these piles of rubble. The rubble was so big, the machines looked like Tonka Toys. The smell and the smoke was still in the air. People were working there 24/7.

It was really emotional. I don't think there was a dry eye down there.

Jack McGowan, Flight for Freedom organizer and spokesman, executive director of SOLV, 52, Helvetia

There was a quiet offer to the leaders of the Flight for Freedom and Vera, of course, and they picked us up by police escort at the front of the Waldorf and brought us through roadblock after roadblock into World Trade Center. They dropped us right adjacent to the pit and we stood there in sorrow and awe, watching the firemen and construction workers go through the mounds, the gigantic mounds of debris still looking for those that had passed . . . . On one of the buildings that was overlooking the pit, the mound, they had erected a massive banner that said "We will never forget." And there are photographs of that.

Two years after the Flight for Freedom, Mayor Katz described how she felt amidst the devastation:

It reminded me of the scenes I saw in Paris when I was a little girl, but at the same time as I saw the horror, I knew New Yorkers would get through it, I knew it would be rebuilt, I knew it would provide a memorial for the world and certainly a memorial for the lives that were lost.

Lance and Marla Nuttman, 20s, McMinnville

Lance: Walking up out of the subway, the change in venue is evident immediately. We're about four blocks or so from Ground Zero, and the first thing that hits you is the smell . . . . The second thing that grabs your attention is the security. The site is a crime scene, and it is treated thus by the multitudes of NYPD, National Guardsmen, and various other uniformed men and women in the area. The third thing you notice is the quiet . . . . There are hundreds of civilians, tourists, and locals alike, who make a sort of procession across about a six-block area. Makeshift memorials can be found on every chain-link fence and street corner.

Marla: You could smell it the whole time—you could smell the smell of that burning plastic that was coming up from the sewers. New York has a smell, but what we were smelling, under the wreckage? That awful smell.

It was a month after; they had put up fencing so we couldn't get up too close, but we could—we were walking through streets that we'd seen on the TV that had been evacuated and buildings that were empty because of the event and what happened afterwards and so when we finally got up there as close as could get, it was pretty solemn.

I even felt that the workers who were stopping people, everything was pretty solemn and quiet. It felt like even the traffic was quiet. Everybody was reserved and respectful because it was a mass grave. But it was pretty amazing, even as far away—as close as we could get, was too far away.

Lance: After spending two full days go-go-go screaming people in the [Columbus Day] parade, you can't sleep on the sixteenth floor because you can hear Fifth Avenue constantly honk-honk-honk—

You step out of the subway it was silence. It was bizarre. The ash—everywhere. I have a really cool picture of just a building. Scaffolding everywhere, ash everywhere, people writing "Make Love Not War" with their finger on the ash. [PHOTO 5]

Marla: It was—

Lance: —reverential.

Marla: Yes. Everybody felt that way. It seemed very reverential.

Krista Vasquez, 29, Portland; Scott Williams, 20s, Portland

The KGW reporters, who had traveled with the mayor the day before, made Ground Zero their first stop on Sunday morning and that was the focus of their coverage that day, said Vasquez: "Here's why we made this trip."

> I remember not being able to see a lot of the destruction. But I remember seeing all of the people, I remember it being incredibly quiet, and I remember seeing the signs of support written on a bus shelter. Words of encouragement from people all over the world. We're with you New Yorkers, their name and unit in Germany. Wherever they were, words on encouragement on bus shelters, walls, a lot of the buildings were boarded up.

> There was just a tremendous amount of compassion and feeling there. I don't know how to describe it. I remember the feeling of, "We are here, we're paying our respects, we're in awe." I remember that sense of solitude and quietness and silence, and it was powerful, too.

Scott Williams:

> Until you get to a place—and let's face it, nobody else has had that sort of incident, you can't really imagine. And there wasn't a lot of video shot of surrounding buildings that I saw . . . . But just the amount of damage to surrounding buildings and neighborhood places that were closed.

Joy Scherz, 51, Corvallis (Pop. 78,158)

> There are these huge buildings and there's no lights on, no movement, and dust is two inches thick.

What I wasn't ready for was the desolation so far out from the actual destruction, to see that for blocks out there was no movement. We saw people dragging suitcases across the Brooklyn Bridge. It was another level of terror to see how it had really destroyed these people's lives.

Elaine Edgel, 41, Gresham (Pop. 90,205)

Bank Supervisor Elaine Edgel of Gresham had gone with her family to the New York Stock Exchange earlier that morning, where they received a bag with an NYSE T-shirt inside.

> While we were taking pictures at Ground Zero, the bag with the NYSE T-shirt fell out into the dust. I picked it up and started to brush it off. All of a sudden I stopped and put the shirt close to me and held it. I rolled the shirt up and to this day it's put away, still with the dust on it. I guess it became kind of sacred to me.

Glennis McNeal, 63, Portland

> Ground Zero leaves its autograph on nearby streets and buildings and even on the washcloth you wipe across your face at the end of day.

Thomas Wiebe, 49, Portland

> We [he and his wife, Cindy] decided to go down to Lower Manhattan to see the ruins of the World Trade Center, after debating whether it would be proper to do so; in particular, I wanted to see it so as to remember what had happened. It was not possible to get any closer to what is now called Ground Zero than perhaps three blocks; every street was barricaded, and access beyond those points was controlled. It was dusty, and just North of Ground Zero, several blocks of dump trucks were lined up to remove debris from the site. Between the buildings, the twisted metal of the exterior steel frame which remained, perhaps three or four stories high, could be seen. There was still a very heavy smell in the air, a part of which was concrete dust from the remains of the fallen buildings. We walked around the area, with construction vehicles coming and going. As we walked by the City Hall, which was situated just a few blocks from Ground Zero, Mayor Giuliani walked up the street with some of his aides, exhorting and thanking those he passed by.[4]

Martha Seward, 48, Nyssa (Pop. 3,163)

On their own, not part of the Flight for Freedom, the Seward family decided to travel to New York and Washington, DC the week after September 11 to pay their respects and show their support.

We were walking from our hotel towards the World Trade Center. There was hardly anybody out and people who were, wore masks and the ashes were still falling; some would even have umbrellas. The—I felt the somberness of it.

And going down to where it happened, I just could hardly look at it, I just couldn't fathom all that went on.

And they were still bringing parts of people out, what they could find.

And the papers. Papers littered the place. There was all kind of papers and ashes everywhere and people didn't talk. The people who were around the World Trade Center didn't talk. You would say something, but nobody would hold conversations.

The ashes. I clearly remember going into the jeans store and the jeans were still folded on the display and there was like two inches of ashes on all the displays. And the proprietors just standing there in a daze. They didn't know what to do. They opened up their doors to us and we would just start crying.

Bruce Knowlton, 50, Gresham

"People were there to pay their respects," said Knowlton. "No one was there to gawk. It seems that everyone involved in this is of the same mind. It was a patriotic-type thing."

On the subway, Knowlton ran into a New York woman who was also headed to Ground Zero but didn't want to go alone. Several blocks from where the towers once stood, she told him that the street where they were standing had been littered with body parts the day of the attacks.

State Sen. Margaret Carter, 55, Portland

One of the most frightening moments for me was when we went to Ground Zero and to see how deep it was. I didn't want to stand near the fence that surrounded it because I felt so afraid. The fear of all of those people whose lives had been lost and it was down in that deep crevice. That's the first time . . . I felt afraid. I went with Darlene Hooley.

U.S. Rep. Darlene Hooley, 62, Portland

Darlene Hooley was a member of the U.S. House of Representatives from Portland and had previously visited Ground Zero with members of Congress on September 23.

> You can't know how large and awful it is until you've stood there and looked at it. You don't get a sense of all of the smells: the stagnant water and the acrid smell of the air. Everyone had a face mask on. It is so enormous. The metal girders are so huge, and yet there literally was no concrete; it was all powder.
>
> I talked to search-and-rescue workers who had been working eighteen-hour days, and I saw dogs that were near exhaustion. The dogs were getting dressed because they weren't finding people. So they had other people hide from them so they could be rewarded by finding someone.
>
> When I was there the first time, they still were hauling things out in the bucket brigades. They hauled the debris to the landfill, then dumped it out and raked carefully through all of it, looking for personal items, parts of the panels and the body parts.[5]

"I'll never forget how the air tasted. Who tastes air? I still have that taste in my mouth."

—Chris Sullivan, 2021
(reported for KXL Portland in 2001)

What was most surprising about Ground Zero and had the most immediate impact was the odor, Hooley described above. Flight for Freedom participants described it as "rubber-like," " synthetic," "chemical," "acrid burning-plastic-and-wire," "metallic," "electrical," "ash and chemical smell."

"It hits you like a brick wall," **Jack Kostel of Portland** wrote in a memoir in October 2001.

> You have the grey, dirty, gritty picture with the wind blowing all kinds of small particles around, covering all the surrounding buildings and streets. You walk parallel to the site for about seven blocks

and at each intersection you look into the destruction one block away. You see the workers and machinery and trucks clearing away this huge, smoking, dirty pile of rubble. Half the people are observing and moving to the right while the other half are moving to the left. There is a buzz and murmur coming from the people, but it is quiet and respectful. I chose not to stay long, so I returned to the subway and headed for Central Park. I was getting away from that terrible smell, the smell I will always remember.[6]

Jackie Young, 62, Happy Valley (Pop. 4,519)

I was kind of reluctant to go down to the epicenter because everything was still burning and smoldering, and I didn't want to be disruptive.

Somebody asked us if we were going and I said, "I'm not sure if we should go, they're still busy working," and he said, "No, of everybody who should go there, you have to go."

So we went down with this other couple we were traveling with [Don and Jeanine Ford], and we're lost in New York City. We must have looked like deer in headlights. This young guy dressed in a suit with his briefcase came up to us and said, "Can I help you?"

We said, "We feel like we should go to the epicenter."

He said, "I'm going to take you myself." And he forgot about going to work and took us down to the epicenter.

People on the subway—we listened and hugged and prayed. It was amazing.

Jeanine Ford, 56, Portland

As you approach, you begin to see businesspeople on the streets wearing dust masks. Next, you notice the increased police presence. Fences and guards keep you back a distance form where workers still labor to remove debris and recover bodies. An almost reverent stillness enfolds you . . . .

Pictures and messages are posted about, with bouquets of flowers stuck through the chain-link fences. Particles of ash drift down in a continuous flow, so small and light that you don't really see them, except against the glossy black of a building. A light mist falls with ash. An acrid smell of smoke and ash fills the air and your nasal passages. It is so strong you can almost taste it . . . . It is truly like a war zone.

At the guarded gate in the fence, rescue workers walk with tired steps and lowered heads, not inviting conversation or eye contact. A fireman almost bumped into me. I noticed that he was a chaplain. We spoke for a few moments and he told me that he had come from Chicago, to give aid and comfort to those working in the ruins. He asked me who I was there for, so he could add them to his prayer list. I told him the purpose of our trip and asked him to pray for the rescue workers. The toll on them is imaginable! Many search day after day to find and remove the bodies of their friends and coworkers. As he left, I gave him a rose to place at Ground Zero. As he passed, he leaned down and kissed my cheek. A small gesture, but full of expression and our shared human bond.[7]

Judi Henningsen, 58, Portland; Susan Henningsen, 34, Portland

"At Ground Zero walking around, you had to show your ID just to cross the street at that time," said Judi Henningsen, who went with her daughter, Susan.

Our most important destination was to go to "Ground Zero." We went to see the damage and to pay tribute to all those who lost their lives there.

As we walked closer to the site, roads were barricaded. Police and military were everywhere. Blue plastic blocked some of our view. Dust was getting thicker as we walked. Window washers were attempting to clean away the dust. Street cleaners were making passes to clean the streets. Many trucks were parked or ready to carry debris away. Verizon is madly trying to make sense of twisted broken cables. People sweeping all over. There are guards at the doors of many businesses and stores.

In the area, the dust was a quarter of an inch thick. We passed a jewelry store, where the jewelry had been removed. The displays were tipped over on their side and thick with dust.

You could see the imprints that were on the stand from the dust.

So many signs left on buildings that were made by passersby. There were names on posters, candles, flowers makeshift shrines. This was enough to tear your heart.

Once in a while we were able to get a glimpse between buildings. Such devastation. Twisted beams and mortar. There was an indescribable smell in the dusty air. I suppose it was a mix of burning debris, asbestos and perhaps some who were lost.

We stopped at a pub for lunch several blocks away. They told us they had been closed for the first couple of weeks. They were busy making sandwiches for the firemen that were working so hard to find people buried in the rubble.[8]

Marilyn Slizeski, 48, City Councilor, Philomath (Pop. 3,898)

Visiting Ground Zero was haunting, especially because it was so reminiscent of the aftermath of Mount St. Helen's, with thin veils of ash covering everything. Buildings facing the explosions were tinted black on the one side. Ash was still falling nearly a month after the incident. What was most dramatic is that the sidewalks of Manhattan, usually shadowed by the huge buildings, are now exposed to the sun.[9]

Vic Rini, 68, Aloha (Pop. 41,741), native New Yorker

Behind us was a store window covered with photos, drawings, and messages . . . . I also remembered walking these same streets as a young man right out of high school. And now I was looking at such destruction.

Suddenly, from the stillness came the high-pitched cries of a woman in pain, lamenting that she never wanted this to happen, that she was a Muslim and that she was for peace. "I'm sorry," she kept repeating, "I'm sorry!" We were statues and none of us responded. It was a strange encounter.[10]

Edd and Debbie Pedro, 42 and 41, Hermiston (Pop. 13,154)

Edd and Debbie Pedro told the *East Oregonian* about their visit, seeing the bright orange netting that keeps building debris from falling on workers below. They also noticed the stores, closed immediately with the blast. Looking through the windows of a shoe store, they saw a thick layer of dust.

"You could see the clean spots where people were helping the customers try on the latest styles in shoes," said Edd. "There were boxes of shoes on the floor. Just waiting."[11]

Rob Platt, 50, Portland

Within a block, maybe half a block, you see all the storefronts that are like frozen in time. You'd see high heels, shoes on display in the front window and they were all covered with soot and dust—I mean a lot. And it was like a nuclear explosion or something, it was just eerie. Store after store after store. All the glass was gone and all the inventory was just completely dusted. It was all where it was supposed to be. It didn't get blown away, it wasn't a mess. All the stuff inside was covered with dust. I've got to think the glass got broken.

And then the night, the evening when they had the spotlights. When they were doing twenty-four-hour shifts and the whole thing was like it just rose in the sky out of Wall Street. Wherever you were in New York you'd see it. Not only would you see the spotlights but you'd see the plume of dust that was rising from the site.[12]

Tahn Amuchastegui, 32, Portland

As we got closer we could see firemen and others combing the structure looking for any trace of the victims of the tragedy. I felt it all in my gut and I was awestruck for quite some time. Disbelief at the magnitude of destruction that had been wrought. The silence of those around me and the only sounds being those of the recovery teams and an occasional vehicle noise on the site. Eerie quiet is not what one pictures when one thinks of NYC.[13]

Debra-Diane Jenness, 46, Crystal Lake (Pop. 400)

[Going to Ground Zero] . . . was something we had to do; I mean, we HAD to, you were drawn to it like a magnet, not as a tourist attraction, but because of what had happened there to us as a Nation and to New York as a City.

. . . As we got about five blocks away, news filtered thru the air that the attack on Afghanistan had begun. You could see security pick up immediately in areas all over the city . . . .

I cannot write much about what we saw and the pictures we took; words do not do it justice. It is difficult, if not totally impossible to describe what it was like. Of course, we all had the TV images to look at, but the reality of BEING THERE; well, you just didn't know what to say. It took your breath away. It was awesome to think that ANYONE survived in the entire area, as we walked for blocks and blocks with damaged buildings and dust and soot. It was something you had to FEEL. I guess this is one of those times where you have to say, "you hadda be there" and mean it.

We were quiet even to each other the rest of the day, it was hard to talk about it. Yet at the same time, seeing it, being there, helped give a part of healing in each of our hearts.[14]

Sandra Kempel, 53, Portland

I was standing behind a group of people when they first walked into the area and I just sort of tapped someone in front of me on the shoulder. They were a couple and they were looking up.

I'm going, "This is my first time in New York, and could you please first tell me where the towers would have been?"

And they pointed out where they would have been had they still been standing. It's just incredible . . . [The cranes were] stories and stories high, something you could not comprehend just seeing it on television.

Flight for Freedom participants also shared the memory of the quiet, how despite heavy equipment moving mountains of rubble and crowded sidewalks, people walked by silently.

Clarice Schorzman, Colton (Pop. 5,116*)

"Nothing can prepare one for the carnage there," Colton Middle School Principal Clarice Schorzman wrote to Colton School District Superintendent Steve Dickenson. In walking around Ground Zero, Schorzman was repeatedly touched on the shoulder, arm, or hand by policemen who said, "Thank you for coming."

At Wall and Broad . . . with Trinity Church looming over us, three policemen stopped me and asked if I'd help a Berkeley cop (in town for the first time, volunteering) find the Waldorf-Astoria. Everyone knows who we are and where we're staying. The Wall Street subway entrance is now reopened, so it was up to Grand Central, transfer, up to Lexington to 51st. It felt so good to be of help.[15]

*Based on 2019 U.S. Census. Numbers are not available for 2000 U.S. Census.)

Lana Cupper, 50, Portland

The Cuppers' son had taken a job in the World Trade Center months before the attacks.

"We had been back there when the Towers were still standing when the kids first moved and about a year before. We walked all around the Towers and there were some near little places we looked at close by where the Towers stood. And we wanted to go back to that spot and see if we could remember anything and what was left.

There was still smoke or something, smoking off the top of the rubble. And the other thing I remember was that they had a lot of chain link fencing going around it. And I remember going on the back side of some little place, the same shop the kids had taken us into. And there were people posting posters of missing people.

There was a lady who was crying. I reached out and touched her shoulder. I said, "I'm sorry, did you lose someone?"

She turned around and wrapped her arms around me. I was just holding her. I didn't know her.

She said, "She's missing. Will you help me look?"

She just bawled, she was just sobbing. I had tears running down my face. But the whole experience of people, with the posters up there, and people were still holding hope that people were in this wreckage.

. . . That was the most profound moment, that lady who came up to me by the chain-link fencing that I remember . . . .

. . . She had a black cape on and it wrapped around her like she was cold.

I was like, "Oh, the poor thing."

That was most profound moment for me of the whole experience. I held her it seemed like a long time. I bet at least five minutes. And then we talked for quite a while. I told her that I would look. She was insisting that we help her find that person.

I remember what that person looked like. She was a young person—I'm sure she said it was her daughter. Because it was a young person, a person in her mid-to-late twenties that was lost.

Just a stranger doing that to you was just like, "Oh my God."

That's when it really hit me. She was just a small—a number compared to how many people were doing the same thing, knowing that they lost somebody.

The picture was of a young person in her mid-to-late twenties. She might have been standing somewhere in the city, I can't remember what was in the background. She was a beautiful girl. She was smiling in the picture and she looked really happy. I'm sure it was somewhere in the city, come to think of it.

I mostly remember the lady that I held for such a long time when she was pouring her heart out.

I told her we'd look. I told her also why we were there, that our son, he didn't work there, but he went there many times a week for business meetings so we were very concerned about what had happened.

And then she knew—I told her that we were on this Flight for Freedom. I don't know that she was registering what I was saying, she was so much in her own pain and grief at the time.

And it was rainy that day. She was kind of bundled up. I don't know, it was meant to be that we touched each other that day and at that time.

When I think about it, I now wish I would have reached out more and tried to see if there was anything—if we could keep in touch or if I could anything else while I was in town. And then just her reaching over and falling apart. It was probably what she needed at that second to be touched.

. . . That was a painful, painful city . . . .

George Haight, 52, Woodburn (Pop. 20,100)

Haight told the *Woodburn Independent*, "Well, the low point, and I made a mistake here, was that I went to Ground Zero by myself. I wasn't prepared for how overwhelmed I would become.[16]

The devastation isn't just over the 16-acre site. I was walking through canyons of skyscrapers that are blackened by soot sixteen stories high, office paper is still flying around on the streets, it's very eerie and spooky. I needed to get out of there.

I hadn't expected myself to be quite so overwhelmed by it. In fact, a woman came jogging by me, she just lived a couple blocks from the towers and she said, "Are you okay?"

"Actually not. We're supposed to be here to give you folks a hug from Oregon and say we're in the same boat here, but by golly, I'm the one who needs a hug."

She just threw her arms around me and just blubbered and hugged and walked a couple three blocks. For the last twenty years, she's been jogging around the Trade Center. It was her route. People that she lost and would not see again, and it got me. I thought, "I've got to get a little further away from here."

I walked into Battery Park, which was set up like a National Guard camp. They had all these army vehicles and troops and guns and tents and latrines . . . .

I was kind of overcome by the whole massiveness of it and I just wanted to get out of there finally. And I walked up to this police-woman who was standing by the ferry slip and I told her that I want to know where to go to get a cab to get back to the Waldorf, I just wanted to go back home and to my room and call Oregon and call my wife. She reached in her pocket and gave me her cell phone and I called my wife from Battery Park . . . .

When I got home, I still had the cell phone number and I called her, Officer Garcia. She was just delighted. I said, "Your generosity needs to be recognized by someone. Who would you like me to write a letter to?"

My sergeant would be really appropriate," she said, and she gave me the name and I wrote a note and sent the picture of her I'd taken. The fact that she let me use her cell phone was above and beyond.

Gerry Frank, Honorary Chair of the Flight for Freedom, 77, Salem (Oregon State Capital, Pop. 347,214)

What you see on television is one thing, but I think you have to see it with your own eyes. It is hard to grasp its scope until you are involved. The atmosphere and smell are things I cannot describe." Frank was escorted by police and a Federal Emergency Management Official.[17]

Rick Love, 39, Portland
Rick Love of Azumano Travel was adamant that he did not want to go to Ground Zero. "I was all but forced to go by my other friends from Azumano and once I got there, I did not want to leave."

Rob Oster, 20s, Gresham

Former Long Islander Rob Oster described the scene itself for the *Gresham Outlook*:

Pictures cannot do justice to the size and scope of the devastation. The naked skyline of Lower Manhattan as you approach New York City is your first real indication of the impact of the attack. The smell finds you quickly once in Lower Manhattan. It's an odd combination of burning electrical wires or plastic burning. The air is thick with a chalky dust that sneaks up on you. You don't really notice it for a few minutes until you can't clear your throat. The taste of vaporized concrete never leaves your mouth.

As you get within three or four blocks of Ground Zero, you begin to notice the dust. It's everywhere. Buildings and streets are covered in a white film. New buildings are shrouded in gray—and then you see the destruction. Face to face with the largest attack on American soil. It truly takes your breath away . . . .

Walking along Chambers Street, I encountered bus shelters, store windows, lamp posts and more, all transformed into makeshift memorials by victims' families, school children and people from around the country . . . .

I was halfway across Greenwich when I froze in my tracks, unable to obey a police officer's command to keep moving and stop blocking the street. My throat tightened and my eyes moistened.

About three blocks away, a 10-story high pile of debris sat amid neighboring buildings. It was peculiar to see a beautiful blue sky stretching above the wreckage in place of the two mighty structures that dominated the Manhattan skyline for most of the past four decades and all 34 years of my life.

It was also as close to Hell as I care to be in my lifetime . . . .

Vehicles leaving the devastation were hosed off by workers to keep wreckage dust from spreading throughout the city. The odd person still sported doctors' masks as they made their way through city streets . . . .

Jack McGowan

I saw when I was in New York during that period of time, that New York was a city that was split in two geographically. What

I mean by that—around the Waldorf-Astoria, Grand Central, Midtown, the city was starting, barely but starting to get back into to some type of rhythm. You would hear the occasional honk of the car, you would see people walking to and fro at the typical brisk pace.

And what I saw was that the city was divided in two at Canal St. anything south of Canal, the city was still frozen in time. There was no banter in the streets, no cars honking, people were going to work in somewhat of almost a daze.

The smell was so permeable and so lasting that when you emerged from the subway anywhere south of Canal, the scent that knocked you out in my estimation—it came at me, I didn't think about it. Three scents. The first scent was the scent of something burning, the second scent was the scent of sweat, concrete dust, and the third scent was the scent of decomposing life. To my dying day, I will never forget that scent.

Words can't describe it. The closest analogy I can think of is "Dante's Inferno . . . . To see two proud buildings, part of New York's skyline, reduced to twisted metal eight stories high, the visual aspects were amazing. And there were quick blasts of smoke and steam that burst out, then disappeared just as quickly, from fires burning still a month later.

For native New Yorkers like McGowan the shock may have been the greatest. "What you saw was what you didn't see: two very tall buildings," said Eldon Mains, who grew up in the Bronx and owned Hills Florist and Gifts in Hillsboro.[18]

Toni Epperson, candidate for Josephine County Commissioner, 55

At Ground Zero, Epperson had an encounter with firefighters whose colleagues were buried under the rubble. "They're waiting for the bell to ring so that they can go get their firemen." During the recovery work, a fire department bell signaled the discovery of the remains of a fallen firefighter.[19]

"What you can't see, you can hear and smell and taste. You get an overwhelming feeling of emptiness," said Barbara Shaw of Scio.

"Could not figure out why we were coughing, and then we realized it was the dust and the smell. Will never forget the empty feeling," wrote Connie Hawk of Salem.

Baruti Artharee, 48, Portland

Artharee was deputy director of the Portland Development Commission and the board chairman of the Urban League of Portland.

Another burning memory that I have. One of the guys in our group was Roger Hinshaw, who at that time was the president for Oregon and Southwest Washington for Bank of America. I had worked with him on charitable foundations. And another guy was a Latino gentleman and his name was Jesse [Carreon] and he was the president of Portland Community College at the time.[20] And then the fourth guy was Bernie Kronberger, the community outreach person for U.S. Bank. The four of us ended up walking together down to Ground Zero. We walked and had a chance to talk and all of a sudden you've got people from different diverse backgrounds, different classes, everyone had their own story.

And this site. It was a very moving experience. We saw the destruction. As close as we could get to the barriers we saw the destruction. But the one thing that has been ingrained in me that I haven't heard anybody talk about, and when I think of 9/11, this is one of the emotions that comes back. It was the smell of death at Ground Zero. At the time we were there, and there was that odor in the air, and you knew it was the odor of death. It was something I have never smelled before or since.

Billie Jean Morris, Greater Hermiston Chamber of Commerce Director, 55

After a while, breathing the air made your voice hoarse and it felt like you had grit in your eyes. All of the workers there had red eyes from being in it after so long . . . . The American Red Cross workers, National Guardsmen, police officers, and firefighter had rashes on their foreheads where their helmets and hats hit their seat-beaten brows.

Chris Sullivan, KXL Radio, 32, Portland

I'll never forget how the air tasted. Who tastes air? But the air, I still have that taste in my mouth. I can still feel that taste in my mouth of concrete and dust. You couldn't see it, but the air had a taste, and I'll never forget that. As you walked around, you're always smacking your lips, like what is all that?

Jane and Steve Ditewig, 50s, Longview, Washington (Pop. 34,660)

On October 7, both Jane and Steve recorded their impressions of Ground Zero in their Flight or Freedom journal.

Jane: The odor and congestion in our throats were disturbing—surreal.

Steve: Very little noise, aside from periodic police, ambulance, or fire sirens. People's eyes are glued to the glimpses you get of terrible piles of rubble and debris out of which rise pieces of buildings and tall cranes all illuminated by bright lights. Adjacent buildings that are still standing are draped from top to bottom in rec material—perhaps as a dust shield. Security personnel and vehicles are everywhere. Very sad and depressing feelings about this area—a lot of people died.

Dave and Linda Holley, 60s, Sweet Home (Pop. 8,016)

After seeing reports on TV and having trouble separating movie images from reality, it finally hit home how absolutely terrible it must have been for the people.

The noise of the buildings collapsing would have been horrible, and the ash and dust cloud that enveloped everything would have been horrific.

Standing and looking up at the tall buildings around the Trade Center site, I was seeing again the people jumping from the buildings and finally knew that this was real people and not scenes from a movie. The mind can finally accept just how God-awful it must have been . . . .

The impression gotten from looking at one of the towers was like you see in a salvage yard where cars have been compacted together . . . .

We thought we both knew how we felt about it. We both thought that we were pretty well informed, but you really have to be there to really feel the emotional impact of it (having been so far removed from the scene of the attack at home.) . . .

Linda and I laid in bed the second night sharing our thoughts and agree that we are taking back with us things that we didn't think would happen . . . .[21]

Bill Cooper, KPAM radio, Portland

It was completely silent. We're standing there and I remember I was in a little store alcove, entryway so I wasn't directly on the sidewalk and people were crossing back and forth in front of me to the site. It was hushed reverence, nobody was talking. I was there for fifteen or twenty minutes before I moved on.

A bunch of us ended up on a side street [nearby] . . . I think I was getting some people—on-the-street interviews to use on the air and there was a window opened above us, four or five stories above us . . . . Somebody leaned out and yelled out to us, "Hey, we're bombing the shit out of Afghanistan."

. . . I saw some workers coming off the site and I was able to do an interview with some of them. "What are your feelings as you're digging through?" They were pretty emotional about it. I got the sound of the backhoes and you could hear the pickaxes and shovels on the concrete.

And then I did stand-up and I wrote a script and had the natural sound behind me as I read a thirty-second radio piece with the natural sound of Ground Zero behind me.[22]

Joyce Willing, 38, Portland [PHOTO 6-7]

Where the towers had been, and seeing the flowers and the memorials that were there, it really hit home what a tragedy many, many people faced. I didn't lose anybody in the towers, but I certainly had even people in Oregon who had lost people or seven degrees of separation, that you might know, but to have such a devastation. It made me feel like we were in the middle of Afghanistan or Iraq. Luckily, we had not experienced those kinds of attacks before.[23]

Stephanie Hinshaw, 15, Portland

Hinshaw had felt "a breeze of loss that hung over everything" in the city, but going to Ground Zero was a different experience.

[In SoHo] the area was alive and bustling. After awhile the stores started to look less interesting and many of them were boarded up. There were few cars on the road and less people yelling. The only people we saw were walking quickly, their heads aimed at the pavement.

Ground zero was blocked off along with all the surrounding blocks. No vehicles were allowed entrance to the financial district, all roads were blocked off. Police stood in the middle of the road motioning the cards to either turn left or right. I wondered how long they would have to stay there for . . . .

The only people there were there for the same reason we were, to get a view of what wasn't there. The silence was eerie. People weren't yelling. They didn't even appear to be talking. One lady walked by wearing a gas mask. Everybody looked down instead of straight ahead. There was a gloomy sense of despair that filled the air and seemed to pound on you as you walked.

The air almost seemed thick with pain and death. It was like no place I had ever been. It was so unnatural, it felt as if we were in a weird book where the earth had been destroyed and was now sitting still and rotting, supporting no life because all the people had moved underground. Yes, that sounds insane. But that's how it felt. It felt like we weren't supposed to be there, like the ground hadn't been stepped on for some time . . . .

We joined a crowd standing across the street from the remains, and could peer through the empty space between two buildings. The police kept telling us to move along, please walk quicker. Please don't stand in the middle of the street, they say. Many people were taking pictures. I didn't see the point. I felt like I had been hit with an airplane and it made me mad that they were taking pictures of my remains. It wasn't respectful. I felt bad for the policemen who had to tell the crowd to move along. It wasn't a tourist site. I wanted to tell everyone to stop. My head was swirling . . . .

I raised my eyes to the top of the building that sat right next to the rubble. It was mountainous and seemed to reach into the heavens. I tried to imagine the point at which a building almost twice that size would end. I couldn't find one in the sky . . . .

There was a small sushi place right next to the huge empty square that the police were guarding. It was also covered in ash, and locked up. I wondered if they would ever get any business again. I thought of all the people that had died.

The whole thing was so massive—the event so huge. The proportion of it couldn't be contemplated completely until it was put right under your nose. I wanted to leave, I felt horrible, inappropriately alive. Ground zero gave off the clear shock and helplessness of the community. Sure America was strong. But no matter how strong you are, when you're hit, you realize that you have no control over things. And that every person is just as weak and helpless as the next in terms of fate. I cried for the helpless child that was America. I cried for the people, for the death, for the destruction. I suddenly gained an immense respect for the firemen and the rescue workers. I felt their pain. I felt everyone's pain. The pain is indistinguishable from person to person when you look at two giant holes in an infrastructure that used to serve as symbol for everything . . . .

I think we were all in shock as we walked away from ground zero. As I walked and contemplated I heard the faint tone of the national anthem seep into my ears and cut into my soul. That song had never meant anything to me before, anything. But suddenly I couldn't hold back the tears as they fell and I felt an amazing and overwhelming passion and pride for our country and what we had lived through. That life still goes on. That I'm still alive. I was grateful and proud. But I was also full of hate, hate so passionate that it scared me.

I found myself no longer opposed to a war. I wanted to hurt the people that did this to us, to me.

"In a sick and twisted way," my mom said, "That's the same way they felt."[24]

Michele Longo Eder, 47, of Newport

Though I went to Union Square and Washington Park, I stayed away from the site of the bombing. It was, I felt, a mass grave, a place I ought not to go. Instead, I took a boat tour around the southern tip of Manhattan and for me that view was enough. The destruction of the Twin Towers left a massive breach in the skyline. Smoke plumes still rose from the site. Our boat went under the Brooklyn Bridge, up the East River, turned around, and came back again. I took a city bus back to Grand Central Station, then walked back to the Waldorf. I was done in.[25]

1. Wes Loucks working at the World Trade Center site. Photo courtesy of Wes Loucks.

2. Portland Firefighters in Far Rockaway, Queens, New York. Left to right: Dwight Englert, Ed Hall, Wes Loucks, Neil Martin. Photo courtesy of Wes Loucks.

3. Portland firefighters working "the pile" with Billy Quick (center). Photo courtesy of Wes Loucks.

4. Portland Mayor Vera Katz at Ground Zero. Left to right: Mayor Katz in brown coat, Frank Klejmont, Melody Madison, Cliff Madison. Photo by Cliff Madison.

5. "Make Peace Not War. Heroes Live Forever." Dust-covered storefront near the World Trade Center site. Photo courtesy of Lance and Marla Nuttman.

erhaps a formal memorial will be built someday. For now, there are the walls and windows of Lower Manhattan, where thousands of messages have been inscribed in the gray snow of destruction that fell two weeks ago today, when the World Trade Center collapsed in the wake of a terrorist attack.

—The New York Times, September 25, 2001[20]

World Trade Center, New York, New York. Interior. Large arched windows, 1976. Photographer: Balthazar Korab Studios, Ltd. Collection of the Library of Congress.

Towers of the World Trade Center in Lower Manhattan Seen From West Street 05/1973. Windows at the bottom; note the size of the people. Photographer: Wil Blanche. Collection of the U.S. National Archives.

Photos of the windows after the attacks taken by Portland Police Officer Cliff Madison from the World Trade Center site. Photos: Cliff Madison.

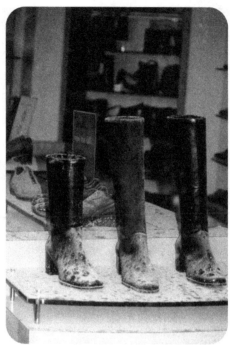

Photo by Alice McElhany

Photo by Alice McElhany

Photo by Alice McElhany

Photo by Alice McElhany

Photo by Cliff Madison

Photo courtesy of Loen Dozono

Photo courtesy of Loen Dozono

Photo courtesy of Loen Dozono

Photo courtesy of Loen Dozono

Photo by Alice McElhany

Photo by Cliff Madison

Photo by Cliff Madison

Photo by Cliff Madison

Photo by Cliff Madison

Photo by Cliff Madison

Photo by Cliff Madison

Photo by Cliff Madison

Photo by Cliff Madison

Photo by Cliff Madison

Photo by Bill Cooper

Photo by Cliff Madison

Photo by Al O'Brien

Photo by Pat Goodrich

BEARING WITNESS

"Originally, I thought the most important thing was to get people to fly again and to get the economy moving, but I don't think it's as important as reaching out to people in anguish. —*Eugene Mayor James Torrey*

Flight For Freedom participants made history themselves and they may know more New Yorkers' stories of September 11 than any others on the planet. It seemed as though, to New Yorkers, the "Oregon ♥ NY" T-shirts and buttons were invitations. First, they offered the Freedom Fliers gratitude, and then they offered their stories of where they had been on September 11 and what had happened to them.

These impromptu interactions occurred numerous times every day for every Oregonian. It was in these connections, the New Yorkers shaking their hands, saying thank you, wanting a hug, and giving in return the painful and poignant gift of a story or memory, that evoked from the Freedom Fliers a depth of heartfelt giving far beyond what they had ever anticipated.

That the Flight For Freedom directly contributed to New Yorkers' economic well-being was proved repeatedly. The washroom attendant at the Waldorf told **Medford City Councilman Ed Chun** that if the Oregonians had not come, he would not have been working.

Dundee Postmaster James Lane and his family described for the *Newberg Graphic* an encounter with a man who approached him and

361

his family in Columbus Circle: "He asked if we were from Oregon and said, 'Can I give all of you guys a hug?' He said if people spend money he can keep his job."

At the Waldorf-Astoria, the woman who cleaned **Barbara Shaw**'s room asked for her autograph.

Even the shadier elements in New York were happy to see us.

—Marla Nuttman of McMinnville

Nancy Waples and her family were startled when they heard a loud, "Hey Oregon, thanks for coming!" over a loudspeaker as they were walking down the street. They looked around and discovered it was a policeman using his voice amplification to good purpose. The people around them thought so, too, because they started clapping.

"No matter where we went, police officers, dignitaries, the average citizen on the street, television teams and cameramen, came up to us to say thank you for coming," said **Celia Wiebe**.

I personally was interviewed four times, by the BBC, Chinese television, French television and a local New York station. The New York reporter was in tears after I finished my impassioned speech and said, "Tell the people of Oregon we are so glad you came and we love you."

In her article for *Galley Proofs*, journalist **Glennis McNeal** recalled similar encounters:

We were cheered, hugged, thanked, and praised.

Our hotel maid cried. "Last week I worked one day. This week, because of you guys, I'm working four," she said.

The Central Park carriage driver said, "Where have you been? We've been waiting for you since September 12!"

A young couple brought hot coffee to my friend as we waited in line for theater tickets. And, when we stood up to stretch during the play intermission, an audience member brought us a box of chocolates. "This is for your trip home. Thank you for coming to New York." . . .

This was not my first visit to New York City, but by far the most memorable. Never again do I expect to be hugged and kissed by a Park Avenue doorman and told, "Thank yez for coming from Are-ee-gone. I mean it, sister."

Mary Kelso of Beaverton said, "I would go back in a New York minute. If I could have stayed longer, I would have . . . . I tried to spread my money around. I had my shoes shined and my hair cut."[1]

Jeanine Ford of Portland, whose son was a Portland police sergeant:

> When we went to the beautiful and famous Tavern on the Green, the manager served us complimentary champagne to show his appreciation. The waiters told us that before the Flight for Freedom arrived, the restaurant had been "like a morgue."

Jackie Young of Happy Valley, a college friend of Jeanine, had gone there with Jeanine and her husband, Don (JJ).

> He then brought out two whole bags filled with matchbooks with the Tavern on the Green logo. He said, "This is all I have to give you to take back."

I still have some matchbooks [almost twenty years later].[2]

Bill Cooper of KPAM Radio, Portland:

> The people in New York really embraced us. They loved having us there. I was having dinner with Chris Sullivan [KXL Radio] at a little Irish pub not too far from the Waldorf-Astoria hotel. We were sitting at the bar, we were eating a steak and having a beer and talking. We were wearing our "Oregon heart New York:" buttons. A couple of guys came up to us and shook our hands, thanked us for supporting New York . . . . And they left. We finish our dinner and we ask the bartender for our check.
>
> He said, "The two guys you were talking to paid for your dinner." Apparently, that happened a lot to people . . . . They really took us under their wing and appreciated us being there.[3]

Al O'Brien of Portland remembered how devastated the people were. "The train station (subway) with no one but the Oregon people waiting for the next train."

364 | Oregon ♥ New York   Sally Ruth Bourrie

After GMA I tried to go some places and give some people some money. I had dinner at a place for 250 and I was one of ten.

I was trying to be a customer of these little places—seven dollars for a cup of coffee. When I was at the site, I went into a deli; it was narrow and deep. The guy saw me wearing the T-shirt and he said, "Let me buy you a cup of coffee." I asked him about how much business he lost. He said he used to sell lunches to people from the towers. They didn't have time to come down, we delivered them to the floors. Over 1,000. The place wouldn't have seated twenty-five people, but he sold 1,000 lunches on a daily basis. There were ten people in there and people couldn't get them out very fast.

He found a way to do things—preorder. A lady came in from Tribeca. She hadn't been home yet—the deli guy asked.

She said, "Our building had to be evacuated so I can't go home." She was walking around [on September 11] and her feet were getting so hot. The sidewalks were so hot that they burned the soles off her shoes.

The area beneath the towers was as big as Grand Central.[4]

Kathi Karnosh of Portland: [PHOTO 1]

I didn't know a soul. I went up to the concierge there at the hotel and there was a group of people standing by and I inquired where to go for dinner and the news crew from Portland said, "Why don't you join us?" . . . I just tagged along.

A couple, Mary is her name, and her husband grew up in Brooklyn, and we just kind of hooked up and Mary and her husband, whose name escapes me, said, "Why don't you just join us? We're going to walk across the Brooklyn Bridge, we're going to have lunch at Katz's Deli.

Jane and Steve Ditewig, Longview, Washington: [PHOTO 2]

Jane: Rupert's Hello Deli. We tried to get on the Letterman show and couldn't so we went to Rupert's Deli and I gave him my T-shirt and he gave us all hot chocolate. It was just a really, really neat experience. There are so many wonderful experiences that we had. It's feeling like we were doing something.

Steve: He invited us in for hot chocolate and we talked with him for several minutes about all that had happened, what fun Dave was, how much we were getting out of our visit, and he was very appreciative of our being there.

SOLV Executive Director and Flight For Freedom organizer Jack McGowan:

❝This was relayed to me and I didn't see it per se, but there was one night where a family from Eastern Oregon. They decided to go and they had never flown before. It was . . . just a regular restaurant and it was very close to the Waldorf and they were staying at the Waldorf. I believe it was the family of four: mom, dad, and two children. And they were wearing their "Oregon Loves New York" pins. They walked into the restaurant and this was a few days after the media had picked up and *USA Today* and the *Times* and we were on *GMA*, the *NBC Nightly News*. It permeated the city.

And they walked into the restaurant and the maître d' saw them and turned around to the restaurant—and there weren't many people in the restaurant, but it had a very sizeable amount of clientele and he said to the patrons, "Ladies and gentlemen, these people are from Oregon."

And there was this applause from everyone in the restaurant. And I heard that people were vying for the bill to pay for this family's dinner.

Connie Hawk of Salem, who had been to New York many times before:

❝The highlight was just touching base with the locals. I went to this upscale, family restaurant, Fresco, that we had been to before, a short walk from the Waldorf-Astoria. I had my Oregon Loves New York shirt and as soon as I walked in, I was treated like royalty. The women in the diamonds came up to hug me, the owner and his family couldn't let me know how much the people coming from Oregon meant to them. I know before the 9/11, dressed as I was, I would have been out of place.

Also, restrooms, as funny as it may seem, were now opened to the public, even if you were not buying stuff at the store. That was the biggest culture shock.

There were no horns honking, and the streets were empty on the way to the airport. The cab driver could not stop talking about how great it was that we came.

Rich and Nancy Dorr of Lake Oswego got the ride of their lives in Manhattan:

> We were walking through an upscale residential area on our return to the hotel when we happened on an apartment building under renovation. We stopped to chat with two construction workers who had noticed our "Oregon Loves New York" buttons. I asked them about the difficulty of transporting building materials through Manhattan and they replied that the different trades took care of their own material.
>
> One of the men asked us if we had ever been up an outside construction elevator. We told him we hadn't and he asked if we would like to go. So up the outside of the twenty-plus-story building we went. What a view! The East River to the East, the United Nations and one of the Trump towers to the South and numerous skyscrapers to the North and West.
>
> One of the men had been erecting construction elevators for forty years and the other was an engineer. The elevator man said he took Harrison Ford the movie star up to look at the apartment on top where we were. I asked him what the apartment would go for when completed and he replied "19 million." On the trip down they taught Nancy to operate the elevator.

The kindness and gratitude of New Yorkers when they saw her button astounded **Betsy Holzgraf**—in coffee shops, the Museum of Modern Art gift shop where, after the cashier asked, "Are you with that group from Oregon?" everyone clustered around her at the cash register and told her how grateful they were that the Oregonians had come. She heard from other Freedom Fliers that a homeless man had even stopped them and thanked them. And when they stood in line for day-of-show theater tickets and people saw her button, they insisted she go to the head of the line. It was a nice experience, but it gave her an interesting perspective. "This is a tiny taste of being a celebrity and I wouldn't want to live like this."

Martin Fisher of Bend, who went with his wife and daughter:

> There's like 12 million people there. A couple hundred people from some Podunk state that I bet most of them couldn't find on a map showed up and all of a sudden, it's actually important. When people would talk to you, you could just tell that it was like that just talking about it was at the same time painful for them but also cathartic.
>
> You couldn't say anything when they're talking to you about what's happened and what they've seen. What do you say? You just kind of sit there looking dumbstruck and nodding in sympathy or something because you can't say anything. You can't say, "Gee, I understand," or even "I'm sorry." That just doesn't cut it.

Susan
Hey I just want to thank you for all those great pictures. The one in the card I framed and put it on my mantle. You're a very beautiful woman. Hey Hoss and I were just having a regular day until you show up and brought up our spirts, sorry it made you cry. I am glad you guys had a great time here. You helped our city alot and we all thank you. If you need NYC patches I will send them to you no problem. Next week Hoss and I should be up in the Bronx for the World Series. Do you like the Yankees. Hey not everyones perfect. In the Decemeber Issue of Horse Illustrate Magazine there is going to be an article on the NYPD Mounted Police. Maybe Hoss will be in it. Well I just want to say thank's to you and all the people of Oregon. NY LOVES OREGON TOO!!!!
THANK'S
JOHN

Susan Henningsen with New York police and their thank you note to her. Photo and note: Judi Henningsen.

Mary Platt of Portland:

We went to some little café for breakfast and . . . they said, "You don't understand. We're a very tight community here and we're completely dependent on the bridges for food to come here. And so this has been a horrific experience and the food shortage is a real concern and issue."

That kind of conversation [was typical] . . . . We were wearing those shirts that indicated who we were and people would stop us in the street routinely. From one part of the block to the next, people would come up to us and I remember one man telling us that his wife was pregnant. They didn't know if they should stay or go—what do we think?

People would either thank us or just pour out their stories. It really did feel like a walking ministry or something.[5]

Debra-Diane Jenness of Crescent Lake:

Saturday morning, October 6th, we woke up to a light rain falling. Being Oregonians, I had brought my umbrella along. . . . We stopped off at the "Flight for Freedom" registration desk and got maps, schedules and Oregon Loves New York buttons.

Well, we took off walking up to and then down along Fifth Avenue, heading towards the Empire State Building. We were stopped many times along the way by New Yorkers yelling at us, "Hey, Oregon, way to go, thanks for coming!", "Hey Oregon, we're so glad you're here, we love you!" and so on. It made you feel absolutely incredible. . . . [B]y the time we got to the Observation Deck, the clouds had broken and the sun was shining through. It was a little breezy and cool, but really pretty.

We walked all over the deck, taking pictures of various sites that were visible; Madison Square Garden, Macy's, and then, The Site. It was very, very quiet on that side of the deck. So much smoke still coming out from the hole in the ground. So much emotion that it stirred up inside of you. You wanted to photograph it and you didn't; hard to balance, because of all that had happened there, the massive loss and destruction, and the anger that you also felt to those responsible. It was hard to deal with the emotions. Made them very raw.

But still, you felt you HAD to be there, you HAD to be a part of this history in the making. We stayed there and stayed. Spoke with one of the police officers, who wanted a picture with us. Said for us to be safe when we were in town, and we thanked him. It was hard to leave there. After we finally did, realized that the line of people waiting to get in went for several blocks; there had been no outside line when we arrived, so guess we timed that just right . . . .

I had to do one "New York" thing; I walked up the street two blocks to Saks 5th Avenue. Had to go in and say I had been there! We were all wearing our "Oregon Loves New York" T-shirts at this time also. So I was well-received in Saks, and had several sales ladies call me over, thank me for coming and give me samples of cosmetics for a souvenir. The best one was them putting it all in a "Saks 5th Avenue" bag! Which I will treasure forever![6]

Portland Firefighter Allen Oswalt:

When we wore our "Oregon Loves New York" buttons, we would get handshakes, pats on the back, thumbs up, just walking down the street. And the seven of us went to BB King's Blues Bar at Times Square in the evening. We got a table and we have our "Oregon Loves New York" T-shirts, the women had buttons on, and our table literally filled up with drinks. There was no way we could drink it all. Everyone in the bar wanted to buy a round for us. They could see our table was jampacked full and they still kept comin'. We didn't visit among ourselves at all, we were visiting with New Yorkers. They wanted a picture of them with Oregonians.

Portland Area Theatre Alliance President Julie Stewart met with Alan Eisenberg, Association Executive Director of the Actors Equity, who stressed his gratitude to the Oregonians because they were going to Broadway and Off-Broadway shows. Stewart also noted that the Broadway firehouse, like all the others in Manhattan, had become a shrine for flowers, candles, and messages. And, she added, "As a ladder truck returned from the day's funerals, I noticed that it is graced with the masks of Tragedy and Comedy."

Proving that it's a small world, Stewart ran into her cousin at the Waldorf:

We celebrated our family reunion with a carriage ride throughout New York City and became fast friends with our carriage driver. In a strange twist of fate, he turned out to be an actor, director, and playwright. I gave him lots of information about the New Rave festival,

JAW West and other theatre opportunities in Portland. Perhaps we will see more of him.[7]

When she couldn't reach Azumano Travel, **Pat Klum of Neotsu** made reservations for herself and her husband, and when Azumano representatives ran into them on the plane to New York, they immediately invited the Klums to join the group. On their return, Pat and Bob wrote the Dozonos about their experience, enclosing a leftover traveler's check to be donated to the Salvation Army:

> We visited with a West African man who brought his daughter, Veronica, to see the Elton John-Tim Rice musical *Aida* for her thirteenth birthday. It was her first Broadway play. She proudly told us her father was going to Washington, D.C., to receive an award for excellence in business.
>
> We sat next to two young men at *42nd Street* who were out-of-work actors. They were using tickets from Kansas family members who were afraid to fly to New York. We stood in a line for an hour-and-a-half and spoke at length about war and peace with an orthodox Jewish couple from New Jersey while we hoped for tickets to *The Producers*. Stewardesses from Germany shared their concerns about their first flight to the United States after the World Trade Center attack. We laughed with a British couple from Oxford about the "King's English." They informed us that they didn't want "Charley" to succeed to the throne and were waiting for "young William." . . .
>
> Everywhere we went, we stodgy old Oregonians were treated like royalty. Our doorman, seeing our Oregon buttons, held back others seeking cabs, telling them, "Oregon first." Limo drivers in between corporate jobs stopped when no cabs were available, offering to take us anywhere for a nominal flat fee or told us to just pay them what we thought the trip was worth.
>
> We met a high school girl from St. Mary's Academy in Portland who traveled to New York City with her older sister, a student at Southern Oregon. They made no plans for entertainment but spent their day volunteering with the Salvation Army at Ground Zero passing out cold drinks to the workers. A man about our age was planning to help there the next day. I wished we could have done the same . . . .
>
> We hope we reflected the spirit of caring and sharing of our Oregon heritage by taking pictures to send to Veronica and her Dad, the

choreographer and her parents, and some others who did not have a camera handy at important events and by inviting the two young actors to come visit Oregon and stay with us.

Martin Fisher of Bend:

So we got checked in and almost right off the bat that first night we went to dinner at some Italian restaurant right around the corner from the Waldorf. And in this whole restaurant, which had like three floors, there were maybe five people in it. And we ate there and they were telling us about the fact that on a Friday night they should be full. And it was just totally empty. And they talked about how their business had fallen off something like 80 percent.

And then our waiter talked to us about having actually seen the towers fall. That was the first sense you got that being there meant something to the people there. He apparently lived toward the south end of Manhattan and I guess he saw it on his way into work. In fact, [he was] the first person who we had talked with who said they'd seen anything. And all through the evening, he was really happy and jovial and what-not, except when he was talking about that. He clammed up, he talked about it, but he wasn't very jovial.

When we were in there and when we were leaving, all kinds of random staff people would come up to us and say, "Thank you for coming." They had given us those pins, "Oregon loves NY," and some of them had seen a story on the news or something and had figured it out so they came up and thanked us nicely.

"Thank you for coming here because no one else is."

In all my life the place I was sure I wouldn't visit was New York. It has the reputation of being not safe, not clean, rude to visitors, and so I was sure I would never go there.

I think the attitude of people was maybe as shocking at first as anything else there. I honestly had no desire whatsoever to ever go there . . . . [Fisher had interacted with about three people from New York previously in his life.]

And this first impression in the restaurant was not at all what I expected . . . .

The following day, on Saturday we went to the Empire State Building right away and got caught in the only rain of the entire weekend, was the thirty minutes we were standing outside on the top. There was a 40 mph gust of wind; it was awful, but it was a lot of fun. I think it was the first weekend the building had reopened to the public and we actually ran into another group of people from Roseburg who apparently had planned the trip like a year or so ago and they came anyway. They weren't part of this group. We ran into them because I was wearing my U of Oregon jacket and they yelled, "Go Ducks." That was something I wasn't expecting in New York, was somebody yelling "Go Ducks" at me.

Then we went to Macy's and contributed our fair share to the New York economy. That was expensive. But it was the same at Macy's. People were randomly coming up to us and saying, "Thank you for coming."

We had lunch in this large cafeteria-ish thing at Macy's and we sat with some people who lived like forty minutes outside of town and had come into the city for the first time since the crash. They talked about actually a friend of theirs who escaped from—I think they said he came out of like the eighty-first floor of the first tower. It was the first people who knew someone who was actually inside. They were very thankful.

We had either the button or the shirt on all the time. In part, I suppose it was kind of a selfish thing. You quickly realized that wearing the button or the shirt was kind of this ticket to people coming up to you and being nice. I'm not sure how else to say it. And they would stop us all over the place . . . .

Every cabbie wanted ones [one-dollar bills] because so few people were riding that they couldn't make change.

On the next Sunday, we had stopped in this coffee shop/ bagel house thing who couldn't make change because there was no one coming in. We walked all around at Times Square a couple of times, I think, saw a play and did the shopping thing, and it was just amazing. People were just constantly stopping us. Some people would come up with tears in their eyes and just hug you and say, "Thank you."

The police officers were wearing buttons that people had given them.

I remember we walked up to a pasta restaurant and the people by the window knocked on the glass and waved at us. We were walking down the same street and someone in a car went past and shouted out their window, "You guys are heroes." I was like, "Who, what?"

So it quickly became something else entirely. And you started realizing that just being there meant something . . . .

Others from Oregon talked about being given free food and other items when New Yorkers saw the button on their shirts. This felt a little strange to me because one objective of the organizers was to stimulate the economy. So I think that sort of sent the message that, notwithstanding the mayor's plea to come in and spend money, the people there really just wanted people to show up for the sake of showing up.

We went to *Les Misérables*; we went to the Russian Tea Room; we walked around Times Square; once in the day, once at night; Rockefeller Center, saw all the places that you see on TV, which I thought was really cool. Because now when I see TV, I go, "I've been there, I know where that is."

It's much larger in life [than on TV]. I don't think TV captures the size of Times Square. The size of some of those signs is just amazing. You don t really see that on TV, at least that I notice now. Les Miz, that was the third time I've seen it, but I thought that seeing it on Broadway would be something significantly different than seeing it at the civic auditorium, and it was. Have you ever seen it?

This time, in the context of what was going on then, it took on a completely different meaning. The story's impact and its message was different this time. I've got it actually just about memorized. I could tell you almost every line in it, I've read it, I know the story inside and out and the first time I saw it, it was an emotionally powerful story. The second time I saw it, I was able to enjoy it for the play. And I kind of thought the third time I saw it I would start thinking, this is the same old, I know this story, I know all the words. I was kind of thinking really that my daughter would enjoy it more than I would.

But and I was surprised. I hadn't thought of this, but when they start singing about lost friends killed at the barricade and the struggle to add meaning to that, it really hits home during the song. The empty chairs at the empty tables where he was singing about his friends who all got killed at the barricades and he's singing about how his friends would come there and sing there and talk and drink and they are gone now and as he's singing, the ghosts of his friends are coming up behind him. I always thought that song was the saddest song in the play anyway, that was just unbelievably powerful.

Likewise, at the very end of it when all of the people who died show up and the last song is about how sort of notwithstanding how dark things are now, it's going to be better because they're going to keep pushing forward. It just changed the show's entire context. I'd have never thought that, but it was a completely different show.

[My daughter] got up that morning [September 11] with us and we were watching and she came in and saw it going on. They talked about it at her school so she understood what had happened. When she got there, she was really just impressed by the size of everything; the incredible number of taxicabs really impressed her to the point where, when a couple of times we had walked around for a long time and she finally said, "Let's just get a cab. It's really easy, watch," and she'd stick her thumb out. And ever since then, in fact, she's asked to go back. She really enjoyed the play, she liked going up on the Empire State Building, liked the subway . . . . She even, I think, appreciated going on Sunday to the Trade Center area. She saw it and was trying to understand that that's where the Twin Towers once stood.

ST. PATRICK'S CATHEDRAL AND THE FUNERALS

Chris Sullivan of KXL Radio, Portland:

At one point just as I was walking along on my own, going by St. Patrick's because that was my mother's favorite cathedral when she was alive. When I'd go to New York, I'd check it out. There was a random firefighter's funeral going on day and night . . . . It was important for me to go to St. Patrick's because my mom and I enjoyed the cathedral so much. Being Catholic, there was a ceremony going on, didn't want to be too intrusive.

Retired Portland schoolteacher Patty Deines did attend one fireman's funeral at St. Patrick's Cathedral; she was invited by the fire-fighter guarding the door who said, "You're from Oregon, you're one of us. We'd be honored if you'd come in."

SOLV Executive Director and Flight For Freedom organizer Jack McGowan:

It was near St. Patrick's Cathedral and I was walking down the block and I just needed time to myself to walk through my birth-place. I came upon a policeman, a big, burly cop, and he looked at me and he came up and he must have been six feet, three inches and he put his arms around me and hugged me. We hugged on a New York City street corner. I remember that today, the look in his eyes, the tears in his eyes . . . .

The memorial masses, the funerals were daily, and multiple areas all across the metropolitan area. It was Rockaway, Queens, it was Long Island, and it was New Jersey. It seemed like every church of every denomination was having funeral services every single day. And the memorial at Saint John the Divine.

Oregon State Senator Margaret Carter of Portland:

I went to two of the firefighters' services there. That was incredible because as a Christian woman, I felt that I needed to show support, even though I knew no one. That was not a time of show-off and people knowing who you are. It was a time of solemnity, of showing support for the grieving people of that city. To be able to economically help and to help those who were grieving. That was the highlight of my trip, being there to support those who were grieving.

Those services were so solemn . . . . There was a hush in the audience. The solemness of those services. The only time I talked to New Yorkers was shopping—people would recognize us in that way and we would talk, but no substantive conversations about why we were there and anything else.

They let anyone into the services; it tells you that even though it was a catastrophic event, people were still cognizant of support from around the country so they didn't seem uptight about it. I just walked in and sat in the back.

Dundee Postmaster James Lane and his family also saw a funeral. "A couple of thousand people were watching. There were hundreds of firefighters. There were a couple of women telling us they'd had nightmares—."

Jane Ditewig of Longview, Washington:

St. Patrick's Cathedral. There were the daily funeral processions for the firefighters and the police, too, but especially firefighters. They had bagpipes and you'd hear the bagpipes and the procession. They were doing that every day. And we went to a special mass there. It was part of the Oregon group at seven o' clock that morning after we got there. That was part of the experience.

John Webster of Hood River:

"Having arrived early Thursday, with no sleep, I readily hit the streets anticipating the vigorous sights and sounds of Manhattan.

When I came to Sixth Avenue between 49th and 50th where St. Patrick's Cathedral is located, I was stuck in my tracks at the deafening silence in the air. Lined along the street were many hundreds of onlookers watching the memorial service being held for one of the many heroes, a policeman, killed while serving in the tragedy. No horns, no taxis roaring by.

It was an incredible sight if not an unsettling eeriness. Many were crying, holding pictures of loved ones lost or missing.

My thoughts turned to almost despair: 'Will the city ever be the same? How will these people ever get back to normal?'

Walking farther toward 42nd Street [the theater district] I was again amazed by the silence—the once-bustling crowded Times Square was empty—no lines at the ticket offices, restaurants, or movie theaters. Walking from theater to theater, shows that were normally sold out had many tickets available.

I gladly ponied up the ticket price and went to *Chicago*. At the end of the performance the entire cast sang "America the Beautiful." I don't think there was a dry eye in the theater . . . .

I'll never forget how empowering the bus drivers were, thanking everybody.[8]

THE FIRE STATIONS

Portland firefighter Allen Oswalt worked on the hazmat team. His station east of Portland was one of the city's busiest. Twenty runs in a twenty-four-hour period was not unusual. [PHOTO 3]

"We went to Grand Central Station, me and one of the guys I went with, just to see the architecture. We're standing on one of the upper concourses. There was a fire in one of the subway tunnels and firefighters were going across the floor of Grand Central Station and they got a standing ovation. We got grandstand seats on that . . . .

We wanted to hear those stories of New Yorkers, especially the fire-fighters. After 9/11 there were so many firefighters in midtown and Manhattan that were killed that firefighters from Brooklyn were having to fill those shifts . . . .

We had firefighters coming to receptions that the Waldorf held for us—I must have heard forty-five or fifty different stories, but we were seeking them out. When we went to the fire station near the Waldorf, we wanted to hear the stories in the station, anyone that wanted to come talk to you. I think the firefighters wanted to talk to us because we were firefighters.

I think they looked down on us a little because we're not FDNY. We're like suburban firefighters. They're on a little higher pedestal than we are. I don't like to get more than ten floors up (laughs).

Oswalt and his friends went to a fireman's wake—at least he presumed that's what it was. The bars were so crowded it wasn't possible to go in and talk to anyone.

Once they've found evidence that someone had died, then they can do the funeral and stuff. The guys that were in uniform would get like two fingers of beer—because they're on duty—and they would raise it up.

I think the family was somewhere inside. We couldn't get that far because there was a steady stream of mostly on-duty firefighters in their turnouts trying to get to the family. We really had no business there . . . We were just amazed at what was going on.

They're so dense with firefighters in Manhattan—there are so many of them—we don't even have a fire station near mine [in Portland], it's four miles away. In four miles, they'll have six fire stations in Manhattan. It was a big crowd and we were drawn to it by the firetruck parked down front. At times, there were three of them out there. They either came by purposely or coming back from a run, they stopped by.[9]

Joe Seward of Nyssa on the Idaho border did not go on the Flight for Freedom but actually took his family—wife, daughter, and son-in-law—to Washington, DC, and New York City on his own at the end of September because he felt so strongly about showing support and bearing witness to what had happened.

FDNY is broke up into ladders . . . and the other stations are like the underground firefighter-type people. [There are] hundreds of those little stations that have maybe twenty people a shift. They're not very big, they're just hole-in-the-wall stations. That station that was just across Times Square from us. They lost two shifts—one shift going off went down to the fires and the shift coming on went down to those fires. And 90 percent of those died. They were some of the first guys there. The flowers were piled up.

Joe's wife, **Marty Seward**:

We went to a couple of fire stations [including] the one that lost most of the firemen. We went and hugged the one that was left, one or two that was left and we cried with him. And then on the outside of that fire station were the pictures of the firemen that were lost, and there were flowers everywhere, mementos, notes, and people would just come and stand there and some would put their hands on the pictures and that was one of my impressions.

Everybody was quiet at the station, people were crying. All their pictures, the ones that died were on the wall, teddy bears. It makes me cry now. Teddy bears and flowers and pictures of their families.[10]

Organizer Bruce Samson of Portland:

My daughter, who is a teacher and was born in Portland and now is teaching in Bellevue, Washington, was able to bring greeting cards from her fifth grade to the firemen. She and I paid a private visit to one the firehouses and we were treated extremely well by the captain who was in charge.

He took us into their gathering room where they drink coffee. There were three or four of the firemen who sat with us and talked about what it was like. That private time with those firemen was really special.

I asked the captain what it's like now and he says it's very disorienting because the men that were killed were doing what we all are expected to do and yet obviously somehow it turned into a disaster for them personally as well as for the people in the building. It was disorienting for them because they were going into a building that probably—had they known the dynamics of the collapse or the potential dynamics of the collapse, the way it pancaked down to the ground—they probably would have been forbidden from doing what they were doing, [which was] going up the stairs at the time the top of the building was coming down on them . . . .

"Our job when there's a fire in a high-rise is to go up and get people out and put the fire out."

Engine 54, Ladder 4, Battalion 9
[PHOTO 4]

That Midtown Manhattan firehouse was the hardest hit in all FDNY on September 11. An entire shift—fifteen firefighters—were killed. They were among the very first to respond and go into the World Trade Center and none of them made it out alive. The remains of some of them would never be found. Twenty-eight children were left fatherless.[11]

In 2003, **Sandra Kempel of Portland** remembered: [PHOTO 5-7]

Visiting the firehouse and meeting some of the firemen who lost friends. It was tremendously overwhelming to be there and shake their hands and tell them what a great job they had done and know what they had had to deal with because they lost friends and relatives.

The gentleman who was marketing representative of Grayline tours of New York suggested it. We were standing at GMA, at the little island of Times Square, because their office was right across the street from the firehouse. He thought that they would really appreciate some Oregonians coming by and greeting them personally. It wasn't planned on my part. In a conversation just standing there, he said, "You're coming to the firehouse after, aren't you?"

In 2020, she added:

We went to two fire stations—they had both lost a significant number of their people and they had their own memorials set up with the pictures. That was heart-wrenching.

They were probably feeling pain and I don't know—they were polite enough, but I can remember the expression on one of the guys' faces. Who knows what he'd gone through? He was just sort of deadpan. I have a picture of him and wow, if his eyes could tell the story, it would be incredible.

Beth Faulhaber of Molalla, director of the Police Activities League, and **Portland School Police Officer Jerry Cioeta** brought Portland middle school students **Alisha Santos, twelve, and Sarah Loftis, eleven.** They visited Engine Company 8, Ladder Company 2, on 51ˢᵗ St. between Lexington Ave. and Third Ave. "We had some cards and letters that some of the Molalla Elementary School kids had written to firemen at the fire station," Faulhauber told *The Molalla Pioneer.* "They lost ten people at that station."[12]

Professor and playwright Michael Phillips: [PHOTOS 8-9]

I'm walking south on Eighth Avenue toward 42ⁿᵈ Street and, suddenly, I see a huge, 6-foot-by-6-foot bronze statue sitting on a trailer on the side of the street. Alongside it are two six-foot tall plaques. They've been donated to the city by a sculptor in Pennsylvania. The statue is of a fireman, down on one knee, his hat off and held in one hand. He is holding his head in the other hand. A look of exhaustion, sadness, grief. The two plaques show NYC police, firemen, and rescue workers. People walking down the street in full conversation suddenly stop, grow silent, stare. Many begin to cry.

I finally move on from the statue and suddenly come upon a fire station. Outside, all around the front of the building, are flowers, candles, cards, large posters and banners, all expressing condolences and support. The centerpiece is a large picture of fifteen firemen from that station, none of whom came home on 9/11.

George Haight of Woodburn: [PHOTO 10]

I walked through Greenwich Village on the West Side. (I thought I needed to get close to something a little more natural than all these buildings.) I saw the Hudson River.

I could see about twenty people standing around on the meridian of the highway and an oil drum that they were burning stuff in. I thought, "What a strange place to have a fire." I walked over and they were holding banners up thanking the firemen and policemen.

It was the West Side Highway and all the emergency vehicles were coming and going to the center. [Volunteers around Greenwich Village] had been there since the day of the attack and had manned that little meridian in the middle of the highway twenty-four hours a day. The fire trucks would go by and the firemen would be waving and honking their horns and the little group would be standing there with their banners and their handwritten signs and say, "Thank you," "Our thoughts are with you," and they wanted to name the highway the "Heroes Highway."

I got to visiting with this chap who lived in the Village, and he said, "Oh, you're one of those, we're so proud to have you in our city . . . .What are you doing for the next couple of hours?"

I said, "Whatever you want me to."

He said, "I want to show you my end of the city."

So, off we went on a hiking tour of Greenwich Village, and he wanted to show me, in particular, his neighborhood fire station. It was another real tearjerker. We spent about a half hour there. They'd lost six firemen, and so there were all the handwritten notes and flowers and teddy bears and right in the middle of the display and right at the firehouse door was a little evergreen tree with "Oregon Loves NY" stickers all over it.

This guy and I just hugged and cried and shook hands with the firemen . . . And we've talked a couple of times since.

Barbara Shaw of Scio:

To walk amongst the dust and the fire station that lost the most men. That trip is in my heart. Processions—they didn't even have enough chapels to take care of everybody. There were just constant people in the street. Constant funerals. It was just an amazing trip . . . . I know what a beautiful gift to the world it was.

Rob Platt of Portland:

One of the many powerful moments of the trip was we went out to Staten Island on the ferry and . . . on the way back there were one firefighter and maybe two or three, but I talked to one firefighter who was on the way to a funeral for some of his guys that he worked with that were casualties of the whole 9/11 thing and I had a conversation with him. That was pretty heartbreaking.

It was what he didn't say that kind of sticks with me. He said, "This is really tough." And it's one of those moments . . . . Because we were just there and the boat was going back to Manhattan and he was—grief was pouring off him.[13]

The whole trip was like that.

Lynn Lundquist of Powell Butte—rancher, teacher, and former **Speaker of the Oregon House of Representatives**—stood on a street corner across from a funeral for a New York City firefighter:

> New York cared we were there . . . . Thousands of people were there, standing silent. Thousands more firefighters stood shoulder to shoulder for blocks and blocks.

> Taking a picture would have been sacrilegious . . . . The hurt is going to be there for a long time and I didn't see that as much until I got there . . . .

> It was one of those demoralizing and uplifting situations that many times in life you cannot find.[14]

Cinquantacinque

Connie Hawk's daughter and five-year-old granddaughter from Stamford, Conn., came in to New York to see her. Together they brought cookies she'd baked in Salem to Engine 55, known as "Cinquantacinque" (Italian for "Fifty-Five"), which was formed in Lower Manhattan's Little Italy in 1887. "They were so nice. They showed us the pictures of the brothers they had lost; their boots, helmets, and everything were left waiting for them to be found. They had only found one, and on the day we visited he had been put to rest," she wrote.[15] [PHOTOS 11-12]

Portlander Jane Meskill also visited that fire station with her friend, **Alexia Halen**:

> **Jane:** Fire stations who'd lost so many people. That was harrowing. Just even that they have these little, tiny—they're like carriage houses. Just as wide as a regular storefront, but they have the fire engine in there. Then they draped the fire stations with this black cloth over the top and they had pictures of all the firemen that had deceased and the firemen were there accepting condolences. Kind of like at a wake. They were in deep, deep mourning. It was so dark. So sad. It was very silent, very quiet.

> **Alexia:** It was like an altar. People weren't talking. I think the firehouse we were at was one of the firehouses that got hit really hard. A lot of the men were in the buildings and died that day. It was the one that lost most of its members. At that time, we were all together

with one common enemy. In solidarity, because somebody attacked us. We'd never experienced anything like that to that magnitude . . . . We could not be in a more different time right now [2021]. It's pretty striking.

Debra-Diane Jenness of Crescent Lake. On Sunday, the Jenness family walked to Ground Zero after the Union Square service, stopping at the renowned fire station Engine 24, Ladder 5 in the South Village along the way:

This particular station had lost eleven brothers from their midst. Their pictures were on display. It was heartbreaking.

We were quietly reflecting and taking a few photos when a young girl came up on roller blades and started to weep deeply and uncontrollably; I went to her, gave her a hug and some Kleenex. She said she lives only four blocks from there, but she had been on safari in Africa at the time, and it had taken her the last three weeks to get home; this was the first time she'd been down since she just got home late the last evening. She knew the people from this station; she knew the dead; she cried some more.

I could do nothing but hold her, and it seemed to help. The station crew was out when we got there, but they returned while we were still there. After they backed their rigs in, they all came out to shake hands with us and give us hugs and thank us for coming. It made you feel incredible . . . .

Down by the New York Stock Exchange we met a young man wearing a New York Rangers hockey jersey. Being hockey fans ourselves, we stopped to chat. His name was Martin, and he asked for our address; we have since exchanged Christmas cards and phone calls to stay in touch. He said it meant so much to New York to have the group from Oregon come out. We told him it meant as much to us as well . . . .

Chinatown Firehouse

Mayor Katz visited the Chinatown fire station, and made them a gift of a 9/11 cartoon by Portland's award-winning editorial cartoonist, Jack Ohman. [PHOTO 13]

Washington State University student firefighters Brent Olson and Jeff Siemers lived and worked at the Washington State University fire station, one of only a handful of such campus fire departments in the country. [PHOTO 14] As student volunteer firefighters, they responded to fire and medical calls, along with the City of Pullman Fire Department. Brent, the son of Port of Portland Commissioner Mary Ann Olson, had traveled to New York during his freshman year and become friends with members of Ladder 16. He planned to visit his friends there. They also toured Engine 9, and Ladder 6.[16]

Billy Quick

One legendary firefighter, and much beloved in the FDNY, became well-known in Portland when Azumano Travel brought him and other FDNY members out to Portland for the 2002 Rose Parade. (See Appendix A: The Aftermath.) Billy Quick worked tirelessly at Ground Zero and died ten years later from the toxicity to which he was exposed. Sho Dozono was among those from Portland who returned to New York for Billy Quick's funeral.

Portland firefighter Wes Loucks, 51, Gladstone (pop. 11,438): The only reason we got to go [work at Ground Zero] was because of my friend, Billy Quick. He was well-known and well-respected in the department so if you knew him, you were accepted. He had come to Oregon ten years earlier, him and a friend of his who was a friend of his, a detective out of Nassau county. They came out to climb Mount Hood and they came to our fire station. I worked at the Lloyd Center. We got to know them pretty well.

Billy Quick at the 2002 Portland Rose Parade. The firefighters signed a newspaper article and gave it to Sho and Loen Dozono. Courtesy of Sho and Loen Dozono.

For myself, being able to be back there within days, when it's still a disaster scene, when they're still looking for survivors, and then having a friend there who had suffered through it.

My friend, Billy Quick was his name, he worked there seven days a week for months, and they told us when we were back there, they warned us, there's going to be some repercussions for working on this dust-filled site. You're breathing in glass, dust. He worked there and doctors warned that within 10 years there are going to be people dying because of this. My friend died almost ten years to the day from the attacks. He died of kidney failure, of lung disease. His name got put on the wall with the other firefighters that were killed the day of. They had a saying back there, "They're still dying." It was the ten-year anniversary was when he died, and there was a lot of firefighters dying from cancer, tissue failure, a number of things.

There are still people who are suffering. I was back there three or four different times in that year's period from 9/11 all the way to the memorial in 2002, plus the trip on St. Patrick's Day when we all went on the St. Patty's Day parade.

David Morkal, Battalion Chief, Executive Officer to the Chief of Operations, FDNY: Billy was a big fan of Portland and used to go back there all the time. When he had a chance to go out there, he was all over it.

When he went back to Portland [one time], he said, "What's up with that?"

"[It's] Mt. Hood [elevation: 11,250 ft.]. You've got have some skills [to climb that]."

So he went and climbed it. He would just do whatever he wanted to do. He hadn't done a lot of mountain climbing, he just climbed Mt. Hood and he came back and said, "That was pretty fun."

Before he passed, he was in such bad shape, he couldn't go back there. Two guys from Portland were staying with him the night that he died. He had to sleep on his side so he could breathe and while he was sleeping he rolled over on his back and suffocated . . . . Billy gave a lot to the department and to humanity and it took a lot from him.[17]

POLICE VISITS

Portland Police Public Schools Captain Cliff Madison and Portland Police Public Schools Director of Security Lieutenant Frank Klejmont, a former New York City police officer, had brought their uniforms, which they planned to wear to one event, but they ended up wearing them every day. Before they left, they purchased New York tribute pins made by the Portland Police Foundation to give to their peers on the other coast. [PHOTO 15]

Instead of sightseeing, they visited about ten downtown precincts. Along with their wives, they gave out the pins with the message that "Your brothers and sisters in Portland are thinking about you," Madison said. "The whole precinct came out to shake our hands. People were in tears in the precincts because two cops stopped by to say hi . . . . Traditional New York cops—you're not thinking about warm and fuzzy."

They also brought a signed poster from the Portland 911 [emergency] center, where Madison had once worked, and with Mayor Katz went to a Manhattan police station and presented the poster. [PHOTO 16] Madison:

They were really open and warm and saying thank you. The operators took 3,000 calls in the first twelve minutes [after the first tower was hit].

After the second tower was struck, the city then started figuring out they were under attack. They started trying to remove people from places that could be potential targets, [but] they couldn't close down the 911 Center. If you take out the 911 Center, you take out the city. They were operating under that call load and wondering if that next call would be aimed at them . . . .

At the Port Authority police station precinct, they experienced an overwhelming gesture of the sincere gratitude their colleagues in New York felt regarding their visit. Madison:

This one sergeant said, "I have something to give you." Frank and I walk to a locker room. In the locker room, there was a black plastic bag. This sergeant was in the subway and there's an explosion in the subway and it blew him down the subway—and there's a train that should be coming down the line. He got on his radio and said to make sure this train gets stopped—because of all the debris.

He opens this bag. It's got his uniform he was wearing that day.

Klejmont (who had been in the Twin Towers with his wife and daughter the previous July, just two months before):

The uniform he wore that day was coated in ash. He had been walking in the subway heading towards the Twin Towers when it collapsed and it showered him with dust and then it was nonstop for twenty-four hours.

Madison added:

He started taking off the collar pin on his shirt for his precinct. I said, "I can't take those. Those are your good-luck charms." He said "No, I want you to have it. It's a good luck charm and it already worked for me."

Klejmont:

He gave Cliff his collar insignia as a memento and Cliff didn't want to take it.

Cliff said, "This means so much to you."

He said, "You coming here meant more."

I think he was knocked down in the blast when the buildings collapsed.

Madison: [PHOTOS 17-18]

You show your love to the city and they show it back. People used to say Parisians or New Yorkers are rude. I've been to both. In New York, you show you have respect for the city and they'll open up their hearts to you . . . .

As a police officer, [the Flight for Freedom] made me better.

Alexia Halen and her friend Jane Meskill visited the Tenement Museum during the trip:

Alexia: We went to the Tenement Museum. It's on the Lower East Side and when we went it was not that well-known. It's these old tenement buildings that they've set up to look like they did when immigrants came over. All these families lived in one room—twenty people lived in one tenement room. It's my favorite museum hands-down because—and I think really what made it so special—was that it really captured who we are as a country. We are people from all over the world and we all belong here and we all worked hard to do our best and start a new life for ourselves and our families. The whole museum—there are some videos at the beginning and a guide who takes you through and it was such an interesting thing to do, given what was going on. Especially with people who were discriminating against anybody with dark skin at that moment. People were afraid of people and just that—to go through that museum and think we're all human beings and we're all mostly really good people. And it was just such a sad statement of people wanting—profiling and people being afraid.

Jane: When it first opened, I took my mom. Her family came from Ireland. Her mother's parents came from Ireland. Her mom's mom got sick on the way—just for a visit they came, and they refused to get back on the boat. They were in the Lower East Side at the turn of the century when there were 1,000 people per block . . . .

It was just as people had left it. They found people who had lived there and they have recordings of the people in the rooms . . . . The ground floor was a bar and behind the bar were three outhouses and behind the bar where people lived—12 ft. x 28 ft.—and in one room they would sleep and they would also bring in the clothes from the garment district. They were sewing, [they had] a little room/kitchen and the back room was the bedroom. A family of six would live there, have a staff of sewers [seamstresses] during the day and they'd go up and down with their chamber pots and everything went up and down these stairs—for hundreds of people. And the bar used the same outhouses.

Lana Cupper of Portland, whose son and wife lived in New York City:

[It was] just so profound the way people connected with you. Strangers. That lady who just fell into my chest [at Ground Zero].

. . . It mostly was sad, but I remember going into Grand Central Station. It was like a group of local kids were singing some kind of

"Amazing Grace" or something. It was a beautiful—I cried. I can't remember exactly what it was. And they were all holding hands. They finished as we kind of walked up to the group and the leader of the group and saw and our badges and our shirts and came up and said, "Thank you for coming."

So many people reached out . . . .

[There were so many] emotions there: sick to your stomach, grateful that your whole family wasn't hurt . . .

I remember meeting up with the kids a lot of times at the end of each day we were there and telling them what people were saying to us on the street corners and they were like, "Yeah." They could see it, too, a change from what they lived with prior to this happening.

Brian McCartin of Portland: The essence of Brian McCartin's Flight for Freedom trip is captured in a twenty-year-old golf ball. "Every time I reach into my bag, I'll pull one out and that'll be the Paperloop ball." It goes right back in the bag, he says: "That's got too much meaning." [PHOTO 19]

Portland Oregon Visitors Association (now Travel Portland) Vice President of Sales and Marketing Brian McCartin and Public Relations and Communications Director Deborah Wakefield, the trip was an opportunity to do some marketing and public relations.

"While I was talking to business and potential clients, Deborah was talking to the media. They were all curious about Portland," said McCartin, adding that they were able to get time with New Yorkers who may have been too busy to talk with them before. "We weren't sexy enough . . . . We weren't known as a big corporate town, compared to San Francisco, Seattle, Boston." He added:

We looked at an opportunity to try to reach out to people that we'd been talking to about business, but let them know there's another human spirit in Oregon . . . . We think more about relationships, being Oregonians.

I think that because of what happened there, they [New Yorkers] put down their guard a little bit . . . and could be human and meet with us and I think they were all somewhat in awe that we were there. There was an opportunity . . . to connect with potential clients that we were trying to build relationships with . . . .

They were probably still in shock and what's next, and looking for someone to talk to. And also curiosity—"What is this Portland?"

Also, McCartin said, "I think we were sensitive." If the people they met with wanted to talk about their 9/11 experiences, they were there to listen. "We were there to help lift their spirits and let them know, we were there to be there for them."

Among the companies McCartin met with was Paperloop, which owned magazines and other media sources devoted to the paper, pulp, forest, and allied industries. With the Pacific Northwest's history of wood and paper products, he thought Paperloop would be "a natural." He met with Leo Nadolske, who ran Paperloop's New York office, which had had a "beautiful" view of the Twin Towers.

On Tuesday, September 11, Nadolske was flying to New York from Norfolk, Virginia. While changing planes in Atlanta, he learned that a plane had hit the World Trade Center and that flights were grounded. All the televisions in the airport were turned off except for the ones at the bars. "Everybody was jamming the bars," said Nadolske. "We went to customer service and they said a flight just hit the Pentagon." Nadolske and his colleague were fortunate to be able to get a hotel room in Atlanta; their luggage remained at the airport. Two days later, on Thursday, September 13:

> We wound up getting the last train ticket and we took a train back—twenty-three stops.
>
> We pulled into Penn Station and we're getting off the train, we hear all these people applauding . . . . And here comes a bunch of Philadelphia firefighters, and they were covered in soot with all their equipment and they got on the train going back to Philly.

The Paperloop office was shut down and power was out. Many of the staff had watched the second plane hit the tower from Nadolske's office. "That was when they decided to leave," said Nadolske. "Trains were out, cell phones were out. The only way out they had was to walk across the Fifty-ninth Street Bridge."

Nadolske was in a bar in Atlanta when the second plane hit. "You're like, 'Oh my God, that's Tower One,' and you go into a little bit of shock." Leo had everyone's home phone numbers; he called them all, and stayed in touch with the office via the hotel phone. And when the hotel bill was $800, which he paid, the Westin in Atlanta sent him a refund check of $600 because they understood the problems that day.

"The Westin Atlanta Peachtree Center did a great thing," says Nadolske.

Going back to work when the office reopened, the atmosphere on the subway was different. Instead of avoiding eye contact, "Everybody looked at each other. We all knew what we had gone through," said Nadolske. "We have to move on. The world doesn't stop."

That day he took the whole office out to lunch and the topic of conversation was: "Who did you know who passed?" Nadolske knew one woman whose husband had left her a voicemail saying that it didn't look good and how much he loved her.

No other city came to New York to support them, Nadolske said.

[Portland] *was the only city with the exception of Milwaukee sending the Harley Davidsons, bringing one hundred motorcycles into the city— that was something to see—and then Portland.*

My mother said, "Pick yourself up by your bootstraps," and that's what people were doing. I think I was responsible for a show we did out there, a trade show at the convention center.

Say whatever you want to say about New Yorkers, when the chips are down they are a resilient people. We don't take shit from anybody. And you can print that.[18]

"He met me in his office, gave me a sleeve of golf balls, and I brought him a slew of stuff," said McCartin, who walked quite a way to Nadolske's office, which was in the barricaded part of the city. Twenty years later, McCartin still treasures those golf balls.*

---

*See Appendix F for Leo Nadolske's full interview about his experience on 9/11.

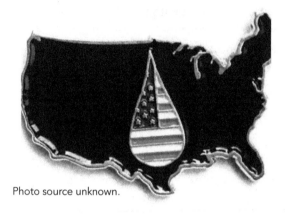

Photo source unknown.

9/11 STORIES

Joyce Willing of Portland:

> It might have been easier for somebody to share a little bit because they knew they weren't going to be triggering for me."[19]

Portland Police Captain Cliff Madison:

> I had an attorney [next to me] on the plane coming back. His offices in Manhattan were closed [on September 11] and one of his secretaries from the Middle East said, "You should take the day off." And finally he decided to come in late. She's nowhere to be found. [20]

Michael Phillips:

> I talked to a friend who lives in Pennsylvania. She said she was driving into New York on the morning of the attack. She was approaching the Lincoln Tunnel when she noticed the Trade Towers on fire. As she watched, the first tower crumbled. She pulled over to the side of the road, and sat there in shock for a few minutes. Then, she simply tuned her car around and went home.

Molly Cunningham of Milwaukie told the *Clackamas Review*:

There was such joy in being able to make contact with folks, but there was such an overwhelming feeling of sadness from the moment we arrived. I went into a shop that was about two doors down from the barricade . . . and the shop owner was talking about what happened on that day. He didn't hear anything. It's just that one moment everything seemed normal, and the next minute he couldn't see anything in front of him—his whole shop was filled with white, thick dust. Pretty soon, the door opened and people just started coming in droves, their eyes full of stuff, their mouths full of stuff, to get cleaned up.

He told us, "I'm just so glad to be alive."

Rebecca Webb and Kam Kimball of Portland went to Battery Park on Sunday, where they had a profound experience with residents there. [PHOTO 20]

> **Rebecca:** We met this older couple. They saw our buttons and they had these extremely strong Brooklyn accents. They came up and they said, "Ore-gone, we love Ore-gone."
>
> **Kam:** [Their son] lives in Rhododendron [Oregon].
>
> **Rebecca:** And so we just started chatting with them. They told us they had been separated the morning of 9/11.
>
> **Kam:** [He had had] like an 8:00 [doctor's] appointment and they didn't see or hear from each other for several days.
>
> **Rebecca:** They hadn't had cell phones before that, but they were carrying their little bags and they explained that they'd gone to get cell phones . . . . They poured their hearts out to us and opened up to us.
>
> **Kam:** There was no one else around. The city was so quiet. I don't remember anybody else on that sidewalk. It was just us and them.
>
> **Rebecca:** They were completely comfortable talking to us because their son lived in Oregon . . . and they happened to mention that they lived nearby; literally, their view out the front window was the Trade Center towers. And they said, "We live on the twenty-ninth floor. Would you like to come up?"
>
> **Kam:** It was the first day that they were allowed back in that building.
>
> **Rebecca:** We had to go through a gauntlet of security with them holding our hand and saying they're with us. They took us up to their apartment, which was still pretty dusty.
>
> **Kam:** The windows were filthy.
>
> **Rebecca:** They'd been blown out and replaced . . . . We couldn't quite believe it. It was almost surreal going up there. If you looked out the

window, you were looking at the hell of the aftermath, still emitting pollution.

Kam: And workers down there. Also the buildings surrounding that area that were blown out.

Rebecca: I think that was the pit of the second tower. She told us the story. They had floor-to-ceiling mirrors on one side and floor-to-ceiling windows on the Trade Center side.

She was blow-drying her hair at the mirror and glanced at out her window when a plane went by and she saw it crash into the first tower and her mind wouldn't accept it. She said to herself, they must be making a movie and kept doing her hair. And when she saw the second plane hit the tower that was directly out her window—

Kam:—She said it was almost eye level from where she was.

Rebecca: She said it was some kind of suction, but it seemed like the pressure must have sucked her into the hallway and there were military people who took her at that point. There was either security or military presence in that building; between the first plane and the second plane they came to get the residents.

Kam: Her husband was already gone, in Queens, I think, or Brooklyn. They ferried her off. I was trying to remember where they took her to—Staten Island?

Rebecca: She was evacuated with a bunch of other people. The residents there were evacuated because by then, by the second plane, people knew that these older folks needed to be rescued. They were taken out immediately, but she was taken care of, and then she realized that she didn't know where her husband was.

Kam: I thought it was three days.

Rebecca: They were so sweet.

Kam: They offered us doughnuts.

Rebecca: It was a classic little New York apartment that had a passthrough, a kitchen where you could see their pots. They made us coffee and doughnuts and told us their story.

Kam: It was small, but I'm sure it was a premium, because it had a view of the World Trade Center.

Rebecca: It made it real. It was already real, but it was so human. It was the personal story that humanizes a story like that. I don't know if I wrote down their name at the time. But I'll never forget going up, having them invite us into their home.

Kam: And that was also so nontypical of New Yorkers to be so welcoming and chatty. Like Rebecca said, everywhere we went, it was such a different world there.

Rebecca: That was exactly right. It was very compelling. When they said, "Do you want to come up to the apartment?" It was like, "We want to show you what we've been through." And it was remarkable. I can still picture how she described she was standing there blow-drying her hair when the first plane hit. The way she put it was her mind would not accept it—they must be making a movie. The reality set in with the second plane. I'm sure it was terrifying and she was in shock. This is just me speculating. For somebody in their elder years, shock could protect you from having a heart attack. They seemed fine. Physically they were fine.

Kam: I do remember her standing there and showing us how it happened to her. And because it was so recent. It wasn't six months later. I think that they were still experiencing the trauma of not knowing where each other was. He was so worried that she was dead, that was his fear. And then not being able to reach her.

Rebecca: Because of where they lived they didn't let them in right away. It was days before they could go home. I don't know how they found each other.

Kam: I think they both were taken to different shelters—Red Cross shelters.

Rebecca: They would have also ended up in some kind of care. They would have stopped—just like the security that would have stopped when we were trying to enter. I feel like there were tarps.

Kam: I just remember it being so dirty. And the smell was horrible.

Rebecca: It was really palpable pollution.

Kam: It was a nice day for a walk. I do remember just the streets being so quiet and eerie.

Rebecca: It was very eerie. It's absolutely eerily vacant. You could sit anywhere. Restaurants and the shopping—it was like we were VIPs everywhere we went because there were so few people there at all. They knew why we were there.

Portland playwright/professor Michael Phillips:

Because I was wearing an "Oregon Loves NY" button, at every restaurant I went into someone from New York came up and talked to me, thanking me for coming. In almost every case, within five minutes they were telling me where they were when the attack happened, and whether they had lost anyone in the towers. And, almost without exception, tears welled in their eyes. I hardly had to talk at all—I just listened, and shared their grief.

I had a drink with a former student of mine who lives in Hoboken, but works in Manhattan. She saw the second tower fall.

Again, after just a few minutes of talking about it, she began crying, and in the midst of her crying looked up and said, "I've had nightmares every single night since then. I don't know when they'll stop."

Sitting in a theatre before the play began, the young woman sitting next to me, along with her parents, thanked me for coming to New York and once again began talking. She's buying an apartment up on 76th Street, but has to go downtown to sign the final papers. She's put it off for three weeks now, because she can't bring herself to go down there. At intermission, another couple comes up to me (I'm wearing my button, and they've seen it from a few rows away), just to say thank you . . . .

Sunday night, I'm sitting in a restaurant, getting ready to leave, when two young women come up to me. About five minutes later we're joined by another of their friends. It turns out that both of the women live down near where the trade towers used to be. One left her windows open, and when she was finally able to get back to her apartment she found over a foot of soot and debris. As she began to clean it up, she found stationery and other papers from the trade towers buried in her living room. The other woman had her windows shut, but the soot hit with such force that it came in every crack and her apartment was filled with an inch of soot. Because she works in some kind of emergency management down in that area, she had to stay the entire day of the attack, even though the rest of building was evacuated. She saw the entire attack, and the collapse of both buildings, from her office window. Later that day, she walked all the way out of south Manhattan, covered head to toe in soot, with no place to stay for the night. An off-duty police officer saw her and offered to take her somewhere.

She tells me all of this without tears. I say, "You seem to be doing remarkably well after all that."

To which she says, "Give me six months."

In his 2002 play, *Voices from a Sunlit Shadow,* Phillips captured beautifully the experience many Freedom Fliers had in New York:

ONE: People would see the button and rush up to talk to me. Everywhere I went. And they'll all say the same thing.

THREE: Thank you.

TWO: Thank you.

FOUR: Thank you so much.

FIVE: Thank you.

ONE: And then they'd tell me their stories.

FOUR: Where they were when it happened.

THREE: I was in my office, very near the trade towers.

TWO: I was in my car, near the Holland Tunnel.

ONE: I was at work.

THREE: I was having breakfast.

TWO: I was . . .

FOUR: And they'd talk about whether or not they had friends or family who didn't get out in time . . . .

FIVE: If all I can do is listen, then I'll listen.[21]

Police Activities League Activities Director **Beth Faulhaber of Molalla, fellow chaperone Jerry Cioeta, Alisha Santos, 12, and Sarah Loftis, 11,** connected with their waiter at a theme restaurant called Jekyll and Hyde. He lived in an apartment three blocks away from the World Trade Center. Faulhaber told his story to *The Molalla Pioneer*:

> He said he was at home the day it happened and everyone got evacuated "with the clothes on your back" and then they had to walk over the Brooklyn Bridge. He said they probably walked twenty miles that day. For two weeks they couldn't get back into their apartments. He's back in his apartment now, but he has to go through security checkpoints to get in and out of his apartment every day.[22]

Jackie Young of Happy Valley:

I like Fendi perfume and I thought I'm going to do my Christmas shopping. On Broadway there's a big Fendi store. It was before the parade and we were going around town.

I walked in there and there was nobody in there, it was just dead empty . . . so empty . . . . I could hear my own footsteps . . . .

Over in a distant corner, there was a group of five salesgirls huddling together in conversation. They were all dressed in black – their store clothing colors. They didn't see me come in. I walked over to them to see if I could get some help to find a bottle of perfume for a gift. When they saw my huge red, white and blue stars-and-stripes bag and my "Oregon Loves New York" T-shirt they got the floor manager to serve me.

She immediately got tears in her eyes and said, "Oh, you are one of the people from Oregon. I was praying I would get to meet one of you to thank you for coming here!"

My own eyes filled with tears as I certainly couldn't understand why everyone was so thankful; it seemed like the least we could do. I was kind of embarrassed.

Then she told me the incredible story of how she was tormented not knowing where her son was when she heard that the towers had fallen. She said, "My son works in the buildings. When they were coming down, there was no way we could contact each other. I waited and waited and hoped and prayed."

Five hours later he burst through the door covered with ash from top to bottom and sobbing, fell into his mother's arms. He said all he could think of was, "I have to get to my mom." . . . It took him five hours to run all the way from the World Trade Center to Fendi on Broadway.

I just gave her a big hug and one of the Max Lucado prayers and thanked her for sharing her story. We both cried . . . .

LETTERS

The Oregonian, Mayor Katz, and the Dozonos all received thank-you letters from New Yorkers. From *The Oregonian*:

Craig Acklen, Bangor, Pennsylvania:

The crowd standing near me on Fifth Avenue was obviously appreciative of the gesture made by the group that traveled more than 3,000 miles to show their support of New York City in its effort to recover from the terrorist attacks. They still may not know for sure where Oregon (Ar-y-gahn) is, but they know it's a long way to travel.

I have lived within 90 minutes of New York City ever since I graduated from Grants Pass High School in 1965 and fell in love with it. We travel into Manhattan regularly for shows, sporting events, and just to be there.

Shortly after the attacks on the World Trade Center, I wanted to go there just to be reminded that there was still life in "The City." Seeing fellow Oregonians with the same idea was a real bonus. On behalf of everyone who loves New York, I'd like to express my thanks to all the Oregonians who helped to make this gesture of friendship.[23]

Delia McQuade Emmons, New Jersey:

"On Monday, Oct 8. I stepped out of the Pierre Hotel on New York's Fifth Avenue to find the Columbus Day Parade in full swing.

I made my way to the curb to find a contingent of Oregonians about 100 strong, decked out in shorts, proclaiming I Love New York. For a solid month, I have mourned friends, attended heartrending memorial services and tried to put one foot in front of the other to get through the days. I was born and raised in Brooklyn, worked for more than 30 years in the shadow of the Twin Towers. I like to think I'm pretty tough—"never let 'em see you cry" is my motto.

Although I make my home now just across the river in New Jersey, I'm a New Yorker in my soul. As I stood at the curb, several women came over to talk. A silver-haired lady told me that she and her colleagues just had to come to help us out. She said that the whole country was standing beside us and that we would pick up the pieces and move forward.

Suddenly, on a bright, blustery afternoon on the corner of 60th Street and Fifth Avenue, something happened to me that has never happened before: A grandmother from Oregon made me cry. She also made my day![24]

THE MISSING

One of the most pervasive wallpapers of that moment in New York were the posted notices that were taped everywhere. The Kinko's near the Waldorf was using its windows as a massive billboard. The notices were for the missing from the people who loved them. The tragic paradox of a snapshot of a person in a happy moment of life in counterpoint to the language on the flyer was one of the most heartbreaking insights into what life had become for New Yorkers. [PHOTOS 21-23]

THE MOST HAPPY ENDING

Leslie Krueger, who worked for the Oregon state government in Salem, had gone on the Flight for Freedom alone. While on the trip, she learned about Mercy Corps' request for volunteers to help put comfort kits together for children directly impacted by the events of September 11, and decided to try to stay an extra day to help. In a conversation recorded in 2021, she and David Parker recalled the day they met.[25]

> **Leslie:** I called work and asked for an additional vacation day, which was no problem. The wonderful people at Azumano Travel took care of the flight and accommodation changes so that I could leave on Wednesday. Since Mercy Corps did not need the volunteers until evening, I had the day to do whatever. My niece said, "You have to take a tour around New York City." So I decided, "Why not? I've got some time to kill." And I went and booked on the Circle Line cruise.
>
> We were running around with those big [Oregon Loves New York] buttons. So I get on the Circle Line boat and in the back and I'm sitting there taking it in and I noticed the crew guy starts coming up and doing his thing.
>
> And at one point he said to people, "Don't stand here, you're going to block other people's view." So what do other people do? Stand there.
>
> I looked at him, like, "Do you believe this?" He then asked people to move.

David [Circle Line tour guide]: The senior-most tour guide had called me up the day before and he said in light of everything—the site is still smoldering—and he said, "Dave, I just can't do it right now. Can you do the day?" I said, "Yeah, sure." We knew this group was in town so we fully expected to see them, I guess.

I hadn't worked since September 1. I had an appendicitis attack on the boat and I was rushed to the emergency room and I had surgery immediately, which is why I was out on September 11.

I saw her go up the steps—she's very striking—and I was just grabbing a quick lunch and I took a note of which side of the boat she was on. I thought, "Why am I bothering? She's from Oregon." I saw the big button on a black coat—

Leslie: It was sage.

David: You were wearing black, trust me on this. I'd normally do a Gilligan [pose], but I would have ripped out the stitches. So I do something else, which Letterman did, a fashion model pose. I waved her off taking photos because if you pose for one photo at the beginning of the tour, you have to pose for everybody on the boat until they get their photo, but I felt bad about it. [PHOTO 24]

Leslie: So we got through this whole thing [the tour]. It was very entertaining.

David: And during the tour she has a very distinct laugh. She laughs like Betty Rubble. I'm a laugh man. When she really gets going, she's like her dad, just air comes out. That's comedy gold. So I ran with that, but—"We love it when you take pictures, we don't love it when you block people's views." . . .

Leslie: At the end, I wanted to thank him and I asked how to get to the Upper West Side to make the comfort kits. He said, "You take this bus," but all I had was bills and I didn't have change. The buses didn't take bills, they only take change. He was helping me get change so I could get on the bus.

David: I felt that bad that I'd waved her off the photo, I explained why. When the trip was over, we had this conversation: I will send you a photo of something I can't do right now because I just got my appendix out. What's your work address?

Leslie: I told him I worked for the state and I can't get mail at work. I'll give you my home address.

David: I'd get in trouble with HR for that, but anyway, that piece of paper was lost in a grant application for financial aid that I was supposed to fill out after I lost three months of salary from Circle Line, three months of salary from another job I had in the winter doing proofreading work for a leading financial magazine. When I went back to that magazine job, by the way, my first job was to read names—"Such-and-such name One World Trade," "Such-and-such name Two World Trade." There was no way to ever forget it. It's still difficult for me to go by the site.

At one point during the pandemic Gov. [Andrew] Cuomo talked about how every New Yorker has some sort of PTSD because of September 11th. I do not disagree. The amazing part of that—I had no idea how many people I knew worked down there. They were all fine . . . .

Leslie: I get to the airport and was sitting there, hardly anybody's at the airport. I thought, you know, I thought that I was really impressed with the tour guide's presentation and so while I was waiting there I said I'd like to leave a message for him and I really wanted to thank him.

David worked at the Circle Line only five days after September 11. When he returned to work in November, he found a surprise waiting for him.[26]

David: It's November. I'm cleaning out my locker, and there was a yellow post-it note taped to the locker and it said, "Dave, Leslie called to thank you for everything you did yesterday." They didn't even write down who took the note. Because she has a distinct name that I have an association with (Krueger), that was enough to jar my memory to her last name and where she lived. So I called up information and I said, "How many first initial 'L' Kruegers do you have in the 503 area code?"

She said, "Three."

I said, "Give me all three."

Leslie: Time goes by and I'd gone out and bought myself a computer and I was waiting for the [computer guy] to call. It was the tour guide, not the computer guy.

David: I said, "Hi, this might be a strange phone call. My name is David and I'm a tour guide for Circle Line, did you take a boat tour about a month ago?"

She said, "Oh my god."

Leslie: When I told people at work I'd given him my personal address, they couldn't believe it. They said, "What's he going to do—" We talked for quite a while. It was a series of phone calls, many emails.

David: Leslie, not that many because it took me forever to type an email. The phone bill was horrendous. We would talk a half an hour, an hour.

Leslie: We were talking on the phone at least once a week on the phone and one or two emails a week.

David: At that time I had no computer and there was a thing in Times Square called an internet cafe. It was the biggest thing and their colors were orange and white. So I would rent time and I only hunt and peck in terms of typing, only thirty words a minute.

These were deep conversations, things you would normally do on a date, we did on the phone.

Leslie: On December 28th, I flew to New York for our first date.

David: I invited her to the city to see Patrick Stewart in his one-man show, *A Christmas Carol*. He plays all the parts.

Leslie: He came to Oregon for Valentine's Day.

David: I had the opportunity to meet her family . . . . Leslie went back to New York in April for her birthday and met my parents [who came in from Pittsburgh]. We went to the Japanese cherry blossom festival in Prospect Park. In June, I went to Portland. I had my maternal grandmother's ring in my pocket. I wasn't interested in wasting a lot of time at that point.

Leslie: We were in downtown Portland. There's a place called Pioneer Square, there's a sidewalk that has all these quotes . . . .

David: My grandmother's name was Nora Wendt. It's her ring in my pocket. "I'm here, you're there, and that's fine." Nora Wendt. That quote was on the sidewalk. [PHOTO 25]

Leslie: He got down on one knee. And this cute couple with a baby just down the street said, "Did you guys get engaged?" That was on

Flag Day, June 14. By September 11, the first year anniversary, I was in New York.

David: I don't have computer skills. I'm a nontraditional personality. I've worked in an office, I've done OK with office work, and it's not something I'm enamored with. I'd invested all this time trying to get seniority [at Circle Line], which I still don't have. Years ago when I took the Circle Line job — I was convinced to take the job, the guys are in their sixties, you're going to move up in seniority. Only three have left, mostly because they died. Many of my coworkers are in their eighties, they're still there. So let's say that I started off as number, eight, number nine; I'm still only number five.

The senior-most tour guide has been doing the job longer than I've been on the planet. The second is his son, about my age, but everybody between us is much older.

Leslie: I said I would move, so that's what I did. It's been culture shock, to say the least. The sugar granules are so much bigger here. That was one of the weirdnesses.

David: We got married on December 28, the one-year anniversary of our first date. And we saw a Broadway show, *A Christmas Carol* with F. Murray Abraham. He was my acting teacher in graduate school at Brooklyn College. [PHOTO 26]

Leslie: When I got home, my niece said, "I meant a *bus* tour, not a boat tour."

In 2021, David said the pandemic has left New York much the way it felt after 9/11.

When you walk in Times Square nobody's there—now is like it was then. [After 9/11] hotel occupancy in the city had gone down from 98 percent to less than 50 percent in two weeks, not unlike what you might see now. In terms of economically, it's the worst year to hit New York since September 11, 2001.

1. Kathy Karnosh with Katz's deli co-owner Alan Dell. Photo courtesy of Kathi Karnosh.

2. The Ditewigs and Betsy Holzgraf at Rupert's Hello Deli. Left to right: Jane Ditewig, Rupert, Steve Ditewig, family friend, Betsy Holzgraf. Photo courtesy of Jane and Steve Ditewig

3. Portland firefighter Allen Oswalt, at left, had the honor of presenting a "freedom quilt" to FDNY firefighters. Photo courtesy of Allen Oswalt.

4: Engine 54, Ladder 4, Battalion 9.
Photo: Alice McElhany.

5. Sandra Kempel and Glenn Kloster took his models to this fire station as he had planned. Photo: Barbara Shaw (left). 6. Photo: Sandra Kempel (right)

7. Memorial to firefighters of Battalion 9 lost in the 9/11 attacks. Photo: Sandra Kempel (above).

8. and 9. Portland Police Officers Frank Klejmont (left) and Cliff Madison at the Kneeling Fireman statue, which was brought in on a flatbed truck and parked in front of the Milford Plaza Hotel on Eighth Avenue at West 44th Street on September 19. One of New York's first memorials to 9/11, the bronze statue happened to be at JFK International Airport on its way to the Firefighters Association of Missouri from Parma, Italy. Its manufacturer, Matthews International Corporation of Pittsburgh, donated the statue to the city of New York with the blessing of the Missouri firefighters. The statue is permanently located at 6 East 43rd Street. Photos courtesy of Cliff Madison.

10. Engine 24 "Red Rover" in Greenwich Village. Photo: Kathi Karnosh.

11. Cinquantacinque patch. Property of Sally Bourrie.

12. Engine 55, known as "Cinquantacinque." Photo: Jane Meskill.

13. Mayor Vera Katz donates a political cartoon by Oregonian political cartoonist Jack Ohman to the Chinatown firehouse. Photos: Betsy Ames

Photo: Betsy Ames

14. Washington State University student firefighters Brent Olson and Jeff Siemers at Ground Zero. Photo is the property of Oregonian Publishing Co.

15. New York tribute pins made by the Portland Police Foundation Portland Police officers Frank Klejmont and Cliff Madison gave to police at the stations they visited. Photo: Cliff Madison.

16. (above) and 17. (below) Mayor Vera Katz presents a signed poster from the Portland 911 [emergency] center to a Manhattan police precinct. At the back, Portland Police Officers Frank Klejmont (left) and Cliff Madison (right). Photos courtesy of Cliff Madison.

18. Cliff Madison trades patches at a New York City police station. Photo courtesy of Cliff Madison.

19. Ever since he received this gift from New Yorker Leo Nadolske during the Flight for Freedom, Brian McCartin has kept this golf ball—unused—in his golf bag. Photo: Brian McCartin.

20. Rebecca Webb purchased this print from a street vendor when she was in New York in 2001 and keeps it where she sees it every day. Photo courtesy of Rebecca Webb.

21. and 22. People view flyers of the missing.
Photos: Alexia Halen

23. Photos by Library of Congress, Prints & Photographs Division, photograph by David Finn

24. The "Gilligan" by David Parker. Photo courtesy of Leslie Parker.

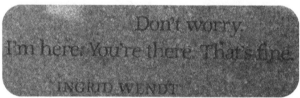

25. Photo courtesy of Leslie Parker.

26. Photo courtesy of Leslie Parker.

THE IMPACT

“I expect to hear that all of our lives were changed by our visit. — *Portland Mayor Vera Katz*

The Freedom Fliers were officially recognized by President George W. Bush, Transportation Secretary Norman Mineta, Governors George Pataki (New York) and John Kitzhaber (Oregon), Mayors Vera Katz (Portland) and Rudolph Giuliani (New York), and many others. The mission garnered worldwide publicity and earned Sho and Loen Dozono and the staff of Azumano Travel the prestigious American Express "Great Performers" award and the American Society of Travel Agents "Travel Agent of the Year" award, among many others.

In terms of business, the trip was very productive, said SOLV Executive Director and Flight for Freedom organizer Jack McGowan soon after the trip:

> “Community leaders met with New York leaders, and our tradespeople met with their tradespeople. They tried to arrange for some conventions to come to Oregon. This put Oregon front and center in the nation's mind. This wasn't good for Oregon just from a publicity standpoint, but it bore fruit in the number of relationships built.[1]

What's clearer than ever twenty years later is that the trip's most important legacy is that participating in the Flight for Freedom profoundly affected those who participated in it. Many felt more connected to others. Many believed more strongly in their ability to make a difference because they experienced it firsthand by traveling 3,000 miles to comfort complete strangers in a city whose way of life was so different from theirs. Some found themselves making new choices about how they wanted to spend their time. Some, like Leslie Krueger, even made major life decisions based on their experience of the trip.

Sadly, **Mayor Vera Katz** (1933–2017), who so courageously battled her own fears to lead the group, is no longer with us. But she spoke and wrote at length about the trip and it is clear that her spirit informed much of the trip as did her physical presence. For Mayor Katz to participate on this trip, she had to get on a plane—something she hated and feared—and return for the first time to the city that she had left in 1964. This meant confronting the shattering and destruction of the place that had been her family's safe haven, and the launching pad for her American Dream. "The reason I didn't want to go is because it was shattered. There wasn't any safe place," she said. But being in New York, leading Oregonians, appearing on television, in the end was, she said, "probably one of the most positive experiences I've had in my life, both personal, and as part of a community."

In 2003, she spoke at length about her experience of the Flight for Freedom, what it meant, and how her battle with breast cancer had informed her interactions.

> I don't think we spent that much money. We were treated like royalty and the prices were depressed anyway, but because of the work done on the media, they all knew who we were and that my god, there's a group of 1,000 Oregonians 3,000 miles away coming to literally give us hope and heart . . . .
>
> I came back and it was very clear that we weren't safe anywhere. Our safety is threatened. And yes, we're not New York, but we could have our own terrorist attack.
>
> I'm a Jew, I had very strong political leanings, I didn't have a sense of personal safety, and I was in awe that a lot of the citizens in this community didn't feel that there was safety issue. Why are you spending

the time, spending the money covering reservoirs? We don't have a problem, and yet in Laurelhurst you have a domestic terrorist that held a community hostage, and their animals and their families.

I was very confused that a lot of the Portlanders that I talked to thought well, this isn't going to impact their own lives.

. . . We weren't ready at that time. I don't think anybody was ready. We're far more prepared right now.* . . .

We went to a fire station and we went to the 911 and I did a lot of the public appearances, "Regis and Kelly" and all of that, ABC Radio, so I did not get to do a lot of the visits to schools, for example, but we did get to Ground Zero, and then we went to St. John the Divine . . . I [had] lived two, three blocks away from St. John the Divine so it was like truly going home.

I had not visited that address in all the years after we left and we left in 1964 and I would see St. John the Divine every time I would come home from school. Going there to this feast, that was just an extraordinary experience, and then to have the son of the man who really was my motivator in getting involved in the public arena give an incredible presentation. And all I needed to do was close my eyes and I could hear Robert Kennedy speaking, the same sound, the same passion . . . . Not only did they rip my heart out for the city but my home as well . . . I got over that part, realizing that change does happen and that's life and move on . . . .

As you get older, you begin to see how these things come, serendipitously in many cases, and in other cases, you plan it that way . . . . . . It was sixty years ago and I knew that I would never come back in that position again, sort of a closure to my childhood in New York.

Q: Did the fact that this happened after you'd battled breast cancer bring up any emotions or have any effect on how you thought about the trip at all?

No, the trip was just basically, "Oh my god, how—my heart just went out to New York. There's still a part of me that will always be there. Selfishly, what it means to me personally and then, "OK, let's gather people up and let's do something and let's show them that there are people who care." . . .

---

*The Flight for Freedom moments for Mayor Katz were not only ceremonial photo ops. She and others went to the New York City 911 center and spent time learning how they prepared for and handled emergencies.

I had to think a little bit about the message for the group, not for me personally. For the group, here's a part of America who thought that it was important to show the support and to show the love and to give people back the power that was taken away from them. Give them back the power, give them the energy. I truly believe you can pass energy from one soul to the other . . . .

With a city of over eight million people, everywhere the little groups went—I didn't have time to go to dinner—but when they went to dinner and they wore the button or they made out the check, they got a free bottle of wine, anything you want, it was unbelievable. And it gave others the power to make some change, to begin to create change. We're usually pretty powerless in making those kinds of change connections and I think it gave the woman living in Hermiston or the woman living in Bend, wherever they all came from, their families, the power to make some change or to change somebody's life for maybe a small minute in time or maybe for a long period of time . . . .

I think what it was, it showed that this community, as much as I think New York is special, I think Portland, even with those folks who drive me crazy with their ugly emails, is a very special community. And if we can do this, we can do anything. Just call the group out—we can do anything.

It's one of those memorable events in people's lives that tie people to each other. My relationship with people that I spent time with, it'll always be different than anything I had prior to the trip or with other folks. It's like the Robert Kennedy campaign. If you know that somebody had worked on the Robert Kennedy campaign, there's a tie there that no matter what happens in professional, political, personal lives, that tie stays and you forgive them if they do something that annoys you, but that tie is very strong.

How has it changed your life?

There's the tie with the breast cancer. I don't get a chance in this public arena to build very personal relationships in split seconds. I have a few friends I spend time with, but it's that kind of split-second connection where I, in the breast cancer, I acknowledge, I understand and I give the way I can through my energy through a physical hug of somebody or holding them a little tighter than normal and saying, "I understand . . . Because we went through the same thing—it's a parallel, what happened in New York. "I understand the pain you're feeling." It sensitized me even more to do that kind of personal outreach when somebody would come to me and say, "By the way, I have cancer." . . . .And I will go out of my way most every time to either call people I don't even know or offer to go with them to see the physician if they don't have anybody to go, or give them counsel, or just give them a hug. The trip built on that . . . .

Interestingly enough, I got an email from somebody that reminded me that I did something like that for a member of their family and I had no clue of who it was and somebody who emails me on a regular basis reminded me the other day what I had done and it's nice.

It's kind of America, you know, it's what this country was to me, what it is to a lot of people and we sort of forget to celebrate what this country really means. We were the Vietnam War, the Reagan administration, the Watergate, and you sort of remove yourself, and sometimes . . . not terribly proud of what's going on at the heart of government in America. And here was an opportunity to just take the flag and show your emotions on your sleeve and be proud to be an American.

How does this one-on-one contact compare to your achievements as a public figure, in government?

That's why it's very special because I don't get a chance to do that in my daily routine. I sit, trying to negotiate a deal or sit and try to make sure people are working together.

There was another memorable time. It was an ecumenical ministry service at the Rose Quarter and I was asked to speak and we had people from all religions speak. We had a pretty good crowd. It was just after 9/11, probably before we came to New York, and the ceremony was over. I had walked close to the front of where people were sitting. We were elevated, like on a stage and hoards of people came toward me and I felt that I needed to respond. And they were tearful and they were thankful and I didn't know where all of that emotion came from, from Portlanders, and I felt like I was playing almost a religious role in being there to give them that hug, that holding of the hand. Terribly empowering, but you have to be careful you don't take this too seriously that you can really change people's lives. But just knowing that the mayor of the city was there to comfort them. A lot of them were from New York, a lot of them had family that were impacted and they didn't have anybody to turn to. I just happened to have hesitated and not gone back to the car and I just kind of opened up this floodgate of folks . . . . I've never experienced anything like that before in my life.

Is there anything about people, your feelings about people, that changed or grew from this trip?

> I hope you understand that I get some of the meanest, ugliest letters and emails. And you almost begin to feel that there isn't any goodness on some days or some weeks. And now I understand how police officers feel because they see the ugliness on the street most of the time. They don't see the joy, they don't see the goodness, and I realized after all of this that I'm too close to some of these issues, that there's goodness and hope out there and I need to recognize that and to honor it and be there when people need me.[2]

In responding to a New Yorker who had emailed her, Mayor Katz wrote:

> The Flight for Freedom's trip to New York City was a moving and exhilarating experience. There have been formal and informal reunions of participants, many stories and laughs shared, and tears cried. Other Oregonians, some returning from recent visits, have shared stories like yours. It is a gentle reminder of how we, each in our own way, has an opportunity to touch history.[3]

Eric Long, General Manager, The Waldorf-Astoria

> Given my decades in the hospitality industry, I thought I had seen it all . . . until September 11th. I don't have to tell you about the immediate effect on New York and on the country. But when I say I thought I had seen it all, I don't mean just the attacks, I am also referring to the amazing resilience of this great city, as well as the extraordinary outpouring of support for it. Witness Oregon's "Flight for Freedom," which brought about 1,000 people to New York and to the Waldorf-Astoria for the sole purpose of demonstrating their solidarity with the city by spending over $1 million here.
>
> The Oregonians came early in the recovery process, less than a month after the disaster However, they blazed a trail that many others have followed . . . .[4]

♥

For **Stephanie Hinshaw, 15, of Portland,** the impact would be felt on many levels, particularly when she and her family visited Ground Zero. This was her first time on the East Coast and New York City was vastly different than anywhere she'd been before and she discovered she liked it:

> The city was huge, and freezing. I had to resist the temptation of looking up and up and up at all the huge buildings, at the risk of looking like a tourist. I loved the taxis, they were everywhere. The people were from all over. The city felt old and well worn-in, which gave you a sense of being grounded to something more secure. It seemed so much rawer, so much more real than any city I had been to on the West Coast. I absorbed the rawness of the city until I myself felt real and at home. I felt like a different person here. I felt like I had the power to be whatever I wanted. I felt no barriers. There was none of that same sense of conformity that hung around back home. I loved it here.[5]

The Dozonos received many, many thank you notes. One, from Aleck and Mary Edra Prihar, included a sentiment shared by many Freedom Fliers: "Many of us received more than we gave."[6]

Jesus "Jess" Carreon had moved to the Portland area in July to become president of Portland Community College. He wrote an essay for the *Lake Oswego Review* and talked about visiting his friend and colleague, Dr. Antonio Perez, president of the Borough of Manhattan Community College. In the end, he wrote:

> The lesson for me, for us in Oregon, for all Americans, is that whatever occurs, we have the strength of character not only to survive this type of calamity, but also the fortitude and kindness to support each other and become an even greater and more inclusive democracy.[7]

Soon after the trip, the *Gazette-Times* in Corvallis reported on the impact felt by participants in the area:

"Did we make a difference economically? Unless other states copy us, probably not," said Joy Schertz of Corvallis. "But at least emotionally, I think we did."

. . . Philomath City Councilor Marilyn Slizeski spoke with folks on the streets, taxi drivers, anyone she thought needed a chance to discuss their experiences.

"Everyone was touched by it," she said. "They all had things to say. One of the things is that everyone matters."

"I didn't expect that we could make as a big a difference as we did," she said. She said the group that participated grew very close in the short time its members were together.

"There was an emotional bonding between the participants that's something indescribable," she said . . . . Slizeski hopes that the group can continue to work together in some capacity, and do additional work.

"I can't think of a better thing Oregon could have done to make a connection to New York." . . . Slizeski may take her family to New York City for Christmas, something that hadn't even occurred to her before the attacks.[8]

In southern Oregon on the California border, the *Daily Courier* in Grant's Pass, the county seat of Josephine County, talked with its local Freedom Fliers:

"It's not Oregon [and] New York. We were all one," said Josephine County Clerk Georgette Brown, who traveled with her husband, Larry, and daughters Monique and Martie. Brown, who's originally from New York and used to work on Wall Street, said that the taxi driver who took her family to the airport on the way home was wearing a turban, but it doesn't make sense to fear someone because of that, or to assume all Arabs are part of the terrorist group.

"You can't just put everyone in one basket." While it was a difficult trip, Brown also said about New York, "There is hope here."[9]

Ryan McAninch of Portland, a seventeen-year-old senior at Jesuit High School, said this in an *Oregonian* opinion piece not long after his return:

> [P]erhaps this horrible event will make us stronger, causing us to rethink our priorities. In a matter of a few moments on the morning of Sept. 11, we all became aware of how suddenly our world can be turned upside down, how precious life is—and how much we need each other.
>
> . . . The beauty of America is that we have the ability to get knocked down and then stand up even stronger than before. God bless America.[10]

Jeanine Ford of Portland wrote an article for her husband's newsletter about the events of the trip and concluded by capturing its greater meaning:

> Words cannot convey the things we felt and experience on this trip. It was a moment in history where the time, place, and intermingling of peoples created a love and unity that can only be described as miraculous! As Oregon hastened to comfort New York, West was joined to East, wrapping all of the country "from sea to shining sea" in a bond that was unimaginable a month ago.[11]

Hood River native John Webster, who went on the Flight for Freedom and coincidentally would be moving to New York City on November 1, told the *Hood River News* in October 2001:

> I had started the trip apprehensively, but my apprehension turned to gratitude after seeing the hundreds of New Yorkers—from all walks of life—thanking us for being there, taxi drivers giving thumbs up in support (even free rides), waiters coming over to our table, personally thanking us for traveling all that way.
>
> My faith has been restored in that people—all Americans—have a great determination to survive in the midst of catastrophe, anguish and despair. I am proud to be an American.[12]

♥

Billie Jean Morris, Greater Hermiston Chamber of Commerce Director, 55

Soon after the trip, in the "Watermelon Capital" of Hermiston in northeastern Oregon, Morris received an email from a fifteen-year-old New York teenager who had thanked her and her friends for coming and had gotten her photo taken with them while at a Broadway show. The teen wanted Morris to know that the last time she went into Burger King she asked the employee if she knew Morris, since the fries that they made there could have come from Hermiston.

Morris will never again drive by a shoe store or pass a lost shoe along the road without thinking of the shoes that must have littered New York City streets as people ran to safety. But every time she sees a New York headline or surfs past *The New York Times* Web site, she'll stop and see what progress the clean-up effort has made.

"I'm connected now," she said. "It's my city now too."[13]

Beverly Harkenrider, Hermiston. Beverly and her husband, Frank, the former mayor of Hermiston, were among the most upbeat and recognizable people of the trip, for their continual joy in being in New York. Beverly was also known for the watermelon pin on her lapel, proclaiming her origin with pride.

Little did most Freedom Fliers know, Beverly had more than one pin, and she had given one to one of the people from Delta Air Lines. That woman was a colleague of Deb, a woman from New York, who wanted to find "a little elderly couple" who went on the trip because she wanted to thank the Oregonians for coming to New York. She contacted the Hermiston newspaper and found them. Beverly told the *East Oregonian* how, over the year since the trip, she and Deb became friends. Just as Beverly and the other Freedom Fliers had listened in Manhattan, she continued listening through their email correspondence.

In Deb's first email to Beverly she wrote, "I was so touched by your caring and concern. The wonderful people from Oregon made us feel understood and cared for. I cannot express how touched and comforted I felt."

Deb also told her story of 9/11—and the at least eleven people she knew who died there, from an NYPD officer (colleagues and friends of her husband) to FDNY firefighters (including a close friend's husband), to flight attendants to a Cantor Fitzgerald employee (her next-door neighbor), to her daughter's friend's parents (who called her first to say they were sorry but there was no way out; they jumped holding hands), and others. Over days, she would learn of more and more who had died and think of the families they left behind.

Deb described how, on Saturday when she went back to work at JFK Airport, passengers from Rome on the first inbound international flight since the attacks entered the airport singing "God Bless America," and hugged the airlines employees and thanked them for keeping them safe.

> That is when I lost it. Everyone was crying, including the pilots and crew. Upon returning upstairs, I ran into another friend who was crying and saying "I can't believe Lisa is gone" . . . . [Lisa] went to work for American Express in the WTC. She was thirty-three and had just returned to work after the birth of her baby girl. Her body was never recovered.

Soon after, Deb came down with ear and sinus infections and asthmatic bronchitis and was away from work for three weeks. When she returned, she learned of yet another loss. Beverly said that Deb and her husband, Tom, were coming to visit them at the end of September (2002).

> Deb has endeared herself to me. Besides this heart-rendering account of the 9-11 attack, she has written of her family, her friends, and her work. She has a marvelous sense of humor and has many interesting stories to tell. I treasure the friendship we have formed as a result of this terrible tragedy and continue to believe that out of everything bad, some good will come. There have been many acts of kindness and caring expressed and a new awakening for love and loyalty to our country.[14]

♥

Debbie Pedro, 41, Hermiston (Pop. 13,154). Debbie Pedro will remain connected after she and a New York police officer traded pins—her "911" remembrance pin made in Oregon for his precinct pin, reading "Midtown North."[15]

Rachel Gerber wrote about Sho Dozono, Azumano Travel, and the trip:

> We were exposed to the kind [of "class"] that shows dignity in the face of emotional drought, faith when gripped with fear, and love and healing replacing inconceivable hatred. We saw it reflected in the faces of New Yorkers; I saw it in my fellow travelers . . . .
>
> The dream—to help heal a hurting city. But we got so much more—proof that we are indeed the home of the brave. Five days ago, I really hadn't "seen nothin' yet." Now, though, I swear I've seen it all.[16]

Melvin "Pete" Mark, Jr. (1926–2017), Chairman of Portland-based Melvin Mark Companies, who had grown up in Philadelphia and New York, wrote to Sho Dozono after he and his wife Mary returned. His words express the gratitude of every Flight for Freedom member towards the Dozonos—but his last sentence applies to every person who had the courage to get on a plane and fly across the country on Columbus Day weekend 2001:

> As you know, we go to New York once a year, but I've never experienced anything like last weekend. It was well organized and superbly done. Each reception was excellent and you spoke so beautifully and so sincerely that it was truly an emotional experience. Everyone with whom we spoke in New York—from the cab driver to the restaurateur to the shopkeeper—was so grateful for us being in New York.
>
> You should take such pride in what you've accomplished for Oregon.[17]

"I think it's impacted the people of New York City in realizing that everybody from other parts of the country really do care about (them)," **Dave Holley** told his local Sweet Home newspaper, *New Era*, when they got home. "Everybody was in it together . . . It was just an emotional experience."

Going beyond the devastation and the loss of life at Ground Zero, "You don't think about the domino effect on other people," Holley said. "People have not only been injured or lost their jobs, some are without homes. In one nearby apartment building, two-thirds of the apartments were closed. In midtown New York, there is still quite a bit of security."

What the Holleys took away from New York is not the usual . . . . "We leave thinking that maybe we didn't do the things we were supposed to do, like visit the Empire State Building and take a harbor cruise or take a carriage ride in Central Park, but other things became more important . . . We're not taking home a lot of souvenirs, but we're taking home images and impressions and, I think, leaving a bit of us in New York.

"As glad as I was to be able to head home today," **Linda Holley** said, "I was sad too. I learned New Yorkers are friendly people and even though the attack took place in their city and broke their hearts, once we saw what they saw, part of us was left in New York."[18]

Bernie Kronberger (1946–2016), regional community affairs manager for Wells Fargo, told the *Daily Journal of Commerce* that the trip had had a major impact on his life. He helped organize the first flight and participated in both the first and second trips. "What it showed to me is that people are more resilient, compassionate and stronger than they realize," he said. "There are heroes on every street."

On its most basic level, Kronberger noted, the Flight for Freedom began as a professional network of business leaders working together to organize a complex logistical strategy on a rapid timeline. They had to set goals, delegate tasks, and work collaboratively—all skills they continue to use today—to accomplish their mission. And, over the years, those professional relationships have grown into lifelong friendships.

Kronberger had arrived in the Port of New York in 1951 as a five-year-old immigrant from Austria. For him, the 9/11 attacks and visits to New York City reinforced the importance of family, friends, home and freedom. "We can never forget how fortunate we are to live in this great country," Kronberger said.[19]

George Haight of Woodburn. As George Haight prepared to leave for the one-year anniversary Flight for Freedom trip to New York in 2002, Haight told the *Woodburn Independent* that his first experience in New York had become an "emotional benchmark." In Woodburn, the trip's impact on his life had been palpable, he said. "[I]t made me a little more aware of my civic responsibilities locally, even after living here for thirty years. Maybe I can help make the community a little more cohesive."[20] For the second trip, his wife went too.

George Haight died in 2013. When Haight returned from the 2001 trip, his local paper, the *Woodburn Independent*, ran an editorial that summed up what may be the greatest implication of the trip for every Freedom Flier, I hope :

> George Haight made a difference . . . . If nothing else comes from the destruction the terrorist attacks visited on our shores, the one thing we can all grasp is that little things do make a difference. Ask the people of New York.
>
> Or, better yet, ask Haight. He can tell you that his presence in New York, not the money he came to spend, was what the New Yorkers shook his hand and gave him hugs for . . . .
>
> Haight is a prime example that it's not always dollars and cents that rebuilds a community. It's caring folks willing to share the emotion of a moment, willing to be the wall others lean on, willing to simply say, "you are not alone in this," that will help New York and this country arise from the terrorist attacks of Sept. 11 . . . .
>
> George Haight made a difference. So shall we all. In the end, the large acts will get the publicity, but it will be these small acts of kindness that will mend the hurt we all feel.[21]

Some in the communities where Freedom Fliers lived were deeply impacted upon learning of their neighbors' experiences. Allen Pembroke's October 24, 2001 letter to the editor of the *Woodburn Independent* provides a glimpse:

George Haight is one of those unsung heroes for taking a step of faith and traveling with other Oregonians to New York as part of the Flight for Freedom program . . . . Kudos should also go to John Baker for covering this story with two great stories on Mr. Haight's mission . . . . Your description of Haight's time in New York, coupled with his own words, truly painted a picture of contrasting emotions. The joy of being able to help versus the emotional toll the trip took upon viewing the remains of what was once the World Trade Center.

Mr. Baker's story was well-written, honest, emotional, and left me feeling proud of Mr. Haight's contributions, as well as those of all Oregonians who undertook this mission of hope.

Congratulations to Woodburn and the Northwest for being the first to step forward with the kind of help that New York so desperately needs. We've always been leaders out here, and now the world knows it.[22]

♥

Organizer Bruce Samson of Portland (2003)

You always hear . . . [that] one person could make a difference if you really work on something. I've been involved in a lot of community stuff, but never at the ground floor like this where two or three or four of us decided that something was a good idea and it took off like this. It makes you realize that if you do have something that you think is worthwhile and you go for it, it can make a difference. And then the other thing is, I think it made me feel really more like we were all in it together. We are all in this thing together, New Yorkers, Oregonians, Californians, it is a large community, this country, not just a group of separate states or cities. That's what it felt like and that's what it felt like to the New Yorkers that we talked to also.[23]

Organizer Nick Fish (1958–2020) of Portland (2003)

That event changed my life here in Oregon. All those people became dear friends. The Flight for Freedom started marching in various parades, we did a reunion at which I had a chance to speak and the folks who went as part of the thousand strong, we all got to know each other and run into each other and the folks that planned it became very close. And everything I've done since, I've had that core group of people helping me and guiding everything that I've been doing in Portland so it would not be an exaggeration to say that it was a transforming event in my life.

That experience for [my wife and me] crystallized for us why we love being here . . . . That experience of coming together with people that you don't know around a common cause, working your butt off, working together with leadership like Sho and Loen who are selfless leaders, who are people who never seek the limelight but facilitate these kinds of things, a chance to meet all those people and be part of something that just grew well beyond what any of us imagined, was one of the unique experiences of my life. All of those people have become almost like family members. It's almost like we went to war together . . . .

I don't know that I'll ever have an experience that comes close to the intensity of that experience outside of having my daughter.[24]

In 2011, Portland City Commissioner Nick Fish told the Oregon *Daily Journal of Commerce* that, as one of the Flight for Freedom organizers, he had been inspired by Sho Dozono's leadership style. "The original flight was a life-changing event, and it was done on a shoe-string and in record time," he said. "The Dozonos welcomed everyone and allowed people to do their thing. They were very comfortable with a decentralized leadership system."

Fish noted that the Flight for Freedom let people channel their anxiety into something positive. A sense of community has grown among the participants, he added.

"It's a little microcosm of a Leadership 101 experience for me," Fish said. "Everyone who participated in the Flight for Freedom felt like they were involved in something special. I've often reflected on that experience in my current job, and there were many important lessons: set a vision and establish clear goals; empower people to do their job and get out of their way; and the more people who you inspire to give their best, the better the outcome."[25]

Michael Phillips of Portland

I'm on the Board of Directors for the Portland Area Theatre Alliance, and intended to spend much of my time in New York supporting live theatre. I did that but the things that I will remember for the rest of my life have to do with the people of New York. I have never seen an entire city in such collective pain, and in such collective need of support. While many of us on the trip spent a lot of time going to the theatre, eating in restaurants, shopping, and generally lending our financial support to the city, I think what we did was ultimately much more important than that. We connected with human hearts, and we shared their grief. I'll never forget this trip.

♥

George Haight of Woodburn

❝It wasn't just a trip. I think maybe just the sense of community, not just Portland, not just Oregon but nationally, is a feeling that I'll never question. I mean, I've always been a proud native Oregonian but I've never been prouder of Oregon than I was on this trip. I felt like I was an ambassador for Oregon back there and an ambassador for New York back here.

It gave me perspective that will last for the rest of my life . . . . We all have our own little lives and concerns and biases and political bents and sadly, it often takes a tragedy to cut though all that and get down to the basic emotions and this certainly did. So, it's a sense that I could touch somebody's heart 3,000 miles away and certainly further than that away from my reality of the world and just have an immediate affinity and a common ground . . . . I have stopped by the Beechwood Ocean Front Motel in Lincoln City to say hello [to the woman with whom he went to the press conference in Chinatown.].

There were so many little human connections, little, tiny things that reminded me how easy a gesture can be remembered, a little extra kindness means a lot to people and it spurred me to perform other random acts of kindness on an almost daily basis. Those things do stick with people. They stick with me when they happen to me. They reminded me to be a little bit more thoughtful about little things . . . .

It was somewhat unstructured so we all just kind of fanned out and did our own little things, but when you got back into the lobby and sat down and started visiting with people, the same feelings were there from all different perspectives and all corners of the city and it was just delightful.[26]

♥

Martin Fisher of Bend

I think you come away with the sense that just being fellow Americans is important . . . a sense of community that's country-wide, that's national in scope maybe, that people who live in New York aren't foreigners. It's something that people always say but take for granted but don't understand what it is until you have to step up and act like it [Americans].[27]

Alice McElhany of Portland

Though I thought the trip was over when I arrived safely at home, I found my thoughts stayed with New York for months to come. I kept in touch with fellow travelers. And I wanted to return to the exciting city with wonderful people. Smelling smoke, whether it be from a cigarette a match or a fireplace, reminded me of the site of the World Trade Center, which burned for months after the attack. Hearing sirens or seeing a fire station reminded me of those who lost their lives and I would stop and pray for the safety of those who carry on. I like to watch television shows and movies that are filmed in New York just to get a little taste of the City. I can't even describe my feelings, which include love, anger, sadness, and joy over New York's loss and struggle to recover.

To wrap the trip up in a few words I would just say, "Oregon, and especially I, love New York!"[28]

State Treasurer Randall Edwards and his wife, Portland School Board member Julia Brim-Edwards had such a fun and moving experience that they decided to take their two oldest children (ages eight and seven) to New York the following month, for Thanksgiving. In 2003, he shared the impact of the trip.

It was . . . a great experience for them, and what a small world: one of the police officers who I met there when I was there in October, I happened to run into him again near Rockefeller Center . . . and he actually remembered meeting me.

. . . Even though it wasn't the same experience in the sense of being with a big group, it was really important for us to try to explain for our kids what had happened there and also for having them see. We took them down to where the towers were . . . . We went on a fireboat while we were there and these firemen from this boat told us an enormous amount of stories and they gave us a trip around Manhattan.

Part of what touched me was to try to give my kids to firsthand understand what happened. They're still young, but they got a huge amount out of this. Of course, they also enjoyed just being in New York. Through their eyes, it was so fun to watch them experience New York, like any time you go to New York for the first time, adult or child, it just is an amazing city . . .

For both Julie and I, it forever has touched our lives, just the experience, the knowing that we in our own way, made a statement. We are both very engaged citizens in Portland and the state and it just kind of renewed your faith that you can play a part and make a change . . . .Whether or not we changed New York, I think just the fact we went—people went out of their way, it just showed a level of humanity that you don't see in New York, or hadn't. New Yorkers will say, "Well, it's always been there," but most people who come from the outside that go there who are not from New York or native New Yorkers, it can be a pretty walled-off place. People don't necessarily want to talk to you or say anything to you.

. . . That whole experience has proved to me that there was a great connection between a world-class multimillion-populated city and a state that's on the far reaches of the same country and for those who'd never been to New York or even those who had, the fact was, the event drew us together and I think that was really the intent of the whole trip . . . .

It's got to be one of the most spontaneous happenings this state's ever been involved in and having it be so successful . . . . I think we did play a role in helping New York realize and maybe even the country, that there was a reason why we needed to support the city . . . .

Nancy Waples of Gresham. Nancy Waples's mother, in her seventies, wrote about the Flight for Freedom experience in a creative writing class, "about how a little old lady from Oregon became a VIP."

In addition to the organized events, Waples and her family met with a friend who worked at St. Vincent's Hospital and needed to find her mother who lived in Battery Park, and another friend who had worked near the World Trade Center. For Waples, who is from Gresham, the trip's impact was immense:

> I think it gave me a stronger feeling of community, being part of a community. It's hard to explain . . . I guess it just, last year we were in the Portland parade—the Spirit parade—and just being able to express that community feeling of being part of that. That was just something that I'd never experienced before. Being an Oregonian . . . . It was a highlight of my life, I'll always remember it.
>
> We kind of all went, "It's a free trip to New York," but it was so much more than that. I really felt that that really did something, that we really helped those people. Even during that parade, they felt better, they felt good about us being there. One lady said, "I never thought the rest of the country would care. I can't imagine that you would come all this way to help us." But I really think we accomplished that.[29]

Burt Behm of the Southern Willamette Valley

> As Americans, we are all pulling in one direction, and if there is some good that comes out of this I believe it's the fact that as Americans we're all going one direction now. [To KXL Radio after visiting Ground Zero.]

Lance Nuttman of McMinnville

> The camaraderie . . . . You couldn't just check your cell phone, we had it on a map. We looked at Zagat's and this is how we explored this monstrous city. We did it safely.
>
> And then the shift, almost literally. We were there less than a month after 9/11 and the shift of the world was changing. We didn't know how, but it was important for us to be there to support everybody.[30]

Elaine Edgel of Gresham

> I think the greatest feeling I walked away with was the knowledge of how strong each one of us really are. How we all, every race, every religion, from every different social background came together

and cried as a Nation and grew up together. The way it should have
been from the beginning.[31]

Connie Hawk of Salem

I went back because I needed to, not realizing how much the
people of New York needed us to. I really can't express how much the
trip meant to me as it took me a long time to sleep through the night
after 9/11. I know the trip was the start of the healing process for me.[32]

Joy Cavinta, Tigard*

In 2003, Joy Cavinta, a single mother who worked in a custom
film-processing lab, made her first-ever trip to New York City with
the Flight for Freedom. As a volunteer with the sheriff's department,
Joy returned to New York on two more trips, beginning in March
2002, when she rode in the St. Patrick's Day parade.

The city itself, she said, "took a hold of me" from the first visit. She
visited Ground Zero and met her volunteer New York counterparts at a
private party in a tavern called Badges of Honor in Farmingdale, on Long
Island. Badges of Honor is owned by a retired police detective who is
now Assistant Chief of the Farmingdale Fire Department, says Cavinta.
She returned for the September 2002 memorial trip as a law enforcement
representative, where she met a man in whom she was interested. She
returned in January of 2003 to spend time with him and see the things she
had not seen on her previous trips, like the Empire State Building and the
Statue of Liberty. "He turned out to be a jerk," she says, but in the course
of returning to Badges of Honor to catch up with her colleagues, she met
someone else. They visited each other in New York and Portland . . . .

His cousins worked at the World Trade Center and died in the
attacks and so he has a pretty direct connection to the World Trade
Center stuff. His family, which is big, is very close. There was just one
night that we just sat and talked in depth about it and his feelings and
everything and it was kind of like the release needed to be there with
somebody who was neutral with somebody who had no ties to the
bombing, who didn't lose a family member or a friend. I looked at him
and said, there's one thing you can look at from before this incident

*I have not located Joy Cavinta more recently for this book.

had happened. I look at it, I made an extraordinary friend. Osama bin Laden didn't win and something good came out of it. You and I became friends. We never would have met had this not have happened. He may think he won. He did a lot of damage, but he didn't win.[33]

Debra-Diane Jenness of Crescent Lake

It was the most emotional of weeks. A grand vacation? Absolutely not. But probably the best trip we have ever taken. As a homeschooling parent, my son will read about this in his history books before his high school days are thru. He watched the news unveil on TV. (And we thought it was history in the making with the Presidential election the previous November!!) But what better opportunity could I give him for his History class than to take him there and let him share it, be a part of it, feel it? It was the best feeling he ever had, he said. We have never felt more needed or appreciated anywhere. And I hope we are able to return to offer whatever comfort we can again. Hugs meant a lot, even to complete strangers. Which, when you really look at it, we are not strangers in this world, really; just friends who haven't been introduced yet.[34]

♥

Merrit Marthaller of Gresham

When reading about the trip there was no question of my not going. I was one of the earliest to sign up. The need for people of the world to give hugs and pray together, let alone help their economy, was of the utmost importance. It was my first trip to NY and the people will always be the most vivid memory of my travels. I truly believe their saying if Oregon ever needs help they will be here.[35]

Tahn Amuchastegui of Beaverton (2003)

When my Dad and I were in New York my Dad hung his Oregon Loves NY T-shirt on the memorial wall at St. Paul's. I was on the other side of the street and managed to get a couple pictures of him doing this and it is a good memory for us. We returned home and life has slowly returned to "almost" normal.

My son is five and attends preschool half days. Last month he brought home the school newsletter. There was a story written by a family who had to go to New York for a funeral (not World Trade Center-related). When they decided to go to Ground Zero they came upon St. Paul's. Almost immediately they were drawn to the "Oregon Loves NY" T-shirt. It was still there on the wall two months later through all the wind, rain, and snow. They were able to sign the shirt and leave messages of hope for others to read.

No one at the school knew [that] my Dad and I had been in New York or that my Dad left his shirt on the wall. What a wonderful surprise it was for us to find that someone so close had been touched by something we did so far away.[36]

Hawaii, 2021:

My dad passed in 2015 and this trip was one of the best memories he and I shared for many years.* . . . .

Tahn had created a memorial website that was lost, but he plans to get it up and running again.

I look forward to standing a memorial page back up for the 20th anniversary. I also intend to travel to New York City this year, but I haven't decided if I will go in September or in October while we were there so many years ago.[37]

Al O'Brien of Portland (2003)

The most lasting effect from the Flight For Freedom is the experience of being in New York at a most memorable time in history. I was impressed with the way the people of New York and all the different governments were handling this terrible tragedy. I came away with a better understanding of what other countries have gone through in their times of war and terrorism. It will now be forever firmly embedded in my mind what a blessing it is to have been born

---

*Tahn's father, Tim, was quoted by *The New York Times* when he was in the parade, and he began by saying, "I think it's important that we aren't afraid." You can read his comments in the "I Love a Parade" chapter.

here and what it is to be a citizen of this great country.[38] The Flight for Freedom will and is having a lasting effect on my life.[39]

2021:

> You don't hear all the right stuff on the news. I found that out because of that trip. They enhance things and slide over things I think are important . . . . I don't watch a lot of news and I don't have a lot of faith in the national news. I did at the time.

When he was working at a rental-car company in Portland, he'd tell people about the trip and "They're flabbergasted. It's patriotic. They wish they'd done it."[40]

Portland Public Schools Police Captain Cliff Madison of Portland. In 2003, Madison said:

> That whole few days, it was one emotional high point after another. It's almost like when you were done, the withdrawal. We got off the plane in Portland, it was like, "I don't want this to be done." I can still picture the faces of the New Yorkers on the parade line. They were crying, expressing that emotion . . . . After the trip you needed a vacation physically and emotionally.
>
> Sho Dozono and the rest of the group, what they put together was a great opportunity for us to experience, a once-in-a-lifetime experience. I don't expect in all my travels to take a trip that will have this emotion . . . .
>
> You never want to forget where you're from. I was raised that way. As Americans, we want to never forget the feeling from that event. You don't appreciate what you have unless you have that feeling. There will be new buildings there in a couple years, there will be memorials, that feeling has to stay in our hearts.
>
> Somebody from Southern Oregon said usually it's just Portlanders that do these kinds of things. They were glad to have the opportunity to do this.
>
> I heard "God bless you" and "You don't know what this means to us" so many times.[41]

In 2020, Madison, who now lives in Palm Springs, California, said about the Flight for Freedom, "That's what it's about, you can care for each other and come together."

2021

Flight for Freedom Media Director John Ray's life changed profoundly:

> Like most of us, my life changed when I returned from the Flight for Freedom. Looking back, these twenty years of professional successes began when I attended that first organizing meeting on that Sunday in late September 2001. In due time my new PR business exploded with offers to do work because of new friends Sho and Loen Dozono, Nick Fish, and Len Bergstein.
>
> With an eye on New York City and a personal promise to myself, I arrived in August 2006 with a new family that started because of a dotted line connection to Flight for Freedom.
>
> I lived back east for fourteen years, the first ten in the city and as a commuter from Connecticut. I got to know New York City very well, as my new job at the City University of New York required me to be in all five boroughs frequently. Often I was in as many as three.
>
> I do not feel ashamed or sorry that my life took a forward and positive path after that horrible day. The new open doors gave me a new sense of myself, a confidence that was shaken when I fired from an industry that sustained me for twenty-three years. And I made professional friends who I love and some, who are gone, I try to honor their encouragement to me.
>
> I have returned to Portland, which has lost some of its luster. But it will always be where a new beginning can start with the single seed planted in possibilities.

Attorney and former U.S. Congressman David Wu of Washington, DC

> George [Azumano's] tone and imagination, Sho's leadership. It was a win-win for everybody. The Oregonians brought money, but New Yorkers more than anything needed moral support. It was an economic shot in the arm.[42]

Joe Weston of Portland. Weston, principal of Weston Investment Co., LLC, brought his family on the Flight for Freedom in 2001 and participated in the Flight of Friendship to Thailand, where he and friend George Passadore, at that time president of Wells Fargo in Portland, washed an elephant! They brought their families on the 2005 trip to New York as well, where they opened the New York Stock Exchange. Passadore also organized a sister-city trip to Bologna through Azumano Travel.

> People were appreciate, and especially the merchants. Lots of people asked, "Where is Oregon?" And I'd tell them, "It's on the West Coast, between Seattle and San Francisco."

Weston also remembered the wide variety of people on the trip: "It was a congenial group of people . . . and we all got along."[43]

Betty Long of Beaverton. Betty Long was strongly impacted by the Flight for Freedom.

> I decided to take a Community Emergency Response Team (CERT) class . . . . Each member of the class was given a name tag and certified that we were OK to help before the First Responders arrived.
>
> Then I implemented a September 11th program at our American Legion Post 104 in Aloha, Oregon. Our American Legion Auxiliary members invited our local firemen and spoke [about] how brave and dedicated they are to their job.
>
> When Sho Dozono ran for Mayor of Portland, I decided to volunteer for his election. I went to various fundraisers and drove around and placed lawn signs at approved addresses all over Portland. At one fundraiser, a senator from Hawaii, Daniel Inouye, was there to support Sho. I got involved in the political circle as I met various people. I wanted to volunteer my help for all his time and efforts in the Flight for Freedom trip.
>
> Our theme was Oregon loves New York, but we left feeling as if New York loves Oregon.[44]

She participated in many subsequent Flight for Freedom and Flight of Friendship trips. She also volunteered for Sho Dozono's campaign for mayor.

Portland firefighter Allen Oswalt.

I think that maybe I had a preconceived notion of New Yorkers as rude. Everyone thinks that, but that is not the impression I got when I was there. So that changed 180 degrees. The people were so kind and they were so welcoming. Even the guy that carried our luggage up. He wants a tip, but he said, "We have been waiting for you guys to get here."

Oswalt and his wife normally go to nature for their vacations. New York is not a place he had any desire to see, and he was not a big fan of flying.

Never would I fly and never would I stay at the Waldorf. I wouldn't drive to New York just to see the town. And it changed my way of thinking about New Yorkers. They're fellow countrymen, they're Americans.

Cameron Platt of Portland. Cameron Platt was sixteen when he participated in the Flight for Freedom.

I think of that trip's importance in terms of seeing New Yorkers a little bit more as people. Growing up in Oregon, the image of New York is everybody is mean and impersonal and always in a hurry. Even at the age of sixteen that was what I thought . . . . more than anything, it just changed my perspective on New York as a city and New Yorkers as a people as being very kind and having empathy and being grateful for others coming to do whatever we could to help in some small way.

I think understanding 9/11—I don't think at the time I realized how much of a world event it would be to change the trajectory of wars and political geopolitics, security, homeland security, all of the stuff that kind of came after 9/11. It was too soon to realize that, but I think our story falls in that bucket where it was like, "Oh, New Yorkers are people and they want to talk to us." We're there to even just listen. It felt kind of important to be there and to be seeing New Yorkers, if you will, and hearing their experience . . . .

I remember thinking that was so cool about the collaboration between a mayor, a travel agency director's idea, and an airline gets involved, and the Waldorf-Astoria got involved—a confluence of partnerships. To this day, I'm fascinated by how public sector/private sector can forge partnership: this is all possible. If somebody takes leadership and takes it happen, then all the other organizations will participate and make it happen . . . .

It's a very relatable. Looking back, it's inspiring that you really can make a huge impact with a pretty simple idea, and it's executing against it, which I think is cool.[45]

Frank Shiers, KLSY, of Bellevue, Washington, led a trip to New York around the same time as the Flight for Freedom, selling out all forty available seats in an hour, with a thirty-person waiting list. He delivered hundreds of teddy bears to the Red Cross for the children of the attack victims.

> The biggest thing that I took away from it was how solemn it was and how traumatizing it was for New York and for the people of the country. My wife and I, when we were on Cape Cod three weeks before, which was literally days after it happened, there was a candlelight vigil at Provincetown where we were staying. That kind of stuff was happening from the time that it happened.
>
> Everybody talks about how the country came together at that time and there was a period when everybody put aside their political differences and came together as a country in response to this thing, this horrible tragedy. That was evident at the time, that was a component of what we observed.
>
> There was a sense of, we're all New Yorkers, we're all touched by this tragedy and it was important and valuable to share that with the people of New York.
>
> I guess I would say that we were a very small, tiny component of what happened post-9/11. What we did was good, it was valuable. The flip side of that is that I think it was an important experience for the people that went on the trip, a very tangible one. That there were people that went, it gave them an opportunity to see what was going on and to be a part of that history.

♥

♥

Baruti Artharee of Las Vegas

That quote of mine from *The Oregonian* at the time of the trip—
"They weren't trying to kill white people, or brown, yellow or red.
They were there to kill Americans"—it just rang a bell with me currently with what's going on with the George Floyd trial. And it hit
me the same way.

We're still in that same situation. Who's being attacked? We are
Americans and we're being attacked, for ethnic reasons, religious
reasons, from disabilities to sexual orientation. We're seeing attacks
on the Asian people and rising anti-Semitic attacks. People are being
killed, beaten by the police. People are being attacked for ethnic
reasons, religious reasons, and so are liberal-leaning white people
who stick up for less advantaged people. So it is a stark realization
of what has happened.

And when I think about Biden's election. Who elected Biden? They
are Americans. The Trump supporters—I certainly question them.

. . . When I think about the walk to Ground Zero, who I was with; the
Sunday ceremony; the Waldorf-Astoria, some of my personal profiling, and then everyday camaraderie and fellowship. Everybody on
the plane, it didn't matter your political party, if you were urban or
rural. There were a lot of things that became more meaningless. The
common theme was, we as Americans, we're not going to take this.
We're going to stand up, show up and speak up . . . .

For me personally, the only other time I've seen a coming-together
like that was the election of President Obama. I saw people come
together from every walk of life. The Flight for Freedom would rank
right up there with me in regard to the cross section of people who
came together. We are Americans and we have to do what's right
for our country. And in the election cycle, getting that ineffective
and unbalanced Donald Trump and the circus he has created out
of there. This is a danger to our republic. I saw the cross-section of
people to get Trump out of the office. I saw the cross-section before,
to get Obama elected—and the elation, the camaraderie across all
races and classes. The Flight for Freedom ranks right up there with
that.

Sarah Bott, who was Mayor Katz's communications director; she now lives in Hawaii.

> We didn't know what was going to happen. [Mayor Katz] was getting death threats for being Jewish. She was brave, man. I miss her a lot. I miss her leadership very, very much. Sho Dozono is a brilliant genus. Couldn't love that guy more. And Jack McGowan. Real leaders, real leadership, people working together and making it happen. Right down to the Oregonians that came from Joseph and Banks. . . .
>
> She was trailblazing and that's what leadership is all about. She worked with people's strengths and brought people together and her vision was bigger than all of us.

Lana Cupper of Portland

> I felt like I was on the same team. It was just a community of love right then. I was not part of their pain, but part of it in a different way. It's really hard . . . unless it's happened to you, no matter if we're talking about cancer, losing a spouse, unless it's happened to you—your heart goes out to somebody, but you really don't know unless you've been through it. Everybody processes their pain in different ways . . . .
>
> I'm very grateful that we were part of [the trip] . . . . It's stirring up a lot of remembering for me right now. Which is a good thing. It's something I'll never forget and especially that lady that came up to me with the poster of that missing person. The pain, but you really did feel the love and the appreciation of the city, the people that did reach up to you and would come up to you on a street corner and reach out and thank you for coming. That I was a part of something epic.

Todd Davidson was Executive Director of the Oregon Tourism Commission (Travel Oregon) in 2001, and was named Chief Executive Officer in 2004.

> I'm forever indebted to Sho and Loen for coming up with the idea, for sharing the idea, for affording the privilege to be part of it.

Some were just wearing their T-shirts on the street, not even in the parade. People were just stopping them on the street and how much it meant to them that we as Oregonians . . . Nobody stopped to say what's your race, your religious background, your political affiliation. Those things fall away because it's that human-to-human contact and that's what was most important. They were hurting and we could help them out and we did.

How many times have we all heard in grief counseling in those situations where you have a friend or family member who's lost a loved one and you're reluctant and don't know what to say. I'm sorry sounds so trite and simple . . . I read a piece about the power of just being there. Just go and sit with them. You don't need to know what to say. Just your presence can be healing. That's what Flight for Freedom was, that willingness and desire to be with them when they're hurting. There's power in that. We think we have to have the right words to say.

I'm looking back over a thirty-three-year career in the tourism industry in Oregon and if you were to ask me to name the most memorable moments, this is one of those most memorable moments. [See his encounter with a New York woman in the parade chapter.] This is one of those times that it all came together. I do what I do because I believe in the power of the tourism industry to create good jobs for Oregonians. That's important to me . . . . To be able to share this beautiful place with the world, that's the power for me . . . To go to New York to stand there on the street being held by her and me holding her,* that's where it all comes together. The power of the travel and tourism industry is through that human connection . . . .

Most people think I can say $1.2.billion and 112,000 jobs [tourism brings Oregon], and those are important numbers and the legislature does care about them, but the two stories I tell the most—this is one, and the other involves an inner city down in L.A.

Jane and Steve Ditewig, Longview, Washington, have not been back to New York since 2001.

Steve: It wasn't a vacation. We are very proud to be a part of it.

Jane: We were good ambassadors for Oregon and New York because how many times did you tell your story afterward because people were so interested that we did that. Particularly with my students,

---

*See Parade chapter.

too, because I was teaching high school at the time. I was gone for a day or two, which I also want to thank my principal because he saw the value in it and let me go. Just having the conversations with the kids at the time, and to this day. It's how we all feel a little bit of attachment to that horrible thing that happened because we were there.

Alexia Halen of Portland

    I think it did [have an impact on my life]. How important it is to give people hope and to not be fearful and to come together and stand strong . . . .that experience just sort of solidified that. You got to visually and emotionally feel how important that was.

Mary Platt of Portland

    It was a month, no time at all. All of us came back feeling profoundly impacted, profoundly changed, with such a heart connection. It's like somebody having fallen into swift water, you reach a hand out and pull them up to shore a bit. And yet it was a tiny gesture in the larger scale of what was going on.[46]

Judi Henningsen of Portland

    I think of our freedom and how we need to cherish it and I think sometimes people are letting it slip through their fingers and that's sad, that they didn't have opportunity to see that and understand what had happened and how people rallied to support other people. It showed how much we support people.

It seems all connected—my sister grew up with and was a close friend with Loen Azumano. It didn't register to me until I was on the bus with the Azumanos. Oh my gosh, my sister and Loen were always competing for first place and stuff . . . .

Things have changed in New York City since we were there the first time, the second time and now. Things have certainly changed . . . I'm referring to the coronavirus. There's whole lot more unrest in the United States. I think it's scary if it continues this way because of the polarity of the people in the United States. People are getting more violent and more guns. It's not as complacent as it used to be. It's sad.

We just felt we needed to do that . . . . We didn't even think about it, it wasn't even an issue. It was just let's go do it, let's go support New York, they needed it. We've never been there and we're going with a group.

Shortly after the trip, Henningsen wrote a memoir and in it she wrote, "I feel in my own small way, I might have made a difference. A difference to make a few people smile and maybe feel a little bit better. Funny how disasters and crisis can bring people together. United we stand."

When she was reminded of what she'd written almost twenty years ago, she said:

> Truth be told, I'd forgotten it. But it's true, and knowing that the young woman who videotaped George Floyd's murder, it's a great reminder: I will never again doubt that one person or one small act can make a difference.

Betsy Holzgraf of Portland. "What I didn't realize when I went was how much I would get out of it. I just thought I was doing it for the people there."

Holzgraf teared up when she remembered the thank-you notes the children in New York sent to Mayor Katz to thank Oregonians for coming that were reprinted in *The Oregonian.*

> One of them was how brave we were to come. I hadn't thought about it except that one time, that our country's going to war [when the bombing of Afghanistan began]. The letter was something to the effect of, "They broke our buildings, but they didn't break us." A little kid. Just those kinds of things.
>
> The inspiration and the strength that people there were showing. The resiliency. How many people did we walk by and didn't know who had lost friends, family? And the people's pictures still up—have you see this person, have you seen this person?
>
> The outpouring from the whole world that we actually squandered, but how everybody for once, we were the strong country, but the world reached out to us. From the planes that had to land in Newfoundland and everybody was put up in people's homes. Outpouring, aid, all that kind of thing. I'll always be grateful that I did that.

The personal connection, one-on-one with people there, was the legacy for me. Those are the things that choke me up still, that I was able to be part of that. I never thought of it that way [as being brave] until I read that article that the child wrote and I thought maybe it was, but at the time I didn't feel like it. It just felt like something I needed to do. I didn't go into it expecting to get anything out of it per se, other than supporting. Who knew that 1,000 of us were going to go?

Ann Nice of Portland

It was just so heartwarming. There were no moments that weren't. I cry easily anyway and I was on the verge of tears constantly. It was such a life-altering experience for me on so many levels.

Radio journalist Rebecca Webb of Portland is now, in 2021, co-founder of the award-winning Portland Radio Project (PRP.fm). She likens the world of the COVID-19 pandemic and saving PRP.fm to the September 11 experience.

When the COVID-19 first hit, I didn't know if we would make it a few weeks. We didn't know; we were dependent on live events and podcasting that was sponsored. We decided on the advice of a business coach, his advice was don't think about any of those things. Think about how you can use your platform to serve the public right now. It changed my whole outlook—we did creative programming—[things people needed to know like] are businesses open or are restaurants open for takeout—new programming that covered the twin pandemic of the COVID disparities for people of color and Black Lives Matter and we had people step up who'd never given money before, and people gave back to the station. And we got money, including from the CARES Act. We're going to come through it better, stronger.

And that's what happened after 9/11 too.

Webb and **Kam Kimball,** who went together on the Flight for Freedom, talked about how that post-9/11 experience was reassuring to remember after the trauma of 2020 in Oregon:

Rebecca: It's really wonderful to think back at how that inspiration by those few individuals just flourished into such a partnership, this outpouring, and it reminds me when I think back to 2020 the community standing up during the wildfires in northern California and in Oregon . . . . You saw these communities rise up and go directly toward the fires to help.

Kam: It's the best of human nature.

Rebecca: Especially with what Oregon has been through this year, it's heartwarming to reflect on it. That we can do it, we can rise above it.

Kam: And the country really came together during that time, too . . . . and to know that it [that coming together] can exist.[47]

Joyce Willing of Portland

It just made me a little more aware of how—and the pandemic has . . . brought it up—how fragile life can be. We go around in our daily business, the Capitol event, riots in Portland, and the pandemic has and you don't know if you're going to be around the next day. And also that you saw everybody in New York pull together, and the country, to get us going. That has to happen for any major emergency and including the pandemic. We all need to be on the same page, pull together, whether you're a Trump believer, and a staunch Democrat. And what's going to make it healthier, happier . . . .

We don't know what the country's going to be facing, we need to be looking way forward and doing what's best for our country.

I remember stories even of the Civil War and the Revolutionary War the women weren't allowed to fight, but they were doing their best to provide care for soldiers and stuff and food. It's time to do that again. Some of the rhetoric you see on social media—are you kidding me? Let's focus on moving forward.

Jackie Young of Happy Valley

I think about how it impacted us. Because it really, really did impact us. Because I have a scrapbook for my family and us to see. Now so many years have gone past and there's a whole generation of kids who see it as something that's in a history book, and to have contact with somebody who saw the aftermath, went through the wake-up calls all over the country in regards to what was happening. The shock we went through, and disbelief we went through, and coming together—I get kind of choked up talking about it even now.

The lasting impression I have of the whole thing was of seeing Congress on the steps of the Capitol all joining hands and singing "God Bless America." Oh my god . . . .

There is so much division going on right now. Right now we don't have the strength to fight an enemy without; we've got an enemy within . . . .

I'm eighty-two in May and I've lived through many presidencies, the Cuban crisis, the polio epidemic, the Vietnam War, you name, it, but I don't think there's ever been a time when I've ever felt that as a country that we're more threatened. I think it's we the people that are going to bring the peace. It isn't going to be the president. It's going to be the hearts and soul of the people.[48]

Chris Sullivan, KIRO Radio, Seattle (KXL Radio, Portland, at the time of the trip):

> . . . You could definitely tell that the people from the Fire Department or the Police Department—so many of their brothers had died and you could tell that there was definite, "Thanks, guys, for coming, we needed a shot in the arm." There was definitely appreciation to be there and to have made such a grand kind of gesture for what it was worth, just to let them know that people from the Northwest cared about them . . . .

Especially if you think of a place like New York, it's never not packed, and it hasn't been in the last year [2020] and it certainly wasn't in the month near 9/11. Let's be honest, flying—we were all a little concerned because we were [only] a month away from [September 11]. Flying and going to New York had a little bit of a risk to it. We didn't know what was going on.

It showed, OK if these 800 people from a place you never heard of—Oregon, where's that? It's somewhere near California. These people got on planes and found their way here just to spend money in our town. Maybe somebody in Alabama or Florida will do this. It was kind of risky when you see what happened in four planes.

I'm always a nervous flyer. I think at that point if anybody had looked sideways at anybody on a plane, it would have been much different. These were charters, essentially, everybody knew who they were. But to be flying wasn't exactly comforting. I flew back from New York on September 10. One my college roommates had gotten married. And it was kind of interesting. I think I picked up something [flu bug] and I took 9/11 off. My wife was like . . .

We had a really funny tour guide. He was really happy that people came out to spend money and show love. I was thirty-two, thirty-three and it didn't sink it until later how important this was for the psyche of New York, even in some small way, and I'm really happy to have been a part of it.

We're cleaning out a lot of our stuff now that we're empty nesters. I found signed stuff from Vera, I found some pins from police officers that had a map of America but with a heart in the center of it, a lot of little things like that I found. Looking back, it was a pretty impactful thing and I think for the people we touched when we got there.

Kristen Dozono spent a great deal of time at Azumano Travel answering the phones and working the hospitality desk at the Waldorf-Astoria. After the 2001 trip, she became acquainted with the firefighters who came to Portland for the 2002 Rose Parade.

. . . showing up, showing up means something. Standing on the same ground and being there for people. The firefighters we got involved with from there; we had long-term relationships with Billy Quick, who passed away from lung damage.

How devastated everybody was, how heavy the world was, and to see and feel the hope and the connections that were made is something that anybody that went on that trip could never forget. And then to see and understand the opportunities that you have to be there for someone in need, to tell them they're not alone, to grab somebody's shoulder.

Nobody was flying. New York City was literally on its knees, emotionally, physically, and financially.

People being too scared to fly—who would have thought to bring in hundreds and hundreds of Oregonians less than a month after when people are still in such shock—that we would coalesce and do this. And number two, striking the responsive chord that we did. People came out of the woodwork saying, "We want to go."[49]

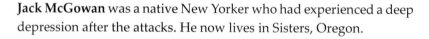

Jack McGowan was a native New Yorker who had experienced a deep depression after the attacks. He now lives in Sisters, Oregon.

> I'm still trying to get my head around it . . . . everybody wanted so bad to be able to do something, and this was a vehicle for that something to be done. I think that was one of the things and also it was such a cross-section of people from the Northwest. You really had rural people and corporate executives and political leaders. And it just built and built and I think that's the thing that was so shocking to me, to look around at that ballroom at the Waldorf at that first night, be at the microphone in that ballroom that was absolutely packed. To say to yourself not what a feeling of pride, it was just this feeling of awe. The sorrow was so palpable and the shock was still so with us and yet all these people coalescing of diverse backgrounds came together because they believed that this could be done.

Sociologists would have field day with this. It was a moment in time where there was still a certain degree of naïveté . . . We're approaching in today's world . . . is catastrophe burnout. Where you have the shooting du jour, this ridiculous void of political extremes.

Who had heard of Isis or the Taliban or—all of a sudden, names like Osama bin Laden became noteworthy or as such a broad understanding of the name. It was like a president. He became this horrific symbol of what could be done to America and I think it just—it absolutely was the fracturing of the last vestige of naïveté in this country.

It started with John Kennedy and then the Vietnam War, and then Bobby Kennedy and Martin Luther King and Selma and Montgomery and this fracturing of what defines America and then for this to occur. Then you had the Oklahoma City bombing. It was like one thing after the other that fractured the underpinnings of what the American belief system was about. Because of that, people looking for grounding, looking for something to build upon. Albeit, it was such a small—when you look at the population of the United States—it was about 1,000 people, to tell them they're not alone, to make contact when people are isolated and alone . . . It was such an incredible experience. I sound almost selfish in this regard, but it was such a lifeline. If I hadn't done this, if I had just stayed, I would have missed a huge time of my life that helped me immensely.

Kathi Karnosh of Portland

I worked in a dental office at the time, I'm retired now. I took advantage of an opportunity I thought was historic.

Since then, Northwest Medical Teams, I've been an active volunteer with that organization. It's now known as Medical Teams International. I've had an opportunity to travel all over the world as part of the dental teams. I've assisted a lot of dentists and done a lot of oral surgeries on trips all over. I made my first trip with them to Vietnam and Thailand in October of 2000.

So I got kind of a big travel bug from that trip and so it was less than—it was almost a year later that this opportunity presented itself and I found myself raising my hand and since then I've kept raising my hands. I've had many adventures and travels to many countries and I've been pretty fortunate to be able to do that, utilize my skills.

Also we had trauma counselors with Northwest Medical Teams that went back to that Ground Zero area. Remember the fence with all the photos and all the messages? And they would just camp out there and offer their services to people who were grieving. And a couple of the ladies who went there also went to—remember the earthquake and tsunami that hit after Christmas day in Indonesia? I spent five weeks there and I'm trying to recall their names. I have them written down and have photos. Somehow that conversation about the trip to New York went up. They said, "We went back." They were one of the first trauma counselors that traveled 3,000 miles across the country just to offer their services to people who were struggling during that time.

I was just fifty-one back then. I can't believe I'm now seventy, but I keep really active. I volunteer on a mobile dome van once or twice a week and have been very involved in Medical Teams International now. I live just a couple miles up the road from the corporate headquarters so . . . I guess it's just in me to utilize my skills and be of service and see if there's some place for me to help.

I've been very blessed by my willingness to risk going to places that some people would say I wouldn't go there. I didn't hesitate at all when I saw the opportunity to go to New York . . . .It was a statement that we Oregonians aren't afraid—1,000 of us weren't afraid to make this trip and show our support and I think the country was really grieving still and it was a time of community and support that is rather lacking in these days.

Jane Meskill of Portland

I'm surprised I went, too, but it does seem to be something I have a push to do. I went to the Women's March in DC after Trump was elected . . . . I know it's COVID, but I'm planning on going to DC for the inauguration. There won't be gatherings and stuff like that . . . .

That's the only thing I learned. I think it's important to show up. And so I did find that out about myself. I felt like I wasn't showing up because I had kids—I can't go. But I have this real draw to go— to Sarajevo as well, and do some art therapy with kids who were traumatized.

I think it's sort of like making sure they were going to be all right. I think that's what I needed, to see for myself that life goes on and things were going to be OK. That's why I need to go to DC, too. This has been so traumatic. Just to be held down and not to be able to change things.

It was much more stressful than I thought it was going to be. I didn't know what I thought it was going to be like, but it was stressful. The amount of sorrow there was stressful and coming to terms with why this happened. [Unnamed] showed up the last night we were there. He's a New Yorker and he was talking about as an American we brought this on ourselves for meddling in other people's business. It's like telling a rape victim you shouldn't have worn that. Of course you have to look at yourselves and see your part in being in that conflict, but it was so raw then, it was pretty stressful to hear all that.

We're in that situation now, but . . . this collective sorrow of where we were is similar. But it was the first experience I'd had of that as well.

Krista Vasquez of Portland

When I was at KGW, I covered thousands of stories and there's only a few that I will continue to remember. That was one experience that I will never forget. It's just being overcome by what was actually going on in NY, the fact that we were so close to Ground Zero, and the love that Oregonians were showing to New Yorkers, taking pictures with New Yorkers. I was at the Waldorf and walking back from the Waldorf-Astoria to Rockefeller Center to do our live shots and people wearing their pins, and seeing stickers on telephone poles and fire hydrants—We're here and we're here to support you and we hope New Yorkers know that we want to help you, we want to help get life back . . . .

There were just so many emotions in that trip. First, you're completely shocked by what you're seeing at Ground Zero, but then you're completely overwhelmed by reading the messages written on the bus shelters, and then you come back to your hotel and you hear about the first retaliation strikes happening [in Afghanistan], and then you're marching in a parade with people yelling how much they love you.

And then when you leave, you're like, "We did it. We helped boost the spirits of New Yorkers; we were impacted in ways that nobody else could ever experience."[50]

For twenty years, **Brian McCartin**, now president and CEO of the Tempe Tourism Office in Arizona, has kept the American flag he carried in the Columbus Day parade with the pin designed and donated to the Freedom Fliers by Cordelia Wilkes in the glove compartment of his car. When his staff asked him, "What's going on with the flag?" He said it honored his son, who serves in the Marine Corps.

But more importantly, he told them, "It was the Flight for Freedom. You should Google search it; you'll be amazed what you see."

Photo by Brian McCartin

TIMELINES: 9/11 AND ITS AFTERMATH

will never forget the Oregonians. I got to meet and speak to them in the lobby of the Waldorf. It was like they were witnesses. It was extremely cathartic. To have people interested, because I wanted to talk about my experience, to get it out of me so I would not have to think about it or talk about it again.

—Lisa Sokoloff, Acting Supreme Court Justice in New York County and 9/11 Survivor

A TIMELINE OF THE SEPTEMBER 11 ATTACKS

All times are Eastern Daylight Time—Ireland was five hours ahead (9 a.m. in New York was 2 p.m. in Dublin); Portland, Oregon, was three hours behind (9 a.m. in New York was 6 a.m. in Portland).[1]

It is election day in New York City.

8:46 a.m. American Airlines Flight 11 from Boston to Los Angeles slams into the 110-story North Tower of the World Trade Center in New York. The North Tower and its twin, the South Tower, are the city's tallest buildings, and the fourth-tallest in the world. Between 50,000 and 60,000 people are estimated to be in the buildings and its train stations.

The plane crashes in between floors 93 and 99, immediately killing hundreds of people, including all those onboard.

Almost immediately, emergency responders are sent to the building.

9:03 a.m. United Airlines Flight 175 from Boston to Los Angeles flies into the South Tower, between floors 77 and 85.

If they weren't before, people across the country and around the world are now glued to their television sets. Many people started the day when they received this telephone call from a friend or loved one "Turn on your TV."

They would stay glued to their sets for days, as the major networks played nothing but news for more than 90 hours, the longest news-only, commercial-free marathon in U.S. history, outlasting the President John F. Kennedy assassination and its aftermath.

"We were looking out the window and the entire sky was filled with paper," a New Yorker who was nearby told *The New York Times*. "We thought it was a ticker tape parade." Three miles away, across the East River in Brooklyn, sheets of office paper fluttered out of the sky.

"Fireballs were falling to the ground, which I now know were people," says one onlooker.

9:05 a.m.   President Bush, who is in Sarasota, Florida reading to second graders at the Emma E. Booker Elementary School, is told by Chief of Staff Andrew Card that a second plane has struck the World Trade Center, and that "America is under attack." Parts of the school immediately become a makeshift command center.

9:25 a.m.   The Federal Aviation Administration (FAA) bars all civil aircraft in the United States from taking off.

9:28 a.m.   President Bush makes a short address to the nation: "Terrorism against our nation will not stand."

9:36 a.m.   U.S. Vice President Dick Cheney is evacuated to the Presidential Emergency Operations Center located under the White House.

9:37 a.m.   American Airlines Flight 77 from Washington, DC to Los Angeles crashes into the west side of the Pentagon just outside Washington, DC. The Boeing 757 has 58 passengers and a crew of six. 24,000 people work in the Pentagon—for hours, it's not clear whether the plane actually hit the Pentagon or not; pieces of the plane that can be easily seen are quite small, less than three feet long.

The children at the Pentagon's day care center are successfully evacuated.

9:42 a.m.   The FAA orders all civil aircraft (4,546 of them) currently flying in U.S. airspace to land. This is the first national grounding of all commercial planes in U.S. history, and it would last for two days.

9:48 a.m.	The Capitol and the West Wing of the White House are evacuated.
9:49 a.m.	The FAA bars aircraft takeoffs in the United States. International flights in progress are told to land in Canada.
9:55 a.m.	President Bush departs Florida on Air Force One. His destination is not made public. On Air Force One at that time, radio and phone connections were sketchy ("Can you hear me now?"), email wasn't available, and TV reception was inconsistent.
9:59 a.m.	The South Tower of the World Trade Center collapses. People run for their lives as a tsunami of soot, smoke, and debris rolls across Lower Manhattan.
10:00 a.m.	FDNY orders firefighters to evacuate the North Tower. Many do not hear this order and continue to climb up inside the tower.
10:03 a.m.	United Airlines Flight 93 from Newark, NJ, to San Francisco crashes into a field in Shanksville, Pennsylvania, about 75 miles southeast of Pittsburgh, killing everyone (42) on board. It was not immediately known that these crashes were connected, nor that its destination had likely been Washington, DC. The crash left little evidence of the plane: all that remained was a crater about eight to 10 feet deep, 30 to 50 feet wide, and pieces of debris described as "no larger than a phone book."
10:28 a.m.	The North Tower collapses. Once again, massive, opaque clouds of soot, smoke and debris roll across Lower Manhattan. Once again, people run for their lives.
11:02 a.m.	New York City Mayor Rudolph Giuliani orders the evacuation of Lower Manhattan.
10–11:30 a.m.	Government buildings around the country are evacuated. The United Nations closes. The Securities and Exchange Commission (SEC) closes all U.S. financial markets. The District of Columbia government shuts down.

People flee Lower Manhattan, trying to get on boats to carry them to Staten Island and New Jersey; hundreds of people answer the U.S. Coast Guard's call for "all available boats" to come to New York Harbor. The nation's largest domestic maritime evacuation rescued 300,000 people with all manner of vessels, including, ferries, tugboats, and |

even historic boats—in a U.S. version of the World War II evacuation of Dunkirk.

Streets surrounding the Capitol Mall in DC become paralyzed as people try to get away from the federal buildings, worried that they would be targeted next.

DC federal workers race into the Metro (the DC subway), only to be greeted by a flashing sign: "Security alert! The Metro is closed until further notice. Please try to call a relative or a taxi if you need a ride."

The DC subway reopens by midday.

1:04 p.m.   After landing at Barksdale Air Force Base in Louisiana (information that was not known to viewers until he had left there), President Bush appears on television. He states that the government is doing everything they can to protect the American people and vows to "hunt down and punish those responsible."

2:35 p.m.   New York Governor George Pataki and Mayor Giuliani hold a press conference that relayed the first bits of news of New York, along with a lot of unknowns and "not sures."

Mayor Giuliani says they had just spoken with the President.

They "believe" the cause of the collapse of the buildings was the impact of the planes, not bombs.

Giuliani: "We will strive now very hard to save as many people as possible and to send a message that the city of New York and the United States of America is much stronger than any group of barbaric terrorists, that our democracy, that our rule of law, that our strength and our willingness to defend ourselves will ultimately prevail."

Where did the planes come from? They would leave it "up to the federal government to release that information," says Giuliani.

Giuliani reports that 1,500 "walking wounded" had been evacuated to Liberty State Park in New Jersey, about 600 in local hospitals and of them, 150 were critical.

When asked what he saw that morning at the Trade Center site, Giuliani responds: "I don't know that I'm really able to describe it. It was the most horrific scene I've ever seen in my whole life. We saw the World Trade Center in flames, a big gaping hole all the way on the top of it. We could see people jumping from the top of the building."

"Hundreds" of firefighters and police are on the scene to rescue survivors, and more than 1,000 rescue workers, says the mayor. They knew some had been lost and some they were "very worried about." Gov. Pataki states that about 2,000 National Guard and state police would arrive by evening.

Two warships are on their way into the port of New York.

When asked about casualty numbers, the mayor responds, "I don't think we really want to speculate about that. The number of casualties will be more than any of us can bear ultimately."

Throughout the day

In New York and DC, people line up at phone booths to try to reach loved ones to let them know they are alive. Cell phones are not ubiquitous as they are today—and networks are down or overloaded.

The long ordeal of not knowing about friends' and family's survival begins. Some would be reassured within hours of their loved ones' safety. For others . . .

New York Waterway spokesman Pat Smith tells *The New York Times* that its 24 boats normally carried 32,000 people a day but would probably carry 200,000 passengers by the end of the night. The Circle Line, the city's beloved Manhattan- circumnavigating tour boats, dedicates its six vessels to ferrying people off the island. By 6 p.m., lines of people hoping to board one of the Circle Line boats at the company's 42nd Street dock stretch all the way to 50th Street, with thousands waiting to get aboard.

And they walk. Thousands of people clog New York City bridges, refugees clad in the concrete, steel, and glass dust that had been the World Trade Center. While buses continued operating north of Houston Street—a "savior," says *The New York Times*. Ferries waive their fees and fill to capacity as long as they are needed, taking people to New Jersey, Queens, Brooklyn.

Tales of passenger calls to loved ones from the burning towers begin to be told on television. A glimmer of what might have been a heroic effort of self-sacrifice of passengers on the Shanksville plane, which saved the country from a second attack on Washington, starts to be reported.

People watching television start hearing the name "Osama bin Laden."

3:25 p.m.   CNN's John King reports that the President is now in Nebraska and receiving a National Security Council briefing. Getting the President back to the White House is a priority, says King, but the President's security is the top priority.

5:20 p.m.   Seven World Trade Center collapses. The occupants of its 47 stories had been evacuated earlier. Its major tenant was the Salomon Smith Barney investment bank, but other, smaller tenants included the SEC, the Internal Revenue Service, the U.S. Secret Service, the New York City Office of Emergency Management, the Central Intelligence Agency, and the Department of Defense.

6:54 p.m.   President Bush arrives at the White House.

7:45 p.m.   After evacuating the Capitol earlier in the day, roughly 150 Members of Congress come together on the building's East Front for a press conference. Senators stand by Representatives, Democrats next to Republicans, and the leadership of both houses. Spontaneously at the end of the press conference, they sing "God Bless America."

By day's end, bridges and tunnels into Manhattan are closed, in the biggest shutdown of transportation services in the city's history.

The federal government in Washington and the financial markets in New York were shut down.

All airports in the country were closed for the first time in the nation's history. Some Amtrak rail lines in the Northeast were halted.

The primary election in New York City was delayed.

Disneyland was closed. So was Disney World.

Major League Baseball was shut down for a day, as had only happened before during World War I when the Secretary of War issued a "work or fight" order shutting down baseball completely, and on D-Day.

High-rise buildings from Boston to Seattle, Atlanta to Los Angeles, were shut down, as were high-rises in Europe.

Security was tightened at U.S. borders, embassies, and military sites around the world. The National Guard patrolled Washington and New York.

Patrols increased along the trans-Alaska oil pipeline.

In an unprecedented move, the U.S. Health and Human Services Department (HHS) activated a national medical emergency system that dispatched roughly 7,000 volunteer doctors, nurses, pharmacists, and other medical staff to the scenes of the attacks.

8:30 p.m.   President Bush addresses the nation: "[T]terrorist attacks can shake the foundations of our biggest buildings, but they cannot touch the foundation of America. These acts shatter steel, but they cannot dent the steel of American resolve . . . . The search is underway for those who are behind these evil acts . . . . We will make no distinction between the terrorists who committed these acts and those who harbor them."

Near the closing of his speech, he uses a term that will become commonplace: the war on terrorism. "America and our friends and allies join with all those who want peace and security in the world and we stand together to win the war against terrorism."

By evening, the international response

Governments around the world offer condolences and pledge solidarity in the fight against terrorism.

Condolences sent to the President come from British Prime Minister Tony Blair and England's Queen Elizabeth II, Canadian Prime Minister Jean Chrétien, Chinese President Jiang Zemin, and Israeli Prime Minister Ariel Sharon. Mexico's President Vicente Fox releases a statement rejecting "all forms of violence" and expressing "horror" at the news of the terrorist attacks on the United States. Cuban Foreign Minister Felipe Perez Roque offers airspace and airports to any aircraft from the United States or elsewhere.

Palestinian leader Yasser Arafat says he is horrified by the attacks. But in the West Bank town of Nablus, about 3,000 people took to the streets, chanted "God is great" and handed out candy in celebration. From Gaza, Islamic Jihad official Nafez Azzam says "What happened in the United States today is a consequence of American policies in this region."

Russian President Vladimir V. Putin calls the attacks "terrible tragedies." China says it is "horrified." Pope John Paul II condemns the "unspeakable horror" and prays for the victims and their families.

The North Atlantic Council of NATO expresses its solidarity with the United States.

Members of the United Nations Security Council unanimously condemn the attacks and call for the perpetrators to be brought to justice.

In Iran, about 200 people gather spontaneously in Madar Square, on the north side of Tehran, in a candlelight vigil of sympathy and support for the American people.

Sheikh Yassin, leader of the Islamic militant group Hamas, says "No doubt this is a result of injustice the U.S practices against the weak in the world."

10 p.m.   In a press conference, exhausted and "visibly shaken," Mayor Giuliani reveals the news that many first responders died. When asked how many, he says, "A lot, it's a lot."

"We lost the deputy chief of the fire department and the chief of the FDNY," he says. Also lost were the beloved chaplain Father Mychal Judge, and FDNY icon (known as "God" and "Master of Disaster") Ray Downey, for whom the mayor had just given a party at Gracie Mansion for his years of service, including leading the Oklahoma City bombing rescue for the United States.

The big question for reporters: How many casualties of the attacks? "That will be in the thousands, but there is no way of knowing at this point."

"Mr. Mayor, is there still hope?

"Yes, there is still hope that there are people who are still alive," he says.

Giuliani names the shelters that are open for displaced people.

There had been no looting or any other problems, he says. The New York medical examiner got hurt, but they're ready to deal with thousands and thousands of bodies.

There is no power in the western part of Lower Manhattan.

"Stay home, if you work in Manhattan," the mayor says.

Muslim Americans will receive extra protection, says Giuliani. "Nobody should blame any group of people or any nationality or any ethnic group . . . . If citizens get involved in this they're just participating in the kind of activity we just saw. They'll be arrested."

"People tonight should say a prayer for the people that we lost and be grateful that we're all here."

Police Commissioner Bernard Kerik says that the NYPD had suffered losses, a "contingent of cops" with him and the mayor at the Trade Center. He and the mayor had left them for 10 minutes; while they were gone, a portion of the building fell, and they haven't been found yet.

Kerik says they know people are still in the buildings that are alive and they're making every effort to get to them, including some police officers.

"We're still hopeful that we'll find people," says Giuliani. Some people were pulled from the rubble and taken to the hospitals.

Throughout the night

Explosions at the WTC building site and in cars on the streets continue. Fires also burn at the World Trade Center site and at the Pentagon.

AS IT HAPPENED: SEPTEMBER 12-26

Below you will find a day-by-day account of what we knew in the two weeks after the September 11 attacks, as people in Portland were planning the Flight for Freedom. These moments are based largely on the encyclopedic coverage provided by *The New York Times* and focus primarily on New York City because that was the destination of the Flight for Freedom.

This section is included to help put you in the shoes of the Freedom Fliers and the New Yorkers who suffered the attacks.

With the hindsight of twenty years, it's easy to think we knew more than we did.

No one knew what was going to happen next.

SEPTEMBER 12, 2001

"It wasn't a dream" was the realization with which many people around the world began their day. Many New Yorkers were missing. "Have you seen" was becoming a New York refrain. "Ground Zero" was already the term used for Lower Manhattan by many workers.

Work had continued through the night at Ground Zero; lights were installed so that rescue work could continue. One thousand firefighters and rescue workers worked around the clock at the site of the blast to find survivors. More than 200 missing firefighters and nearly 100 police officers were unaccounted for. Those firefighters included the FDNY's leadership.

No one had claimed responsibility and how these attacks, which all happened within 50 minutes, could have happened remained unknown.

New York City ordered 11,000 body bags, but the death toll from the attacks was unknown. "It could eclipse the loss of life the country suffered in the Japanese attack on Pearl Harbor, when more than 2,300 perished," wrote *The New York Times*.[1] Hospitals and triage centers were prepared for the dead and injured, but neither appear. "There have to be thousands there and we have seen only a few hundred," St. Vincent's Manhattan Hospital Chief Anesthesiologist George G. Neuman told *The New York Times*.* The number would likely rise dramatically once rescue workers started digging into the rubble.

Hospitals discover that the injured from the Twin Towers don't exist. They were prepared to help the injured and they didn't show up. People across the country line up to give blood, the only thing they know to do. But the blood turns out not to be needed because there are so few injured.[2]

Firefighters fought the fire at the Pentagon throughout the night. The extent of the damage remained unknown, as was the number of people killed and injured, though estimates ranged from 100 to 800. Fortunately, the section of the 6,500,000 square-foot, 150-acre building—the world's largest office building—where the plane hit had just been renovated and was not heavily occupied; it had been fitted with

---

* Dan Barry, "A DAY OF TERROR: HOSPITALS; Pictures of Medical Readiness, Waiting and Hoping for Survivors to Fill Their Wards," The New York Times, September 12, 2001, https://www.nytimes.com/2001/09/12/us/day-terror-hospitals-pictures-medical-readiness-waiting-hoping-for-survivors.html.

explosion-resistant windows, which may have safeguarded others in the five-story building.

FBI investigators had gone to South Florida, stating that terrorists had possibly been pilots.

While the World Trade Center and Pentagon tragedies seemed to have been coordinated attacks, what happened with the Shanksville crash remained unclear.

Hyman Brown, a University of Colorado civil engineering professor and the construction manager for the World Trade Center, said that flames fueled by thousands of gallons of aviation fuel melted the towers' steel supports. "This building would have stood had a plane or a force caused by a plane smashed into it," he told the *Los Angeles Times*. "But steel melts, and 24,000 gallons of aviation fluid melted the steel. Nothing is designed or will be designed to withstand that fire."[3]

Some of those still in the rubble reportedly called officials or family members on their cell phones, and some trapped police officers made radio contact with headquarters.

President Bush visited the Pentagon crash site late in the day.[4]

Flags flew across the country.[5] In Portland, stores ran out of flags and Mayor Vera Katz went on TV to teach kids how to draw their own flags.

Hundreds of volunteers and medical workers converged on triage centers, offering help and blood. Across the country, people overwhelmed blood donation centers.

Around the world, U.S. embassies became shrines, with people bringing candles and flowers to express their sympathy. Policy disagreements were forgotten as the world rallied to support the United States.[6] The United Nations held emergency meetings of the General Assembly and the Security Council and condemned the attacks. NATO Secretary General Lord Robertson would officially inform the

UN Secretary-General Kofi Annan that the North Atlantic Council met and agreed that the attack on the United States was equal to an attack on all members.[7]

And in the United States, police began guarding mosques in many communities.

SEPTEMBER 13, 2001

With speculation quickly flaring after it was learned that the city had 30,000 body bags available, Mayor Giuliani sought to reassure the public with the city's first estimate. It put the missing count at 4,763 based on he said "a list that is as inclusive as we can make it." The figure included the passengers and crew members from the two hijacked planes as well as the thousands of people who worked in the towers and had not been heard from. He also said that ninety-four bodies had been found in the wreckage and that forty-six of them had been identified. This would be the practice going forward, reporting the numbers missing, found and identified. At the site, the mission was still considered one of rescue, not recovery.[8]

It was widely reported that a group of firefighters had been found trapped alive in a vehicle, and calls from families of the missing flooded a Fire Department hotline. But late in the day, the story was rescinded, a rumor that had begun after rescuers fell into a hole in the rubble and were pulled out. Such stories, said reporters, can happen because the news media is not allowed into the site because it's so dangerous and rumors gain traction among those inside and passed along to reporters.[9]

At the Pentagon, they, too, were hoping to find survivors in the rubble. Firefighters had been working round the clock to stop the fires, but their efforts were hampered by repeated evacuations because radar had detected airplanes headed toward the Pentagon. "We were there about 14 hours straight, battling smoke in the dark. But the most frustrating thing was we had to keep dropping our gear and running for our lives when we wanted to stay and save other lives," said Andrea

Kaiser, a firefighter from Arlington County. The fire flared after 9:30 that night, but was contained by 10:20.

Fire officials said they were close to recovering the voice and data recorder, or "black box," from Flight 77, but fears that parts of the badly damaged building would collapse prevented them from reaching it. "If we pull out the wrong cable, the whole building could collapse and then we'd lose our rescue workers," said Chief Edward Plaugher of the Arlington County Fire Department.

About 40 percent of the building remained closed, though most of the Pentagon's 24,000 workers returned to work, doubling up in offices either in the Pentagon or in spaces nearby. The scope of the damage remained unclear.

Authorities announced that 126 service members and civilians were missing and, officials said, presumed dead, raising the death toll from Tuesday's terrorist attack near Washington to 190. The numbers included the 64 passengers and crew members aboard American Airlines Flight 77. While the number seemed low, in comparison to the thousands feared lost in New York City, officials reminded the public that it exceeded the 168 deaths in the Oklahoma City bombing in 1995, which had been the worst terrorist bombing on American soil.

Pentagon officials identified the deceased by military branch of service, with the Army suffering the heaviest losses at twenty-one soldiers and officers and fifty-three civilians killed; the Navy reported thirty-three sailors and officers lost, along with nine civilians.

In Washington, families of the missing could be found at a counseling center in a nearby hotel searching for information, many clutching photos of their missing loved ones.[10]

Officials in Washington elaborated on the "real and credible information" that that the American Airlines Boeing 757 that slammed into the Pentagon may have originally been headed for the White House. On Wednesday, a Bush administration official described a chilling threat to the Secret Service after the plane had hit the Pentagon. "Air Force One is next," the caller had said.[11]

As they continued the round-the-clock labor that had begun on Tuesday, at the World Trade Center, the rescue workers—construction workers and other volunteers who were helping firefighters, police officers, paramedics and others—described the painstaking process of picking through the rubble by hand, filling buckets in six-to-twelve-hour shifts, even as earth-moving machines did their work and repeatedly a klaxon horn sounded to signal a possible collapse and send workers running for safety. The hope of finding survivors remained, though body parts were more likely discoveries. Hundreds of persons working in bucket brigades removed debris that had been hand-sifted, bucket-to-bucket in a straight line, one bucket at a time handed off to a line of dump trucks waited in the southbound lanes of the West Side Highway at the southern tip of Manhattan island.

The workers on the site said they had been plagued by what appeared to be fiberglass particles in the air, which rubbed against their collars and ate away their socks. The machine operators wore respirators with filters and goggles. Many of the volunteers wore paper dust masks. At night they worked under lights powered by oil or gas generators. [See also the interview with Portland firefighter Wes Loucks, who was in "the pile" within days.][12]

For the public, environmental officials and doctors said, the persistent pall of smoke wafting from the remains of the World Trade Center poses a very small, and steadily diminishing, risk to the public.[13]

Four thousand federal agents and 3,000 support personnel had been in a worldwide investigation, which identified eighteen hijackers from the four airplane manifests—the hijackers were all ticketed passengers. Attorney General John Ashcroft said that as many as fifty people may have been involved, who may have provided housing, rented cars, airline tickets, information and other support. It even included airport workers. Authorities thought it possible that additional potential hijackers who arrived from the Middle East attended flight schools and were still out there. A nationwide manhunt for these accomplices continued and intensified. At the time, it was a major discovery because unlike the terrorists implicated in the 1993 attack on the World Trade Center, who plotted in secretive cells, many of these men went out of their way to live openly and to blend in, living in the suburbs and sending their kids to public schools.[14] The operation was well-financed, out of bin Laden's $300 million fortune; it had been a year or two in the making, in Germany, Canada, Massachusetts, New Jersey, Florida and other places.

The public learned that the CIA had warned top officials in August about the bin Laden threat, following up on reports in June and July that bin Laden planned an attack over the Fourth of July. The threat of a domestic attack by bin Laden had been repeated by the CIA many times in recent years.

In Lower Manhattan, buildings were being inspected to make sure they were safe and could withstand the vibrations of the subway so that people could return to their homes safely.

Investigators unearthed the data recorder from United Airlines Flight 93. The recorder was found at 4:20 p.m. in the large crater gouged into a reclaimed strip mine by the impact of the Boeing 757, killing all 45 on board. The recorder was the only one to be recovered from any of the four hijacked planes. Cellular telephone calls from two passengers to their wives suggest that passengers might have tried to overcome the hijackers to keep them from slamming the jet into a Washington landmark.

"Like a nuclear bomb," said Jim Brant, the owner of the Indian Lake Marina a mile and a half downwind from the crash. Mr. Brant said he watched the fireball mushroom as high as 500 feet. Later on, just as in Lower Manhattan, bits of paper began to rain down, and John Fleegle, the marina service manager, noticed bits of clothing, a shirt, underwear, pieces of paper, wiring and a four-foot piece of what appeared to be the aluminum skin of the plane. He climbed the roof of a nearby cabin and snuffed out the fire caused by the remnants of a seat cushion. Bits of what appeared to be bone and flesh washed up at the marina.[15]

President Bush announced that he would travel to New York City
on Friday after leading a prayer service at the National Cathedral in
Washington.

New York airports reopened for the first time since Tuesday and then
closed after ten people were taken into custody and one arrested at
Kennedy International and La Guardia Airports. Mostly, the three airports filled with stranded passengers, as continual cancellations and
reschedulings took place, with only a few arrivals and departures actually taking place. A man wearing a pilot's uniform and discovered to have
false pilot's identification was arrested. In Italy, investigation reopened
on a pilot's uniform and credential that had been stolen four months
before, an incident that became of interest only since the U.S. terrorist
attacks. At Newark International Airport, two men on a Saudi aircraft
were detained after being identified on a terrorist watch list.[16]

Timed to coincide with the full-scale resumption of American commercial air traffic, the mobilization order for up to 50,000 military
reservists, the largest number since the 1991 Persian Gulf War against
Iraq, initially to support air patrols over New York and Washington
and on alert elsewhere in America went from the Pentagon to President
Bush for his signature.[17]

Phoenix, Orlando, and San Francisco airports were evacuated temporarily. All three New York airports were closed by evening. Only a small
fraction of a regular day's 35,000 to 40,000 flights took off, and some airports and airlines did not allow passenger flights at all.

Under the FAA's new security directive, passengers could not bring
such items as nail files onboard, needing a paper ticket to get through
security, and those without such tickets being prohibited from going
near the gate. The Federal Aviation Administration said there were
about 250 commercial aircraft aloft at 4:30 p.m.; on an ordinary day,
there would have been about 6,000 flights in the air. Passengers were
urged to stay away unless they could confirm that their flight was
going to take off. Those that were at the airport scanned the faces of
those on their flights, knowing that passengers had hijacked the last
planes in the air, on Tuesday.

The first flight to arrive was Alitalia Flight 622, which landed at Los Angeles International Airport from Calgary, Alberta, where it had been diverted on Tuesday. The flight had originated in Milan. All but two major airports, Logan in Boston and Ronald Reagan National Airport in Washington, were cleared by aviation officials to open, although some did not do so. New security steps included eliminating curbside check-in, preventing people without tickets from venturing past security, and banning knives, including cutlery, from airplanes. In the rush to implement the new security measures, each airport interpreted them differently. In Wichita, Kan., airline employees emptied and searched suitcases at the check-in counter. In Miami, security guards searched cars entering the airport. In Omaha, one passenger said that airline security workers had removed nail clippers, a sewing kit and a corkscrew from his bag, but that once on board, he was served a meal with a plastic knife. International airlines were not allowed into the United States until they complied with the new security standards.[18]

The Federal Aviation Administration had implemented a new ban on cargo on passenger planes, which threatened to severely disrupt the electronics industry and other businesses for weeks to come, particularly for transpacific shipping.[19] FedEx put its first plane back into the sky at 2 p.m. Central time. For the first time since it started business in 1973 as an overnight delivery service, for the past fifty-two hours FedEx had had to rely solely on trucks to keep its packages moving. It tripled the size of its truck fleet, to more than 950 trucks, by contracting with various trucking concerns. In response to an idea from delivery drivers, American flags were allowed to fly on their delivery vans.[20]

The New York Times reported that people were no longer allowed to go to the gates to welcome passengers: "At Hartsfield International Airport in Atlanta, people waited for arriving passengers behind a yellow line well away from the terminal gates. Employees at an information booth said more people than usual were holding flowers and many meetings were very emotional."[21]

Broadway theaters, which had closed on Tuesday and Wednesday, reopened. Many schools and businesses reopened as well.

Traffic was a mess, as millions of commuters tried to get into work, many using the roads as alternatives to the destroyed Lower Manhattan subway lines. Automobile traffic all the way back to Staten Island was tied up—and a bomb scare even isolated Staten Island for a time. Officials warned that getting around the New York region would not return to normal again for a long time. The train lines and stations that remained open were dangerously swamped with passengers, and some were so packed that police moved in barricades to control the crowds.[22]

Thousands of people who lived in Lower Manhattan remained exiled. Officially, a five-mile stretch remained off limits, and residents struggled to get behind police lines to pick up clothing and other belongings.[23] The subway in that area was extremely damaged by broken water mains that had flooded tunnels while water supply was cut off as well. About 12,000 commercial and residential buildings remained without electricity, 1,400 without gas and nearly 300 without steam and no estimate of when power would be restored.[24]

As people returned to work in New York City, flags flew ubiquitously, including on taxicabs. Still, all was not back to normal in any way. Call volume had nearly doubled and phone service was unreliable. Verizon was still providing free intracity phone calls from its 4,000 pay phone in Manhattan. Approximately ninety bomb threats in the late morning and early afternoon led to evacuations across many landmark buildings in the city as well as bridges and tunnels, affecting tens of thousands of people already traumatized and taking a risk to come back into the city after the nation's largest terrorist attack on its own soil, in their home. In Washington, DC, bomb threats shut down the Capitol temporarily and the American University campus, and work stopped work at the Pentagon. Miami; San Francisco; and Wilmington, Delaware, also experienced scares.

What perhaps set the tone more than anything was the city's new wallpaper, the flyers. Flyers heartbreaking in the juxtaposition of their photos of weddings and vacations and the times happy times everyone wants to capture on film (this was 2001, after all)—always titled something like "MISSING" and "HAVE YOU SEEN?" with names and descriptions of where that person worked in the World Trade Center.

In windows of restaurants, stores, they were taped everywhere, the most painful evidence of the humanity that seemed to have vaporized in the rubble of Ground Zero.[25]

For those who think of New York City as a heartless, anonymous place, donation centers, often made of ad-hoc volunteers demonstrated a place where humanity had put itself center stage. Children brought the contents of piggy banks and Pokémon wallets, doctors and nurses drove in from Kentucky with supplies, a boss radioed his ice delivery truck to make a detour, and a guy drove up with his van, in case somebody needed it. And by the next day, corporations would donate $100 million, plus matching employee contributions. The Firefighters Widows' and Children's Fund would need it by December, they said, because so many had been killed. The group estimated that the attacks had probably left 1,000 children to care for.[26]

Attacks on mosques and other hostile acts against Arab-Americans and others from South Asia prompted Attorney General John Ashcroft to hold a news conference. "Such reports of violence and threats are in direct opposition to the very principles and laws of the United States and will not be tolerated." Separately, President Bush said, "We should not hold one who is a Muslim responsible for an act of terror." *The New York Times* reported that interfaith religious services bringing together Christians, Jews, Muslims and others to emphasize spiritual common ground had been growing.[27,28]

Congress, despite some misgivings from lawmakers over granting President Bush open-ended authority to conduct an undeclared war — it is, after all, Congress's constitutional role to declare war and control expenditures, was moving swiftly to give the administration $40 billion to wage its antiterror initiative. The administration had asked Congress for an immediate $20 billion to begin building the military and intelligence force required to start the antiterror campaign.[29]

Secretary of State Colin L. Powell named Osama bin Laden, a Saudi fugitive and Islamic militant who is said to be located in Afghanistan, a prime suspect in the attacks, the first public accusation of bin Laden by a top administration official. The administration made clear that they planned a comprehensive military campaign to demolish terrorist networks, "removing the sanctuaries, removing the support systems, ending states who sponsor terrorism," said Paul D. Wolfowitz, the deputy secretary of defense.

President Bush today called the attacks on the World Trade Center and the Pentagon "the first war of the 21st century."[30] The campaign against terror "is now the focus of my administration," he said.

Already the administration focused diplomatic and military strategy on Russia and Pakistan, the (logical places geographically) to begin. The Soviet Union had occupied Afghanistan from 1979 to 1989 with the United States waging a proxy war against them using mujahadeen rebels (guerrilla fighters). State Department officials plan a meeting in Moscow next week to learn more about the country and to try to gain access to Russia's military facilities.[31]

NATO won Russian support for a campaign against global terrorism. In a joint statement, NATO and Russia declared they were "united in their resolve" that those who carried out the attacks would not "go unpunished."[32]

The National Football League put off its entire schedule of games this weekend, the first stoppage in its history not arising from a labor dispute. Nearly every major college football game was postponed or canceled, as were professional golf tournaments. Major League Baseball extended its postponements through the weekend.

New York City's primary election was rescheduled for September 25.

Now I'm wondering, is it Thursday or Friday? And I'm thinking, who cares?

—Chuck Meara, who walked down sixty-eight floors of 1 World Trade Center, his second escape, including the 1993 Trade Center bombing[33]

Stock markets announced plans to resume trading on Monday after the longest shutdown since the Great Depression, when President Franklin D. Roosevelt ordered a national bank holiday in March 1933 to halt bank runs. President Bush, who went to the Washington Hospital Center this morning to visit survivors of the attack on the Pentagon, said he would go to New York on Friday after attending a prayer service at the National Cathedral in Washington.[34]

The President proclaimed Friday a National Day of Prayer and Remembrance for the Victims of the Terrorist Attacks on September 11, 2001. He asked that places of worship have noontime memorial services, ring bells, and hold candlelight remembrance vigils in the evening. He "encouraged" employers to permit time off for their workers during lunch hours to attend services and he invited people around the world who share America's grief to join.[35]

Flags fly at half-staff across the Continent, hours-long lines back up before official condolence books, towns and cities come to a halt to observe moments of silence, churches are filled with mourners, blood banks are swamped, political contests are toned down, concerts are reprogrammed to honor the dead, and sports events that stir national passions are being postponed. Around the world, expressions of sympathy for Americans were enormous:

- In Beijing, funeral wreaths pile up.
- A London police support office was overwhelmed with calls from people seeking to give blood of house stranded travelers.
- At Buckingham Palace, a special Changing of the Guard dedicated to victims of the attacks was held. A military band played "The Star-Spangled Banner" while onlookers holding American flags wept in silence.[36]

SEPTEMBER 14, 2001

Mayor Giuliani said fifty-nine bodies had been found and identified, and thirteen body parts had been identified. There were also fifty-two unidentified bodies, he said, and 408 unidentified body parts. The list of the missing stood at 4,717. The mayor also said that ninety-four bodies had been found in the smoking wreckage and that forty-six had been identified.[37]

More than 300 firefighters are officially listed as missing or dead and that includes five of the department's most senior officials and a dozen battalion chiefs. The overall toll is nearly thirty times the number of firefighters ever lost before by the department in a single event—a statistic that puts into perspective the dangers professional firefighters face and the catastrophic nature of Tuesday's terrorist attack. Missing too, and presumed dead, are about forty New York City police officers, and at least thirty members of the Port Authority police.[38]

A temporary morgue of refrigerated trucks surrounds the sixteen-acre site. Mostly body parts are being found, although some gruesome passengers and a flight attendant have been found with their airline seats, the flight attendant, hands bound. The day's rain raised concern, not because the site became slippery but because cavities where people might be alive were being filled with water. A semblance of order seems to be arising, as volunteers, even those highly qualified, are being turned away, abandoned office buildings and hotels are becoming dormitories and empty restaurants used to prepare and serve food to workers.[39]

Even as the search is still called a "rescue" operation, loved ones of those missing were quietly confronting another possibility. David Vincent of Rochester stood outside the armory on Lexington Avenue at 26th Street, waiting for family members to arrive with a toothbrush or strands of hair from his daughter Melissa, something that held a DNA sample that could be used to match against remains being removed. She worked on the 102nd floor of the north tower, and had not been heard from in three days. "You can't do anything but stay focused on finding her," he told *The New York Times*. "You have to block the world out and concentrate."[40]

In Washington, teams uncovered the flight data and cockpit voice recorders in the rubble of the section of the Pentagon hit on Tuesday. The charred boxes were handed over to the Federal Bureau of Investigation, officials said, and then sent to the National

Transportation Safety Board laboratory in Washington. This is the first voice recorder found from the four hijacked aircraft.[41]

Around 9.a.m. the three broadcast networks broke a record for covering one news event for more consecutive hours than any previous event in American history. The previous news event had been the John F. Kennedy assassination in November 1963, which had been covered for seventy hours. The three networks had broadcast more than ninety hours straight — without commercials, which advertising executives said was costing the networks about $30 million per day in advertising revenue. The first planned break was not scheduled until sometime Saturday morning. Initial ratings for the first four days of coverage indicated that an average of 30 million to 50 million viewers a day watched network coverage in prime time, a far higher average than normal.[42] Television was the major source of news for the public.

Justice Department officials disclosed the names of nineteen men who they said had commandeered the four commercial jets in Tuesday's terror attacks, and said they wanted to question more than 100 other people associated with the hijackers. Most of the men, if not all, had Middle Eastern origins.[43]

Yesterday, city officials moved the northern boundary of the "frozen zone" — the section of the city off-limits to all but those who live there — south from 14th Street to Canal Street, freeing businesses in that swath of downtown — a northern border of Chinatown, the largest concentration of Chinese people in the western hemisphere, to open and workers to resume making a living. On Canal Street, a man passed out American flags. A young man on a bicycle stuck one in his hair and rode out into traffic. A man walked down Walker Street shouting curses to no one in particular, about no one in particular. Things were getting back to normal one bit at a time, *The New York Times* reported.[44]

With only one opponent in both houses, the House and Senate approved a joint resolution authorizing military action by President Bush ("all necessary and appropriate force") against the terrorists who attacked the United States on Tuesday.[45] Congress was also to vote on an allocation of $40 billion — twice the administration's $20 billion request. The Senate also approved a $40 billion package for counterterrorism activities, search and recovery efforts in New York and other related projects.

The airlines had hoped that Congress would grant them $12.5 billion in loan guarantees and $2.5 billion in direct aid as part of the $40 billion emergency benefits package, but Congress did not appropriate the money for them.[46]

Ansett Airways of Australia was abruptly grounded, stranding thousands of passengers and leaving 60,000 employees in shock.[47]

Despite long lines, delays, and constant security concerns the National Air Traffic Controllers Association reported that airliner activity was about 50 percent of normal, which was much higher than the day before.[48]

Airlines were warning that they would go bankrupt, estimating losses at $100 million to $275 million a day since Tuesday.

President Bush gave the Pentagon authority to activate up to 50,000 reserve troops to maintain aerial patrols over American cities and to strengthen security at crucial military and civilian installations. Some reservists could also be deployed overseas to provide security at American bases or perform other support missions, Pentagon officials said.

William J. Burns, assistant secretary of state for Near East affairs, met with the Arab envoys and delivered what a senior administration official called a simple message: "The time has come to choose sides." Either declare their nations members of an international coalition against terrorism, or risk being isolated in a growing global conflict.[49]

Over the last three days, American officials had engaged in secret discussions with Pakistan. The country's ruling generals have been told that they must allow they must allow the United States to use Pakistan's airspace, its military airfields, and its military intelligence apparatus (that is assumed to be knowledgeable about bin Laden's networks), for attacks against targets in Afghanistan, and block resources to the Taliban.[50]

The National Day of Prayer and Remembrance began in Washington, DC, in a nationally televised service at Washington National Cathedral. It was an extraordinary assemblage of the nation's leadership, past and present, particularly given the reason for the service, which was attended by former Presidents Clinton, George H.W. Bush, Jimmy Carter and Gerald Ford, as well as former Vice President Al Gore, who flew back from a meeting in Austria on Thursday at Bush's request. (Less than a year before, Gore had lost a close presidential election to Bush through a decision by the Supreme Court.) Members of Congress, the Cabinet, chairman of the Joint Chiefs of Staff and other military leaders, and dignitaries and officials from all over the nation and the world also attended. Only Vice President Cheney was absent, for security reasons.

President Bush said, "In every generation, the world has produced enemies of human freedom," the president said, glancing at his father, a fighter pilot in the Pacific in World War II and a symbol of another generation's heroic battles. "They have attacked America because we are freedom's home and defender. And the commitment of our fathers is now the calling of our time.

"Our responsibility to history is already clear. To answer these attacks and rid the world of evil."

The president left the cathedral accompanied by Senators Charles E. Schumer and Hillary Rodham Clinton, Acting Gov. Donald T. DiFrancesco of New Jersey and other members of the New York and New Jersey Congressional delegations. Together they boarded Air Force One and arrived over the trade center wreckage at 3:30 p.m.

But the day would be remembered most for what happened that afternoon, when President Bush, accompanied by Mayor Rudolph Giuliani, Gov George Pataki and members of Congress, traveled to Ground Zero, where the search continued for survivors in the rubble. Standing atop a charred fire truck, someone yelled out that they couldn't hear him. He grabbed a bullhorn, and what he said became a rallying cry for the country and sent his popularity soaring: "I can hear you. The rest of the world hears you. And the people who knocked down these buildings will hear all of us soon."

The New York Time's description of the president's visit foreshadows what was the most surprising and enduring experience of those who participated in the Flight for Freedom. He spoke "only occasionally as if his presence was the message, not his words."

"The nation sends its love to everybody who is here," Mr. Bush said. And at another point, he shouted: "May God bless America."[51]

Candlelight vigils and other observances took place across the country that evening.

SEPTEMBER 15, 2001

Balbir Singh Sodhi, a Sikh American man, is shot and killed outside of his gas station in Mesa, Arizona. He is the first person to be murdered in a hate crime following 9/11.[52]

The New York Times Pulitzer Prize-winning "Portraits of Grief" appear in the newspaper for the first time. These are portraits of the missing—of the more than 4,000 persons missing at the time, few had been identified as deceased. In fact, few of the missing had even been identified for certain. As the newspaper described it, "For days after 9/11 the numbers of the dead defied calculation, and even the names of the missing only slowly accumulated—all while the paper's cry for some kind of accounting grew stronger." To begin, reporters collected the flyers that surviving families made about their missing loved ones and had taped on every surface across the city and began to make phone calls to gather their recollections. On September 15, they were called, "After the Attacks: Among the Missing," a title that was changed the following day. The 200-word profiles with photo appeared daily through December 31 (1,910 in a death toll that eventually rose to more than 2,750), regularly through September 2002, and then sporadically through 2003, as more information was released, often because surviving families later chose to provide it. *The Times* called these pieces "snapshots of their lives with family and at work." *The Oregonian* began to publish them on September 17, on a page even more prominent than that of *The Times*: inside the front page. These very human, very personal, and even intimate portraits erased any view of the tragedy as one of only numbers of "casualties." As *The Times* described them: "The normal trappings of an obituary generally were absent; few credentials or other signs of status were included, beyond the jobs they held, and family descriptions. The portraits identified one aspect of life—a woman gardening, a man taking his daughter to ice-skating lessons, or perhaps indulging in a fondness for cigars. For many people across the country and around the world, these snapshots became a ritual. *The Times* received "hundreds" of e-mails and letters from readers who said they read them religiously, "rarely missing a day. For some, it was a way of paying homage. Others said it was a means of connecting, a source of consolation.[53]

In New York, the first three funerals were held for those lost in the attacks on Tuesday, three top officials of the city's fire department: Chief Peter Ganci; First Deputy Fire Commissioner William Feehan; and Father Mychal Judge, the department's chaplain. Hundreds of firefighters and police officers from New York and surrounding communities attended. "Today was a very solemn and difficult day in New York City news conference, with the three funerals we had for Bill Feehan, for Pete Ganci and for Father Judge," Mayor Giuliani said at a news conference that evening. "Unfortunately, it is an indication of what we are probably going to face in the future." About 300 New York firefighters are still unaccounted for and as many as 5,000 are still missing.

A memorial service for former federal prosecutor and conservative TV commentator Barbara Olson took place in Arlington, Virginia. Olson was one of the passengers on American Airlines Flight 77, which crashed into the Pentagon. Before she died inside the doomed airplane, she made two telephone calls to her husband and, said CNN, "kept her cool." Supreme Court Justice Clarence Thomas eulogized her. As services began to take place, they were memorials, not funeral services because families did not want to wait for recovery of a body.[54]

SEPTEMBER 16, 2001

The New York Times reports that donations have been received from every state in the union, clothing, food, including tons of dog food for the canines helping at Ground Zero. New clothing now fills warehouses as far as 90 miles away in Poughkeepsie, N.Y. No more donations and no more volunteers are needed. Still, "It doesn't feel right to be at home, and just not do anything," said fourteen-year-old Stuyvesant High School sophomore Shunpei Okochi, who had witnessed the collapse of the towers when his school was being evacuated. He and a friend had come to volunteer while school was closed and were loading Red Cross trucks.[55]

SEPTEMBER 17, 2001

The Oregonian begins publishing *The New York Times'* "Portraits of Grief" on page A2 (inside the front page). In October, the paper would publish a column in which its ombudsman, Dan Hortsch, raised the question of when *The Oregonian* should stop. When he checked his voice mail that afternoon, he found sixty-eight messages. Hundreds followed. The gist was: Don't stop.[56]

The official number of deaths in the destruction of the World Trade Center stood at 201, and the medical examiner has identified only a few dozen victims; almost 5,000 are listed as missing.[57]

President Bush says we want bin Laden "Dead or Alive."[58]

Wall Street reopens.

Major League Baseball resumes after six days away. Schedule interruptions had occurred only twice before, due to World War I and D-Day.[59]

The subway trains were running downtown again. The Staten Island Ferry crisscrossed the harbor. The mayor reoccupied City Hall. But on this sunny late summer day when tens of thousands of workers returned to their Lower Manhattan offices for the first time since the World Trade

Center attack, little, in fact, was normal, *The New York Times* reported. Commuters stood on the bow of the Staten Island ferries, some tearing up as, for the first time, they faced the jolting view of Lower Manhattan without the glistening towers that have dominated the skyline. A lawyer politely asked a Supreme Court justice downtown to adjourn his civil case because the defendant was missing and the small import-export office where he had worked in the World Trade Center no longer existed. A woman went to the Health Department headquarters at 125 Worth Street, seeking to get a birth certificate for her 16-year-old son, whose last name she intended to change, at his request, from Mohammad to Smith. She was turned away, since the headquarters office remained closed.[60]

President Bush visits the Muslim American Society in Washington, DC.

David Letterman returns to his CBS late night show, marking the first late-night show to go back on the air. Those in the audience saw Letterman, hands occasionally shaking, and wiping tears from his eyes. The show focused on the tragedy and his monologue was not comedic.[61]

SEPTEMBER 18, 2001

Mayor Giuliani stated that the likelihood of finding survivors "is very, very small. We still hope and pray, but the chance is very, very small."[62]

The count of the missing stands at 6,030.[63]

The New York Times runs a long feature story about Afghanistan.[64]

In the last week, mosques in at least six states had been attacked—four in Texas—as have Muslim taxi drivers in several cities. President Bush condemned attacks on Muslims, Sikhs, and others who appear to be Middle Eastern. Murder charges were brought against an Arizona man accused of the September 15 hate killing. Middle- and high-school students have been harassed.[65]

The Pentagon began activating thousands of National Guard and Reserve troops across the nation today, "a strong symbol of this nation's resolve," said President Bush. The first guardsmen and reservists would help in cleanup operations from last week's terrorist attacks and in securing the nation's borders by flying air patrols over New York City and Washington, inspecting ships entering major harbors and serving as police at military bases and airfields.[66]

Major airlines saying they expected the layoffs to reach 100,000. And the Boeing Company, whose fortunes are tied to the industry, said tonight that it would lay off 20,000 to 30,000 workers by the end of 2002 because of fewer orders for aircraft. The federal government promised aid the following week.[67]

The Bush administration announced a major expansion of its power to detain immigrants suspected of crimes, including new rules allowing legal immigrants to be detained indefinitely during a national emergency. Previous rules placed the Justice Department under a twenty-four-hour deadline on whether to release detained immigrants or charge them either with a crime or with violating the terms of their visa. Under the new rules, the department said it would continue to hold seventy-five immigrants arrested in connection with the attacks on the World Trade Center and the Pentagon.[68]

The memorial service planned for Sunday in Central Park, which had been expected to attract one million people, was called off, in part because of safety concerns around large crowds.[69]

SEPTEMBER 19, 2021

With layoffs mounting in the airline industry, the stock market skittish and the world economy weakening, the president and Democratic and Republican leaders made clear that the government was moving toward some concrete response—beyond a multibillion-dollar bailout for the airlines that could be passed this week.

"Not only has someone conducted an act of war on us," President Bush told reporters before meeting with the Congressional leaders, "our economy has slowed way down, and this is an emergency."

"I'm going to work with Congress," he said, "to send a clear message to America, American workers, American businesspeople, that this government will respond to this emergency."[70]

President Bush ordered bombers to within striking distance of Afghanistan and insisted that the Taliban turn over Osama bin Laden and others suspected of attacking New York and Washington. The following night the president will address a joint session of Congress on what he has called "a global war on terrorism" and sacrifices that might be asked of the American public.[71]

SEPTEMBER 20, 2001

Mayor Giuliani announced that the estimate of the missing had risen to 6,333 from 5,422. The number of the injured, including both those injured in the attacks and those injured in the rescue efforts totaled 6,291. The mayor attributed the sharp increase to the delayed reporting of more than sixty nations.[72]

President Bush addressed the nation and a Joint Session of Congress, and made his case for U.S. actions in response to the attacks in New York and Washington. He provided an overview of who the attackers were, organizations and names that very likely were new to many/most Americans—Al Qaeda and Osama bin Laden—their goals, and his plan for using the $40 billion provided by Congress on what he called the "war on terror." He explained how this war would be different than other wars, that it was a new kind of war, not for territory, not against one nation. He explained the Taliban's repression in Afghanistan and pledged an attack unless Afghanistan surrendered bin Laden.

- He spoke to Muslims, saying that Islam's "teachings are good and peaceful, and those who commit evil in the name of Allah blaspheme the name of Allah."
- He took pains to make clear that "The enemy of America is not our many Muslim friends. It is not our many Arab friends. Our enemy is a radical network of terrorists and every government that supports them."
- "From this day forward, any nation that continues to harbor or support terrorism will be regarded by the United States as a hostile regime."
- "Either you are with us, or you are with the terrorists."

The president also announced a new Cabinet-level Office of Homeland Security. His speech was interrupted thirty-one times by applause.[73]

Battery Park residents begin to be allowed to return home.[74]

SEPTEMBER 21, 2001

Congress passed a $15 billion package to bail out the airlines and agreed to set up an open-ended federal fund to compensate victims of the terrorist attacks. The plan passed 96 to 1 in the Senate and 356 to 54 in the House. It now goes to President Bush, who is supportive. The legislation sets no limits on the amount of money a victim can receive in economic damages and pain and suffering from the victim compensation fund the legislation establishes. The fund is intended to protect the airlines from liability for damages and deaths on the ground, and offers victims and their families a choice of suing United Airlines and American Airlines or avoiding years of litigation by instead seeking compensation from the fund.[75]

Law enforcement officials said that the tape from the Flight 93 cockpit voice recorder revealed a massive struggle that seems to have led to the crash in Pennsylvania. Earlier speculation was that the plane was on its way to the White House.[76]

The Bush administration told Congress that it would waive economic sanctions against Pakistan and India that were imposed after they tested nuclear weapons in 1998. The action rewards Pakistan, which is an ally in the war on terrorism. European allies endorsed an American military response to the terrorist attacks.[77]

A benefit concert to raise money for the victims and their families, especially New York City firefighters and police officers was produced by the four American broadcast networks: ABC, CBS, Fox, and NBC. Actor George Clooney organized celebrities to perform and staff the phone bank to take donations. Broadcast live and commercial-free, *America: A Tribute to Heroes* won a Peabody Award and an Emmy.

SEPTEMBER 23, 2001

The New York Times reports that Democratic leaders in the House and Senate said a federal takeover of airport security was the best way to restore public confidence in air travel after the September 11 terrorist attacks, and Republican leaders raised no objection. This will change the previous system in which airlines paid private contractors.[78]

"A Prayer for America," New York City's official prayer service to remember the missing and the dead at the World Trade Center took place at Yankee Stadium. The interfaith event was primarily for family members of the dead and missing as well as rescue workers, Twenty-thousand mourners gathered for the city-sponsored service, which was simulcast on scoreboard screens in Brooklyn and Staten Island. The afternoon combined interfaith religions and patriotism.

At the door, guests received free stuffed animals affixed with notes and crayoned drawings from children across the country. They also received American flags and flag-emblazoned T-shirts and bandanas and the Red Cross provided tissues and roses. Hot dogs and soda were served. The tone for the afternoon, a combination of solemnity and patriotism was struck by James Earl Jones, who began the day by saying, "Our nation is united as never before," to which the audience cheered. "We are united not only in our grief, but also in our resolve to build a better world. At this service, we seek to summon what Abraham Lincoln called 'the better angels of our nature.'"[79]

SEPTEMBER 24, 2001

President Bush ordered an immediate freeze of all assets in the United States of suspected Islamic terrorist groups and individuals and gave the treasury secretary broad new powers to impose sanctions on banks around the world that provide them access to the international financial system.

President Vladimir V. Putin offered the United States broad support for antiterrorist operations in Afghanistan, including opening Russian airspace to relief missions, taking part in some search-and-rescue operations, and arming anti-Taliban forces inside Afghanistan.

Attorney General John Ashcroft says that there is a "clear and present danger' of more terrorist attacks.

SEPTEMBER 25, 2001

The official number of bodies found at the World Trade Center site was 276; the city medical examiner had identified 206. In all, 6,453 could be missing.[80]

Already 115,000 tons of debris had been cleared, everything from airplane parts to steel girders.

The mayoral primary that had begun on September 11 took place today. Michael Bloomberg wins on the Republican side.

The New York Times reported that rumors and misinformation were rampant: "from the mundane to the ridiculous, from the fantastic to the sad. Born out of chaos and sent speeding along by gossip and e-mail, the new urban legends are throwing up false hopes to the needy, diversions to the melancholy and roadblocks to the rescuers.

The news often reports them, the Internet repeats them, and before long the wackiest theories seem plausible."[81]

The latest New York Times/CBS News Poll shows that Americans favor going to war even if that means thousands of casualties for U.S. armed forces, yet they say that the United States should wait to act until it is certain who is responsible for the attacks.

- For the first time since 1990, a majority of Americans say the economy is worsening.
- Eighty-nine percent approve of the way President Bush is doing his job, up from 50 percent in late August.
- Eight in ten say Americans will have to forfeit some of their personal freedoms to make the country safer, an increase even from a week ago.
- Ninety-five percent approve of how Mayor Giuliani has handled the attacks.[82]

The Travel Industry Association meets with the Commerce Secretary to plead for government action to try to restore confidence. "Our industry is in dire straits," said Betsy O'Rourke, senior vice president of the trade group. "If the American people don't get back to traveling, to normal life, a number of these companies won't be there to serve them,"[83]

"I hope we don't let a handful of people dictate how we live," said Mary Ujhelyi of Park Ridge, IL, who was still planning an annual golf trip with her friends.[84]

Defense Secretary Donald H. Rumsfeld renamed the war against terrorism "Operation Enduring Freedom."

Duane Woerth, a 747 pilot and president of the Air Line Pilots Association, told Congress that his members should be allowed to take an FBI training course and then be deputized as federal law enforcement officers, which would permit them to carry guns in the cockpit. But the idea got mixed reviews from other aviation experts and from members of Congress, said *The New York Times*.[85]

SEPTEMBER 26, 2001

The official number of bodies found the World Trade Center site stood at 300; the city medical examiner had identified 232. In all, 6,347 could be missing.[86]

With Delta's announcement today, the total number of job losses in the aviation industry had surpassed 100,000. Delta Air Lines, the nation's third-largest carrier, said yesterday that it would cut up to 13,000 jobs worldwide and reduce its flight schedule by 15 percent because of a plunge in the demand for air travel. Last week, Continental Airlines announced 12,000 job cuts; 11,000 by US Airways; 20,000 by the AMR Corporation, the parent company of American Airlines and Trans World Airlines; and 20,000 by UAL, the parent company of United. Among the major carriers, only Southwest Airlines has not announced job cuts.[87]

The New York Times reports on the many ideas for replacing "the hole in the city . . . . The transformed human meaning of the World Trade Center site . . . has become the driving force," say experts the *Times* consulted. A memorial to the victims must be the top priority in any plan, said Richard Sennett, a sociologist and Manhattan resident who is also the chairman of the Cities Program, an urban design program at the London School of Economics. Commercial uses such as a New York Stock Exchange/Guggenheim have been floated, but Sennett and others say commercial use should be adapted to a memorial to the victims. "This space, almost regardless of what we do, will become a pilgrimage site. It cannot be just a standard-issue commercial real estate deal or we will not be living up to the expectations of the world," said Robert D. Yaro, the executive director of the Regional Plan Association, a non-profit economic and land-use planning group in Manhattan.[88]

Toys "R" Us announces its "Make A Flag. Make A Difference" campaign, September 27–30. For each American flag kids make in Toys "R" Us stores, the corporation will donate $1 to the Toys "R" Us Children's Fund 9/11 Emergency Relief Fund. Flags will be "proudly" displayed at the front of the stores. "In addition to our other efforts, nothing would thrill us more than to display millions of kids' flags knowing that, together, we can make even more of a difference. It's our way of honoring the thousands of families affected by our nation's recent tragedies. It's also a reminder that in difficult times, it's more important than ever to spend time with your kids."

The $15 billion airline bailout approved overwhelmingly by Congress has lobbyists for other industries and groups—insurance, travel agents, pilots, restaurant workers, and others—lining up now to make the case that their clients, too, need federal aid.[89]

The Department of Transportation is asking state law enforcement agencies to pull over every truck with hazardous materials placards and to check the drivers' credentials and paperwork, officials said yesterday.[90]

SOME NOTES ON OREGON
OR
IF OREGON CAN DO IT, ANYONE CAN!

Feeling Adventurous? How Oregonian of you.

—*The Oregon Encyclopedia's search engine*

THE LAND

I t's the land, the environment, that was, and maybe still is, the basis of the Oregon identity. As we've seen, Oregon is highly diverse geographically. The Cascades, one of Oregon's many mountain ranges, define the state. Spanning from British Columbia through Washington and Oregon to California, the Cascades separate the lush, rainy Willamette Valley (where Portland is) and its neighboring coast from the dry, high elevation of the regions to the east. West of the Cascades, Oregonians receive up to 130 inches of rain a year, while their eastern counterparts are lucky to get 20 inches. So while Portlanders are growing moss between their toes, east of the Cascades it's the dry American West: wide open spaces, cattle rangelands, mining, wheat, and more mountains.

West of the Cascades, particularly along the Willamette Valley, population is more dense. That's where you'll find Oregon's major cities. In 2019, Portland proper was home to 645,291 people, with Salem, the capital, a distant second at 169,259. But cities in the eastern part of the state are far smaller. Ontario, near the Idaho border, is the largest, with nearly 11,000 people. In the central Oregon region, which is east of the Cascades, the largest city is Bend, with a current population of about 101,000.

This divide is more than geographical; it's cultural and political as well, and has even been recognized by Oregonians and their leaders, to the extent that a "Toward One Oregon" discussion across a wide range of fields took place more than a decade ago, as the state explored ways they could work together in the new millennium. The conflicts and issues that have arisen are the same ones confronted in the rest of the United States: the loss of jobs and being left behind by globalization, whether the environment or the economy should come first, or whose stories even get told, as the national conversation becomes increasingly dominated by our urban areas.

More than half of Oregon is owned by the federal government. Of the state's 61 million acres, the Forest Service administers about 15.5 million. The state is also home to thirteen national parks—some of our oldest and most spectacular—plus 256 state parks on 109,000 acres.

Historian Thomas Cox calls eastern Oregon a "mosaic"; he tells us that all of eastern Oregon cannot be lumped into one category. But he says these largely rural Oregonians do share one thing: an identity "deeply rooted in the land and the peculiar characteristics thereof, an identify that grew out of the prolonged and ongoing dance between Eastern Oregon's people and their environment."[1] Both, he writes, "stand in sharp contrast to the better-known story of the Oregon that lies west of the Cascades."

Of course, attachment to the land originated with the Native Americans, who began human habitation of Oregon in, as historian William G. Robbins describes it, "time immemorial." The story of the Native Americans in Oregon typifies that of tribes across the United States; they were displaced, lost much of their land, often due to broken treaties with the U.S. government, and spent much of the last century fighting to regain what had been promised to them. Many of those who came after, whether cattlemen or farmers or miners, also felt the tug of that land and that's why they stayed, even as, for many, the livelihoods that had sustained them disappeared.

Needless to say, these issues are complex. To understand them and to find a way forward, it is essential to be open to some of the inherent contradictions and to hold them consciously.

> Do I contradict myself?
> Very well then I contradict myself.
> (I am large, I contain multitudes.)
> —*Walt Whitman, "Song of Myself"*

The "Oregon mystique" was built in the 1970s and is linked intimately with the legacy of Republican Governor Tom McCall (1967–1975), who used that term often in his references to the state. McCall was born to a wealthy family in Massachusetts but grew up on a ranch near Prineville, in central Oregon, in less prosperous circumstances. His connection to the land was authentic.[2]

It was McCall who gave the state a clear and distinct identity.[3] But it brought together—in fact, it required—both Republicans and Democrats who wanted to protect the state from exploitation and preserve the environment.* A popular journalist in print, radio and television before becoming governor, one of McCall's greatest strengths was his ability to capture public spirit with populist language and to garner media support for an issue or legislation.

McCall, who ultimately left the Republican party and became an Independent, was perhaps most famous for his interview with the "CBS Evening News" in 1971, when he said, "Come visit us again and again. This is a state of excitement. But for heaven's sake, don't come here to live."

Oregonians loved it. It became the unofficial state motto—and growth rates were above the national average throughout the 1970s.[4]

Three McCall administration policies gave Oregon an identity that lasted through the final years of the twentieth century and continues to this day to some degree. The "Beach Bill" (1967) made all the beaches in Oregon public, asserting the state's ownership from the water's edge to the dune. Most people had assumed the state government owned Oregon's beaches until a local motelier blocked off the beach behind his establishment in 1966. In 1913, the state legislature, led by Governor Oswald West, had taken the slick action of

---

*Oregon was known for moderate, socially progressive Republicans during the post-World War II era. Senators Wayne Morse and Mark Hatfield were critics of American foreign policy, especially the Vietnam War. Early in his career, Hatfield had successfully led the legislature in outlawing racial discrimination in public accommodations in Oregon; raised the discussion of the connection between livability and conservation within the state; and was outspoken in his condemnation of Senator Joseph McCarthy's anti-communist witch hunt. (Barbara Mahoney, "Mark O. Hatfield (1922-2011)," *The Oregon Encyclopedia*, https://www.oregonencyclopedia.org/articles/hatfield_mark_o_1922_/, last updated January 21, 2021.)

designating state beaches as a public highway, which in truth meant nothing at all in terms of ownership. But it worked until the motel owner staked his claim more than fifty years later. Governor McCall fought back and the end result was that the beaches were preserved for everyone's use.

The 1971 "Bottle Bill," whose purpose was to reduce litter and conserve resources, was probably the most famous of its time; it garnered national attention. This landmark bill required a five-cent deposit on malt and soft-drink glass bottles* and cans. That Oregon succeeded in passing such a bill was an enormous accomplishment. Container and beverage manufacturers lobbied intensely—and that kind of pressure had killed a similar bill in Washington state the year before.[5]

While the Bottle Bill was perhaps the most well-known of Oregon's environmental measures, S.B. 100 (1973), has had the greatest long-term impact of the McCall-era legislation. "We don't have a 'no growth' policy. We have a wise growth policy," said McCall, who his biographer, Brent Walth, calls a "conservationist" rather than an "environmentalist." The state's economy was dependent on its natural resources; McCall knew that timber and agriculture would be decimated by runaway growth, and pollution would follow. The concern, which McCall was able to capture in rhetoric that enabled him to gather popular and media support, was "sagebrush subdivisions, coastal condomania, and the ravenous rampages of suburbia" that would destroy the areas on which the state's economy and beauty relied. S.B. 100, which had bipartisan authorship and sponsorship, defined the public interest at the state level while preserving land-use decision making at the local level. Under S.B. 100, farmlands received statewide protections and every city and county in the state was required to prepare a comprehensive plan in accordance with state goals.

Calling S.B. 100 "the nation's most progressive land-use planning legislation," Robbins wrote in 2020:

> Fly the length of the Willamette Valley, across the rich irrigated lands
> in central and eastern Oregon, or the great reclamation district in the

---

*Plastic was not used for these containers in 1971.

Klamath Basin, and you will see contiguous agricultural lands and an absence of urban sprawl. Although there have been problems implementing statewide land-use goals and there has been some attrition, the DLCD [Department of Land Conservation and Development] has mandated urban-growth boundaries, protected farmlands and forests, and preserved recreational and national areas. The effects of S.B. 100 are visually scripted across Oregon's landscape.[6]

In 2001, this land-use planning was still strong, and it remains so twenty years later.

ECONOMIC TRANSITION

The Oregon story mirrors that of the United States economically in many ways. Much of the economy of the United States has been based on its natural resources and the transition away from that economic base as resources have declined is the story of many parts of the United States. The repercussions of that transition on the lives of Oregonians is a major story in the second half of the twentieth century and was peaking—or perhaps more accurately, reaching a nadir—around the time of the Flight for Freedom.

After the Europeans arrived in the eighteenth century, the Oregon economy was based on extracting resources, processing them, and shipping them elsewhere. The fur trade—"the earliest and longest-enduring economic enterprise that colonizers, imperialists, and nationalists pursued in North America"[1]—drew the Europeans to the West Coast in the late eighteenth century after about 250 years of trapping on the East Coast. Europeans came by sea; many resources moved from the inner parts of the state to the west for shipping. When Americans arrived later, by land, they, too, harvested wealth from the interior areas of the state and moved them west.

In time, Oregon's economy diversified and for much of the nineteenth and twentieth centuries, timber, fishing and agriculture—and mining for a time—were the state's sustenance. According to Oregon State University Professor Emeritus William G. Robbins, this transition took place much later than that of other states, with lumber and agriculture dominating economic activity through the 1970s.[2] But with globalization, timber processing no longer needed to take place locally, which put Oregon lumber mills out of business. Not only did this mean the elimination of local jobs, it also weakened or even severed the relationship between eastern and western, urban and rural parts of the state.

By the time the Freedom Fliers took to the skies, one-fifth of the state's workforce was employed in the manufacturing of forest products, down from nearly two-thirds in 1950s. Forest products' share of the economy had declined, too. And the size of trees available to cut had shrunk within living memory. Old-timers remembered when the trees were such large caliper that only one could fit on a semi-truck bed. The Post World War II building boom had taken Oregon's vast stands of old-growth timber[3] and what remained were younger, smaller trees as candidates for harvest. The U.S. Forest Service, whose role had been to safeguard the timber in our national forests began to sell off acreages to satisfy the postwar demand.

Fishing is an Oregon staple, but populations of the most valuable products—shellfish chinook, silver, chum, and pink salmon—in the wild have declined greatly. To replenish the population the state has implemented a program to build hatcheries, where salmon are grown and released to the ocean to begin their upriver journey.[4]

High-tech manufacturing had started in suburban Portland after the war, with Beaverton-based Tektronix an early player. Intel gave a major boost to the sector when it arrived in the 1970s and by the early 2000s, it was the largest private employer in the state.[5] Biotechnology and the manufacture of plastics and software were also growth industries.

One result of this transition was the loss of good-paying manufacturing, timber, and fishing positions that don't require a college education—jobs through which a wage-earner could support a family. These jobs were not replaced. High-tech jobs require college degrees.

Those in rural areas have been hit hardest compared with those along the I-5 corridor just west of the Cascades, which is the more developed, urban part of the state. As agriculture became more mechanized, people were replaced machines, eliminating jobs, along with the declines in timber production.[6] A look at 2000 unemployment rates by county shows the disparities. At that time, the national unemployment rate was 4.0 percent and Oregon's overall rate was higher, at 5.2. Washington County, where much of the tech employment and the Nike Corporation reside, had the state's lowest unemployment rate, at 3.9 percent, while Grant County in Eastern Oregon, home of the Malheur National Forest and the John Day Fossil Beds, experienced the highest unemployment, at 9.7 percent.*

This disparity exemplifies how Oregon, perhaps surprisingly, mirrors trends in the United States as a whole.

Around the time of the Flight for Freedom, Oregon had the nation's highest rate of hunger, according to a US Department of Agriculture report, and one of the highest rates of "food insecurity."

Hungry, yes, but Oregon was nowhere near the top in terms of poverty. Its $6.50 minimum wage was one of the highest, and the state was nineteenth in household income.

One problem was that cost of living in the state continued to go up, even as wages did not. Housing costs had risen twice as fast as income since the mid-1980s. From 1978 to 1998, the proportion of Oregon jobs paying less than $25,000 increased from 30 percent to 35 percent. A 1999 study by the Northwest Policy Center at the University of Washington calculated Oregon's livable wage at $34,000 for a family of three; the federal poverty standard was $17,050 for a family of four.[7]

It's a story that is familiar in many other places twenty years later.

In rural areas especially, many looked to tourism to fill the void. While tourism would become an important industry in Oregon, particularly in the new millennium, service jobs do not pay what a timber job paid. A 1993 study by the Bend Chamber of Commerce and the City of Bend, which was growing fast, found that part-time and seasonal employment accounted for 49 percent of jobs with a combined payroll of $33 million vs. $74.7 million for the same number of jobs in the timber industry.

These economic changes brought cultural changes as well, and they reflect some of the divide we see in the country today, in exacerbated form. As new people came into rural communities, either

*While the numbers look good in 2000, Oregon was entering a recession at the time of the Flight for Freedom and even high-tech jobs were dwindling.

to work in the service economy or as tourists or owners of vacation homes (boosting real estate prices—and property taxes), a clash ensued. This clash brought into conflict not simply attitudes or politics but deeply held values.

"Citizens long present could make a living off the tourist trade, but in effect were reduced to the servant class, 'not so much fearing the [new arrivals] as despising them.'" Cox reports.[8]

This cultural divide can be seen across the United States today. While it may appear to be a Pollyanna concept amid what seem like toxic polarities in 2021, the example of the Flight for Freedom demonstrates that even in small ways it may be possible for Americans to begin to coalesce around a common purpose.

THE MOST POLITICALLY POLARIZED STATE

B ased on 2004 president election exit data—only three years after the Flight for Freedom—Oregon was the most politically polarized state in the country. Not surprisingly, the Cascades were the demarcation.

By far, the nation's most liberal Americans were west of the Cascades and the most conservative citizens lived to the east.

To understand the data, Nate Silver of 538 created what he called a "Liberalness Score." A high score = more liberal. The lower the score, the more conservative.

The average Kerry voter in Oregon had a Liberalness Score of 7.17. At 2.11, Vermont Kerry voters were a distant second. On the conservative side, the gap was tighter. The average Bush voter in Oregon had a Liberalness Score of 2.01, the lowest score in the country. Tennessee voters followed close behind at 2.02.

"This is how," writes Silver, "you wind up with the weird political soup wherein Oregon has decriminalized marijuana but has also passed a gay marriage ban, or how it allows assisted suicide but also has one of the nation's lowest effective tax rates."[1]

Oregon politics has been divisive between metro areas and rural parts of the state since the nineteenth century, states Oregon State University Professor Emeritus of History William G. Robbins, a phenomenon paralleled in its neighbor to the north, Washington state, which has also experienced tensions between areas east and west of the Cascade Range. Robbins notes that:

> In western Oregon there are pockets and counties that have common political inclinations with those east of the Cascades. Southwestern Oregon, in particular, has clusters of counties that are low-tax, conservative Republican, and cutting budgets to the point that counties (Josephine) have virtually no law-enforcement in the field.

So rather than dividing politics between east and west, urban and rural is more accurate.[2]

When the call went out for Oregonians to fly to New York City, nobody who participated thought for a second about political views. Everyone was an American and regardless of politics, they were going to that bastion of liberalism New York City to help their fellow Americans. Approximately one in every 3,000 Oregonians joined the Flight for Freedom.

WATER

For many months before the Flight for Freedom, an armed confrontation in the Klamath Basin near the California border brought national attention to the state—and the only thing that put the conflict to rest (for the moment) was a terrorist attack a continent away. The 2001 Klamath Basin water crisis was a bellwether for actions, attitudes, and issues that have grown almost commonplace in the United States over the past twenty years. In 2021, as the region experiences its worst drought in 1,200 years, it is possible that we will see a replay of what happened twenty years ago.[1]

The question that incited one of the first mass antigovernment protests organized on the internet was simple: Water is a limited resource and who gets it? This is a question that will become even more urgent across the twenty-first century American West.

In 2001, the protagonists were farmers, fishermen, Native tribes, environmentalists, birds, fish, and the government—and from our vantage point today, we recognize them as recurring players in recurring confrontations. Wildlife and wildlands have no speaking parts. And the government decides.

The conflict began with well-intentioned government action around the turn of the last century. Ironically, that government action resulted in antigovernment ire and problems that are unresolved to this day.

The seeds were sown (so to speak) in 1902, when agriculture meant taming a land of unending abundance—and before the Dust

Klamath Marsh, Oregon. Photo: Dave Menke, USFWS.

Bowl that devastated the nation's Midwestern farms called for a new way of thinking about how to keep farmland healthy. In 1902, President Theodore Roosevelt signed the National Reclamation Act to turn the nation's arid lands to agricultural production.

The Klamath Basin, which spans southern Oregon and northern California, was a prime candidate. The Basin's main city, Klamath Falls (population approximately 20,000) sits near an enormous marshland fed by rivers in the midst of high desert, poised so it seemed to the men of the day, for man's genius and technology to wrest and tame the Earth for the benefit of mankind.

In 1906, the Klamath Project began, turning the "Everglades of the West" into arable farmland by draining the rivers, marshes and lakes. A raised railroad bed cut the wetlands off from the river.

Almost simultaneously, just two years later in 1908, the same President Roosevelt designated 81,000 acres of marsh and open water in Lower Klamath Lake as the first National Wildlife Refuge for waterfowl, now called Lower Klamath National Wildlife Refuge. Twenty years later, his cousin Franklin added 37,000 acres: the Tule Lake National Wildlife Refuge. Later on, four more wildlife refuges in the Klamath Basin were established.

Why the Klamath Basin? Among bird lovers in particular, the Klamath Basin was and is renowned as a haven for migrating birds. It is the major stopping point on the Pacific Flyway that stretches from Alaska to Argentina, a resting place for approximately eighty percent of migrating waterfowl—seven million of 350 species in the early twentieth century, down to one million after a century of farming in the area. The Basin is also the winter home of the largest population of Bald Eagles in the lower forty-eight states, who hunt in the refuges and surrounding agricultural lands.

In 1917, the Bureau of Reclamation held a public drawing for forty-two new tracts that attracted 175 would-be farmers. Later offerings gave preference to World War I and in years to come, World War II veterans, who also needed to show that they were likely to farm successfully. Under the National Reclamation Act, They received for 160-acre homesteads and subsidized water to grow crops like potatoes to feed the growing population of California. (Originally, farmers were to pay the cost of building the irrigation infrastructure, but that requirement was never enforced.)[2]

Swans in flight at Klamath Basin National Wildlife Refuge Complex. Photo: George Gentry, USFWS.

Over the first half of the twentieth century, approximately 80 percent of the area was drained and dams were built to generate hydroelectricity for the region. And even though the population of birds had declined substantially, 2001 — the driest season on record for the Klamath Basin — was the first time fish got the government's vote.

On April 30, courts ruled that no Upper Klamath Lake water could be diverted to irrigate the 240,000 acres of farmland in the Klamath Basin Irrigation Project. This was the first time in history that the Project's more than 1,000 farmers had not received any water at all. The Lost River sucker and shortnose sucker (locally known as mullet) who live exclusively in the Klamath Basin and whose survival is regulated by the Endangered Species Act, and Coho salmon who live in the Klamath River and are also endangered, got priority. The mullet lives in Upper Klamath Lake and to spawn, it migrates up the tributaries as well as along the lake's shoreline where there are springs. The Endangered Species Act mandates a certain level of water in the lake for the mullet to survive.

The decision was projected to cost hundreds of millions of dollars in losses for the farmers, and even potentially cost them their land and their livelihood. The farmers believed that they and their ancestors had lived up to the terms of the contracts, which many believed promised them water forever.

"There's a remarkable similarity between what the farmers say about the impact of the drought and what the Indians have been feeling," said Bud Ullman, director of the water adjudication project for the Klamath Tribes, told *The Boston Globe*. "The farmers say that the US betrayal of water promises is hurting their community. Indians say, `That's just what happened on to us. We understand what you're going through.'"

The tribes were supposed to have senior water rights based on who was there first. The legal standard, determined by the nation's courts is called the Doctrine of Prior Appropriation, or "first in time, first in right." The population of the endangered shortnose sucker, which is sacred in the tribes' religious heritage, had declined from the millions in the 1920s to about 250, and the tribes were allowed to catch one fish each spring for ceremonial purposes only.*

---

*For these tribes, writes Robbins, "the *first in right* doctrine has deep personal meaning." To understand the position of the Klamath tribes in this ongoing water struggle, it is important to understand the thread of their history,

The fishermen were less sympathetic. "There are plenty of places that you can raise potatoes, but the salmon only have one Klamath River," said Glen Spain, spokesman for the Pacific Coast Federation of Fishermen's Association, whose lawsuit triggered the government's new set of priorities that spring. "We're family food providers just like [the farmers] who've been there for just as many generations as they have and they're putting us out of work."[3]

Just one week after the court decision—on May 7—the "Bucket Brigade" rallied 13,000–18,000 supporters from around the West who passed water from the lake to the irrigation canals by buckets. A protestor from Elko, Nev., brought in a 10-foot-tall bucket topped by an American flag to immortalize the action. The bucket stood in front of the Klamath County Government Center until 2014 and the Bucket Brigade is recognized as a major historic event in the area. The name "Bucket Brigade" was also taken by an organization that established a relief fund for farmers in economic distress due to the drought.

Support on-site arrived from other states, thanks to pleas via the internet, whose power and utility for communications among likeminded people was just beginning to be understood. At the headgates, protesting farmers set up a trailer with four phone lines and a website that received more than 100,000 hits in a single month. They organized a "Klamath T Party," established a cavalry with dozens of horses, and put up a sign reading, "Call 911—Some sucker stole our water." Another protestor bore a sign, "Feed the Feds to the Fish."

---

particularly since the mid-nineteenth century. First, the Euro-Americans entered their homelands, then they were assigned reservations. In the case of the Klamath, their "trust property totaled 590,000 acres of rich timberland, which had the potential of producing 3.8 billion board feet of lumber, and the government believed that the distribution of per capita payments to enrolled tribal members would make them financially independent." The U.S. government "terminated" that trust in 1956 and took the property away from them, concerned, in the midst of the Cold War and Communist that sovereign nations existed within the United States. After fighting for restoration, the U.S. government restored the trust relationship in 1986, the law did not restore all of their former lands, but left them "a dozen small areas of about 300 acres in Klamath County." Donald Fixico, "Termination and Restoration in Oregon," *The Oregon Encyclopedia*, https://www.oregonencyclopedia.org/articles/termination_and_restoration/#.YLNUS6EpAc9, last updated January 20, 2021.

Witticisms aside, this was no joyride. "In July, anti-federal militants joined farmers at the headgates to install and guard pumps and
pipes that sent Klamath River water directly into the main irrigation
canal."[4] Vandals broke into the headgates of the irrigation canal and
turned on the water three times, including using a blow torch and
chain saw, until federal marshals arrived. (Local police, who supported the farmers, did not intervene.)

The protest evolved into an antigovernment, anti-Endangered
Species Act movement with high-profile involvement by members
of the Patriot movement, which was a militia amalgam of survival-
ists; the Common Law movement, which denies the authority of
all governmental institutions above the level of the county; white

The 10-foot-tall bucket commemorating the "Bucket Brigade" protests in defiance of
federal orders to divert water to the wildlife refuge near Klamath Falls. Photo: Gino
Rigucci.

supremacists; armed opponents of taxes and abortion; and others.[5] Environmentalists received death threats drove far from their area to do their grocery shopping.

Over the summer, several Western Congressional representatives introduced bills to amend the Endangered Species Act, but none went far. US Senator Ron Wyden presented a plan to restore some tribal lands, assure farmers of certain water levels each year, and purchase some of the land.

By late summer, while mediation talks continued, farmers remained unsatisfied. They wanted water for their crops. To make their point, they announced "Freedom Day" for Tuesday, August 21. Via phone and the Internet, farmers teamed with other organizations to host convoys of antigovernment protestors, which made their way through Montana, Nevada, Idaho, Washington, California and Oregon and converged on Klamath Falls.[6] Threats of violence escalated and some local residents expressed the belief that their cause had been hijacked by outsiders.

"We've been contacted by the Freemen," said Klamath County resident Stan Thompson, referring to a well-known common-law group. "We don't need those jerks in here."

Congress allocated $20 million in disaster relief and several million dollars from the state of California.[7] For several weeks, Interior Secretary Gail Norton opened the head gates, allowing irrigation at one-seventh of capacity.

And negotiations continued.

Then 9/11 happened. Federal agents were needed elsewhere. The local community, itself grieving the attacks, understood. The government and the protesters agreed to keep negotiating, and to end the demonstrations, at least until Jan. 1. (The following year, a new plan resumed water to farmers.)

"We feel like we've been under siege here in Klamath, but we realize that the national emergency takes precedence over our cause," Bill Ransom of the Klamath Relief Fund, which raised money to help farmers hurt by the drought, told a reporter. "We're not antigovernment. I think you'll find some of the most patriotic citizens in the country in the farmlands."[8]

In 2002, the Bureau of Reclamation provided a generous water allotment to the farmers, restoring flow through the canal without regard to the needs of aquatic wildlife That fall, about 80,000 mature salmon died shortly after entering the Klamath River to spawn, and thousands of juvenile salmon died as well. Bacterial infections in the lower river were caused by warm water due to low water levels. "This ecological calamity led to severe curtailment of commercial salmon fishing along 700 miles of the West Coast in 2006 and 2007. Klamath Project farmers responded by supporting federal disaster relief for the commercial fishing industry."[9]

The conflict over water in the Klamath Basin, has been, writes Robbins:

> . . . epic and ongoing, pitting tribes on the upper river contesting for water in Upper Klamath Lake and tribes on the lower river wanting adequate water for the survival of salmon. Farmers want their share of water, two national Klamath wildlife refuges need water, and the tribes in the upper and lower basin argue endangered-species status for their respective fishes. The situation is the ultimate Catch-22.

Precipitation in southern and southwestern Oregon is at record lows today.* The Bureau of Reclamation turned water off on May 5 to "A Canal," which diverts water from the Upper Klamath Lake to irrigators in Klamath County as well as Siskiyou and Modoc counties in California. Klamath Project irrigators [the farmers] will have no water in 2021.[10]

Two California law professors summed up the challenges of the Klamath soon after:

> [H]ow to move beyond a long history of inefficient irrigation, remedy the ecosystem degradation that system has produced, and make the transition from a colonial commodity-production economy to a modern, globally integrated one. The Klamath is a classic degraded, unsustainable basin, exhibiting all the environmental and economic woes of the "new" West.[11]

---

*A *New York Times* story on the Klamath Basin drought includes a photo that shows just how dire the situation has become. Mike Baker, "Amid Historic Drought, a New Water War in the West," *The New York Times*, https://www.nytimes.com/2021/06/01/us/klamath-oregon-water-drought-bundy.html, Published June 1, 2021, updated June 8, 2021.

LEWIS AND CLARK

On the road with Thomas Jefferson's Corps of Discovery, or even standing alongside the trail as they pass by, we meet ourselves, and more important, we meet people who are not ourselves. —*Historian James P. Ronda*[1]

If you ask people what they know about Oregon history, they may know about two events: the Lewis and Clark Expedition and the Oregon Trail. These are the first major events of Americans entering the "Oregon Country," which became the states of Oregon and Washington, plus portions of Idaho, Montana, and British Columbia.

They were coming to a land that had been inhabited by humanity for at least fifteen thousand years. Over time, many, many Native tribes with distinct cultures could be found there, living according to the rhythms of the seasons and the available resources. In open marsh areas, they conducted managed burns in the autumn that encouraged growth of the camas bulbs that were a major source of food. In about 1800, the native population of the Pacific Northwest was about 300,000, a number that may have been much larger before the first smallpox epidemics in the 1770s, brought by the Spanish along the coast.

The first Imperial claim to Oregon Country by the United States took place in May 1792, when Captain Robert Gray's Columbia Rediviva landed near the mouth of a river he named the "Columbia." Gray traded in sea otter pelts to trim luxury garments in China, the predecessor to the beaver trade that would explode in the coming decades.

For the next fifty years, the Oregon Country would be up for grabs by empire builders, with the United States—a small country with a small military—taking whatever action it could to stake its claim to the area and searching for a way to reach the northwest tip of the continent by land from the east. At the same time, the British were active fur traders, arriving by sea along the West Coast, engaging in peaceful commerce with the Native tribes as long as the tribes did the traders' bidding. They intermarried and relied on their role as merchants to make their claim.

In the quotation above, historian James Ronda is describing the Lewis and Clark Expedition, but that description applies equally to the Flight for Freedom. In that sense, these two efforts, 200 years apart, are kin. The self-selected, diverse group of individuals who joined the Flight for Freedom in the fall of 2001 shared one quality: they cared for people who were not themselves. That they cared enough to fly 3,000 miles to a city still traumatized by the attacks of 9/11; that they cared enough to fly when many were still afraid to fly, and to stand with people they did not know and who were in many ways not at all like them. Because to the Freedom Flyers, the important thing was that they were people in need.

In terms of empire building, the Lewis and Clark Expedition, officially called the "Corps of Volunteers for North West Discovery," was the most successful North American land exploration in U.S. history. The expedition came on the heels of perhaps the greatest land deal in world history, the Louisiana Purchase (1803). The Louisiana Purchase by President Thomas Jefferson doubled the size of the United States with 828,000 square miles to the west for the bargain price of $15 million.

Before talking a bit about the impact and import of the Louisiana Purchase, it is essential to understand that this was a deal between imperial powers, writes William G. Robbins, professor emeritus of history at Oregon State University and one of the most important experts in the history of Oregon. "Indigenous people had no voice."[2]

"History is always written by the winners. When two cultures clash, the loser is obliterated, and the winner writes the history books—books which glorify their own cause and disparage the conquered foe," wrote Dan Brown in the *DaVinci Code,* popularizing a concept that has been understood for at least two centuries. This needs to be considered as we understand our own country's history as well. Only relatively recently have the voices of the indigenous and marginalized peoples in our country been understood to be relevant to our nation's story.

The 8,000-mile Lewis and Clark expedition, which took place from 1804 to 1806, was the inspiration of Jefferson, who had wanted for decades to locate the infamous (and mythical, Lewis and Clark ultimately confirmed) Northwest Passage to the Pacific Ocean, to map this uncharted part of the continent that was now part of the new nation, and document its flora and fauna. The maps were the first detailed topographic representations of this territory made by non-Native people. The Corps, which Jefferson sent to "Oregon," identified at least 120 animal specimens and 200 botanical samples and carried on peaceful relations with dozens of Native American tribes whose cooperation was essential to the explorers' survival. (While it was not exactly "cooperation," the explorers benefited from stealing a canoe from the Clatsop tribe when the expedition departed from the lower Columbia River in 1806.)

In fact, Ronda tells us, at every step of the way, women and/or Native Americans were key to the expedition's progress. While their experience with Native peoples was peaceful, expedition journals stereotyped the Indians in a way that was typical of the time—was negatively—which, writes historian William Robbins, "contributed to fixing in our historical literature fundamental notions of superiority and dominance over Native Americans."

The expedition leaders, Lewis and Clark, selected a surprisingly diverse corps of about thirty, made up mostly of unmarried soldiers. Most prominent among them was Sgt. John Ordway, who wrote a journal entry every day of the journey. The group also included a French-Canadian boat crew; George Drouillard, a French-Indian interpreter and the highest paid after the leaders; a one-eyed fiddle player named Pierre Cruzatte (part French and part Omaha Indian); German-born Pvt. John Potts, a miller by trade; and the oldest member, French-Canadian trader Toussaint Charbonneau, who was hired as an Indian interpreter, and who brought along one of his wives, a pregnant Shoshone woman named Sacagawea.

"Imagine the sounds around the campfire," Ronda writes, "William Clark's Virginia-Kentucky drawl, Sgt. John Ordway's New Hampshire inflections, George Drouillard's Shawnee-flavored French, and the cries and first words of Jean Baptiste, the baby born to Sacagawea on the trip."

York, Clark's enslaved manservant, is the second documented Black person in Oregon history, and he quickly proved why Clark had brought him along. Trusted with a rifle (unusual among enslaved people), York was a crack shot and supplied the group with many a meal. Expedition journals also document him finding many new species. The first Black person Native tribes had seen, they called him "the big Medicine," a term signifying "that in which the power of god is manifest." Lewis and Clark used that admiration of York to smooth their encounters throughout the journey. Unlike others in the party, York received nothing extra for his contributions when it was all over, and Clark did not mention him in a missive to lawmakers that gained celebrity for all who participated. Clark repeatedly refused to free him or even to allow York to live with his wife and work in Louisville, Kentucky, and send his earnings back to Clark.[3]

After the leaders, the most famous Corps member today is Sacagawea, whom Charbonneau had purchased as a slave from the Hidatsa Indians who had kidnapped her as a child. Lewis and Clark allowed her to come along in the hope that she could communicate with Shoshone they came upon and that having a woman along would signal to the Native tribes that the expedition was not a war party. This was prescient because Sacagawea and her baby did just that. She served as an interpreter and provided valuable insights when in the familiar geography of her homeland (Montana and Idaho). She is also known to have supplemented their diet by foraging for roots and berries that prevented scurvy, along with tasks such as dressing hides and making moccasins. The captains lucked out, too, when they needed horses to cross the Bitterroot Mountains and her brother was the chief of the tribe that had them.[4]

For this country's history, the Lewis and Clark Expedition's importance was far more than a president's scientific flight of fancy. Jefferson's project was strategic; this was a way for the small, new, and relatively weak country militarily to stake an international claim on the Pacific Northwest for the United States. By finding a way into the

Oregon Country, Americans could follow and populate the region, another non-military claim. The United States needed to get people into the Oregon Country to bolster its claim to the resource-rich region. Possession is, after all, nine-tenths of the law.

William Appleman Williams (1921–1990), Oregon State University professor and one of the most important voices in the study of American diplomacy in the twentieth century, called Jefferson the great democrat and the great American empire builder.[5]

Ronda tells us that Lewis and Clark "aimed at making it safe for cows, corn and capital at the expense of bison, prairie grasses and cultures not fitting the expansionist agenda." They painted a picture of plenty composed of fur, agriculture, and Indian trade, along with a way to get to the Pacific from the East. The Oregon Country was hyped by politicians, missionaries, and others based on the expedition's reports so that Americans would move there and allow the United States to claim those lands. It was the beginning of Oregon as the "land of milk and honey" that would entice the rugged, the optimistic, and the adventurous for the next seven decades.

As we shall see in the article about the Oregon Trail, hundreds of thousands of people came West in a relatively short period of time. We must keep in mind the flip side of the heroic celebration of their achievements: they came at the expense of the people whose homelands they were occupying. In addition, the negative, dehumanizing language regarding the indigenous people found in the expedition's journals was broadcast across the country and both the language and the actions vicious and racist. Robbins writes:

> In a brief news item, "Bounties For Scalps" in March 1866, a writer for the *Albany Democrat* praised white settlers in far southeastern Oregon's Owyhee country for their strategy to rid the area of Indians. The local community was offering "bounties for scalps— $100 for a buck's, $50 for a squaw's." The *Democrat* reported that a troop of twenty-five men were "actively engaged in hunting for the red wretches."

Just as personal healing requires rigorous, honest self-examination, so does national healing. We are all imperfect and we are all in some way broken. Our whole country in some way lives with the injuries caused by our ancestors to our fellow Americans. Even if we weren't there when atrocities happened, we must, if we are to heal, see the dark side and be willing to be present without judgment for those living with the trauma, just as members of the Flight for Freedom stood in the pain of those survivors of the September 11 attacks.

THE OREGON TRAIL

The people who cast their lot to walk—yes, that's right, they walked, unless you were ill or elderly—the Oregon Trail to the Pacific Northwest certainly were adventurous (and maybe a little crazy).

The Oregon Trail is the longest and was the most heavily used route in the nation's resettlement of western North America. Between 1840 and 1860, 300,000 to 400,000 traveled along and reinforced its ruts, making the U.S. destiny manifest overland from sea to shining sea. This sense of entitlement, this idea of destiny of an exceptional people, was the mindset as the United States expanded across the continent, hundreds of thousands of people obliviously (at best) marching across the homelands of Native people.

The mapwork done by Lewis and Clark's Corps of Discovery was useful for those who came later. In 1812, Robert Stuart, a Pacific Fur Company man returning from Fort Astor (present-day Astoria, on the Oregon Coast), discovered a route over the Continental Divide called the "South Pass," actually two close-together passes at about 7,400 feet elevation.[1] In 1813, the *Missouri Gazette* predicted that "a journey to the Western Sea will not be considered (within a few years) of much greater importance than a trip to New York."[2]

By 1818, the United States and Great Britain had jointly claimed sovereignty over the Oregon Country in the "Treaty of Joint Occupation of Oregon."* In 1846, under treaty, the U.S. and Great Britain agreed to go their separate ways, so to speak, and established the 49th parallel (today's border) as the northern border between the United States and present-day Canada.

Oregon became a region of white immigrants in the 1830s, historian William G. Robbins tells us, displacing the Native people, first in the western part of the territory and after 1860, in the eastern part as well. The newcomers in the west, particularly, were "oblivious" that they were displacing others as they claimed their land and set up their farms and missions and towns.

By the early 1840s, the pace had accelerated. "Oregon Fever" started to catch on, particularly in the Midwest. From 1840 to 1846, the non-Indian population in the Willamette Valley grew from 150 to 6,000.³ They came for free land, they came to escape Midwestern floods, they came to start over after the Panic of 1837 (financial crisis). When gold was discovered in California in 1848, at the forks in the trails in Wyoming and Idaho, many chose to go south rather than to journey into the Pacific Northwest.

Virtually all the emigrants to Oregon came from states west of the Mississippi such as Iowa and Missouri. A large proportion of them went west for their health. Tuberculosis, or "consumption," was the leading cause of death in the nineteenth century and for most of that period physicians attributed the disease to heredity. Treatment was a "favorable climate" with fresh air and a proper diet—which would be found in the West. "[O]ne of the most significant by-products of the medical belief in the efficacy of climate was western settlement."⁴

As a saying of the time went, they also walked 2,000 miles "to see the elephant," a nineteenth-century phrase that meant embracing the uncertainty and the adventure, enduring whatever hardships came in order to experience the unbelievable.

People walked the Oregon Trail in small groups, alongside converted farm wagons made as watertight as possible for river-fording and topped with big, canvas-covered hoops—"covered wagons"

---

*The following year, a treaty with Spain made the 42nd parallel the southern boundary of Oregon; it remains the border between Oregon and California to this day.

Oregon National Historic Trail. Map courtesy of the National Park Service.

usually pulled by oxen or donkeys (both sturdier than horses) who walked in the ruts carved by previous pioneers.

Sustained attacks by Indians on emigrant wagon trains were rare; mutual aid between Indians and overlanders was far more typical than violent hostility. Not surprisingly, however, as the number of emigrants crossing the Oregon Trail increased during the 1850s, Indian-white relations deteriorated.

As more and more people arrived, settlers decided they needed to form a government. In 1843, they created the Provisional Government, which initially comprised four counties. The most important element of the new "Organic Code" they created was how land ownership would be managed. Each person was limited to one claim, which could be no larger than 640 acres or one square mile. Every free male descendant of a white man (which included the sons of Indian mothers and white fathers) could be a citizen. Slavery was prohibited and black settlers were excluded from living within the provisional government's borders.

For those with land claims, securing territorial status under the United States government was critical. But how new states and territories came into the Union was contentious due to the slavery debate – would they be slave or free? As a result, Oregon's transition to territorial status would be a protracted process.

What happened next was one of the key determinants in Oregon's history.

In 1848, when the U.S. created the Oregon Territory, it upheld the assurances to tribes the federal government had made under the Northwest Ordinance of 1787, which stated that, "the utmost good faith shall always be observed towards Indians; their land and property shall never be taken from them without their consent."*

In actuality, then, the 640 acres assigned by the Provisional Government to the more recent emigrants violated those 1787 rights.

To settle the issue of the land grants, the "first prerequisite step," Oregon's Territorial Delegate Samuel Thurston told Congress, was to eliminate Native title to land. As a result, Congress passed legislation authorizing commissioners to negotiate treaties with the Indians, remove tribes "and leave the whole of the most desirable portion open to white settlers." Treaties were dictated and the Indians had no voice in the legislation that was passed by Congress, the Oregon Donation Land Law of 1850.

To those who arrived after 1850, the law cut in half the amount of land to 320 acres. Only American citizens or those with the intention of becoming American citizens, and who were white or "half-breed Indians" were eligible. The Oregon Donation Land Law assumed that tribes would automatically surrender rights to the United States government.

Historian William G. Robbins captures how the future unfolded cogently, "The Oregon Donation Land Law benefited incoming whites and dispossessed Indians."[5]

> The Donation Land Law was significant in shaping the course of Oregon history. By the time the law expired in 1855, approximately 30,000 white immigrants had entered Oregon Territory, with some 7,000 of them making claims to 2.5 million acres of land. The overwhelming majority of the claims were west of the Cascade Mountains. Oregon's population increased from 11,873 in 1850 to some 60,000 by 1860.[6]

---

*The Northwest Territory includes the region south of the Great Lakes, north and west of the Ohio River, and east of the Mississippi River. This was the first official territory of the United States and in creating the Oregon Territory this model for treatment of tribal rights was part of the language included.

IMMIGRANTS OF COLOR IN OREGON

If you give all the land in Oregon to one population, to the exclusion of all other populations, they will use that land to prosper, to gain financial advantage. That financial advantage will be transferred from generation to generation down into the generation that we live in today. So to understand the Oregon of today, you have to understand the public policy of Oregon of yesterday. —*Darrell Millner, Portland State University professor emeritus of Black Studies*[1]

Policy toward people of color in Oregon is a unique combination of state and federal law. Oregon's Japanese were forced to walk away from everything they owned when they were incarcerated during World War II, in one of the most shameful actions in our history under a presidential Executive Order. It meant that these people lost everything and had to start all over from nothing rather than being able to hand down to their progeny any wealth they had accumulated.

When it entered the union, Oregon's constitution prohibited Blacks from living there. (Nevertheless, Black people lived in Oregon throughout its history.) To this day, only about 2 percent of Oregon's population is Black, compared to 13.4 percent of the U.S. population.[2]

In 2020, the term "systemic racism" entered the mainstream media with a strength and frequency it had not had before. Systemic racism refers to structures actively put in place in order to privilege

531

a race or races and disadvantage a race or races. An examination of Oregon's history shows how systemic racism is built and implemented, and while Oregon's history is unique, it is emblematic of our nation's history. As we walk through the experience of immigrants of color in Oregon, note not only how policy and law reflect the vicissitudes of the economy and an area's need for labor but how people's fears around employment can be exploited to incite antagonistic attitudes towards populations of color.*

Millner sums up a situation that began more than a century ago, with results not unlike the situation in the rest of the country:

> As you look around Oregon today, racially speaking, you notice that populations of color are overrepresented in poverty, they're underrepresented in political power, and those kinds of realities that we see today, can be traced easily to the kind of political decisions that were made in the Pioneer Generation.[3]

Still, as Oregon State University Emeritus Distinguished Professor of History William G. Robbins explains, the racial prejudices of Oregon's early white settlers were not unique. These settlers beliefs paralleled the racial prejudices of the states from which they emigrated: Missouri, Iowa, Indiana, Ohio, Illinois, and other Midwestern and border states. There was little to distinguish Oregon from other Western states during the nineteenth century.[4]

A look at the history of the Latinx, Black, Chinese, and Japanese immigrant populations in Oregon is revealing.

BEFORE THE OREGON TRAIL

The first Latinos arrived in Oregon in the sixteenth century with Spanish exploration, although their numbers in the area remained

---

*According to the 2000 U.S. Census as reported by ABC News, Oregon didn't even make it into the top ten "whitest" states in the country. They were: Maine, Vermont, New Hampshire, West Virginia, Iowa, Wyoming, Idaho, Montana, Kentucky, and North Dakota. ABC News, "Census Finds Least Diverse Part of Nation," abcnews.go.com, January 7, 2006, https://abcnews.go.com/US/story?id=93608&page=1.

minuscule until well into the nineteenth century.[5] Unlike the British who came for commerce, the Spanish were focusing on expanding their territory. By 1821, Mexico had achieved independence from Spain and its territory stretched from the present-day Oregon-California state line to Central America.

Black people could be found in Oregon throughout much of its history. In the 1820s and 1830s, Black men came to Oregon country as slaves to work for fur traders; free Black men became successful fur traders in their own right and valued wagon train guides.

THE OREGON TRAIL PERIOD AND STATEHOOD

When the United States took possession of Mexico's northern territory—today's California, Arizona, New Mexico, Nevada, Texas, Colorado, and part of Oklahoma—after the Mexican-American War of 1848, it incorporated Spanish, Mexican, and Indigenous cultures that were hundreds, if not thousands, of years old. That cultural heritage included skilled *vaqueros* (horsemen and cattle herders) and mule packers, who were hired by American cattlemen to help with cattle drives north to the Oregon Territory. Some of these *vaqueros* became pioneers of eastern Oregon.

Mexican mule packers were used by Americans during the Indian Wars. During the Rogue River War (1855–1856), they supplied army troops with food and other necessities. Thirty-seven Mexicans also served as support troops with the Second Regiment Oregon Mounted Volunteers.

The first person of Latinx origin listed in an Oregon census was a thirteen-year-old boy in Oregon City, in 1850, and twenty Mexicans, including five women, lived in Oregon City in 1860.

At the height of Oregon Trail immigration between 1840 and 1860, under jurisdiction of the U.S. and the U.K., the Provisional Government, and statehood (1859), Oregon voters banned slavery. At the same time, exclusion laws that prohibited Blacks from residing there—which were all rescinded and not strictly enforced—nevertheless made it clear that Blacks, neither free nor enslaved, were welcome. Under these exclusion laws, "African American immigrants were officially excluded, but those already present were generally allowed to stay."[6]

When Oregon became a state in 1859, the third exclusion law (1857) was in its Bill of Rights. Blacks were prohibited from owning property, voting, using the legal system, making contracts, and even just being in the state.[7]

This was no accident. For some farmers, the issue was primarily economic. They had not owned slaves, but they came from slave states and had struggled to compete against the free labor used by slaveowners. Others were afraid that having Blacks in the country would lead to racial conflict, which they had experienced in the states from which they had come. Others, wrote Jesse Applegate, among the most racially tolerant of early white settlers, "hated slavery, but a much larger number of them hated *free negroes* worse even than slaves."[8]

While these laws affected only Black people, other laws like the Oregon Donation Land Law of 1850, a federal law that applied only to Oregon, more broadly affected people of color. This law allocated 320 acres to each unmarried white male (or "half-breed Indian") or 640 acres to every married couple who arrived in the Oregon Territory before December 1, 1850, and half that amount to those who arrived by 1854. This was one of the first laws that allowed married women to own property. (See the "Oregon Trail" article for more information on the Oregon Donation Land Law.)

The first Chinese immigrants in Oregon settled in the southwestern part of the state, primarily in Jackson and Josephine counties. Small groups of bachelor miners arriving in 1850–1853, they were Cantonese, the population that would dominate Oregon's Chinese-American history for the next century. They were the first Chinese to venture beyond California. For the next ten to twelve years, Oregon's Chinese were the miners and the merchants who "mined the miners." Their numbers fluctuated according to the boom-and-bust cycle of mining, and because they were always hoping to find the next pot of gold. Just how many people this involved is not clear: Douglas Lee writes in *The Oregon Encyclopedia* that especially in the early 1860s, the number of these immigrants could have ranged from a few dozen to a few hundred.[9]

CIVIL WAR–1882

Until 1885 when Seattle surpassed it, Portland was a transportation and communications hub, and a financial center for the Pacific Northwest, thanks in large part to its strategic location between the Columbia and Willamette Rivers. It also served as a key routing center for the migration of Cantonese workers across the Pacific Northwest.

During the Civil War (1861–1865), the Oregon legislature approved a five-dollar annual poll tax on Blacks, Chinese, Hawaiians (Kanakas), and Mulattos. The state also prohibited whites from marrying Blacks, Chinese, South Pacific Islanders, and any person with more than half Indian parentage. This law also punished the person who performed any such marriage ceremonies with a fine and prison.

In 1866, the state legislature ratified the Fourteenth Amendment, which gave all people—including Blacks—the full rights of citizenship. When Democrats won the legislature, they withdrew the state's ratification of the amendment, but soon after, the amendment became federal law. In 1869, Congress passed the Fifteenth Amendment, which stated, "The right of citizens of the United States to vote shall not be denied or abridged by the United States or by any State on account of race, color, or previous condition of servitude." Oregon was one of five western states that rejected the amendment, but the following year the Oregon Supreme Court ruled that Blacks could vote because the amendment was the law of the land. Oregon did not formally ratify the Fifteenth Amendment until 1959.[10]

The State of Oregon quietly ratified the Fourteenth Amendment in 1973.[11] Historians have often stated that Oregon's delay in ratifying the Fourteenth Amendment was because two votes had been cast by House members who were illegally elected to the 1866 Legislature, a minor administrative issue that had been overlooked for a century. In 2004, author Cheryl A. Brooks argued in the *Oregon Law Review* that the delay in ratification was "an accurate gauge of the white majority historical views about granting equal protection and full citizenship rights to people of color." When a state sees itself as having an identity of equality and liberty, the idea that prejudice could have been involved in ratifying the Fourteenth Amendment can be difficult to consider, but Brooks tells us that "selective omission" can enter the picture as a society's values change, making it difficult to accept that values had been different in the past.[12]

The first Japanese person settled in Oregon in 1880, the result of Japan's relaxation of 200 years of isolationist policies. Miyo Iwakoshi arrived with her Scottish husband, Andrew McKinnon, and their five-year-old adopted daughter. McKinnon built a steam sawmill called Orient. Today Orient is an unincorporated community near Gresham.

Cantonese Chinese began arriving directly from Gwongdung as well as from California. While many had expected to go home relatively quickly, instead, many of them made permanent homes in Oregon. During this period, they moved away from mining and into commercial agriculture, salmon canneries, railroad construction, domestic service, and work in laundries, for ranchers or as cooks in lumber camps. Those who could afford to started their own businesses, such as cafes, laundries, general stores, and laborer brokerages.

This was the era, from 1865–1880, of transcontinental railroad construction, and regional feeders, or spurs, were needed. After 1865, the number of Chinese immigrants grew extensively—from 3,330 in 1870 to 9,510 in 1880—and they could now be found across the state, but primarily across southwest Oregon, central and northern Willamette Valley, in northwest Oregon, and on the Columbia Plateau. Mexicans, too, worked as laborers on the railroads as the need arose—often to maintain sections of the rails—and in agriculture.

In Portland, the Chinese population grew substantially, from twenty-two in 1860 to 2,480 in 1880—the largest Chinese community between San Francisco and Vancouver, British Columbia. But as the community grew, so did anti-Chinese sentiment in Oregon and across the West. During the 1870s, Oregon's labor and political leaders called for both the expulsion of current Chinese residents and the exclusion of future Chinese immigrants. Portland had an anti-Chinese club that held rallies with speeches, fundraising, brass bands, and dancing.

1882-1929

Throughout the American West, anti-Chinese sentiment continued to escalate, culminating in the first federal Chinese Exclusion Act (1882), which banned Chinese laborers from entering the United States for ten years—though in reality, the law banned nearly all Chinese from coming.

Ten years later, the exclusion was renewed (Geary Act). The Chinese Exclusion Law became permanent in 1902 and remained in force until 1943 when China was a World War II ally of the United States against the Japanese occupation of China.

The Chinese in Oregon were discriminated against in housing, commercial opportunities, and medical and social services; banned from attending public schools, entering professions, and serving on juries; and not allowed to vote or hold office. Oregon also banned interracial marriage from 1866–1951 so men of color had these options: (1) remain celibate; (2) engage prostitutes; or (3) seek out common-law marriages or consensual arrangements with Black, Native American, Hispanic, or white women. (Very few Chinese women had come to the United States.) The Chinese population in the state declined after peaking at 10,397 in 1900. By 1940, there were only 2,086 Chinese persons in the state.

During this period, most Cantonese-Chinese lived in Portland, and as in other large cities nationwide, they were segregated from whites, though they left their neighborhoods for work. In many ways, they became almost invisible, both in Portland and in rural parts of the state, Douglas Lee writes in *The Oregon Encyclopedia*. They also continued to interact with mainstream whites as well as other ethnic groups, either for business or when others came as visitors and tourists. Still, the Chinese were not allowed to live in other areas except when employment required it, as in the case of live-in domestics, for example.

Still, anti-Chinese violence occurred. In the mid-1880s, two large buildings in Chinatown were burned down and eighty masked men raided Chinese woodcutters' camps near Albina, a small town later incorporated into Portland, to scare the Chinese into leaving. The *Oregonian* newspaper reported that police made no arrests and the white men involved reported that they "had a hell of a fine time."[13] The most egregious act of violence took place in 1887, when a small group of white men massacred thirty-four Chinese miners in Hells Canyon in Wallowa County in the northeastern corner of the state.

With the Chinese Exclusion Act in place, the railroads turned for their labor to the Japanese, who began to move to Oregon.[14] Like the Chinese before them, the Japanese were bachelors and intended to send their money home. An 1894 treaty with Japan allowed free immigration of Japanese workers to the United States.

All Japanese workers came through Portland so a community to support the immigrants, or *Issei*, who spoke only Japanese and knew little about their new country, evolved. Called "Japantown" (Nihonmachi) this community of hotels, restaurants, bathhouses, and other enterprises arose through the initiative of Japanese entrepreneurs and was a major support for the Japanese community from 1890–1942, when all Japanese were expelled from Portland. By 1910, Portland's Japantown had grown to more than 100 enterprises.[15]

By 1910, the 3,418 *Issei* in Oregon had fulfilled their contracts and many of them decided to stay in America, but they were still bachelors and they needed wives. They were limited to Japanese wives, though, because in addition to Oregon's ban on interracial marriage, under the 1907 Expatriation Act, women who married non-citizens lost their citizenship. (After women received the vote in 1920, the 1922 Cable Act removed that penalty.)

In 1907, in response to rising anti-Japanese sentiment due to the influx of Japanese workers, particularly in San Francisco, the United States and Japan concluded the "Gentlemen's Agreement." The Chinese Exclusion Act loomed large, and the Japanese did not want a law targeting them; President Theodore Roosevelt, for his part, viewed Japan positively and wanted good relations with them to counter Russia's expansionist plans in Asia. So the agreement was simply a note from Japan. It largely eliminated new Japanese worker immigration to the United States. In turn, the United States agreed to allow Japanese immigrants already in the country to remain, and to permit their wives, children, and parents to immigrate.

The Gentlemen's Agreement open the door to "picture brides" from Japan. *Issei* bachelors who couldn't afford to return to Japan to wife-hunt in person sent flattering photos of themselves and selected brides from the photos of Japanese women they received in return. As a result, the number of *Issei* women in Oregon increased from 294 in 1910 to 1,349 in 1920.

By the 1920s, these families had children, *Nisei*, who were American citizens. Parents and children communicated using a mixture of Japanese and English, and children went to Japanese school after class in the public schools.

Japanese families could be found in rural areas because they had invested their earnings and purchased land or, in the case of Hood River, they had received stumpland and marshland in exchange for clearing it. By 1909, more than one-quarter of the 3,873 Oregon *Issei* were involved in farm labor, and from 1907 to 1910, the number of Japanese farmers increased from 71 to 233.

About 60 percent of Oregon's Japanese population was involved in agriculture and with growth and success came a backlash. An Anti-Asiatic Association formed in Hood River 1919 that pledged not to sell or lease land to Japanese. Anti-Japanese bias in Hood River would receive national attention shortly after World War II.

After three failed attempts, in 1923 the Oregon legislature passed the Alien Land Law, which prohibited *Issei* from operating farm machinery or owning or leasing land—but a loophole allowed their citizen children to be landowners.[16]

Oregon's attitudes reflected nativism in the United States that was on the rise. Over time, federal immigration restrictions had been tightened; the Immigration Act of 1924 focused on curbing immigration from southern and eastern Europe (Italians, Poles, Slavs, and especially Catholics), and had a broad impact on immigration to the United States for forty years. The Japanese government protested because the law because it violated the Gentleman's Agreement; tensions grew between the two nations.[17]

Economic needs determined exemptions. Mexicans were exempted from the law because World War I had increased the need for Mexican labor, especially in agriculture. By 1920, 569 "foreign-born" Mexicans appeared in the census, a number that would triple within the decade. Official numbers aside, it is known that approximately 80,000 Mexicans worked in agriculture, railroads, mines, and canneries in the United States and many of them were in Oregon, along with part-time migrant workers in agriculture.

While Black men could be found in small numbers working in ranching, mining, and logging for short periods, Black communities were found in urban areas primarily and railroads were a major employer, both in large cities like Portland and in small towns in eastern Oregon.[18]

In 1906, the Oregon Supreme Court ruled in *Taylor v. Cohn* that a Black man could not be refused a box seat in a theater because of his race, but in an identical case in 1917, *Allen v. People's Amusement Park,* was lost in the Oregon Supreme Court, sanctioning racial segregation in public places and services. The ruling remained in place until Oregon's legislature passed an anti-discrimination law in 1953. As in many other U.S. cities, restrictive covenants, redlining, and prohibitions in the real estate handbook limited Blacks' ability to purchase property in the inner northeast section of Portland. Outside Portland, many rural towns—even those with a small Black population or even none at all—enforced Sundown Laws that required Blacks to be out of town by nightfall or encounter hostile action by the police, private citizens, or both.

In the 1920s, Oregon was home to the largest Ku Klux Klan (KKK) chapter west of the Mississippi River and had the highest per-capita Klan membership of any state.[19] Its primary targets were Catholics and Jews, not Blacks, in part because Oregon's Black population was so small and relatively isolated. Governor Walter Pierce was elected in 1923 with KKK support and subsequently served in the U.S. House of Representatives from 1932 to 1942.

In 1914, Portland became home to the first National Association for the Advancement of Colored People (NAACP) chapter west of the Mississippi, and it remains active to this day. The Portland NAACP fought KKK propaganda through educational campaigns and protest. The community also had a weekly newspaper, *The Advocate*. The community was small, geographically isolated, and artificially confined by the practices of the city's white power structure. Still, like Japantown and Chinatown, it was a fully functional community. It had its own infrastructure, with hotels, restaurants, and other small businesses, social organizations, and clubs. The Black church was also a source of support and camaraderie.

THE GREAT DEPRESSION

With the coming of the Great Depression and employment at a premium, the idea that white people should take priority for jobs reached the highest levels of the federal government. President Herbert Hoover's administration promoted the slogan, "American jobs for real Americans." With unemployment skyrocketing, whites who had lost their jobs took work they would not have considered earlier and many people of color were pushed out of their jobs.

The Depression revealed Latinos' vulnerability, but it also reinforced the need for Latinx labor, as Latinos were willing to do work that even in the Great Depression whites would not take on.[20] Employers in Oregon began to hire "white workers only" regardless of their legal status, but a significant number of Latinos remained employed in the Pacific Northwest. Latinos retreated to the rural areas, where they were railroad laborers. They also worked in the orchards and fields in Hood River and the Willamette Valley. Mexicans remained in demand for hard labor in the fields, which was called "stoop labor" and racialized as Mexican labor, because it was the kind of work white people still did not want to do.

The Great Depression also affected the Black community deeply. Black businesses were often underfunded and run on a shoestring, so during this precarious period, many businesses failed, shaking the community's economic stability.

WORLD WAR II

The economic boom of World War II brought with it nearly unprecedented employment opportunities for people of color. But for the Japanese in Oregon, it brought the loss of everything they owned and they were imprisoned for no reason except their race. The majority of those imprisoned were American citizens.

The war also changed the Chinese experience in America dramatically. In 1940, the U.S. instituted the country's first peacetime draft. When war was declared in December 1941, Chinese Americans were among the first to be called. Almost 20,000 Chinese-American men and women fought—nearly one in every five Chinese people in the

United States and Hawaii, although Hawaii did not become a state until 1959.* About 40 percent who served who were not U.S. citizens due to the nation's laws prohibiting their naturalization. In 1943, by executive order, President Franklin D. Roosevelt repealed the Chinese Exclusion Law,[21] which made it possible for Chinese to become naturalized citizens and many did.

With the end of the Chinese Exclusion Act, the numbers of American-Born Chinese (ABC) in Oregon grew dramatically, and emigrants arrived from California and elsewhere as well. Since Chinese immigration had not been allowed for sixty years, those Chinese in the United States had largely been born, raised, and educated in America or had immigrated (legally and illegally) when they were young so they were culturally assimilated. As a result, they successfully competed in both classrooms and the job market.

Portland became a center of the wartime shipbuilding industry. The city's Black population exploded from about 2,000 in 1940 to a high of 22,000 in 1944, as Black shipyard workers, many with families, were recruited to Portland from other parts of the country. The jobs they could hold were limited, however, because they were not allowed to join the union, which also made them more vulnerable to layoffs.

The nation's largest temporary federal housing project, Vanport (between Vancouver and Portland), was built on the Columbia River to house wartime workers. About a quarter of its residents were Black. Many Blacks left Oregon when the war ended and shipyard jobs disappeared, but many stayed, giving the state a Black population six times larger than its prewar population.

On the military side, "The Triple Nickles," which was the all-Black 555th Parachute Infantry Battalion, was stationed at Pendleton Field; the U.S. Air Force base in Klamath Falls attracted a small Black population as well.

---

*In December 2020, Chinese American World War II veterans were awarded a Congressional Gold Medal. Adam Stump, "Chinese-American WWII Veterans receive Congressional Gold Medal," *Vantage Point Official Blog of the Department of Veterans Affairs*, December 10, 2020, https://blogs.va.gov/VAntage/82179/chinese-american-wwii-veterans-receive-congressional-gold-medal/.

For the Latinx population, World War II brought new demand for workers and those who had previously supported deportation now advocated bringing Mexicans to the United States. The Bracero Program (1942–1947) brought 15,000 Mexican men to Oregon as *braceros*, for farm labor and railroad maintenance. *Braceros* are seasonal Mexican workers. The program guaranteed transport to and from Mexico, a minimum wage, decent working conditions, and protection from military service.

Mexican Americans were also migrating to Oregon, and growers used them after the Bracero Program ended. In addition, many Oregon growers preferred to hire undocumented workers.

"Nineteen forty-one was the year that changed the lives of almost all persons of Japanese ancestry living in the United States," writes George Katagiri in *The Oregon Encyclopedia*. The destruction of Japanese-American lives in the United States during World War II is one of the most shameful episodes in our history. They were told they would be imprisoned and could keep only what they could carry. There were no criminal charges, no trials. No person of Japanese ancestry living in the United States was ever charged with an act of sabotage or disloyalty. They were given no channels for appeal of their losses.

On December 7, 1941, the Japanese attacked the U.S. naval base at Pearl Harbor near Honolulu, Hawaii, and killed more than 2,400 Americans, including civilians. Another 1,000 people were wounded. The next day, President Franklin D. Roosevelt asked Congress to declare war on Japan.

Little more than two months after the attack, on February 19, 1942, President Roosevelt signed Executive Order 9066, "to prescribe military areas in such places and of such extent as he or the appropriate Military Commander may determine, from which any or all persons may be excluded."[22] Under the order, Lt. Gen. John DeWitt, commander of the Western Defense Command, ordered all persons of Japanese ancestry to be removed from a zone he designated approximately 200 miles wide along the West Coast (roughly Highway 97 in Oregon). Those east of the delineation were not affected.

"The Japanese race is an enemy race," DeWitt said. At another point, he was more succinct: "A Jap is a Jap," he said.

More than 60 percent of the Japanese sent to internment camps were American citizens (70,000 of the 112,000 evacuees). More than 3,000 were already serving in the U.S. military when they were reclassified as "enemy aliens."*

Oregon was on the front lines of American history. Bear in mind that Loen Dozono, who first had the idea of the Flight for Freedom as a way to provide help and support to New Yorkers, was a member of a family who was incarcerated. Her father, George Azumano, was serving in the U.S. military, sent home as an "enemy alien" and had to help his family give up their business, their home, and everything they owned.

The exclusion order issued on April 28, 1942, in Portland required all Portland residents to report in one week—by May 5—to the temporary staging center with only what they could carry. Japanese from Hood River and Marion counties were sent to Pinedale in Northern California. They disposed of their pets, livestock, furniture, homes, businesses, and farms for pennies of their worth.

People did not know where they were ultimately going or when they would return.

More than 3,600 people stayed in whitewashed livestock stalls in the Pacific International Livestock Exposition Facilities in Portland. A plank floor was laid over the dirt, plywood partitions and barbed wire put in place, and internees were watched by armed guards. While they were there, they organized a small city with a post office, security department, fire brigade, mess hall, and publishing office, along with churches and recreational and educational activities.

---

*The same executive order applied to smaller numbers of U.S. residents who were of Italian or German descent. About 3,200 resident aliens of Italian background were arrested and more than 300 interned. About 11,000 German residents—including some naturalized citizens—were arrested and more than 5,000 were interned. "Yet while these individuals (and others from those groups) suffered grievous violations of their civil liberties, the war-time measures applied to Japanese Americans were worse and more sweeping, uprooting entire communities and targeting citizens as well as resident aliens." (George Mason University, *History Matters*. See endnote for full citation.) It is notable and perhaps not as well known that Canada and Mexico implemented their own versions of this incarceration.

The most memorable incident took place one day when the assembly center was like an oven. The Fire Department hosed down the hallways, thinking they could cool the facility as the water evaporated. But they forgot one thing: the manure under the plank floors. The wet manure gave off a stench and attracted hordes of flies. Thousands of rolls of flypaper hung indoors for days.

By early September, ten "permanent" "relocation camps" had been completed in desolate desert areas in several western states. "Ironically," writes Craig Collisson in *The Oregon Encyclopedia*, "by the time the camps were constructed, the United States had turned the tide of the war in the Pacific at the battle of Midway, eliminating the threat of a Japanese invasion of the West Coast."

The War Relocation Authority (WRA) moved the Portland contingent to the Minidoka camp near Twin Falls, Idaho. Oregonians from Pinedale went to Tule Lake in Northern California. Each person received only an army cot and mattress, so internees built furniture from scrap lumber. Barracks were not insulated, which meant heat in summer and freezing cold in winter. They had no running water or electrical outlets. Latrines were open-pit toilets. As at the assembly centers, the internees organized fire and police departments, newspapers, dances, baseball teams, planted "victory gardens" and offered classes.[23]

In 1943, federal authorities encouraged the Japanese in the camps to move to eastern cities. But most remained, primarily because they no longer had homes or businesses.

Authorities also allowed Japanese to serve in the military again. Two major all-*Nisei* military units formed. Around 4,500 served in the Military Intelligence Service (MIS) after studying Japanese language at Fort Snelling, Minnesota. The MIS became "America's secret weapon" in the South Pacific. They eavesdropped behind enemy lines, translated Japanese documents, and interrogated prisoners of war.*

---

*Hood River's Frank Hachiya, who died on January 3, 1945, was a member of the MIS, who was killed on Leyte and posthumously awarded the Silver Star. The Defense Language Institute in Monterey, California, has dedicated a building in its Asian language complex in his honor. To learn more about Hachiya, see William G. Robbins, "Frank Hachiya (1920–1945)," *The Oregon*

The 442nd Regimental Combat Team (RCT) saw combat in Italy and France and became the most decorated unit in the history of the United States Army for its size and length of service. It also suffered the highest combat casualty rate of any unit that served.

In 1944, Californian Mitsuye Endow successfully challenged the constitutionality of E.O. 9066 before the U.S. Supreme Court. The War Department declared that as of January 2, 1945, the Japanese were free to leave camps, but by March only 100 had returned to Oregon. Knowing the challenges the Japanese would face on the West Coast, the WRA urged those in the camps to head east. Almost 69 percent of Japanese Americans in Oregon returned to their former hometowns.

They were seldom welcomed back and sometimes faced vandalism and violence. In February 1945, the Oregon House passed Joint Memorial No. 9, urging President Roosevelt to "prevent the return of said Japanese aliens and said citizens of Japanese extraction to the west coast states for the duration of the present war with Japan."

In Hood River, almost every store displayed a "No Japs Allowed" placard in their windows, but a group of citizens there also formed the League for Liberty and Justice to help the Japanese resettle. And in 1944, when the Hood River American Legion Post No. 22 voted to remove the names of sixteen *Nisei* from a plaque honoring those who had served in World War II, criticism poured in locally and nationally. The following year, the names were returned to the plaque under pressure from American Legion national headquarters.

By war's end, the Japanese held title to only 25 percent of the land they had held prior to incarceration. While the trauma of the war had changed them, its trials had brought the Japanese community closer together.

THE POST-WAR ERA

At this writing in 2021, much of downtown Portland is still boarded up after months of Black Lives Matter protests. A friend reported that

---

Encyclopedia, last updated February 1, 2019, https://www.oregonencyclopedia.org/articles/hachiya_frank_1920_1945_/#.YLL52qEpAc8.

his white son and Black daughter-in-law often hear the "n" word as they walk together in the city. Sadly, in Oregon, as in other places across the country, anti-Asian hate has been on the rise as well.

While there is a long way to go, the post-war era has been marked by increased activism among all the people of color in Oregon. The Latinx community, is now the largest and fastest-growing minority group in Oregon, followed by Asian Americans.

Latinos have continued to play a central role in Oregon's economy. Their advocacy and activism has led to improved safeguards at work, as well as citizenship and educational opportunities.

But during the 1950s, Operation Wetback, a military operation, rounded up a million undocumented Mexicans nationwide for deportation, including in Oregon.[24] At the same time, Tejano Julian Ruiz arrived with his father with the goal of moving their Texas labor contracting business to the state. In 1954, they settled in Woodburn (twenty-seven miles southwest of Portland), where their labor-contracting business recruited hundreds of Latinos for jobs.

Over time, a large Latinx community has grown in that city. KWRC in Woodburn began Spanish radio programming in 1965. Centro Chicano Cultural, established in 1969 between Woodburn and Gervais, was a cultural center for the state's Latinx community.

During the 1960s, Oregon Latinos began to engage in the civil rights movement at every level, Latinx entrepreneurs started more businesses, and the United Farm Workers of Oregon, established in 1968, worked to improve conditions for Latinx farmworkers. Three years earlier, the Oregon Council of Churches formed the Valley Migrant League to provide social services for Latinos in six Oregon communities and to work with the government on social and economic issues.

During the 1970s, a new wave of Latinx immigrants arrived, most of them from Michoacan and Oaxaca, Mexico. They often worked on tree farms and in canneries, and as migrant farmworkers. By the 1990s and 2000s they also served on contract crews fighting forest and range fires.

Mexican crews also worked in the forest industry during the 1970s and 1980s, replanting logged-over areas (*pineros*). Founded in 1985, Pineros y Campesinos Unidos del Noroeste (Northwest Tree Planters and Farm Workers United, PCUN) brought together forest and farm workers. PCUN has combined direct action in the fields, solidarity with other groups, and legislative advocacy to sign up undocumented immigrants for legal amnesty, to eliminate the use of toxic pesticides, and to advocate for increasing the minimum wage and granting collective bargaining rights to farmworkers, who are exempt from the rights to organize given to other workers under the National Labor Relations Act. The group also helped to found the Farmworker Housing Development Corporation (1990), which provides affordable farmworker housing in Woodburn.[25]

By the early 1980s, growers had come to rely on undocumented workers. In 1986, Congress passed the Immigration Reform and Control Act (IRCA) and established the Special Agricultural Workers program (SAW), which gave legal status to undocumented Latinos who had been in the country since 1982.

Between 1980 and 1990, the Latinx population in Oregon grew by 70 percent as civil wars in Nicaragua, El Salvador, and Guatemala caused people to flee; the rate would increase to 144 percent between 1990 and 2000. By 1990, about two-thirds of Oregon's Latinos lived in cities.

In the twenty-first century, Latinos are the largest minority population in Oregon. By 2013, the 500,000 members of the permanent Latinx community were the fourteenth largest number of Latinos in the nation. Of those who identify as Latinx, 63 percent were born in the United States. According to the Pew Hispanic Center, about 5 percent of Oregon's workforce in 2010 comprised unauthorized workers, or about 110,000 people.

Five cities in Oregon now have majority Latino populations, all of them small and in traditional agricultural and ranching areas: Gervais (67 percent), Boardman (62 percent), Nyssa (61 percent), Woodburn (59 percent), and Cornelius (50 percent). Many cities have seen significant increases in the Latinx population in the twenty-first century, including those in the Portland metro area, Bend in central Oregon, and the eastern Oregon towns of Hermiston and Umatilla. Ontario, Oregon, on the Idaho border is now 44.8 percent Latinx.

During the post-war period, the Japanese largely assimilated. The English-speaking *Nisei* started their own families. Culturally more American than the *Issei*, they had more options in life. Portland's Japantown had disappeared with the World War II evacuation, and Japanese foodstuffs were becoming available at grocery stores. Eventually, the third and fourth generations appeared; most of their friends were Caucasians and intermarriage became the norm. In 2000, 31 percent of Japanese Americans identified themselves as multiracial.

Attempts have been made to acknowledge the damage done to the Japanese during World War II, as Americans' view of the camps changed, thanks to the civil rights and ethnic power movements of the 1960s and 1970s.[26]

At the federal level, in 1970 the Japanese American Citizens League (JACL) supported a resolution by activists demanding that the government compensate *Nikkei** incarcerated during World War II. By 1983, the Congressional Commission on Wartime Relocation and Internment of Civilians acknowledged that "race prejudice, war hysteria, and a failure of political leadership," not military necessity, had led to Japanese incarceration. In 1988, President Ronald Reagan signed legislation that provided $20,000 for each former prison. Two years later, the first nine *Nikkei* received their checks along with an official apology from President George H.W. Bush.

Portland's Japanese American Citizens League held its first Day of Remembrance at the site of the former stockyards on the anniversary of the signing of Executive Order 9066, February 19; other observances have been held in Hood River and Eugene. Over the years, the Day of Remembrance has grown to speak out for the civil rights of others, including Arab Americans and Native Americans.[27] Speakers have also included Oregonian Minoru Yasui, who unsuccessfully challenged the constitutionality of the order in 1942 by breaking curfew. Thanks to Portland attorney Peggy Nagae, his conviction was vacated in 1984 and he was awarded the Presidential Medal of Honor posthumously in 2015. The Minoru Yasui Legacy Project holds many events,

---

*"Japanese emigrants and their descendants living outside (and sometimes inside) Japan." "Nikkei," *Densho Encyclopedia*, last updated March 19, 2013, https://encyclopedia.densho.org/Nikkei/.

a writing contest, and other activities that embrace his values and the fight for justice.

After World War II, Portland Mayor Terry Schrunk was inspired to build a Japanese garden in Portland's Washington Park to commemorate the growing ties between Oregon and Japan and heal the wounds of World War II. The 5.5-acre site was dedicated in 1961 and the Portland Japanese Garden opened in 1967. Originally conceived as five gardens that displayed the many styles of Japanese garden design, a tea house built in Japan and assembled in Portland arrived in 1968, and in 2017 the garden added the Cultural Village, which features three new structures by architect Kengo Kuma.

Dedicated in 1990, the Japanese American Historical Plaza at Waterfront Park in Portland is composed of thirteen engraved stones of basalt and granite to tell the story of Japanese incarceration and reiterate the importance of the Bill of Rights.

And in 2001, Japanese American Oregonians, Sho and Loen Dozono, who spearheaded the Flight for Freedom.

With the Chinese Exclusion Act a thing of the past, after the war, foreign-born Cantonese who were veterans could either send for or find Cantonese-Chinese wives in the U.S. Scores of Chinese began to relocate beyond Portland's Chinatown, and live and work in mainstream white society. These Cantonese-Chinese, along with American-born Japanese and Korean Americans, became known as "model minorities." Many became physicians, lawyers, architects, engineers, educators, social workers, scientists, and other professionals.

Still, the United States limited the number of Chinese who could immigrate by passing the McCarran-Walter Act in 1952, which capped annual Chinese immigration at 105. This quota, combined with the rapid increase in the number of American-born Cantonese-Chinese, significantly changed the demographics of Chinese in Oregon and in the rest of the country. From 1945 into the 1960s, most Chinese in America were born, raised, and educated in the United States.

Under an Executive Order early in his administration, President John F. Kennedy updated the number of immigrants who could come in from different countries, so that they no longer reflected the disproportionately high number of Western Europeans from fifty years earlier. Under these new quotas more Chinese could come into the country, which made it possible for Oregon Congressman David

Wu's family to join his father in the United States after years of separation, for example.

With the passage of the Immigration and Nationality Act of 1965 (known among Asian Americans as the Pan Asian Immigration Law), U.S. immigration eliminated the quotas that had been in place since the 1920s with the aim of promoting immigration from Northwestern Europe. Chinese received a new quota of 20,000 (vs. 105) immigrants per year; with those seeking reunification with family members the number reached about 100,000 by 1968. While few came directly to Oregon, a significant community with pride in its culture has developed there over the years. After 1980, many Chinese immigrants were not Cantonese, but were Chinese from Taiwan, Burma, Singapore, Malaysia, Indochina (Vietnamese Chinese, Cambodian Chinese), and ultimately from Mainland China as well. As a result, Oregon's Chinese have become much more diverse in their ethnolinguistic, socioeconomic characteristics and in their settlement patterns.

In 2000, Portland opened the Portland Classical Chinese Garden, now the Lan Su Chinese Garden, which is one of the most authentic Chinese gardens outside of China. Architects, landscape designers, and artisans from Portland's sister city, Suzhou in China's Jiangsu province, which is known for its Ming Dynasty gardens, designed and built the Walled Garden in collaboration with American counterparts. Artisans from Suzhou lived in Portland for nine months and built the hardscape on site.

While conditions seemed to improve for other immigrants of color in Oregon over time, the ability for Blacks to get ahead has continued to be difficult. The state's origins of exclusionary policies, a theme that is unspoken and likely unknown by many Oregonians, informs the treatment of Blacks to this day. Nevertheless, in Oregon after the war, every city or town with a university or college had Black residents, scholars, students, and athletes.

Activism and persistence resulted in the passage of a fair employment law (1949), Oregon's first statewide anti-discrimination legislation. The law barred racial discrimination in hiring, promotion, and working conditions. Oregon was the sixth state in the country to pass such legislation. Four years later, a law outlawing racial discrimination in the use of public accommodations, was followed by a fair housing law (1957; expanded 1959).[28] However, enforcement of the fair housing law seldom happened. Only in Portland's Albina neighborhood were Blacks allowed to buy homes.

In Albina, a Black community was created—poorer than other places in the city, but it was a cohesive community. Beginning in the 1950s, the community was severed by Interstate 84, Memorial Coliseum, the Rose Quarter, and other developments. During the 1970s and 1980s, redlining was commonplace; displaced Blacks could not get loans to buy or repair homes in Albina so the neighborhood went even further downhill, which made it ripe for gentrification. By 1999, Blacks owned 36 percent fewer homes than they had a decade earlier, while whites owned 43 percent more.[29] Gentrification, which is ongoing, forced many Blacks out of the city and into low-income housing in the suburbs.

In 1954, the U.S. Supreme Court ruled in *Brown v. Board of Education* that racial segregation in public schools was unconstitutional. The Portland school board attempted to comply in the 1960s and 1970s by busing Black students and recommending that Black schools be closed while allowing white students to attend their closest neighborhood school. Problems like the achievement gap between Black and white students, uneven application of discipline to students of color, and graduation rates continue to be unsolved in the twenty-first century.

Another major issue for Blacks in Portland was the relationship between the Black community and the police. Many Blacks accused the police of brutality and racism. In the summers of 1967 and 1969, race riots exploded along Northeast Union Avenue, the main thoroughfare of the Black community in Albina. Police and their supporters attributed the riots to "outside agitators" and lawless militants. Many Blacks laid the blame on police incitement and the harassment of Black youth.[30]

In the 1970s and 1980s, high-profile police shootings of young Black men in Portland and other incidents exacerbated the Black community's relationship to the police. The police department was investigated in the 1980s after police officers put dead possums in front of Black-owned restaurants.

In the late 1980s, when a violent skinhead movement identified Oregon, and particularly Portland, as one of several locations in the Pacific Northwest suitable for creating a white homeland; Portland became a very real danger zone for Blacks. In November 1988,

Ethiopian exchange student Mulugeta Seraw was murdered, and his murderer was found to be a member of the skinhead community. Kenneth Mieske, a member of East Side White Pride, was convicted for the crime. The California-based founders of White Aryan Resistance (WAR), were convicted in a civil trial for encouraging violence against Blacks.

Only in the 1980s, did Portland start to become a progressive city.[31] "Portland was firmly in the hands of the status quo—the old, conservative, scratch-my-back, old-boys white network," Professor Millner told *The Atlantic* in 2016. The following year, a Portland jury awarded a Black former employee of Daimler Trucks in Portland $750,000, over racist harassment that occurred at its manufacturing plant over the course of years. Other employees had been part of a $2.4 million settlement in 2014, over incidents that included an employee threatening a Black worker with a noose and saying he'd drag the man behind a truck, a noose found hanging over a production line, graffiti including a swastika in the restroom, and use of the n-word.[32]

But there were also steps forward. William A. Hilliard (1927–2017) became editor of *The Oregonian* newspaper in 1987, a post held by few African Americans in the United States. He immediately expanded the paper's reach into the suburbs and encouraged diversity in hiring and news coverage. Five years later, he instructed the paper's Sports department not to use Indian-themed nicknames for professional and college sports teams. He also embraced the LGBTQ+ community. "It is imperative that our newspapers reflect the multiculturality of America," he said in 1993. "Let's respect the sexual orientation of others." That year, he became the first African American to serve as president of the American Society of Newspaper Editors. In 1998, Hilliard was named to the Oregon Newspaper Hall of Fame.[33]

Doctor DeNorval Unthank (1899–1977) arrived in Portland in 1929, just three years after Oregonians voted to allow Blacks to live permanently in the state. Despite harassment and obstacles from white Portlanders, he became a leader in advocating for improved race relations and equality for Blacks. He had been recruited to serve the Union Pacific Railroad's Black employees. After 1931, Unthank became Portland's only Black doctor. During the Depression he expanded his practice to Asians, loggers, and whites. Unthank was a cofounder of the Portland Urban League in 1945 (donating his examination room

for the League office) and he served as president of the Portland
chapter of the NAACP. He was also active in the passage of Oregon's
1953 Civil Rights Bill. After a lifetime of awards and honors, in 1969,
the city of Portland dedicated a park to Dr. Unthank for his years of
activism in humanitarian efforts. At that time, he was the only living
Portland citizen to have such a space named after him.[34]

For twenty-three years, from 1980–2003, longer than any other
maestro, Music Director James DePreist built the Oregon Symphony
"into a virtuoso band more than able to hold its own in any international company," *Gramophone* magazine wrote in 2001. *Oregonian*
Music Critic David Stabler called him "the moral center of Oregon's
artistic community." DePreist, who overcame polio just as he was
beginning his conducting career, was one of the few black conductors
to lead major orchestras in the United States and abroad. His brilliant
career was filled with awards recognizing his talent and achievements
(thirteen honorary doctorates, to name just a few). He took the symphony on its most extensive tours to reach as many people as possible
across the state, playing in ice rinks, tennis courts, parks, the state
fair, convention centers, sports arenas, community centers and a renovated Safeway store. He also took it to the Hollywood Bowl and led
it in its first recordings. The Symphony's free memorial concert on
September 14, 2001, epitomized the balm that music can provide and
demonstrated how an orchestra can serve the community in its greatest time of need. Carried live on television and radio, the performance
reached a record 250,000 people. Hundreds of Portlanders who could
not be among the 2,700 that packed "the Schnitz" could listen outdoors because the Symphony had installed speakers so that everyone
could grieve together. "They sit on benches or sprawl on the grass,
letting the muted beauty of Tchaikovsky wash over them," wrote
Stabler. "I would never want to be denied the opportunity to conduct
because I'm Black, but neither would I want to be engaged because
I'm Black," said DePreist.[35]

ACKNOWLEDGMENTS

This book is a labor of love, as was the Flight for Freedom for everyone who participated. While I am thanking those who helped me professionally, I realize that a big part of what these acknowledgments will acknowledge is the love of many people who kept me going to reach the finish line with a book whose content truly serves the Freedom Fliers and their achievement.

As I reread the acknowledgments for the book I wrote for participants in 2003, it's like acknowledgments déjà vu because many people were just as supportive twenty years later.

The fact is, as Vera Katz told me in 2003, the people who went on this trip have a bond, a bond she compared to the one shared by the people who worked on the Robert F. Kennedy campaign. I believe wholeheartedly that she was right. Every single Freedom Flier I contacted was deeply moved through their participation in the Flight for Freedom. They wanted to share their experiences with me and they wanted to help in any way they could. Those who answered my ads and reached out to me with their memories made things so easy, and I am grateful. They all told me they believe this is an important project.

"John Ray was instrumental in getting the ball rolling and in making me believe I could take an impulse and make it bound." I wrote that in 2003 and it's just as true in 2021. John was the first person I contacted with the current book idea and for nearly two years I've have gone back to him repeatedly with questions and requests for contacts and information. He's been enormously generous with his time in the midst of massive changes in his own life. And perhaps most importantly, he told me I'm a good writer and provided encouragement at this project's very incipience.

Jackie Young and Phil Young hosted Sho Dozono and me for lunch in their beautiful home and Jackie shared her extensive scrapbook, which she shows her family every year on September 11, especially making sure that young people understand what happened and how Oregonians made a difference. There I met the Fords, and Jackie and Jeanine Ford have been unfailingly supportive with not just information but kind words and prayers. Jackie said that day that as you get older, you see that things in life have a way of weaving together in a meaningful way (my paraphrase). I feel very much that my time in Portland was meant to be, in no small part because of the opportunity to be part of the Flight for Freedom. And with Jackie and Jeanine I feel that I made some true friends.

Brian McCartin, now in Tempe, Arizona, trusted me with his files from the Portland Oregon Visitors Association. His organized, annotated documentation has been essential to my understanding of how the trip developed and he's provided some of the most valuable visuals as well. In addition, I was the beneficiary of the goodwill he generated during the trip when, twenty years later, one of the New Yorkers he met with, Leo Nadolske, was willing to spend time with me and talk through his traumatic 9/11 memories.

Charles Gibson, formerly of ABC News, went out of his way to get me a transcript of the Flight for Freedom appearance on *Good Morning America*, and the staff there responded to the request instantly. Scott Williams of KGW, who went on multiple Flight for Freedom trips, has provided me with video of the group's appearances and his enthusiasm about the trips has meant a great deal.

My greatest admiration goes to those who, twenty years later, can find their photos! Many, many Freedom Fliers sent me their pictures, and you will see the list in the photo credits list at the back of the book. Many, many, many thanks to all of you. I couldn't use all of them, unfortunately, but I am thrilled to have had such an extensive selection to choose from.

Cliff Madison, Barbara Shaw, and Jackie Young all made trips to scanning shops to get their photos digitized and this book is the better for it. I will also put in a plug for "DPSDave" in Corvallis, Oregon— superb end products at very reasonable prices, although the place looks a little shabby, according to Barbara. I feel as though she and I developed a further bond through our DPSDave experience.

I have been fortunate to have other cheerleaders. Kelly Sturtevant has helped me to connect to and accept that core of identity and spirit inside us that is the compass—no, I'll be more twenty-first century—GPS that helps us to live the life we are uniquely equipped for, make the contributions we're suited to make, and welcome the blessings that surround us and that we so deserve.

My friend Murry Sidlin, whom I met in Portland almost twenty years ago when I covered his "Defiant Requiem" concert drama for *The Boston Globe*, has encouraged me every step of the way.

For more than forty years, I have known Laurel Mueller. We met first at Vassar College. We have seen each other through a lot and we have watched each other grow. Whether we're even the same people we were lo, those many decades ago, I have no idea. As with other key times in my life, I know that when I need a pep talk, she's the one to call and she will give me a good one.

Almost on the eve of surgery this year another college classmate, Lisa Sokoloff, shared the story of her 9/11 horror with me. I am thrilled that I can include it in this book because I hope it will help young people who know little about the real jeopardy people in Lower Manhattan were in when the World Trade Center was attacked. Lisa's story is harrowing. Lisa is connected to the Flight for Freedom directly because she was homeless and living in the Waldorf-Astoria when we were there. Twenty years ago, in the hotel lobby, she shared her story with Freedom Fliers, who in turn are sharing their recollections of that moment in this book, too. Lisa is eternally grateful to us for coming to the city at that time, and to those who listened to her so many years ago. You were witnesses. As Oregonian Mary Platt told Lisa then, "This is what we came for."

Yet another college classmate, New Yorker Eric Marcus, joined us at the dinner in Chinatown, and he has been kind enough to let me interview him twice about the Flight for Freedom, in both 2003 and now. I saw Ground Zero with him on our trip in 2001.

My editor, Janet Hulstrand, has come through over and over and over on tight deadlines and with her plate filled with other work to give this text care and attention. She consistently encouraged me to take the time I could to make it as good as I could, even if it meant she would have to push harder to get the editing done in less time. She's also been enormously supportive, which has made a difference at some crazy hour of the morning as I worked to get the next chunk of copy complete. Her combination of expertise and kindness has made all the difference in my confidence in the finished volume.

Thanks to Janet, I connected with book designer Nita Congress and her husband, Steve, who came in at the eleventh hour after it became clear that my designer would not meet the schedule on which we had agreed months before. And then, at 11:59 p.m., Kathleen Capshaw not only offered her services, which polished every page, but brought with her Mary Rike, who created a lovely cover that conveys the spirit and meaning of this trip. This book exists for the twentieth anniversary of the 9/11 attacks because of Nita and Steve and Kathleen and Mary. Not only that, they provided me with a more beautiful book than I imagined possible.

Oregon State University Emeritus Distinguished Professor of History William G. Robbins peer-reviewed the "Notes on Oregon" section and could not have been more helpful. He, too, worked on a tight deadline and I am not only honored that he was willing to undertake this review, but he shared his expertise generously and constructively. He is the world's leading expert on the history of Oregon and to be able to take advantage of his encyclopedic knowledge of seemingly every aspect of the state has been a rare treat. Above all, the book is infinitely better for it.

I had expected to travel to Portland multiple times to research this book, interview people, and see scrapbooks and photos, but COVID got in the way. I ended up making only one very quick trip not long before the manuscript was due to the publisher. I am grateful to Sho and Loen Dozono for opening their files to me, which made a huge difference in understanding how the trip developed, and to Sho for saving me hundreds of dollars by being my driver while I was there. Sho and Loen opened their home to me and hosted the organizers and me at their table. Patricia Schechter, who was overwhelmed with commitments, made the time to meet with me and then later allowed me to interview her to expand my understanding of her late husband, Nick Fish, whose contributions to the Flight for Freedom were incalculable. I also met Len Bergstein, who helped me to understand some key reasons why only this team was able to orchestrate a big group trip to New York after 9/11. Nobody else ever figured out how to pull it off.

I am grateful to the many people who made the time to see me, including Nancy Parrott, whose insights on how the Azumano Travel staff ticketed and then, in a week, created a travel group out of 1,000 random people. A special shout-out to David Zielke who was critical in helping me to understand the elements of successful group travel, but mostly because he ran over to the Dozonos' house just to say hello—and give me some very cool Port of Portland socks. George Passadore was an excellent host and I am grateful to him and Joe Weston for sharing their memories and for George, his 2006 speech. I must be honest, though; I'm not sure what was most important that day, all I learned about the Flight for Freedom or getting to see and even sit in his DeLorean!

I learned more about successful project management from Elaine Franklin in the first ten minutes of our interview than I have in any other endeavor or professional coursework. Jack McGowan ensured that the Zoom call with organizers was recorded, that I had a session with them together, and that I sent them my notes to pique additional memories, which demonstrates his understanding of the historical value of this work. I also greatly appreciated that he made an effort to look me in the eye and say, "You are our leader." That gesture and his respect was deeply empowering. I see why SOLV grew exponentially under the custodianship of him and Jan.

I am grateful that Kerry Tymchuk has been supportive of creating room in the Oregon Historical Society for this important effort by Oregon's people.

Finally, I would like to thank my cousins, Margaret Huntsman and Jacque Bourrie, who always listen and always care. My cat, Angel, and my dog, Raji, who are happy to stay up late and sleep until whenever, always listen attentively to stories about the Flight for Freedom and never criticize my work.

Sally Ruth Bourrie
July 2021
Silver Spring, Maryland

APPENDIX A:
THE AFTERMATH

" I will remember it forever. It was people trying to make the world better." —*Len Bergstein, on the "Flight to Friendship" to New Orleans in 2007*[1]

When the group returned, a reunion was held at the Portland Hilton on October 28. About 400 people attended. On a wide-screen television set, the group saw some of their news clips, leaders, including Mayor Katz and Nick Fish, spoke, and light refreshments were served. Mayor Katz read letters she had received from participants and grateful New Yorkers.[2] [PHOTO 1]

The spirit of the trip led many people to say they'd like to continue the effort. Jan Woodruff, director of marketing for Portland State University, and Philomath City Councilor Marilyn Slizeski tried to start a small group to continue the spirit, and captured just how profoundly many of the people on the Flight for Freedom were moved. Their invitation to the first meeting on November 11 stated:

" Sho was quoted as saying about the trip, "I want this to be infectious and contagious so that the rest of the country will pick up on it." Well, many of us were infected, and now suffer a vague, disquieting sense of obligation to use our gift of wisdom for the benefit of humanity. The question is, "How?"

After much discussion, we realized that our best hope lies in gathering together a small group of kindred souls to discuss how we might transform our gift into actions that improve the world. You struck us as someone with the kind of heart and spirit needed to help create such a vision.

In remembrance of the tragedy, we decided to gather nine flight-for-freedom alumni to "break bread" on the eleventh of every month ("9-11") . . . . to explore this idea.

And in closing they added:

PS Until we meet, we invite you to draw inspiration from the following:

"Never doubt that a small group of thoughtful committed citizens can change the world; indeed, it is the only thing that ever has." — Margaret Mead

"The pure love of one person can offset the hatred of thousands." —Gandhi

" . . . we are challenged to rise above the narrow confines of our individualistic concerns to the broader concerns of all humanity . . . . We have before us the glorious opportunity to inject a new dimension of love into the veins of our civilization." —Dr. Martin Luther King, Jr. (1960s)

" . . . the most serious problems we face as a nation are not actually solvable through traditional political means because they are the wounds of an internal disease . . . . No amount of military might can ultimately control the bonfire of ethnic hatred . . . . The bridge to a better world . . . will not come from our political system as it now exists. It will come from deep within us." —Marianne Williamson, *Healing the Soul of America*

Some members met in November, but Woodruff closed down the effort in January due to lack of interest.[3]

On October 10, the day after most of the group had returned, an editorial in the Portland *Skanner* encouraged continuation of another thread of the trip, the economic one:

Dozono's Freedom Flight is such a good idea, in fact, why don't we build on it? Our state economy is slipping into a recession, but for Oregon's rural communities, this has been true ever since the decline and slow death of the timber economy. Many talk about Oregon's "urban-rural divide," but so far no one has found a solution.

Imagine a caravan of Oregonians booked to take weekend tours of our own beautiful rural areas? We could time such tours to take advantage of local events that celebrate so well the heart of each community . . . .

Our friends on the Freedom Flight to New York have shown that proactive and compassionate support can make a lasting difference. Let's take this wonderful idea and build on it.[4]

The following month, in the *Portland Tribune*, Sho himself encouraged Oregonians to spend their "kicker" tax rebate checks in Oregon.* Comparing it to the Flight for Freedom, in which Oregonians wanted "to do something that might make a difference," Sho wrote: "That kind of spirit appears time and again as Oregonians come through when they are challenged. Investing in Oregon is something we can all do. It can be another example of Oregon's spirit that makes this place so special . . . . Let's start growing Oregon's recovery now."[5]

On November 15, Mayor Vera Katz awarded all participants in the Flight for Freedom a "Spirit of Portland Award," "which were awards presented annually to Portlanders who have made outstanding contributions to the community over the past year." Mayor Katz presented the award to Sho and Loen Dozono on behalf of all participants.[6] [PHOTO 2]

The Mayor's office provided a certificate that each Freedom Flier could personalize: [PHOTO 3]

Azumano offered a trip to New York in November for firefighters and other first responders to attend the firefighter memorial service planned by the city for November 18, but that trip was postponed when the memorial service was canceled after firefighters withdrew after the city reduced the number of firefighters working at the World Trade Center site from 300 to twenty-four in late October.

After the September 11 attacks, New York Mayor Rudolph Giuliani had said, "We will be at the site to recover your loved ones until the last brick is removed."

---

*Since 1980, Oregon's "kicker" has been enshrined in law. If the state brings in at least 2 percent more tax revenue than it budgeted for, that excess money is returned to taxpayers proportional to the amount of tax they paid. (Tim Knopp, "Opinion: Defend the Kicker as Oregonians' Last Hope for Tax Relief," *The Oregonian*, May 26, 2021, https://www.oregonlive.com/opinion/2021/05/opinion-defend-the-kicker-as-oregonians-last-hope-for-tax-relief.html.)

A November 7 press release from the firefighters unions stated, "[Giuliani's] decision broke faith with New York fire fighters by limiting their ability to recover the bodies of their fallen brothers, a long-standing tradition in the fire service dating back more than 200 years."

Firefighters believed the mayor's decision turned the recovery process into a "scoop-and-dump operation." Rubble was now being shipped directly to the Fresh Kills landfill on Staten Island. According to the firefighters' unions, "at least one victim's torso has already been hauled to the dump on Staten Island."

The firefighters had protested Giuliani's decision at the World Trade Center site on November 2, resulting in fistfights between fire-fighters and police officers and the arrest of eleven active firefighters. Of the 343 firefighters missing, only twelve of their bodies had been recovered.*

"The fire fighters of FDNY, the widows of our fallen brothers, and thousands of civilians expect the bodies of the fallen fire fighters, police officers, and civilians to be removed from that site in a dig-nified manner, not dumped with debris in a Staten Island landfill," International Association of Fire Fighters (IAFF) General President Harold Schaitberger said.

"Our members are still grieving," said Kevin Gallagher, president of the Uniformed Firefighters Association Local 94 (UFA). "Our people were traumatized once on Sept. 11 and they have been re-traumatized in the last few days. In the memory of our fallen brothers and in honor of their grieving families, we must postpone the Memorial service."[7]

The trip "for Oregon and Washington firefighters, their friends, and family" was postponed until St. Patrick's Day. Gordon Hovies, vice president of the firefighters Local 43, and retired Portland Fire & Rescue Lieutenant Wayne Winter, coordinated information on

---

*As of Friday, 3,923 presumed victims were missing and another 547 were confirmed dead. "Scaled Back Recovery Prompts Scuffle between Police, Firefighters," CNN.com, November 2, 2001. http://www.cnn.com/2001/US/11/02/rec.firefighter.protest/.

Ground Zero,* the St. Patrick's Day Parade, funerals, and tours hosted by the New York firefighters.[8]

In February or March 2002, an unnamed Freedom Flier, along with Alice McElhany and Mike Getsiv organized a "small, informal gathering" of people to share photos and experiences. The organizers shared an update on the clean-up at the World Trade Center site, and the address of Engine 54, Ladder 4, Battalion 9, which had experienced the recovery of the body of one of its brothers in the past week. A recent *Oregonian* article on the fire station, addresses of places to donate and write to in New York, websites, and an email from fourteen-year-old Connor Geraghty, an FDNY firefighter's son who lost his father in the attacks and was routing a petition to start a National Firefighters Day on September 11. Whether additional small gatherings such as this one took place is not known.[9]

On May 8, Loen and Sho returned to New York to visit P.S. 6 on Staten Island, whose second graders had written thank-you notes to Azumano Travel for the Flight for Freedom. [PHOTO 4] Their teacher, Mrs. Denise Tessitore, explained the background of the trip in the school's May 2002 newsletter:

> The Oregon Freedom Fliers wrote a lovely letter to my class in response to the cards they received from us. Mrs. Dozono, a Japanese American mother of five, wrote to us separately expressing

---

*Hovies reported that while he and the other Portland firefighters were in New York, they "had the opportunity" to work at the World Trade Center site to recover bodies:

"While there the body of a brother from Ladder 25 was recovered. We were asked in the commissary to serve as honor guards. We were up for the task. This was a sight to behold, seeing all the firefighters lined up along both sides of the bridge in place with some Police and EMS personnel.

"When a body is located, a search is concentrated around the area to check for additional bodies After the search is done, before the body is being taken out of the area, there is a prayer recited over the radio channel. The body is placed into a Stokes basket, with a flag draped over it. The group then walks to the base of the bridge where another prayer is given over the radio channel. All persons in attendance are asked to salute. The Honor Guard then salutes members of the procession as they proceed up the bridge to place the body into an ambulance. Many tears were shed during this somber moment." Gordon Hovies, "St. Patrick's Day Parade," *The Straight Stream*, XXII, no. 2 (July 2002): 9.

an interest in visiting the class, and doing an origami demonstration. The children and I are very excited about this and have invited her to our Mother's Day Tea on May 8th. My students are learning about modern day patriotic Americans, and how the United States is one diverse family that stands together—especially in times of crisis.[10]

Loen did give an origami demonstration and the kids performed as well. [PHOTO 5] In turn, the Dozonos invited Tessitore of P.S.6, to be in the 2002 Portland Rose Parade in June, and to bring a friend. Tessitore brought Jackie Venezia, whose brother, Paul Barbaro, had worked for Cantor Fitzgerald investment bank, which lost all 658 employees who worked in its World Trade Center headquarters—nearly 70 percent of the firm's employees—in the attacks.[11] [PHOTO 6]

Along with Tessitore, the Dozonos brought seventeen firefighters to Portland for the parade, and they built a big multicar" float called the Freedom Train filled with Azumano Travel employees and Flight for Freedom organizers, along with the New Yorkers.[12] [PHOTOS 7-8] The experience had an enormous impact on the New York firefighters. David Morkal, who is now [2021] battalion chief and executive officer to the chief of operations, had invited the New York firefighters. He had been promoted to lieutenant on September 16: [PHOTO 9]

> One week [after September 11] . . . I worked my regular forty-eight hours of shift work and seventy-two hours of overtime in one week . . . .
>
> My involvement [with Flight for Freedom] was when I ran into Gordon Hovies at a funeral* and I saw his Portland Fire Department uniform and I went over and talked to him and a few other guys from Portland. He had my contact information and several weeks later or months, he reached out to me and said they were trying to bring some people from New York to Portland for the Rose Festival parade . . . . My sister lives out there and my niece and so I said "Yeah, I'll go," and grabbed a friend of mine from one of my first firehouses. He had never been west of New Jersey so flying across the Rockies to Oregon was a whole new experience for him.
>
> And then just a whirlwind of experiences in Oregon.

---

*Likely the St. Patrick's Day trip.

I remember being in the parade and they told us, "Just stay on the float, don't get off," and as we're going down the road, it was almost like the wave—people would stand up and applaud us as we drove by and would sit back down. And at one point I saw my sister and my niece and jumped off and gave my sister a hug and my niece a kiss and it was at that point that a woman had a rose lapel pin and she pinned it onto my uniform. I still wear that, it's still on my uniform. [Since] June of 2002 . . . .

There was a period of time when the chief of the department was against [non- official pins on the uniform], but it stayed in my pocket. [When rules changed] It went back on my uniform.

I think that it was such a subtle sign of respect and it was such a minor little giving moment that I felt that it was important. And I remember the look in her face of just kind of compassion, I guess, and so it became part of my uniform.[13]

Sal Chillemi was the firefighter Dave invited to come with him. He didn't know anything about the Flight for Freedom before going to Portland:

Dave Morkal was a fireman in my firehouse. I was there . . . a few years before Dave got hired as a fireman. And when he came to the firehouse he was on probation and became a fireman there so I knew him for a few years . . . . When he moved, I helped him move upstate with his wife and a couple firemen. Then Dave, he studied and became a lieutenant. Once you become an officer you have to leave the firehouse that you're in. You have to bounce around the city and work at different firehouses and he had to leave my firehouse, Engine 260. So during 9/11 Dave was not in my firehouse . . . . I had not seen Dave in four or five years, we'd have a casual conversation here and there through the years . . . .

Out of the blue, I was working at the firehouse and Dave calls up my firehouse, he says, "Sal, this is Dave Morkal. Hey Sal, how would you like to go to Portland, Oregone?"

I'm saying, "What?"

"How would you like to go to Portland?"

"To live?" I said.

He met some people who were trying to get together with some firemen that worked on 9/11 and they would love to sponsor a trip for some firemen who worked on 9/11 to go to Portland, Oregone.

"When is this going to happen?"

"In two days."

"What?"

"I think they want everyone to leave on Friday and come back on Wednesday."

It was very quick. I said, "Dave, let me call you back. Let me get in touch with my wife and make sure there's nothing going on at home."

I said I'd love to do it and I called him right back and I said, "I'm going, I'm coming with you." They wanted somebody that was there when the buildings collapsed. And Dave had found out that I worked that tour of 9/11, that morning tour. I was there for twenty-four hours after that tour; I stayed on the scene.* He knew that I was there and in touch and had seen what happened firsthand. I was honored that he reached out me after not speaking with Dave for two years. That was awesome. I loved the guy.

. . . The hospitality—the Rose Festival barbecue was tremendous. I have so many pictures of the mayor of Portland. FLIR Systems sponsored this. They did a tribute to firefighters from the FLIR Systems based in Portland. FLIR makes special instruments and they

---

*I was practicing yoga with my wife a few years before 9/11 and when 9/11 happened, I was working that day, I was there in front of the building when it came down. Me and a bunch of guys were working towards the building and as it was coming down, we were like, "Oh my God." I didn't turn and run. I put my mask on, put my helmet on, went down on my knees, head on chest and I just prayed that I wouldn't get hurt.
    I was yelling to guys who were dropping their oxygen masks—I was yelling to them, "Put your mask on and then run." I didn't want them to inhale that cloud of dust that came my way. I was able to go down on my knees and just pray and for some reason, my calmness and meditation that I did throughout the years [helped me]. Thank God, He was with me and I didn't get hurt. That was a tribute to the yoga." Sal Chillemi, interview with the author, February 24, 2021. In 2003, Chillemi and his wife opened a yoga studio, which she ran while he continued to work as a firefighter. The studio was open for eighteen years, until February 2021, when the economic effects of COVID shut them down.

donated an instrument that detects fire in the walls . . . and gave it to FDNY . . . .

The mayor of Portland, she was with us. It was very touching . . . . We met the president of the Rose Festival Parade . . . The parade goes on for like a mile. So what happened was –when we were on this float in our uniforms, all the firemen from New York, . . . [for the usual floats] going down the street people were all sitting down and in lawn chairs and little chairs on the curbside, waving to the floats as they're passing by, very nice, normal stuff. But when we passed people with our float, nobody sat down. Everybody stood up. It was like a wave. Everybody was sitting down and as our float passed, everybody stood up and as our float passed them, they all sat down then. It was so emotional.

I remember telling Dave, "Davy, look at this, this is crazy what's happening here. People are standing" —they didn't do that for any other float. Just our float as we passed them by. So beautiful, so emotional and so touching. And that's how they made us feel that day. I'll never forget that. I'll never ever forget that.

[He has a VHS tape of the parade.] I don't even know who took this video. It's very long, it's two hours. It came from a fireman there and asked if I'd like to have it. So he mailed it to me from Portland . . . .

We were on an aircraft carrier, and I'm standing next to Miss America. All these aircraft carriers and firemen. I've met an Admiral Brown* and he was in charge of the Coast Guard and then I met an Admiral LaFleur,** who was in charge of the fifth fleet of the Navy. And they honored us —we were so humbled, me and Dave.

They closed the street down that night we were there at Rogue [a craft brewery and pub in Newport]. People came from everywhere to meet us and to talk to us and it was so beautiful.

I remember a group of guys, they were Navy Seals, working, and [one says], "Sir, I'm so honored to meet you. Would you sign my T-shirt?"

---

*Likely Vice Admiral Manson Brown, who was U.S. Coast Guard Deputy Commandant for Mission Support and Commander of Coast Guard Pacific Area.

**Likely Vice Admiral Tim LaFleur who was commander, Naval Surface Force, U.S. Pacific Fleet.

I said to him, I remember introducing myself to him and he introduced himself to me. I said, "I'm honored to meet you. You are a
Navy Seal for this country. You're out there four years, giving your
life, across the world, you're doing special tactics to keep our country
free. You want you to sign my T-shirt?"

It was so heartfelt, Sally. I never seen anything like it in my life, I
never felt anything like it.

Six months or a year later, they wanted us to get together at the
Waldorf-Astoria. And they had like a cocktail party, like on the top
floor of the Waldorf. I went, I met Dave there. Not all the firemen
that went on the trip were there. A few of us were, we were in the
FDNY uniform. My wife came with me and I remember . . . being
interviewed by somebody from Portland, Oregone . . . .

I remember being interviewed in the hallway of the Waldorf-Astoria
and I was on the 6:00 news, I believe, to say the hospitality of the
Oregonians and what had happened there was beautiful to me, I'll
never forget it.[14]

On the first anniversary of the September 11 attacks, Flight for
Freedom participants were invited to two events. In Portland, at 9:11
p.m., the Oregon Convention Center's (OCC) two towers would be
illuminated, with light rising more than 1,000 feet, a "light memorial"
representing the height of the towers of the World Trade Center.*
Freedom Fliers were invited to meet nearby at the Japanese American
Historical Plaza at Tom McCall Waterfront Park. Sho Dozono had
developed the idea for the memorial, according to the OCC website,
and worked to raise the money for the new lighting system, which
was brought in from Venice, Italy.[15] Flight for Freedom organizers Jack McGowan of SOLV and John Ray of JRay Media Solutions
were instrumental in creating a daylong community observance and
a call to volunteerism on the anniversary of the 9/11 attacks called
"Celebrate our Community."[16] Portland Police Captain Cliff Madison
remembers another important event of the day at which he and others

---

*The lights had been installed that summer. The beams would shine every
night from dusk to midnight through Veteran's Day. The convention center's website also showed the memorial as part of an "Internet vigil" held
here on OCC's website. The light memorial shone from September 11 through
Veterans' Day, November 11.

spoke: "Sho and Nick Fish and Bruce [Samson] put together an event in Pioneer Square in downtown Portland . . . . 'America under the worst times shows its colors, we can come back.'"[17]

Azumano Travel also sponsored an anniversary trip called the "9-11 Memorial Trip" to New York. This time the trip took place from September 7 or 8—September 12, with the choice of staying at the Waldorf-Astoria or the Doral Park. No organized events were planned.

> An October Columbus Day trip is not being planned due to lack of available hotel and air space. Plus, the City of Portland will be hosting former New York City Mayor Rudolph Giuliani on October 14, so we need to be here at that time to welcome him to the Rose City.[18]

Sandra Kempel of Portland participated:

The reason I personally went back was to pay homage to everyone who was lost that day and to all those who worked so hard to reclaim the site and reclaim the remains of those they could find. We stayed in the Waldorf at the same time the president [Bush] was there. Secret servicemen everywhere and not only that, across the street at the Intercontinental Hotel, Hamid Karzai, the new president of Afghanistan, was staying, because they were addressing the U.N. And I fell right on my face. I tripped on uneven pavement right out in front of Trinity Church and fell against a metal street construction plate they put down over a hole in the pavement so I had to go to the emergency hospital where the first victims were taken, got five stitches—that was the ninth of September.

They were making preparations for the commemoration, they've got streets blocked off, and the taxi driver is trying desperately to get to the hospital. That was an experience, and I also had time to reflect while I was there, victims of 9/11 lay on this very gurney or bed or whatever and just looked around at the people working there and wondering, what if it had been them?

You wouldn't believe what I looked like. Black eyes, black chin, scraped up back of whole hand. It was not a pretty sight and it was like 100 degrees in the subway and we're traveling by subway a lot, and people are looking at me like, you got mugged in New York, didn't you? I was on GMA like that. The president had the audacity to talk to the UN and it was pre-empted on the West Coast. It was the first time in GMA history in this studio, that they invited the studio audience to be in the studio with them, on the second floor. They took us up in the freight elevator. They had a lot of police there, and they got very nervous. It was Diane [Sawyer] and Charlie [Gibson] and Robin [Roberts] and Tony [Perkins] who said, "Bring 'em on up, what the heck?" I was standing right behind them.[19]

George Haight of Woodburn also went back to New York for September 11, 2002. This time he brought his wife, Toni. It was an opportunity to exorcise some feelings that had haunted him, said *The Woodburn Independent*:

> Since his trip to Gound Zero shortly after the Sept. 11 terrorist attacks on the World Trade Center, Woodburn's George Haight has carried a little emptiness in the pit of his stomach.
>
> Every video snippet of a plane crashing into one of the towers or every reference read in a newspaper reminds him of the acrid smell and twisted metal he experienced from the viewing platform.
>
> Now, nearly a year later, Haight is hoping to lay down some new, more pleasant memories of New York City.[20]

The 9-11 Memorial trip included almost 400 Oregonians. The majority, reported the *Statesman Journal*, were Oregon police and firefighters to help their colleagues heal and to show respect for the dead.

> "This time, I think it will go right back to the emotion of the first trip" said retired firefighter Wayne Winter, who was part of a group called Tribute of Honor, which was formed after the attacks. "The whole city will be emotional and brought to its knees." Three funerals for emergency workers killed in the twin towers' collapse will take place the week of the September 11 anniversary. Unlike the previous trip, this one would cost participants from $800 to $1,000, Winter said.[21]

In 2006, on the five-year anniversary of the attacks, Azumano Travel created a full-fledged Flight for Freedom trip that its website tagged, "Here's Your Second Chance at a Once-In-A-Lifetime Experience." [PHOTO 10] Mayor Michael Bloomberg had invited the group to come to New York again.[22]

About 300 Oregonians participated from October 6–10, 2006. Once again, they stayed at the Waldorf-Astoria, went to the morning shows, marched in the Columbus Day parade, and attended two particularly special events: a memorial service at the Cathedral of St. John the Divine, and leaders once again rang the opening bell at the New York Stock Exchange. [PHOTO 11] Many of the same organizers were involved; Nick Fish was again key, and this time he was able to stay for the whole thing!

An observance at the American Express Building next to the World Trade Center site was also powerful, with beloved New York firefighter Billy Quick speaking to the crowd. There, George Passadore, retired Wells Fargo regional chairman, gave a powerful and moving remembrance as well. Excerpts of his comments were published in the *Portland Business Journal*:

Back in 2001, when Sho and Loen organized the first Flight for Freedom, they had two goals in mind: They wanted to lend support to the grief-stricken residents of New York City and they also wanted to bolster the economy here.

Each person had their own reason for being part of the original flight. Many posted their comments on the Flight for Freedom Web site.

One person wrote: "This is Oregon's way of declaring a peaceful war on the evil of terrorism."

Others wrote that they saw the flight as a teaching opportunity for their children, while others said they participated because they wanted to show the world that they were not afraid to fly.

No one could have predicted back then that our simple gesture of making a four-day trip would generate worldwide attention.

With five years having passed since the attacks, Americans are no longer afraid to fly. And New York's economy is strong again.

So what is it about our feelings for America that drives our desire to still be heard some five years later? The answer can be found in one word: spirit.

The terrorists thought that by killing our citizens, they killed our spirit. They failed miserably. In the aftermath of the attacks, we saw patriotism rise to a level we had not seen since World War II.

We saw this country turn from 50 states into one nation, indivisible. We saw peoples of all colors become citizens of one country, under God.

We saw Africans, Asians, Australians, Europeans, Mexicans, Russians and people from countries all around the world become Americans. And, for four days, we saw a group of Oregonians become New Yorkers. No, the terrorists did not kill the spirit of the American people. In fact, they pinpointed the exact spot where that spirit will rise again: a place we now call Ground Zero.

Ground Zero is not a place where life ends. It is a place where our spirit begins, where it starts from zero, and climbs to the heavens.[23]

New Orleans saxophonist Devin Phillips, who had been displaced the year before when Hurricane Katrina devastated the city, joined the group and performed at the Cathedral of Saint John the Divine.*

Five years later, New Yorkers remembered Oregonians from the first trip, said Kristen Dozono. "People would be like, 'I remember that, I remember that.' It was so amazing."

Many people who had not participated in the first trip were able to attend this one; Passadore was one of them. Ann Nice, retired and now president of the Portland Association of Teachers, gave herself the gift of the 2006 trip. Those two Flight for Freedom trips were the only times she's been to New York.

Five years later, in 2011, on the tenth anniversary of what was well-known as "9/11," Azumano Travel organized another Flight for Freedom trip, which would be the last. Sho announced the trip in *The Oregonian*:

We are going back this weekend in observance of the ten-year mark. We will not march in a parade or be a part of the solemn ceremonies at ground zero. We will watch from some distance the observances and take part in our own tribute to the fallen heroes at a concert in the Cathedral of St. John the Divine. With a theme of "Peace and Unity," the Portland Gay Men's Chorus, joined by the New York Gay Men's Chorus, will perform. It will be the highlight of our trip.[24]

---

*Philips still lives in Portland, where he leads jazz and funk bands, and is the artistic director of the American Music Program Jazz Orchestra for young jazz performers.

At St. John the Divine, the Portland Gay Men's Chorus performed Robert Seeley's anti-war cantata "Brave Souls and Dreamers," and were joined in closing the concert by the New York City Gay Men's Chorus, conducted by Gene Robinson, the first openly gay Episcopal bishop.[25]

KGW video journalist Scott Williams covered the original trip and the 2011 effort:

> Ten years later, it was almost back to normal. That just showed the resiliency of New York City folks and the effort of everyone to cope with the disaster, tragedy, and then moving on to making things normal. After the initial shock, I think the overriding purpose for most people in New York was, "We're New York and we're not going to let this get in the way of our future. Just seeing all that stuff had an impact."

> What I remember ten years later is that . . . we went all the way down to Battery Park and there was a memorial for folks from 9/11 so they had American flags set out in the park. We walked through there and I think at that point the raw wound of the 9/11 attack was pretty much closed as compared to the first trip, but now we're getting into the realization and that ability to grasp the scope of what happened and what happened afterwards . . . .

> The first trip there were notice boards with picture after picture and note after note, "Where are you?" "If you get this, call me here." "I know you were downtown, I'm staying here until things get better."

> Ten years later, you have a situation where people can take a minute to realize, to reflect, and so the Battery Park trip was interesting.

> The Portland Gay Men's Chorus . . . that was really something because they did sort of a requiem piece and so they sang in this beautiful church cathedral and it gave people a chance to sort of—beyond reflect, an opportunity to share grief, deep memories. There were a lot of tears and people being able to sort of purge a lot the deep, dark emotions that they'd had from this whole experience . . . .

> [Trying to get from Battery Park at the very bottom of Manhattan to almost the top of the island] To get almost to the Bronx by subway was a whole adventure. We had an incident there—I went with [KGW reporter] Tracy Barry that time, but we still laugh about how these two bumpkins from Portland were trying to navigate the subway system.

At one point we're on the platform trying to decide where we're going to go, debating. The train operator's window flies open and she says, "Where are you trying to go?"

[They told him.] "Get on here and then take this route."

So there was that and we got off the train at the wrong spot going to this concert, so now we're walking in this neighborhood and I've got all my camera gear and which way are we supposed to go? "I think we got off at the wrong place."

We were in a sketchy neighborhood maybe, [and] this big, black town car crosses three lanes right in front of us. The driver says, "What are you doing? You shouldn't be walking in this neighborhood with all this stuff."

She said, "I'm off the clock. Where are you going?"

By this time, we were like, "I hope we make it to this concert."

We got there five minutes ahead.[26]

The Flight for Freedom trips were not the only such forms of "civic therapy" (as *The Oregonian* called it) organized by the Dozonos and their team at Azumano Travel. In 2004, they embarked on a series of "Flight of Friendship" trips, first to Thailand (in February and April 2005), after the 2004 tsunami hit south and southeast Asia,[27] then to New Orleans in 2007 to support rebuilding after Hurricane Katrina — on-site projects that were organized by the Pacific Northwest's Mercy Corps.

In 2011, the same year as the final Flight for Freedom, the last Flight of Friendship, this time to Japan, took place in response to the devastating earthquake there. From May 29–June 4, the trip took people to Sendai, the largest city in the affected region, with three days in that city and two nights in Tokyo. The mission was simple, said *The Oregonian*: "Assess the devastation, pitch in at homeless shelters, and spend some tourist money in the affected areas."

1. Nick Fish speaks at reunion. Photo
Courtesy of Loen Dozono

Spirit of Portland Awards

*"We have demonstrated in the past, and will continue to do so in the future, that
we are creative and resourceful, persevering and pragmatic." --MAYOR VERA KATZ*

MAYOR'S SPIRIT OF PORTLAND AWARD
SHO AND LOEN DOZONO, on behalf of all who participated in the "Flight for Freedom" from Oregon to New York
City. Participants gained national attention for their show of
economic and emotional support in the aftermath of the terrorist attacks on September 11. By getting on airplanes, attending Broadway shows, dining out, shopping, marching in
the Columbus Day Parade, and filling up an entire hotel in
Manhattan, the nearly one thousand Oregonians who made up
the "Flight for Freedom" touched the hearts of New Yorkers
and became known throughout the country as being residents
of the City that Cares.

The Mayor's Award was given to ALL
participants in the Flight For Freedom

2. Photo courtesy of Jackie Young

2. Photo courtesy of Jackie Young

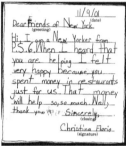

4. New York children's thank-you notes to the Freedom Fliers. Photos courtesy of Sho and Loen Dozono

5. Left: Children in Denise Tessitore's class at P.S. 6 on Staten Island when Sho and Loen Dozono visited. In May 2002. Right: Sho and Loen Dozono receive quilt from Denise Tessitore's class at P.S. 6. Denise Tessitore is at far right. Photos courtesy of Loen Dozono

6. Staten Island Schoolteacher Denise Tessitore and her friend, Jackie Venezia, who the Dozonos had invited to be on the Azumano Travel Freedom Train float after Tessitore's second-grade class had sent thank-you notes to the Oregonians for coming to New York. Photo courtesy of Loen Dozono

7. Riders of the 2002 Azumano Travel "Freedom Train." Photo courtesy of Loen Dozono

8. The Freedom Train float created by Azumano Travel for the 2002 Portland Rose Parade. The float featured Flight for Freedom organizers, New York firefighters, and a Staten Island schoolteacher and her friend, who had lost her brother in the September 11 attacks. Photos courtesy of Loen Dozono

9. FDNY Battalion Chief David Morkal has worn a Portland rose pin on his uniform's lapel since 2002. Photo courtesy of David Morka

Mission

In the aftermath of the horrifying events of September 11, one thousand Oregonians boarded planes for New York City to lend support to its grief-stricken citizens and bolster an economy left dazed by the devastating blow it had been struck. Their trip became known as the Flight For Freedom, and in four short days these goodwill ambassadors from the Pacific Northwest came to understand the power of a simple gesture.

Flight for Freedom 2006 is an opportunity to renew friendships. To reflect on how mere minutes can dramatically alter lives and change a city, how four days can last forever. More importantly, it is an opportunity to rededicate ourselves to freedom, to celebrate our diversity, to recapture a spirit of unity and rejoice in the strength that is America, from sea to shining sea.

›About us

In putting together Flight For Freedom 2006, Honorary Co-Chairs Sho and Loen Dozono are joined by many of the same organizers, supporters and distinguished political leaders who were the driving force behind the original Flight For Freedom.

›Latest news

May 30, 2006
New York City is welcoming Oregonians back this October with a special invitation from Mayor Bloomberg. read more

›In their own words

"When I read the newspaper story about "Flight For Freedom" and the overwhelming response of Oregonians I was filled with pride, and not in the least bit surprised. Oregonians have hearts as big as the Pacific Northwest." read more
J.A., Arlington, VA · September 2001

Here's Your Second Chance at a Once-in-a-Lifetime Experience...

10. Screenshot retrieved by the author June 27, 2021.

11. Flight for Freedom participants ring the opening bell at the New York Stock Exchange. From left to right, unidentified, prolific Portland developer and major partner at Hoyt Street Properties Joseph Weston, Nick Fish, unidentified, Sho Dozono, Randall Edwards's son (who rang the bell), Oregon State Treasurer Randall Edwards, Randall Edwards's son, unidentified women, Attorney and Flight for Freedom organizer Bruce Samson, retired Wells Fargo regional chairman George Passadore. Photo courtesy of Patricia Schechter.

APPENDIX B: FORMER NEW YORK GOVERNOR GEORGE PATAKI

Interview with the author, May 13, 2021

When my longtime friend Mary Ann Fish made me aware that Oregon was trying to put together a trip to New York in October 2001, I knew right away that it would be an important event for the entire city. And I knew I would make the time to see them and speak to them while they were in Manhattan.

On September 11 and in the days and weeks after, people from all over the country were incredibly gracious in their outpouring of help in every way imaginable. But as the media thread about the attacks themselves ended and the effort to return normal began, one of the biggest problems was that people were afraid.

They were afraid to go to New York City—and the economy of New York was being devastated. Even people in the metropolitan area were afraid to come into Manhattan. The hotels were vacant, workers were unemployed, restaurants were empty, and theaters were dark. Tens of thousands of people had lost their jobs through no fault of their own because after the attacks people were afraid to come into the city because they were afraid they could be attacked again.

So when 1,000 Oregonians said we're going to go—and in a highly visible way—go to restaurants, stay in hotels, attend theaters, walk on the streets, and let the rest of the world know that it's OK to be in New York, the meaning of that act was far beyond the economic benefit, although that was significant.

The symbolic commitment to be a part of the recovery of New York from these horrible attacks meant a great deal to all New Yorkers and sent a very positive message to the entire nation. The Flight for Freedom demonstrated that people from 3,000 miles across the continent felt comfortable and safe in the streets, and that message got out in the rest of the country.

There were a number of symbolic things that I remember as key turning points in letting people know that New York was going to be OK. A major one was President Bush throwing the first pitch when the World Series returned to Yankee Stadium in October 2001. The fact that 55,000 people could be there and the President was out in public in front of them in New York was an incredibly positive and inspiring message that meant a lot.

And the people from Oregon were also an important part of that recovery. It was another one of those periodic, high-visibility events that convinced people ultimately that it was OK to come back.

Speaking to hundreds of those Oregonians in the Waldorf-Astoria's Grand Ballroom, my message was simple: Thank you. This is the spirit of America and this is the message we have to send, that we're Americans and even in the aftermath of this horrible attack, we're not going to be cowed, afraid to gather in groups, or to gather at the theater or at dinner. We need to live free of fear across the entire country, including in New York City not far from where the events occurred.

It was a slow process for people to feel that they could go to New York for the first time, but the Flight for Freedom was an important step in that process. It literally took a couple of years, but within a couple of years New York was thriving as never before. The Oregonians' trip will always be remembered by New Yorkers because it was courage and graciousness at a time of uncertainty that helped us to begin to build back to where we are today.

Citation

Whereas, all Americans and freedom-loving people of the world continue to join with New Yorkers in rebuilding in the aftermath of events that occurred on September 11th -- another tragic day that will live in infamy; the world has witnessed in other times of loss New Yorkers' ability to find a greater strength that enables us to stand up and restore our lives, and we will again this time; and

Whereas, with gratitude, we recognize our fellow Americans who have been inspired by our Country's leadership from President George W. Bush, the citizens of New York State and those from across our Country who have contributed so much to our State and continue to serve as a foundation of strength during our time of need; as a Nation, we must all join together in an effort to reclaim our lives and cherished American way of life; and

Whereas, all New Yorkers are grateful to those individuals and organizations that have demonstrated a remarkable show of support since that fateful Tuesday; in that regard, it is especially heartwarming to applaud the efforts of the outstanding citizens from the State of Oregon who took part in the recent "Flight For Freedom" to visit the greatest City in the world -- New York -- and to witness all of its glory; and

Whereas, in early October, more than 900 Oregonians traveled by air to New York City as a show of support for the victims of the tragic events of September; this mission was also undertaken in an effort to bolster America's airline industry and to help jumpstart our State and Nation's economy; through their actions and admirable goals of contributing to our tourism industry, these individuals truly illustrate the generosity and caring spirit of all Americans; and

Whereas, it is my pleasure to extend greetings to all taking part in the Reunion for the "Flight For Freedom" participants, which will take place on October 28, 2001; this event will give these caring and patriotic citizens the opportunity to reflect and reminisce about their wonderful experiences in the Big Apple, and will serve as a springboard for future events of this kind in other cities and states; and

Whereas, events such as the "Flight For Freedom" clearly illustrate that Americans will rise to meet the challenges that face us and, in doing so, disavow efforts to diminish our invincible spirit of freedom; all New Yorkers thank the people of Oregon who came to our State with love in their hearts and to offer a helping hand to us and, we are proud to once again join those assembled in the spirit of strength and unity that has come to define us as a State and Nation;

Now, Therefore, I, George E. Pataki, Governor of the State of New York, do hereby recognize the members of

"FLIGHT FOR FREEDOM"

and offer our sincere thanks to them for their efforts in bringing comfort to those have suffered great losses, in supporting our State and Nation's economy and, most importantly, in lifting the spirit of the greatest City in the world.

Governor
October 28, 2001

APPENDIX C: OREGON'S SENATORS PRAISE THE FLIGHT FOR FREEDOM

Congressional Record Vol. 147, No. 132 (Senate—October 4, 2001)

The PRESIDING OFFICER. The Senator from Oregon . . . .

Mr. WYDEN. One last point: Something that I and Senator Smith are together on is the pride in our State and our citizens. A number of Oregonians, strong-willed people in our State, are mounting an operation that they call Flight for Freedom, answering the national call for all of us to get on with our lives and come to the aid of those hurt in the attacks of September 11. In a show of solidarity with their fellow Americans, more than 700 Oregonians are making the statement this weekend by heading to the hotels and Broadway shows and restaurants in New York City that are fighting for economic survival in the aftermath of the attack. With Oregonians' Flight for Freedom, the people of my State are standing shoulder to shoulder with the citizens of New York in an effort to make clear that no terrorist can break the American spirit.

I congratulate Sho Dozono and the other organizers and participants in Oregon's Flight for Freedom for their generous efforts. I urge all Americans to follow their example. Oregonians are showing this weekend that we are going to stand against terrorism by reaching out to fellow citizens and enjoying what American life has to offer in our centers of commerce across this great Nation. Because of these kinds of efforts, we can send a message that terrorists can't extinguish the American spirit.

I yield the floor.

Congressional Record Vol. 147, No. 138 (Senate—October 15, 2001)

FLIGHT FOR FREEDOM

Mr. SMITH of Oregon. Mr. President, ever since the days of the pioneers, when folks would gather from miles around to participate in community barn raisings, the spirit of neighbor helping neighbor has been an Oregon tradition.

I rise today with great pride in my State to tell you that the tradition of neighbor helping neighbor reached new heights these past few days in a remarkable project entitled "Flight for Freedom."

Spurred by New York City Mayor Rudy Giuliani's call that New York City was open for business, Portland Mayor Vera Katz and Portland businessman Sho Dozono came up with the idea of sending a delegation of Oregonians to New York City to lend whatever support they could to the residents of the Big Apple.

It wasn't too long before 100 Oregonians signed up, and then 200, and then 500, and then 750, and when all was said and done, over 1,000 Oregonians from every corner of my state boarded planes and traveled to New York City last weekend.

This delegation brought a great deal of business to New York hotels, restaurants and stores. But more important than that, they brought a great message. A message that we are one Nation. A message that the 3,000 miles between New York City and Oregon was made non-existent on September 11. A message that as New Yorkers move forward in the days and weeks ahead, Oregonians and Americans will stand with them.

It was a message expressed in the tee-shirts that members of the Flight to Freedom wore and distributed as they marched in the Columbus Day Parade. The shirt said simply "Oregon loves New York."

Many participants in the Flight for Freedom have described the trip as the most moving and most memorable of their life. They will always remember the gratitude New Yorkers extended to them. They will always remember the words of a New York policeman who said, "The gap in the New York skyline is incredible. It can't ever be replaced. But we'll bounce back with the help of people like you in Oregon."

I know my colleague Senator Wyden joins with me in saying to Senator Schumer and Senator Clinton that we share the sentiments expressed by our fellow Oregonians last weekend. We, too, love New York, and we, too, will stand with you every step of the way.

The State motto of Oregon is "She flies with her own wings." And it seems to me that Oregon, New York City, and all of America are flying just a little bit higher today because of the spirit and leadership of Mayor Vera Katz, Sho Dozono, and all those who made the Flight to Freedom such a remarkable success.

Congressional Record Vol. 148, No. 64 (Senate—May 17, 2002)

OREGON HERO OF THE WEEK

Mr. SMITH of Oregon. Mr. President, I am proud to rise today to pay tribute to a true American Patriot from my home state of Oregon. This week, I want to recognize the service and compassion of Sho Dozono, of Portland, OR.

Mr. Dozono, President and CEO of Azumano Carlson Wagonlit Travel and the Azumano Group, is a respected member of the Portland business community. He continually tries to improve his community and has served on a number of boards and commissions including the Portland Metro YMCA, Portland Multnomah Progress Board, and was recently elected to serve as the chair of the Portland Metropolitan Chamber of Commerce board of directors.

But like so many employers, after September 11, 2001, Mr. Dozono was forced to lay off employees and watch as the effects of the terrorist attacks spread across the country to his west coast home. Mr. Dozono and his wife Loen decided that they would not allow their own financial difficulties to keep them from showing their love and support to the victims in New York City. What started as an idea of a bus convoy across the United States grew into an inspirational display of patriotism and compassion, aptly named the "Flight for Freedom."

Mr. Dozono brought together over 1,000 Oregonians to answer the call of Mayor Rudy Giuliani for tourists. Not only did the group lend a healing hand to the broken economy of New York City, but the "Flight for Freedom" was instrumental in convincing Americans everywhere to travel again. The week-long trip, which included marching in the Columbus Day Parade, attracted worldwide publicity and earned recognition from New York and national officials. At a crucial time, Dozono persevered to share his belief in the American dream with those whose light had been tragically dimmed.

I rise to salute Sho Dozono, not only for his inspirational efforts after 9/11, but because his desire to improve his community is a life-long commitment. In 1997, Dozono traveled to Philadelphia to represent the City of Portland at the Presidential Summit on Volunteerism in America, chaired by then-retired General Colin Powell. He is a former chair of the Portland Public Schools Foundation and co-chaired a march that raised over $11 million to save teaching positions that would have otherwise been cut because of reduced funding.

This month as we honor and celebrate Asian Pacific American Heritage Month, I find it very appropriate to rise and recognize the efforts of Sho Dozono. I believe Mr. Dozono is to be commended for his ongoing efforts to serve his community and country, and I salute him as a true hero for Oregon.

APPENDIX D:
LETTERS OF ACCLAMATION

THE WHITE HOUSE
WASHINGTON

October 5, 2001

I am pleased to send warm greetings to the more than 750 Oregonians who have traveled to New York City by air as part of the "Flight for Freedom." I appreciate your show of support for America's airlines and for the victims of the September 11 tragedy.

Your efforts to contribute to New York's economy and assist with relief efforts represent the generous and caring spirit of America. You also show the world that the strength of our Nation is not only in our economy or in our buildings. America's strength lies in her people.

I commend you for your compassionate service to the city and the people of New York. Laura joins me in sending best wishes.

THE SECRETARY OF TRANSPORTATION
WASHINGTON, D.C. 20510

October 6, 2001

Dear Oregonians:

Congratulations on being a "Flight For Freedom" participant and for doing something very positive and good for your country.

By accepting Mayor Giuliani's invitation to fly to New York, you have shown that the American spirit is alive and well in Oregon. You have also sent a strong message to the rest of the country—that it's okay to fly again, that we will not allow terrorists to take away our freedom of mobility. You, and all the "Flight for Freedom" organizers and sponsors back in Oregon are doing a wonderful thing to get America moving again physically, financially, and emotionally.

On behalf of President Bush and Vice President Cheney, thank you for your contribution to the nation. You are champions of the American spirit. You are a credit to us all as we return our transportation system to the way it should be. Thanks a million everybody. Have a great Columbus Day and a great visit to New York.

Sincerely yours,

Norman Y. Mineta

United States Senate
WASHINGTON, DC 20510-3704

October 8, 2001

My Fellow Oregonians,

Like most Americans, I have never experienced a horror equal to that of the terrorist attacks of September 11. After seeing the destruction first-hand as I have, you now know that words, photographs, and even the imagination fail to capture the devastation visited upon us on that horrible day. But today is a day not only to reflect on this tragedy, but also to celebrate the spirit of our great nation. Your visit here is a visible sign that life in America will go on stronger than ever in the wake of this tragedy.

Some people may say that terrorists prey on innocents because they are incapable of waging war on our military. But they know America better than that. In reality, terrorists do not attack our armies because they know that America's power has never resided in its planes, its tanks, or its guns. Rather, the people and their liberty define our nation and give us our true strength – and that is what they seek to destroy. Only by forcing us to live in fear and restrain our own freedom can they achieve their objectives. And while terrorists may understand the source of our strength, they also underestimate us.

That is why it is not enough for our soldiers to hunt down the murderers and for our diplomats to array the nations of the world against terror. Each of us, as ordinary citizens, plays an even more important role, not just as firemen, policemen, or volunteers, but as a people determined to live free of fear. Each of you, in answering Mayor Giuliani and President Bush's call for a return to normalcy, have become a shining example of the indomitable spirit that has distinguished us as Oregonians and as Americans.

By coming to New York, you have shown the terrorists that they may murder our citizens and destroy our buildings, but they can never truly defeat the American people. At this moment, I can remember few times that I have been more proud of our great state; for your presence here today shows that 3,000 miles of land may separate Oregon and New York, but that there is no distance between Americans. Thank you again for coming.

Warmest regards,

Gordon Smith

October 6, 2001

Welcome to New York!

Your visit is a wonderful reminder of the compassion and caring that the people of Oregon have extended to New Yorkers following the traumatic events of September 11th. New York is ready to give back by sharing with you the rich diversity of experience that is a hallmark of the City. Wherever your explorations take you - - East Side, West Side, SoHo, NoHo, Brooklyn or the Bronx - - our theatres, museums, merchants, and restaurants have a warm welcome waiting. We are delighted that you are here and hope that you will return again and again.

With appreciation and thanks,

Charles E. Schumer
United States Senator

Hillary Rodham Clinton
United States Senator

THE CITY OF NEW YORK
OFFICE OF THE MAYOR
NEW YORK, N.Y. 10007

October 2, 2001

Mr. Sho Dozono
Chair
Portland Metropolitan Chamber of Commerce
221 N.W. Second Avenue
Portland, OR 97209

Dear Mr. Dozono:

On behalf of the City of New York, I want to extend a warm welcome to the participants of the Flight for Freedom. Your decision to make New York City your destination of choice has special meaning to the residents of this City. It is a symbol of solidarity in these difficult times and a demonstration that Americans will not be held captive in their homes by the senseless acts of a few.

New York City suffered a terrible loss, as did the nation. But out of that loss grew a sense of unity and goodwill unprecedented in our time. We saw this in the relentless search for survivors conducted by our uniformed emergency services, and in the brave acts of our law enforcement and fire fighters, many of whom made the ultimate sacrifice to save their fellow man.

Your trip to New York is part of a healing process. As you walk our streets know that we are appreciative of the outpouring of support, hope and love that you, our neighbors, have given. New York City remains stronger than ever.

Sincerely,

Rudolph W. Giuliani

APPENDIX E:
NICK FISH (1958-2020)

Interview on July 31, 2003

For me, the thing began in the typical Portland way, which is, I had been developing a relationship with Sho—I had met Sho Dozono through some JASO (Japan-America Society of Oregon) events, so he was someone who was sort of on my radar. He and I had talked about doing a trip to New York, which would be a benefit trip, which we'd put together and would be used by a charity. I would use my knowledge and experience about New York to help tailor a terrific long weekend. And that was a reaction of mine that whenever I read about trips to New York in the Travel section of the newspaper, it semed to me like they did the cliché, touristy thing and they missed the focal things.

And the context for 9/11 is, I had moved here from New York City, had family in New York City, and 9/11 for me was devastating. I had a lot of people I knew living in Manhattan who were directly affected, so I had a personal connection to the city in addition to feeling the horror that we all felt.

I read in the paper one day that Sho Dozono and others were planning something called the Flight for Freedom. It was just a little box in the paper and my first reaction was, "Why didn't Sho call me?" And then, when I got over that and realized that these things happen quickly and who the hell am I, I called Sho and said, "I read about this thing you're doing and sign me up in any capacity to help."

"What do you think?" he said.

I said, "I think there are probably just three things"—and I was brainstorming—"I could help you with immediately." 1. If you're going to some kind of a memorial service while you're there I think Union Square is the place to do it, and I used to chair the local community board and we could quickly pull together all the pieces to have the city, the community board, and . . . . 2. I told him that there was an important event on Sunday, which was something that I try to go to every year was the Blessing of the Animals at the Cathedral of St. John the Divine, which is my home church. For the big ticket events like their New Year's Eve service, for things like summer and winter solstice and for Easter and St. Francis Day, that was the place that I enjoyed going and I had friends who also went. I mentioned to Sho that there was this extraordinary service, the Blessing of the Animals and I had a sense that it was going to be a big event this year because of 9/11. And then I told him that to the extent that he wanted to do a big gala at the Waldorf, I had some very good connections both with the theater community and with Gov. Pataki's office. My ace in the hole there was that my stepmother, Mrs.. Hamilton Fish, works for Gov. Pataki. So I said, if you want to get the governor there and you want to get some stars from Broadway, that could be helpful. That was just nervous energy, threw out three ideas that came to me.

Typical Sho, and it's one of the things that make him a gem—he said, "We're having a meeting this afternoon, can you swing by?" He may have said, "We're having a meeting in five minutes."

I walk into the room and it's a room filled with people whose names I was familiar with but I had not met. I moved here in November of '96 so I'm still feeling my way around. I knew Sho but not well, never met Bruce Samson but knew of his reputation, knew of Elaine Franklin, I'd heard of Jack McGowan but never had met him. Had heard of Len Bergstein, I'm not sure we had met. Had never met John Ray or the Dozono children. There were some other folks in the room who played leadership roles, people I'd met at that time. So for me it was pretty new, very exciting. Jack McGowan was on the speakerphone and the press piece that Jack and Len and John did was just so brilliant in connecting with all the venues and kind of drawing an enormous amount of attention to this trip. Ultimately, it became such a huge thing that Vera, who I understand was sort of on the fence because of other obligations, cleared her schedule to come, which was huge. It was an enormous statement.

We went around the room, Sho introduced me: "This is Nick Fish. Nick has some ideas. Why don't you share them?" I gave out ideas as a transplanted New Yorker.

Sho said, "That sounds good, Nick. I want you to work on those."

I quickly realized that I had been drafted and I had my assignment. It was a little daunting, not because I didn't think I could deliver. This thing was happening very quickly, I hadn't worked with most of the people in the room, I had to figure out protocol.

It was because of a little box in The Oregonian and I put two and two together and got excited.

I just carved out some time, kind of dropped what I was doing and started working with the governor's office [New York Governor Pataki] and Mary Ann Fish, my stepmother, to work on the governor's piece; called both the head of Actors' Equity and the head of the League of Theaters and asked them if they would consider supplying some stars from Broadway to a gala. My community board covered the theater district so I was deeply involved.* They were bullish, which was good because I was calling friends.

In the Fourteenth Street Union Square Business Improvement District, the president was a dear friend of mine. He listened to me for about five minutes and said, "It's done, we'll make it happen."

Then I called my friend Stephen Facey, executive vice president of programs at St. John the Divine, and when I told him that we had this delegation that may include the mayor and may come to the service on Sunday, he said that Bobby Kennedy [Jr.] was going to be speaking, the guide dogs from the search and rescue process were going to be part of the processional and that the mayor of Portland, a former New Yorker, would come speak, would be the icing on the cake. Steve and their people worked together to work out some of the kinks.

I had some friends in the mayor's office that I was able to touch base with. It kind of quickly fell together and because again, because of Sho's leadership style and because of the extraordinary people he pulled together, everyone was focused on getting things done. He had

---

*Fish had spent a decade on Community Board Five, said his wife, Patricia Schechter (May 13 2021).

delegated this to me. I think my enthusiasm in pitching—people got on board.

After some hard work, the three events began to come together. I flew to New York with Jack McGowan and others, and it was like to be with the Beatles. The people I was sitting next to asked to sit next to him, knew him from his media days.

We got a lift from someone who was going to a premiere for a Danny Glover film. We crashed somebody's limo that was sent by the studio. When we got to the Waldorf, there was a war room, and I got on the phone to firm things up—the Pataki thing was not yet firm, we were pushing, pushing, pushing, pushing. But I got things firmed up.

Fortune shined on us and it happened that the principal violinist from the Portland Symphony was on board, I tracked him down.* Henry Stern decided that the was going to come officiate. The Business Improvement District set up an amazing event headed by the guy who owns the restaurant on the square—Eric Petterson from Coffee Shop, although Danny Meyer was very supportive, but Eric Petterson provided some of the logistical stuff and so that was the first piece and when we got there, they had set up a beautiful soundstage and cordoned off the norther part of the park and they kind of helped us at the restaurant before it started. And the violinist performed. I asked my friend Baruti Artharee, who's now the head of the Urban League, if he would be able to speak at the event.

Bruce was the MC, and he did a fine job, and we had a mob, plus we had all this press. At that point for me, that was the first taste that this thing was huge, that there was something happening here beyond just Oregonians coming to New York. There was a connection that was being made; we were in the middle of this media frenzy. That was Sunday morning and we were then put into police escorts with the mayor and whisked up to the Cathedral of St. John the Divine and my friend Stephen greeted us at the sidewalk level. The cathedral was filled with 3,000 people, we had VIP seats at the front of the cathedral. Vera gave the speech of her life and was so moved to be on the same podium with Bobby Kennedy that she put her speech aside and she spoke from the heart—the place rocked. It was staggering.

---

*It was Roy Stilwell, retired Oregon Symphony violinist.

Howard and Alice Shapiro, Peter and Mary Mark, and Betsy Ames—to be there with someone who had roots in New York but now called Portland my home. It was one of the most emotional moments I can think of in my life, really, and [then] the guide dogs and other animals came through. The service is very unconventional thing filled with gospel and jazz and dance and poetry and theater and it is the highlight of what the cathedral does and it's just a gem and it's probably my favorite event, period. I'm not a deeply religious person, but . . .

There are so many amazing coincidences serendipity, it was for me just an endless set of connections and unexpected things and add to that that I didn't know most of these people so we were thrown into this intense experience, we were bonding, we were in New York at a time when the city was totally down, streets were quiet at night, the hotel we stayed in was empty but for us and there was a very strong, powerful odor in the air of fire and burning metal and other things which we can only imagine. And the city had never been as somber. I experienced a tremendous range of emotions that I shared with Jack McGowan and I returned as sons of New York who had relocated to Oregon.

Monday morning I was invited to join the state treasurer and his delegation to Wall Street and I watched as Randall and all—they bounced the Majority Leader and Speaker of the U.S. Congress for the Oregon delegation. The whole thing lit up around Oregon Loves New York. We met the head of the Stock Exchange, who was as childhood friend of Jack McGowan's.

I had to go home that afternoon because I had to be in court Tuesday afternoon. I was so focused on my piece and I didn't see the forest for the trees. I made some phone calls to hear that the governor was rearranging his schedule to meet the event, confirmed that the Broadway stars would be there, and went to the airport. To this day, I kick myself for having had that conflict. The farewell event was a beautiful way to finish the event, but unfortunately, I couldn't be there. But to get the governor—at that time, the governor was managing the crisis and was in the middle of the firestorm himself and for him to change his schedule so he could be at the benefit at the Waldorf was huge. I think it would have been easier to get the president at that time.

That event changed my life here in Oregon; all those people became dear friends. The Flight for Freedom started marching in various parades, we did a reunion at which I had a chance to speak and the folks who went as part of the thousand strong, we all got to know each other and run into each other. And the folks that planned it became very close, and everything I've done since, I've had that core group of people helping me and guiding everything that I've been doing in Portland so it would not be an exaggeration to say that it was a transforming event in my life.

But I didn't think it up, I didn't put the pieces together, I didn't have anything to do with the travel plans, the beautiful website, the overall planning, I didn't have to worry about any of the sort of those critical things. I just had two events on Sunday and one on Monday night, which I was responsible for coordinating and because I had relatively fresh connections to the city of my birth and a place where I had worked professionally where I had moved to Oregon, I was in the unique position to get my friends and support group in New York to help Sho and his team to fill out the schedule for the trip, but it was all about Sho and Loen and Bruce and others, but I was very proud to play a part.

I wore the button. Being someone who grew up in New York, it was doubly sweet. I wore my button all the time. Saturday night I went to the St. Mark's Church in the Bowery to a dance recital that was a hauntingly beautiful thing with a cello and a solo performer. The church is downtown, and the area around the church had a very strong pungent smell of post-9/11 and that was an intense experience. I wore the button to that and to the dinner I went to afterwards.

That experience for us crystallized why we love being here [Portland]. My father, when he was in Congress, we lived in DC, I went to college and law school in Boston, and I was born in New York City and raised in the Hudson Valley. But that experience—and it hasn't happened at the same level since I've been here because nothing will be as charged as that immediate aftermath of 9/11—but that experience of coming together with people that you don't know around a common cause, working your butt off, working together with leadership like Sho and Loen who are selfless leaders, who are people who never seek the limelight but facilitate these kinds of things—a chance to meet all those people and be part of something that just grew well beyond what any of us imagined, was one of the unique experiences of my life.

All of those people have become almost like family members. It's almost like we went to war together. Since I didn't know most of them before and to go to New York, come back to my hometown as an Oregonian—I hope to have a full life, but I don't know that I'll ever have an experience that comes close to the intensity of that experience outside of having my daughter. And so it is why we are very, very bullish on Portland because it does seem to be a place that you can still do these kinds of things and come together with people. If I ever get a chance to get into elective office this will be my model.

If you had been in the room as I was looking around that table at that meeting, I think that it was largely because it was a room filled with people that are doers and who are skilled at executing a game plan and who had real conspicuous strengths they brought to the able. Sho and Loen were the inspiration for this thing and everyone in the room loved and respected them, and I came to love them. Jack McGowan has been involved in the media in one way or another for a very long time and had a very strong sense of how to do these things; John Ray was tireless in performing his role. Even Mrs. Bob Packwood who I had never met before, I knew the caricature I read about, she was hugely skilled at executing the game plan, had operated at a very high level. The guys at the chamber of commerce were very good. Bruce Samson is a guy who will constantly deflect attention for what he's done. But Bruce and Sho together have done some of the heavy lifting for the education funding in the state and never get the credit they deserve. But all the other people who gravitated and offered to help. It was a very strong team, it was a dynamite idea, the execution was almost flawless, and the timing was just right, and it happened to be a weekend that was a down weekend in terms of press so we were the only show in town until the end of the service at the cathedral.

You couldn't make this up. At the end of the service at the cathedral, here you are at the religious venue that day, the oldest and the larges cathedral of its kind in the world and one of the most spectacular sites/venues in New York, packed with ordinary citizens mourning and grieving over this whole thing and as the dean got ready to end the service, he announced that he had just gotten word that we had started to bomb Afghanistan and so from up until Sunday noon we were almost like one of the biggest stories in the country and it captured the imagination.

I saw Vera on CNN just before I got in a plane flying to New York. Aaron [Brown] was interviewing her and she was just extraordinary. We were first out of the box. It was beautifully organized, serendipity, beautiful stories being told. There was serendipity around the Hilton people and we could cram everybody into the hotel, they owned the Waldorf. It was almost like it was just destined to be a success. There was serendipity on our time, timing, quality of the people, strength of the idea, execution of the plan, the intense emotional neediness of people in New York who were just staggered, it all came together.

But to me, the indispensable parts were Sho and Loen and Jack and Bruce and others. And I have tremendous respect for what Sho and Loen did and they always resisted getting attention for it and credit and I think they just did a helluva job and the timing couldn't have better.

[On the Union Square service] One thing about New York, when the city and those various entities commit to doing something right, it's pretty remarkable because of the high caliber of people working on these things. They had it, with a sound system, to the flowers, to a podium with "City of New York," to the press management—and there were two or three people there making sure that it was being done as a professional thing. It didn't hurt that I had developed a strong relationship with the chief of police at Lower Manhattan.

Bruce walked into this thing thinking, '"Good God, I hope this works out," doesn't know who I am, hasn't worked with me; but everybody stepped up and it came together in ways that nobody anticipated.

[Baruti Artharee's speech at Union Square] When they attacked the World Trade Center, it was indiscriminate and the people that paid the price were black and brown and yellow and . . . when America responds to this attack, they will do it black and white and brown working together. And he was roped into it at the last minute, very graciously agreed to do it, but you could tell that he was moved by the moment. We all finally overlooked the fact that that marvelous violinist missed a few notes, but it was so poignant as he was playing.

APPENDIX F:
LEO NADOLSKE

Interview with the author on March 24, 2021

Among the companies Portland Oregon Visitor Association's Brian McCartin met with during the Flight for Freedom was Paperloop, which owned magazines and other media sources devoted to the paper, pulp, forest, and allied industries. He met with Leo Nadolske, who ran Paperloop's New York office, which had had a "beautiful" view of the Twin Towers. I spoke with Nadolske for this book and while much of his story is not directly related to the Flight for Freedom, I felt his 9/11 experience could provide insight into the emotional state of New Yorkers when the Oregonians came to the city.

I was out of town when it happened. I had just landed in Atlanta. We were flying from Norfolk, Virginia . . . and we're getting off the plane in Atlanta to change over and the director of sales was on the phone with our office. And they said a plane had hit the World Trade Center. At that time, we thought it must have been a small plane. One of the best flights I ever took was from Toronto to La Guardia, and the pilot turned the plane sideways and he pivoted around the South Building and you can see the guy changing the light bulbs. That doesn't happen anymore since 9/11.

We got off the plane [in Atlanta] and there was a bit ruckus going on. He [Nadolske's traveling partner, the director of sales] said, "I don't think we're going anywhere."

They turned all the televisions off in the airport except in the bars. Everybody was jamming the bars. We went to customer service and they said a flight just hit the Pentagon . . . . They told us at customer service they couldn't get out baggage out. The best thing to do, they said, was to try to go downtown and get a hotel room. We got our hotel guy to get us a hotel room in Peachtree Center connected to Macy's. So we had to go buy new clothes for the day, and then there was nothing else to do but sit and wonder. All cell phones were out. All communication had to be via the hotel phone. That was another story. Hotel phones charged lots of money when they realized what was happening. The Westin Hotel, they did a fantastic job.

So Thursday comes, they said the planes were going. We walked into Atlanta Hartsfield airport and it's empty. So we walk up to a skycap and we give him our claim stubs and he said that will be about forty-five minutes. We believe we are never going to see our bags again. Forty-five minutes later, sure enough—we were the second and third bags. It turned out that they had 55,000 people stranded in Atlanta.

Delta did a fantastic job. We got on a line to get back to New York City. We've got flights, but La Guardia, Kennedy, and Newark are still closed. We wound up getting the last train ticket and we took a train back. Twenty-three stops. We pulled into Penn Station and we're getting off the train, we hear all these people applauding. And we're like, "Why are people applauding?" And here comes a bunch of Philadelphia firefighters. And they were covered in soot with all their equipment and they got on the train going back to Philly.

I jumped in a cab and going down Fifth Avenue to Grand Central, there was an F-16 flying overhead. I was like, "Jesus Christ, it's like a war zone." I got on a train, went home, my wife and my two little boys got out of the car and ran up to me. It was one of the sweetest moments of my life.

Harley-Davidson donated police motorcycles and they rode across the George Washington Bridge, took the Harleys all the way to City Hall, and turned them over to Giuliani. Say whatever you want to say about New Yorkers, when the chips are down, they are a resilient people. We don't take shit from anybody. And you can print that.

On the other side of the coin, our office was shut down. I had called the CEO of the company when I was in Atlanta, they were in San Francisco. I said, "If you get a chance, check in on the New York office."

I had a big office and one of the editors for one of the magazines was walking by my office and he happened to see I had the windows open, blinds up. You could see the twin towers. And he said, "There's smoke coming out of the twin towers." So they turned on the news and they're hearing all about it. It's like twenty-some people standing in my office listening to the stereo and watching the building.

Joan Rosenblatt. She was like my assistant. I used to call her my little Jewish buddy. I'd say, "Jo, I took care of that yesterday." She'd say, "How did he know what I was going to say?" At that time, she was probably sixty-five [years old]. She, Joan, goes, "What's that other plane doing?" And as the plane starts turning around and crashing into the building, that's when it hit.

Jane McDermond grabbed Joan and buried her head in her shoulder so she couldn't see it. That's when they decided to leave. Trains were out, cell phones were out. The only way out they had was to walk across the 59th St. Bridge. Then we tried to stay in touch when everything was going to get up in running. I had to get in touch with the facility to see when we could get back in because there was no power.

We knew when we were in Atlanta watching TV in the bar when the one building collapsed how you just freaked out. "You're like, "Oh my God, that's Tower One," and you go into a little bit of a shock. That's when they left. When the first building came down, that's when my building closed. I had all [the employees'] home phone numbers and I called everyone. I used the hotel phone to stay in touch with the office. The hotel bills were like $800 for the phones. And in a hotel survey afterward, I said, "You guys were spectacular, you did a job, couldn't get better, but you soaked us on the phone bills." A guy sent me a check for $600. From the Westin. The Westin Atlanta Peachtree Center did a great thing.

Eventually, you've got to move on. I did go down [to the site] a month after. The guy I was on the trip with, Jay Gorga, he and I jumped on the train and went down to the towers and it was surrounded with chain link fence and it smelled about a block and a half away, it smelled like a freshly extinguished fire in the fireplace. That was something.

We had a guy, he supposedly, ironically, was the first person to die at the top of the twin towers. His name was Father Judge. He was the chaplain—he was a good guy. He was about two blocks from our office and we'd see him once in a while. We were across the street from the firehouse, on 34th. They presented the pope with his fire helmet.

I had a beautiful office, if I looked downtown I could see the twin towers. When the fog was rolling in, I couldn't see the towers anymore. Ironically, I came back from Japan and I took pictures of the twin towers. So I do have pictures of it since they've been gone. I haven't had a chance in twenty years to put them together in a collage.

Going back to the office for the first time. Commuting-wise—you don't look at the other guy, like in the elevator. Certain trains, you do look at another guy, you think, "I can't believe somebody'd go out of the house like that." But nobody ever talks to anybody on the subway. When you got on the subway everybody was going back to work [for the first time], everybody looked at each other, we all knew what we had gone through. We have to move on, the world doesn't stop.

I got into the office, welcomed everybody back. There was a conundrum. I think I took everybody out to lunch, the whole office. And then you start talking: "Who did you know who passed?" I didn't know anybody except I used to work with a gal years ago, her husband was there. He left her a message, he told her this didn't look good, and how much he loved her.

Then I went to a conference in Washington, DC, and heard this group of firemen who were there that day and they were giving their version of what had happened. The guy was standing in the rubble. His friend called him: "I'm in stairwell number two, can you get there to assist us?" Father Judge died from somebody falling from the building [on him]. Somebody picked him up—they knew he was dead, they knew who he was and they carried him to a church right near where it happened. There was a Catholic church there and they laid him at the altar.

I went downtown, like with this pandemic,* all the stores went bankrupt. I'll never forget it. There was a cross made of steel beams [from the World Trade Center] that had been torn down. It's in the 9/11 Museum and I complained to the people that led the museum. I said, "You guys have a lot of guts. You've got the cross that was standing there on the basement floor?" I don't know if they ever moved

---

*This interview took place during the COVID-19 pandemic.

it. I remember seeing that for the first time. Oh my God, I don't f-in' believe it. It's unbelievable.

It was a weird day, a weird time.

I was the senior executive in New York. [Brian McCartin] said he came in to support New York. It's like the only city with the exception of Milwaukee sending the Harley Davidsons, bringing 100 motorcycles into the city, that was something to see. And then Portland.

My mother said, "Pick yourself up by your bootstraps" and that's what people were doing. I think I was responsible for a show we did out in Portland, a trade show at the convention center out there. They were very nice people out there.

The stories. There are nine million stories in the Naked City and that's mine. I could only imagine people in the office, watching them [the towers] come down. There are people crossing the 59th Street Bridge. There's no subways, I don't think the buses were running. But it was a strange time.

The New York Yankees playing for the first time after 9/11 was a milestone for New Yorkers.

The first time after 9/11 they were in Cleveland. They came out on the field, they played the national anthem and a guy [sorry, error in my transcription, perhaps an announcer at the stadium] said to our opponents, seeing the New York Yankees, "Please remember that on 9/11 we were all New Yorkers." The place went crazy.

And then you had that home game with the Mets. It was kind of weird because if I'm not mistaken, it was like the top of the 11th inning, a home run.*

And when the Yankees came back—you can go on YouTube and see it, President Bush came in town and threw out the first pitch. He

---

*The Mets jersey 2016 Hall of Fame electee Mike Piazza wore on Sept. 21, 2001, in the first game played in New York after tragedy befell the United States, continues to serve as an inspiration for fans around the globe. That night, Piazza's dramatic eighth inning home run propelled the Mets to a 3-2 victory over Atlanta at Shea Stadium. "Piazza jersey from first game after 9/11 continues to inspire," National Baseball Hall of Fame, https://baseballhall.org/discover-more/news/hall-of-fame-to-honor-baseball-after-911-with-exhibit, retrieved June 19, 2021.

talked to Derek Jeter, "Got any pointers for me?" [Jeter says] "Yeah, whatever you do, don't bounce it or they'll boo you."

"We don't want that," President Bush said, and then he threw out the first pitch and he hummed it right in there. Everybody was chanting, "USA, USA."

A lot of the doctors from Westchester, the Bronx, Long Island, were rushing to the hospitals in the city volunteering their services and sure enough, there was nobody to bring in. There were no patients, they were all gone. Everybody was jumping in to help anyway—it was personal. In New York, you don't take a lot of things personally, but when it's personal, it's personal. [paraphrasing him]

APPENDIX G:
ORGANIZERS, SUPPORTERS AND VOLUNTEERS

Organizers
Honorary Chair
Gerry Frank, Author of *Where to Find It , Buy It, Eat It in New York*

Co-organizers
Sho Dozono, Chair, Portland Metropolitan Chamber of Commerce
Jack McGowan, Executive Director, Stop Oregon Litter and Vandalism (SOLV)
Bruce Samson, Former General Counsel, NW Natural, and Former Chair, Portland Metropolitan Chamber of Commerce

Finance
George Passadore, President, Oregon Region –Wells Fargo
Jim Rudd, CEO, Ferguson Wellman, Inc.

Media & Public Relations
Len Bergstein, Northwest Strategies
Elisa Dozono, Port of Portland
Elaine Franklin, Political Consultant
John Ray, Media Consultant
Karen Winder, Public Relations Consultant

Meeting & Event Coordination
Val Hubbard, VH Productions

Supporters
Vera Katz, Mayor of the City of Portland

Platinum Corporate Sponsors
American Express   Waldorf Astoria

Major Corporate Sponsors
Delta Air Lines   Intel
United Airlines   Nike
Hilton Hotels   Columbia Sportswear
Azumano Travel/American Express   Evergreen International Airlines

Corporate Sponsors

US Bank
Regence BlueCross BlueShield
 of Oregon
Ater Wynne, LLP
Bank of America
Advantage Sales & Marketing

Ferguson Wellman, Inc.
Wells Fargo
PacifiCorp
RB Pamplin Corp.
IBM-Oregon Division

Corporate and Civic Supporters

Portland Metropolitan Chamber
 of Commerce
Portland Oregon Visitors
 Association (POVA)
Stop Oregon Litter and Vandalism
 (SOLV)
Portland State University
Mayor James D. Torrey,
 City of Eugene
Bend Chamber of Commerce
Medford/Jackson Chambers
 of Commerce

Portland Area Theatre Alliance
 (PATA)
Portland Association of Teachers
The Urban League of Portland
NW Natural
Diane Linn, Chair, Multnomah
County Commission
Melvin Mark Companies
National Conference for Community
 and Justice
Portland Community College
Portland Public Schools
Port of Portland

Local Media Participants

KATU (Ch. 2)	KOIN (Ch. 6)	KXL (AM 750)
KEX (AM 1190)	KPDX Fox 49	Asian Reporter
The Portland Observer	KNRK (FM 94.7)	The Oregonian
KGW (Ch. 8)	KPAM (AM 860)	

New York Protocol Liaison

Nick Fish

Diversity Committee

Gov. Victor Atiyeh (1978-1986)   State Sen. Margaret Carter

Congressional Delegation

Congressman David Wu   Congresswoman Darlene Hooley

State of Oregon

Randall Edwards, Treasurer

Volunteers

Vanessa Blake	Tony Fuerte	Tammie Offia
Bobbie Bond	Sonja Gabriel	Nancy Parrott
Terry Bracy	Bill Harmon	Jeri Plantico
Jessica Brown	Tina Harmon	Lynne Porter
Marilyn Bruner	Jeri Hunt	Cathy Rudd
Maureen Denny	Ari Inayama	Barbara Rummel
Kathy Donikowski	Lynn Koepke	LaVonne Scheckla
Kristin Dozono	Rick Love	Kim Simmie
Loen Dozono	Gregg Macy	Marty Voruz
Jo Earle	Christine Manning	Linda Winter
Cindy Forgue	Judy Myers	

NOTES

"Introduction"

1 Kristen Dozono, interview with the author, April 18, 2021.
2 Courtenay Thompson, "Oregonians Will Travel to N.Y. to Lend Support," *The Oregonian*, September 28, 2001, B7.

"Where They Were: Geography and Emotions"

1 Carl Abbott, "Portland," *The Oregon Encyclopedia*, https://www.oregonencyclopedia.org/articles/portland/#.YLgoSEwpAc8, last updated January 20, 2021; Chet Orloff, "Portland Penny," *The Oregon Encyclopedia*, https://www.oregonencyclopedia.org/articles/portland_penny/#.YLgp3UwpAc8, last updated September 19, 2019; Ann Curry-Stevens and Amanda Cross-Hemmer, *The Native American Community in Multnomah County: An Unsettling Profile*, Executive Summary, 2011, https://www.portlandoregon.gov/civic/article/505489.
2 Carl Abbott, "Columbia River Gorge National Scenic Area," *The Oregon Encyclopedia*, https://www.oregonencyclopedia.org/articles/columbia_gorge_national_scenic_act/#.YLg_cEwpAc8, last updated March 17, 2018.
3 Robert W. Hadlow, "Columbia River Highway," *The Oregon Encyclopedia*, https://www.oregonencyclopedia.org/articles/columbia_river_highway/#.YLhC9UwpAc8, last updated March 17, 2018.
4 David Lewis, "Willamette Valley Treaties," *The Oregon Encyclopedia*, https://www.oregonencyclopedia.org/articles/willamette_valley_treaties/#.YLhepEwpAc9, last updated January 20, 2021.
5 The Willamette Valley Visitors Association, "Willamette Valley Food Trails Showcase the Region's Bounty," *Willamette Valley Oregon Wine Country*, retrieved June 3, 2021, https://www.oregonwinecountry.org/food-trails-showcase-regions-bounty.
6 "Oregon Economic Mainstays in the Late 1800s," Oregon Secretary of State, https://sos.oregon.gov/archives/exhibits/constitution/Pages/after-economy.aspx, retrieved on June 3, 2021; Emilly Prado, "Explore Northeast Oregon's Indigenous Cultures," *TravelOregon*, May 22, 2019, https://traveloregon.com/things-to-do/trip-ideas/favorite-trips/explore-northeast-oregons-indigenous-cultures/.

National Park Service, "John Day Valley Rock Formations, John Day Fossil Beds National Monument," nps.gov, https://www.nps.gov/media/photo/view.htm?id=cd3bed45-1d4c-4cfd-8207-2c938584ec41, retrieved June 3, 2021. The site provides the following description and history:

Prior to Euro-American settlement of the John Day Valley in the late nineteenth century, the area between the Southern Columbia Plateau and the Northern Great Basin was occupied and used by several American Indian peoples, including the Tenino and Umatilla, who were historically part of the Columbia Plateau peoples, and the peoples of the northern Great Basin, the Northern Paiute. Territories claimed by these groups in the upper John Day Valley were frequently disputed and boundaries fluctuated over time. However, documentation indicates that the most recent pre-contact occupant of the Picture Gorge area was the Hunipui band of the Northern Paiute, who wintered in the area and had a seasonal hunting, fishing, and gathering economy..

7   Barbara Tricarico, *Oregon* (Atglen, PA: Schiffer Publishing Ltd., 2020): 104–105; "Your Smith Rock State Park Guide," SmithRock.com, https://smithrock.com/, retrieved June 3, 2021; Central Oregon LandWatch, "How we are helping Jefferson County farming families," October 23, 2018, https://www.centraloregonlandwatch. org/update/2018/10/23/how-we-are-helping-jefferson-county-farming-families.

8   Not wet like the Willamette Valley, neither is Southern Oregon as parched as Eastern Oregon; average annual precipitation is about thirty inches, and that includes a bit of snowfall. But in the summer, it's hot. As the rest of the state, Southern Oregon offers lots of outdoor activities. Joanne B. Mulcahy, "Southern Oregon [Oregon Folklife: Our Living Traditions Folklife in Oregon]," *Oregon History Project*, https:// www.oregonhistoryproject.org/narratives/oregon-folklife-our-living-traditions/ folklife-in-oregon/southern-oregon/#.YLl-bUwpCOs, 2005, updated and revised by OHP Staff, retrieved June 3, 2021.

9   The OSF grew out of the late-nineteenth-century Chautauqua movement to bring culture and entertainment to rural areas. In 2012, the OSF's "New Theatre" became the Thomas Theatre (effective 2013) after donors made a generous contribution in memory of Peter Thomas, longtime OSF Development Director, who died in March 2010. The OSF wrote that Thomas "graced us with his presence and skill as a leader of our development department for twenty-one years." I went to high school with then "Pete" Thomas, who was a leader and hero to us younger students even then—I, a lowly freshman and he, a senior. Thirty years later when I was living in Oregon, I caught up with him again in Ashland and he could not have been nicer. I am so grateful to have reconnected with him. Oregon Shakespeare Festival, retrieved before February 19, 2021, https://www.osfashland. org/en/company/our-history/performance-spaces/thomas.aspx. For the history of the Oregon Shakespeare Festival, see Oregon Shakespeare Festival, "Ashland and the Festival," *Oregon Shakespeare Festival*, retrieved before February 19, 2021, https://www.osfashland.org/en/company/our-history/ashland-festival.aspx.

"By the Numbers: Oregon and New York"

1   Sources for table data: U.S. Department of Commerce, Economics and Statistics Administration, U.S. Census Bureau, Profiles of General Demographic Characteristics 2000 Census of Population and Housing (New York, May 2001), https://www2.census.gov/library/publications/2001/dec/2kh36.pdf. U.S. Department of Commerce, Economics and Statistics Administration, U.S. Census Bureau, Profiles of General Demographic Characteristics 2000 Census of Population and Housing (Oregon, May 2001), https://www2.census.gov/ library/publications/2001/dec/2kh41.pdf. According to the 2000 U.S. Census, New York City (all boroughs) was the largest urban center in the country. Its population density was extremely above average; Oregon's population density was below average, as was Portland's. United States Census Bureau, Decennial Census Historical Facts (2000), retrieved April 20, 2021, https://www.census.gov/ programs-surveys/decennial-census/decade/decennial-facts.2000.html. Portland State University. Population Research Center; Cai, Qian; and Hough, George C. Jr., "2001 Oregon Population Report" (2002). Oregon Population Estimates and Reports. 3. https://pdxscholar.library.pdx.edu/populationreports/3.

"An Idea Becomes Reality"

1 Sally Donnelly, "The Day the FAA Stopped the World," *Time*, September 14, 2001, http://content.time.com/time/nation/article/0,8599,174912,00.html.

2 Robert Goldfield, "Chamber directors OK combination with APP," *Portland Business Journal*, January 13, 2002 Updated Jan 13, 2002, 9:00pm PST, https://www.bizjournals.com/portland/stories/2002/01/14/story8.html; Danielle Frost, "Sho Dozono retires after 21 years from Community Fund Board of Trustees," *smok signӘlz*, December 28, 2018. https://www.smokesignals.org/articles/2018/12/28/sho-dozono-retires-after-21-years-from-community-fund-board-of-trustees/.

3 Much of the discussion of the Dozonos' development of the Flight for Freedom in this chapter is based on Loen Dozono's notes and journal from that period, which are in her possession.

4 Jeri Hunt memo to All Azumano and Azumano/Away Staff, "Terrorist Attacks," September 11, 2001. Photocopies in author's files.

5 Azumano Travel/American Express memo to All Corporate Accounts, "Important Notice," September 11, 2001. Photocopies in author's files.

6 Sho Dozono, "Memo to Staff," September 12, 2001. Photocopies in author's files.

7 NATO press release, "Statement by the North Atlantic Council," 11 September 2001, https://www.nato.int/docu/pr/2001/p01-122e.htm.

8 NATO press release, "Statement by the North Atlantic Council," 12 September 2001, https://www.nato.int/docu/pr/2001/p01-124e.htm.

9 Suzanne Daley, "After the Attacks: The Alliance; For First Time, NATO Invokes Joint Defense Pact With U.S," September 13, 2001, https://www.nytimes.com/2001/09/13/us/after-attacks-alliance-for-first-time-nato-invokes-joint-defense-pact-with-us.html; European Union, Special Council Meeting General Affairs, Brussels, September 12, 2001, p. 3.

10 Warren Hoge, "After the Attacks: West; Outpouring of Grief and Sympathy for Americans Is Seen Throughout Europe and Elsewhere," *The New York Times*, September 14, 2001, https://www.nytimes.com/2001/09/14/us/after-attacks-west-outpouring-grief-sympathy-for-americans-seen-throughout.html

11 Agencies, "Worldwide chaos as airlines struggle to maintain services," September 12, 2001, https://www.independent.companyuk/news/world/americas/worldwide-chaos-as-airlines-struggle-to-maintain-services-9153433.html, retrieved February 29, 2020.

12 Other speakers at the service whose contributions Loen described: "A woman spoke of having lived in the Middle East for many years and how the name "bin Laden" to her meant one of the wealthiest, most generous families in that country, very respected. And the tragedy that one son had possibly brought such shame to them all. Yet, the need to pray for all of them . . . There were maybe five speakers. Most had words of hope and forgiveness."

13 Minidoka is now a National Historic Site. The Pearl Harbor attack intensified existing hostility towards Japanese Americans. As wartime hysteria mounted, President Roosevelt signed Executive Order 9066 forcing over 120,000 West Coast persons of Japanese ancestry (Nikkei) to leave their homes, jobs, and lives behind, forcing them into one of ten prison camps spread across the nation because of their ethnicity. National Park Service, "Minidoka National Historic Site. History & Culture," NPS.gov, https://www.nps.gov/miin/index.htm https://www.nps.gov/miin/learn/historyculture/index.htm, accessed March 10, 2021; Craig Collisson, "Japanese American Wartime Incarceration in Oregon," *The Oregon Encyclopedia*. https://www.oregonencyclopedia.org/articles/japanese_internment/, retrieved March 8, 2021. Under the administration of President George H.W. Bush and the Civil Liberties Act of 1988, Japanese received reparations and a formal apology from the U.S. government.

14   "Japanese Envoy Feted At Oregon Trade Talks," *The New York Times*, February 12, 1974, https://www.nytimes.com/1974/02/12/archives/japanese-envoy-feted-at-oregon-trade-talks-jokes-about-governor.html.

15   Richard Read," George Azumano, founder of Azumano Travel, dies at 95 after a life working to improve U.S.-Japan relations," *The Oregonian/OregonLive*, posted December 11, 2013, updated January 10, 2019, https://www.oregonlive.com/business/2013/12/george_azumano_founder_of_azum.html.

16   Rose City Funeral Home, "George I. Azumano June 9, 1918–December 9, 2013 (age 95)," https://www.rosecityfuneralhome.com/notices/George-Azumano, retrieved March 8, 2021.

17   George Azumano, "Epworth United Methodist Church (Portland), *The Oregon Encyclopedia*, https://www.oregonencyclopedia.org/articles/epworth_united_methodist_church_portland_/#.YEcEptxOkc8, retrieved March 9, 2021.

18   "Alpha Delta Phi Fraternity: Building the Entire Man: Social, Moral, Intellectual," Alpha Delta Phi website, https://www.alphadeltaphi.org/, retrieved May 22, 2021.

19   Thomas Boyd, "Money Issues Linger from Dozono's Past," *The Oregonian*, posted April 24, 2008, updated March 27, 2019, https://www.oregonlive.com/oregonianextra/2008/04/money_issues_linger_from_dozon.html; Nigel Jaquiss, "Sho Dozono's Rules," *Willamette Week*, https://www.wweek.com/portland/article-1426-sho-dozonos-rules.html, published October 29, 2002, updated January 24, 2017; Laura Del Rosso, "Oregon agent's 'Freedom' trip brings 900 to NYC," October 4, 2001. https://www.travelweekly.com/Travel-News/Travel-Agent-Issues/Oregon-agent-s-Freedom-trip-brings-900-to-NYC; Courtenay Thompson, "Dozono leads Oregonians to New York," *The Oregonian*, October 4, 2001.

20   In 1990, Oregonians had voted for a new property tax cap that shifted education funding away from local property taxes to the state, which began a decline in school funding. Two years later they voted down a sales tax dedicated to funding schools. (The state has never had a sales tax.) Even though lottery revenues went, in part, to education, Oregon's school system was declining. In 1996, the city was facing a $15 million education-budget shortfall.

       In 1995, Sho co-founded the Portland School Foundation with former gubernatorial candidate Ron Saxton and Cynthia Guyer, who became its executive director. As Saxton tells the story, late one Friday night in 1996 Sho called him, upset about [looming] teacher layoffs. "Sho couldn't wait; he called a breakfast Saturday morning at Zell's," Saxton recalled. "He said, 'We're going to have a march a month from now with 30,000.'"

       The others thought that after four to five months of planning, they might be able to attract 2,000 people. But Dozono persisted in his belief that they could attract 30,000 people. (The word "persistent" may be the adjective most commonly attached to Sho.) A month later, Governor John Kitzhaber and his predecessors led 30,000 people through Portland for more than making up the shortfall.

       "We just wanted to show the community not only how individual teachers and parents and grandparents support the school—we had corporate sponsors as well," Sho told *The Portland Tribune* in 2006. Sponsors included Nike and Wells Fargo & Company, along with the Michael Jordan Foundation. The $11 million they raised saved more than 200 teaching positions, said Guyer.

       Jennifer Anderson, "School-Funding Pros Go for the Bucks Again," *Portland Tribune*, January 10, 2006, https://sparkaction.org/content/school-funding-pros-go-bucks-again; Meg Sommerfeld, "30,000 Rally for More Aid in Ore.," *Education Week*, June 12, 1996, https://www.edweek.org/policy-politics/30-000-rally-for-more-aid-in-ore/1996/06.

21   Joe Sharkey, "After the Attacks: The Travelers; Tighter Airport Security Will Slow Business Fliers," *The New York Times*, September 13, 2001, https://www.nytimes.com/2001/09/13/us/after-attacks-travelers-tighter-airport-security-will-slow-business-fliers.html.

22 Pam Belluck, "After the Attacks: Getting There; Renting Wheels and Riding Rails as Skies Stay Off Limits," *The New York Times*, September 13, 2001, https://www.nytimes.com/2001/09/13/us/after-attacks-getting-there-renting-wheels-riding-rails-skies-stay-off-limits.html.

23 Michael Harrison, "Airline collapses amid $10bn industry losses," *The Independent*, September 15, 2001, https://www.independent.companyuk/news/uk/home-news/airline-collapses-amid-10bn-industry-losses-9131330.html.

24 After the Attacks: Getting There; Renting Wheels and Riding Rails as Skies Stay Off Limits, Pam Belluck, September 13, 2001, Section A, Page 22, https://www.nytimes.com/2001/09/13/us/after-attacks-getting-there-renting-wheels-riding-rails-skies-stay-off-limits.html

25 Joseph B. Treaster, "After the Attacks: The Liability; Airlines Seek to Limit Lawsuits Over Attacks," *The New York Times*, September 14, 2001, https://www.nytimes.com/2001/09/14/us/after-the-attacks-the-liability-airlines-seek-to-limit-lawsuits-over-attacks.html.

26 James Barron, "Bush Says Attack Was 'First War of the 21st Century,'" *The New York Times*, September 13, 2001 (online only), https://www.nytimes.com/2001/09/13/nyregion/bush-says-attack-was-first-war-of-the-21st-century.html.

27 "Silence as Europe Mourns Dead," CNN.com, September 14, 2001, Posted: 6:22 AM EDT, http://edition.cnn.com/2001/WORLD/europe/09/14/europe.mourning.0610/index.html.

28 Dan Barry, "After the Attacks: The Vigils; Surrounded by Grief, People Around the World Pause and Turn to Prayer," September 15, 2001, https://www.nytimes.com/2001/09/15/us/after-attacks-vigils-surrounded-grief-people-around-world-pause-turn-prayer.html. Also Paul Vallely, "A Silent World, United in Grief," *The Independent*, 15 September 2001. https://www.independent.companyuk/news/world/americas/a-silent-world-united-in-grief-5364173.html.

29 *Irish America* Staff, "Irish National Day of Mourning," December / January 2002, https://irishamerica.com/2001/12/irelands-national-day-of-mourning/.

30 Independent News and Media, one of the nation's largest media conglomerates, donated its newspaper sales that day to a fund for the families of the victims, which amounted to more than 120,000 punts.
   "National Day of Mourning for Victims of 911," Ireland XO, 14, 2001, https://irelandxo.com/ireland-xo/history-and-genealogy/timeline/national-day-mourning-victims-911. (From the website: "Ireland Reaching Out (Ireland XO) is a volunteer-based, non-profit initiative which builds vibrant, lasting links between the global Irish Diaspora and parishes of origin in Ireland."); A short news clip from Irish television with interviews of Irish people at the Embassy that day is touching: https://www.rte.ie/archives/2016/0830/812866-national-day-of-mourning/.

31 Ian Christopher McCaleb, CNN Washington Bureau, "Bush Tours Ground Zero in Lower Manhattan," CNN.com, September 14, 2001, http://edition.cnn.com/2001/US/09/14/bush.terrorism/; Robert D. McFadden, "After the Attacks: The President; Bush Leads Prayer, Visits Aid Crews; Congress Backs Use of Armed Force," *The New York Times*, September 15, 2001, https://www.nytimes.com/2001/09/15/us/after-attacks-president-bush-leads-prayer-visits-aid-crews-congress-backs-use.html; Dean E. Murphy, "After the Attacks: The Reaction; Front-Line Workers Are Happy to See the Commander in Chief," *The New York Times*, September 15, 2001, https://www.nytimes.com/2001/09/15/us/after-attacks-reaction-front-line-workers-are-happy-see-commander-chief.html.

32 David Stabler, "James DePreist: Scenes from a musical life," *The Oregonian*, posted February 8, 2013, updated January 10, 2019, https://www.oregonlive.com/performance/2013/02/james_depreist_scenes_from_a_m.html.

33 Murry Sidlin, Email to the author about the September 14 Oregon Symphony "In Memoriam" concert, May 23, 2021. See also "Behind the Scenes of the In Memoriam Concert," Oregon Symphony Orchestra *The Reprise* newsletter, undated, fall 2001.

34 Kim Campbell, "New York Times Portraits Resonate Coast to Coast," *The Christian Science Monitor*, December 6, 2001, https://www.questia.com/read/1P2-32592670/new-york-times-portraits-resonate-coast-to-coast. "In October, the paper published a column in which its ombudsman, Dan Hortsch, raised the question of when The Oregonian should stop. When he checked his voice mail that afternoon, he found sixty-eight messages. Hundreds followed. The gist was: Don't stop."; Janny Scott, "A Nation Challenged: The Portraits; Closing a Scrapbook Full of Life and Sorrow," *The New York Times*, December 31, 2001, https://www.nytimes.com/2001/12/31/nyregion/a-nation-challenged-the-portraits-closing-a-scrapbook-full-of-life-and-sorrow.html.

35 "Portraits of Grief" interactive feature, *The New York Times*, https://archive.nytimes.com/www.nytimes.com/interactive/us/sept-11-reckoning/portraits-of-grief.html#/portraits-of-grief/P/1626, retrieved on May 27, 2021.

36 Sho Dozono, "Update for Staff," memo, September 18, 2001. Photocopy in author's files.

37 R. W. Apple Jr., "A Nation Challenged: News Analysis; A Clear Message: 'I Will Not Relent,'" *The New York Times*, September 21, 2001, Section A, Page 1 https://www.nytimes.com/2001/09/21/world/a-nation-challenged-news-analysis-a-clear-message-i-will-not-relent.html; Elizabeth Bumiller, "A Nation Challenged: The Overview; Bush Pledges Attack on Afghanistan Unless It Surrenders bin Laden Now; He Creates Cabinet Post for Security," *The New York Times*, September 21, 2001, https://www.nytimes.com/2001/09/21/world/nation-challenged-overview-bush-pledges-attack-afghanistan-unless-it-surrenders.html; eMediaMillWorks, "Text: President Bush Addresses the Nation," *The Washington Post* online, September 20, 2001, https://www.washingtonpost.com/wp-srv/nation/specials/attacked/transcripts/bushaddress_092001.html.

38 Sho Dozono, "The Plan," memo, September 21, 2001. Photocopy in author's files.

39 Jack McGowan, interview with the author, April 10, 2021. Unless otherwise noted, all quotations by Jack McGowan are taken from this interview.

40 Len Bergstein, group interview with the author, May 13, 2021. Unless otherwise noted, all quotations by Bergstein are taken from this conversation.

41 John Ray, interview with the author, July 22, 2003. Unless otherwise noted, all quotations by John Ray are taken from this interview.

42 Gerry Frank, interview with the author, February 27, 2021.

43 Sho Dozono, "Thank You!," memo to Corporate Accounts, September 24, 2001. Photocopy in author's files.

44 Elaine Franklin, interview with the author, April 27, 2021.

45 "New York Airlift: Draft of Presentation Speech," Hilton Hotel, Portland, September 24, 2001, 3:00 p.m. Photocopy in author's files. Speech for presentation by Sho Dozono.

46 Maureen Denny, email to Jeri Hunt, "FW: about the people," October 4, 2001. Photocopy in the author's files.

47 Jack McGowan, Sho Dozono, Elaine Franklin, and John Ray, interview with the author, April 29, 2021. Recording in author's files.

48 Milt Freudenheim, "Empty Hotels and Ships Offering Lots of Discounts," September 25, 2001, https://www.nytimes.com/2001/09/25/business/nation-challenged-destinations-empty-hotels-ships-offering-lots-discounts.html.

49 Myriam DiGiovanni, "Flight for Freedom touches down in the Big Apple with Oregon CU staffers," *Credit Union Times*, October 16, 2001, https://www.cutimes.com/2001/10/16/flight-for-freedom-touches-down-in-the-big-apple-with-oregon-c-staffers/.

50 Sho Dozono, "Recovery," memo, September 25, 2001. Photocopy in the author's files.

51 Themes included, "'Flight for Freedom' is both symbolic and practical," "[W]e will not be cowered [sic: cowed] by atrocity." Len Bergstein, "Themes," memo to Communications Team, September 25, 2001. Photocopy in author's files.

52 Loen's notes also state, "Ray Mathes, the executive director of the Citizens Crime Commission also said he was on board, and that it would be safe."

53 Courtenay Thompson, "Memories Amid the Ruins," *The Oregonian*, October 11, 2001.

54 Vera Katz, interview with the author, July 25, 2003.

55 Gordon H. Smith, interview with the author, March 15, 2021.

56 Doug Irving, "Portland Plans NYC 'Flight for Freedom,'" kgw.com, September 26, 2001, http://www.kgw.com/kgwnews/terrornorthwet_story.html?StoryID=27591.

57 "News Conference, Wednesday, September 26, 10 AM, Remarks for Sho Dozono," photocopy in author's files.

58 John Ray, Len Bergstein; Loen and Sho Dozono, and Nancy Parrott, group interview with the author. May 13, 2021.

59 Chris Sullivan, interview with the author, February 20, 2021.

60 Bill Cooper, interview with the author, June 17, 2021.

61 G. Jeffrey MacDonald, "This Christmas, Some See Virtue in Buying Sprees," *The Christian Science Monitor*, December 5, 2001, https://www.csmonitor.com/2001/1205/p1s4-ussc.html.

62 Mitch Goldstone, "From Irvine CA For: To Gerry Frank and Sho Dozono," email to Gerry Frank and Sho Dozono, October 11, 2001. Photocopy in the author's files.

63 George Pataki, interview with the author, May 13, 2021.

64 "Portland ♥ New York," *The Oregonian*, September 29, 2001, www.oregonlive.com/printer/printer/ . . . xsl?/base/editorial/10017645232326691.xml, retrieved on October 2, 2001.

65 Nancy Parrott, interview with the author, March 3, 2021.

66 Rick D. Love, email to the author, July 23, 2003.

67 Debra Diane-Jenness, email to the author, April 19, 2002. She stated that she was writing "for the Jenness Family, Gordon, Debra-Diane and Tyler."

68 Patricia Schechter, interview with the author, May 28, 2021.

69 Rachel Monahan, "Commissioner Nick Fish's Death Leaves Portland Grieving— and City Hall Changed," *Willamette Week*, January 8, 2020, https://www.wweek.com/news/city/2020/01/08/commissioner-nick-fishs-death-leaves-portland-grieving-and-city-hall-changed/.

70 Anna Griffin, "Portland Commissioner Nick Fish Dies at 61," Oregon Public Broadcasting, January 2, 2020, https://www.opb.org/news/article/nick-fish-portland-dead-obituary/.

71 Ann Nice, interview with the author, December 9, 2020.

72 Cliff Madison, email to the author, May 31, 2021.

73 John Ray and Jack McGowan; also Sho Dozono, Elaine Franklin; group interview with the author. April 29, 2021. Recording in the author's files.

74 "Flight for Freedom Exceeds Expectations: Over 600 Oregonians on 62 Flights to Travel to New York City Weekend of Oct. 6," press release, September 30, 2001, photocopy in author's files.

75 Amy Solomonson, interview with the author, October 3, 2001.

76 Paula Becks, email to flightforfreedom@azumano.com, October 13, 2001. Photocopy in the author's files. Becks added an idea that she "heard from a gal on our trip": "Perhaps some NYC folks would like to visit us, and we could make room in our homes for them."

77 Joseph Spinnato, interview with the author, c. October 3, 2001.

78 Jack McGowan, group meeting April 29, 2021.

79 Marla Nuttman, interview with the author, January 24, 2021.

80 Senator Ron Wyden, speaking on the Flight for Freedom, 107th Congress, 1st sess., *Congressional Record* 147, No. 132 (October 4, 2001): S10271–2.

"Why They Went"

1   Barbara Shaw, email to the author, April 27, 2021.
2   Associated Press, "800 Oregonians Converge on Big Apple," CNN.com, October 3, 2001, http://www.cnn.com/2001/TRAVEL/NEWS/10/03/rec.attacks.ny.trip.ap/index.html.
3   Melissa Goodwin, interview with the author, October 4, 2001.
4   Joseph E. Weston, interview with the author, May 14, 2021.
5   Allen Oswalt, interview with the author, March 19, 2021.
6   Merritt Marthaller, fax to the author, November 12, 2001.
7   Al O'Brien, interview with the author, November 23, 2020.
8   Courtenay Thompson, "From Oregon, with Love," *The Oregonian*, October 7, 2001, D6.
9   Baruti Artharee, email to the author, May 11, 2021.
10 Kathleen and Philip Peters, interview with the author, July 31, 2003.
11 John Baker, "East Coast Help Takes Flight," *Woodburn Independent*, October 3, 2001, 1 and 2.
12 John Baker, "Mission Accomplished," *Woodburn Independent*, October 17, 2001, 1 and 2.
13 Genevieve Voorhees, interview with the author, October 4, 2001.
14 Alexia Halen, interview with the author, November 28, 2020.
15 Jane Meskill, interview with the author, November 25, 2020.
16 Don Yule, interview with the author, October 4, 2001.
17 Thomas Wiebe, "Oregon loves New York: memories of 9/11," *The Oregon Scribbler*, September 11, 2011, https://oregonscribbler.com/remembering-911-oregon-loves-new-york/, September 11, 2011, retrieved June 12, 2021.
18 Bill Cooper, interview with the author, June 17, 2021.
19 Glenn Kloster, interview with the author, October 4, 2001.
20 Sandra Kempel, interview with the author, July 25, 2003.
21 Myriam DiGiovanni, "Flight for Freedom Touches Down in the Big Apple with Oregon CU Staffers," *Credit Union Times*, October 16, 2001. https://www.cutimes.com/2001/10/16/flight-for-freedom-touches-down-in-the-big-apple-with-oregon-cu-staffers/, retrieved March 31, 2021.
22 Joel Gallob, "Local residents head to New York City," *News-Times* (Newport, Ore.), October 5, 2001, A1 and A9.
23 Ann Nice, interview with the author, December 9, 2020.
24 Judith Spitzer, "Molalla, Colton Contingent Arrives Back from New York Mission," *The Molalla Pioneer*, October 13, 2001, 1.
25 Lance and Marla Nuttman, interview with the author, January 24, 2021.
26 Gregg Zoroya, "Tourist spending defies terrorism," *USA Today*, October 3, 2001, 1D, 6D.
27 Stephanie Hinshaw, essay on the Flight for Freedom, October 15, 2001; contained in Margaret Hinshaw, email to Cindy Forgue, October 26, 2001, in the author's files.
28 []Interview with the author, July 25, 2003.
29 "Oregon Delegation and Dollars Headed to New York," *Hells Canyon Journal* (Hells Canyon, Ore.), October 10, 2001, 14. Also press release, "State Treasurer Joins Delegation to New York," October 3, 2001.
30 Ron Saxton, "New York City Greets Oregon Family Visitors with Wide-Open Arms," *Portland Tribune*, October 9, 2001.
31 Doug Irving, "Portland Plans NYC 'Flight for Freedom,'" KGW.com, September 26, 2001.
32 Rachel Gerber, "Life-Changing Visit to the Streets of New York," *The Oregonian*, October 10, 2001.

33 "Hundreds of Oregonians Sign Up for Flight for Freedom," *The Portland Business Journal*, October 1, 2001, page number unknown.
34 Cameron Platt, interview with the author, June 6, 2021.
35 Mary Platt, interview with the author, May 24, 2021.
36 Kathi Karnosh, interview with the author, February 23, 2021.
37 Joyce Willing, interview with the author, January 9, 2021.

"The Adventure Begins"

1 Ten years later, *The Oregonian* would publish a guest column by Sho and Loen Dozono, and Bruce Samson, which was actually letter they had written to New York Mayor Michael Bloomberg, who had received criticism for strongly supporting a Muslim community center and mosque to be constructed two blocks from Ground Zero. Their letter included the following:

"Three weeks after 9/11, when a group of Oregonians flew to New York to show moral support at a time when the rest of the country was paralyzed in fear, our efforts were appreciated in a broad way. In the mad scramble of organizing those 1,000 travelers, several of the group leaders felt it important to our mission to include a member of the local Muslim community to travel with us.

"Even though it wasn't publicized, it was an important element of what we felt needed to be part of our expression of caring and hope. We are in the planning stages of a return trip to New York for the 10th anniversary 9/11 commemoration next year.

"In the midst of this planning and among the inquiries to participate in such an event has come an e-mail expressing strong negative opinions about the new construction project.

"In the days after 9/11 the local and national Japanese American communities (of which we are a part) undertook to support the Muslim and Arab American community when there was a national debate that even touched upon rounding up and incarcerating that group.

"During WW II, when war-time hysteria caused 110,000 West Coast Japanese Americans to be incarcerated—it was a seizure of civil rights under the rationale of fear. We took a stand with them so that it would not be repeated.

"We saw the Flight for Freedom as a statement against the fear that terrorists count on creating . . . not as a statement against a religious or ethnic group. We hope that most of the 1,000 Oregonians who traveled with us nine years ago would share this same value.

"We commend you for your stand. We stand with you.

"Sho and Loen Dozono, and Bruce Samson are co-chairs of the Flight For Freedom project."

Sho Dozono, Loen Dozono, and Bruce Samson, "NYC Muslim Center: Bloomberg Stand Deserves Support," *The Oregonian*, https://www.oregonlive.com/opinion/2010/08/nyc_muslim_center_bloomberg_st.html. Posted August 18, 2010, updated January 10, 2019.

2 Loen Dozono notes and photocopy of note in binder of Flight for Freedom documentation in Sho Dozono's private papers. This note states that Cordelia Wilkes would be selling the rest of the pins she was making and donating the proceeds; no organization for donation stated.

3 Stephanie Hinshaw, essay on the Flight for Freedom, October 15, 2001; contained in Margaret Hinshaw, email to Cindy Forgue, October 26, 2001, photocopy in the author's files.

4 Alexia Halen, interview with the author, November 28, 2020.

5 Debra-Diane Jenness, email to the author, April 19, 2002. All quotations taken from this email.

6   Bill Cooper, interview with the author, June 17, 2001.
7   Courtenay Thompson, "From Oregon, With Love," *The Oregonian*, October 7, 2001.
8   Elaine Franklin would say later that among some of the organizers it was determined that the most dangerous place to be in New York City during the Flight for Freedom trip—despite the terrorist threat—was between Rep. David Wu and a camera.
9   Rebecca Webb, "Charitable Passengers Board Flight with Case of Nerves, Good Will," *Portland Tribune*, October 9, 2001.
10   Jackie Young, interview with the author, January 31, 2021.
11   Mary Platt, interview with the author, May 24, 2021.
12   Elaine Franklin, interview with the author, April 27, 2021.
13   Todd Davidson, interview with the author, February 11, 2021.
14   Leslie Parker, interview with the author, February 3, 2021.
15   Clarice Schorzman, "A Letter Home," *The Molalla Pioneer*, October 13, 2001, 2.
16   Jack McGowan, Sho Dozono, Elaine Franklin, Jack McGowan, and John Ray. Group interview with the author, April 29, 2021. Recording in the author's files.
17   Rob Platt, interview with the author, May 30, 2021.
18   Lance and Marla Nuttman, interview with the author, January 24, 2021.
19   Barbara Ross and William Sherman, "972 Oregonians Fly Here 'Cuz They Love N.Y.," *New York Daily News*, October 7, 2001, page number unknown.
20   Jack McGowan, interview with the author, April 10, 2021.
21   John B. Webster, "Oregonians Made True Friends in New York," *Hood River News*, October 13, 2001, page unknown.

"Mourning, Feasting, and an Unexpected Challenge"

1   Courtenay Thompson, "From Oregon, With Love," *The Oregonian*, October 7, 2001, D6.
2   Amy Waldman, "After the Attacks: The Memorials; Grief Is Lessened by Sharing and Solace From Strangers," *The New York Times*, September 14, 2001, https://www.nytimes.com/2001/09/14/us/after-attacks-memorials-grief-lessened-sharing-solace-strangers.html.
3   Harriet Senie, "Mourning in Protest: Spontaneous Memorials and the Sacralization of Public Space," in J. Santino, *Spontaneous Shrines and the Public Memorialization of Death*, (US: Palgrave Macmillan), 2006, 47 and 48. Senie captures the importance of Union Square and the activities there after 9/11:
     "There were personal expressions in poetry and prose written on the ground or on the huge rolls of paper provided for that purpose. American flags, which soon became ubiquitous throughout the city, appeared draped in front of the statue of George Washington and in his hand. Henry Kirke Brown's sculpture, the second equestrian monument to be cast in the U.S. and the city's first outdoor bronze sculpture, dedicated on July 4,1856, functioned as the symbolic locus of the state and national power. Covered with comments of love and peace, the statue conveyed a decidedly mixed message.
     "The crowds that gathered around the clock at Union Square appeared intent to create a communal space, a place providing comfort in numbers in the most uncertain and frightening of times. As one young man remarked, "You get a little hope in togetherness." In a few days the nature of the gathering at Union Square changed, becoming more of a festival reminiscent of 60s happenings. Early on the Department of Parks in consultation with the Art Commission decided to remove the graffiti from George Washington and restore Union Square to its pre-9/11 state. This process of desacralization, what Kenneth E. Foote calls the rectification of a site, implies "no lasting positive or negative meaning" will be associated with it. And, indeed, that has been the case."

For more on the ubiquity of the American flag after 9/11, which was evident not only in New York City but across the country, see photos in *The New York Times*, September 14, 2001, A1, A14–15, with the captions: "Flying the Colors: Americans responded to the attacks by displaying the flag"; "A Symbol Offers Comfort On New York's Streets;" "Americans at home and overseas confronted this week's terror attacks with one simple gesture, flying the flag. The displays seem as much acts of defiance as of patriotism."

4   Michael Kimmelman, "In a Square, A Sense of Unity," New York Times, September 19, 2001, https://www.nytimes.com/2001/09/19/arts/in-a-square-a-sense-of-unity-a-homegrown-memorial-brings-strangers-together.html?searchResultPosition=3.

5   Debra-Diane Jenness, email to author, April 19, 2002. All quotations taken from this email.

6   Jack McGowan, interview with the author, June 19, 2021.

7   Cliff Madison, interview with the author, January 18, 2002.

8   Personal notes in author's files taken while attending the service.

9   Sally Ruth Bourrie, notes taken at Union Square service, October 7, 2001.

10   Courtenay Thompson, "Childhood's Memories of War Arise Amid the Ruins," *The Oregonian*, October 11, 2001, B7.

11   St. Francis of Assisi, "Canticle of the Creatures," 1225, as quoted in *Franciscan Seculars: From Gospel to Life—From Life to Gospel*, http://franciscanseculars.com/the-canticle-of-the-creatures/, retrieved June 19, 2021. "While suffering intensely from his physical infirmities, he announced: 'I wish to compose a new hymn about the Lord's creatures, of which we make daily use, without which we cannot live, and with which the human race greatly offends its Creator.'" Regis J. Armstrong, *Francis of Assisi, Early Documents: Vol. 1, The Saint* (Hyde Park New York: New City Press, 2002), 113, quoted in *Franciscan Seculars*, above.

12   In his 1990 Message for World Day of Peace, St. John Paul II described his purpose:
      "In 1979, I proclaimed Saint Francis of Assisi as the heavenly Patron of those who promote ecology. He offers Christians an example of genuine and deep respect for the integrity of creation. As a friend of the poor who was loved by God's creatures, Saint Francis invited all of creation—animals, plants, natural forces, even Brother Sun and Sister Moon—to give honour and praise to the Lord. The poor man of Assisi gives us striking witness that when we are at peace with God we are better able to devote ourselves to building up that peace with all creation which is inseparable from peace among all peoples.
      "It is my hope that the inspiration of Saint Francis will help us to keep ever alive a sense of "fraternity" with all those good and beautiful things which Almighty God has created."
      John Paul II, "Peace with God the Creator, Peace with All of Creation," Message for World Day of Peace, January 1, 1990, as quoted in Cathal Duddy, OFM, "St. Francis—A Guide for Nature Lovers & Ecologists," *Praying Nature with St. Francis of Assisi*, http://www.praying-nature.com/site_pages.php?section=Guide+for+Nature+Lovers, retrieved June 19, 2021.

13   Kennedy, Robert F. Jr., sermon at the Feast of St. Francis, Cathedral of St. John the Divine, October 7, 2001; recording provided by Cathedral archives, June 17, 2021.

14   Courtenay Thompson, "Childhood's Memories of War Arise Amid the Ruins," *The Oregonian*, October 11, 2001, B7.

15   Marianne Garvey, "A Blessing on Rescue Dogs," *New York Post*, October 8, 2001, https://nypost.com/2001/10/08/a-blessing-on-rescue-dogs/.

16   Dani Dodge, "Oregonians March in New York," *Mail Tribune*, October 9, 2001, page number unknown.

17   Lance Nuttman, "Lance and Marla's Website," and www.geocities.com/lmnyc5/. Retrieved in 2003 and no longer online.

18   Chris Sullivan, "Flight for Freedom: Day Two in Manhattan," KXL.com, October 7, 2001.

19 Associated Press, "Oregonians Learn of Airstrikes While in New York," *Daily Astorian*, October 8, 2001, unknown page number.
20 Courtenay Thompson, "Trip of Hope Turns to One of Anxiety," *The Oregonian*, October 8, 2001, C7.
21 John Ray, interview with the author, July 25, 2003.
22 Jackie Young, email to the author, July 29, 2003.
23 Lance and Marla Nuttman, interview with the author, January 24, 2021.
24 David Wu, interview with the author, March 11, 2021.
25 "Congressman David Wu to Host Dinner for Oregonians in New York," press release from David Wu's office, October 5, 2001.
26 Eric Marcus, interview with the author, July 30, 2003.
27 Eric Marcus, interview with the author, April 23, 2021.
28 Judi Henningsen, memoir of the Flight for Freedom written very soon after completing the trip, 2001.
29 Ron Saxton, "New York City Greets Oregon Family Visitors with Wide-Open Arms," *Portland Tribune*, October 9, 2001.
30 Julie Stewart, "A Journey to the Heart of New York," *PATA*, http://www.pataweb.net/archives/Flight.html, retrieved July 26, 2003

"America Wakes Up to Oregon"

1 Editorial, "Mr. Feelgood," *Woodburn Independent*, October 17, 2001, page number unknown.
2 Associated Press, "Strikes raise specter of retaliation vs. U.S.," *Baltimore Sun*, October 8, 2001, file:///C:/Users/sbour/AppData/Local/Temp/newsarchives100801.htm.
3 Diego Ibarguen, (Associated Press writer) "Patriotism on parade in N.Y.," *The Columbian*, October 9, 2001, A6.
4 Chris Sullivan, "Flight for Freedom: Day Three," KXL.com, October 8, 2001.
5 Ellis Henican, "America Strikes Back/Commentary/ Still in Step with Holiday," *Newsday*, October 9, 2001.
6 "Parade gives New Yorkers a reason to cheer," *Tampa Bay Times*, October 9, 2001, published September 10, 2005. https://www.tampabay.com/archive/2001/10/09/parade-gives-new-yorkers-a-reason-to-cheer/, retrieved June 27, 2021. Note: the URL for this story lists a date of 10/9/2001, which I believe is the original date of publication, though the website itself gives the "published" date in 2005.
7 Lisa L. Colangelo and Corky Siemaszko, "New York still loves a parade," *New York Daily News*, October 9, 2001, 18.
8 Joe Mauriello, email to Azumano Travel Flight for Freedom address, August 26, 2002, printed out by the author July 24, 2003. Copy in the author's files.
9 Flight for Freedom website guest book, printed out by the author, 2003. Photocopy in the author's files.
10 Joe Mauriello, interview with the author, January 22, 2021.
11 Joe Mauriello, email August 26, 2002.
12 Sandra Kempel, interview with the author, July 25, 2001.
13 Author's notes from Wu's comments at the dinner, October 7, 2001.
14 Transcript of "Good Morning America" visit by Oregonians on October 8, 2001, provided courtesy "Good Morning America," ABC News; thanks to Charles Gibson for facilitating this acquisition.
15 Lance Nuttman, "Lance and Marla's Website," www.geocities.com/lmnyc2. Downloaded 2003, no longer available online.
16 Doug Irving, "Freedom Flyers Head Back to Portland," kgw.com, October 9, 2001.
17 John Ray, interview with the author, July 22, 2003.
18 Julie Andersen, interview with the author, October 9, 2003.

"Ringing the Bell"

1   Randall Edwards, interview with the author, July 25, 2003.
2   *Daily Shipping News*, October 16, 2001.
3   Nick Fish, interview with the author, July 31, 2003.
4   Randall Edwards, interview with the author, July 25, 2003.
5   Michael Brick, "Mood on the Exchange Floor Somber on Second Day of Attacks," *The New York Times*, Business section, October 8, 2001. "It's not anything like the mood the first day," said Bernard L. Madoff, the chairman of Bernard L. Madoff Investment Securities, who was in his midtown office juggling two telephones, one connected to a trader on the floor and one connected to a reporter in the member's gallery of the exchange. "Everybody is calm. Nobody's anticipating a real market change."
6   Loen and Sho Dozono, interview with the author, July 21, 2003.
7   Jack McGowan, interview with the author, April 10, 2021.
8   Jim Hart, "'Ground Zero' Fills Hooley with Disbelief," *West Linn Tidings*, October 11, 2001, A1 and A16.
9   Jack McGowan, interview with the author, April 10, 2021.
10 Chris Sullivan, interview with the author, February 20, 2021.
11 Brick, "Mood on the Exchange Floor Somber on Second Day of Attacks."
12 Brick, "Mood on the Exchange Floor Somber on Second Day of Attacks."
13 Chris Sullivan, "Flight for Freedom: Day Three," KXL.com, October 8, 2001.
14 Brick, "Mood on the Exchange Floor Somber on Second Day of Attacks."
15 Randall Edwards, interview with the author, July 25, 2003.
16 Chris Sullivan, "Flight for Freedom: Day Three," KXL.com, October 8, 2001.

"I Love a Parade!"

1   Dawn Taylor, "The Wartime Tourist," *Clackamas Review*, October 25, 2001, A1 and A6.
2   Bryan Virasami, "Big Patriotic Showing at Columbus Day Parade," Newsday.com, October 9, 2001.
3   Lisa L. Colangelo and Corky Siemaszko, "New York Still Loves a Parade," *New York Daily News*, October 9, 2001, 18.
4   Doug Irving, "Freedom Flyers Head Back to Portland," kgw.com, October 9, 2001.
5   Irving, "Freedom Flyers Head Back to Portland."
6   Robert D. McFadden, "One Part Columbus Day, and One Part 4th of July," *The New York Times*, October 9, 2001. https://www.nytimes.com/2001/10/09/nyregion/one-part-columbus-day-and-one-part-4th-of-july.html?searchResultPosition=1.
7   Jackie Young, interview with the author, January 31, 2021.
8   Doug Irving, "Freedom Flyers Head Back to Portland."
9   Kristen Dozono, interview with the author, April 18, 2021. Azumano Travel announced that free replacement shirts would be available for pick-up from October 15–19 at the office, and that the travel agency would be willing to mail them for the cost of postage. Additional shirts and buttons could also be ordered.
10 Nancy Waples, interview with the author, July 24, 2003. Waples said her brother said, "'I'm not going to go.' And I said, 'Oh yes, you are.' We probably forced him to do it. And he was mad at me, but he had so much fun, and I have so many pictures of him shaking hands with people and talking with people along the route. He said it was the most fun."
11 Judith Spitzer, "Molalla, Colton Contingent Arrives Back from New York Mission," *The Molalla Pioneer*, October 13, 2001, 1–2.
12 Vic Rini, "City of Heroes," *Northwest Italian News*, manuscript emailed by Rini to author on November 2, 2001.

13 Kathleen and Philip Peters, interview with the author, July 31, 2003.
14 Courtenay Thompson, "Hugs and Cheers on Fifth Avenue," *The Oregonian*, October 9, 2001.
15 Michele Longo Eder, *Salt In Our Blood*, Newport, Oregon: Dancing Moon Press, 2008, p. 192.
16 Cliff Madison, interview with the author, January 18, 2002.
17 Lance Nuttman, "Lance and Marla's Website," and www.geocities.com/lmnyc7. No longer available; printed out by the author in 2003.
18 Todd Davidson, interview with the author, February 11, 2021.
19 Courtenay Thompson, "Hugs and Cheers on Fifth Avenue," *The Oregonian*, October 9, 2001.
20 Randall Edwards, interview with the author, July 25, 2003.
21 Vera Katz, interview with the author, July 25, 2003.
22 Debra-Diane Jenness, email to author, April 19, 2002. All quotations taken from this email.
23 Thompson, "Hugs and Cheers on Fifth Avenue."
24 Scott Williams, interview with the author, March 23, 2021.
25 Mary Platt, interview with the author, May 24, 2021.
26 Jackie Young, interview with the author, January 31, 2021.
27 Courtenay Thompson, "Hugs and Cheers on Fifth Avenue," *The Oregonian*, October 9, 2001.
28 Nancy Mechaber, interview with the author, January 17, 2021.
29 Jeri Hunt, Azumano Travel Flight for Freedom scrapbook, 2002.
30 Mac Chiulli and Bob Moore, email to Mayor Vera Katz, October 11, 2001.
31 John Barell, email to Mayor Vera Katz, October 18, 2001.
32 Casey Walker, email to Mayor Vera Katz, November 30, 2001.
33 Sandra Kempel, interview with the author, July 25, 2003.
34 "Lance and Marla's Website."

"All Oregon Reception"

1 Gov. George Pataki, interview with the author, May 13, 2021.
2 Randall Edwards, interview with the author, July 25, 2003.
3 George Haight, interview with the author, July 26, 2003.
4 Brian Berusch, "Oregon Travel Agency Leads New York City Solidarity Tour." *Travel Trade News Edition*, October 15, 2001, 18.
5 Chris Sullivan, "Flight for Freedom: Day Three," KXL.com, October 8, 2001.
6 Kathleen Peters, interview with the author, July 31, 2003.

"Last Moments"

1 Ellis Henican, "America Strikes Back/Commentary/ Still in Step With Holiday," *Newsday*, October 9, 2001, page A.26.
2 Elaine Franklin and John Ray, group meeting April 29, 2021. Meeting notes in author's files.
3 Sho Dozono, email to the author, July 31, 2003.
4 Myriam Bourjolly, "Putting Their Money Where Their Hearts Are: Flight for Freedom Touches Down in the Big Apple with Oregon CU Staffers," *CU Times*, date and page number unknown.
5 Sandra Kempel, interview with the author, November 10, 2020.
6 Sandra Kempel, interview with the author, July 25, 2003.
7 Myriam DiGiovanni, "Flight for Freedom touches down in the Big Apple with Oregon CU staffers," *Credit Union Times*, October 16, 2001, https://www.

cutimes.com/2001/10/16/flight-for-freedom-touches-down-in-the-big-apple-w
ith-oregon-cu-staffers/, retrieved March 31, 2021.

8   Ann Nice, interview with the author, January 29, 2021.
9   Randall Edwards, interview with the author, July 25, 2003.
10 Betsy Holzgraf, interview with the author, January 29, 2021.
11 Nancy Waples, interview with the author, July 25, 2003.
12 Debra-Diane Jenness, email to author, April 19, 2002. All quotations taken from this email.
13 Clyde Haberman, Like St. Vincent's Itself, Missing Wall Means Much," *The New York Times*, February 1, 2010, https://www.nytimes.com/2010/02/02/nyregion/02nyc.html. The discussion of the Wall of Remembrance at St. Vincent's is taken from this article. After the flyers were taken down, expense made it unfeasible to create the display hospital staff had hoped, but *The Times* reported that they had kept the flyers in binders that they brought out at their annual September 11 chapel service. The publication captured the trauma of those working in St. Vincent's as well. For Dr. Steven Garner, chief medical officer f Bourjolly, Myriam. "Putting Their Money Where Their Hearts Are: Flight for Freedom Touches Down in the Big Apple with Oregon CU Staffers," *CU Times*. date and page number unknown. For the medical centers, last year's most vivid scene was this: "I was standing next to a secretary whose husband was a firefighter. We were watching TV and saw him run into a building. She said, 'There he is,' and it was a moment of exhilaration. Three minutes later, it fell," Garner said. "There were no words to be spoken."
14 Debra-Diane Jenness, email to the author, April 19, 2002.
15 "Special Tribute to 9/11 McDonald's Owner Operator Hero Lloyd Frazier at Annual Stony Brook University's 'Give Kids a Smile' Day," LongIsland.com, September 19, 2017, https://www.longisland.com/news/09-19-17/special-tribute-to-911-mcdonalds-owner-operator-hero-lloyd-frazier-at-annual-stony-brook-universitys-give-kids-a-smile-day.html.
16 Scott Williams, interview with the author, March 23, 2021.
17 Tahn Amuchastegui, email to author, April 9, 2021.
18 Lance Nuttman, "Lance and Marla's Website," www.geocities.com/lmnyc2, which no longer exists. Printed out by the author in 2003.
19 Marla Nuttman, interview with the author, January 24, 2021.
20 Nancy Parrott, interview with the author, March 3, 2021.
21 Tahn Amuchastegui, email to author, April 9, 2021.
22 Lance Nuttman, "Lance and Marla's Website," www.geocities.com/lmnyc2, which no longer exists. Printed out by the author in 2003.
23 Kostel, "Flight for Freedom Memories."
24 Betty Long, email to the author, June 20, 2002.
25 Barbara Shaw, interview with the author, n.d., 2021.
26 Jane Meskill, interview with the author, February 23, 2021.
27 Chris Sullivan, "Flight for Freedom: Day Three," KXL.com, October 8, 2001.
28 Sho and Loen Dozono, interview with the author, July 21, 2003.
29 Michael Phillips, email to friends on October 11, 2001, sent to the author on July 26, 2003.
30 Marla Nuttman, interview with the author, January 24, 2021. All other commentary from Lance Nuttman, "Lance and Marla's Website," www.geocities.com/lmnyc2, which no longer exists. Printed out by the author in 2003.

"Ground Zero"

1   Michael Phillips, *Voices from a Sunlit Shadow*, 2002, 8.
2   Wes Loucks, interview with the author, March 5, 2021.

3   Mary Platt, interview with the author, May 24, 2021.

4   Thomas Wiebe, "Oregon loves New York: memories of 9/11," *The Oregon Scribbler*, September 11, 2011, https://oregonscribbler.com/remembering-911-oregon-loves-new-york/, September 11, 2011, retrieved June 12, 2021.

5   Jim Hart, "'Ground Zero' Fills Hooley with Disbelief," *West Linn Tidings*, October 11, 2001, A1 and A16.

6   Jack Kostel, "Flight for Freedom Moments," October 2001, photocopy in the author's files.

7   Jeanine Ford, "Flight for Freedom," newsletter, no date, 13. Scan in the author's files.

8   Judi Henningsen, journal, October 9, 2001.

9   Theresa Hogue, "Flight for Freedom Returns to Oregon," *Gazette-Times* (Corvallis, Ore.), October 13, 2001, A1 and A11.

10   Vic Rini, "The City of Heroes," *Northwest Italian News*. Manuscript emailed by Rini to author on November 2, 2001.

11   Teri Meeuwsen, "From Hermiston to New York, with love," *East Oregonian* (Pendleton, Ore.), October 16, 2001, 1A and 3A.

12   Rob Platt, interview with the author, May 30, 2021.

13   Tahn Amuchastegui, email to the author, April 9, 2021.

14   Debra Diane-Jenness, email to author, April 19, 2002.

15   Clarice Schorzman, "A Letter Home," *The Molalla Pioneer*, October 13, 2001, 2.

16   This discussion is a compilation of interview I did with Haight and John Baker, "Mission accomplished," *Woodburn Independent*, October 17, 2001, 1 and 2.

17   Peter Wong, "Gerry Frank loves New York—still," *Statesman Journal*, October 11, 2001, 1A and 2A. Interestingly, the newspaper also notes that several restaurants in the Mid-Willamette Valley were taking part in the Oregon Restaurant Association-Red Cross project called Dine for America or the Windows of Hope effort. Participating restaurants were donating a percentage of that day's sales to the relief efforts.

18   Ian Rollins, "Freedom Flight was 'Moving Experience,'" *Hillsboro Argus*, October 13, 2001, 1A.

19   Patricia Snyder, "Locals Deeply Moved by New York Visit," *Daily Courier*, October 13, 2001, unknown page number.

20   Carreon had moved to Portland only a few months before to assume his position as president of Portland Community College, which began on July 30, 2001.

21   Sean C. Morgan, "Freedom Flight Visit to New York City Creates Lasting Images for S.H. Couple," *The New Era* (Sweet Home, Ore.), October 17, 2001, 1, 3.

22   Bill Cooper, interview with the author, June 17, 2021.

23   Joyce Willing, interview with the author, January 9, 2021.

24   Stephanie Hinshaw, essay on the Flight for Freedom, October 15, 2001; contained in Margaret Hinshaw, email to Cindy Forgue, October 26, 2001, in author's files.

25   Michele Longo Eder, *Salt In Our Blood*, Newport, Oregon: Dancing Moon Press, 2008, 192.

26   Dan Barry, "A Nation Challenged: Messages; From a World Lost, Ephemeral Notes Bear Witness to the Unspeakable," *The New York Times*, September 25, 2001, https://www.nytimes.com/2001/09/25/nyregion/nation-challenged-messages-world-lost-ephemeral-notes-bear-witness-unspeakable.html.

"Bearing Witness"

1   Mary Kelso, Interview with the author, October 9, 2001.

2   Jackie Young, interview with the author, January 31, 2021.

3   Bill Cooper, interview with the author, June 17, 2021.

4   Al O'Brien, email to author, July 26, 2003.

5   Mary Platt, interview with the author, May 24, 2021.
6   Debra-Diane Jenness, email to author, April 19, 2002. All quotations taken from this email.
7   Julie Stewart, "A Journey to the Heart of New York," *PATA*, October 2001, www. pataweb.net/archives/Flight.html, retrieved July 26, 2003.
8   John B. Webster, "Oregonians made true friends in New York," *Hood River News*, October 13, 2001, page unknown.
9   Allen Oswalt, interview with the author, March 19, 2021.
10   Joe Seward, interview with the author, March 21, 2021.
11   ABC7 New York, "Hardest hit firehouse still recovering 10 years later," September 11, 2011, https://abc7ny.com/archive/8349429/.
12   Judith Spitzer, "Molalla, Colton Contingent Arrives Back from New York Mission," *The Molalla Pioneer*, October 13, 2001, 1.
13   Rob Platt, interview with the author, May 30, 2021.
14   Ted Taylor, "Goodwill trip boosts the spirits of New Yorkers, locals," *Bend Bulletin*, October 13, 2001, page number unknown.
15   Connie Hawk, email to the author, July 25, 2003.
16   Elisa Dozono, "About the People," email, October 4, 2001; "Two of WSU's Finest Travel to Ground Zero in New York," *WSU Public Safety Newsletter*, October 2001, pp. 1 and 2. Photocopies in the author's files.
17   David Morkal, interview with the author, January 22, 2021.
18   Leo Nadolske, interview with the author, March 24, 2021.
19   Joyce Willing, interview with the author, January 9, 2021.
20   Cliff Madison, interview with the author, January 18, 2002.
21   Michael Phillips, *Voices from a Sunlit Shadow*, 2002, pages 6 and 8.
22   Spitzer, "Molalla, Colton," 1.
23   Craig Acklen, "Letters: Gesture of friendship treasured What a thrill for this Oregon native to witness the reception the large contingent of Oregonians marching in the New York City Columbus Day parade received from New York City residents," *The Oregonian*, October 13, 2001. Also appeared in the *Daily Courier*, Grant's Pass, Ore., October 12, 2001.
24   Delia McQuade Emmons, "Oregonian Makes Her Day," Letters, *The Oregonian*, October 13, 2001, page number unknown.
25   Leslie and David Parker, interview with author, February 24, 2021.
26   Leslie Parker email to the author, September 25, 2003; Leslie Krueger is the return email name.

"The Impact"

1   Ian Rollins, "Freedom Flight Was 'Moving Experience,'" *Hillsboro Argus*, October 13, 2001.
2   Vera Katz, interview with the author, July 25, 2003. Other excerpts from this interview can be found throughout this book.
3   Mayor Vera Katz, email to Katie Kirk, July 15, 2002.
4   Eric Long, *At Your Service: A Newsletter for Guests of The Waldorf-Astoria and The Waldorf Towers*, Winter 2001, 1.
5   Stephanie Hinshaw, essay on the Flight for Freedom, October 15, 2001; contained in Margaret Hinshaw, email to Cindy Forgue, October 26, 2001, in author's files.
6   Aleck and Mary Edra Prihar, email to Azumano Travel, October 9, 2001.
7   Jesus 'Jess' Carreon, "PCC President, Old Friend Link Up at 'Ground Zero.' *Lake Oswego Review*, October 11, 2001, A1 and A2.
8   Theresa Hogue, "Flight for Freedom Returns to Oregon," *Gazette-Times* (Corvallis, Ore.), October 13, 2001, A1 and A11.

9   Patricia Snyder, "Locals Deeply Moved by NY Visit," *Daily Courier* (Grants Pass, Ore.), October 13, 2001.
10 Ryan McAninch, MY TURN: Events Alter Atmosphere in New York," *The Oregonian*, October 25, 2001.
11 Jeanine Ford, "Flight for Freedom," newsletter, no date, 13. Scan in author's files.
12 John Webster, "Flight for Freedom Oregonians Made True Friends in New York," *Hood River News*, October 1, 2001. "John Webster is a native Hood Riverite who works for Sprint Communications. In an odd twist, Webster is about to fulfill a long-time desire to reside in New York. Six months ago, he requested transfer to his company's repair division in New York; he starts work there around Nov. 1."
13 Teri Meeuwsen, "From Hermiston to New York, with love," *East Oregonian* (Pendleton, Ore.), October 16, 2001, 1A and 3A.
14 Beverly Harkenrider, "Bond of friendship forged between NYC, Hermiston women," *East Oregonian*, September 10, 2002, https://www.eastoregonian.com/opinion/bond-of-friendship-forged-between-nyc-hermiston-women/article_7b8a6be8-42c3-5f8c-b1a3-a5a7d701c777.html.
15 Teri Meeuwsen, "From Hermiston to New York, With Love," *East Oregonian* (Pendleton, Ore.), October 16, 2001, 1A and 3A.
16 Rachel Gerber. "Life-Changing Visit to the Streets of New York," *The Oregonian*, Commentary, October 10, 2001.
17 Letter, October 12, 2001, Sho Dozono files.
18 Sean C. Morgan, "Freedom Flight Visit to New York City Creates Lasting Images for S.H. couple," *The New Era* (Sweet Home, Ore.), October 17, 2001, 1 and 3.
19 Melody Finnemore, "In Wake of Sept. 11, Local Group Soared," *Daily Journal of Commerce*, September 2, 2011, https://djcoregon.com/news/2011/09/02/in-wake-of-sept-11-local-group-soared/.
20 John Baker, "Remembering 9-11, Going Back," *Woodburn Independent*, September 11, 2002, 1 and 3. The second trip, organized by Azumano Travel, took place from September 8-12, 2002.
21 "Mr. Feelgood," editorial, *The Independent* (Woodburn, Ore.), October 17, 2001.
22 Allen Pembrooke, "Trip of Woodburn Man Was Important One," *Woodburn Independent*, October 24, 2001, page number unknown.
23 Bruce Samson, interview with the author, July 31, 2003.
24 Nick Fish, interview with the author, July 31, 2003.
25 Melody Finnemore, "In Wake of Sept. 11, Local Group Soared," *Daily Journal of Commerce*, September 2, 2011, https://djcoregon.com/news/2011/09/02/in-wake-of-sept-11-local-group-soared/.
26 George Haight, interview with the author, July 26, 2003.
27 Martin Fisher, interview with the author, March 13, 2002.
28 Alice McElhany, email to the author, July 26, 2003.
29 Nancy Waples, interview with the author, July 24, 2003.
30 Lance Nuttman, interview with the author, January 24, 2021.
31 Elaine L. Edgel, email to the author, July 27, 2003.
32 Connie L. Hawk, email to the author, July 24, 2003.
33 Joy Cavinta, interview with the author, July 27, 2003.
34 Debra-Diane Jenness, email to the author, April 19, 2002.
35 Merritt Marthaller, email to the author, July 26, 2003.
36 Tahn Amuchastegui, email to the author, March 22, 2002.
37 Tahn Amuchastegui, email to the author, April 9, 2021.
38 Albert O'Brien, email to the author, July 31, 2003.
39 Albert O'Brien, email to the author, July 26, 2003.
40 Albert O'Brien, interview with the author, January 29, 2021.
41 Cliff Madison, interview with the author, January 18, 2002.
42 David Wu, interview with the author, March 13, 2021.
43 Joseph E. Weston and George Passadore, interview with the author, May 14, 2021.

44 Betty Long, letter to the author, November 19, 2020.
45 Cameron Platt, interview with the author, June 6, 2021.
46 Mary Platt, interview with the author, May 24, 2021.
47 Rebecca Webb and Kamlynn Kimball, interview with the author, January 29, 2021.
48 Jackie Young, interview with the author, January 31, 2021.
49 Kristen Dozono, interview with the author, April 18, 2021.
50 Krista Vasquez, interview with the author, February 5, 2021.

"A Timeline of the September 11 Attacks"

1 Sources for this timeline:
- "CNN Breaking News America Under Attack: Bush Holds Press Briefing," CNN. com, aired September 11, 2001—14:20 ET, retrieved February 9, 2020, http://transcripts.CNN.com/TRANSCRIPTS/0109/11/bn.35.html.
- "CNN Breaking News New York's Governor And Mayor of New York City Address Concerns of the Damage," CNN.com, aired September 11, 2001—14:35 ET, retrieved February 9, 2020, http://transcripts.CNN.com/TRANSCRIPTS/0109/11/bn.42.html.
- Jim Dwyer and Ford Fessenden, "One Hotel's Fight to the Finish; At the Marriott, a Portal to Safety as the Towers Fell," *The New York Times*, September 11, 2002, https://www.nytimes.com/2002/09/11/nyregion/one-hotel-s-fight-finish-marriott-portal-safety-towers-fell.html.
- Matea Gold and Maggie Farley, Los Angeles Times Staff Writers, "World Trade Center and Pentagon attacked on Sept. 11, 2001," September 12, 2001, https://www.latimes.com/travel/la-xp.m.-2001-sep-12-na-sept-11-attack-201105-01-story.html.
- Matt Kelly, "On Account of War," National Baseball Hall of Fame online, https://baseballhall.org/discover-more/stories/short-stops/1918-world-war-i-baseball, retrieved June 20, 2021. Randy Kennedy, "A Day of Terror: Transportation; With City Transit Shut Down, New Yorkers Take to Eerily Empty Streets." September 12, 2001, Section A, Page 8, https://www.nytimes.com/2001/09/12/us/day-terror-transportation-with-city-transit-shut-down-new-yorkers-take-eerily.html Advertisement.
- Joe Klein, "Shadow Land" *The New Yorker*, February 10, 2002 (February 18, 2002 print issue), https://www.newyorker.com/magazine/2002/02/18/shadow-land.
- 9/11 News Coverage: 7:45 PM: Congress Sings "God Bless America," CNN headline news footage, retrieved June 13, 2021, https://www.youtube.com/watch?v=IH_6EUCILew.
- Office of the Historian, United States House of Representatives, "The Singing of 'God Bless America' on September 11, 2001," retrieved February 8, 2020, https://history.house.gov/Historical-Highlights/2000-/The-singing-of-%E2%80%9CGod-Bless-America%E2%80%9D-on-September-11,-2001/.
- Staff and Wire Reports, "Timeline in Terrorist Attacks of Sept. 11, 2001," washingtonpost.com, September 12, 9:04 p.m., https://www.washingtonpost.com/wp-srv/nation/articles/timeline.html.
- Text of Bush's address, CNN.com, September 11, 2001, posted: 11:14 P.M. EDT (0314 GMT) Retrieved January 19, 2020, https://edition.CNN.com/2001/US/09/11/bush.speech.text/.
- Amy Tikkanen, "Timeline of the September 11 Attacks," britannica.com, retrieved January 20, 2020, https://www.britannica.com/list/timeline-of-the-september-11-attacks.

• "World Shock Over U.S. Attacks," CNN.com, September 11, 2001, posted: 9:31 P.M. EDT, retrieved February 28, 2020, https://www.CNN.com/2001/WORLD/europe/09/11/trade.centre.reaction/.

"As It Happened: September 12–26"

1 Jim Dwyer and Lawrence K. Altman, "After the Attacks: The Morgue; Loads of Body Bags Hint at Magnitude of Grisly Task," *The New York Times*, September 13, 2001, https://www.nytimes.com/2001/09/13/us/after-the-attacks-the-morgue-loads-of-body-bags-hint-at-magnitude-of-grisly-task.html.
2 Michelle Boorstein, "Thousands of Doctors, Nurses Called to Help," The Associated Press, September 12, 2001, https://old.post-gazette.com/headlines/20010912nyhospitalsnat6p6.asp.
3 Matea Gold and Maggie Farley, Los Angeles Times Staff Writers, "World Trade Center and Pentagon attacked on Sept. 11, 2001," *Los Angeles Times*, September 12, 2001, https://www.latimes.com/travel/la-xp.m.-2001-sep-12-na-sept-11-attack-201105-01-story.html.
4 Office of the Press Secretary, "Remarks by the President While Touring Damage at the Pentagon," White House archived website, September 12, 2001, https://georgewbush-whitehouse.archives.gov/news/releases/2001/09/20010912-12.html.
5 R. W. Apple Jr., "After the Attacks: News Analysis; No Middle Ground," *The New York Times*, September 14, 2001, https://www.nytimes.com/2001/09/14/us/after-the-attacks-news-analysis-no-middle-ground.html.
6 Warren Hoge, "After the Attacks: West; Outpouring of Grief and Sympathy for Americans Is Seen Throughout Europe and Elsewhere," *The New York Times*, displays as September 13, 2001 in the TimesMachine, and in the September 14, 2001 print newspaper, Section A, Page 21, https://www.nytimes.com/2001/09/14/us/after-attacks-west-outpouring-grief-sympathy-for-americans-seen-throughout.html.
7 Suzanne Daley, "After the Attacks: The Alliance; For First Time, NATO Invokes Joint Defense Pact With U.S.," *The New York Times*, September 13, 2001. https://www.nytimes.com/2001/09/13/us/after-attacks-alliance-for-first-time-nato-invokes-joint-defense-pact-with-us.html; "Members of Security Council condemn 'horrifying' terror attacks on US.," *UN News*, September 11, 2001, https://news.un.org/en/story/2001/09/13932-members-security-council-condemn-horrifying-terror-attacks-us.
8 James Barron, "Bush Says Attack Was 'First War of the 21st Century,'" *The New York Times*, September 13, 2001 (online only), https://www.nytimes.com/2001/09/13/nyregion/bush-says-attack-was-first-war-of-the-21st-century.html.
9 Robert D. McFadden, "After the Attacks: The Overview; A Shaken Nation Struggles to Regain Its Equilibrium, but Remains on Edge," *The New York Times*, September 14, 2001, https://www.nytimes.com/2001/09/14/us/after-attacks-overview-shaken-nation-struggles-regain-its-equilibrium-but.html.
10 Steven Lee Myers and Elizabeth Becker, "After the Attacks: The Pentagon; Defense Department Says 126 Are Missing, Raising Total of Crash Victims to 190," *The New York Times*, September 14, 2001, https://www.nytimes.com/2001/09/14/us/after-attacks-pentagon-defense-department-says-126-are-missing-raising-total.html.
11 James Barron, "Bush Says Attack Was 'First War of the 21st Century."
12 Susan Sachs, "After the Attacks: The Site; A Delicate Removal of Debris, With Monstrous Machines and Gloved Hands," *The New York Times*, September 14, 2001, https://www.nytimes.com/2001/09/14/us/after-attacks-site-delicate-removal-debris-with-monstrous-machines-gloved-hands.html.

13   Andrew C. Revkin, "After the Attacks: The Chemicals; Monitors Say Health Risk From Smoke Is Very Small," *The New York Times*, September 14, 2001, https:// www.nytimes.com/2001/09/14/us/after-attacks-chemicals-monitors-say-health -risk-smoke-very-small.html.

14   McFadden, "A Shaken Nation Struggles to Regain Its Equilibrium"; James Risen and Don van Natta Jr., "After the Attacks: The Suspects U.S. Says Hijackers Lived in the Open With Deadly Secret," *The New York Times*, September 14, 2001, https://www. nytimes.com/2001/09/14/us/after-attacks-investigation-authorities-have-learn ed-identities-18-hijackers.html.

15   Jere Longman and Jo Thomas, "After the Attacks: The Pennsylvania Crash; Recorder Found; May Reveal a Struggle," *The New York Times*, September 14, 2001, https://www.nytimes.com/2001/09/14/us/after-the-attacks-the-pennsylvania-crash -recorder-found-may-reveal-a-struggle.htmlSEARCH.

16   Clifford J. Levy and William K. Rashbaum, "After the Attacks: The Airports; Bush and Top Aides Proclaim Policy of 'Ending' States That Back Terror; Local Airports Shut After an Arrest," *The New York Times*, September 14, 2001, https://www. nytimes.com/2001/09/14/us/after-attacks-airports-bush-top-aides-proclaim-polic y-ending-states-that-back.html.

17   Thom Shanker and Eric Schmitt, "After the Attacks: Mobilization; Rumsfeld Ordering Call-Up Of Up to 50,000 Reservists," *The New York Times*, September 14, 2001, https://www.nytimes.com/2001/09/14/us/after-attacks-mobilization-rumsfel d-ordering-call-up-up-50000-reservists.html.

18   Pam Belluck with Laurence Zuckerman, "After the Attacks: Transportation; Flights Are Cleared to Resume, but the Skies Remain Largely Empty," *The New York Times*, September 14, 2001, https://timesmachine.nytimes.com/timesma chine/2001/09/14/182184.html?pageNumber=23;; McFadden, "A Shaken Nation Struggles to Regain Its Equilibrium."

19   Mark Landler With Richard A. Oppel Jr., "After the Attacks: The Cargo Trade; Ban on Airliners' Freight Has Businesses Scrambling," *The New York Times*, September 15,   2001,   https://www.nytimes.com/2001/09/15/us/after-attacks-cargo-trad e-ban-airliners-freight-has-businesses-scrambling.html?searchResultPosition=1.

20   Emily Yellin, "After the Attacks: The Overnight Shipper; Back in the Air Again, And Feeling a Special Rush," *The New York Times*, September 15, 2001, https://www. nytimes.com/2001/09/15/business/after-attacks-overnight-shipper-back-air-a gain-feeling-special-rush.html

21   Pam Belluck, "After the Attacks: Transportation; More Planes Take to Skies, But Plenty of Kinks Remain," *The New York Times*, September 15, 2001, https:// www.nytimes.com/2001/09/15/us/after-attacks-transportation-more-pl anes-take-skies-but-plenty-kinks-remain.html.

22   Randy Kennedy, "After the Attacks: The Commuters; Closings Snarl Travel to Manhattan Again," *The New York Times*, September 14, 2001, https:// www.nytimes.com/2001/09/14/us/after-the-attacks-the-commuters-closings -snarl-travel-to-manhattan-again.html.

23   James Barron, "Bush Says Attack Was 'First War of the 21st Century."

24   Terry Pristin, "After the Attacks: Utilities; Phone Service Improving, But Many Still Lack Power," *The New York Times*, September 14, 2001, https://www. nytimes.com/2001/09/14/us/after-the-attacks-utilities-phone-service-improving- but-many-still-lack-power.html.

25   John Kifner and Susan Saulny, "After the Attacks: The Families; Posting Handbills as Votive Offerings, in Hope of Finding Missing Loved Ones," *The New York Times*, September 14, 2001, https://www.nytimes.com/2001/09/14/us/after-attack s-families-posting-handbills-votive-offerings-hope-finding-missing.html.

26   Elissa Gootman, "After the Attacks: Charity; A Range of Donors Help Those in the Rescue Effort," *The New York Times*, September 14, 2001, https://www. nytimes.com/2001/09/14/us/after-the-attacks-charity-a-range-of-donors-help

-those-in-the-rescue-effort.html; Tamar Lewin, "After the Attacks: Financial Aid; Companies Pledge $100 Million In Relief," *The New York Times*, September 15, 2001, https://www.nytimes.com/2001/09/15/us/after-the-attacks-financial-aid-co mpanies-pledge-100-million-in-relief.html.

27 Laurie Goodstein and Gustav Niebuhr, "After the Attacks: Retaliation; Attacks and Harassment of Arab-Americans Increase," *The New York Times*, September 14, 2001, https://www.nytimes.com/2001/09/14/us/after-the-attacks-retaliatio n-attacks-and-harassment-of-arab-americans-increase.html; Associated Press, After the Attacks: The Vigils; In Silence And Prayer, Remembering The Victims," *The New York Times*, September 14, 2001, https://www.nytimes.com/2001/09/14/us/ after-the-attacks-the-vigils-in-silence-and-prayer-remembering-the-victims.html.

28 McFadden, "A Shaken Nation Struggles to Regain its Equilibrium."

29 Elisabeth Bumiller and Jane Perlez, "After the Attacks: The Overview; Bush and Top Aides Proclaim Policy of 'Ending' States That Back Terror; Local Airports Shut After An Arrest," *The New York Times*, September 14, 2001, https://www. nytimes.com/2001/09/14/us/after-attacks-overview-bush-top-aides-proclaim-polic y-ending-states-that-back.html. [Note: the title of this article is shared by two different articles by different authors published on the same day and they have different URLs. This article includes October 7, 2002 correction, which is quoted here.]

30 Barron, "Bush Says Attack Was 'First War of the 21st Century."

31 Bumiller and Perlez, "Bush and Top Aides Proclaim Policy of 'Ending' States That Back Terror." [Note: the title of this article is shared by two different articles by different authors published on the same day and they have different URLs. This article includes October 7, 2002 correction, which is quoted here.]

32 *The New York Times*, Reuters, AP, Agence France-Presse (Sources), "After the Attacks: Around the World," *The New York Times*, September 14, 2001, https://www.nytimes.com/2001/09/14/us/after-the-attacks-around-the-world. html?searchResultPosition=1.

33 33 Jim Dwyer, "AFTER THE ATTACKS: CLOSE CALLS; Survivors Who Barely Made It Out in Time Try to Cope With Grim Fact That Others Did Not," The New York Times, September 14, 2001, https://www.nytimes.com/2001/09/14/us/ after-attacks-close-calls-survivors-who-barely-made-it-time-try-cope-with-grim. html.

34 Barron, "Bush Says Attack Was 'First War of the 21st Century.'"

35 Office of the Press Secretary, "National Day of Prayer and Remembrance for the Victims Of the Terrorist Attacks on September 11, 2001 By the President of the United States of America A Proclamation," White House archived website, September 13, 2001, https://georgewbush-whitehouse.archives.gov/news/ releases/2001/09/20010913-7.html.

36 Hoge, "Outpouring of Grief and Sympathy.

37 Richard Pérez-Peña, "After the Attacks: The Mood; Glimpses of the Normal Even as Obstacles Grow Clearer," *The New York Times*, September 15, 2001, https://www. nytimes.com/2001/09/15/us/after-the-attacks-the-mood-glimpses-of-the-norma l-even-as-obstacles-grow-clearer.html.

38 "Heroes Amid the Horror," *The New York Times*, September 15, 2001, https://www. nytimes.com/2001/09/15/opinion/heroes-amid-the-horror.html?searchResultPosi tion=1. Among those listed as missing or dead are 350 New York City firefighters, including some of the department's top leaders—William Feehan, the first deputy commissioner; Peter Ganci, the chief of department; Raymond Downey, the chief of special operations; and the Rev. Mychal Judge, the department chaplain.

39 Susan Sachs, "After the Attacks: The Trade Center; Heart-Rending Discoveries as Digging Continues in Lower Manhattan," *The New York Times*, September 15, 2001, https://www.nytimes.com/2001/09/15/us/after-attacks-trade-center-heart-rend ing-discoveries-digging-continues-lower.html.

40   Richard Pérez-Peña, "Glimpses of the Normal."

41   Elizabeth Becker, "After the Attacks: the pentagon; As Rescue Work Continues, Flight Recorders Are Found in Pentagon Rubble," *The New York Times*, September 15, 2001, https://www.nytimes.com/2001/09/15/us/after-attacks-pentagon-rescue-work-continues-flight-recorders-are-found-pentagon.html.

42   Bill Carter and Jim Rutenberg, "After the Attacks: Television; Viewers Again Return To Traditional Networks," *The New York Times*, September 15, 2001, https://www.nytimes.com/2001/09/15/us/after-the-attacks-television-viewers-again-return-to-traditional-networks.html?auth=login-email&login=email.

43   Neil A. Lewis and David Johnston, "After the Attacks: The Investigation; Justice Dept. Identifies 19 Men as Suspected Hijackers," *The New York Times*, September 15, 2001, https://www.nytimes.com/2001/09/15/us/after-attacks-investigation-justice-dept-identifies-19-men-suspected-hijackers.html.

44   Rick Bragg, "After the Attacks: Canal Street; Shops Raise Shutters, But Barriers Remain," *The New York Times*, September 15, 2001, https://www.nytimes.com/2001/09/15/us/after-the-attacks-canal-street-shops-raise-shutters-but-barriers-remain.html.

45   "After the Attacks; Text of Joint Resolution Allowing Military Action," *The New York Times*, September 15, 2001, https://www.nytimes.com/2001/09/15/us/after-the-attacks-text-of-joint-resolution-allowing-military-action.html.

46   Laurence Zuckerman, "After the Attacks: Financial Struggle; Airlines, in Search of Relief, Warn of Bankruptcy," *The New York Times*, September 15, 2001, https://www.nytimes.com/2001/09/15/us/after-attacks-financial-struggle-airlines-search-relief-warn-bankruptcy.html. Gordon M. Bethune, the chairman and chief executive of Continental Airlines, the fifth largest carrier, said in a telephone interview, referring to the industry. "We all are going to be bankrupt before the end of the year. There is not an airline that I know of that has the excess cash to handle this."

47   Michael Harrison, "Airline Collapses Amid $10bn Industry Losses," *The Independent*, September 15, 2001, https://www.independent.co.uk/news/uk/home-news/airline-collapses-amid-10bn-industry-losses-9131330.html.

48   Pam Belluck, "After the Attacks: Transportation; More Planes Take to Skies, But Plenty of Kinks Remain," *The New York Times*, September 15, 2001, Section A, Page 19, https://www.nytimes.com/2001/09/15/us/after-attacks-transportation-more-planes-take-skies-but-plenty-kinks-remain.htmlAdvertisement. According to the F.A.A., at 5:50 p.m., after the ban on private planes was lifted, there were 4,111 flights aloft, compared with 6,000 on a normal day. Federal transportation officials took steps today to bring air travel back to normal, announcing late in the day that private planes would be allowed to fly, as long as they did not come within 25 nautical miles of New York City or Washington.

49   Jane Perlez, "After the Attacks: The Overview; U.S. Demands Arab Countries 'Choose Sides,'" *The New York Times*, September 15, 2001, https://www.nytimes.com/2001/09/15/us/after-the-attacks-the-overview-us-demands-arab-countries-choose-sides.html.

50   John F. Burns, "After the Attacks: In Pakistan; U.S. Demands Air and Land Access to Pakistan," *The New York Times*, September 15, 2001, https://www.nytimes.com/2001/09/15/us/after-the-attacks-in-pakistan-us-demands-air-and-land-access-to-pakistan.html. Osama bin Laden was killed in Pakistan on May 2, 2011.

51   Ian Christopher McCaleb, CNN Washington Bureau, "Bush Tours Ground Zero in Lower Manhattan," CNN.com, September 14, 2001, http://edition.cnn.com/2001/US/09/14/bush.terrorism/; Robert D. McFadden, "After the Attacks: The President; Bush Leads Prayer, Visits Aid Crews; Congress Backs Use of Armed Force," *The New York Times*, September 15, 2001, https://www.nytimes.com/2001/09/15/us/after-attacks-president-bush-leads-prayer-visits-aid-crews-congress-backs-use.

html; Dean E. Murphy, "After the Attacks: The Reaction; Front-Line Workers Are Happy to See the Commander in Chief," *The New York Times*, September 15, 2001, https://www.nytimes.com/2001/09/15/us/after-attacks-reaction-front-line-worke rs-are-happy-see-commander-chief.html.

52 Deepa Iyer, author of We Too Sing America: South Asian, Arab, Muslim and Sikh Immigrants Shape Our Multiracial Future (The New Press 2015), email to the author, July 8, 2021.

53 Roy J. Harris Jr., "'Portraits of Grief' 10 years later: Lessons from the original New York Times 9/11 coverage," Poynter.org, August 31, 2011, https://www. poynter.org/reporting-editing/2011/portraits-of-grief-10-years-later-lessons-from-the-original-new-york-times-911-coverage/; David W. Chen, Jan Hoffman and Tina Kelley, "Portraits Of Grief: The Victims; A Driver With Size 15 Boots, a Stealth Joker and a Spiritual Diner," *The New York Times*, March 9, 2003, https://www.nytimes.com/2003/03/09/nyregion/portraits-grief-victims-drive r-with-size-15-boots-stealth-joker-spiritual-diner.html.

54 "New York remembers firefighters in first funerals," CNN.com, September 16, 2001, https://www.cnn.com/2001/US/09/15/vic.terror.funerals/; Robert D. McFadden, "After the Attacks: The Funerals; For the Fire Department, the First Three Farewells," September 16, 2001, https://www.nytimes.com/2001/09/16/us/ after-the-attacks-the-funerals-for-the-fire-department-the-first-three-farewells. html.

55 Jim Dwyer, "After the Attacks: donations; Donated Goods Deluge the City And Sit Unused," *The New York Times*, September 16, 2001, https://www.nytimes. com/2001/09/16/us/after-the-attacks-donations-donated-goods-deluge-the -city-and-sit-unused.html.

56 Kim Campbell, "New York Times Portraits Resonate Coast to Coast," *The Christian Science Monitor*, December 6, 2001, https://www.questia.com/read/1P2-32592670/ new-york-times-portraits-resonate-coast-to-coast; Janny Scott, "A Nation Challenged: The Portraits; Closing a Scrapbook Full of Life and Sorrow," *The New York Times*, December 31, 2001, https://www.nytimes.com/2001/12/31/nyregion/a-nation-challenged-the-portraits-closing-a-scrapbook-full-of-life-and-sorrow.html

57 Diane Cardwell, Glenn Collins, Winnie Hu, Andrew Jacobs, Dean E. Murphy, Lynda Richardson and Janny Scott, "A Nation Challenged: Portraits Of Grief: The Victims; Parties, Love Notes and Other Small Memories That Now Loom Large," *The New York Times*, September 18, 2001, https://timesmachine.nytimes.com/times-machine/2001/09/18/219142.html?pageNumber=42.

58 ABC News, "Bush: bin Laden Wanted Dead or Alive," ABC News, September 17, 2001, updated January 7, 2006, 10:24 a.m., https://abcnews.go.com/US/ story?id=92483&page=1.

59 "Baseball heals America," foxsports, October 20, 2016, https://www.foxsports. com/mlb/gallery/september-11-10-year-anniversary-look-back-at-baseball-ml b-comeback-082711.

60 Eric Lipton, "A Nation Challenged: The Scene; Returning to the Office On the First Monday Since the City Changed," *The New York Times*, September 18, 2001, https://www.nytimes.com/2001/09/18/nyregion/nation-challenged-scene-returnin g-office-first-monday-since-city-changed.html.

61 Bill Carter, "Letterman Leads Talk Show Hosts Back on the Air," *The New York Times*, September 19, 2001, https://www.nytimes.com/2001/09/19/arts/ letterman-leads-talk-show-hosts-back-on-the-air.html.

62 Susan Sachs, "A Nation Challenged: The Site; At the Site, Little Hope Of Uncovering Survivors," *The New York Times*, September 19, 2001, https://www. nytimes.com/2001/09/19/nyregion/a-nation-challenged-the-site-at-the-site-l ittle-hope-of-uncovering-survivors.html.

63 Eric Lipton, "A Nation Challenged: The Toll; Taking Account of the Dead, Feeling Weight of History," *The New York Times*, https://www.nytimes.com/2001/10/06/nyregion/nation-challenged-toll-taking-account-dead-feeling-weight-history.html.

64 Barbara Crossette, "A Nation Challenged: History; Afghanistan, for Ages an Affliction to Mighty Empires, Is Not Easily Subdued," *The New York Times*, September 18, 2001, https://www.nytimes.com/2001/09/18/world/nation-challenged-history-afghanistan-for-ages-affliction-mighty-empires-not.html.

65 Tamar Lewin and Gustav Niebuhr, "A Nation Challenged: Violence; Attacks and Harassment Continue on Middle Eastern People and Mosques," *The New York Times*, September 18, 2001, https://www.nytimes.com/2001/09/18/us/nation-challenged-violence-attacks-harassment-continue-middle-eastern-people.html.

66 James Dao and Steven Lee Myers, "A Nation Challenged: The Military; Pentagon Activates First Wave of Guardsmen and Reservists," *The New York Times*, September 18, 2001, https://www.nytimes.com/2001/09/18/us/nation-challenged-military-pentagon-activates-first-wave-guardsmen-reservists.html.

67 Laura M. Holson and Laurence Zuckerman, "A Nation Challenged: The Industry; Boeing and United Plan to Lay Off Thousands," *The New York Times*, September 19, 2001, https://www.nytimes.com/2001/09/19/business/a-nation-challenged-the-industry-boeing-and-united-plan-to-lay-off-thousands.html.

68 Philip Shenon and Robin Toner, "A Nation Challenged: Policy And Legislation; U.S. Widens Policy on Detaining suspects; Troubled Airlines Get Federal Aid Pledge," *The New York Times*, September 19, 2001, https://www.nytimes.com/2001/09/19/us/nation-challenged-policy-legislation-us-widens-policy-detaining-suspects.html.

69 Richard Pérez-Peña, "A Nation Challenged: Reporter's Notebook; Huge Memorial Service In Central Park Is Put Off," *The New York Times*, September 19, 2001, https://www.nytimes.com/2001/09/19/nyregion/nation-challenged-reporters-notebook-huge-memorial-service-central-park-put-off.html.

70 Alison Mitchell and Richard W. Stevenson, "A Nation Challenged: Congress; Bush and Leaders Confer on Way To Bolster Weakened Economy," September 20, 2001, https://www.nytimes.com/2001/09/20/us/nation-challenged-congress-bush-leaders-confer-way-bolster-weakened-economy.html.

71 David E. Sanger, "A Nation Challenged: The Overview; Bush Orders Heavy Bombers Near Afghans; Demands bin Laden Now, Not Negotiations," *The New York Times*, September 20, 2001, https://www.nytimes.com/2001/09/20/world/nation-challenged-overview-bush-orders-heavy-bombers-near-afghans-demands-bin.html.

72 Jennifer Steinhauer, "A Nation Challenged: The Tally; Giuliani Reports Sharp Increase in the Number of Those Listed as Missing," September 21, 2001, https://www.nytimes.com/2001/09/21/nyregion/nation-challenged-tally-giuliani-reports-sharp-increase-number-those-listed.html.

73 R. W. Apple Jr., "A Nation Challenged: News Analysis; A Clear Message: 'I Will Not Relent,'" *The New York Times*, September 21, 2001, https://www.nytimes.com/2001/09/21/world/a-nation-challenged-news-analysis-a-clear-message-i-will-not-relent.html; Elisabeth Bumiller, "A Nation Challenged: The Overview; Bush Pledges Attack on Afghanistan Unless It Surrenders bin Laden Now; He Creates Cabinet Post for Security," *The New York Times*, September 21, 2001, https://www.nytimes.com/2001/09/21/world/nation-challenged-overview-bush-pledges-attack-afghanistan-unless-it-surrenders.html; eMediaMillWorks, "Text: President Bush Addresses the Nation," *The Washington Post* online, September 20, 2001, https://www.washingtonpost.com/wp-srv/nation/specials/attacked/transcripts/bushaddress_092001.html.

74 Susan Saulny, "A Nation Challenged: Battery Park City; The Displaced Begin to Make Their Way Back Home," *The New York Times*, September 21, 2001, https://www.nytimes.com/2001/09/21/nyregion/nation-challenged-battery-park-city-displaced-begin-make-their-way-back-home.html.

75   Lizette Alvarez with Stephen Labaton, "A Nation Challenged: The Bailout; An Airline Bailout," *The New York Times*, September 22, 2001, https://www.nytimes.com/2001/09/22/business/a-nation-challenged-the-bailout-an-airline-bailout.html.
76   James Risen and David Johnston, "A Nation Challenged: The Investigation; Tape Reveals Wild Struggle On Flight 93," *The New York Times*, September 22, 2001, https://www.nytimes.com/2001/09/22/us/a-nation-challenged-the-investigation-tape-reveals-wild-struggle-on-flight-93.html.
77   Jane Perlez, "A Nation Challenged: Cooperation; U.S. Sanctions On Islamabad Will Be Lifted," *The New York Times*, September 22, 2001, https://www.nytimes.com/2001/09/22/world/a-nation-challenged-cooperation-us-sanctions-on-islamabad-will-be-lifted.html.
78   Matthew L. Wald, "A Nation Challenged: The Airports; Democratic Leaders Say They Back a Government Takeover of Security," *The New York Times*, September 24, 2001, https://www.nytimes.com/2001/09/24/us/nation-challenged-airports-democratic-leaders-say-they-back-government-takeover.html; "Federal Role Sought For Airport Security," *The New York Times*, September 24, 2001, https://www.nytimes.com/2001/09/24/us/federal-role-sought-for-airport-security.html.
79   Robert D. McFadden, "A Nation Challenged: The Service; In a Stadium of Heroes, Prayers for the Fallen and Solace for Those Left Behind," *The New York Times*, September 24, 2001, https://www.nytimes.com/2001/09/24/nyregion/nation-challenged-service-stadium-heroes-prayers-for-fallen-solace-for-those.html; "Union Square Park, Yankee Stadium Hosts 'A Prayer for America," *The Daily Plant*, September 25, 2001, https://www.nycgovparks.org/parks/union-square-park/dailyplant/10920; "'Prayer for America' embraces many faiths," CNN.com, September 23, 2001 Posted: 11:15 a.m. EDT, http://www.cnn.com/2001/US/09/23/vic.yankee.memorial.service/index.html.
80   Terry Pristin and Leslie Eaton, "A Nation Challenged: The Unemployed; Disaster's Aftershocks: Number of Workers Out of a Job Is Rising," *The New York Times*, September 26, 2001, https://www.nytimes.com/2001/09/26/nyregion/nation-challenged-unemployed-disaster-s-aftershocks-number-workers-job-rising.html.
81   Dexter Filkins, "A Nation Challenged: Rumors; As Thick as the Ash, Myths are Swirling," *The New York Times*, September 25, 2001, https://www.nytimes.com/2001/09/25/nyregion/a-nation-challenged-rumors-as-thick-as-the-ash-myths-are-swirling.html.
82   Richard L. Berke and Janet Elder, "A Nation Challenged: The Poll; Poll Finds Support for War and Fear on Economy," *The New York Times*, September 25, 2001, https://www.nytimes.com/2001/09/25/us/nation-challenged-congress-lawmakers-tap-brakes-bush-s-hurtling-antiterrorism.html. According to this article, xix in ten respondents say the nation is in a recession and two in ten say the nation is near one. Asked whether they had more confidence in President Bush or his advisers, 70 percent said they had equal confidence in both. Of those who chose, 22 percent expressed greater confidence in President Bush's advisers; 5 percent said they had more confidence in the president. More than seven in ten Americans consider themselves very patriotic, a substantial rise since the question was last asked a decade ago. Eighty-four percent of Americans say they have a good image of New York City, up from 61 percent when the question was last asked in early 1998. Sixty-one percent of people who do not live in New York City said they would take a trip there in the next six months if they could afford it or had the time off.
83   Milt Freudenheim, "A Nation Challenged: The Destinations; Empty Hotels and Ships Offering Lots of Discounts," *The New York Times*, September 25, 2001, https://www.nytimes.com/2001/09/25/business/nation-challenged-destinations-empty-hotels-ships-offering-lots-discounts.html.
84   Freudenheim, "Empty Hotels and Ships Offering Lots of Discounts."

85 Matthew L. Wald, "A Nation Challenged: Airline Security; Proposal to Arm Pilots Gets Mixed Reaction," *The New York Times*, September 26, 2001, https://www.nytimes.com/2001/09/26/us/a-nation-challenged-airline-security-proposal-to-arm-pilots-gets-mixed-reaction.html.

86 Glenn Collins, Robin Finn, Winnie Hu and Floyd Norris, "A Nation Challenged: Portraits Of Grief: The Victims; At Work and at Home, Lives Filled With Aspirations and Inspirations," *The New York Times*, September 27, 2001, https://www.nytimes.com/2001/09/27/nyregion/nation-challenged-portraits-grief-victims-work-home-lives-filled-with.html.

87 Sherri Day, "A Nation Challenged: The Airlines; Delta Announces Job Cuts and Reductions in Service," *The New York Times*, September 27, 2001, https://www.nytimes.com/2001/09/27/business/nation-challenged-airlines-delta-announces-job-cuts-reductions-service.htmlRetrieved 1/21/2020.

88 Kirk Johnson and Charles V. Bagli, "A Nation Challenged: The Site; Architects, Planners and Residents Wonder How to Fill the Hole in the City," *The New York Times*, September 26, 2001, https://www.nytimes.com/2001/09/26/nyregion/nation-challenged-site-architects-planners-residents-wonder-fill-hole-city.html.

89 Leslie Wayne, "A Nation Challenged: Aid To Business; Airline Bailout Encourages Other Industries to Lobby for Government Assistance," *The New York Times*, September 27, 2001, https://www.nytimes.com/2001/09/27/us/nation-challenged-aid-business-airline-bailout-encourages-other-industries-lobby.html.

90 Andrew C. Revkin, "A Nation Challenged: Hazardous Materials; States Are Asked to Pull Over Any Truck Allowed to Carry Hazardous Cargo," *The New York Times*, September 27, 2001, https://www.nytimes.com/2001/09/27/us/nation-challenged-hazardous-materials-states-are-asked-pull-over-any-truck.html.

"The Land"

1 Thomas R. Cox, *The Other Oregon: People, Environment, and History East of the Cascades* (Corvallis: Oregon State University Press, 2019), xvi and xvii.

2 Brent Walth, "Thomas William Lawson McCall (1913–1983)," *The Oregon Encyclopedia*, https://www.oregonencyclopedia.org/articles/mccall_thomas_l/#.YLNEtKEpAc-, last updated January 22, 2021.

3 William G. Robbins, peer-review commentary, May 2021, in the author's files.

4 Brent Walth, *Fire at Eden's Gate: Tom McCall & the Oregon Story*, Portland, Oregon: Oregon Historical Society Press, 1994, 5–6. Also Cox, page 243. During McCall's administration, the filthy Willamette River got cleaner and the Oregon Department of Environmental Quality was established. The Oregon Forest Practices Act of 1971 was the first of its kind, requiring that natural resources—including streams and wildlife—be protected during logging operations.

5 According to the Oregon Department of Environmental Quality, "In 1971, before the bottle bill passed, beverage containers made up as much as 40 percent of roadside litter. By 1973, they were only 10.8% and by 1979 they were down to 6%." Judy Henderson, "Fact Sheet: The Expanded Bottle Bill," Oregon Department of Environmental Quality, http://www.deq.state.or.us/lq/pubs/factsheets/sw/ExpandedBottleBill.pdf, last updated: June 26, 2007.

6 William G. Robbins, *Oregon: This Storied Land*. Seattle: University of Washington Press, 2020, p. 154. The discussion of S.B. 100 is informed by Carl Abbott, "Senate Bill 100," *The Oregon Encyclopedia*, last updated March 17, 2018, https://www.oregonencyclopedia.org/articles/senate_bill_100/#.YHNmYT8pAc8; and Oregon Planning, Department of Land Conservation and Development, "History of Land-Use Planning," https://www.oregon.gov/lcd/OP/Pages/History.aspx, retrieved on April 11, 2021.

"Economic Transition"

1   Barton Barbour, "Fur Trade in Oregon Country," *The Oregon Encyclopedia*, last updated January 20, 2021, https://www.oregonencyclopedia.org/articles/fur_trade_in_oregon_country/.

2   William G. Robbins, "Sally Bourrie's *Flight for Freedom* Project" peer review commentary, May 2021, in author's files.

3   Robbins, "Sally Bourrie's *Flight for Freedom* Project."

4   Robbins, "Sally Bourrie's *Flight for Freedom* Project."

5   Sarah Paulson, "Intel Bunny Suit," *The Oregon Encyclopedia*, last updated March 17, 2018, https://www.oregonhistoryproject.org/articles/historical-records/intel-bunny-suit/#.YHOxkT8pCOs.

Also of interest in terms of Oregon's current economic strengths:

Founded in 1964 as "Blue Ribbon Sports," the Nike Corporation based in suburban Portland (Beaverton) is perhaps Oregon's most famous company. In the 1980s, Nike broke new ground with its endorsement deal with Chicago Bulls basketball rookie Michael Jordan and the Air Jordan sneaker, which created a new category: "luxury" basketball shoes.

Trade with Asian countries accounts for a substantial proportion of the state's export revenue. George Azumano was key to growing agricultural exports to Japan, and Sho Dozono, who was born in Japan, was integral to growing Japanese tourism to Oregon as well as in economic development for the state. Japan is Oregon's largest overseas market.

6   Robbins, "Sally Bourrie's *Flight for Freedom* Project."

7   Sally Ruth Bourrie, "Fully employed, but hungry: More in Oregon face hard choices," *The Boston Globe*, December 17, 2000, at A8. The USDA report, which covered 1996–1998, classified 12.6 percent of Oregon households as "food insecure," meaning that families could barely meet their food needs, which ranked seventh-highest in America. Oregon was first in the more severe category, "food insecurity with hunger," in 5.8 percent of Oregon households. These are households in which nutritional needs are not being met, and parents and children may be skipping meals for financial reasons.

8   William Kittredge, *Hole in the Sky* (New York: Knopf, 1992), 228, quoted in Thomas R. Cox, *The Other Oregon: People, Environment, and History East of the Cascades* (Corvallis: Oregon State University Press, 2019), 246.

"The Most Politically Polarized State"

1   Nate Silver, "Oregon: Swing State or latte-drinking, Prius-driving lesbian commune?," FiveThirtyEight, May 17, 2008, https://fivethirtyeight.com/features/oregon-swing-state-or-latte-drinking/.

2   William G. Robbins, "Sally Bourrie's *Flight for Freedom* Project" peer review commentary, May 2021, in author's files.

"Water"

1   Gillian Flaccus, "Drought along the Oregon-California border could mean water cuts for farmers, tribes," Associated Press, April 12, 2021, https://www.oregonlive.com/pacific-northwest-news/2021/04/drought-along-the-oregon-california-border-could-mean-water-cuts-for-farmers-tribes.html.

2   Thomas R. Cox, *The Other Oregon: People, Environment, and History East of the Cascades* (Corvallis: Oregon State University Press, 2019), page 133. This discussion of the history of the Klamath Project was also informed by the following

sources. Klamath Basin Audubon Society, "Our Unique Habitat," https://www. klamathaudubon.org/basin-birds, retrieved June 2, 2021. William G. Robbins, "National Reclamation Act (1902)," *The Oregon Encyclopedia*, last updated March 14, 2019, https://www.oregonencyclopedia.org/articles/national_reclamation_ act_1902_/#.YDGoU3lOmUk. Stephen Most, "Klamath Basin Project (1906)," *The Oregon Encyclopedia*, https://www.oregonencyclopedia.org/articles/klamath_ basin_project_1906_/#.YDGrWHlOnVh, last updated February 6, 2020; Water Education Foundation, "Klamath River Basin Chronology," https://www.water-education.org/aquapedia/klamath-river-basin-chronology, retrieved February 20, 2021. The Klamath River flows 253 miles from Southern Oregon to the California coast, draining a basin of more than 15,000 square miles.

3   Sally Ruth Bourrie, "A Shortage of Water Pits Farmer Against Fish in Ore., Tensions Rise as US Rations Dwindle," *The Boston Globe*, August 17, 2001, A2.

4   Most, "Klamath Basin Project."

5   Southern Poverty Law Center, "Conflict in Klamath, 2001," *Intelligence Report*, Winter Issue, November 29, 2001, https://www.splcenter.org/fighting-hate/intelligence-report/2001/conflict-klamath. Associated Press, "Drought-relief fund for farmers in southern Oregon is drying up," April 28, 2002 Updated: March 11, 2011, https://www.seattlepi.com/news/article/Drought-relief-fund-fo r-farmers-in-southern-1086222.php. According to the SPLC story: "Sheriff Timothy Evinger stood by as protesters trespassed on federal land and illegally opened the head gates. In a speech naming local environmental activists, Klamath Falls police officer Jack Redfield said, 'It won't take much from [them] to spark an extremely violent response. I am talking about rioting, homicides and destruction of property.'" Redfield was temporarily put on administrative leave and the environmentalists sued the city. Ryan Pfeil, "The Battle of the Bucket: Commissioners, Residents disagree on what to do with water crisis symbol," *Herald and News*, September 19, 2008, http://www.klamathbasincrisis.org/bucket/battle091908.htm.

6   William F. Jasper, "Klamath Falls Freedom Day," *The New American*, September 24, 2001, https://www.thefreelibrary.com/Klamath+Falls+Freedom+Day.-a079789132.

7   Congressional Research Service, "Klamath River Basin Issues: An Overview of Water Use Conflicts," EveryCRSReport.com, June 13, 2002, https://www.every-crsreport.com/reports/RL31098.html.

8   Southern Poverty Law Center, "Conflict in Klamath, 2001."

9   Most, "Klamath Basin Project."

10 William G. Robbins, "Sally Bourrie's *Flight for Freedom* Project" peer review commentary, May 2021, in author's files. Also, on May 19, 2021, the Klamath Water Users Association, which represents the farmers, put out a press release telling people to stop intimidating tactics against the Bureau of Reclamation employees, which included publishing their names and addresses on social media. "KWUA Urges a stop to unacceptable behaviors, Klamath Falls News online, May 19, 2021, https:// www.klamathfallsnews.org/news/kwua-urges-a-stop-to-unacceptable-behaviors.

11 Holly Doremus and A. Dan Tarlock. "Fish, Farms, and the Clash of Cultures in the Klamath Basin." *Ecology Law Quarterly* 30, no. 2 (2003): 279. Accessed May 30, 2021. http://www.jstor.org/stable/24114216.

"Lewis and Clark"

1   James P. Ronda, "Why Lewis and Clark Matter: Amid all the hoopla, it's easy to lose sight of the expedition's true significance," *Smithsonian Magazine*, August 2003, https://www.smithsonianmag.com/history/why-lewis-and-clar k-matter-87847931/. The discussion of Lewis and Clark is also informed by the following: William L. Lang, "Lewis and Clark Expedition," *The Oregon Encyclopedia*,

retrieved February 17, 2021, https://www.oregonencyclopedia.org/articles/lewis_and_clark_expedition/#.YC3qdHlOkc8.

2   William G. Robbins, "Sally Bourrie's *Flight for Freedom* Project" peer review commentary, May 2021, in author's files.

3   Hannah Natanson, "An enslaved man was crucial to the Lewis and Clark expedition's success. Clark refused to free him afterward," *The Washington Post*, January 12, 2020, https://www.washingtonpost.com/history/2020/01/12/york-slave-lewis-clark-expedition/.

4   Stephenie Ambrose Tubbs, "Sacagawea," *The Oregon Encyclopedia*, last updated March 16, 2021, https://www.oregonencyclopedia.org/articles/sacagawea/. Irving W. Anderson, "Sacagawea," *Lewis and Clark the Journey of the Corps of Discovery*, https://www.pbs.org/lewisandclark/inside/saca.html. Accessed March 24, 2021.

5   William G. Robbins, "Sally Bourrie's *Flight for Freedom* Project."

"The Oregon Trail"

1   William G. Robbins, "Sally Bourrie's *Flight for Freedom* Project" peer review commentary, May 2021, in author's files.

2   William L. Lang, "Oregon Trail," *The Oregon Encyclopedia*, last updated January 20, 2021, https://www.oregonencyclopedia.org/articles/oregon_trail/.

3   William G. Robbins, *Oregon: This Storied Land* (Seattle: University of Washington Press, 2020), 49.

4   Jeanne Abrams, "On the Road Again: Consumptives Traveling for Health in the American West," *Great Plains Quarterly*, 30 no. 4 (fall 2010): 273–274. The tubercle bacillus would not be discovered until 1882.

5   This discussion of the Oregon Donation Land Law is based on William G. Robbins, "Oregon Donation Land Law," *The Oregon Encyclopedia*, last updated February 2, 2021, https://www.oregonencyclopedia.org/articles/oregon_donation_land_act/#.YLLMrKEpAc8.

6   Robbins, "Oregon Donation Land Law."

"Immigrants of Color in Oregon"

1   Hanna Anderson, "How Portland's Black History is Made," *PSU Vanguard*, February 3, 2021, https://psuvanguard.com/how-portlands-black-history-is-made/.

2   David Peterson del Mar, "14ᵗʰ Amendment," *The Oregon Encyclopedia*, https://www.oregonencyclopedia.org/articles/14th_amendment/, last updated September 16, 2020

3   Anderson, "How Portland's Black History is Made."

4   William G. Robbins, "Sally Bourrie's *Flight for Freedom* Project" peer review commentary, May 2021, in author's files.

5   The discussion of Latinx history in Oregon is based largely on the following entry in *The Oregon Encyclopedia*: Jerry Garcia, "Latinos in Oregon," *The Oregon Encyclopedia*, https://www.oregonencyclopedia.org/articles/hispanics_in_oregon/#.YC4VonlOkc8, last updated January 20, 2021. Garcia's note to the entry: "Latino refers to persons who live in the United States and trace their ancestry to Latin America or, in some cases, the Caribbean or Spain. The term "Latino" was included for the first time in the 2000 census. In that census, people of Spanish/Hispanic/Latino origin could identify as Mexican, Puerto Rican, Cuban, or "other Spanish/Hispanic/Latino." In the 2010 census it was noted that, "for this census, Hispanic origins are not races." This information was gleaned from Lynn Stephen,

The Story of PCUN and the Farmworker Movement in Oregon. Revised edition. Eugene, Ore.: Center for Latino/a and Latin American Studies, 2012, p. 6.

6   Cheryl A. Brooks, "Race, Politics, and Denial: Why Oregon Forgot to Ratify the Fourteenth Amendment," *Oregon Law Review* 83 (2004), 735; Much of the discussion of the history of Blacks in Oregon is based on Darrell Millner, "Blacks in Oregon," *The Oregon Encyclopedia,* https://www.oregonencyclopedia.org/articles/blacks_in_oregon/, last updated January 20, 2021.

The Provisional Government, created in May–July 1843, was the first governmental structure created by non-Natives on the Pacific Coast of North America. Barbara Mahoney, "Provisional Government," *The Oregon Encyclopedia,* last updated September 16, 2020, https://www.oregonencyclopedia.org/articles/provisional_govt_conference_in_champoeg_1843/.

7   Darrell Millner, "Blacks in Oregon," *The Oregon Encyclopedia,* https://www.oregonencyclopedia.org/articles/blacks_in_oregon/, last updated January 20, 2021. Greg Nokes, "Black Exclusion Laws in Oregon," *The Oregon Encyclopedia,* https://www.oregonencyclopedia.org/articles/exclusion_laws/, last updated July 6, 2020.

8   Jesse Applegate, Views of Oregon History 74 (1878) (unpublished manuscript on file with the University of California Berkeley Bancroft Library), as quoted in Brooks, "Race, Politics, and Denial," 736.

9   Douglas Lee, "Chinese Americans in Oregon," *The Oregon Encyclopedia,* https://www.oregonencyclopedia.org/articles/chinese_americans_in_oregon/#.YGF0Zz8pAc8, last updated January 26, 2021.

10   "Black in Oregon 1840–1870 National and Oregon Chronology of Events" *Oregon Secretary of State Shemia Fagan,* retrieved May 30, 2021, https://sos.oregon.gov/archives/exhibits/black-history/Pages/context/chronology.aspx; David Peterson del Mar, "15th Amendment," *The Oregon Encyclopedia,* https://www.oregonencyclopedia.org/articles/15th_amendment/#.YLMkCKEpAc8, last updated January 21, 2021.

11   By David Peterson del Mar "14th Amendment," *The Oregon Encyclopedia,* https://www.oregonencyclopedia.org/articles/14th_amendment/, last updated September 16, 2020.

12   Brooks, "Race, Politics, and Denial," 759. True healing comes from facing, coming to terms with, and reconciling the past with the present, says Brooks.

13   Douglas Lee, "Chinese Americans in Oregon"; Tim Greyhavens, "Oregon Albina, Approximate Site of the Former Chinese Community," *The No Place Project,* 2020, https://www.noplaceproject.com/albina, retrieved April 17, 2021.

14   The discussion of the Japanese as well as the context around their entry into the United States based on the Exclusion Act can be found in George Katagiri, "Japanese Americans in Oregon," *The Oregon Encyclopedia,* last updated January 26, 2021, https://www.oregonencyclopedia.org/articles/japanese_americans_in_oregon_immigrants_from_the_west/#.YC4FB3lOkc8; History.com Editors, "Japanese Internment Camps," *History,* last updated March 17, 2021, https://www.history.com/topics/world-war-ii/japanese-american-relocation; "Japanese-American Internment During World War II," *National Archives,* last reviewed March 17, 2020, https://www.archives.gov/education/lessons/japanese-relocation; "Asian Immigration," ImmigrationHistory.org, retrieved March 28, 2021, https://immigrationhistory.org/lesson-plan/asian-migration/.

15   According to Katagiri, they included Teikoku and Furuya grocers, Ota Tofu, S. Ban Mercantile, the Royal Palm Hotel, Kobayashi express company, Yabuki Laundry, Oshu Nippo newspaper, Tokio Sukiyaki restaurant, and dentists Dr. Kei Koyama and Dr. Kiyofusa Katayama.

16   Cherstin M. Lyon, "Alien Land Laws," *Densho Encyclopedia,* last updated Oct. 8, 2020, https://encyclopedia.densho.org/Alien_land_laws/. Dr. Jacqueline Peterson-Loomis, "Immigration and Exclusion Time Line Oregon History 101,"

The Oregon Encyclopedia, retrieved April 17, 2021. https://www.oregonencyclope-dia.org/media/uploads/Oregon_History_101_Timeline_12-1-14.pdf.

17   Office of the Historian, Foreign Service Institute, United States Department of State, https://history.state.gov/milestones/1921-1936/immigration-act, retrieved March 28, 2021.

18   See Quintard Taylor, *In Search of the Racial Frontier: African Americans in the American West 1528–1990* (New York: Norton, 1998). Taylor states that while Black cowboys and Buffalo Soldiers, for example, have been popularized, African Americans primarily could be found in urban areas in the West.

19   Eckard Toy, "Ku Klux Klan," *The Oregon Encyclopedia*. last updated September 19, 2019. https://www.oregonencyclopedia.org/articles/ku_klux_klan/#. YHsiez8pAc8. Because the KKK was so large in Oregon during the 1920s, it has been the subject of much study, beginning with Toy's first examination in the 1950s. See also Alana Semuels, "The Racist History of Portland, the Whitest City in America," *The Atlantic*, July 22, 2016, https://www.theatlantic.com/business/archive/2016/07/racist-history-portland/492035/.

20   "Repatriation raids" that unexpectedly put Latinx people on trucks buses or trains bound for Mexico took place across the United States (and continued during the Roosevelt administration); research shows that about sixty percent were American citizens. Becky Little, "The U.S. Deported a Million of Its Own Citizens to Mexico During the Great Depression," History.com, January 12, 2019, https://www.history.com/news/great-depression-repatriation-drives-mexico-deportation.
      Oregon did not make the repatriation raids a practice, though Mexicans were removed in less aggressive ways. Recent research has shown that these deportations made no difference in the ability for white people to make a living during this time. In fact, research shows no change or even a decline in employment rates and a decrease in wages for the remaining people during the period of deportations. Jongkwan Lee, Giovanni Peri, and Vasil Yasenov, "The Employment Effects of Mexican Repatriations: Evidence from the 1930's," Cambridge, Massachusetts: National Bureau Of Economic Research Working Paper No. 23885, September 2017. https://www.nber.org/system/files/working_papers/w23885/w23885.pdf.

21   James C. McNaughton, "Chinese-Americans in World War II," U.S. Army Center of Military History, 16 May 2000, https://history.army.mil/html/topics/apam/chinese-americans.html. Matthew Daly, "Chinese Americans who served in WWII honored by Congress," *Military Times*, December 9, 2020, https://www.militarytimes.com/military-honor/salute-veterans/2020/12/09/chinese-americans-who-served-in-wwii-honored-by-congress/.

22   Center for History and New Media at George Mason University and American Social History Project/Center for Media and Learning, The Graduate Center, City University of New York, "Executive Order 9066: The President Authorizes Japanese Relocation," *History Matters: The U.S. Survey Course on the Web*, http://historymatters.gmu.edu/d/5154, retrieved March 28, 2021.

23   Craig Collisson, "Japanese American Wartime Incarceration in Oregon," *The Oregon Encyclopedia*, https://www.oregonencyclopedia.org/articles/japanese_internment/, last updated March 22, 2021.

24   The May 15, 1953, *Oregonian* reported: "Agents Sweep Rising Tide of Mexican Illegals South to Border." Quoted in "Latinos in Oregon," *The Oregon Encyclopedia*.

25   David Woken, "Pineros y Campesinos Unidos del Noroeste (PCUN)," *The Oregon Encyclopedia*, last updated August 28, 2018, https://www.oregonencyclopedia.org/articles/pineros_y_campesinos_unidos_del_noroeste_pcun/.

26   Collison, "Japanese American Wartime Incarceration in Oregon."

27   Mitzi Loftus, "Day of Remembrance," *The Oregon Encyclopedia*, last updated March 17, 2018, https://www.oregonencyclopedia.org/articles/day_of_remembrance/#. YHunXT8pAc8.

28 In a 1960 study of the effects of the law by Portland State University and University of Oregon researchers funded by the Portland League of Women Voters "Two findings were particularly important, though not surprising to many. First, the study found that 'they [African Americans] have lower incomes than whites with a similar educational level and the housing they find available to them is in neighborhoods which are of a lower economic class than neighborhoods where whites of a similar educational level live.' Second, findings from the study also suggested that 'increased contact with people of a different race leads to increased understanding.'" Quoted in Joshua Binus, "Fair Housing in Oregon Study," Oregon History Project, © Oregon Historical Society, 2003. https://www.oregonhistoryproject.org/articles/historical-records/fair.

29 Alana Semuels, "The Racist History of Portland, the Whitest City in America," *The Atlantic*, July 22, 2016, https://www.theatlantic.com/business/archive/2016/07/racist-history-portland/492035/.

30 Trudy Flores, Sarah Griffith, "Albina Riots, 1967," *Oregon History Project*, © Oregon Historical Society, 2002, https://www.oregonhistoryproject.org/articles/historical-records/albina-riot-1967/#.YF_29j8pCOs. Also "Blacks in Oregon" Oregon Encyclopedia entry. Also Flores and Griffith, "African American Community Protests School Board," *Oregon History Project*, © Oregon Historical Society, 2002. last updated March 17, 2018. https://www.oregonhistoryproject.org/articles/historical-records/african-american-community-protests-school-board/#.YF_4ej8pCOs.

31 The era began under Mayor John Elwood "Bud" Clark, Jr., who owned the Goose Hollow Inn tavern As mayor from 1985–1992, Clark created a nationally recognized 12-Point Homeless Plan, supported the growth of mass transit, including MAX Light Rail, and earned an award from the AMBAC Corporation as the best managed city of its size in the United States.

32 Steven Dubois, "Bias complaints at Daimler Portland plant settled for $2.4M," the Associated Press, updated February 4, 2015, https://www.seattletimes.com/business/bias-complaints-at-daimler-portland-plant-settled-for-24m-2/; Aimee Green, "Jury awards $750,000 to black worker for racist incidents at Daimler Trucks," *The Oregonian/OregonLive*, updated February 23, 2017, https://www.oregonlive.com/portland/2017/02/jury_awards_750000_to_black_wo.html.

33 David Sarasohn, "William A. Hilliard (1927-2017)," *The Oregon Encyclopedia*, last updated October 12, 2020, https://www.oregonencyclopedia.org/articles/hilliard_william_a_1927_/.

34 Sara Piasecki, "DeNorval Unthank (1899-1977)," *The Oregon Encyclopedia*, last updated December 12, 2020, https://www.oregonencyclopedia.org/articles/unthank_denorval_1899_1977_/#.YMWId0wpAc8.

35 Tim Mahoney, "James DePreist (x-2013)," *The Oregon Encyclopedia*. last updated February 10, 2020, https://www.oregonencyclopedia.org/articles/depreist_james_1936_/; David Stabler, "James DePreist: scenes from a musical life," *The Oregonian*, posted February 8, 2013, updated January 10, 2019, https://www.oregonlive.com/performance/2013/02/james_depreist_scenes_from_a_m.html; Elaine Woo, "James DePreist, celebrated conductor, dies at 76," February 10, 2013, https://www.washingtonpost.com/entertainment/music/james-depreist-celebrated-conductor-dies-at-76/2013/02/10/a3a60cce-7397-11e2-8f84-3e4b513b1a13_story.html.

"Appendix A: The Aftermath"

1 Len Bergstein, with the author, May 13, 2021.

2 Many of the emails received by Mayor Katz are in the author's files. John Baker, "Remembering 9-11, Going Back," *Woodburn Independent*, September 11, 2002, 1

and 3. " I got to see my interview on the plane for the first time. My wife had taped it, but I hadn't been able to watch it. It had been kind of emotional for me," said George Haight.

3   Jan Woodruff, email to Barbara Baker, Eric Schmidt, Loen & Sho Dozono, Marilyn Slizeski, Steve Feltz, Vera Katz; "F4F Alumni Group Update," January 04, 2002, photocopy in author's files.

4   "Freedom Flight Should Keep on Flying," editorial, *Skanner*, October 10, 2001, page number unknown.

5   Sho Dozono, "Kick Your Kicker Back to Oregon," *Portland Tribune*, November 27, 2001, unknown page. Checks averaged $157.

6   In addition, Sho Dozono was the recipient of many honors for his leadership of the Flight for Freedom. In 2002, he received the following awards: American Society of Travel Agents' highest national award, ASTA 2002 Agent of the Year; American Express Great Performer; and CelebrAsian 2002's Excellence Award from the US Pan Asian American Chamber of Commerce (USPAACC). He also received the Portland Award, which annually recognizes the greatest overall contribution to the visitor industry by the Portland Oregon Visitors Association (POVA). Joe D'Alessandro, POVA's president and CEO said: "Following the attacks, the travel industry suffered significant economic losses. We needed to do something to help restore confidence in the travel industry, which accounts for 78 million American jobs and $582 billion in economic impact. The Flight for Freedom helped encourage people to start traveling again for both band vacation purposes. POVA is very proud that Oregonians were behind this effort." Dozono also received the 2002 Governor's Freedom Award "For turning a vision into reality through the Flight For Freedom which sent 1,000 Oregonians to New York City October 4-9, 2001, Flight For Freedom united Oregonians and New Yorkers, brought positive, international exposure to Oregon's economic efforts and sent a message to our nation that we will remain strong and free."; and Oregon Hero of the Week, named on the Senate floor by Oregon Senator Gordon H. Smith.

In 2002, the Dozonos, McGowan, and Samson received a special award for the Flight for Freedom from the Oregon Trail Chapter of the American Red Cross as well.

In 2003, Dozono received the Citizen of the World Award from the Japan-America Society of Oregon, and the Governor's Tourism Award. In presenting the award, Gov. Ted Kulongoski said:

Each year, the Governor's Tourism Award is presented to an individual or organization that embodies a spirit of cooperation and statewide involvement in Oregon's visitor industry development. This year's recipient is so qualified, so impressive that it's difficult to capture the depth of his service to Oregon over the past quarter century.

In 2021, Travel Oregon Chief Executive Officer Todd Davidson said, "Every year there are a series of awards given out and the highest award is the Governor's Tourism Award. They bestowed that on the Dozonos because of the Flight for Freedom . . . . It was a great call." Interview with the author, February 11, 2021.

Sources: "Dozono Named ASTA's Agent of the Year," *Travel Weekly*, May 4, 2002, https://www.travelweekly.com/Travel-News/Travel-Agent-Issues/Dozono-named-ASTA-s-agent-of-the-year; Reed Massengill, "Our Heroes," *Context: Remembering 9/11: How American Express is responding to—and recovering from –the tragic events of September 11, 2001*, undated, unpaginated; Portland Oregon Visitors Association press release, "'Flight for Freedom' Tops List of Tourism Award Winners," June 10, 2002, http://www.travelportland.com/media/news/print_res/freedom_flight_02.html, retrieved July 26, 2003; Senator Gordon H. Smith, Speaking on Oregon Hero of the Week, 107th Congress, 1st sess., *Congressional Record* 148, No. 64 (May 17, 2002): S4534; Gov. Ted Kulongoski,

"Speech by Gov. Ted Kulongski," [Governor's Tourism Award] April 15, 2003, https://en.wikisource.org/wiki/Speech_by_Governor_Kulongoski, retrieved February 26, 2021.

7   "Scaled Back Recovery Prompts Scuffle Between Police, Firefighters," CNN.com, November 2, 2001, http://www.cnn.com/2001/US/11/02/rec.firefighter.protest/; "Fire Fighter Memorial Service Postponed: Healing Not Possible as City Halts Recovery and Arrests Fire Fighters," November 7, 2001, http://daily.iaff.org/memorial2/main.htm.

8   Azumano Travel website announcement, in author's files. Gordon Hovies, "St. Patrick's Day Parade," *The Straight Stream*, XXII, no. 2 (July 2002): 9. Portland firefighters Dwight Englert, Gordon Hovies, Wes Loucks, Deputy Chief Del Stevens, and Bob Woolington worked at Ground Zero. During the trip, Stevens learned later that he'd been chatting with Billy Joel at McSorley's Pub on St. Patrick's Day.

9   Handout, untitled, small informal gathering of Flight for Freedom participants, February or March 2002. In the author's files.

10   Mrs. Denise Tessitore, "Modern Day Patriotic Americans," *P.S. 6 Newsletter*, May 2002, photographs of title page and article in author's files. P.S. 6 is also called the "Corporal Allan F. Kivlehan School."

11   Jessica Pressler, "Cantor Fitzgerald," *New York* magazine, August 26, 2011, https://nymag.com/news/9-11/10th-anniversary/cantor-fitzgerald/.

12   Gordon Hovies, "Vice Presidents' Reports," *The Straight Stream*, XXII, no. 2 (July 2002): 4.

13   David Morkal, interview with the author, January 22, 2021.

14   Sal Chillemi, interview with the author, February 24, 2021.

15   Oregon Convention Center website, https://web.archive.org/web/20021022091143/http://www.oregoncc.org/memorial/memorial_FAQ.htm, retrieved May 13, 2021.

16   Azumano Travel enewsletter, photocopy in author's files; Elizabeth Mitchell, "Marking the date of the terrorist attacks: 9/11: The Experts Recommend," About.com, retrieved May 13, 2021, http://portlandor.about.com/library/weekly/aa091102a.htm

17   Cliff Madison, interview with the author, October 31, 2021.

18   Azumano Travel, "9-11 Memorial Trip" mailer, undated, in the author's files.

19   Sandra Kempel, interview with the author, July 25, 2003.

20   John Baker, "Remembering 9-11 Going back," *Woodburn Independent*, September 11, 2002, pages 1 and 3.

21   Michael Rose, "Group of Oregonians head to N.Y.C. this week," *Statesman Journal*, September 6, 2002, http://online.statesmanjournal.com/sp_section_article.cfm?i=47788&s=2041, retrieved September 28, 2003.

22   Jonathan Nicholas, *The Oregonian*, February 15, 2006.

23   George Passadore, "Ground Zero: Where Our Spirit Begins," *Portland Business Journal*, October 19, 2006, updated October 22, 2006, https://www.bizjournals.com/portland/stories/2006/10/23/editorial4.html. Portland Police Captain Cliff Madison and his wife, Melody, also attended the five-year-anniversary trip, and Madison spoke.

24   Sho Dozono, "Flight for Freedom: Ten Years Later, Oregonians Still Love New York," *The Oregonian*, September 10, 2011, updated January 10, 2019, https://www.oregonlive.com/opinion/2011/09/flight_for_freedom_ten_years_1.html?fbclid=IwAR1CMZgXiTpvyaI6QTKBhRBHUMZyzmijaK2eB1PNcJw-cEwQK5K6eyKkCKd8.

25   David Stabler, "Gay Men's Chorus Will Perform in N.Y. on 9/11," *The Oregonian*, August 25, 2011, E1.

26   Scott Williams, interview with the author, March 23, 2021.

27   "More than 60 people from Oregon and around the United States made up the original 'Flight of Friendship' trip [in early February] to help people in Thailand who work in or are dependent upon the tourism industry for their livelihood.

Tourism is recognized as one of the key industries in the tsunami-affected area." "Flight of Friendship' plans second trip," *Portland Business Journal*, March 14, 2005, 10:41 a.m. PST, updated: March 14, 2005, 11:40 a.m. PST, https://www.bizjournals.com/portland/stories/2005/03/14/daily4.html.   U.S. Representative Greg Walden recognized the Flight of Friendship on the floor of Congress: "Flight of Freedom: A Journey to Save Jobs," *Congressional Record*. 109th Cong., 1st sess., February 1, 2005, Vol. 151, No. 8, E129, https://www.con-gress.gov/congressional-record/2005/2/1/extensions-of-remarks-section/article/e129-1?q=%7B%22search%22%3A%5B%22%5C%22flight+of+friend-ship%5C%22%22%5D%7D&s=2&r=2.

BIBLIOGRAPHY

Transcripts of all interviews by the author available in the author's files.

9-11 Artists Respond, Vol. 1 (January 2002): 154.

Abbott, Carl. "Columbia River Gorge National Scenic Area." *The Oregon Encyclopedia.* https://www.oregonencyclopedia.org/articles/columbia_gorge_national_scenic_act/#.YLg_cEwpAc8. Last updated March 17, 2018.

Abbott, Carl. "Portland." *The Oregon Encyclopedia.* https://www.oregonencyclopedia.org/articles/portland/#.YLgoSEwpAc8. Last updated January 20, 2021.

Abbott, Carl. "Senate Bill 100." *The Oregon Encyclopedia.* https://www.oregonencyclopedia.org/articles/senate_bill_100/#.YHNmYT8pAc8. Last updated March 17, 2018.

ABC News. "Bush: bin Laden Wanted Dead or Alive." abcnews.go.com. September 17, 2001 updated January 7, 2006, 10:24 a.m. https://abcnews.go.com/US/story?id=92483&page=1.

ABC News. "Census Finds Least Diverse Part of Nation." abcnews.go.com. January 7, 2006. https://abcnews.go.com/US/story?id=93608&page=1.

ABC7 New York. "Hardest Hit Firehouse Still Recovering 10 Years Later." September 11, 2011. https://abc7ny.com/archive/8349429/.

Abrams, Jeanne. "On the Road Again: Consumptives Traveling for Health in the American West, 1840–1925." *Great Plains Quarterly* 30, no. 4 (2010): 271-85. Accessed May 30, 2021. http://www.jstor.org/stable/23534371.

Acklen, Craig. "Parade marchers did Oregon proud." Letter to the editor, *Daily Courier* (Grants Pass, Ore.), October 12, 2001. Also appeared in *The Oregonian* on October 13, 2001.

"AFTER THE ATTACKS; Text of Joint Resolution Allowing Military Action." *The New York Times*, September 15, 2001, https://www.nytimes.com/2001/09/15/us/after-the-attacks-text-of-joint-resolution-allowing-military-action.html.

Agencies. "Worldwide chaos as airlines struggle to maintain services." September 12, 2001. https://www.independent.companyuk/news/world/americas/worldwide-chaos-as-airlines-struggle-to-maintain-services-9153433.html. Retrieved February 29, 2020.

Agogino, Cindy. Interview with the author. Fall 2020.

"Alpha Delta Phi Fraternity: Building The Entire Man: Social, Moral, Intellectual." Alpha Delta Phi website. https://www.alphadeltaphi.org/. Retrieved May 22, 2021.

Alvarez, Lizette with Stephen Labaton. "A Nation Challenged: The Bailout; An Airline Bailout." *The New York Times*. September 22, 2001. https://www.nytimes.com/2001/09/22/business/a-nation-challenged-the-bailout-an-airline-bailout.html.

Ambrose Tubbs, Stephenie. "Sacagawea." *The Oregon Encyclopedia.* https://www.oregonencyclopedia.org/articles/sacagawea/. Last updated March 16, 2021.

Amuchastegui, Tahn. Email to the author, March 22, 2002.

Amuchastegui, Tahn. Email to the author, September 10, 2002.

Amuchastegui, Tahn. Email to the author, April 9, 2021.

Andersen, Julie. Interview with the author. October 9, 2003.

Anderson, Hanna. "How Portland's Black History is Made." *PSU Vanguard*. February 3, 2021. https://psuvanguard.com/how-portlands-black-history-is-made/.

Anderson, Irving W. "Sacagawea." *Lewis and Clark the Journey of the Corps of Discovery*. PBS online. https://www.pbs.org/lewisandclark/inside/saca.html. Accessed March 24, 2021.

Anderson, Jennifer. "School-Funding Pros Go for the Bucks Again." *Portland Tribune*. January 10, 2006. https://sparkaction.org/content/school-funding-pros-g o-bucks-again.

Apple Jr., R. W. "After the Attacks: News Analysis; No Middle Ground." *The New York Times*. September 14, 2001. https://www.nytimes.com/2001/09/14/us/after-th e-attacks-news-analysis-no-middle-ground.htmlSupported. by

Apple Jr., R. W. "A Nation Challenged: News Analysis; A Clear Message: 'I Will Not Relent.'" *The New York Times*. September 21, 2001. https://www.nytimes. com/2001/09/21/world/a-nation-challenged-news-analysis-a-clear-message-i- will-not-relent.html.

Applegate, Jesse. Views of Oregon History 74 (1878) (unpublished manuscript on file with the University of California Berkeley Bancroft Library), as quoted in Brooks, "Race, Politics, and Denial," 736.

Armstrong, Regis J. *Francis of Assisi, Early Documents: Vol. 1, The Saint*. Hyde Park New York: New City Press, 2002. Quoted in *Franciscan Seculars: From Gospel to Life— From Life to Gospel*. http://franciscanseculars.com/the-canticle-of-the-creatures/. Retrieved June 19, 2021.

Artharee, Baruti. Email to the author. May 11, 2021.

Artharee, Baruti. Interview with the author. April 16, 2021.

"Asian Immigration." ImmigrationHistory.org. https://immigrationhistory.org/ lesson-plan/asian-migration/. Retrieved March 28, 2021.

Associated Press. "After the Attacks: The Vigils; In Silence And Prayer, Remembering The Victims." *The New York Times*, September 14, 2001, https://www.nytimes. com/2001/09/14/us/after-the-attacks-the-vigils-in-silence-and-prayer-rememberi ng-the-victims.html.

Associated Press. "Drought-Relief Fund for Farmers in Southern Oregon is Drying Up." April 28, 2002 Updated: March 11, 2011. https://www.seattlepi.com/news/ article/Drought-relief-fund-for-farmers-in-southern-1086222.php.

Associated Press. "800 Oregonians Converging on NY." October 3, 2001. Also "800 Oregonians Converge on Big Apple." CNN.com, October 3, 2001. http://www.cnn. com/2001/TRAVEL/NEWS/10/03/rec.attacks.ny.trip.ap/index.html.

Associated Press. "Flight For Freedom Sold Out." October 2, 2001.

Associated Press. "From Oregon . . . With Love." October 4, 2001.

Associated Press. "Harkenriders Join NYC Parade." *East Oregonian* (Pendleton). October 10, 2001.

Associated Press. "None of Us Will Ever Forget." *Seattle Post-Intelligencer News Services*. https://www.seattlepi.com/news/article/None-of-us-will-ever-forget-1065529. php. September 11, 2001, updated: March 15, 2011 2:35 p.m.

Associated Press. "Northwest Response Varies After Bombing of Taliban." October 8, 2001. (Appeared in *The Register-Guard*, Eugene, Ore.)

Associated Press. "Oregonians Learn of Airstrikes While in New York." *Daily Astorian*. October 8, 2001.

Associated Press. "Oregonians Visiting New York Cheered." October 9, 2001. (This is the *Oregonian* story of the same date.)

Associated Press. "Strikes raise specter of retaliation vs. U.S." *Baltimore Sun*. October 8, 2001. file:///C:/Users/sbour/AppData/Local/Temp/newsarchives100801.htm.

Associated Press staff. "IN THE NEWS: Freedom Flight Organizers Get Awards." November 12, 2001.

Azumano, George. "Epworth United Methodist Church (Portland)." *The Oregon Encyclopedia*. https://www.oregonencyclopedia.org/articles/epworth_united_ methodist_church_portland_/#.YEcEptxOkc8. Retrieved March 9, 2021.

Azumano Travel enewsletter c. spring 2002. Photocopy in author's files.

Azumano Travel Flight for Freedom website, www.azumano.com/flightforfreedom/. No longer in existence. Printed out by the author in 2003 and in the author's files.

Azumano Travel/American Express memo to All Corporate Accounts. "Important Notice." September 11, 2001. Photocopies in the author's files.

Baker, John. "East Coast Help Takes Flight." *Woodburn Independent*. October 3, 2001, 1 and 2.

Baker, John. "Mission Accomplished." *Woodburn Independent*. October 17, 2001, 1 and 2.

Baker, John. "Remembering 9-11 Going Back." *Woodburn Independent*, September 11, 2002, 1 and 3.

Baker, Mike. "Amid Historic Drought, a New Water War in the West." *The New York Times*. https://www.nytimes.com/2021/06/01/us/klamath-oregon-water-drought-bundy.html. Published June 1, 2021,updated June 8, 2021.

Barbour, Barton. "Fur Trade in Oregon Country." In *The Oregon Encyclopedia*. https://www.oregonencyclopedia.org/articles/fur_trade_in_oregon_country/. Last updated January 20, 2021.

Barell, John. Email to Mayor Vera Katz. October 18, 2001. Copy in the author's files.

Barron, James. "Bush Says Attack Was 'First War of the 21st Century.'" *The New York Times*. September 13, 2001 (online only). https://www.nytimes.com/2001/09/13/nyregion/bush-says-attack-was-first-war-of-the-21st-century.html.

Barry, Dan. "A DAY OF TERROR: HOSPITALS; Pictures of Medical Readiness, Waiting and Hoping for Survivors to Fill Their Wards." The New York Times, September 12, 2001. https://www.nytimes.com/2001/09/12/us/day-terror-hospitals-pictures-medical-readiness-waiting-hoping-for-survivors.html.

Barry, Dan. "After the Attacks: The Vigils; Surrounded by Grief, People Around the World Pause and Turn to Prayer." September 15, 2001. https://www.nytimes.com/2001/09/15/us/after-attacks-vigils-surrounded-grief-people-around-world-pause-turn-prayer.html.

Barry, Dan. "A Nation Challenged: Messages; From a World Lost, Ephemeral Notes Bear Witness to the Unspeakable." *The New York Times*. September 25, 2001. https://www.nytimes.com/2001/09/25/nyregion/nation-challenged-messages-world-lost-ephemeral-notes-bear-witness-unspeakable.html.

"Baseball heals America." Foxsports. October 20, 2016. https://www.foxsports.com/mlb/gallery/september-11-10-year-anniversary-look-back-at-baseball-mlb-comeback-082711.

Beason, Tyrone. "Northwest does its part to boost The Big Apple." *The Seattle Times*, October 3, 2001.

Becker, Elizabeth. "After the Attacks: The Pentagon; As Rescue Work Continues, Flight Recorders Are Found in Pentagon Rubble." *The New York Times*. September 15, 2001. https://www.nytimes.com/2001/09/15/us/after-attacks-pentagon-rescue-work-continues-flight-recorders-are-found-pentagon.html.

Becks, Paula. Email to flightforfreedom@azumano.com. October 13, 2001. Photocopy in the author's files.

"Behind the Scenes of the In Memoriam Concert." Oregon Symphony Orchestra *The Reprise* newsletter. Fall 2001, n.p.

Belluck, Pam. "After the Attacks: Getting There; Renting Wheels and Riding Rails as Skies Stay Off Limits." *The New York Times*. September 13, 2001. https://www.nytimes.com/2001/09/13/us/after-attacks-getting-there-renting-wheels-riding-rails-skies-stay-off-limits.html.

Belluck, Pam. "After the Attacks: Transportation; More Planes Take to Skies, But Plenty of Kinks Remain." *The New York Times*. September 15, 2001. https://www.nytimes.com/2001/09/15/us/after-attacks-transportation-more-planes-take-skies-but-plenty-kinks-remain.htmlAdvertisement.

Belluck, Pam with Laurence Zuckerman. "After the Attacks: Transportation; Flights Are Cleared to Resume, but the Skies Remain Largely Empty." *The New York*

Times. September 14, 2001. https://timesmachine.nytimes.com/timesma-chine/2001/09/14/182184.html?pageNumber=23;.

Bergstein, Len. "Themes." Memo to Communications Team. September 25, 2001. Photocopy in the author's files.

Bergstein, Len; Dozono, Loen and Sho Dozono; Nancy Parrott; John Ray. Interview with the author. May 13, 2021.

Berke, Richard L. and Janet Elder. "A Nation Challenged: The Poll; Poll Finds Support for War and Fear on Economy." *The New York Times.* September 25, 2001. https://www.nytimes.com/2001/09/25/us/nation-challenged-congress-lawmakers-tap-brakes-bush-s-hurtling-antiterrorism.html.

Bernsohn, Bill. "Portland Sends Comraderie [sic], and Money, Top NYC." kpam.com, October 6, 2001.

Berusch, Brian. "Oregon Travel Agency Leads New York City Solidarity Tour." *Travel Trade News Edition,* October 15, 2001, 18.

Binus, Joshua. "Fair Housing in Oregon Study." Oregon History Project, © Oregon Historical Society, 2003. https://www.oregonhistoryproject.org/articles/historical-records/fair.

"Black in Oregon 1840–1870 National and Oregon Chronology of Events" Oregon Secretary of State Shemia Fagan, https://sos.oregon.gov/archives/exhibits/black-history/Pages/context/chronology.aspx, retrieved May 30, 2021.

Blake, Wendy. "Oregonians Come To NY." *Crain's New York Business,* undated.

Boorstein, Michelle. "Thousands of Doctors, Nurses Called to Help." The Associated Press. September 12, 2001. https://old.post-gazette.com/headlines/20010912nyhos-pitalsnat6p6.asp.

Bott, Sarah. Interview with the author. January 28, 2021.

Bott, Sarah. "NEWS COVERAGE: KXL Stories About Trip to NYC." October 10, 2001, in author's files. See stories under "Sullivan, Chris" below.

Bourjolly, Myriam. "Putting Their Money Where Their Hearts Are: Flight for Freedom Touches Down in the Big Apple with Oregon CU Staffers." *CU Times.* date and page number unknown.

Bourrie, Sally Ruth. "Flight for Freedom." *Northwest Woman.* Spring 2002, 18–19.

Bourrie, Sally Ruth. "Fully Employed, But Hungry: More in Oregon Face Hard Choices." *The Boston Globe.* December 17, 2000, A8.

Bourrie, Sally Ruth. Interviews with Flight For Freedom passengers on return flight to Portland. October 9, 2001.

Bourrie, Sally Ruth. "950 from Oregon heed plea to visit." *Chicago Tribune,* October 6, 2001.

Bourrie, Sally Ruth. "Pacific Northwest Delivers Patrons and a Pick-Me-Up." *Boston Sunday Globe,* October 7, 2001, A22 and A23.

Bourrie, Sally Ruth. "A Shortage of Water Pits Farmer Against Fish in Ore., Tensions Rise as US Rations Dwindle." *The Boston Globe.* August 17, 2001, A2.

Boyd, Thomas. "Money Issues Linger from Dozono's Past." *The Oregonian.* https://www.oregonlive.com/oregonianextra/2008/04/money_issues_linger_from_dozon.html. Posted April 24, 2008, updated March 27, 2019.

Brady, Ignatius Charles and Lawrence Cunningham. "St. Francis of Assisi." *Encyclopedia Britannica,* https://www.britannica.com/biography/Saint-Francis-of-Assisi. Retrieved June 19, 2021.

Bragg, Rick. "After the Attacks: Canal Street; Shops Raise Shutters, But Barriers Remain." *The New York Times.* September 15, 2001. https://www.nytimes.com/2001/09/15/us/after-the-attacks-canal-street-shops-raise-shutters-but-barriers-remain.html.

Brick, Michael. "Mood on the Exchange Floor Somber on Second Day of Attacks." *The New York Times,* Business section, October 8, 2001.

Brooks, Cheryl A. "Race, Politics, and Denial: Why Oregon Forgot to Ratify the Fourteenth Amendment." *Oregon Law Review* 83 (2004), 735.

Bumiller, Elisabeth. "A Nation Challenged: The Overview; Bush Pledges Attack on Afghanistan Unless It Surrenders bin Laden Now; He Creates Cabinet Post for Security." *The New York Times.* September 21, 2001. https://www.nytimes.com/2001/09/21/world/nation-challenged-overview-bush-pledges-attack-afghanistan-unless-it-surrenders.html.

Bumiller, Elisabeth and Jane Perlez. "After the Attacks: The Overview; Bush And Top Aides Proclaim Policy of 'Ending' States That Back Terror; Local Airports Shut After An Arrest." *The New York Times.* September 14, 2001. https://www.nytimes.com/2001/09/14/us/after-attacks-overview-bush-top-aides-proclaim-policy-ending-states-that-back.html. [Note: the title of this article is shared by two different articles by different authors published on the same day and they have different URLs. This article includes October 7, 2002 correction, which is quoted here.]

Burns, John F. "After the Attacks: In Pakistan; U.S. Demands Air and Land Access to Pakistan." *The New York Times,* September 15, 2001, https://www.nytimes.com/2001/09/15/us/after-the-attacks-in-pakistan-us-demands-air-and-land-access-to-pakistan.html.

"Business Briefs." *Portland Tribune,* September 28, 2001, page D2.

"CNN BREAKING News America Under Attack: Bush Holds Press Briefing." CNN.com. Aired September 11, 2001—14:20 ET. http://transcripts.CNN.com/TRANSCRIPTS/0109/11/bn.35.html

"CNN BREAKING NEWS New York's Governor And Mayor of New York City Address Concerns of the Damage." CNN.com. Aired September 11, 2001—14:35 ET. http://transcripts.CNN.com/TRANSCRIPTS/0109/11/bn.42.html.

Campbell, Kim. "New York Times Portraits Resonate Coast to Coast." *The Christian Science Monitor.* December 6, 2001. https://www.questia.com/read/1P2-32592670/new-york-times-portraits-resonate-coast-to-coast.

Cardwell, Diane, and Glenn Collins, Winnie Hu, Andrew Jacobs, Dean E. Murphy, Lynda Richardson and Janny Scott, "A Nation Challenged: Portraits of Grief: The Victims; Parties, Love Notes and Other Small Memories That Now Loom Large." *The New York Times,* September 18, 2001, https://timesmachine.nytimes.com/timesmachine/2001/09/18/219142.html?pageNumber=42.

Carreon, Jesus 'Jess.' "PCC president, old friend link up at 'ground zero.' *Lake Oswego Review.* October 11, 2001.

Carter, Bill. "Letterman Leads Talk Show Hosts Back on the Air." *The New York Times.* September 19, 2001. https://www.nytimes.com/2001/09/19/arts/letterman-leads-talk-show-hosts-back-on-the-air.html.

Carter, Bill and Jim Rutenberg. "After the Attacks: Television; Viewers Again Return To Traditional Networks." *The New York Times.* September 15, 2001. https://www.nytimes.com/2001/09/15/us/after-the-attacks-television-viewers-again-return-to-traditional-networks.html?auth=login-email&login=email.

Carter, Margaret. Interview with the author. February 24, 2021.

Carter, Steven. "New York's Giuliani thanks Oregon." *The Oregonian.* October 15, 2002, section B.

Casap, Carlos. "A thank you from New York." Letter to the editor. *The Oregonian.* October 10, 2001.

Cavinta, Joy. Interview with the author. July 27, 2003.

Center for History and New Media at George Mason University and American Social History Project/Center for Media and Learning, The Graduate Center, City University of New York. "Executive Order 9066: The President Authorizes Japanese Relocation." *History Matters: The U.S. Survey Course on the Web.* http://historymatters.gmu.edu/d/5154. Retrieved March 28, 2021.

Central Oregon LandWatch. "How we are helping Jefferson County farming families." October 23, 2018. https://www.centraloregonlandwatch.org/update/2018/10/23/how-we-are-helping-jefferson-county-farming-families.

Chen, David W., Jan Hoffman and Tina Kelley. "PORTRAITS OF GRIEF: THE VICTIMS; A Driver With Size 15 Boots, a Stealth Joker and a Spiritual Diner." *The New York Times*. March 9, 2003. https://www.nytimes.com/2003/03/09/nyregion/portraits-grief-victims-driver-with-size-15-boots-stealth-joker-spiritual-diner.html

Chillemi, Sal. Interview with the author. February 24, 2021.

Chiulli, Mac and Bob Moore. Email to Mayor Vera Katz. October 11, 2001. Copy in the author's files.

Colangelo, Lisa L. and Siemaszko, Corky. "New York Still Loves a Parade." *New York Daily News*, October 9, 2001, 18.

Collins, Glenn, Robin Finn, Winnie Hu and Floyd Norris. "A Nation Challenged: Portraits of Grief: The Victims; At Work and at Home, Lives Filled With Aspirations and Inspirations." *The New York Times*. September 27, 2001. https://www.nytimes.com/2001/09/27/nyregion/nation-challenged-portraits-grief-victims-work-home-lives-filled-with.html.

Collisson, Craig. "Japanese American Wartime Incarceration in Oregon." *The Oregon Encyclopedia*. https://www.oregonencyclopedia.org/articles/japanese_internment/. Last updated March 22, 2021, first retrieved March 8, 2021.

Congressional Research Service. "Klamath River Basin Issues: An Overview of Water Use Conflicts." EveryCRSReport.com. June 13, 2002. https://www.everycrsreport.com/reports/RL31098.html.

"Congressman David Wu to Host Dinner for Oregonians in New York." Press release from David Wu's office. October 5, 2001.

Cooper, Bill. "Flight For Freedom Returning Home." KPAM.com, October 9, 2001.

Cooper, Bill. Interview with the author. June 17, 2021.

Cooper, Bill. "Portlanders Flying to New York to Encourage Travel." KPAM.com, September 26, 2001. This story also ran on www.pdxguide.com and on MSNBC the following day, September 27, 2001.

Cox, Thomas R. *The Other Oregon: People, Environment, and History East of the Cascades.* Corvallis: Oregon State University Press, 2019.

Crossette, Barbara. "A Nation Challenged: History; Afghanistan, for Ages an Affliction to Mighty Empires, Is Not Easily Subdued." *The New York Times*. September 18, 2001. https://www.nytimes.com/2001/09/18/world/nation-challenged-history-afghanistan-for-ages-affliction-mighty-empires-not.html.

Cupper, Lana. Interview with the author. December 11, 2020.

Curry-Stevens, Ann and Amanda Cross-Hemmer. *The Native American Community in Multnomah County: An Unsettling Profile*, Executive Summary, 2011, https://www.portlandoregon.gov/civic/article/505489.

Daily Shipping News. October 16, 2001.

D'Alessandro, Joe. Interview with the author. May 6, 2021.

Daly, Matthew. "Chinese Americans who served in WWII honored by Congress." *Military Times*. December 9, 2020. https://www.militarytimes.com/military-honor/salute-veterans/2020/12/09/chinese-americans-who-served-in-wwii-honored-by-congress/.

Daley, Suzanne. "After the Attacks: The Alliance; For First Time, NATO Invokes Joint Defense Pact With U.S." *The New York Times*. September 13, 2001. https://www.nytimes.com/2001/09/13/us/after-attacks-alliance-for-first-time-nato-invokes-joint-defense-pact-with-us.html.

Dao, James and Steven Lee Myers. "A Nation Challenged: The Military; Pentagon Activates First Wave of Guardsmen and Reservists." *The New York Times*. September 18, 2001. https://www.nytimes.com/2001/09/18/us/nation-challenged-military-pentagon-activates-first-wave-guardsmen-reservists.html.

Darling, John. "Two locals participate in visit to boost N.Y." *Mail Tribune* (Medford, Ore.). October 4, 2001.

Davidson, Todd. Interview with the author. February 11, 2021.

Day, Sherri. "A Nation Challenged: The Airlines; Delta Announces Job Cuts and Reductions in Service." *The New York Times.* September 27, 2001. https://www.nytimes.com/2001/09/27/business/nation-challenged-airlines-delta-announces-job-cuts-reductions-service.htmlRetrieved 1/21/2020.

"Defiant Fliers." *People.* October 29, 2001, 145.

Denning, Max. "The Urban-Rural Divide in Oregon Has Become More Pronounced." *The Register-Guard.* February 12, 2019. https://www.registerguard.com/news/20190212/urban-rural-divide-in-oregon-has-become-more-pronounced.

Denny, Maureen. Email to Jeri Hunt, "FW: about the people." October 4, 2001. Photocopy in the author's files.

Detzel, Tom. "Oregon Women Work at Heart of Relief Effort." *The Oregonian.* September 18, 2001, 1.

DiGiovanni, Myriam. "Flight for Freedom touches down in the Big Apple with Oregon CU staffers." *Credit Union Times.* October 16, 2001. https://www.cutimes.com/2001/10/16/flight-for-freedom-touches-down-in-the-big-apple-with-oregon-c-staffers/.

Ditewig, Jane and Steve. Interview with the author. December 16, 2020.

Ditewig, Jane and Steve. Flight for Freedom travel journal, 2001. Images of the journal in the author's files.

Dodge, Dani. "Oregonians March in New York." *Mall Tribune.* Medford, Oregon. October 9, 2001.

Donnelly, Sally. "The Day the FAA Stopped the World." *Time.* September 14, 2001. http://content.time.com/time/nation/article/0,8599,174912,00.html.

Doremus, Holly, and A. Dan Tarlock. "Fish, Farms, and the Clash of Cultures in the Klamath Basin." *Ecology Law Quarterly* 30, no. 2 (2003): 279-350. Accessed May 30, 2021. http://www.jstor.org/stable/24114216.

Dozono, Elisa. "About the People." Email, October 4, 2001. Photocopy in the author's files.

Dozono, Kristen. Interview with the author. April 13, 2021.

Dozono, Loen. Notes and travel journal. September 26–October 9, 2001. Photocopies in the author's files.

Dozono, Loen and Sho. Interview with the author. July 21, 2003.

Dozono, Nadyne Yoneko, 1915-2013. "Oral history interview with Nadyne Yoneko Dozono." Archives West Orbis Cascade Alliance online. http://archiveswest.orbiscascade.org/ark:/80444/xv820889, 1998 January 23–February 5 (inclusive).

"Dozono Named ASTA's Agent of the Year." *Travel Weekly.* May 4, 2002. https://www.travelweekly.com/Travel-News/Travel-Agent-Issues/Dozono-named-ASTAs-agent-of-the-year.

Dozono, Sho. Email to the author. July 31, 2003.

Dozono, Sho. "Flight for Freedom: Ten Years Later, Oregonians Still Love New York." *The Oregonian.* https://www.oregonlive.com/opinion/2011/09/flight_for_freedom_ten_years_l.html?fbclid=IwAR1CMZgXiTpvyaI6QTKBhR-BHUMZyzmijaK2eB1PNcJwcEwQK5K6eyKkCKd8. September 10, 2011, updated January 10, 2019.

Dozono, Sho. "Flight for Freedom Unveils Website." Memo. September 28, 2001. Photocopy in the author's files.

Dozono, Sho. "Kick Your Kicker Back to Oregon." *Portland Tribune.* November 27, 2001

Dozono, Sho. "Memo to Staff." September 12, 2001. Photocopy in the author's files.

Dozono, Sho. "The Plan." Memo. September 21, 2001. Photocopy in the author's files.

Dozono, Sho. "Recovery." Memo. September 25, 2001. Photocopy in the author's files.

Dozono, Sho. "Thank You!" Memo to Corporate Accounts. September 24, 2001. Photocopy in the author's files.

Dozono, Sho. "Update for Staff." Memo, September 18, 2001. Photocopy in the author's files.

Dozono, Sho, Loen Dozono, and Bruce Samson. "NYC Muslim Center: Bloomberg Stand Deserves Support." *The Oregonian.* https://www.oregonlive.com/opinion/2010/08/nyc_muslim_center_bloomberg_st.html. Posted August 18, 2010, updated January 10, 2019.

Dozono, Sho, Elaine Franklin, Jack McGowan, and John Ray. Group interview with the author. April 29, 2021. Recording in the author's files.

Dubois, Steven. "Bias Complaints at Daimler Portland Plant Settled for $2.4M. The Associated Press. https://www.seattletimes.com/business/bias-complaints-at-daimler-portland-plant-settled-for-24m-2/. Updated February 4, 2015.

Dwyer, Jim. "After the Attacks: Donations; Donated Goods Deluge the City And Sit Unused." *The New York Times.* September 16, 2001. https://www.nytimes.com/2001/09/16/us/after-the-attacks-donations-donated-goods-deluge-the-city-and-sit-unused.html.

Dwyer, Jim and Lawrence K. Altman. "After the Attacks: The Morgue; Loads of Body Bags Hint at Magnitude of Grisly Task." *The New York Times.* September 13, 2001. https://www.nytimes.com/2001/09/13/us/after-the-attacks-the-morgue-loads-of-body-bags-hint-at-magnitude-of-grisly-task.html.

Dwyer, Jim and Ford Fessenden. "One Hotel's Fight to the Finish; At the Marriott, a Portal to Safety as the Towers Fell." *The New York Times.* September 11, 2002. https://www.nytimes.com/2002/09/11/nyregion/one-hotel-s-fight-finish-marriott-portal-safety-towers-fell.html.

Earnshaw, Aliza. "Oregon Businesspeople Organize 'Flight for Freedom' to NYC." *The Business Journal of Portland.* September 26, 2001.

Edgel, Elaine L. Emails to the author. July 27, 2003, 11:17 a.m. and 12:59 p.m.

Edwards, Randall. Interview with the author. July 25, 2003.

eMediaMillWorks. "Text: President Bush Addresses the Nation." *The Washington Post* online. September 20, 2001. https://www.washingtonpost.com/wp-srv/nation/specials/attacked/transcripts/bushaddress_092001.html.

Emmons, Delia McQuade. "Oregonian Makes Her Day." Letters. *The Oregonian.* October 13, 2001, page number unknown.

"Federal Role Sought For Airport Security." *The New York Times.* September 24, 2001. https://www.nytimes.com/2001/09/24/us/federal-role-sought-for-airport-security.html.

Filkins, Dexter. "A Nation Challenged: Rumors; As Thick as the Ash, Myths are Swirling." *The New York Times,* September 25, 2001, https://www.nytimes.com/2001/09/25/nyregion/a-nation-challenged-rumors-as-thick-as-the-ash-myths-are-swirling.html.

Finnemore, Melody. "In Wake of Sept. 11, Local Group Soared." *Daily Journal of Commerce.* September 2, 2011. https://djcoregon.com/news/2011/09/02/in-wake-of-sept-11-local-group-soared/.

"Fire Fighter Memorial Service Postponed: Healing Not Possible as City Halts Recovery and Arrests Fire Fighters." November 7, 2001. http://daily.iaff.org/memorial2/main.htm.

Fish, Nick. Interview with the author. July 31, 2003.

Fisher, Martin. Interview with the author. March 13, 2002.

Fixico, Donald. "Termination and Restoration in Oregon." *The Oregon Encyclopedia.* https://www.oregonencyclopedia.org/articles/termination_and_restoration/#.YLNUS6EpAc9. Last updated January 20, 2021.

Flaccus, Gillian. "Drought along the Oregon-California border could mean water cuts for farmers, tribes." Associated Press. April 12, 2021, https://www.oregonlive.com/pacific-northwest-news/2021/04/drought-along-the-oregon-california-border-could-mean-water-cuts-for-farmers-tribes.html.

"Flight For Freedom." *Headlight Herald* (Tillamook, Ore.). October 10, 2001.

Flight For Freedom press releases, in the author's files:

   "Airlines Welcome Oregonians Back to the Skies." October 5, 2001

"Flight For Freedom A Huge Success." October 10, 2001.

"Flight For Freedom Exceeds Expectations." September 30, 2001.

"Flight For Freedom Garners Worldwide Attention." October 5, 2001.

"Flight For Freedom Participants to March in New York Columbus Day Parade." October 4, 2001.

"Oregonians Organize 'Flight For Freedom.'" September 26, 2001.

"Overwhelming Response Fills 'Flight For Freedom.'" October 1, 2001.

Untitled. September 29, 2001.

Flores, Trudy and Sarah Griffith. "Albina Riots, 1967." *Oregon History Project.* © Oregon Historical Society. 2002. https://www.oregonhistoryproject.org/articles/historical-records/albina-riot-1967/#.YF_29j8pCOs.

Flores, Trudy and Sarah Griffith. "African American Community Protests School Board." *Oregon History Project.* © Oregon Historical Society. 2002. https://www.oregonhistoryproject.org/articles/historical-records/african-american-community-protests-school-board/#.YF_4ej8pCOs. Last updated March 17, 2018.

Fogarty, Colin. "Flight For Freedom." National Public Radio, October 7, 2001.

Ford, Don and Jeanine; Young, Jackie and Phil. Interview with the author. May 12, 2021.

Ford, Jeanine. "Flight for Freedom." Newsletter. No date. Scan in the author's files.

Frammolino, Ralph. "Tourists Slowly Returning to New York." *Los Angeles Times.* October 6, 2001, retrieved September 28, 2003.

St. Francis of Assisi. "Canticle of the Creatures." 1225. Quoted in *Franciscan Seculars: From Gospel to Life—From Life to Gospel.* http://franciscanseculars.com/the-canticle-of-the-creatures/. Retrieved June 19, 2021.

Frank, Gerry. Interview with the author. February 27, 2021.

Franklin, Elaine. Interview with the author. April 27, 2021.

Frazier, Joseph B. "Oregonians Pack for 'Freedom Flight.'" Associated Press. October 3, 2001.

Frazier, Joseph B. "From drought to deluge, boom to bust, 2001 was quite a year." Associated Press. January 8, 2002.

"Freedom Flight Should Keep On Flying." Editorial. *The Skanner* (Portland, Ore.). October 10, 2001.

Freudenheim, Milt. "A Nation Challenged: The Destinations; Empty Hotels and Ships Offering Lots of Discounts." *The New York Times.* September 25, 2001. https://www.nytimes.com/2001/09/25/business/nation-challenged-destinations-empty-hotels-ships-offering-lots-discounts.html.

Frost, Danielle. "Sho Dozono retires after 21 years from Community Fund Board of Trustees." *smok signƏlz.* December 28, 2018. https://www.smokesignals.org/articles/2018/12/28/sho-dozono-retires-after-21-years-from-community-fund-board-of-trustees/.

Gallob, Joel. "Local residents head to New York City." *News-Times* (Newport, Ore.). October 5, 2001, A1 and A9.

Gallob, Joel. "Local residents back from New York City." *News-Times* (Newport, Ore.). October 12, 2001, A1 and A2.

Garcia, Jerry. "Latinos in Oregon." *The Oregon Encyclopedia.* https://www.oregonencyclopedia.org/articles/hispanics_in_oregon/#.YC4VonlOkc8. Last updated January 20, 2021.

Garvey, Marianne. "A Blessing on Rescue Dogs." *New York Post.* October 8, 2001. https://nypost.com/2001/10/08/a-blessing-on-rescue-dogs/.

Gehrett, Les. "Linn Resident Loved 'Freedom' Flight." *Albany (Or.) Democrat-Herald,* October 13, 2001, A3.

Gerber, Rachel. "Life-Changing Visit to the Streets of New York." *The Oregonian.* Commentary, October 10, 2001.

Giegerich, Andy. "It's Sho time for activist." *Portland Tribune.* October 9, 2001, pages 1 and 3.

Gold, Matea and Maggie Farley, Los Angeles Times Staff Writers. "World Trade Center and Pentagon attacked on Sept. 11, 2001." *Los Angeles Times.* September

12,   2001.   https://www.latimes.com/travel/la-xp.m.-2001-sep-12-na-sept-1
1-attack-201105-01-story.html.

Goldfield, Robert. "Chamber directors OK combination with APP." *Portland Business Journal.* https://www.bizjournals.com/portland/stories/2002/01/14/story8.html. January 13, 2002 Updated Jan 13, 2002, 9:00pm PST.

Goldstone, Mitch. "From Irvine CA For: To Gerry Frank and Sho Dozono." Email to Gerry Frank and Sho Dozono October 11, 2001. Photocopy in the author's files.

ABC News "Good Morning America." Transcript of "Good Morning America" visit by Oregonians on October 8, 2001. Provided courtesy ABC News "Good Morning America"; thanks to Charles Gibson for facilitating this acquisition.

Goodrich, Pat. "Flight for Freedom." *C.A.R. Newsletter.* Fall 2001. page 3.

Goodstein, Laurie and Gustav Niebuhr. "After the Attacks: Retaliation; Attacks And Harassment of Arab-Americans Increase." *The New York Times.* September 14, 2001. https://www.nytimes.com/2001/09/14/us/after-the-attacks-retaliation-attacks-and-harassment-of-arab-americans-increase.html.

Goodwin, Melissa. Interview with the author. October 4, 2001.

Gootman, Elissa. "After the Attacks: Charity; A Range of Donors Help Those in the Rescue Effort." *The New York Times.* September 14, 2001. https://www.nytimes.com/2001/09/14/us/after-the-attacks-charity-a-range-of-donors-help-those-in-the-rescue-effort.html.

Gould, Stephen Jay. "A Time of Gifts." *The New York Times.* September 26, 2001, A19.

Green, Aimee. "Jury Awards $750,000 to Black Worker for Racist Incidents at Daimler Trucks." *The Oregonian/OregonLive.* https://www.oregonlive.com/portland/2017/02/jury_awards_750000_to_black_wo.html. Updated February 23, 2017.

Greyhavens, Tim. "Oregon Albina, Approximate Site of the Former Chinese Community." *The No Place Project.* 2020. https://www.noplaceproject.com/albina. Retrieved April 17, 2021.

Griffin, Anne. "Portland Commissioner Nick Fish Dies at 61." Oregon Public Broadcasting.   January   2,   2020.   https://www.opb.org/news/article/nick-fish-portland-dead-obituary/.

Haberman, Clyde. "Like St. Vincent's Itself, Missing Wall Means Much." *The New York Times.* February 1, 2010. https://www.nytimes.com/2010/02/02/nyregion/02nyc.html

Hadlow, Robert W. "Columbia River Highway." *The Oregon Encyclopedia.* https://www.oregonencyclopedia.org/articles/columbia_river_highway/#.YLhC9UwpAc8. Last updated March 17, 2018.

Haight, George. Interview with the author. July 26, 2003.

Halen, Alexia. Interview with the author. November 28, 2020.

Handout, untitled. Small informal gathering of Flight for Freedom participants. February or March 2002. In the author's files.

Harkenrider, Beverly. "Bond of Friendship Forged Between NYC, Hermiston Women." *East Oregonian* September 10, 2002. https://www.eastoregonian.com/opinion/bond-of-friendship-forged-between-nyc-hermiston-women/article_7b8a6be8-42c3-5f8c-b1a3-a5a7d701c777.html.

Harmon, Tina. Email to Vera Katz. "Flight For Freedom—Newsletter." August 23, 2002. In the author's files.

Harris, Roy J. Jr. "'Portraits of Grief' 10 years later: Lessons from the original New York Times 9/11 coverage." Poynter.org. August 31, 2011. https://www.poynter.org/reporting-editing/2011/portraits-of-grief-10-years-later-lessons-from-the-original-new-york-times-911-coverage/.

Harrison, Michael. "Airline Collapses Amid $10bn Industry Losses." *The Independent.* September   15,   2001.   https://www.independent.co.uk/news/uk/home-news/airline-collapses-amid-10bn-industry-losses-9131330.html.

Hart, Jim. "'Ground Zero' fills Hooley with disbelief." *West Linn Tidings.* October 11, 2001, A1 and A16.

Hawk, Connie L. Email to the author, July 24, 10:12 p.m.

Hawk, Connie L. Email to the author, July 25, 2003, 7:53 a.m.

Hawk, Connie L. Email to the author, July 25, 2003, 3:35 p.m.

Henderson, Judy. "Fact Sheet: The Expanded Bottle Bill." Oregon Department of Environmental Quality online. http://www.deq.state.or.us/lq/pubs/factsheets/sw/ExpandedBottleBill.pdf. Last updated: June 26, 2007.

Henican, Ellis. "America Strikes Back/Commentary/ Still in Step With Holiday." *Newsday*. October 9, 2001, A.26.

Henningsen, Judi. Interview with the author. January 24, 2021.

Henningsen, Judi. Memoir of the Flight for Freedom written very soon after completing the trip, 2001.

Herbst, Diane. "9/11 Still Claiming Victims: 10,000 With Cancers, Thousands More With Other Illnesses." *People*. September 11, 2019. https://people.com/human-interest/9-11-still-claiming-victims-10000-with-cancers-thousands-more-with-other-illnesses/.

"Heroes Amid the Horror." *The New York Times*. September 15, 2001. https://www.nytimes.com/2001/09/15/opinion/heroes-amid-the-horror.html?searchResultPosition=1.

Hinshaw, Stephanie. Essay on the Flight for Freedom. October 15, 2001. Contained in Margaret Hinshaw, email to Cindy Forgue, October 26, 2001. Photocopy in the author's files.

History.com Editors, "Japanese Internment Camps." History.com. https://www.history.com/topics/world-war-ii/japanese-american-relocation. Last updated March 17, 2021.

Hoge, Warren. "After the Attacks: West; Outpouring of Grief and Sympathy for Americans Is Seen Throughout Europe and Elsewhere." *The New York Times*. Displays as September 13, 2001 in the TimesMachine, and in the September 14, 2001 print newspaper, Section A, Page 21. https://www.nytimes.com/2001/09/14/us/after-attacks-west-outpouring-grief-sympathy-for-americans-seen-throughout.html.

Hogue, Theresa. "Flight for Freedom returns to Oregon." *Gazette-Times* (Corvallis, Ore.). October 13, 2001, A1 and A11.

Holson, Laura M. and Laurence Zuckerman, "A Nation Challenged: The Industry; Boeing and United Plan to Lay Off Thousands." *The New York Times*. September 19, 2001. https://www.nytimes.com/2001/09/19/business/a-nation-challenged-the-industry-boeing-and-united-plan-to-lay-off-thousands.html.

Holzgraf, Betsy. Interview with the author. December 1, 2020.

Holzgraf, Betsy. "New Yorkers Welcomed Group from Oregon." Hebron, New York local newspaper. Holidays 2001. Photocopy in the author's files.

Hovies, Gordon. "St. Patrick's Day Parade." *The Straight Stream*. XXII, no. 2 (July 2002): 9.

Hovies, Gordon. "Vice Presidents' Reports." *The Straight Stream*. XXII, no. 2 (July 2002): 4.

"Hundreds of Oregonians sign up for Flight for Freedom." *The Business Journal of Portland*. October 1, 2001.

Hunt, Jeri. Azumano Travel Flight For Freedom Scrapbook, 2002.

Hunt, Jeri. Memo to All Azumano and Azumano/Away Staff, "Terrorist Attacks." September 11, 2001. Photocopies in the author's files.

Ibarguen, Diego. (Associated Press writer) "Patriotism on Parade in N.Y." *The Columbian*, October 9, 2001, page A6.

"In Memory Remembering September 11." ONE, October 2002, page 5.

Irish America Staff, "Irish National Day of Mourning." December / January 2002. https://irishamerica.com/2001/12/irelands-national-day-of-mourning/.

Irving, Doug. "Portland Plans NYC 'Flight for Freedom.'" KGW.com, September 26, 2001.

Irving, Doug. "Freedom Flyers Head Back to Portland." KGW.com. October 9, 2001.

"Japanese-American Internment During World War II." National Archives online. https://www.archives.gov/education/lessons/japanese-relocation. Last reviewed March 17, 2020.

"Japanese Envoy Feted At Oregon Trade Talks." *The New York Times*. February 12, 1974. https://www.nytimes.com/1974/02/12/archives/japanese-envoy-feted-at-oregon-trade-talks-jokes-about-governor.html.

Jaquiss, Nigel. "SHO DOZONO'S RULES." *Willamette Week*. https://www.wweek.com/portland/article-1426-sho-dozonos-rules.html. Published October 29, 2002, updated January 24, 2017.

Jasper, William F. "Klamath Falls Freedom Day." *The New American*. September 24, 2001. https://www.thefreelibrary.com/Klamath+Falls+Freedom+Day.-a079789132.

Jenness, Debra-Diane, Email to the author. April 19, 2002. She stated that she was writing "for the Jenness Family, Gordon, Debra-Diane and Tyler."

John Paul II. "Peace with God the Creator, Peace with All of Creation." Message for World Day of Peace January, 1, 1990. As quoted in Duddy, Cathal, OFM. "St. Francis—A Guide for Nature Lovers & Ecologists." *Praying Nature with St. Francis of Assisi*. http://www.praying-nature.com/site_pages.php?section=Guide+for+Nature+Lovers. Retrieved June 19, 2021.

Johnson, Kirk and Charles V. Bagli. "A Nation Challenged: The Site; Architects, Planners and Residents Wonder How to Fill the Hole in the City." *The New York Times*. September 26, 2001. https://www.nytimes.com/2001/09/26/nyregion/nation-challenged-site-architects-planners-residents-wonder-fill-hole-city.html.

K., Harry. "N.Y. Loves Oregon, Too; The Back Fence." *The Oregonian*. October 17, 2001.

"KWUA Urges a Stop to Unacceptable Behaviors." Klamath Falls News online. May 19, 2021. https://www.klamathfallsnews.org/news/kwua-urges-a-stop-to-unacceptable-behaviors.

Karnosh, Kathi. Interview with the author. February 23, 2021.

Katagiri, George. "Japanese Americans in Oregon." *The Oregon Encyclopedia*. https://www.oregonencyclopedia.org/articles/japanese_americans_in_oregon_immigrants_from_the_west/#.YC4FB3lOkc8. Last updated January 26, 2021.

Katz, Vera, Mayor. Email to Katie Kirk. July 15, 2002.

Katz, Vera. Interview with the author. July 25, 2003.

Katz, Vera. "Statement." *Observer*, October 3, 2001.

Kelly, Mike. "A Welcome and Healing Sight." Letter to the editor. *The Oregonian*. October 16, 2001.

Kelly, Matt. "On Account of War." National Baseball Hall of Fame online. https://baseballhall.org/discover-more/stories/short-stops/1918-world-war-i-baseball. Retrieved June 20, 2021.

Kelso, Mary. Interview with the author. October 9, 2001.

Kempel, Sandra. Email to the author, November 2, 2001.

Kempel, Sandra. Interview with the author. July 25, 2003.

Kempel, Sandra. Interview with the author. November 10, 2021.

Kennedy, Randy. "A DAY OF TERROR: TRANSPORTATION; With City Transit Shut Down, New Yorkers Take to Eerily Empty Streets." *The New York Times*. September 12, 2001, Section A, Page 8. https://www.nytimes.com/2001/09/12/us/day-terror-transportation-with-city-transit-shut-down-new-yorkers-take-eerily.htmlAdvertisement.

Kennedy, Randy. "After the Attacks: The Commuters; Closings Snarl Travel to Manhattan Again." *The New York Times*. September 14, 2001. https://www.nytimes.com/2001/09/14/us/after-the-attacks-the-commuters-closings-snarl-travel-to-manhattan-again.html.

Kennedy, Robert F. Jr. Sermon at the Feast of St. Francis, Cathedral of St. John the Divine. October 7, 2001; recording provided by Cathedral archives on June 17, 2021.

Kifner, John and Susan Saulny. "After the Attacks: The Families; Posting Handbills as Votive Offerings, in Hope of Finding Missing Loved Ones." *The New York Times*. September 14, 2001. https://www.nytimes.com/2001/09/14/us/after-attack s-families-posting-handbills-votive-offerings-hope-finding-missing.html.

Kimball, Kamlynn, and Rebecca Webb. Interview with the author. January 29, 2021.

Kimmelman, Michael. "In a Square, A Sense of Unity." *The New York Times*. September 19, 2001. https://www.nytimes.com/2001/09/19/arts/in-a-square-a-sense-of-unity-a-homegrown-memorial-brings-strangers-together.html?searchResultPosition=3.

Kittredge, William. *Hole in the Sky*. New York: Knopf, 1992, 228. Quoted in Cox, Thomas R. *The Other Oregon: People, Environment, and History East of the Cascades*. Corvallis: Oregon State University Press, 2019.

Klamath Basin Audubon Society. "Our Unique Habitat." https://www.klamathaudu-bon.org/basin-birds, retrieved June 2, 2021.

Klein, Joe. "Shadow Land." *The New Yorker*. February 10, 2002 (February 18, 2002 print issue). https://www.newyorker.com/magazine/2002/02/18/shadow-land.

Klejmont, Frank. Interview with the author. February 16, 2021.

Kloster, Glenn. Interview with the author. October 4, 2001.

Knopp, Tim. "Defend the Kicker as Oregonians' Last Hope for Tax Relief." *The Oregonian*. May 26, 2021. https://www.oregonlive.com/opinion/2021/05/opinion-defen d-the-kicker-as-oregonians-last-hope-for-tax-relief.html.

Kostel, Jack. "Flight for Freedom Memories." October 2001. Photocopy in the author's files.

Kulongoski, Gov. Ted. "Speech by Gov. Ted Kulongski." [Governor's Tourism Award] April 15, 2003. https://en.wikisource.org/wiki/Speech_by_Governor_Kulongoski. Retrieved February 26, 2021.

La Follette, Cameron and Douglas Deur. "Heceta Head Lighthouse." *The Oregon Encyclopedia*. https://www.oregonencyclopedia.org/articles/heceta-head-light-house/#.YLgXRkwpAc8. Last updated May 22, 2020.

Landler, Mark with Richard A. Oppel Jr. "After the Attacks: The Cargo Trade; Ban on Airliners' Freight Has Businesses Scrambling." *The New York Times*. September 15, 2001. https://www.nytimes.com/2001/09/15/us/after-attacks-cargo-trad e-ban-airliners-freight-has-businesses-scrambling.html?searchResultPosition=1.

Lang, William L. "Lewis and Clark Expedition." *The Oregon Encyclopedia*. https://www.oregonencyclopedia.org/articles/lewis_and_clark_expedition/#.YC3qdHlOkc8. Retrieved February 17, 2021.

Lang, William L. "Oregon Trail." *The Oregon Encyclopedia*. https://www.oregonencyclo-pedia.org/articles/oregon_trail/. Last updated January 20, 2021.

Lee, Douglas. "Chinese Americans in Oregon." *The Oregon Encyclopedia*. https://www.oregonencyclopedia.org/articles/chinese_americans_in_oregon/#.YGF0Zz8pAc8. Last updated January 26, 2021.

Lee, Jongkwan, Giovanni Peri, and Vasil Yasenov. "The Employment Effects of Mexican Repatriations: Evidence from the 1930's." Cambridge, Massachusetts: NATIONAL BUREAU OF ECONOMIC RESEARCH Working Paper No. 23885, September 2017. https://www.nber.org/system/files/working_papers/w23885/w23885.pdf.

Lee, Michael. Email to the author. July 12, 2002.

Levy, Clifford J. and William K. Rashbaum. "After the Attacks: The Airports; Bush and Top Aides Proclaim Policy of 'Ending' States That Back Terror; Local Airports Shut After an Arrest." *The New York Times*. September 14, 2001. https://www.nytimes.com/2001/09/14/us/after-attacks-airports-bush-top-aides-proclaim-polic y-ending-states-that-back.html.

Lewin, Tamar. "After the Attacks: Financial Aid; Companies Pledge $100 Million In Relief." *The New York Times*. September 15, 2001. https://www.nytimes.com/2001/09/15/us/after-the-attacks-financial-aid-companies-pledge-100 -million-in-relief.html.

Lewin, Tamar and Gustav Niebuhr, "A Nation Challenged: Violence; Attacks and Harassment Continue on Middle Eastern People and Mosques." *The New York Times,* September 18, 2001, https://www.nytimes.com/2001/09/18/us/nation-challenge d-violence-attacks-harassment-continue-middle-eastern-people.html.

Lewis, David. "Willamette Valley Treaties." *The Oregon Encyclopedia.* https://www.ore- gonencyclopedia.org/articles/willamette_valley_treaties/#.YLhepEwpAc9. Last updated January 20, 2021.

Lewis, Neil A. and David Johnston. "After the Attacks: The Investigation; Justice Dept. Identifies 19 Men as Suspected Hijackers." *The New York Times.* September 15, 2001. https://www.nytimes.com/2001/09/15/us/after-attacks-investigation-justic e-dept-identifies-19-men-suspected-hijackers.html.

Lipton, Eric. "A Nation Challenged: The Scene; Returning to the Office On the First Monday Since the City Changed." *The New York Times.* September 18, 2001. https://www.nytimes.com/2001/09/18/nyregion/nation-challenged-scene-returnin g-office-first-monday-since-city-changed.html.

Lipton, Eric. "A Nation Challenged: The Toll; Taking Account of the Dead, Feeling Weight of History." *The New York Times.* https://www.nytimes.com/2001/10/06/ nyregion/nation-challenged-toll-taking-account-dead-feeling-weight-history. html.

Little, Becky. "The U.S. Deported a Million of Its Own Citizens to Mexico During the Great Depression." History.com. January 12, 2019. https://www.history.com/ news/great-depression-repatriation-drives-mexico-deportation.

Loftus, Mitzi. "Day of Remembrance." *The Oregon Encyclopedia.* https://www.oregonen- cyclopedia.org/articles/day_of_remembrance/#.YHunXT8pAc8. Last updated March 17, 2018.

Long, Betty. Email to the author. June 20, 2002.

Long, Betty. Email to the author. July 27, 2003.

Long, Betty. Letter to the author, November 19, 2020.

Long, Eric. *At Your Service: A Newsletter for Guests of The Waldorf-Astoria and The Waldorf Towers.* Winter 2001, 1.

Longman, Jere and Jo Thomas. "After the Attacks: The Pennsylvania Crash; Recorder Found; May Reveal a Struggle." *The New York Times.* September 14, 2001. https:// www.nytimes.com/2001/09/14/us/after-the-attacks-the-pennsylvania-crash -recorder-found-may-reveal-a-struggle.htmlSEARCH.

Longo Eder, Michele. *Salt In Our Blood: The Memoir of a Fisherman's Wife.* Newport, Oregon: Dancing Moon Press, 2008.

Loucks, Wes. Interview with the author. March 4, 2021.

Love, Rick D. Email to the author, July 23, 2003.

Lucado, Max. "Do It Again, Lord!" For "America Prays," a national prayer vigil held Saturday, September 15, 2001. https://maxlucado.com/do-it-again-lord/. Retrieved June 18, 2021.

Lyon, Cherstin M. "Alien Land Laws." *Densho Encyclopedia.* https://encyclopedia. densho.org/Alien_land_laws/. Last updated Oct. 8, 2020.

McAninch, Ryan. "MY TURN: Events alter atmosphere in New York." *The Oregonian.* October 25, 2001.

McCaleb, Ian Christopher, CNN Washington Bureau. "Bush Tours Ground Zero in Lower Manhattan." CNN.com. September 14, 2001. http://edition.cnn.com/2001/ US/09/14/bush.terrorism/.

McCartin, Brian. Interview with the author. February 2, 2021.

McCartin, Brian. Interview with the author. February 10, 2021.

McDonald, Bill. "On His Own Art Has a Role in Recession Repair." *Portland Tribune.* October 23, 2001.

MacDonald, G. Jeffrey. "This Christmas, Some See Virtue in Buying Sprees." *The Christian Science Monitor.* December 5, 2001. https://www.csmonitor.com/2001/1205/ p1s4-ussc.html.

McElhany, Alice. Flier for six-month anniversary gathering of some Flight For Freedom participants. March 2002.

McElhany, Alice. Email to the author. July 26, 2003.

McFadden, Robert D. "After the Attacks: The Overview; A Shaken Nation Struggles to Regain Its Equilibrium, but Remains on Edge." *The New York Times*. September 14, 2001. https://www.nytimes.com/2001/09/14/us/after-attacks-overview-shake n-nation-struggles-regain-its-equilibrium-but.html.

McFadden, Robert D. "After the Attacks: The President; Bush Leads Prayer, Visits Aid Crews; Congress Backs Use of Armed Force." *The New York Times*. September 15, 2001. https://www.nytimes.com/2001/09/15/us/after-attacks-president-bus h-leads-prayer-visits-aid-crews-congress-backs-use.html.

McFadden, Robert D. "After the Attacks: The Funerals; For the Fire Department, the First Three Farewells." September 16, 2001. https://www.nytimes.com/2001/09/16/ us/after-the-attacks-the-funerals-for-the-fire-department-the-first-three-farewells. html.

McFadden, Robert D. "A Nation Challenged: The Service; In a Stadium of Heroes, Prayers for the Fallen and Solace for Those Left Behind." *The New York Times*. September 24, 2001. https://www.nytimes.com/2001/09/24/nyregion/nation-challenge d-service-stadium-heroes-prayers-for-fallen-solace-for-those.html.

McFadden, Robert D. "One Part Columbus Day, and One Part 4th of July." *The New York Times*. October 9, 2001. https://www.nytimes.com/2001/10/09/nyregion/one-par t-columbus-day-and-one-part-4th-of-july.html?searchResultPosition=1.

McGowan, Jack. Interview with the author. April 10, 2021.

McGowan, Jack. Interview with the author. June 19, 2021.

McLain, Tara. "George Haight Group Provided Emotional Support." *Statesman Journal*. March 10, 2002, 6A.

McNaughton, James C. "Chinese-Americans in World War II." U.S. Army Center of Military History. May 16, 2000. https://history.army.mil/html/topics/apam/ chinese-americans.html.

McNeal, Glennis. "Choice encounters in New York City." *Galley Proofs*. Winter 2001–2002, page 3.

McQuade Emmons, Delia. Letter to the editor. *The Oregonian*. October 13, 2001.

Madison, Cliff. Email to the author. May 31, 2021.

Madison, Cliff. Interview with the author. January 18, 2002.

Madison, Cliff. Interview with the author. October 31, 2021.

Magee, Mike, MD. *All Available Boats: The Evacuation of Manhattan Island on September 11, 2001*. New York: Spencer Books, 2002.

Mahoney, Barbara. "Mark O. Hatfield (1922-2011)." *The Oregon Encyclopedia*. https:// www.oregonencyclopedia.org/articles/hatfield_mark_o_1922_/, Last updated January 21, 2021.

Mahoney, Barbara. "Provisional Government." *The Oregon Encyclopedia*. https:// www.oregonencyclopedia.org/articles/provisional_govt_conference_in_cham-poeg_1843/. Last updated September 16, 2020.

Mahoney, Tim. "James DePreist (x-2013)." *The Oregon Encyclopedia*. https://www.ore-gonencyclopedia.org/articles/depreist_james_1936_/. Last updated February 10, 2020.

Marcus, Eric. Interview with the author. July 30, 2003.

Marcus, Eric. Interview with the author. April 23, 2021.

Mark, Melvin "Pete" Jr. Letter to Sho Dozono, October 12, 2001, photocopy in the author' files.

Mark, Stephen R. "Mount Mazama." *The Oregon Encyclopedia*. https://www.oregonen-cyclopedia.org/articles/mt_mazama/#.YLml30wpAc8. Last updated March 17, 2018.

Marthaller, Merritt. Fax to the author. November 12, 2001. In the author's files.

Massengill, Reed. "Our Heroes." *Context: Remembering 9/11: How American Express is responding to—and recovering from –the tragic events of September 11, 2001.* Undated, unpaginated.

Mauriello, Joe. Email to Azumano Travel Flight for Freedom address. August 26, 2002. Printed out by the author July 24, 2003. Copy in the author's files.

Mauriello, Joe. Interview with the author. January 24, 2021.

Mechaber, Nancy. Interview with the author, January 17, 2021.

Memo, Sarah Bott of Mayor Katz' office. "Mayor's NYC Trip: Notes from Wed Planning Meeting." September 27, 2001.

Meeuwsen, Teri. "From Hermiston to New York, with Love." *East Oregonian* (Pendleton, Ore.), October 16, 2001, pages 1A and 3A.

"Members of Security Council Condemn 'Horrifying' Terror Attacks on US." *UN News.* September 11, 2001. https://news.un.org/en/story/2001/09/13932-members-security-council-condemn-horrifying-terror-attacks-us.

Meskill, Jane. Interview with the author. November 25, 2020.

"Mr. Feelgood." Editorial. *The Independent* (Woodburn, Ore.). October 17, 2001.

Millner, Darrell. "Blacks in Oregon." *The Oregon Encyclopedia.* https://www.oregonencyclopedia.org/articles/blacks_in_oregon/. Last updated January 20, 2021.

Mitchell, Alison and Richard W. Stevenson, "A Nation Challenged: Congress; Bush and Leaders Confer on Way To Bolster Weakened Economy." September 20, 2001. https://www.nytimes.com/2001/09/20/us/nation-challenged-congress-bush-leaders-confer-way-bolster-weakened-economy.html.

Mitchell, Elizabeth. "Marking the date of the terrorist attacks: 9/11: The Experts Recommend." About.com. http://portlandor.about.com/library/weekly/aa091102a.htm. Retrieved May 13, 2021.

Monahan, Rachel. "Commissioner Nick Fish's Death Leaves Portland Grieving—and City Hall Changed." *Willamette Week.* January 8, 2020. https://www.wweek.com/news/city/2020/01/08/commissioner-nick-fishs-death-leaves-portland-grieving-and-city-hall-changed/.

Morgan, Sean C. "Freedom Flight visit to New York City creates lasting images for S.H. couple." *The New Era* (Sweet Home, Ore.), October 17, 2001, page 1 and 3.

Morkal, David. Interview with the author. January 22, 2021.

Most, Stephen. "Klamath Basin Project (1906)." *The Oregon Encyclopedia.* https://www.oregonencyclopedia.org/articles/klamath_basin_project_1906_/#.YDGrWHlOnVh. Last updated February 6, 2020.

Joanne B. Mulcahy, Joanne B. "Southern Oregon [Oregon Folklife: Our Living Traditions Folklife in Oregon]." Oregon History Project. https://www.oregonhistoryproject.org/narratives/oregon-folklife-our-living-traditions/folklife-in-oregon/southern-oregon/#.YLl-bUwpCOs, 2005. Updated and revised by OHP Staff, retrieved June 3, 2021.

Murphy, Dean E. "After the Attacks: The Reaction; Front-Line Workers Are Happy to See the Commander in Chief." *The New York Times.* September 15, 2001. https://www.nytimes.com/2001/09/15/us/after-attacks-reaction-front-line-workers-are-happy-see-commander-chief.html.

Myers, Steven Lee and Elizabeth Becker. "After the Attacks: The Pentagon; Defense Department Says 126 Are Missing, Raising Total of Crash Victims to 190." *The New York Times.* September 14, 2001. https://www.nytimes.com/2001/09/14/us/after-attacks-pentagon-defense-department-says-126-are-missing-raising-total.html.

Nadolske, Leo. Interview with the author. March 24, 2021.

Natanson, Hannah. "An enslaved man was crucial to the Lewis and Clark expedition's success. Clark refused to free him afterward." *The Washington Post.* January 12, 2020. https://www.washingtonpost.com/history/2020/01/12/york-slave-lewis-clark-expedition/.

"National Day of Mourning for Victims of 911." Ireland XO, 14, 2001. https://irelandxo.com/ireland-xo/history-and-genealogy/timeline/national-day-mourning-victims-911.

National Park Service. "John Day Valley Rock Formations, John Day Fossil Beds National Monument." nps.gov. https://www.nps.gov/media/photo/view.htm?id=cd3bed45-1d4c-4cfd-8207-2c938584ec41. Retrieved June 3, 2021.

National Park Service. "Painted Hills." nps.gov. https://www.nps.gov/joda/planyour-visit/ptd-hills-unit.htm. Last updated May 16, 2020.

NATO press release. "Statement by the North Atlantic Council." 11 September 2001. https://www.nato.int/docu/pr/2001/p01-122e.htm.

NATO press release. "Statement by the North Atlantic Council." 12 September 2001. https://www.nato.int/docu/pr/2001/p01-124e.htm.

"New York Airlift: Draft of Presentation Speech." [for presentation by Sho Dozono] Hilton Hotel, Portland, September 24, 2001, 3:00 p.m. Photocopy in the author's files.

"New York City Mayor Giuliani Delivers Tourism Message." *Our Travel News* September 17, 2001.

"New York Remembers Firefighters in First Funerals." CNN.com, September 16, 2001, https://www.cnn.com/2001/US/09/15/vic.terror.funerals/.

New York Times. "Oregon Tourists Headed to New York." *The New York Times*, October 4, 2001, page B6.

New York Times News Service. "Oregon Delegation Heads to New York." October 4, 2001.

The New York Times. September 14, 2001, A1, A14-15, with the captions: "Flying the Colors: Americans responded to the attacks by displaying the flag"; "A Symbol Offers Comfort On New York's Streets;" "Americans at home and overseas confronted this week's terror attacks with one simple gesture, flying the flag. The displays seem as much acts of defiance as of patriotism."

The New York Times. Reuters, AP, Agence France-Presse (Sources). "After the Attacks: Around the World." *The New York Times*. September 14, 2001. https://www.nytimes.com/2001/09/14/us/after-the-attacks-around-the-world.html?searchResultPosition=1.

"News Conference, Wednesday, September 26, 10 AM, Remarks for Sho Dozono." Photocopy in author's files.

Nice, Ann. Interview with the author. December 9, 2020.

Nicholas, Jonathan. *The Oregonian*. February 15, 2006.

Nicholas, Jonathan. "New York or Bust." *The Oregonian*. September 26, 2001.

"Nikkei." *Densho Encyclopedia*. https://encyclopedia.densho.org/Nikkei/. Last updated March 19, 2013.

9-11 Artists Respond, Vol. 1 Milwaukie, Oregon: Dark Horse Comics, Inc., 2002.

"9/11 News Coverage: 7:45 PM: Congress Sings 'God Bless America.'" CNN headline news footage. https://www.youtube.com/watch?v=IH_6EUCILew. Retrieved June 13, 2021.

Nokes, Greg. "Black Exclusion Laws in Oregon." *The Oregon Encyclopedia*. https://www.oregonencyclopedia.org/articles/exclusion_laws/. Last updated July 6, 2020.

Nuttman, Lance. "Lance and Marla's Website." www.geocities.com/lmnyc2. No longer exists. Printed out by the author in 2003.

Nuttman, Lance and Marla. Interview with the author. January 24, 2021.

O'Brien, Al. Email to the author, July 26, 2003.

O'Brien, Al. Email to the author, July 31, 2003.

O'Brien, Al. Interview with the author. November 23, 2020.

Office of the Historian, United States House of Representatives. "The Singing of 'God Bless America' on September 11, 2001." House.gov. Retrieved February 8, 2020, https://history.house.gov/Historical-Highlights/2000-/

The-singing-of-%E2%80%9CGod-Bless-America%E2%80%9D-on-September-11,-2001/.

Office of the Historian, Foreign Service Institute. United States Department of State. https://history.state.gov/milestones/1921-1936/immigration-act. Retrieved March 28, 2021.

Office of the Press Secretary. "Remarks by the President While Touring Damage at the Pentagon." White House archived website. September 12, 2001. https://georgewbush-whitehouse.archives.gov/news/releases/2001/09/20010912-12.html.

Office of the Press Secretary. "National Day of Prayer and Remembrance for the Victims Of the Terrorist Attacks on September 11, 2001 By the President of the United States of America A Proclamation." White House archived website, September 13, 2001, https://georgewbush-whitehouse.archives.gov/news/releases/2001/09/20010913-7.html.

Onion, Amanda. "September 11: Six Ways Uncertainty Reigned Aboard Air Force One." History.com. September 10, updated September 12, 2019. https://www.history.com/news/september-11-air-force-one-president-bush

"Oregon's Bite of the Apple." Editorial. *The Oregonian*. October 9, 2001.

Oregon Convention Center website. https://web.archive.org/web/20021022091143/http://www.oregoncc.org/memorial/memorial_FAQ.htm. Retrieved May 13, 2021.

"Oregon Delegation and Dollars Headed to New York." *Hells Canyon Journal* (Halfway.com, Ore.). October 10, 2001.

"Oregon Economic Mainstays in the Late 1800s." Oregon Secretary of State. https://sos.oregon.gov/archives/exhibits/constitution/Pages/after-economy.aspx. Retrieved on June 3, 2021.

Oregon Planning, Department of Land Conservation and Development. "History of Land-Use Planning." https://www.oregon.gov/lcd/OP/Pages/History.aspx. Retrieved on April 11, 2021.

Oregon Shakespeare Festival. "Ashland and the Festival." *Oregon Shakespeare Festival*. https://www.osfashland.org/en/company/our-history/ashland-festival.aspx. Retrieved before February 19, 2021.

Orloff, Chet. "Portland Penny." *The Oregon Encyclopedia*. https://www.oregonencyclopedia.org/articles/portland_penny/#.YLgp3UwpAc8. Last updated September 19, 2019.

Oster, Rob. "Trip Home to New York City Prompts Journey to Glimpse Ground Zero." *Gresham Outlook*. October 10, 2001, 1A and 3A.

Oswalt, Allen. Interview with the author. March 19, 2021.

"Parade Gives New Yorkers a Reason to Cheer." *Tampa Bay Times*. October 9, 2001, published September 10, 2005. https://www.tampabay.com/archive/2001/10/09/parade-gives-new-yorkers-a-reason-to-cheer/, retrieved June 27, 2021. Note: the URL for this story lists a date of 10/9/2001, which I believe is the original date of publication, though the website itself gives the "published" date in 2005.

Parker, Jim. "Portland's Flight for Freedom Sold Out." KGW.com. October 1.

Parker, Jim. "PDX update." *Portland Tribune*. October 5, 2001.

Parker, David and Leslie (Krueger). Interview with the author. February 3, 2021.

Parker, Leslie. Email to the author, September 25, 2003.

Parrott, Nancy. Interview with the author. March 3, 2021.

Passadore, George. "Ground Zero: Where Our Spirit Begins." *Portland Business Journal*. https://www.bizjournals.com/portland/stories/2006/10/23/editorial4.html. October 19, 2006, updated October 22, 2006.

Passadore, George, and Weston, Joe. Interview with the author. May 14, 2021.

Pataki, George. Interview with the author. May 13, 2021.

Paulson, Sarah. "Intel Bunny Suit." In *The Oregon Encyclopedia*. https://www.oregonhistoryproject.org/articles/historical-records/intel-bunny-suit/#.YHOxkT8pCOs. Last updated March 17, 2018.

Pembrooke, Allen. "Trip of Woodburn Man Was Important One." *Woodburn Independent*. October 24, 2001.

"People & Places." *TravelAgent*. October 29, 2001, 20.

Pérez-Peña, Richard. "After the Attacks: The Mood; Glimpses of the Normal Even as Obstacles Grow Clearer." *The New York Times*. September 15, 2001. https://www.nytimes.com/2001/09/15/us/after-the-attacks-the-mood-glimpses-of-the-norma l-even-as-obstacles-grow-clearer.html.

Pérez-Peña, Richard. "A Nation Challenged: Reporter's Notebook; Huge Memorial Service In Central Park Is Put Off." *The New York Times*. September 19, 2001. https://www.nytimes.com/2001/09/19/nyregion/nation-challenged-reporter-s-notebook-huge-memorial-service-central-park-put-off.html.

Perlez, Jane. "After the Attacks: The Overview; U.S. Demands Arab Countries 'Choose Sides.'" *The New York Times*. September 15, 2001. https://www.nytimes.com/2001/09/15/us/after-the-attacks-the-overview-us-demands-arab-count ries-choose-sides.html.

Perlez, Jane. "A Nation Challenged: Cooperation; U.S. Sanctions On Islamabad Will Be Lifted." *The New York Times*. September 22, 2001. https://www.nytimes.com/2001/09/22/world/a-nation-challenged-cooperation-u s-sanctions-on-islamabad-will-be-lifted.html.

Peters, Kathleen and Philip. Interview with the author. July 31, 2003.

Peterson del Mar, David. "14th Amendment." *The Oregon Encyclopedia*. https://www.oregonencyclopedia.org/articles/14th_amendment/. Last updated September 16, 2020.

Peterson del Mar, David. "15th Amendment." *The Oregon Encyclopedia*. https://www.oregonencyclopedia.org/articles/15th_amendment/#.YLMkCKEpAc8. Last updated January 21, 2021.

Peterson-Loomis, Dr. Jacqueline. "Immigration and Exclusion Time Line Oregon History 101." *The Oregon Encyclopedia*. https://www.oregonencyclopedia.org/media/uploads/Oregon_History_101_Timeline_12-1-14.pdf. Retrieved April 17, 2021.

Phillips, Michael. Email to friends on October 11, 2001; sent to the author on July 26, 2003.

Phillips, Michael. *Voices from a Sunlit Shadow*, 2002. Manuscript provided to author by playwright.

Piasecki, Sara. "DeNorval Unthank (1899-1977)." *The Oregon Encyclopedia*. https://www.oregonencyclopedia.org/articles/unthank_denorval_1899_1977_/#.YMWId0wpAc8. Last updated December 12, 2020.

"Piazza jersey from first game after 9/11 continues to inspire." National Baseball Hall of Fame. https://baseballhall.org/discover-more/news/hall-of-fame-to-honor-basebal l-after-911-with-exhibit. Retrieved June 19, 2021.

Platt, Cameron. Interview with the author. June 6, 2021.

Platt, Mary. Interview with the author. May 2021.

Platt, Rob. Interview with the author. May 2021.

Political cartoon. *Portland Tribune*. October 5, 2001.

"Portland agent wins 2002 award." *Travel Weekly*. November 9, 2002.

"Portland © New York" editorial. *The Oregonian*. September 29, 2001.

Portland Oregon Visitors Association press release. "'Flight for Freedom' Tops List of Tourism Award Winners." June 10, 2002. http://www.travelportland.com/media/news/print_res/freedom_flight_02.html. Retrieved July 26, 2003.

Portland State University. Population Research Center; Cai, Qian; and Hough, George C. Jr., "2001 Oregon Population Report" (2002). Oregon Population Estimates and Reports. 3. https://pdxscholar.library.pdx.edu/populationreports/3.

"Portlanders Make Symbolic Trip." *Portland Tribune*. October 5, 2001.

"Portraits of Grief" interactive feature. *The New York Times*. https://archive.nytimes.com/www.nytimes.com/interactive/us/sept-11-reckoning/portraits-of-grief.html#portraits-of-grief/P/1626. Retrieved on May 27, 2021.

Prado, Emilly. "Explore Northeast Oregon's Indigenous Cultures." Travel Oregon. May 22, 2019. https://traveloregon.com/things-to-do/trip-ideas/favorite-trips/explore-northeast-oregons-indigenous-cultures/.

"Praising the 'Flight For Freedom." *Observer*. October 10, 2001.

"'Prayer for America' embraces many faiths." CNN.com. September 23, 2001, Posted: 11:15 a.m. EDT. http://www.cnn.com/2001/US/09/23/vic.yankee.memorial.service/index.html.

Pressler, Jessica. "Cantor Fitzgerald." *New York* magazine. August 26, 2011. https://nymag.com/news/9-11/10th-anniversary/cantor-fitzgerald/.

Prihar, Aleck and Mary Edra. Email to Azumano Travel. October 9, 2001.

Pristin, Terry. "After the Attacks: Utilities; Phone Service Improving, But Many Still Lack Power." *The New York Times*. September 14, 2001. https://www.nytimes.com/2001/09/14/us/after-the-attacks-utilities-phone-service-improving-but-many-still-lack-power.html.

Pristin, Terry and Leslie Eaton. "A Nation Challenged: The Unemployed; Disaster's Aftershocks: Number of Workers Out of a Job Is Rising." *The New York Times*. September 26, 2001. https://www.nytimes.com/2001/09/26/nyregion/nation-challenged-unemployed-disaster-s-aftershocks-number-workers-job-rising.html.

Ray, John. Interview with the author. July 22, 2003.

Read, Richard. " George Azumano, founder of Azumano Travel, dies at 95 after a life working to improve U.S.-Japan relations." *The Oregonian*/OregonLive. https://www.oregonlive.com/business/2013/12/george_azumano_founder_of_azum.html. Posted December 11, 2013, updated January 10, 2019.

"Remembering September 11." *One*. [Scottish Power] October 2002, 5.

Revkin, Andrew C. "After the Attacks: The Chemicals; Monitors Say Health Risk From Smoke Is Very Small." *The New York Times*. September 14, 2001. https://www.nytimes.com/2001/09/14/us/after-attacks-chemicals-monitors-say-health-risk-smoke-very-small.html.

Revkin, Andrew C. "A Nation Challenged: Hazardous Materials; States Are Asked to Pull Over Any Truck Allowed to Carry Hazardous Cargo." *The New York Times*, September 27, 2001, https://www.nytimes.com/2001/09/27/us/nation-challenged-hazardous-materials-states-are-asked-pull-over-any-truck.html.

Rini, Vic. "The City of Heroes." *Northwest Italian News*. Manuscript emailed by Rini to author on November 2, 2001.

Risen, James and David Johnston. "NATION CHALLENGED: THE INVESTIGATION; Tape Reveals Wild Struggle On Flight 93." *The New York Times*. September 22, 2001. https://www.nytimes.com/2001/09/22/us/a-nation-challenged-the-investigation-tape-reveals-wild-struggle-on-flight-93.html.

Risen, James and Don van Natta Jr. "After the Attacks: The Suspects U.S. Says Hijackers Lived in the Open With Deadly Secret." *The New York Times*. September 14, 2001. https://www.nytimes.com/2001/09/14/us/after-attacks-investigation-authorities-have-learned-identities-18-hijackers.html.

Robbins, William G. "Frank Hachiya (1920–1945)." *The Oregon Encyclopedia*. https://www.oregonencyclopedia.org/articles/hachiya_frank_1920_1945_/#.YLL52qEpAc8. Last updated February 1, 2019.

Robbins, William G. "National Reclamation Act (1902)." *The Oregon Encyclopedia*. https://www.oregonencyclopedia.org/articles/national_reclamation_act_1902_/#.YDGoU3lOmUk. Last updated March 14, 2019.

Robbins, William G. "Oregon Donation Land Law." *The Oregon Encyclopedia*. https://www.oregonencyclopedia.org/articles/oregon_donation_land_act/#.YLLMrKEpAc8. Last updated February 2, 2021.

Robbins, William G. *Oregon: This Storied Land*. Seattle: University of Washington Press, 2020.

Robinson, Gail. "Everybody Loves New York—For Now." GothamGazette.com. October 15, 2001. http://www.gothamgazette.com/printable.php. Retrieved September 28, 2003.

Rollins, Ian. "Freedom Flight was 'Moving Experience.'" *Hillsboro Argus*. October 13, 2001, 1A–2A.

Ronda, James P. "Why Lewis and Clark Matter: Amid all the hoopla, it's easy to lose sight of the expedition's true significance." *Smithsonian Magazine*. August 2003. https://www.smithsonianmag.com/history/why-lewis-and-clark-matter-87847931/.

Rose City Funeral Home. "*George I. Azumano* June 9, 1918–December 9, 2013 (age 95)." https://www.rosecityfuneralhome.com/notices/George-Azumano. Retrieved March 8, 2021.

Rose, Michael. "Group of Oregonians head to N.Y.C. this week." *Statesman Journal*, September 6, 2002, http://online.statesmanjournal.com/sp_section_article. cfm?i=47788&s=2041. Retrieved September 28, 2003.

"Rose Parade Tickets on Sale Today." *The Oregonian*. November 29, 2002.

Rosso, Laura Del. "Oregon Agent's 'Freedom' trip brings 900 to NYC." twcrossroads. com. October 5, 2001. The same article appeared in *Travel Weekly* on that date as "Oregon agent takes 900 to New York City."

S., Mary Ann. "Live from New York! The Back Fence." *The Oregonian*. October 14, 2001.

Sachs, Susan. "After the Attacks: The Site; A Delicate Removal of Debris, With Monstrous Machines and Gloved Hands." *The New York Times*. September 14, 2001. https://www.nytimes.com/2001/09/14/us/after-the-attacks-the-workers-events-of-day-return-as-ghosts-in-the-night.html. https://www.nytimes.com/2001/09/14/us/after-attacks-site-delicate-removal-debris-with-monstrous-machines-gloved-hands.html.

Sachs, Susan. "After the Attacks: The Trade Center; Heart-Rending Discoveries as Digging Continues in Lower Manhattan." *The New York Times*. September 15, 2001. https://www.nytimes.com/2001/09/15/us/after-attacks-trade-center-heart-rend-ing-discoveries-digging-continues-lower.html.

Sachs, Susan. "A Nation Challenged: The Site; At the Site, Little Hope Of Uncovering Survivors." *The New York Times*, September 19, 2001, https://www.nytimes.com/2001/09/19/nyregion/a-nation-challenged-the-site-at-the-site-l ittle-hope-of-uncovering-survivors.html.

Duddy, Cathal, OFM. "St. Francis—A Guide for Nature Lovers & Ecologists." *Praying Nature with St. Francis of Assisi*. http://www.praying-nature.com/site_pages.php?-section=Guide+for+Nature+Lovers. Retrieved June 19, 2021.

Samson, Bruce. Interview with the author. July 31, 2003.

Sanger, David E. "A Nation Challenged: The Overview; Bush Orders Heavy Bombers Near Afghans; Demands bin Laden Now, Not Negotiations." *The New York Times*. September 20, 2001. https://www.nytimes.com/2001/09/20/world/nation-challenge d-overview-bush-orders-heavy-bombers-near-afghans-demands-bin.html.

Sarasohn, David. "William A. Hilliard (1927-2017)." *The Oregon Encyclopedia*. https://www.oregonencyclopedia.org/articles/hilliard_william_a_1927_/. Last updated October 12, 2020.

Saulny, Susan. "A Nation Challenged: Battery Park City; The Displaced Begin to Make Their Way Back Home." *The New York Times*. September 21, 2001. https://www.nytimes.com/2001/09/21/nyregion/nation-challenged-battery-park-city-displaced-begin-make-their-way-back-home.html.

Saxton, Ron. "New York City Greets Oregon's Family of Visitors with Wide-Open Arms." *Portland Tribune*. October 9, 2001.

"Scaled back recovery prompts scuffle between police, firefighters." CNN.com. November 2, 2001. http://www.cnn.com/2001/US/11/02/rec.firefighter.protest/.

Schechter, Patricia. Interview with the author. May 28, 2021.

Scheckla, LaVonne. Interview with the author. October 3, 2001.

Schorzman, Clarice. "A Letter Home." *The Molalla Pioneer*. October 13, 2001, 2.

Scott, Janny. "A Nation Challenged: The Portraits; Closing a Scrapbook Full of Life and Sorrow." *The New York Times*. December 31, 2001. https://www. nytimes.com/2001/12/31/nyregion/a-nation-challenged-the-portraits-closing-a-scrapbook-full-of-life-and-sorrow.html.

Semuels, Alana. "The Racist History of Portland, the Whitest City in America." *The Atlantic*. July 22, 2016, https://www.theatlantic.com/business/archive/2016/07/racist-history-portland/492035/.

Senie, Harriet. "Mourning in Protest: Spontaneous Memorials and the Sacralization of Public Space." in J. Santino, *Spontaneous Shrines and the Public Memorialization of Death*. US: Palgrave Macmillan, 2006.

Seward, Joe. Interview with the author. March 21, 2021.

Seward, Martha. Interview with the author. March 23, 2021.

Shanker, Thom and Eric Schmitt. "After the Attacks: Mobilization; Rumsfeld Ordering Call-Up Of Up to 50,000 Reservists." *The New York Times*. September 14, 2001. https://www.nytimes.com/2001/09/14/us/after-attacks-mobilization-rumsfeld-ordering-call-up-up-50000-reservists.html.

Sharkey, Joe. "After the Attacks: The Travelers; Tighter Airport Security Will Slow Business Fliers." *The New York Times*. September 13, 2001. https://www.nytimes.com/2001/09/13/us/after-attacks-travelers-tighter-airport-security-will-slow-business-fliers.html.

Shaw, Barbara. Email to the author. April 27, 2021.

Shaw, Barbara. Interview with the author. [].

Shaw, Barbara. Interview with the author. January 26, 2021.

Shaw, Barbara. Interview with the author. April 14, 2021.

Shaw, Barbara. "The Trip." Part 1, April 27, 2021, in the author's files.

Shaw, Barbara. "The Trip." Part 2, May 26, 2021, in the author's files.

Shaw, Barbara. "The Trip." Part 3, May 26, 2021, in the author's files.

Shenon, Philip and Robin Toner. "A Nation Challenged: Policy and Legislation; U.S. Widens Policy on Detaining suspects; Troubled Airlines Get Federal Aid Pledge." *The New York Times*. September 19, 2001, https://www.nytimes.com/2001/09/19/us/nation-challenged-policy-legislation-us-widens-policy-detaining-suspects.html.

Shiers, Frank. Interview with the author. March 23, 2021.

"Sho Dozono Emerges as Top Winner at Awards Breakfast." *Destination*. July/August 2002. 1 and 2.

"Show of Solidarity Makes Its Way to New York." *The Newberg Graphic*. October 6, 2001, page number unknown.

"Show of support." *East Oregonian* (Pendleton, Ore.). October 17, 2001, page number unknown.

Sidlin, Murry. Email to the author about the September 14 Oregon Symphony "In Memoriam" concert. May 23, 2021.

"Silence as Europe Mourns Dead." CNN.com. September 14, 2001 Posted: 6:22 AM EDT. http://edition.cnn.com/2001/WORLD/europe/09/14/europe.mourning.0610/index.html.

Silver, Nate. "Oregon: Swing State or latte-drinking, Prius-driving lesbian commune?" FiveThirtyEight. May 17, 2008. https://fivethirtyeight.com/features/oregon-swing-state-or-latte-drinking/.

Sinclair, Pete. Interview with the author. October 4, 2001.

Smith, Gordon. Interview with the author. March 15, 2021.

Smith, Sen. Gordon. Senator Gordon Smith speaking on Oregon Hero of the Week. U.S. Congress. *Congressional Record*. 107th Cong., 2nd sess., May 17, 2002. Vol. 148, no. 64.

Smith, Sen. Gordon. Senator Gordon Smith speaking on the Flight for Freedom. U.S. Congress. *Congressional Record*. 107th Cong., 1st sess., October 15, 2001. Vol. 147, no. 138.

Snyder, Patricia. "Locals Deeply Moved by NY Visit." *Daily Courier* (Grants Pass, Ore.). October 13, 2001.

Sokoloff, Lisa. Interview with the author. May 8, 2021.

Solomonson, Amy. Interview with the author. October 3, 2001.

Sommerfeld, Meg. "30,000 Rally for More Aid in Ore." *Education Week*. June 12, 1996. https://www.edweek.org/policy-politics/30-000-rally-for-more-aid-in-ore/1996/06.

Southern Poverty Law Center. "Conflict in Klamath, 2001." *Intelligence Report*. Winter Issue. November 29, 2001. https://www.splcenter.org/fighting-hate/intelligence-report/2001/conflict-klamath.

"Special Tribute to 9/11 McDonald's Owner Operator Hero Lloyd Frazier at Annual Stony Brook University's 'Give Kids a Smile' Day." LongIsland.com. September 19, 2017. https://www.longisland.com/news/09-19-17/special-tribute-to-911-mcdonalds-owner-operator-hero-lloyd-frazier-at-annual-stony-brook-universitys-give-kids-a-smile-day.html.

Spinnato, Joseph. Interview with the author. C. October 3, 2001.

Spitzer, Judith. "Molalla, Colton Contingent Arrives Back from New York Mission." *The Molalla Pioneer*. October 13, 2001, 1–2.

Stabler, David. "Gay Men's Chorus Will Perform in N.Y. on 9/11." *The Oregonian*, August 25, 2011, E1.

Stabler, David. "James DePreist: scenes from a musical life." *The Oregonian*. https://www.oregonlive.com/performance/2013/02/james_depreist_scenes_from_a_m.html. Posted February 8, 2013, updated January 10, 2019.

Staff and Wire Reports. "Timeline in Terrorist Attacks of Sept. 11, 2001." washingtonpost.com. September 12, 9:04 p.m. https://www.washingtonpost.com/wp-srv/nation/articles/timeline.html.

Stanford, Phil. "On the Town." *Portland Tribune*. October 19, 2001.

"State Treasurer Joins Delegation to New York." press release from the Oregon State Treasurer's office. October 3, 2001.

Steinhauer, Jennifer. "A Nation Challenged: The Tally; Giuliani Reports Sharp Increase in the Number of Those Listed as Missing." September 21, 2001, https://www.nytimes.com/2001/09/21/nyregion/nation-challenged-tally-giuliani-reports-sharp-increase-number-those-listed.html.

Stewart, Julie. "A Journey to the Heart of New York." *PATA*. October 2001. www.pataweb.net/archives/Flight.html, retrieved July 26, 2003.

Stump, Adam. "Chinese-American WWII Veterans receive Congressional Gold Medal." *Vantage Point Official Blog of the Department of Veterans Affairs*. December 10, 2020, https://blogs.va.gov/VAntage/82179/chinese-american-wwii-veterans-receive-congressional-gold-medal/.

Sullivan, Chris. Interview with the author. February 20, 2021.

Sullivan, Chris. "The Flight For Freedom." KXL.com. October 6, 2001.

Sullivan, Chris. "Flight for Freedom: Day Two in Manhattan." KXL.com. October 7, 2001.

Sullivan, Chris. "Flight for Freedom: Day Three." KXL.com. October 8, 2001.

Sullivan, Chris. "Flight for Freedom: Day Four." KXL.com, October 9, 2001.

Taylor, Dawn. "The Wartime Tourist." *Clackamas Review*. October 25, 2001, A1 and A6.

Taylor, Quintard. *In Search of the Racial Frontier: African Americans in the American West 1528–1990*. New York: Norton, 1998.

Taylor, Ted. "Goodwill Trip Boosts the Spirits of New Yorkers, Locals." *The Bulletin* (Bend, Ore.). October 13, 2001.

"Terror Attacks Hit U.S." CNN.com. Posted: September 11, 2001 5:14 p.m. EDT. https://www.CNN.com/2001/US/09/11/worldtrade.crash/.

Tessitore, Mrs. Denise. "Modern Day Patriotic Americans." *P.S. 6 Newsletter*. May 2002. Photographs of title page and article in author's files.

"Text of Bush's Address." CNN.com. September 11, 2001. 11:14 p.m. EDT. https://edition.CNN.com/2001/US/09/11/bush.speech.text/

"Thirty Days After." Editorial. *The Oregonian*. October 11, 2001.

"Thomas Theatre." Oregon Shakespeare Festival. https://www.osfashland.org/en/company/our-history/performance-spaces/thomas.aspx. Retrieved before February 19, 2021.

Thompson, Courtenay. "Oregonians Will Travel to N.Y. to Lend Support." *The Oregonian.* September 28, 2001, B7.

Thompson, Courtenay. "Dozono Leads Oregonians to New York." *The Oregonian.* October 4, 2001. Also called "Activist Leads Oregonians to New York."

Thompson, Courtenay. "From New York, With Love." *The Oregonian.* January 3, 2002, F1 and F3.

Thompson, Courtenay. "From Oregon, With Love." *The Oregonian.* October 7, 2001, D6.

Thompson, Courtenay. "Hugs and Cheers on Fifth Avenue." *The Oregonian.* October 9, 2001.

Thompson, Courtenay. "Memories Amid the Ruins." *The Oregonian.* October 11, 2001, B1, B7.

Thompson, Courtenay. "Trip of Hope Turns to One of Anxiety." *The Oregonian.* October 8, 2001, C1, C7.

Tikkanen, Amy. "Timeline of the September 11 Attacks." Britannica.com. https://www.britannica.com/list/timeline-of-the-september-11-attacks. Retrieved January 20, 2020.

"Torrey's Goodwill Visit." Editorial. *The Register Guard* (Eugene, Ore.). October 8, 2001.

Toth, Lisa. "Oregonians to travel to New York." *Daily Emerald* (University of Oregon, Eugene), October 5, 2001.

Toy, Eckard. "Ku Klux Klan." *The Oregon Encyclopedia.* https://www.oregonencyclopedia.org/articles/ku_klux_klan/#.YHsiez8pAc8. Last updated September 19, 2019.

Trampush, Amy. "Flight for Freedom: A Warm Welcome." *The Newberg Graphic.* October 20, 2001, A1 and A2.

Treaster, Joseph B. "After the Attacks: The Liability; Airlines Seek to Limit Lawsuits Over Attacks." *The New York Times.* September 14, 2001. https://www.nytimes.com/2001/09/14/us/after-the-attacks-the-liability-airlines-seek-to-limit-lawsuits-over-attacks.html.

Tricarico, Barbara. *Oregon.* Atglen, PA: Schiffer Publishing Ltd., 2020.

"200 Oregonians Plan Flight To NYC." KOIN.com, September 26, 2001.

"Two of WSU's Finest Travel to Ground Zero in New York." *WSU Public Safety Newsletter.* October 2001, pp. 1 and 2. Photocopy in the author's files.

Tymchuk, Kerry. Interview with the author. March 3, 2021.

"Union Square Park, Yankee Stadium Hosts 'A Prayer for America.'" *The Daily Plant.* September 25, 2001. https://www.nycgovparks.org/parks/union-square-park/dailyplant/10920.

United States Census Bureau. *Decennial Census Historical Facts (2000).* https://www.census.gov/programs-surveys/decennial-census/decade/decennial-facts.2000.html. Retrieved April 20, 2021.

U.S. Department of Commerce, Economics and Statistics Administration, U.S. Census Bureau. *Profiles of General Demographic Characteristics 2000 Census of Population and Housing. New York,* May 2001. https://www2.census.gov/library/publications/2001/dec/2kh36.pdf.

U.S. Department of Commerce, Economics and Statistics Administration, U.S. Census Bureau. *Profiles of General Demographic Characteristics 2000 Census of Population and Housing. Oregon,* May 2001. https://www2.census.gov/library/publications/2001/dec/2kh41.pdf.

Vallely, Paul. "A Silent World, United in Grief." *The Independent.* September 15, 2001. https://www.independent.companyuk/news/world/americas/a-silent-world-united-in-grief-5364173.html.

Vasquez, Krista. Interview with the author. February 5, 2021.

Virasami, Bryan. "Big Patriotic Showing at Columbus Day Parade." Newsday.com. October 9, 2001.

Voorhees, Genevieve. Interview with the author. October 4, 2001.

Wald, Matthew L. "A Nation Challenged: The Airports; Democratic Leaders Say They Back a Government Takeover of Security." *The New York Times*. September 24, 2001. https://www.nytimes.com/2001/09/24/us/nation-challenged-airports-democ ratic-leaders-say-they-back-government-takeover.html.

Wald, Matthew L. "A Nation Challenged: Airline Security; Proposal to Arm Pilots Gets Mixed Reaction." *The New York Times*. September 26, 2001. https://www.nytimes. com/2001/09/26/us/a-nation-challenged-airline-security-proposal-to-arm-pi lots-gets-mixed-reaction.html.

Walden, U.S. Representative Greg. "Flight of Freedom: A Journey to Save Jobs." *Congressional Record*. 109ᵗʰ Cong., 1ˢᵗ sess., February 1, 2005, Vol. 151, No. 8, E129. https:// www.congress.gov/congressional-record/2005/2/1/extensions-of-remarks-section/ article/e129-1?q=%7B%22search%22%3A%5B%22%5C%22flight+of+friend- ship%5C%22%22%5D%7D&s=2&r=2.

Waldman, Amy. "After the Attacks: The Memorials; Grief Is Lessened by Sharing and Solace From Strangers." *The New York Times*. September 14, 2001, https:// www.nytimes.com/2001/09/14/us/after-attacks-memorials-grief-lessened-s haring-solace-strangers.html.

Casey Walker. Email to Mayor Vera Katz. November 30, 2001. Copy in the author's files.

Walth, Brent. *Fire at Eden's Gate: Tom McCall & the Oregon Story*. Portland, Oregon: Oregon Historical Society Press, 1994.

Walth, Brent. "Thomas William Lawson McCall (1913–1983)." *The Oregon Encyclopedia*. https://www.oregonencyclopedia.org/articles/mccall_thomas_l/#.YLNEtKEpAc-. Last updated January 22, 2021.

Waples, Nancy. Interview with the author. July 24, 2003.

Water Education Foundation. "Klamath River Basin Chronology." https://www.water- education.org/aquapedia/klamath-river-basin-chronology, Retrieved February 20, 2021.

Wayne, Leslie. "A Nation Challenged: Aid to Business; Airline Bailout Encourages Other Industries to Lobby for Government Assistance." *The New York Times*. September 27, 2001. https://www.nytimes.com/2001/09/27/us/nation-challenged-aid-busines s-airline-bailout-encourages-other-industries-lobby.html.

Webb, Rebecca. "Charitable Passengers Board Flight With Case of Nerves, Good Will; Increased airport security can't stem a fear of flying." *Portland Tribune*. October 9, 2001.

Webb, Rebecca and Kamlynn Kimball. Interview with the author. January 29, 2021.

Webster, John. "Flight For Freedom Oregonians made true friends in New York." *Hood River News*. October 13, 2001.

Weston, Joseph E. Interview with the author. May 14, 2021.

Wiebe, Thomas. "Oregon loves New York: memories of 9/11." *The Oregon Scribbler*. https://oregonscribbler.com/remembering-911-oregon-loves-new-york/. September 11, 2011, retrieved June 12, 2021.

The Willamette Valley Visitors Association. "Willamette Valley Food Trails Showcase the Region's Bounty." *Willamette Valley Oregon Wine Country*. https://www.oregon- winecountry.org/food-trails-showcase-regions-bounty. Retrieved June 3, 2021.

Williams, Scott. Interview with the author. March 23, 2021.

Willing, Joyce. Interview with the author. January 9, 2021.

Woken, David. "Pineros y Campesinos Unidos del Noroeste (PCUN)." *The Oregon Encyclopedia*. https://www.oregonencyclopedia.org/articles/pineros_y_campesi- nos_unidos_del_noroeste_pcun/. Last updated August 28, 2018.

Wong, Peter. "Gerry Frank loves New York—still." *Statesman Journal*. October 11, 2001, 1A and 2A.

Woo, Elaine. "James DePreist, Celebrated Conductor, Dies at 76." February 10, 2013. https://www.washingtonpost.com/entertainment/music/james-depreis

t-celebrated-conductor-dies-at-76/2013/02/10/a3a60cce-7397-11e2-8f84-3e4b513b1a13_story.html.

Woodruff, Jan. Email to the author. November 6, 2001.

Woodruff, Jan. "F4F Alumni Group Update." Email to Barbara Baker, Eric Schmidt, Loen & Sho Dozono, Marilyn Slizeski, Steve Feltz, Vera Katz. January 04, 2002. Photocopy in author's files.

"World Shock Over U.S. Attacks." CNN.com. September 11, 2001, posted: 9:31 p.m. EDT. https://www.CNN.com/2001/WORLD/europe/09/11/trade.centre.reaction/.

Wu, David. Interview with the author. March 11, 2021.

Wyden, Sen. Ron. Senator Ron Wyden speaking on the Flight for Freedom. U.S. Congress. *Congressional Record*. 107th Cong., 1st sess., October 4, 2001. Vol. 147, no. 132.

Yellin, Emily. "After the Attacks: The Overnight Shipper; Back in the Air Again, And Feeling a Special Rush." *The New York Times*. September 15, 2001. https://www.nytimes.com/2001/09/15/business/after-attacks-overnight-shipper-back-air-again-feeling-special-rush.html.

Young, Jackie. Email to friends and family, September 12, 2001. Sent to the author on July 22, 2003.

Young, Jackie. Email to friends and family, including author. July 22, 2003.

Young, Jackie. Email to the author. July 29, 2003.

Young, Jackie. Interview with the author. January 31, 2021.

"Your Smith Rock State Park Guide." SmithRock.com. https://smithrock.com/. Retrieved June 3, 2021.

Yule, Don. Interview with the author. October 4, 2001.

Zielke, David. Interview with the author. May 6, 2021.

Zoroya, Gregg. "Tourist spending defies terrorism." *USA Today*. October 3, 2001, 1D, 6D.

PARTICIPANTS AND OTHER NOTABLES IN THIS BOOK

Craig Acklen
Betsy Ames
Tahn Amuchastegui
Tim Amuchastegui
Jean Andersen
(Julie Andersen
Martin, Kelley
Martin, Kevin
Martin)
Jos Anemaet
Baruti Artharee
Vic Atiyeh
George Azumano
Nobi Azumano
John Barell
Tracy Barry
Paula Becks
Burt Behm
Len Bergstein
Dan Bernstine
Michael Bloomberg
Sarah Bott
Sally Bourrie
Sarah Brightman
Julia Brim-Edwards
Georgette Brown
(Larry, Monique,
Martie)
Jessica Brown
Lucy Buchanan

George W. Bush
William Callahan
Jesse Carreon
Margaret Carter
Joy Cavinta
Sal Chillemi
Eric and Sara
Christenson
Ed Chun
Jerry Cioeta
Eugene Clark
Hilary Clinton
Bryan Coleman
Bill Cooper
Patricia Craugh
Michael Crawford
Molly Cunningham
Lana Cupper
Joe D'Alessandro
Linda Daugherty
Tracy Daugherty
Todd Davidson
Patricia Deines
Maureen "Mo" Denny
James DePreist
Dave and JoAnn
Dewey
Bonnie Dillon
Jane Ditewig
Steve Ditewig

Mark Dodson
Rich and Nancy Dorr
Terry Dorsey
Asazo Dozono
Elisa Dozono
Kristen Dozono
Loen Dozono
Nadyne Yoneko
"Meema" Dozono
Sho Dozono
Michele Longo Eder
Elaine Edgel
Randall Edwards
Toni Epperson
Derek Ewell
Stephen Facey
Beth Faulhaber
Ted Ferrioli
Maryann Fish
Nick Fish
Martin Fisher (Kerrida)
Bridget Flanigan
Don Ford
Jeanine Ford
Gerry Frank
Elaine Franklin
Gary Fuszek (Ashley;
Kimberley
Rockwood)
Rachel Gerber

Pamela Getty
Michael Getsiv
Charles Gibson
Rudolph Giuliani
Neil Goldschmidt
Melissa Goodwin
Richard Grasso
George Haight
Alexia Halen
Shaheed Hamid
Sheila Hamilton
Jeff Hammerley
Mary Ellen Hanson
Beverly Harkenrider
Frank Harkenrider
Bill Harmon
Tina Harmon
Connie Hawk
Ellis Henican
Judi Henningsen
Susan Henningsen
Brad Hicks (Kimberly)
Roger Hinshaw
Stephanie Hinshaw
Dave Holley
Betsy Holzgraf
Darlene Hooley
Mike House
Val Hubbard
Jeri Hunt
Brad Hutton
Doug Irving
Veronica Jaeger
Debra-Diane Jenness
    (Gordon and Tyler
    Jenness)
Gregg Kantor
Kathi Karnosh
Vera Katz
Mary Kelso
Sandra Kempel
Debby Kennedy
Robert F. Kennedy, Jr.
Kamlynn[] Kimball

James Kirkendall
John Kitzhaber
Frank Klejmont
Glenn Kloster
Pat Klum
Artie Rene Knight
Phil Knight
Bruce Knowlton
Jack Kostel
Bernie Kronberger
Leslie Krueger (Parker)
Colleen Kruse
Kim Kunkle
James Lane
Michael Lee
Terry Lee
Jamie Lim
Jonathan Linen
Diane Linn
Sarah Loftis
Betty Long
Eric Long
Wes Loucks
Rick Love
Randy Loveland
Debbie Lowenthal
Lynn Lundquist
Ryan McAninch
Brian McCartin
Don McClave
Alice McElhany
Jack McGowan
Deborah McGuire
Mike McGuirk
Glennis McNeal
Delia McQuade
Gregg Macy
Cliff Madison
Melody Madison
Eric Marcus
Mary Mark
Melvin "Pete" Mark
Guy Markham
Merritt Marthaller

Amanda Martinez
Joe Mauriello
Nancy Mechaber
Laura Meier
Roger Meier
Robin Merlo
Jane Meskill
Danny Meyer
Suzanne Miller
Debra Minchow
Norman Mineta
David Morkal
Billie Jean Morris
Mary Mueller
Leo Nadolske
Ann Nice
Cristyne Nicholas
Jonathan Nicholas
Tracy Nieporent
Lance Nuttman
Marla Nuttman
Al O'Brien
Mary Olson
Rob Oster
Allen Oswalt
David Parker
Leslie Parker (Krueger)
Nancy Parrott
George Passadore
George Pataki
Debbie Pedro
Edd Pedro
Allen Pembroke
Neal Penland
Tony Perkins
Cheryl Perrin
Kathleen Peters
Philip Peters
Eric Petterson
Devin Phillips
Michael Phillips [or
    Philips?]
Cameron Platt
Mary Platt

Rob Platt
Lynn Porter
Aleck and Mary Edra
  Prihar
Cecil Pulliam
Billy Quick
John Ray
Vic Rini (Dodie)
Dylan Rivera
Kimberley Rockwood
  (Gary Fuszek)
Jeff Rodman
Maria Rojo de Steffey
Cathy Rudd (Hilary)
Jim Rudd
Bruce Samson
Alisha Santos
Ron Saxton
Diane Sawyer
Patricia Schechter
LaVonne Scheckla
Joy Schertz
Clarice Schorzman
Charles Schumer
Joe Seward
Marty Seward
Alice Shapiro
Howard Shapiro
Barbara Shaw
Darryl[sp] Sherman

Frank Shiers
Ron Shiftan
Murry Sidlin
Pete Sinclair
Kai Skye
Marilyn Slizeski
Amy Solomonson
Gordon Smith
Lisa Sokoloff
Joseph Spinnato
Henry Stern
Julie Stewart
Fred Stickel
Roy Stilwell
Greg Strech
Chris Sullivan
Diane Teelan
Denise Tessitore
Scott Thomason
Courtenay Thompson
Craig Thompson
James Torrey
Pamela Treecer
Tom Turner
Kerry Tymchuk
Bobby Valentine
Elizabeth Vargas
Krista Vasquez
Nydia Velázquez
Jackie Venezia

Genevieve and David
  Voorhees
Kay and John "Jay"
  Voorhees
Greg Walden
Jay Waldron
Casey Walker
Cherryl Walker
Mark Walkley
Nancy Waples
Ed Washington
Rebecca Webb
John Webster
Joseph Weston
Celia Wiebe (Tony)
Thomas Wiebe
Eileen Wiedrich
Cornelia Wilkes
Scott Williams
Joyce Willing
Karen Winder
Wayne Winter
Jan Woodruff
Linda Wright
David Wu
Ron Wyden
Jackie Young
Phil Young
Don Yule
David Zielke

ABOUT THE AUTHOR

Sally Ruth Bourrie has been a writer for more than thirty years. Sometimes it's paid well enough to put a roof over her head and sometimes it's been "only" vital mental and emotional sustenance.

She began her career at the J. Paul Getty Museum where she worked as a curatorial assistant in the Exhibitions and Paintings Departments, armed with her new master's degree in Art History and Museum Studies from the University of Southern California. She is proud to have written the first museum exhibition catalogue on the twentieth-century California wood engraver, Paul Landacre, for the Los Angeles County Museum of Art. She came to California from New York, where she had received her bachelor's degree as a double major in Political Science and Art History at Vassar College.

As a full-time freelance writer in Chicago, Denver, and Portland, she contributed heavily to a book on the history of corporate giant Motorola, which gave her an entré to the world of technology, which has been integral to the aforementioned keeping a roof over the head. As a freelance writer, she pitched and sold more than 2,000 features, articles, white papers, advertorials, book, and web content on topics ranging from business and technology to the arts and gardening. Publications included newspapers such as *The Boston Globe*, the *Chicago Tribune*, *The Oregonian*, *The Denver Post*, and *The Dallas Morning News*. Her work also appeared in the *Plain Dealer Magazine*, *Chicago* magazine, *Northwest Woman*, *NASDAQ*, *Colorado Business*, and *Alaska Airlines*; trade publications such as *Cable World* and *Wireless Week* and digital media such as Newsweek.com and Barnes and Noble digital library. She wrote and researched approximately 1,200 artist biographies and objects descriptions for J. Paul Getty Museum website.

Sally served as senior editor for the permanent collections at the National Gallery of Art in Washington, DC, where she oversaw the first new guidebook to the collection in more than twenty years, along with creating the first strategic plan for its award-winning digital catalogues, *Online Editions*, supporting the program in becoming fully sustainable within the institution. She oversaw the editing and production of one of the most complicated catalogues ever produced at the Gallery and which was created both in print and online: *Italian Paintings of the Thirteenth and Fourteenth Centuries* by Miklós Boskovits. Sally was the first editor for internal communications at the University of Virginia Health System as well as magazine editor for the University of Virginia Graduate School and College of Arts & Sciences Communications.

Sally comes from a family in which neither parent graduated from high school, and whose values align with those Chris Arnade has called "back row America": faith, honor, place, and friendship. With the opportunity to live in the world of the elites, whose values Arnade categorizes as wealth and credentials, she has found herself with a capacity that seems increasingly rare in today's divided America: to be able to connect with people in both the front and back rows and to value and celebrate those who are not in the front.

CPSIA information can be obtained
at www.ICGtesting.com
Printed in the USA
BVHW051058110921
616356BV00001B/1